The Tale of Genji

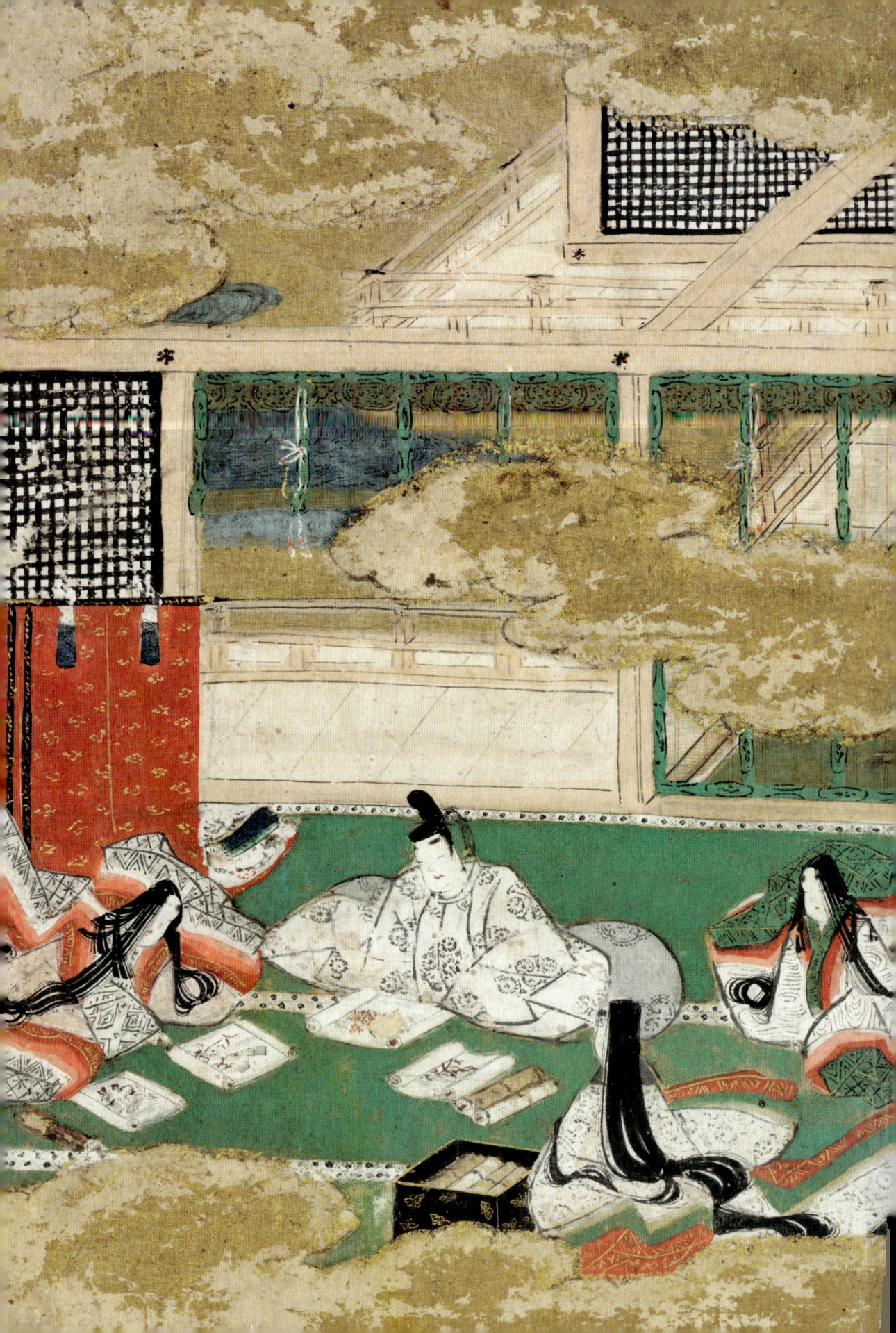

The Tale of Genji

A Visual Companion

Melissa McCormick

Princeton University Press
Princeton and Oxford

Copyright © 2018 by Princeton University Press
Published by Princeton University Press, 41 William Street, Princeton,
New Jersey 08540
In the United Kingdom: Princeton University Press, 6 Oxford Street,
Woodstock, Oxfordshire OX20 1TR
press.princeton.edu

Front matter illustrations: p. ii, detail of image on p. 88; p. vi, detail of
image on p. 232; p. viii, detail of image on p. 68; p. x, detail of image on
p. 160

Jacket illustration: (front) Tosa Mitsunobu, *The Lady at Akashi* (Chapter 13)
from *The Tale of Genji Album*, 1510. Imaging Department
© President and Fellows of Harvard College.

Tale of Genji, translated by Dennis Washburn. Copyright © 2015 by
Dennis Washburn. Used by permission of W.W. Norton & Company, Inc.

Poems from *A Waka Anthology, Volume Two: Grasses of Remembrance, Part
B*, by Edwin A. Cranston. Copyright © 2006 by the Board of Trustees of
the Leland Stanford Jr. University. All rights reserved. Used by permission
of the publisher, Stanford University Press, sup.org.

All Rights Reserved
Library of Congress Cataloging-in-Publication Data
Names: McCormick, Melissa, 1967–
Title: The Tale of Genji : a visual companion / Melissa McCormick.
Description: Princeton : Princeton University Press, 2018. |
Includes bibliographical references and index.
Identifiers: LCCN 2017061368 | ISBN 9780691172682 (hardback : alk. paper)
Subjects: LCSH: Murasaki Shikibu, 978?– Genji monogatari—Illustrations. |
Genji album—Illustrations. | Painting, Japanese—Themes, motives. |
Tosa, Mitsunobu, 1434?–1525. | Arts and society—Japan—History. |
Japanese literature—Heian period, 794–1185—History and criticism.
Classification: LCC ND1059.T6585 T35 2018 | DDC 895.63/14—
dc23 LC record available at https://lccn.loc.gov/2017061368
British Library Cataloging-in-Publication Data is available

Designed by Yve Ludwig
This book has been composed in Dante Pro and Kozuka Mincho Pro
Printed on acid-free paper. ∞
Printed in China
10 9 8 7 6 5 4 3 2 1

Contents

vii   Acknowledgments

ix   Note to Reader

1   Introduction

23   *The Tale of Genji Album* of 1510
      Chapters 1–54

240   Appendix: Album Calligraphy Key

242   Glossary

244   The Album: Works Cited and Consulted

246   Bibliography

247   Index

254   Image Credits

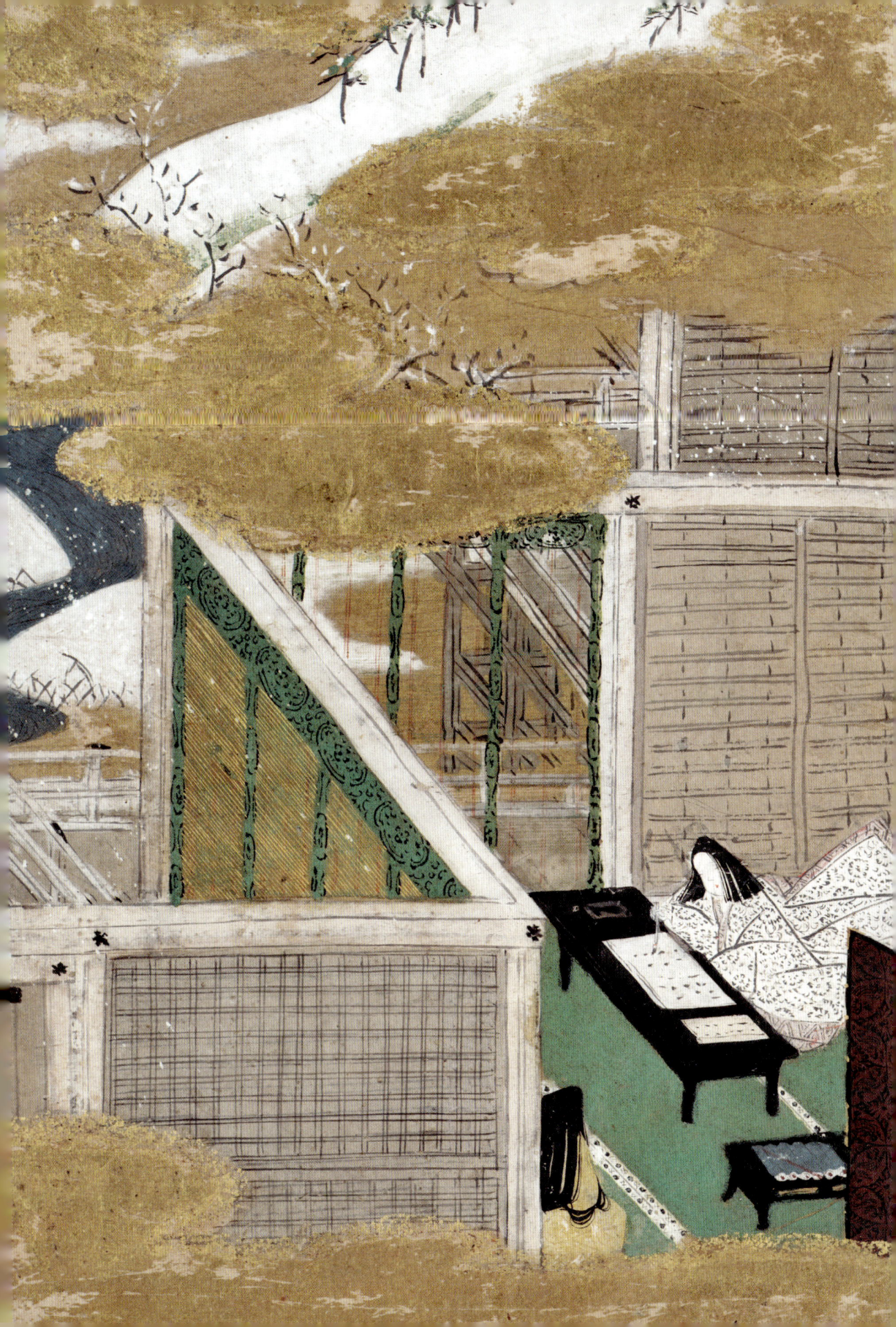

Acknowledgments

Over the years, the students in my seminars and lectures on *The Tale of Genji*, through their questions, insights, skepticism, and wonder over the tale, have been a constant source of inspiration, and this book was written with them always in mind. The ability to teach with the *Genji Album* and to examine it up close on multiple occasions has enriched this project beyond measure. For that, I am indebted to the late Philip Hofer, who bequeathed his collection to the Harvard Art Museums, and to the institution today for making it so accessible. I express my sincere thanks to Rachel Saunders, Abby Aldrich Rockefeller Associate Curator of Asian Art, and to Mary Lister, Manager of the Art Study Center at the Harvard Art Museums, for accommodating numerous requests and for their dedication to the pedagogical mission of the museum. Likewise, the ability to view the album alongside visiting colleagues, in particular, Takagishi Akira, Ido Misato, Kamei Wakana, and Ikeda Shinobu, deepened my understanding of the work, and I thank them for their insights and intellectual generosity. Conversations with *Genji* scholars also helped shaped this book, with special thanks going to Estelle Bauer, Edwin Cranston, Ii Haruki, Edward Kamens, Kasashima Tadayuki, Kawazoe Fusae, Kojima Naoko, Yukio Lippit, Julia Meech, Mitamura Masako, Sano Midori, Edith Sarra, Haruo Shirane, Royal Tyler, J. Keith Vincent, Dennis Washburn, Watanabe Masako, and especially the late H. Richard Okada and the late Chino Kaori. For their direct engagement with the manuscript I am grateful to Fumiko Cranston, Gustav Heldt, Itō Tetsuya, Kimura Atsuko, Andrew Watsky, and to Christopher Jury, for his meticulous editing. The collections at the Harvard-Yenching Library and the Fine Arts Library at Harvard University, and their respective librarians, Kuniko Yamada McVey and Nanni Deng, were indispensable to this book's completion. At Princeton University Press, Michelle Komie shared my vision for the volume from the beginning and worked tirelessly and with endless patience to see it to fruition. For the production, design, and editing of the book, I wish to thank Mark Bellis, Steve Sears, Dawn Hall, and Yve Ludwig for the professionalism and artistry that they bring to their work. Emily Shelton's careful proofreading during the final stages of the book's production was invaluable, as was Blythe Woolston's thoughtful and expert indexing. Finally, I extend my most heartfelt thanks to my family for their patience and support and their belief in this project. To Kio and Azusa, I am forever grateful.

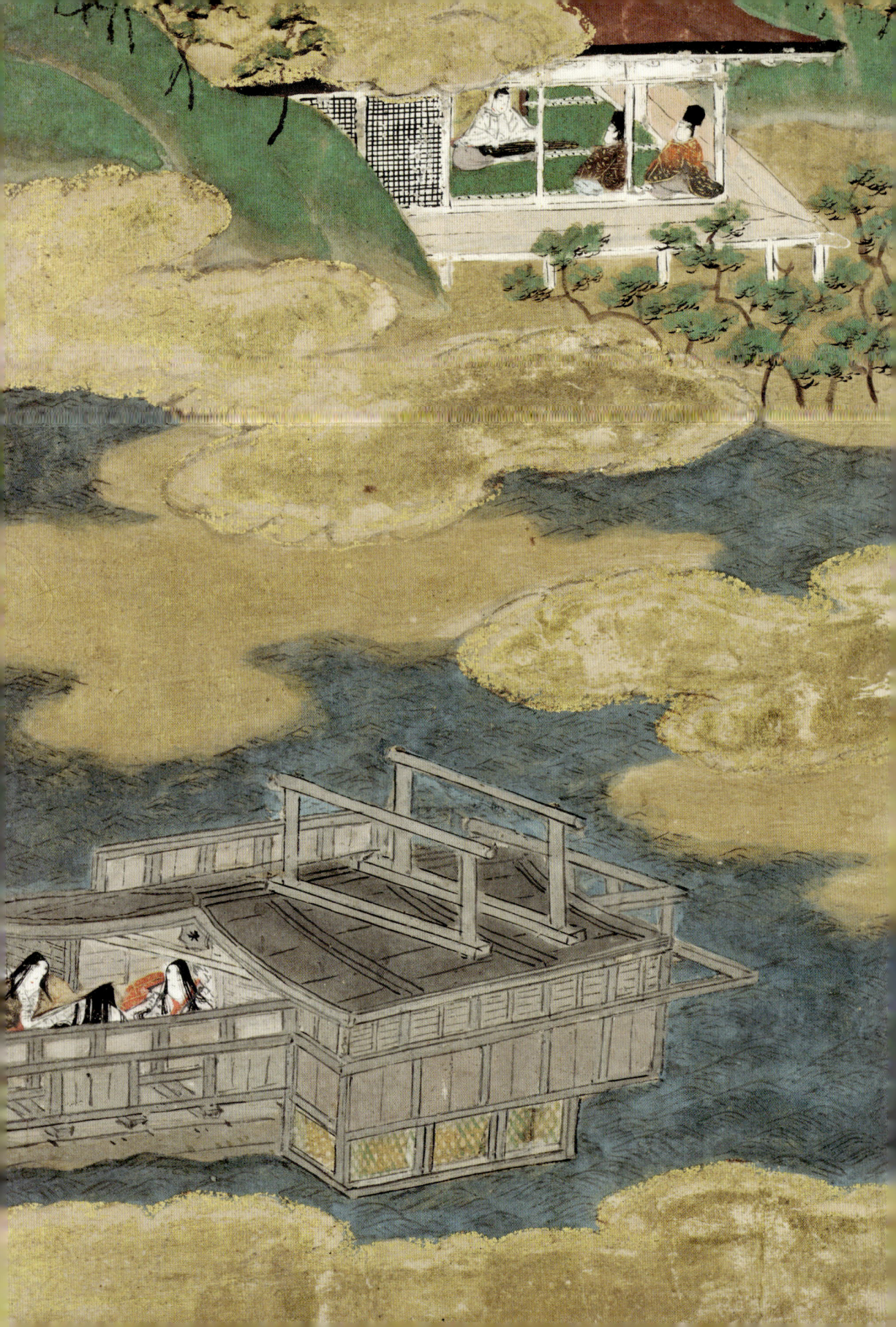

Note to Reader

The pages that follow reproduce for the first time in color all 108 painting and calligraphy leaves of *The Tale of Genji Album* (1510) by Tosa Mitsunobu (act. ca. 1462–1525) in the collection of the Harvard Art Museums, along with English translations of the album's texts. Foundational to the writing of *The Tale of Genji* and integral to its later reception are the 795 *waka* (poems in 5-7-5-7-7 syllabic meter), interspersed throughout the prose, which the album emphasizes by allotting thirty-four of the fifty-four calligraphy leaves to verse rather than prose excerpts. Unless otherwise noted, translations of poems in the book are taken from Edwin A. Cranston, *A Waka Anthology, vol. 2: Grasses of Remembrance* (Stanford, CA: Stanford University Press, 2006). All of the album's texts have been rendered into the modern, standardized Japanese script beneath each calligraphy leaf to make them as accessible as possible, following the transliteration in Fumiko E. Cranston, "Hābādō Daigaku Bijutsukan zō 'Genji monogatari gajō' kotobagaki shakumon," Kokka no. 1222 (1997): 54–57. The romanization of the calligraphy follows modern reading conventions rather than historical orthography, and punctuation marks are based on the annotated edition of *The Tale of Genji* in Shinpen Nihon koten bungaku zenshū (Tokyo: Shōgakkan, 1994–98). Corresponding page numbers in this edition to all of the album's texts are provided in the bibliography. Except for a few modifications and translations of my own to match the album excerpts, all English translations of prose passages and *Genji* chapter titles are taken from Dennis Washburn's translation of *The Tale of Genji* (New York: Norton, 2015).

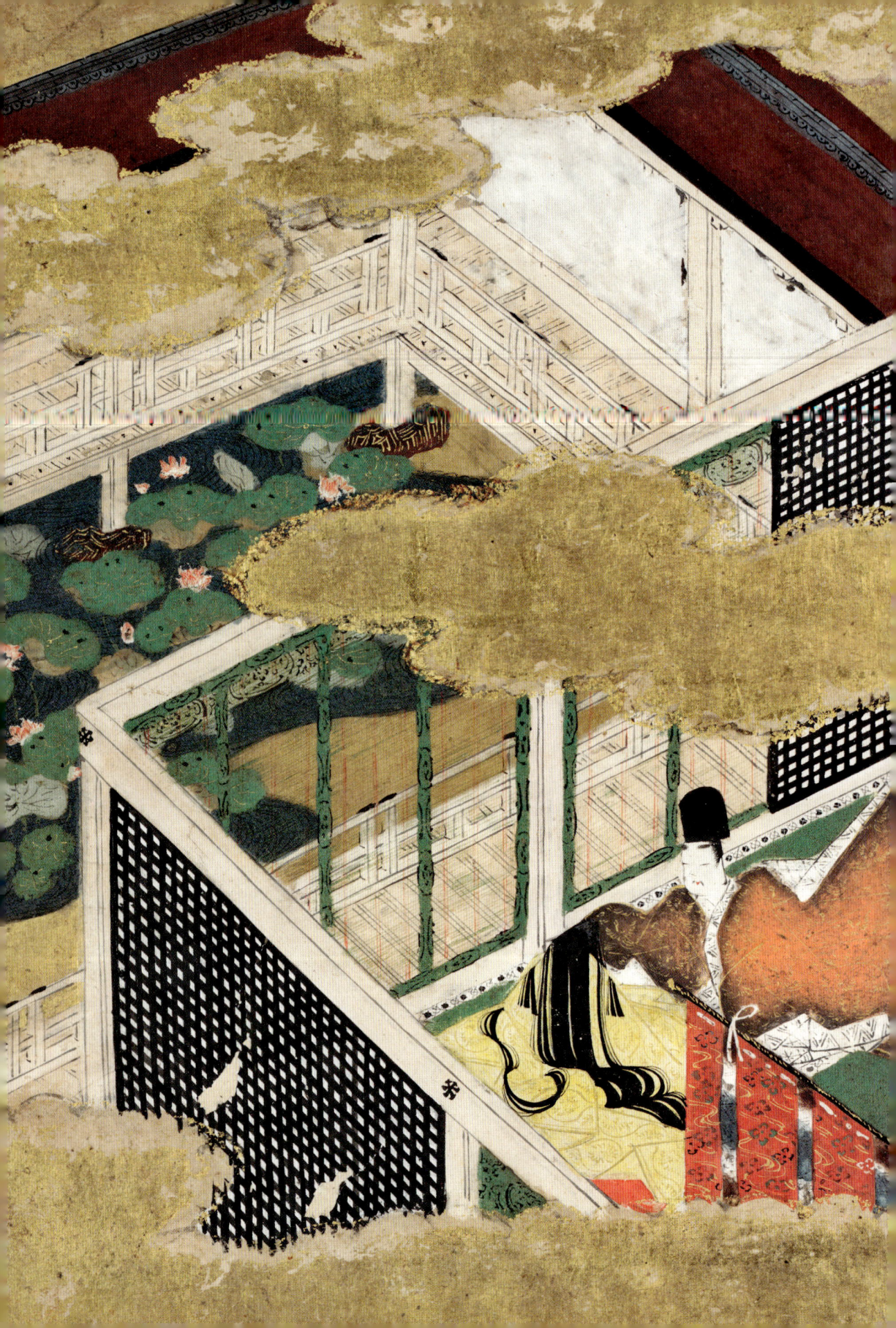

Introduction

In the year 1510, at a private residence in the capital city of Kyoto, two men raised their wine cups to celebrate the completion of an extraordinary project, an album of fifty-four pairs of calligraphy and painting leaves representing each chapter of Japan's most celebrated work of fiction, *The Tale of Genji*. One of the men, the patron of the album Sue (pronounced Sué) Saburō, would take it back with him to his home province of Suō (present-day Yamaguchi Prefecture), on the western end of Japan's main island. Six years later, in 1516, the album leaves would be donated to a local temple named Myōeiji, where the work's traceable premodern history currently ends. In 1957 it came into the possession of Philip Hofer (1898–1984), founder of the Department of Prints and Graphic Arts at the Houghton Rare Book Library of Harvard University.[1] A prolific collector of illustrated manuscripts, Hofer purchased the album along with numerous other Japanese books and scrolls, which were subsequently bequeathed to the Harvard Art Museums in 1985 (fig. 1). This remarkable compendium has survived intact for over five hundred years, making it the oldest complete album of *Genji* painting and calligraphy in the world.

Authored in the early decades of the eleventh century by the court lady Murasaki Shikibu, *The Tale of Genji* is a fifty-four-chapter work of prose and 795 *waka* poems, centered primarily on the life of an imperial son, the "radiant Genji," who is denied his chance to ascend the throne. The tale's popularity began even before Murasaki had completed the work, and by the late twelfth century it had become so widely admired that would-be poets and littérateurs were advised to absorb its lessons. *The Tale of Genji* quickly became a fixture of the Japanese literary canon and centuries later joined the canon of world literature. With its length (over 1,300 pages in the most recent English translation), complexity, sophisticated writing style, development of character and plot, realistic representation of historical time and place, ironic distance, and subplots that extend thematically across the entire work, it meets every criterion that is generally used to distinguish novels from other forms of literature. Although steeped in the complex belief systems and moral codes of its own era, which complicate any simplistic equation of the work with modern fiction, the tale can be read as a monumental exploration of human nature. No matter how characters may triumph or what virtues they may exhibit, all ultimately confront hardships and grapple with their own fallibility, none more so than the eponymous protagonist Genji. To give voice to her characters' internal conflicts and thought processes, Murasaki Shikibu took unprecedented advantage of two hallmarks of classical Japanese literature: the affective power and ironic distancing effect of *waka* poetry, and a mode of prose narration similar to stream of consciousness and free indirect discourse in Western literature. The shifting perspective of the

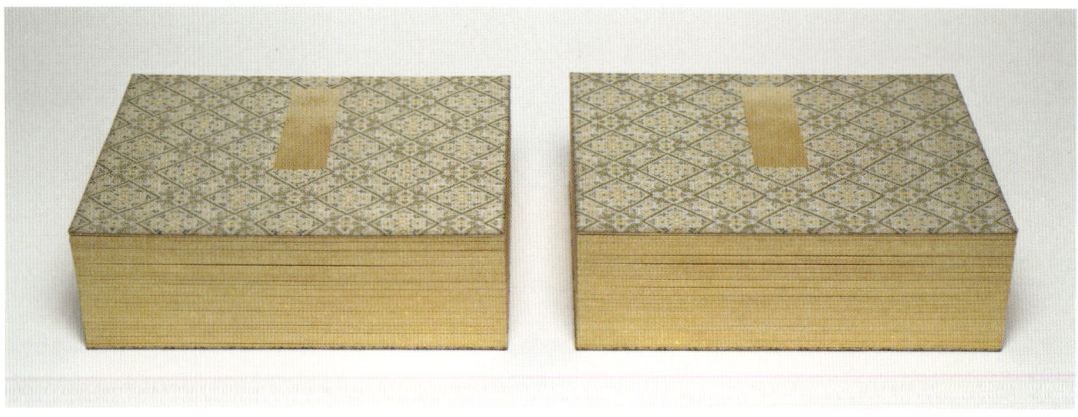

Fig. 1. *The Tale of Genji Album*, 1510. Two volumes, remounted in 1690s. Paintings by Tosa Mitsunobu (act. ca. 1462–1525), calligraphy by Kunitaka Shinnō (1456–1532), Konoe Hisamichi (1472–1544), Sanjōnishi Sanetaka (1455–1537), Jōhōji Kōjo (1453–1538), Reizei Tamehiro (1450–1526), Son'ō Jugō (d. 1514). Overall mounting, each volume: 34.1 × 44.9 cm; 108 album leaves, 24.3 cm × 18.1 cm each. Harvard Art Museums, Cambridge. Credit: Harvard Art Museums/ Arthur M. Sackler Museum, Bequest of the Hofer Collection of the Arts of Asia, 1985.352.

narrator throughout the work also makes for a reading experience surprisingly akin to that of the modern novel.[2] At the same time, the tale's evocative description of the imperial court and the rituals of the aristocracy caused it to be regarded as the embodiment of a golden age of courtly life, especially in later eras when juxtaposed against the nobility's waning political authority.

The history of *Genji* pictures in many ways tells the history of the early illustrated book in Japan. The rich tradition of *Genji* illustration began almost four hundred years before the 1510 album came into being, with the earliest known and most famous extant example being the twelfth-century *Genji Scrolls* (fig. 2). These horizontal handscrolls, with alternating texts and pictures, represent the oldest manuscript of the *Genji* text and suggest how images and texts functioned symbiotically to shape a reader's cognitive experience of the work. Several paintings in these earliest scrolls helped establish a *Genji* iconography that endured through the centuries and informed the 1510 album as well, which even a simple comparison of figure 2 with the album's painting for Chapter Forty-Five (p. 200) makes clear. The extravagant treatment of the paper decoration beneath this earliest *Genji* manuscript, with its dyed sheets, underdrawings, and its surface encrusted with metal in the form of gold dust, and thin slivers of cut silver and gold foil, resembles the sophistication and numinous quality of Buddhist sūtra decoration from the same period. From the thirteenth century, we have vestiges of a more everyday reading experience of *Genji* in the form of small, thread-bound books with scenes from the tale interspersed in their interior pages. As a rule, such books consisted of sets with each of the fifty-four chapters bound separately. This facilitated the circulation of individual chapters for reading and copying, which was essential for creating new manuscript copies before the age of print. Early examples are rare, but one "chaplet" of Ukifune (Chapter Fifty-One) survives partially intact (fig. 3).[3] Its well-thumbed pages convey the enthusiasm of some of the tale's earliest readers, who confessed their preoccupation with the story and who pored over their own cherished copies.[4] Whether extravagantly illustrated scrolls or thread-bound books, both formats tend to reproduce *The Tale of Genji* either in its entirety or in lengthy excerpted passages that approximate the full story.

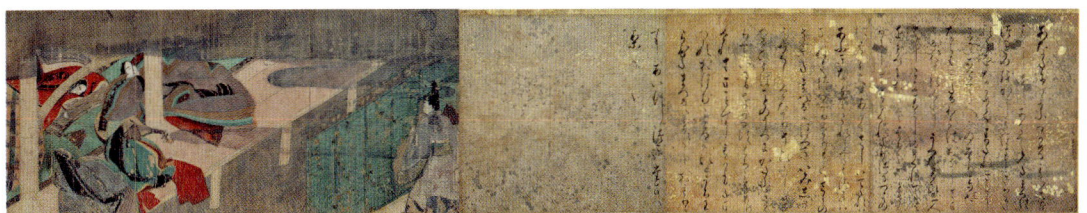

Fig. 2 *The Divine Princess at Uji Bridge (Hashihime)*, Chapter Forty-Five, *Illustrated Handscrolls of the Tale of Genji (Genji monogatari emaki)*. Late Heian period, early twelfth century. Painting: colors, ink, and shell white on paper; calligraphy: gold and silver foil and dust on dyed paper, height 22 cm. Tokugawa Museum of Art, Nagoya.

In contrast, the album format uses only the briefest excerpts from the tale, either short prose passages or one to three poems, to encapsulate the work in a concise manner. Albums are therefore not digests; their short excerpts never explain the plot, characters, or setting as that genre of paratexts had begun to do by the fourteenth century. That is not to say that the producers of the *Genji Album* did not take full advantage of the various digests, commentaries, character charts, dictionaries, and other tools for understanding the universe of the tale. Indeed, as we shall see, the men who made the album were not only consumers, but producers of such texts. The album, however, works best as a supplement to a full *Genji* manuscript, and for readers already knowledgeable about the tale, allows them to visualize scenes more clearly and to understand familiar passages and poems in a new light. The unique selection and coordination of *Genji* texts and images in all formats, whether scroll, book, or album, are always suggestive of how contemporary audiences understood the tale. The *Genji Album* in the Harvard collection offers a particularly important point of view in this regard, both as the sole surviving album predating 1600 and because of the group of individuals behind its creation.[5]

The *Genji Album* was not mass produced but instead made for a specific patron. Thus its 108 texts and images contain a wealth of information about the values, interests, and aspirations of those who commissioned the work and assisted in its creation in the sixteenth century. Its production was a collaborative endeavor, involving a patron, an artist and his painting studio, six calligraphers, and at least two coordinators overseeing the project. The goal was for the selection of scenes and textual passages to encapsulate the story in a compelling and meaningful way for the patron. Most examples of premodern Japanese artworks created before the year 1600 lack documentation, making it hard to say who produced them. In the case of the Harvard *Genji Album*, remarkably, the patron and most details of the work's production are known, having been recorded in the diary of the courtier and one of the coordinators of the project, Sanjōnishi Sanetaka (1455–1537).[6] And because the creators of this album did not simply have a passing interest or superficial knowledge of the *Genji*, but viewed their commitment to the work as a lifelong scholarly endeavor, their curation of these pairs of leaves enriches our own understanding of the tale.

Although *The Tale of Genji* was originally written by a woman in the context of the imperial court of the Heian period (794–1185), and though it centers on the life of an imperial prince, it enjoyed a healthy readership throughout the medieval period among members of the warrior class. From the twelfth century onward, successive military leaders assumed increasing political control over the central government, while the emperor and nobility remained intact in Kyoto, resulting in a fission of the polity that would continue until the nineteenth century. While the institutional and economic power of the imperial court and the aristocracy

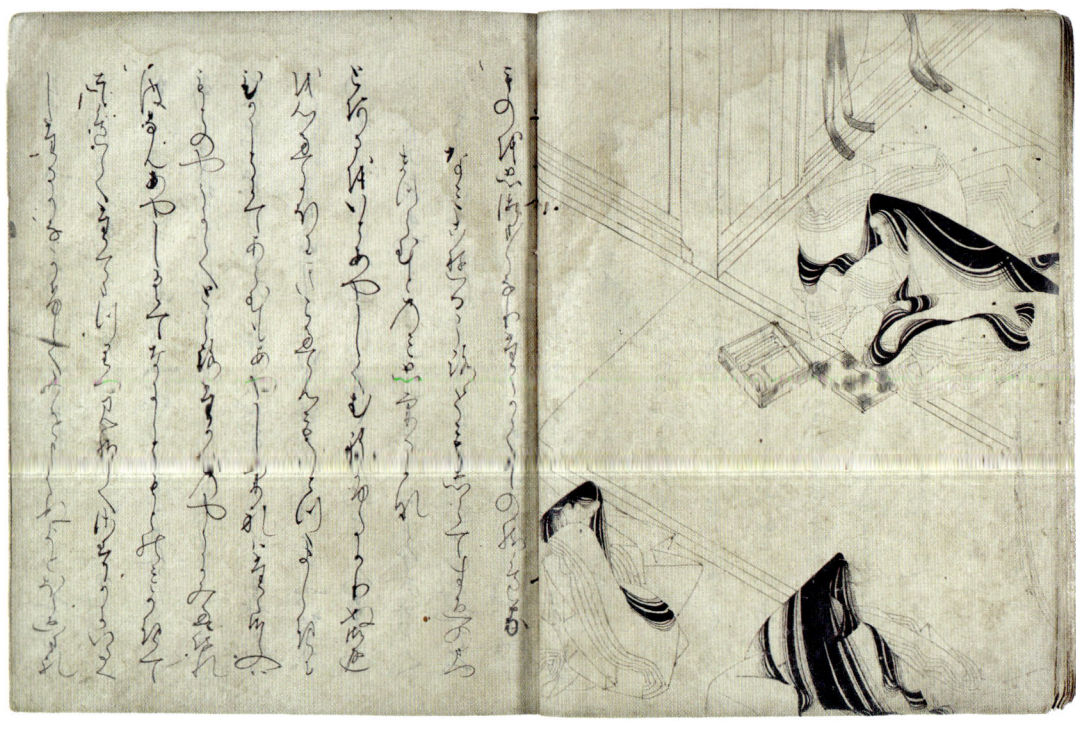

Fig. 3 *A Boat Cast Adrift* (*Ukifune*), Chapter Fifty-One of *The Tale of Genji*. Artist and calligrapher unknown. Kamakura period, thirteenth century. Thread-bound book, with illustrations in ink on paper, 23.7 × 19 cm. The Museum Yamato Bunkakan, Nara.

waned over time, the spiritual identity of the emperor and thus the court's ideological and symbolic influence survived and remained desirable and valuable to those on the outside. Rulers of the Ashikaga Shogunate, for example, belonged to a lineage of imperial princes turned commoners who took the Minamoto (a.k.a. Genji) surname, like the eponymous hero of *The Tale of Genji*. For warlords like the shogun Ashikaga Yoshimitsu (1358–1408), Genji's ability to achieve the exalted status of *honorary* retired emperor (*jun daijō tennō*) as a commoner was aspirational.[7] Murasaki Shikibu's characterization of her commoner hero as a rightful ruler dispossessed, but with the undeniable radiance of a Buddhist monarch, most certainly played a part in earning the shogun's admiration as he sought his own kingly power. Even for men without a professed Minamoto bloodline, however, the dramatic arc of Genji's fortunes, from his privileged position at birth, to his nadir in exile, to his subsequent rise to glory, proved relatable, despite his many flaws, or perhaps because of them.[8] For readers who aimed to be counted among the elite and to engage in cultural discourse, *The Tale of Genji* was simply too important and pervasive to ignore. With its allusions to the Heian and pre-Heian traditions of Japanese and Chinese poetry, prose, folk songs, myths, history, philosophy, and politics, it was a rich source of references and erudition. And as medieval commentators on the *Genji* firmly believed, the tale's underlying narrative structures, if parsed properly, could reveal the profound truths of Tendai Buddhist nonduality, presented in harmony with beliefs in the indigenous gods, or *kami*, that protected the archipelago.[9] With no work of literature before or after approaching it in complexity,

The Tale of Genji was widely viewed as miraculous, authored only with the help of divine intervention.[10] The supernatural aura of the tale should not be discounted when considering the attraction that it held for many. At the same time *Genji* has always made for entertaining reading, in no small part because of its memorable female characters. By the sixteenth century, such characters had taken on lives of their own, transformed into protagonists of their own tales in new forms of fiction and Noh plays, making a knowledge of the tale indispensable for full participation in the culture of the day.

Patrons: Sue Saburō and Sue Hiroaki

The patron of the 1510 *Genji Album*, Sue Saburō, also known as Okinari, hailed from the western province of Suō (present-day Yamaguchi Prefecture), and commissioned the album during a temporary stay in the capital.[11] Although the Sue clan would be remembered for eventually bringing about the destruction of the Ōuchi house, in the early sixteenth century they were still its allies and loyal retainers. The Sue derived countless benefits from their relationship with the Ōuchi clan head, Ōuchi Yoshioki (1477–1528), who in 1508 became one of three military leaders in charge of the government in Kyoto, and who controlled one of only three official trade boats running between the archipelago and the Chinese mainland.

The Sue were also wealthy, and like their Ōuchi lords, had the resources to engage in a range of cultural activities, including the commissioning of paintings and literary works. Sue Saburō arrived in Kyoto in 1508 with Ōuchi Yoshioki and immediately began petitioning the foremost courtier-scholars of the day to mentor him in poetry and classical texts. It was during this time that he commissioned the *Genji Album*, not merely for himself, but on behalf of his father, the estimable warrior and scholar, Sue Hiroaki (1461–1523), who then held the title of Governor of Hyōgo. While the capital continued to be the cultural center of gravity, certain provincial domains had flourished to the point of emerging as "little Kyotos," especially those overseen by men in the Ōuchi sphere with funds to spend and access to exotic goods from trade beyond the archipelago. Sue Hiroaki was one such individual living amid material wealth and immersed in elite culture and scholarship. He had a long history of interaction with litterateurs from the capital, including linked verse (*renga*) poets, and his own scholarly activities are legendary, beginning with his collation and copy of the Kamakura-period military chronicle, *Mirror of the East* (*Azuma kagami*).[12]

By 1516, the *Genji Album* leaves were in Hiroaki's possession, and he declared his intention to dedicate them to Myōeiji, the Buddhist mortuary temple he founded on behalf of his deceased mother. This information appears on the backing papers of the leaves of the *Genji Album* in the form of inscriptions by Hiroaki himself (fig. 4), which were discovered during conservation of the album in 1998.[13] Importantly, it was in that year that Hiroaki hosted at his residence a series of lectures on *The Tale of Genji* (*Genji kōshaku*) by the renowned *renga* poet Sōseki (1474–1533) who was traveling throughout the western provinces.[14] Through their peregrinations, *renga* masters not only disseminated scholarship and transmitted esoteric readings of the tale, but also created a "book network" by which texts and classical works of literature circulated. The point of production was most often the capital, from which *Genji* volumes with title slips brushed by prominent calligraphers made their way to distant provinces, including the domains of Suruga, Echigo, and Suō, at the request of regional daimyo, and often, their wives.[15] Sue Hiroaki enlisted Sōseki for just such deliveries, with one conveyance including a copy of the tenth-century *waka* poetry anthology *Collection of Waka Old and New* (*Kokinshū*), as well as chapter title labels for his own copy of *The Tale of Genji*.[16] The *Genji* lectures of 1516 were thus conducted for a man steeped in the tale and who approached it with a certain reverence; they may even have occurred on the fifteenth of the eighth month, the date that according to ancient legend Murasaki Shikibu was said to have begun writing her tale beneath a full autumn moon at the temple of Ishiyamadera.[17] It was not uncommon for medieval *Genji* scholars and aficionados to submit poetic offerings to commemorate the text's mythogenesis on that date.

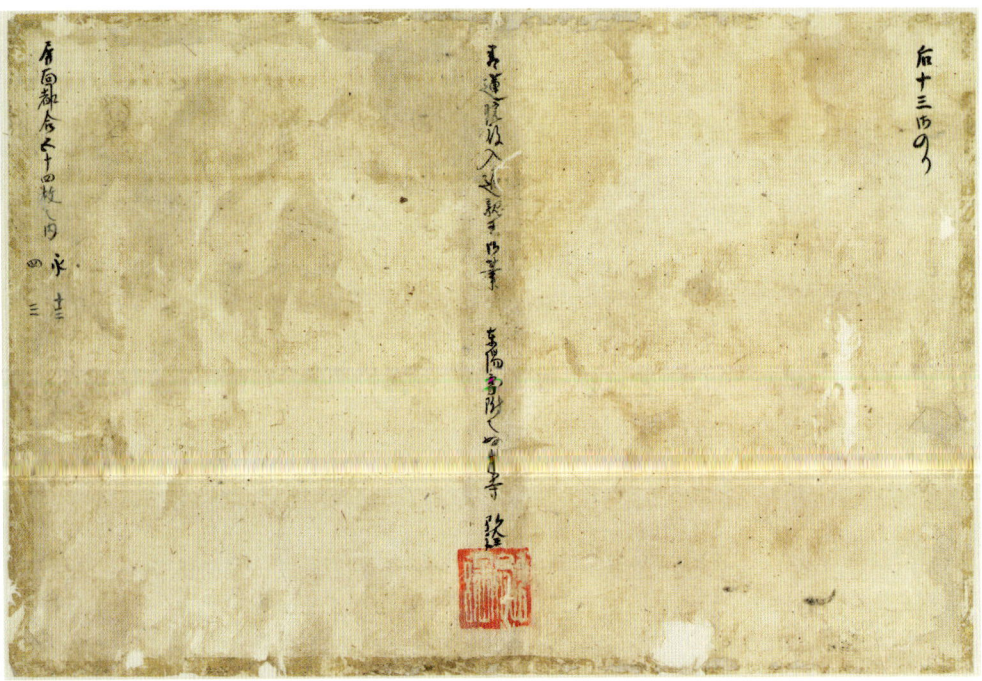

Fig. 4 Backing paper from *The Tale of Genji Album*, 1510; behind the leaves for Rites of the Sacred Law (Minori), Chapter Forty, with inscriptions by Sue Hiroaki and the dedication date of Eishō 13 (1516). 24.2 cm × 36.5 cm. Harvard Art Museums, Cambridge.

The album leaves, so carefully acquired in the capital, could very well have been a centerpiece for the *Genji* lectures of 1516.[18] Inscriptions on the backing papers suggest that Hiroaki had the album leaves remounted onto folding screens not long after he received them, and one possibility is that he had done this in anticipation of Sōseki's arrival in Suō.[19] Thus on the third day of the fourth month of 1516, Hiroaki prepared the leaves for mounting by inscribing pertinent information on their backing papers: he carefully noted the numeric order for each pair of leaves, the chapter title, the date, the name of each calligrapher, and the temple dedication (for later donation), followed by his name and seal.[20] Folding screens displaying the leaves could thus be set up during the lectures as an exquisite backdrop with their vibrant polychrome calligraphy papers and paintings and refulgent gold clouds. The *Genji Album* paintings and texts were surely made for some form of public display. Along with fan paintings, the practice of pasting sets of *shikishi* sheets illustrating courtly tales or verses from poetic anthologies onto screens had existed by the thirteenth century and became more and more common in the fifteenth and sixteenth centuries.[21] As the focal point of a *Genji* exegetical gathering, the leaves were not mere decoration but could be integrated into a culture of discussion and interpretation of the tale, and as such they continue to reward close analysis.

Coordinators: Sanjōnishi Sanetaka and Gensei

For guidance in creating a *Genji* compendium of the highest order there could be no better expert than Sanjōnishi Sanetaka (fig. 5). As a high-ranking member of the court hierarchy with ties through marriage to the imperial court, Sanetaka had direct access to the emperor and was a prolific and renowned poet, scholar, and calligrapher.[22] He is remembered as one of the most remarkable historical figures of the Muromachi period (1338–1573) in large part because of his meticulous sixty-year diary in which, among many other things, he recorded the details of Sue Saburō's *Genji Album* project.[23]

Sanetaka had been a cultural advisor and tutor serving members of the imperial family since young adulthood, and by the time he met the warrior from Suō Province had overseen countless projects involving the coordination of texts and images.[24] To his work on Sue Saburō's album Sanetaka brought years of experience studying the tale and making manuscript copies of the entire work for himself and others. He had also devoted considerable time to authoring works that would help readers understand *The Tale of Genji*, including an explanatory chart of the dizzying number of its characters and their complex interrelationships.[25] Nothing attests

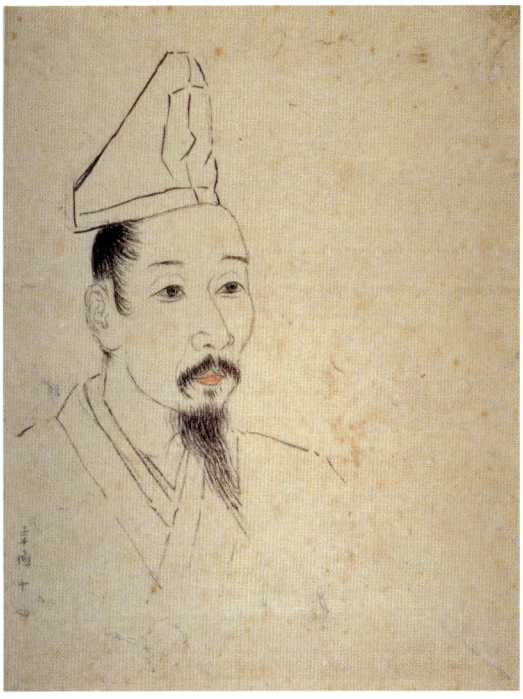

Fig. 5 *Portrait Sketch of Sanjōnishi Sanetaka*. By Tosa Mitsunobu. Dated 1501. Single sheet, ink on paper, 41.2 × 25.8 cm. Historiographical Institute, The University of Tokyo.

to Sanetaka's expertise better, however, than his immersion in the tradition of *Genji* commentaries.[26] These exegetical texts were usually based on previous commentaries as well as *Genji* lectures like those held at Hiroaki's residence, which could consist of several sessions, with a single chapter remaining the topic of discussion for as many as four or five days.[27] The lecturer would usually touch on the biography of Murasaki Shikibu, the genesis of the tale, the origin and meaning of the fifty-four chapter titles, and the structure of the narrative as a whole, as well as carrying out line-by-line readings and exegeses of the text. As mentioned, the album leaves commissioned by Sue Saburō were likely displayed during *Genji* lectures delivered by Jōseki at the Sue residence in 1510, and they may have even been created with this event in mind, which would have made the involvement of a scholar of Sanetaka's caliber invaluable.

Sue Saburō's introduction to the famous courtier came by way of another coordinator overseeing the album's production, the *renga* poet Gensei (1443–1521). Gensei's knowledge of *The Tale of Genji* rivaled that of Sanetaka, and this speaks to the importance of the tale as a source for *renga* poetry.[28] Handbooks provided appropriate "linking" words from *Genji*, boiling the narrative down to discrete units, including chapter titles, character names, and seasonal motifs, that formed the building blocks for new, collectively authored chains of poetry. New genres of *Genji*-specific *renga*, in which poets composed links exclusively related to the narrative and its poetry (*Genji kotoba renga*), came to rival traditional modes of linked verse.[29] There even arose a genre known as "*Genji* province-name *renga*" (*Genji kokumei renga*), in which poets composed verses based alternately on the names of provinces throughout the realm and the titles of the fifty-four *Genji* chapters.[30] At the same time it would be a mistake to overstate the influence of *renga* over *waka* in terms of medieval *Genji* reception, and the album's creation. *Waka* remained the dominant poetic form when it came to the creation of new poetry inspired by Murasaki's tale, and Gensei and *renga* masters like him left countless examples.[31] As the analyses of the texts and images in the pages that follow will attest, an emphasis on the use of specific semantic units (derived from *waka* as well as *renga*) to represent *Genji* scenes and the calligraphy of *Genji* texts helped shape the appearance of the leaves in the 1510 album. At the same time, Gensei's expertise extended to the entire content of the tale. Like Sanetaka, he was well versed in *Genji* commentaries and borrowed volumes of a commentary by Yotsutsuji Yoshinari (1326–1402), *Gleanings from the Rivers and Seas [of Genji Commentaries]* (*Kakaishō*, fourteenth century) at the start of the album project, no doubt to help facilitate conversations with the album's patron or to provide him with instruction on the tale.[??] *Renga* masters like Gensei typically rose from humble backgrounds and proved valuable as instructors to aristocrats as well as members of the military elite like the Ōuchi and Sue; they assisted their patrons in the successful navigation of poetry gatherings and regularly corresponded with them, correcting or sending advice on their written poems.[33] As they were not subject to the protocol that accompanied court rank or military status, they could function as mediators, moving among disparate social groups as go-betweens for a variety of transactions, and traveling throughout the country transporting texts and offering their services in distant provinces. Gensei was a disciple of Sōgi (1421–1502), the medieval period's most famous *renga* poet, who had traveled to the Ōuchi domains in 1480, and again in 1489, and had forged strong ties to the daimyo and their retainers, including Sue Hiroaki. Sōgi even counted among his disciples Sanetaka himself; although Sanetaka had been educated since early childhood in the Chinese and Japanese classics, it was Sōgi who trained him in a closely guarded tradition of exegesis of the first imperial *waka* anthology, the *Kokinshū*, as well as *The Tale of Genji*.[34] The shared connection of Gensei, Sanetaka, and Sue Hiroaki to the venerable Sōgi allowed Gensei to introduce his warrior patron to Sanetaka, which he did within six months of Sue Saburō's arrival in the capital.

Calligraphers: Aristocratic Traces

The album's production began in earnest when Saburō arrived at Sanetaka's residence early in the eighth month of 1509 bearing calligraphy papers (*shikishi*) to accompany a set of *Genji* pictures. These correspond to the fifty-four colorful papers that make up half of the album today. Sanetaka's diary does not mention the preparation of the *shikishi*, but they were certainly decorated by the time Sue Saburō handed them over, painted in five different colors—red, blue, yellow, pink, and green—and embellished with "dragon borders" that appear above, and on the right or left, of each rectangular sheet (fig. 6).[35] The colored papers emulate high-quality imported Chinese paper with similar dragon motifs that had been used primarily in Zen circles since the fourteenth century. Such Chinese-style paper is an interesting choice for the inscription of *The Tale of Genji*, a work of prose fiction (*monogatari*) and *waka* poetry written in *kana*, the phonetic Japanese script, usually considered antithetical to Chinese logographs, which were employed for official writing. The pairing of the five-colored Chinese-style dragon papers with *kana* calligraphy in fact embodies the aesthetic of *wa-kan*, a form of creative expression in art and literature that deliberately juxtaposed Japanese (*wa*) and Chinese (*kan*) cultural objects and practices.[36] In the case of Sue Saburō's *Genji Album*, this aesthetic choice may reflect his family's identity as Ōuchi retainers, men engaged in foreign trade, with claims to continental culture.

Inherent in the juxtaposition of *wa* and *kan* is also an underlying societal and cultural gender structure that associated official Sinitic writing with the masculine gender and vernacular writing in *kana* with the feminine. The latter was literally called "the female hand" (*onna-de*), a gendered mode of writing that, ironically, counted men as some of its most celebrated practitioners.[37] Certain leaves in the 1510 album employ some of the tropes of classical *onna-de* such as "scattered writing" (*chirashi gaki*), in which the *kana* do not appear in syntactical order in regular right-to-left columns but are distributed across the paper in meandering patterns. Chapter Sixteen in the album is the most conspicuous example, with a prose excerpt that begins in the center and zigzags across the sheet in a dizzying manner. But such leaves are relatively rare in the album. The calligraphy of the 1510 album is not in the quintessential *onna-de* style of Heian calligraphy, characterized by gossamer thin brushstrokes that vertically connect multiple phonemes into long flowing ligatures of contiguous lines of script. The writing is of the Muromachi period, and the six calligraphic hands of the album represent distinct calligraphic lineages of the early sixteenth century.[38] Even across these distinctive and identifiable stylistic lineages, however, there is a certain consistency in the use of bold strokes brushed in dark, voluptuous ink. The calligraphers primarily limit themselves to the *kana* syllabary, but strategically employ darkly inked and densely tectonic Sinitic logographs to great visual effect. The ink traces on these *shikishi* represent assertive calligraphic expressions brushed with clarity for maximum legibility, perhaps for screens, and the need to remain discernible when viewed across a room.

It was up to the coordinators of the project to ensure variety in the graphic design of the album's calligraphy. Sanetaka and Gensei both played a role in the organization of the album's texts, which involved selecting the excerpts, procuring the participation of the six calligraphers, and collecting and collating the sheets of writing. They began with the first of these tasks, the selection of texts, which they sent to the various calligraphers, along with instructions or templates.[39] The calligraphers were probably not, in other words, left entirely to their own devices in terms of the layout of their calligraphic assignments. Manuals on protocols for inscription of *shikishi* existed for just this purpose, which the calligraphers themselves may have used.[40] The calligraphers did have some artistic leeway, for example, in the way they responded to the dragon borders of each leaf in a different manner, sometimes ignoring and transgressing them, and other times skillfully using the borders to offset words or phrases of significance. The coordinators did, however, carefully orchestrate the color coordination of the sheets. They sent each of the six calligraphers a total of nine leaves and distributed the colored sheets in such a way that minimized repetition between calligraphic hand and paper hue in the sequence of the completed album.[41] As will be seen in the chapters ahead, the color of a calligraphy leaf often complements the subject matter of the text inscribed on its surface in ways that must have been more than mere coincidence.

The calligraphy of the *Genji Album* is brimming with visual appeal, and yet this effect was no doubt secondary in importance to the sum of the calligraphic and courtly lineages it represented, the "aristocratic body" that is inscribed into the work itself. Each of the hands were as indicative of the identity of the calligraphers as their names and court rank, which in fact endowed the leaves with value. The album becomes, through the hands of its six calligraphers, both a manual reproduction of the *Genji* and a calligraphic representation of

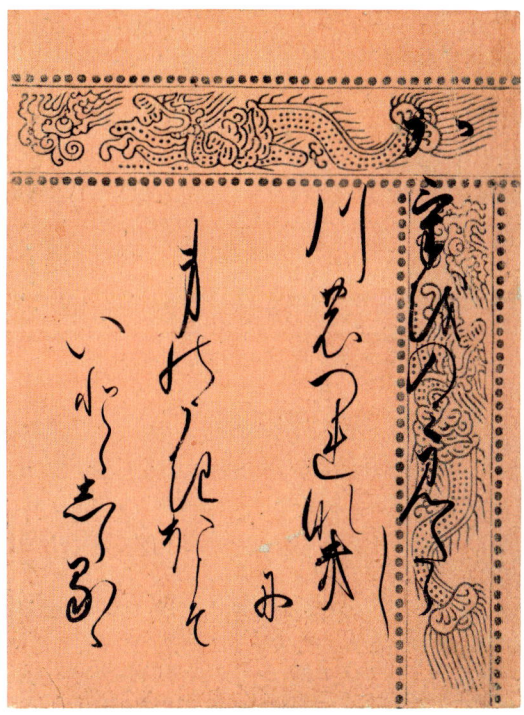

Fig. 6 Sanjōnishi Sanetaka (1455–1537), calligraphy for Leaves of Wild Ginger (Aoi), Chapter Nine from *The Tale of Genji Album*. 1510. Ink on paper, 24.3 × 18.1 cm. Harvard Art Museums, Cambridge.

courtly society that the Sue household could use to possess "the capital," even in the distant provinces.

Painters: Tosa Mitsunobu and the Painting Bureau

Although Sanetaka's diary does not mention the paintings for the *Genji Album*, there is no doubt that they were entrusted to the artist Tosa Mitsunobu (act. ca. 1462–1525), who had been Director of the Painting Bureau (*edokoro azukari*) since 1469.[42] Mitsunobu held that title (bestowed on him by both emperor and shogun) for over fifty years. It was a coveted post for a professional painter that carried a certain amount of financial stability and a steady stream of commissions from a varied clientele beyond the court and shogunate for paintings of all kinds, including Buddhist icons, mortuary portraits, narrative handscrolls, fans, and of course *Genji* paintings. The number of extant works by Mitsunobu show him to be one of the most prolific and successful artists of medieval Japan, and his name is associated with several artistic innovations of the period.[43] As Chino Kaori first demonstrated, the unsigned paintings of the 1510 *Genji Album* are stylistically a perfect fit with Mitsunobu's other known works.[44] Mitsunobu was in many ways the most logical artist to entrust with such a task. His prestigious title and relatively high court rank endowed his paintings with a certain cachet, and to the members of the Sue house his works would have epitomized court culture itself. Mitsunobu was also the painterly counterpart to calligraphers and poets such as Sanetaka and Gensei and had in fact collaborated with both men before.[45] Mitsunobu's interactions with this coterie of courtier-scholars, which included discussions concerning *The Tale of Genji* and frequent participation in poetry gatherings, resulted in paintings that exhibit a sophisticated understanding of the literary canon that he was so often asked to visualize.[46]

The painted leaves of the 1510 album evoke narrative paintings of the earlier Heian period, with their vibrant palette of mineral pigments, shell white for the powdered faces of aristocrats, and fine ink lines for details (fig. 7).[47] While the clothing of figures is gorgeously represented, their faces, namely those of elites, are depicted with an economy of means. The preferred vocabulary that has developed to describe them refers to the "lines" employed for the eyes and the "hooks" that delineate the noses (*hikime kagihana*). One of the most striking elements of these paintings is their abundant use of wafting gold clouds to frame and order each composition, and the interplay between the organic shapes of these clouds and the straight lines and zigzagging diagonals of the architectural components. The paintings are divided between outdoor scenes in which typically a group of figures takes part in a courtly ritual or activity, and indoor scenes in which the roofs are "blown off" (*fukinuki yatai*) to provide full visual access to interiors. This technique of direct access to a scene from a high vantage point is part of a mode of representation that differs from paintings that employ a one-point perspective, or that organize a composition along an imagined horizon line. Thus, rather than depicting the action of narrative scenes within a framework of illusionistic space, in which characters and motifs decrease in size and placement according to a coherent, if unseen grid of seemingly quantifiable spatial relationships, these paintings demonstrate other organizational priorities. A figure's larger size or prominence in any given painted scene is often indicative of a textual emphasis on their interiority in the corresponding narrative passage, or their centrality to the action of the scene. This sliding scale of visual emphasis weighted according to narrative content has been described as a system of "psychological perspective," which emerged out of the symbiosis of word and image in Heian period literature.[48] Such a pictorial system provides an appropriate counterpart to the reading experience of *Genji*, which affords relatively unmediated access to characters' thoughts. It continued to be the primary mode of *Genji* representation with modifications in style and format over the centuries. The paintings in the 1510 album thus employed long-standing techniques of courtly narrative painting and established a *Genji Album* tradition that would continue with members of the Tosa and Sumiyoshi schools among others.

Mitsunobu's paintings stand out, however, as qualitatively different from all *Genji* album paintings that come afterward. These differences are manifest in their use of pigments (relatively light and transparent in certain areas), the sketchy quality of faces and other details, and the prevalence of a wavy line to define rocks, hills, and trees. The approach is unique within so-called *yamato-e* (Japanese-style pictures) of the era, and it signals an artist interested in incorporating certain characteristics of Sino-Japanese ink painting, calligraphic line and wash effects, into the realm of polychrome narrative paintings. The very process by which narrative paintings are made, however, renders this a difficult endeavor. They consist of "built-up pictures" (*tsukuri-e*), for which the lead artist provides a master drawing in ink, usually containing notations about color and other details, that other studio artists then complete (see fig. 10). Layers of mineral pigments and gold foil clouds obscure the artist's hand in narrative paintings and put them at a remove conceptually from ink paintings, which aim to connect viewers viscerally with the energy and persona of the artist through the vitality of exposed calligraphic line. The hand of the master artist could reemerge, however, through the addition of finishing touches in black ink after the color had been applied to the paintings. At this stage, Mitsunobu introduced his signature artistic feature, the tremulous lines that resonate with the indexical brushwork of the ink painting tradition, and they imbue Mitsunobu's paintings with an individuality that seems lacking in many other *Genji* pictures.

Mitsunobu's formal Sinitic pictorial inflections tend to appear only on the margins of the paintings, however, and do not impact the representation of the main characters and motifs, which were expected to maintain the tradition of depicting courtly characters with a degree of sameness. In courtly painting, differentiation occurred through the subtlest of distinctions, like the razor-thin strokes that textured the eyes and eyebrows, the tilt of a character's head, or the relationship of the figure to surrounding figures and motifs. Most importantly, however, difference was *read into* each scene by a viewer informed by an accompanying textual excerpt. Mitsunobu's artistry in the *Genji Album* is most apparent in the way in which he closely calibrates each image with its corresponding inscribed leaf and his larger knowledge of the tale. Such inscriptions, as mentioned, were no longer the long descriptive prose passages excerpted for handscroll illustrations of the *Genji*, as in earlier works, but allusive poems and brief prose passages chosen for their relevance to the body of secondary texts, linked verse gatherings, and Noh dramas that characterized late medieval *Genji* culture. Viewers projected identities onto and thereby individualized the figures within the *Genji Album* by taking cues from the accompanying excerpt and its associations. In other words, while a degree of sameness was integral to Mitsunobu's practice, to informed viewers, these images with their subtle differences were far from repetitive.

The sheer length of *The Tale of Genji* meant that each of the fifty-four chapters offered countless pos-

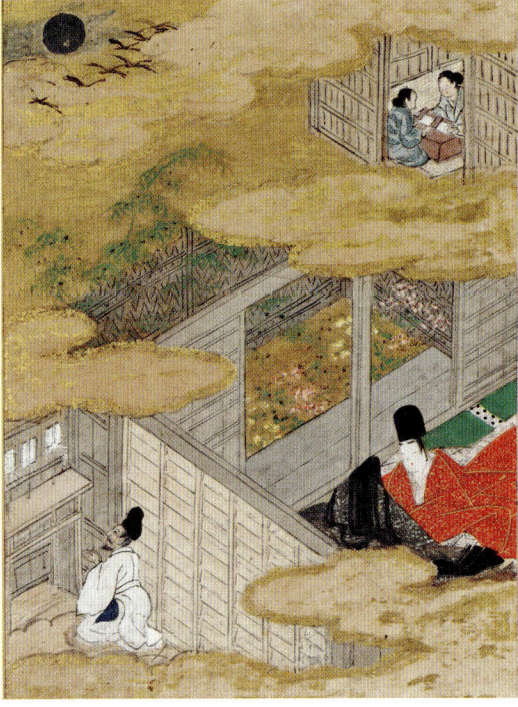

Fig. 7 Tosa Mitsunobu (act. ca 1462–1525), painting for The Lady of the Evening Faces (Yūgao), Chapter Four from *The Tale of Genji Album*. 1510. Ink on paper, 24.3 x 18.1 cm. Harvard Art Museums, Cambridge.

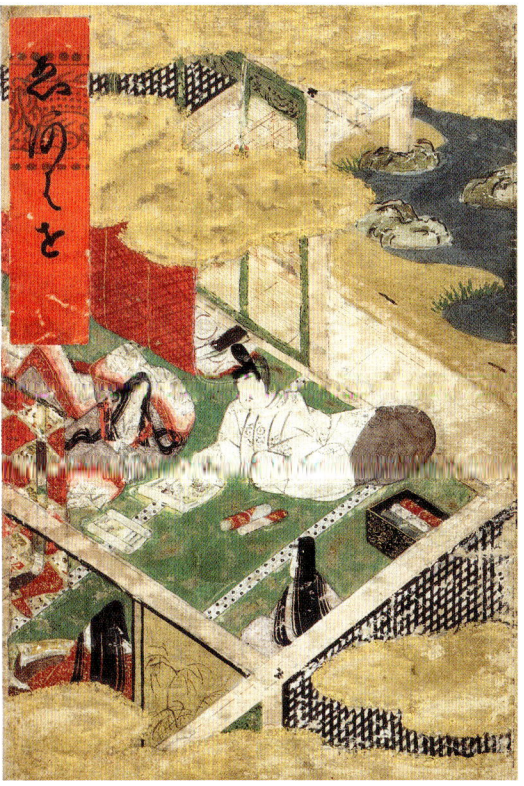 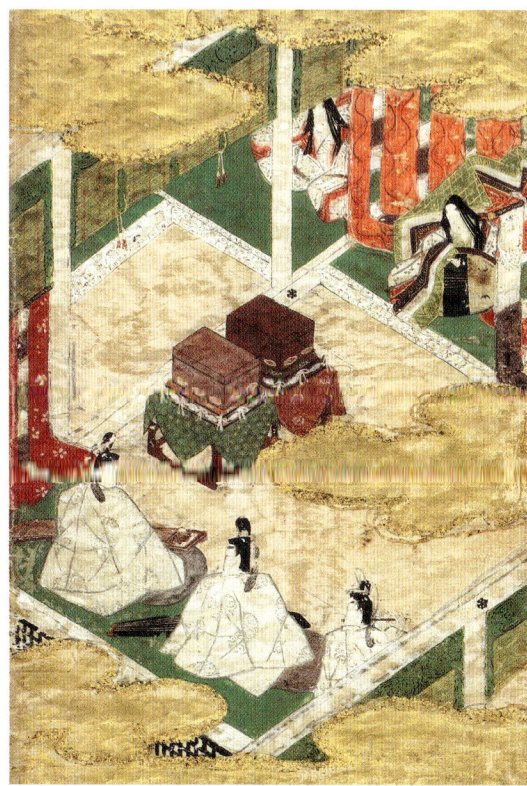

Fig. 8 *A Contest of Illustrations (Eawase)*, Chapter Seventeen of *The Tale of Genji*. By Tosa Mitsunobu. Circa early sixteenth century. One thread-bound book with paintings on front cover (*left*), and back cover (*right*). Ink, colors, and gold on paper, 25.4 × 17.2 cm. Tenri University Library, Nara.

sible scenes for illustration, and though the patron no doubt made his preferences known, he, the coordinators, and Mitsunobu would have worked from preexisting templates. The majority of paintings in the 1510 *Genji Album* in fact depict scenes included in picture manuals and digests of the period, which provided patrons of *Genji* pictures with a menu of text and image options for every chapter in the tale.[49] Sanetaka was known to have borrowed, at least once, a five-volume *"Genji* picture manual" (*Genji eyō sōshi*) for another project years later.[50] Mitsunobu had in fact been catering to patrons and coordinators armed with such manuals since early in his career. In 1476, for example, the courtier Nakanoin Michihide (1428–1494) offered comments on several *Genji* paintings executed by the Painting Bureau (Mitsunobu), having consulted a *"Genji* picture manual" (*Genji no eyō*) and its "esoterica" (*hiji*) on his own.[51] He mentions scenes of the "Hatsune" and "Nowaki" chapters, for example, and the costumes of their painted figures, demonstrating how patrons or coordinators could critique the smallest details of an artist's work. By the time Mitsunobu was commissioned to create Sue's *Genji* pictures, he brought some thirty-five years of experience and feedback from an exacting clientele.

While such manuals gave patrons and coordinators ideas about which scenes and specific elements of *Genji* iconography to request, an artist of Mitsunobu's stature would have had his own store of drawings to be handed down within his studio to represent its unique approach to visualizing the tale.

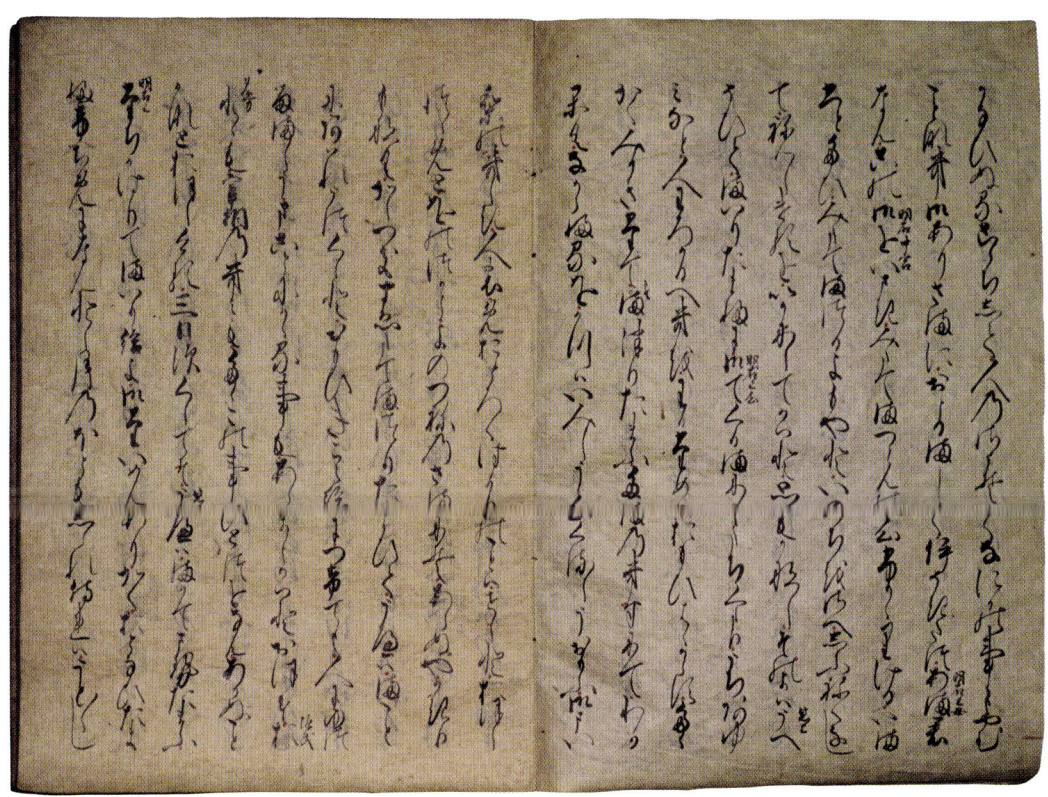

Fig. 9 *Shoots of Wisteria Leaves* (*Fuji no uraba*), Chapter Thirty-Three of *The Tale of Genji*. Calligraphy attributed to Kanroji Motonaga (1457–1527), ca. early sixteenth century. One thread-bound book, ink on paper, 25.4 × 34.4 cm. Idemitsu Museum of Art, Tokyo.

Such templates would have been necessary, moreover, because of the sheer number of paintings his studio was called on to produce. He was asked, for example, to create the front and back cover illustrations for sets of individually bound *Genji* chapters, requiring a total of 108 paintings, two for each chapter. Two volumes from an original set of such fifty-four chapter books with Mitsunobu's cover paintings survive today (figs. 8, 9, and ref. fig., Ch. 33) and provide a glimpse of the luxuriousness of these book sets. The calligraphy on the rectangular title slips in the upper left corner of the front covers appears to be in the hand of Emperor GoKashiwabara (1462–1526), while the interior text of the chapters has been attributed to prominent courtiers active in the early sixteenth century.[52] The text of the Shoots of Wisteria Leaves chapter book (fig. 9) has been attributed to the courtier Kanroji Motonaga (1457–1527), and it shows how the calligrapher added the names of characters, as they had come to be known by the sixteenth century, in the margins, where the original text uses only official titles or elides the referent altogether. The handwritten text thus suggests a reader familiar with *The Tale of Genji*, but one who would have been aided by these notes of identification.[53]

While only two volumes from what was likely an original set of fifty-four survive, copies of the front and back covers of additional volumes by Mitsunobu were made in the seventeenth century (fig. 10).[54] Some of the drawings represent *Genji* scenes that are nearly identical to ones of the same chapter in the 1510 album, while others show alter-

Introduction | 13

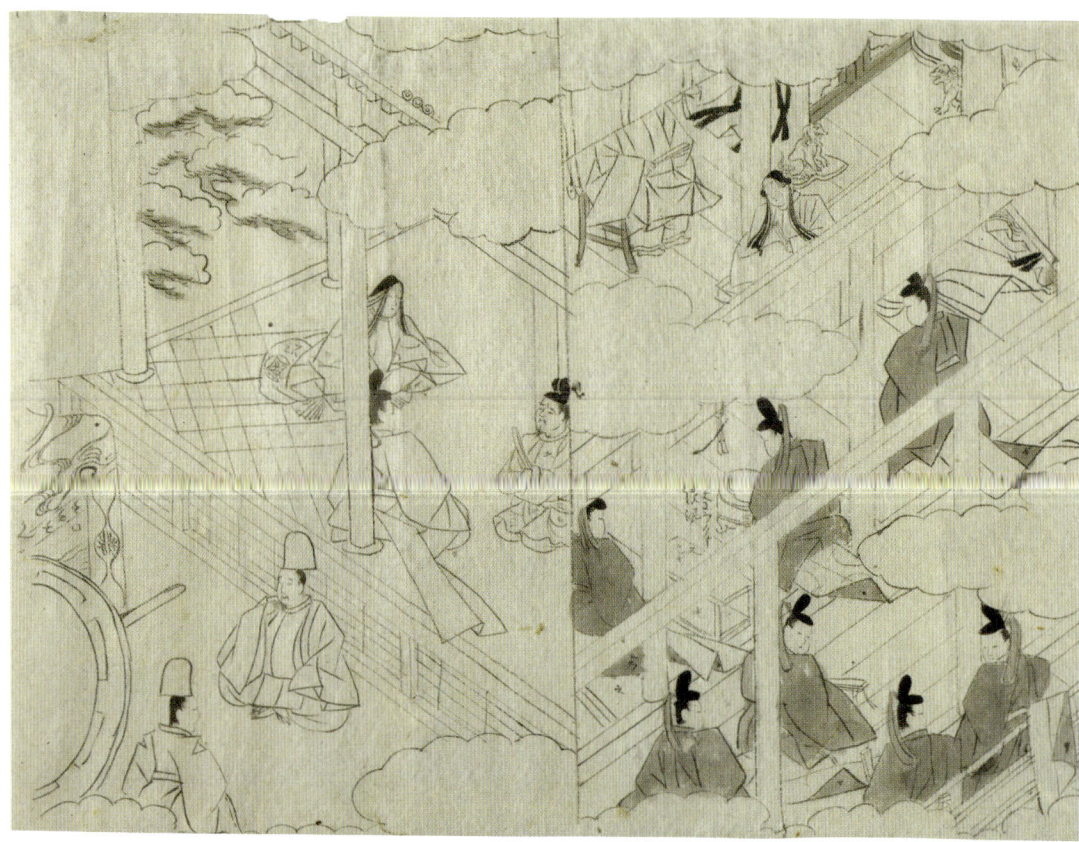

Fig. 10 *Copies of Book Cover Paintings by Tosa Mitsunobu*. By Sumiyoshi Gukei (1631–1705). Dated 1675. Section showing the designs for The Lady of the Paulownia-Courtyard Chambers (Kiritsubo), Chapter One of *The Tale of Genji*, front cover (*left*) and back cover (*right*). Single handscroll, ink and light color on paper, paper sizes differ: sheets 1–10: 27.3 × 348.9 cm; sheets 11–26: 23.5 × 417.3 cm, total width 766.2 cm. Tokyo National Museum.

native compositions. The book-cover drawings also add more to our understanding of what readers in Mitsunobu's day considered to be the most defining moments of a given *Genji* chapter. Take for example the two drawings for the book covers of Chapter One, shown here, where on the front cover we find young Genji meeting the Korean physiognomist whose prognostication about Genji's future hovers over the entire tale. It is in part based on this fortune telling that Genji's father, the Emperor, decides to make him a commoner, and thus his coming-of-age ceremony is held in the private quarters of the imperial residence, rather than the official hall of state, as depicted on the back cover of the book, and in the first painting in the 1510 album. The book covers show these two events in chronological order, front to back, and alert the reader to scenes that deserve special attention while suggesting intriguing associations, and even causal links between the scenes.[55] The patron and coordinators of the 1510 album may have considered both of these painting options out of a menu of designs, but they ultimately selected the image of Genji's coming-of-age ceremony. By doing so they made sure the first image in the album included a view of the iconic Heian palace, the figure of the Emperor, and a composition that hints at the political and interpersonal relationships between the sovereign, the Minister of the Left, and Genji.

Content and Interpretation

Based on these sketches of now lost chapter volumes and extant *Genji* paintings, it becomes clear that scenes that might be construed as inauspicious went unrepresented. As a rule, formal polychrome *Genji* paintings omit scenes depicting episodes of spirit possession, as well as childbirth, or illness (conditions that usually render a person vulnerable to an attacking spirit). The absence of such subject matter hints at the degree to which images were assumed to instantiate the things they represented. Episodes depicting behavior deemed controversial within the world of the story are also avoided in emblematic pictorial representation. Examples include Genji's abduction of the young Murasaki, which shocks the surrounding characters, or his sexual violation of Murasaki four years later at the end of Chapter Nine, the traumatic nature of which is registered through Murasaki's reaction. Given the nature of the function of albums and screens and fans of *Genji*, such complicated scenes might not reflect well on the patrons. And when albums and manuscript sets with illustrated covers were made as part of bridal trousseaus for young women, there arose a need to recast aspects of *Genji* to suit the ideology of marriage and the importance of wifely duties undertaken for the good of a lineage. That is not to say, however, that difficult passages and emotionally complex episodes do not have a place in the 1510 album or other examples; like *Genji* itself, the pictures accommodate different levels of interpretation.

Often artists would adhere to standard iconography, while in other instances, they eschewed common templates altogether to create unique images customized to the interests or demands of specific patrons. Several scenes in the 1510 album seem tailor-made for the Sue house, those for Chapters Six, Twelve, Eighteen, and Twenty-Five, as will be explained. In general, the album's paintings have the cumulative effect of emphasizing Genji as the protagonist; he is often placed front and center in the composition beneath a floating gold cloud that functions as an emphatic rhetorical device. Such an emphasis is not necessarily a given, despite the centrality of Genji in the narrative. The preponderance of fully realized female characters in the tale, as well as women-centered scenes of dialogue and interaction, meant that patrons, if they so desired, could select illustrations that might make Genji seem like a minor character.[56] The album's focus on Genji therefore represents, if not a deliberate choice, then at least a predilection. Scenes of all-male gatherings are also conspicuous in the album, which aligns with the culture of *Genji* lectures and poetry gatherings from which women were almost always excluded.[57] Knowing the historical context of the patron, these choices seem unsurprising. A preponderance of such scenes not only reflects but also helps shape a narrative world in which the patron may, if he chooses, identify with Genji and aspire toward some of his power and privilege and charm, and perhaps even his self-scrutiny.

That is not to say, however, that the presence and voices of female characters, so well-articulated in the tale by its female author, are diminished in the 1510 album's representation of *The Tale of Genji*; quite the contrary. Many scenes in the album feature female

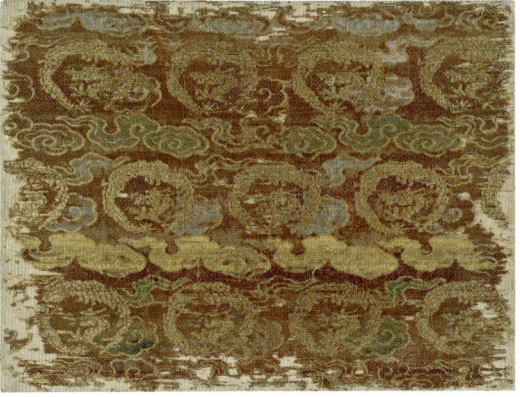

Fig. 11 *The Tale of Genji Album*, previous cover. Edo period (1615–1868), silk lampas, with gold and silver threads, 34.1 × 42 cm. Harvard Art Museums, Cambridge.

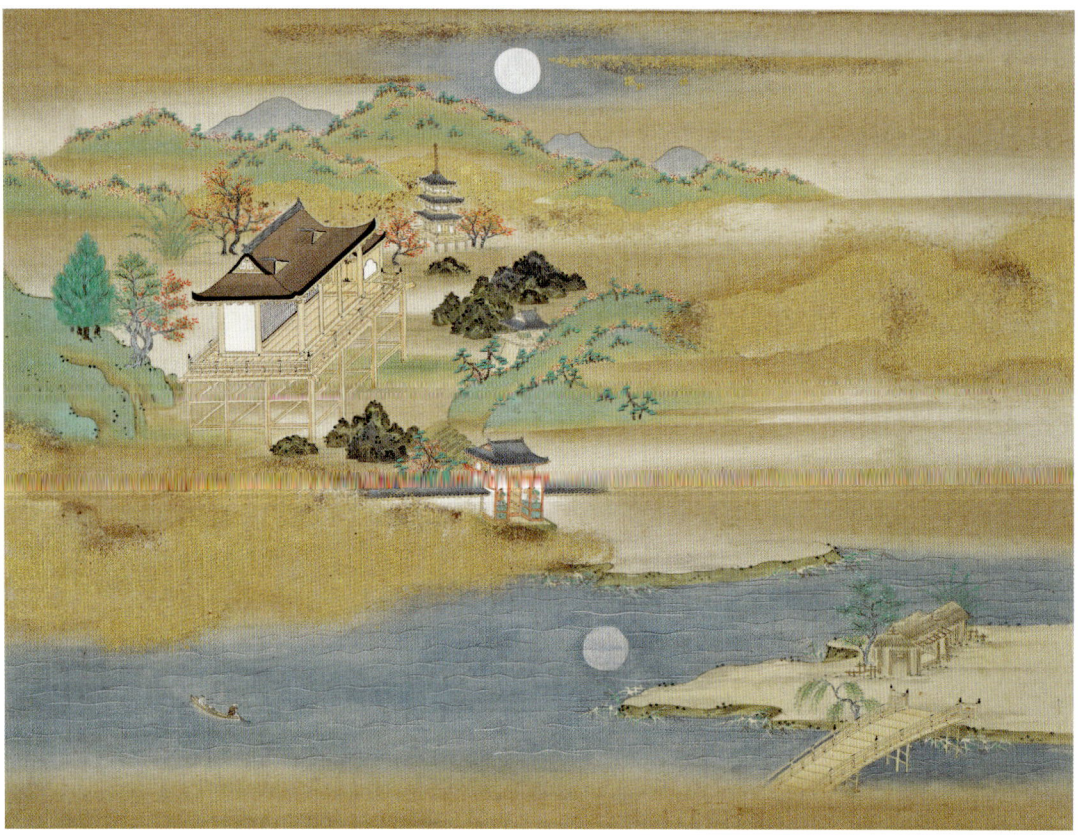

Figs. 12, 13 *The Tale of Genji Album*. Frontispiece (*right*), finispiece (*left*) attributed to Tosa Mitsuoki (1617–1691). Ink, colors, and gold on silk, 34.1 × 42 cm. Harvard Art Museums, Cambridge.

characters on their own, and when read in conjunction with the adjacent prose and poetry excerpts, the pairs of leaves give expression to a panoply of their thoughts, concerns, and actions. The album's producers may not have been especially sympathetic to such characters but may have been simply responding to the centrality of women in the tale and their pivotal role within the marriage politics of the Heian era. It can be just as rewarding therefore to analyze the album's juxtapositions of paintings and texts within the context of Murasaki's eleventh-century tale. In this way, viewers of the album today need not limit themselves to considering only what it meant to its audience in 1510, and it is in this spirit that I offer these analyses of the album's texts and images. While paying close attention to sixteenth-century concerns and how the creators of the album may have interpreted the story, the pages that follow provide synopses of the chapters and interpretations of each scene in the album based on my own understanding of Murasaki's tale, drawing from and building on the rich tradition of scholarship on *The Tale of Genji* that began in the medieval period and that continues to this day.

The 1510 *Genji Album* was remounted during the Edo period, placed between covers of Chinese brocade (fig. 11) and adorned with frontispiece and finispiece paintings on silk that provide an appropriate visual frame for the world of the story (figs. 12, 13). These newly added paintings are attributed to the artist Tosa Mitsuoki (1617–1691), and they

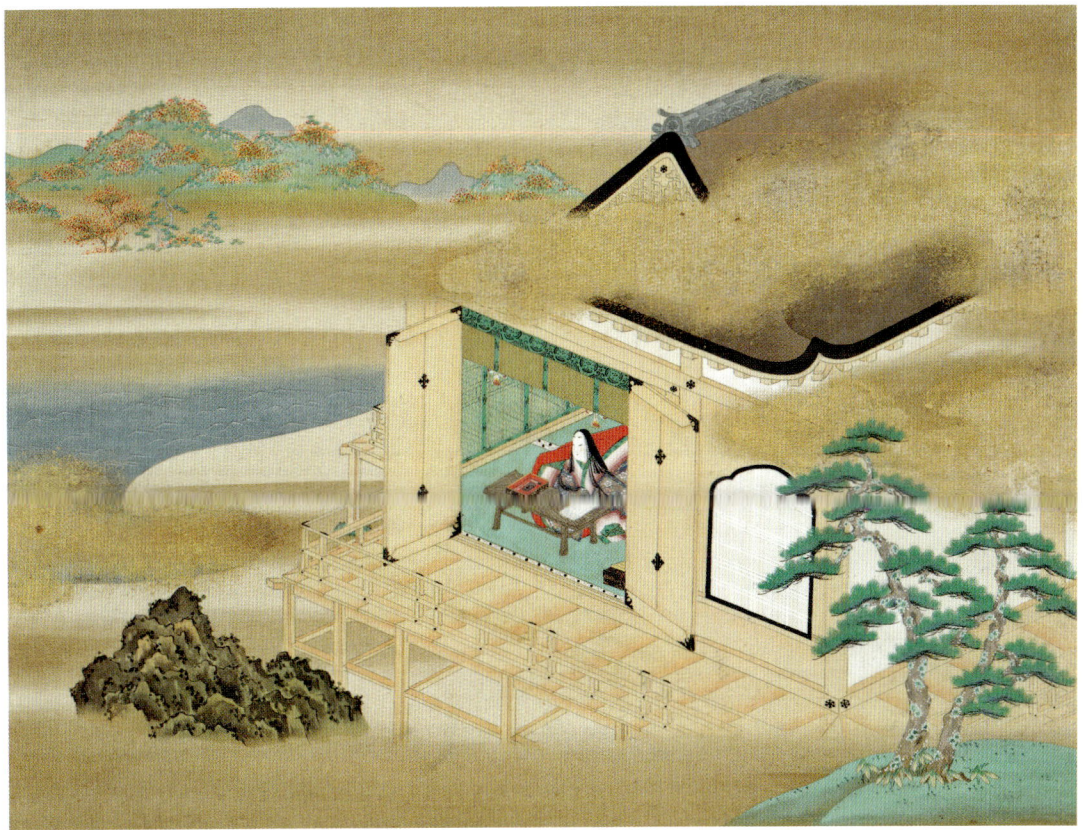

depict the famous legend of the genesis of *The Tale of Genji*, showing Murasaki Shikibu composing her masterpiece at Ishiyamadera. As the story goes, she had been charged by Her Highness the Empress Jōtōmon'in (Fujiwara no Shōshi 988–1074) with the task of writing a new tale and traveled to Ishiyamadera to pray to its famous Nyoirin Kannon for inspiration. On the fifteenth night of the eighth month, the night in autumn when the moon was at its fullest and most luminous, she looked out from her temple perch over Lake Biwa, gazed on the glowing orb reflected on the surface of the water, and suddenly the idea was born. She picked up her brush, but with no paper at hand, reached for the scrolls of the *Great Perfection of Wisdom Sutra* (*Daihannyakyō*) resting on the Buddhist altar, turned them over, and began writing the Suma and Akashi chapters of her tale.

Opening the album today, we first see Murasaki at her desk imagining her tale, then turn the pages to experience all fifty-four chapters of her completed work in microcosm. The source of Murasaki's contemplation, the moon reflected on the waters of Lake Biwa, appears in the finispiece, only visible to us after we have turned over the final leaf of the album. There we find a view of the temple in its landscape with the bright white disc of the moon glowing in the sky while its illusory counterpart floats on the water below. The temple's main hall stands to the left, complete with the Chinese-style window that marks the famous "Genji room" where Murasaki was said to have composed her tale. The figure of Murasaki has disappeared from the painting, but her work lives on. The album beckons us to join centuries of readers who have come before to experience and reimagine her tale.

Introduction | 17

Notes

1. Philip Hofer, "On Collecting Japanese Manuscript Scrolls," *Book Collector* 7 (1958): 369–80; he mentions the *Genji Album* on p. 375.

2. The style of *The Tale of Genji* was thus especially striking for literary modernists at the turn of the twentieth century experimenting with new modes of narration, such as Virginia Woolf and Raymond Mortimer, who in his review of Arthur Waley's translation of the tale described Murasaki's carefully drawn characters as always "wondering what impression they are making and what is going on in other people's minds." Mortimer, "A New Planet," *Nation and Athenæum* 37, no. 12 (1925), 371. Exceptional scholarship in English on the reception of *Genji* in the late nineteenth and early twentieth centuries includes Michael Emmerich, *The Tale of Genji: Translation, Canonization, and World Literature* (New York: Columbia University Press, 2013); Patrick W. Caddeau, *Appraising Genji: Literary Criticism and Cultural Anxiety in the Age of the Last Samurai* (New York: State University of New York Press, 2006); Gaye Rowely, *Yosano Akiko and The Tale of Genji*, Michigan Monograph Series in Japanese Studies 28 (Ann Arbor: Center for Japanese Studies, University of Michigan, 2000).

3. The *Ukifune* booklet in the Yamato Bunkakan Museum consists of two illustrations and thirty pages of text from the latter half of the chapter preserved in book form; another twenty-three pages of text and three illustrations from the first part of the chapter survive in the Tokugawa Art Museum, remounted as a handscroll.

4. The most famous early reader of *Genji* was a woman known as "Sugawara no Takasue's daughter," author of the literary memoir *The Sarashina Diary* (*Sarashina nikki*). She describes receiving all "fifty-some chapters" of the tale at the age of fourteen in the year 1020, then immersing herself in reading "scroll after scroll." The account is not a simple record of reading habits, but deliberately highlights the author's own formation as a writer through her relationship to *Genji*. See *Sarashina nikki*, in *Shinpen nihon koten bungaku zenshū*, ed. Fujioka Tadaharu et al. (Tokyo: Shōgakkan, 1994), 26: 298. For a translation and study of the author's relationship to *Genji*, see Sonja Arntzen and Itō Moriyuki, *The Sarashina Diary* (New York: Columbia University Press, 2014).

5. The era of *The Tale of Genji* painting and calligraphy album truly began in the Edo period (1615–1868), when artists, primarily those of the Tosa school, produced albums in great numbers, often to be a part of bridal trousseau. *Genji* albums by Tosa Mitsuyoshi (1539–1613), Tosa Mitsunori (1583–1638), Tosa Mitsuoki (1617–1691), and Sumiyoshi Jokei (1598–1670) are characteristic examples, and they differ from the 1510 album in appearance and tone. Important studies on several of these albums include: Sakakibara Satoru, "Sumiyoshi-ha 'Genji-e' kaidai: Tsukusho bon kotobagaki," *Suntory Bijutsukan ronshū* 3 (1989): 5–181; Kawada Masayuki, "'Genji monogatari tekagami' kō," 84–115, in *Izumi-shi Kubosō Kinen Bijutsukan Genji monogatari tekagami kenkyū* (Izumi-shi: Izumi-shi Kubosō Kinen Bijutsukan, 1992); Sakakibara Satoru, ed., *Edo meisaku gajō zenshū* 5, *Tosa-ha, Sumiyoshi-ha: Mitsunori, Mitsuoki, Gukei* (Tokyo: Shinshindō, 1993); Inamoto Mariko, "Kyoto Kokuritsu Hakubutsukan hokan 'Genji monogatari gajō' ni kansuru ichi kōsatsu: Chōjirō ni yoru jūfuku roku bamen wo megutte," *Kokka* 1223 (1997): 7–15; and Kano Hiroyuki et al., eds., *Kyoto Kokuritsu Hakubutsukan zō Genji monogatari gajō* (Tokyo: Benseisha, 1997).

6. The connection between the diary entries and the Harvard *Genji Album* was first put forth in Melissa McCormick, "Hābādo Bijutsukan zō 'Genji monogatari gajō' to 'Sanetaka kōki' shosai no 'Genji-e shikishi,'" *Kokka* 1241 (1999): 27–28.

7. Mitamura Masako, "Ashikaga Yoshimitsu no seigaiha 'chūsei Genji monogatari' no ryōiki," *Monogatari kenkyū* 1 (2001): 55–70.

8. A number of individuals throughout time, especially writers preoccupied with the tale and with periods of exile or isolation in their histories, explicitly likened themselves to Genji and understood his story as one of redemption. The sixteenth-century courtier Kujō Tanemichi (1507–1594), author of the *Genji* commentary *Mōshinshō* (1575) and grandson of Sanjōnishi Sanetaka, is one such example, as pointed out by Ii Haruki, "Kujō Tanemichi to 'Genji monogatari kyōenki,'" in *Genji monogatari chūshakushi no kenkyū*, *Muromachi zenki* (Tokyo: Ōfūsha, 1980), 1069. In the Edo period, Kumazawa Banzan used a neo-Confucian reading of Genji's character to interpret the tale as a form of protest literature against the authoritarian Tokugawa regime; see James McMullen, *Idealism, Protest, and the Tale of Genji: The Confucianism of Kumazawa Banzan (1619–91)* (Oxford: Clarendon Press, 1999). At the same time, a male writer's ability to identify with both Genji and Murasaki Shikibu the author could potentially transform his understanding of the self within existing paradigms of gender and literary genre; see J. Keith Vincent, "Purple and White: Shiki and Sōseki's Homosocial *Genji*," forthcoming in *The Tale of Genji: A Norton Critical Edition* (New York: Norton, 2019), edited by Dennis Washburn.

9. Melissa McCormick, "Murasaki's 'Mind Ground': A Buddhist Theory of the Novel," in James McMullen, ed., *Oxford Studies in Philosophy and Literature: Murasaki Shikibu's The Tale of Genji* (Oxford University Press, forthcoming).

10. The legend of the tale's miraculous origins is recounted later in this introduction. For more on the way Murasaki Shikibu came to be worshipped as a bodhisattva, see the analysis of the earliest dated Buddhist portrait-icon of the author in Melissa McCormick, "Purple Displaces Crimson: The *Wakan* Dialectic as Polemic," in *Around Chigusa: Tea and the Arts of Sixteenth-Century Japan*, ed. Dora Ching, Louise Allison Cort, and Andrew Warsky (Princeton, NJ: Princeton University Press, 2017), 181–208. For a comprehensive and insightful account of the reception history of the author see Satoko Naito, "The Making of Murasaki Shikibu: Constructing Authorship, Gendering Readership, and Legitimizing *The Tale of Genji*" (PhD diss., Columbia University, 2010), which includes accounts of how the author was said to suffer in hell for the sin of writing fiction.

11. For more detail on the historical and literary context of the album, which can only be partially addressed here, see Melissa McCormick, "Genji Goes West: The 1510 *Genji Album* and the Visualization of Court and Capital," *Art Bulletin* 85, no. 1 (2003): 54–85.

12. Hiroaki copied the entire chronicle over the course of twenty years, acquiring various recensions to complete his for-

ty-eight-volume manuscript in 1522, one year before his death. Although it currently lacks thirteen years from the eighty-six-year span of the original, Hiroaki's text contains few errors and is considered one of the best surviving versions of the *Azuma kagami*; see Yamaguchi Kenritsu Bijutsukan, *Muromachi bunka no naka ni miru Ōuchi bunka no ihōten* (Yamaguchi-shi: Yamaguchi Kenritsu Bijutsukan, 1989), 140, n. 2.

13. Hiroaki wrote the notations himself on Eishō 13 (1516), 4.3. He carefully recorded in one central line the name of each calligrapher and a statement of donation ("Tōyō dedicates this to Myōeiji"), followed by the name "Hiroaki" and his seal. The same vermilion, intaglio seal appears at the end of Hiroaki's manuscript copy of the *Azuma kagami*. For more details, see the conservation report in Oka Bokkōdō, *Shūfuku*, vol. 6 (Kyoto: Oka Bokkōdō, 2000), 6–16 and 51 for a summary in English.

14. A manuscript copy of *The Tale of Genji* in the Tenri University Library contains a colophon that mentions a written *Genji* commentary (*kikigaki*) based on *Genji* lectures delivered by Sōseki at the residence of "Sue Hiroaki, Governor of Aki Province," in Eishō 13 (1516). Kido Saizō, in his study on the history of *renga* mentions this text in passing, see his *Renga shi ronkō jō* (Tokyo: Meiji Shōin, 1993), 607.

15. It should be noted that despite the predominately male audience of the *Genji Album* and its immediate milieu of poets and scholars, *The Tale of Genji* enjoyed a continued female readership over the course of the medieval period. Women too authored *Genji* commentaries in the sixteenth century, and the first disciple to receive the "*Genji* teachings" from Kujō Tanemichi (see n. 8) was the woman Kyōkōin Nyoshun'ni (1544–1598); Ii Haruki, "*Mōshinshō* no seiritsu," in Nomura Sei'ichi, ed., *Mōshinshō*, vol. 6 of *Genji monogatari kochū shūsei* (Tokyo: Ōfūsha, 1978), 505.

16. This copy of the *Kokinshū* was created at Sue's request by Sanjōnishi Sanetaka, as he records in his diary *Sanetaka kōki* on 7.28 in what was likely Eishō 11 (1514); see Sanjōnishi Sanetaka, *Sanetaka kōki*, 4th ed., ed. by Takahashi Ryūzō (Tokyo: Zoku Gunsho Ruijū Kanseikai, 2000), 10: 673. All subsequent citations refer to this edition. Sōseki may have become Hiroaki's main conduit to the capital after Sue Saburō's return, as he was for other provincial military households, such as the Imagawa. On Eishō 17 (1520) 4.2, Sōseki requests that Sanetaka write a postscript and chapter titles for a copy of *Genji* owned by "Sue, Governor of Hyōgo," (*Sanetaka kōki*, 10: 711), demonstrating that Hiroaki had a complete copy by this time if not earlier.

17. A collection of excerpted *renga* verses by Sōseki called *Gesson no nukiku* includes verses composed at the residence of "Sue, Governor of Hyōgo," another title by which Hiroaki was known, on both the Tanabata festival (the seventh day of the seventh month), and on the fifteenth of the eighth month. Kido Saizō surmised that Sōseki was in the environs of Yamaguchi for at least two months on that occasion; see Kido, *Renga shi ronkō jō*, 606–7. The original manuscript of *Gesson no nukiku* can be found in the Archives of the Imperial Household (MS 353–66).

18. The link between the 1516 *Genji* lectures and the Sue *Genji Album* is discussed in McCormick, "*Genji* Goes West," 65–66, which includes more details on the work's donation to Myōeiji and the familial context.

19. In the upper left corner of each original backing paper for the fifty-four pairs of leaves an inscription reads, "out of the fifty-four total on the screen surface" (*heimen tsugō gojūyon mai no uchi* 屏面都合五十四枚内). Conservators also detected traces of gold leaf on the edges of the backing papers, indicating that they were once pasted onto a ground of gold leaf, common to folding screens; see Oka Bokkōdō, *Shūfuku*, vol. 6 (Kyoto: Oka Bokkōdō, 2000). In addition, Anne Rose Kitagawa determined that the discoloration of certain leaves could only have resulted from their placement on folding-screen panels abutting each other when closed, and posited the placement of the leaves on a hypothetical pair of folding screens; see Kitagawa, "Behind the Scenes of Harvard's Tale of Genji Album," *Apollo* 154, no. 477 (2001): 38–35; Chino, Ikeda, and Kamei also speculated that the leaves were once affixed to folding screens, based on the popularity of the format in this period, as well as the absence of other albums from the early sixteenth century; see Chino Kaori, Ikeda Shinobu, and Kamei Wakana, "Hābādo Daigaku Bijutsukan zō 'Genji monogatari gajō' o meguru shomondai," *Kokka* no. 1222 (1997): 11–24. This publication, a special issue of the art history journal *Kokka*, presented the first substantial research on the album and was spearheaded by Chino Kaori, who invited the participation of twenty-three other scholars.

20. This information appears in the upper right corner on the backing paper of each pair of leaves and reads, for example, "back 13, Sacred Rites of the Law" (*ushiro jūsan Minori*). The leaves for Chapters 1–27 were labeled "front" (*zen*) 1–27, while those for Chapters 28–54 were labeled "back" (*go*) 1–27, thus "back 13" corresponds to Chapter 40. Although the leaves may have been mounted on screens, the numbering system here would have been appropriate for a single-volume accordian-style album with Chapters 1–27 on the front, and Chapters 28–54 on the back. This was the format of the album when it first entered the Harvard Art Museums, thought to be the result of an Edo period remounting. The sequencing of the calligraphers and paper colors also roughly corresponds to this division (see the Album Calligraphy Key in the appendix herein), suggesting that the album was conceptualized as such and that the inscriptions record the original order in anticipation of a future remounting back to the album format, which is indeed what happened.

21. In one well-known early example, *Genji* paintings on *shikishi* were said to have been mounted onto a pair of folding screens for use by the shogun Prince Munetaka (1242–1274) in the mid-thirteenth century. The earliest reference to fans pasted onto folding screens is an example from 1434 in the diary of Prince Fushiminomiya Sadafusa (1372–1456), *Kanmon nikki* (entry for Eikyō 7.6), which mentions that they were of fans with *Genji* pictures. Sanetaka himself records seeing a screen with *Genji* fan paintings, newly commissioned by a member of the Hosokawa family in Entoku 1 (1489), 12.12 (*Sanetaka kōki*, 3:341), while a pair of screens adorned with sixty *Genji* fans dated stylistically to the fifteenth century in the collection of Jōdōji in Hiroshima provides an important extant example of this practice.

22. Sanetaka's ties to the court were through his wife; her older sister served at the court of Emperor Go-Tsuchimikado (1442–1500), while her younger sister, Fujiko, became the con-

sort of Emperor Go-Kashiwabara (1464–1526) and gave birth to Emperor Go-Nara (1496–1557); Haga Kōshirō, *Sanjōnishi Sanetaka*, Jinbutsu sōsho (Tokyo: Yoshikawa Kōbunkan, 1960), 28.

23. For a thorough account of Sanetaka's life and literary works see Miyakawa Yōko, *Sanjōnishi Sanetaka to kotengaku* (Tokyo: Kazama Shobō, 1995). It examines each year of the diary, which Sanetaka kept from 1474 to 1536.

24. Sanetaka's cultural output and his collaboration with Tosa Mitsunobu, the artist of the *Genji Album*, is explored in Melissa McCormick, *Tosa Mitsunobu and the Small Scroll in Medieval Japan* (Seattle: University of Washington Press, 2009).

25. Sanetaka first made a "lineage chart" (*keizu*) of *Genji* characters in 1488 after participating in lectures on the tale by the *renga* poets Sōgi (1421–1502) and Botanka Shōhaku (1443–1527), who assisted him, as did Gensei, the other coordinator of Sue Saburō's album. Sanetaka's *Genji* lineage chart was always in high demand, and he made countless copies of it over the years for various individuals, including Prince Kunitaka, one of the calligraphers of the 1510 album. See Ii Haruki, "Sanetaka no 'Genji monogatari keizu' seisaku," in *Genji monogatari chūsakushi no kenkyū: Muromachi zenki* (Tokyo: Ōfūsha, 1980), 507–63.

26. Two commentaries from the early sixteenth century are attributed to Sanetaka: *Rōkashō*, based on previous commentaries and notes (*kikigaki*) recorded during lectures by leading *Genji* scholars, and *Sairyūshō*, Sanetaka's original commentary completed by his son, Sanjōnishi Kin'eda (1487–1563). See Ii Haruki, ed., *Sairyūshō*, in *Genji monogatari kochū shūsei*, vol. 7 (Tokyo: Ōfūsha, 1980), and Ii Haruki, ed., *Rōkashō*, in *Genji monogatari kochū shūsei*, vol. 8 (Tokyo: Ōfūsha, 1983); and Lewis Cook, "Genre Trouble: Medieval Commentaries and Canonization of *The Tale of Genji*," in *Envisioning* The Tale of Genji: *Media, Gender, and Cultural Production*, ed. Haruo Shirane (New York: Columbia University Press, 2008), 129–53.

27. A list of the appropriate number of days to spend lecturing on each chapter appears at the beginning of *Rōkashō*; see Ii Haruki, ed., *Rōkashō*, in *Genji monogatari kochū shūsei*, 9.

28. Janet Goff touches on the importance of *renga* to the reception of *Genji* in the medieval period, including the creation of *Genji* Noh plays; see her *Noh Drama and The Tale of Genji: The Art of Allusion in Fifteen Classical Plays* (Princeton, NJ: Princeton University Press, 1991).

29. A *Genji-kotobagaki-renga* was held, for example, at the customary ninth-month *renga* gathering at the imperial palace on Daiei 1 (1521) 9.13 (*Sanetaka kōki*, 10:761).

30. A *Genji kokumei renga* was held at the imperial palace on Daiei 5 (1525) 6.3 (*Sanetaka kōki*, 11:290). For a *Genji kokumei renga* manuscript thought to have been composed in 1505, see Ii, *Genji monogatari chūsakushi no kenkyū: Muromachi zenki*, 1131.

31. On the overemphasis on *renga* and neglect of *waka* in scholarship on fifteenth- and sixteenth-century Japanese literature, see Steven D. Carter, "Waka in the Age of Renga," *Monumenta Nipponica* 36, no. 4 (1981): 425–44.

32. Gensei borrowed two volumes of the commentary from Sanetaka on Eishō 6 (1508) Intercalary 8.12 (*Sanetaka kōki*, 9:245), roughly one week before they began organizing the calligraphy assignments. The texts he borrowed covered Chapters One through Four of *Genji*, which Gensei may have used in discussions with Sue concerning the selection of texts for the album.

33. Gensei descended from a warrior clan, the Kawata, and was a retainer of Hosokawa Masaharu, governor of Awa; see Inoue Muneo, *Chūsei kadanshi no kenkyū, Muromachi kōki, kaitei shinpan* (Tokyo: Meiji Shoin, 1987), 194–95.

34. Sōgi transmitted to Sanetaka the "Teachings of Poems Ancient and Modern" (*Kokindenju*) in 1488, along with the "Three Great Matters of *Genji*" (*Genji sanka ji*), as noted in Miyakawa, *Sanjōnishi Sanetaka to kotengaku*, 45.

35. The colored papers appear in the order of red, blue, yellow, pink, and green in the first half of the album (Chapters 1–27), after which the sequence largely follows the order of red, pink, blue, yellow, green, until the end. Exceptions include the two consecutive pink papers of Chapters 34 and 35, which tie these chapters, Early Spring Greens pt. 1 and pt. 2, together. The grouping of the album leaves into two halves of twenty-seven also would have accorded with a double-sided album format.

36. The project seems therefore to pave the way for the blending of "Chinese" and "Japanese" elements in *Genji*-related artworks, which can be seen in the earliest extant portrait-icon of Murasaki Shikibu, dated to 1560 and painted by Tosa Mitsunobu's grandson Tosa Mitsumoto (1530–1569), and commissioned by the grandson of Sanjōnishi Sanetaka, Kujō Tanemichi (1507–1594); see McCormick, "Purple Displaces Crimson."

37. The ability to employ both gendered modes of writing was largely the privilege of men, who wrote official documents in Sino-Japanese characters and personal letters and texts in the vernacular using *kana*, while woman were by and large encouraged to write only in *kana*. For more on these gendered divisions, see Chino Kaori, "Gender in Japanese Art," trans. Joshua S. Mostow, in *Gender and Power in the Japanese Visual Field*, ed. Joshua S. Mostow et. al. (Honolulu: University of Hawai'i Press, 2003), 17–34.

38. Kasashima Tadayuki identified five of the six calligraphers in the album based on stylistic analysis, before the discovery of the diary entries and backing papers that confirmed the names; see Kasashima Tadayuki, "Hābādo Daigaku Bijutsukan zō 'Genji monogatari gajō' kotobagaki no shofū to seisaku nendai," *Kokka* no. 1222 (1997): 53. The Album Calligraphy Key in the appendix to this book is based on the table in his article. Courtly calligraphy during the Muromachi period witnessed the birth of at least seventeen new stylistic lineages; Shimatani Hiroyuki, "Sanjōnishi Sanetaka to Sanjō ryū," *Tōkyō Kokuritsu Hakubutsukan kiyō* 26 (1990): 7–191.

39. Eishō 6 (1509) Intercalary 8.20 (*Sanetaka kōki*, 9:248). It took less than four months to collect all fifty-four completed calligraphy papers, helped by some especially speedy calligraphers, such as Reizei Tamehiro, who brushed and returned his assigned excerpts in two weeks. At least one leaf, Chapter Ten, by Jōhōji Kojō, required a correction, however, slowing down the process. For more on the process of procuring the texts and on the calligraphers, see McCormick, "*Genji* Goes West," 70–71.

40. Tomoko Sakomura examines the history and meaning of *shikishi* inscription and introduces several manuals on calligraphic practice in *Poetry as Image: The Visual Culture of Waka in Sixteenth-Century Japan* (Leiden: Brill, 2015).

41. See the appendix in this book for a chart of the album's calligraphers and their assigned paper colors and chapters. The calligraphy portion of the album was completed by Eishō 6 (1509) 11.19, when Sanetaka and Sue examined all of the papers together (*Sanetaka kōki*, 9:283).

42. Kamei Wakana discusses the meaning of the *edokoro azukari* title in Mitsunobu's day in "Hābādo Daigaku Bijutsukan zō 'Genji monogatari gajō' o meguru shomondai," *Kokka* no. 1222 (1997): 15–18.

43. See McCormick, *Tosa Mitsunobu and the Small Scroll in Medieval Japan* for information on the artist's oeuvre and patronage. Among Mitsunobu's innovations was a new form of narrative scroll for the representation of short stories (*ko-e* or "small picture") as well as the genre of screen painting now known as "Scenes In and Around the Capital" (*rakuchū rakugaizu*), the first known reference to which describes a work made by Mitsunobu in 1506 for the Asakura daimyo of Echizen (the entry for Eishō 3, 12.22 in *Sanetaka kōki*, 8:675).

44. Chino Kaori, "Hābādo Daigaku Bijutsukan zō 'Genji monogatari gajō' o meguru shomondai," *Kokka* no. 1222 (1997), esp. 12–14 for an analysis of his painting style.

45. They all worked on the *Illustrated Legends of the Kitano Tenjin Shrine* (*Kitano Tenjin engi emaki*, 1503), a set of three handscrolls with calligraphy by Sanetaka, title labels by Emperor Go-Kashiwabara, and paintings by Tosa Mitsunobu, all coordinated by Gensei on behalf of the patron. Entries in Sanetaka's diary record the process of production, including discussions between Sanetaka and Mitsunobu that touched on classic examples of scroll painting from earlier periods, providing a glimpse of the presumably numerous conversations that took place regarding the production of the *Genji Album* as well, but that went unrecorded. Entries from Sanetaka's diary related to the *Kitano Tenjin engi* project begin on Bunki 1 (1501) 8.26 and continue until Bunki 3 (1503) 5.12.

46. Mitsunobu discussed *Genji* with the prominent courtier and scholar Nakanoin Michihide (1428–1494), for example, who noted the meeting in his diary in an entry from Bunmei 18 (1486) 6.27; see *Jūrin'in naifu ki*, in *Shiryō sanshū. Kokiroku hen* (Tokyo: Zoku Gunsho Ruijū Kanseikai, 1972), 236. The *waka* gatherings Mitsunobu joined include one in 1491, in which Gensei participated as well, where the focal point was a new Hitomaro portrait painted by Mitsunobu himself. A poem by the artist appears in an original manuscript from the event; see Iwasaki Yoshiki, "Tosa Mitsunobu no bungei katsudō: Yōmeidō Bunko zō 'Sanjō ku' uta to renga," *Gobun* 47 (1986): 36–37.

47. A thorough account of the types of pigments and materials used in the album's paintings and calligraphy papers is Katherine Eremin, Jens Stenger, and Melanie Li Green, "Raman Spectroscopy of Japanese Artists' Materials: *The Tale of Genji* by Tosa Mitsunobu," *Journal of Raman Spectroscopy* 37 (2006): 1119–24.

48. Takahashi Tōru, *Monogatari to e no enkinhō* (Tokyo: Perikan Sha, 1991).

49. One such manual that includes a description of possible scenes for reproduction thought to have been created in the medieval period is translated and discussed in Miyeko Murase, *Iconography of the Tale of Genji* (New York: Weatherhill, 1983).

50. Daiei 6 (1526) 1.20 (*Sanetaka kōki*, 12:130). He borrowed the manual from the courtier Kanroji Motonaga (1457–1527) on behalf of Sago no Tsubune, a female attendant to the Ashikaga Shogunate; for this reference and a historical overview of the process behind *Genji* painting production, see Katagiri Yayoi, "Bijutsu-shi ni okeru Genji mongatari: Genji-e no bamen sentaku to zuyō no mondai o chūshin ni," *Genji monogatari kenkyū shūsei* vol. 14, ed. Masuda et al. (Tokyo: Kazama Shobō, 301–46.

51. For Michihide's letter, see the documents on the reverse of Sanetaka's diary dating to Bunmei 8 (1476) 10.6–8 (*Sanetaka kōki*, 16:156).

52. The calligraphy attributions were made by later connoisseurs but based on stylistic comparison to extant texts by these same individuals, they seem correct.

53. The calligraphy of the text of the Picture Contest, Chapter Seventeen, has been attributed to Nakamikado Nobumasu (dates unknown), the third son of the courtier Nakamikado Nobutane (1442–1525). Nobumasu's participation, combined with his father's well-documented patronage of Mitsunobu, suggests that the project may have been for this aristocratic family. Given the frequency with which women in the provinces requested copies of the tale, one can imagine that the project might have been for someone like Nobutane's daughter, a woman later known as the nun Jukei (ca. 1568), who in 1508 married the warrior Imagawa Ujichika (1471?–1526). If residing far from the capital in the Imagawa-controlled eastern provinces, a copy of *The Tale of Genji* would be something of a lifeline for such a young woman, as a source of entertainment and learning.

54. The copies were done by Sumiyoshi Gukei (1631–1705) in 1675 and consist of forty-one drawings of designs for *Genji* painting book covers and for *shikishi*. The designs appear side by side in a handscroll. For a detailed introduction and analysis, see Ryūsawa Aya, "Tōkyō Kokuritsu Hakubutsukan zō 'Genji monogatari sasshi hyōshi e mohon' ni tsuite," *Museum* no. 643 (2013): 25–50.

55. Ryūsawa Aya considers the logic of narrative painting scene selection on the front and back of painted fans and book covers in "Genji-e no hyō to ura: senmenga to sasshi hyōshi-e o chūshin ni," *Kinjō Nihongo Nihon bunka* 80 (2013): 1–11.

56. One type of premodern *Genji* painting that tends to include such examples are small handscrolls in the monochrome ink (*hakubyō*) often attributed to female artists, and likely made for female readers. See Melissa McCormick, "Genji no ma o nozoku: Hakubyō Genji monogatari emaki to nyōbō no shiza," in *Genji monogatari o yomitoku 1: Egakareta Genji monogatari*, ed. Kawazoe Fusae and Mitamura Masako (Tokyo: Kanrin Shobō, 2006), 101–29; and "Monochromatic *Genji*: The *Hakubyō* Tradition and Female Commentarial Culture," in *Envisioning The Tale of Genji: Media, Gender, and Cultural Production*, ed. Haruo Shirane (New York: Columbia University Press, 2008), 101–28.

57. Before the identity of the patron of the 1510 *Genji* was known, Ikeda Shinobu speculated that it was commissioned by elite men of the courtier or warrior class based on, among other things, the many scenes of homosocial male gatherings in the album; see her essay in "Hābādo Daigaku Bijutsukan zō 'Genji monogatari gajō' o meguru shomondai," *Kokka* no. 1222 (1997): 22.

The Tale of Genji Album of 1510

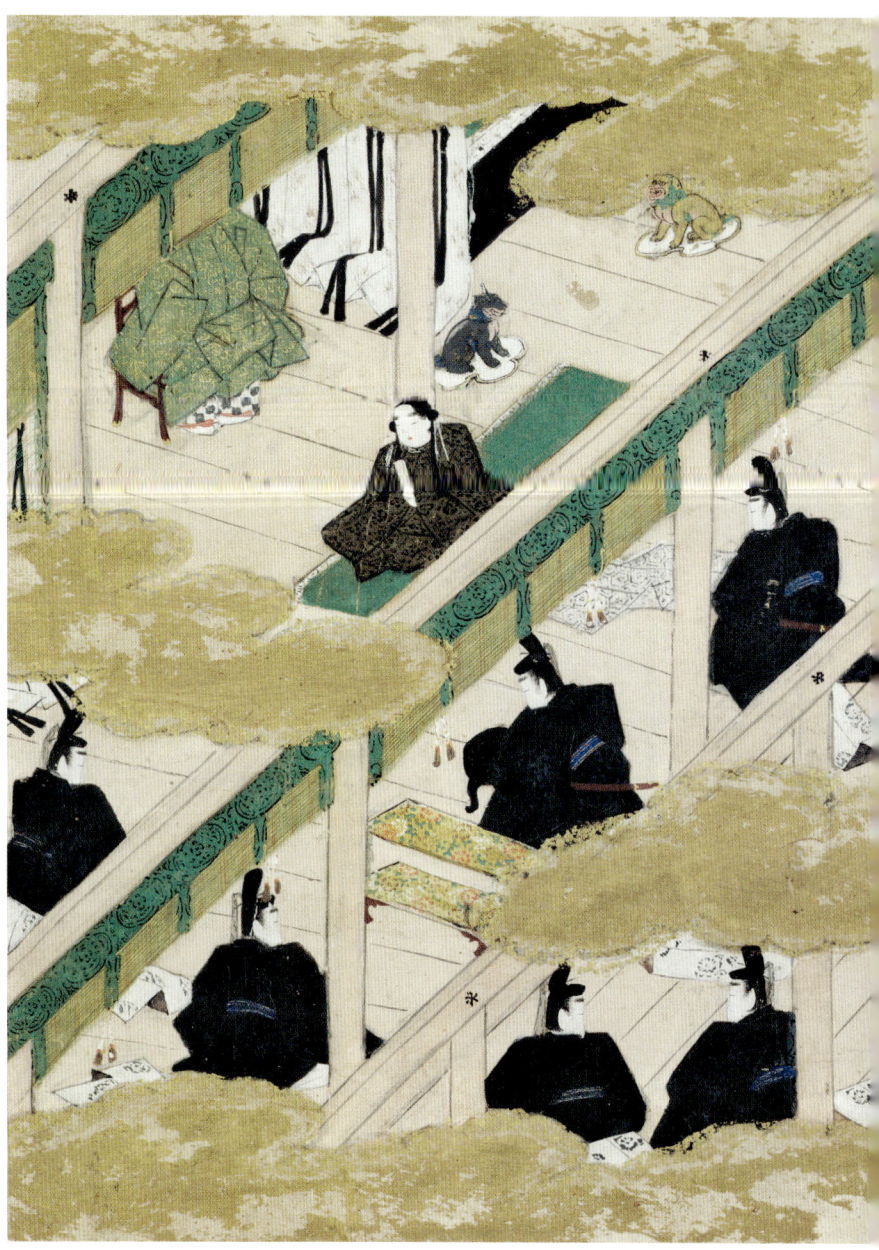

This son's boyish appearance, how bittersweet that it must change, but when the youth turned twelve, His Majesty saw to the initiation himself, attending to various details and adding unprecedented touches to the ceremony.

1

桐壺

The Lady of the Paulownia-Courtyard Chambers

Kiritsubo

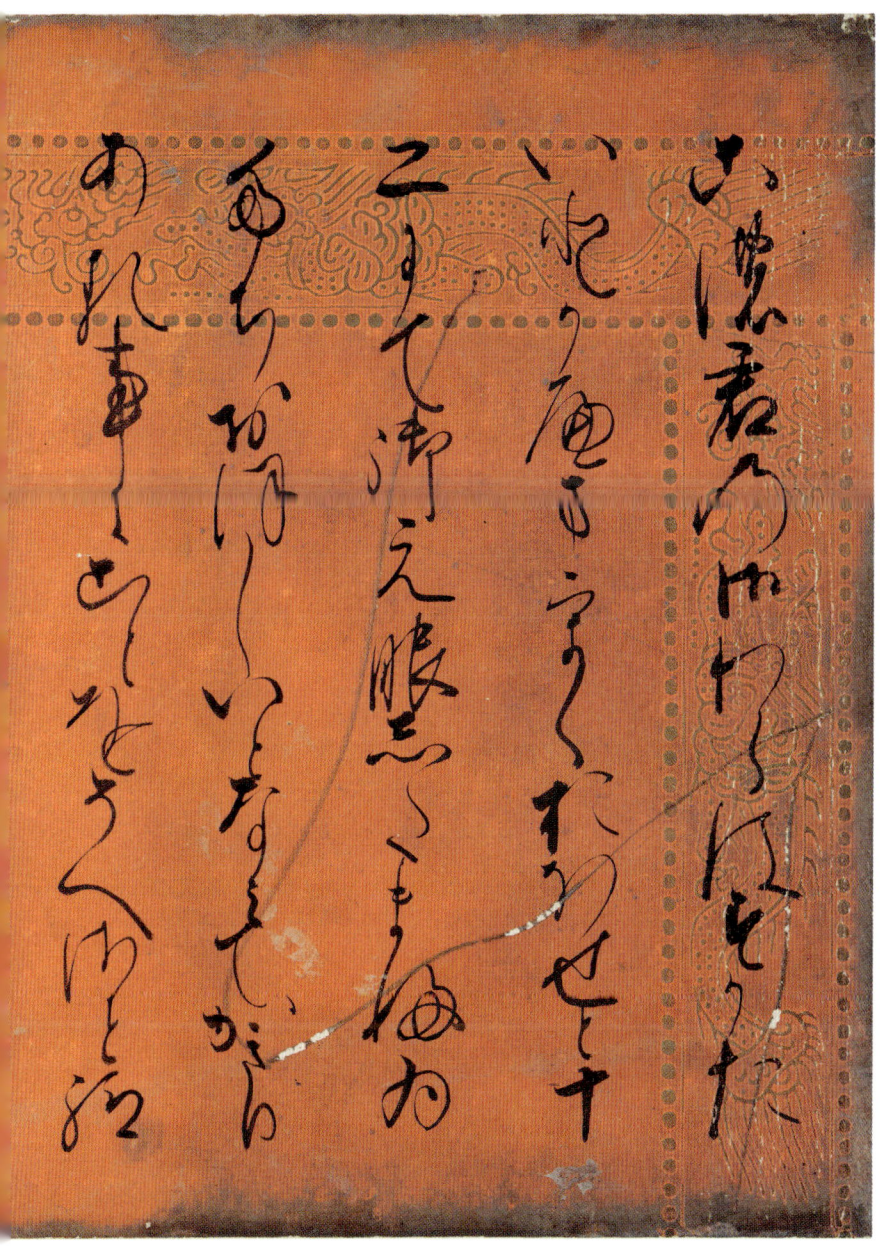

Kono kimi no onwarawa sugata, ito kaemōku oboseto, jūni nite ongenpuku shitamau. Itachi oboshii to namite, kagiri aru koto ni koto o soesase tamau.

この君の御わらはすかた
いとかへまうくおほせと十
二にて御元服したまふぬ
たちおほしいとなみてかきり
ある事にことをそへさせ給

The opening scene of the *Genji Album* captures the final moments of Genji's "boyish appearance," the loss of which is lamented in the accompanying textual excerpt. In keeping with pictorial conventions, gold clouds part and architectural barriers fall away to reveal Genji at his initiation ceremony where his long tresses will be shortened and tucked inside his courtier's cap, modeled by the six men in formal attire who attend to the ceremony. The picture focuses on young Genji and his adolescent hairstyle, showing his hair trailing down his shoulders from loops above his ears tied with white ribbons that frame his innocent-looking face. Genji's countenance demonstrates the artist Tosa Mitsunobu's mastery of the conventions for depicting nobility in courtly narrative painting: white pigment (*gofun*) from ground shells to paint the face, precisely drawn lines for the eyes and nose, with bushy eyebrows and red lips, amounting to an abstract but subtly expressive visage. The solemnity of the occasion is conveyed through details of comportment: the slight tilt of the head, the firmly grasped baton, and the overall compliant pose of the initiate. Furnishings in the picture include a brocade-covered two-tiered shelf with a vibrant floral pattern against a gold ground, and a black lacquered footed basin to receive to the boy's shorn locks, all perhaps alluding to the attention to the ceremony's details paid by the sovereign himself. The Emperor, whose face is hidden behind blinds, as was custom, is seated in the upper left corner. His importance is underscored by the selection of the textual excerpt, which describes the ceremony from his point of view. The courtier to Genji's left, directly in the Emperor's line of vision, is most likely the Minister of the Left, the man who is about to become Genji's father-in-law. Genji's coming of age coincides with his betrothal to the young woman known as Lady Aoi, who, at sixteen, is four years his senior. The scene of initiation, although tinged with sentimentality, pictorializes a consequential political transaction between the Emperor and the Minister of the Left, with Genji in the middle.

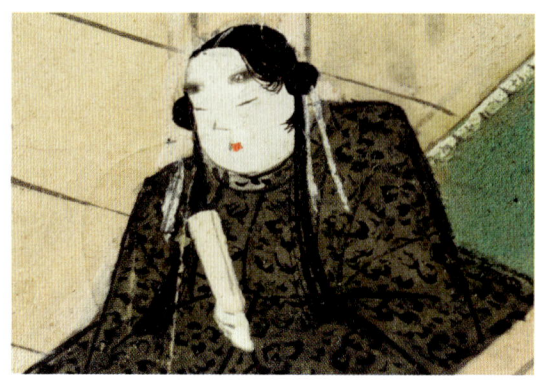

The textual passage for this scene opens with the reflections of the sovereign as he witnesses his son's passage into adulthood. Until this moment Genji had barely left his father's side and had served as a poignant reminder of the Emperor's deceased love known as the Kiritsubo Consort (Lady of the Paulownia-Courtyard Chambers). Much of the opening chapter of *The Tale of Genji* describes an all-consuming love affair between the Emperor and Genji's mother, a woman of lesser social standing than his senior Consort, Kokiden. Their relationship reflects the Emperor's attempt at an assertion of political control over the Kokiden Consort and her powerful Fujiwara family, whose manipulation of the throne curtails direct imperial rule. The birth of Genji to a woman without a controlling Fujiwara patriarch behind her means a potential rival to the throne who would not be subject to control by the Fujiwara Regents. At the same time, without powerful maternal male relatives to occupy influential bureaucratic positions at court to support and protect him, Genji's position is precarious, prompting the Emperor to make him a commoner, thereby removing him as a potential successor. *The Tale of Genji* is thus a tale of the disinherited—the surname "Genji" being designated for such princes removed from the line of succession—in which the reclamation of this birthright and the redemption of Genji's mother's lineage subtends the entire work.

Courtly narrative painting at its best employed architectural settings to convey social relationships, and the album painting for the Kiritsubo chapter is no exception. The Emperor's role as the spiritual and political center of society is expressed by his transcendent position in the upper left, where

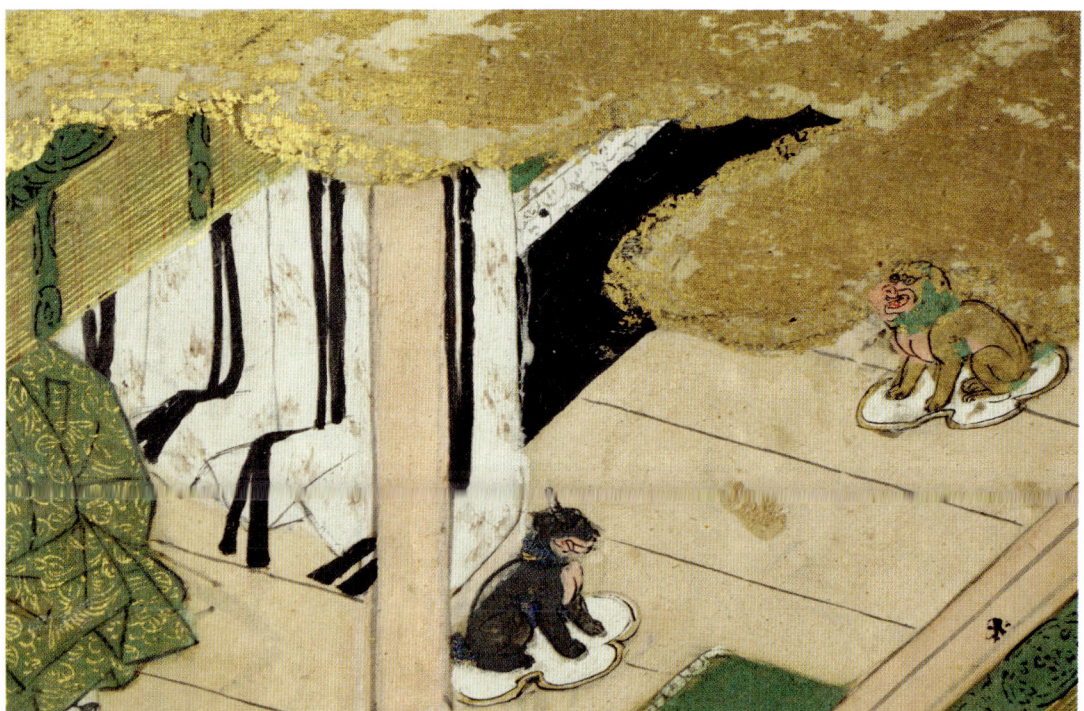

he observes the ceremony from behind the hanging blinds. Out of deference, his body is depicted only from the shoulders down. The three diagonal beams that traverse the picture demarcate separate hierarchical spaces within a building: the inner core (*moya*) in the upper left, the surrounding aisle (*hisashi*), where Genji sits, and the outer aisle, occupied by two courtiers in the lower right. Adjacent to the Emperor, and positioned directly behind Genji, is a curtained dais symbolically guarded by a pair of sculptural lion-dogs placed in front. The ensemble marks the site as the Seiryōden (Hall of Cool and Refreshing Breezes), the Emperor's residence within the palace. The setting is charged with political meaning: the initiation of Genji's half brother, the designated Crown Prince born to the Kokiden Consort, took place in the official Shinshinden (Hall for State Ceremonies). The Emperor's personal involvement in Genji's coming-of-age ceremony, held in his private quarters, implies that for him, Genji takes priority over the Crown Prince, foreshadowing a lifelong rivalry between the half brothers and a theme of public versus private kingship. Genji will never ascend the throne like his half brother, the future Emperor Suzaku, but he will achieve a symbolic form of sovereignty, ultimately rising to the exalted status of "honorary retired emperor" (*jun daijō tennō*). The tale legitimizes Genji's claim to this position in its first pages, using imagery of resplendence and otherworldliness to describe him, calling him the "radiant prince" (*hikaru kimi*). The album's first painting mobilizes the symbolism of architectural settings and the empty imperial dais appearing to float above Genji's head to establish themes of identity, rivalry, and shadow imperial rule that structure the entire tale.

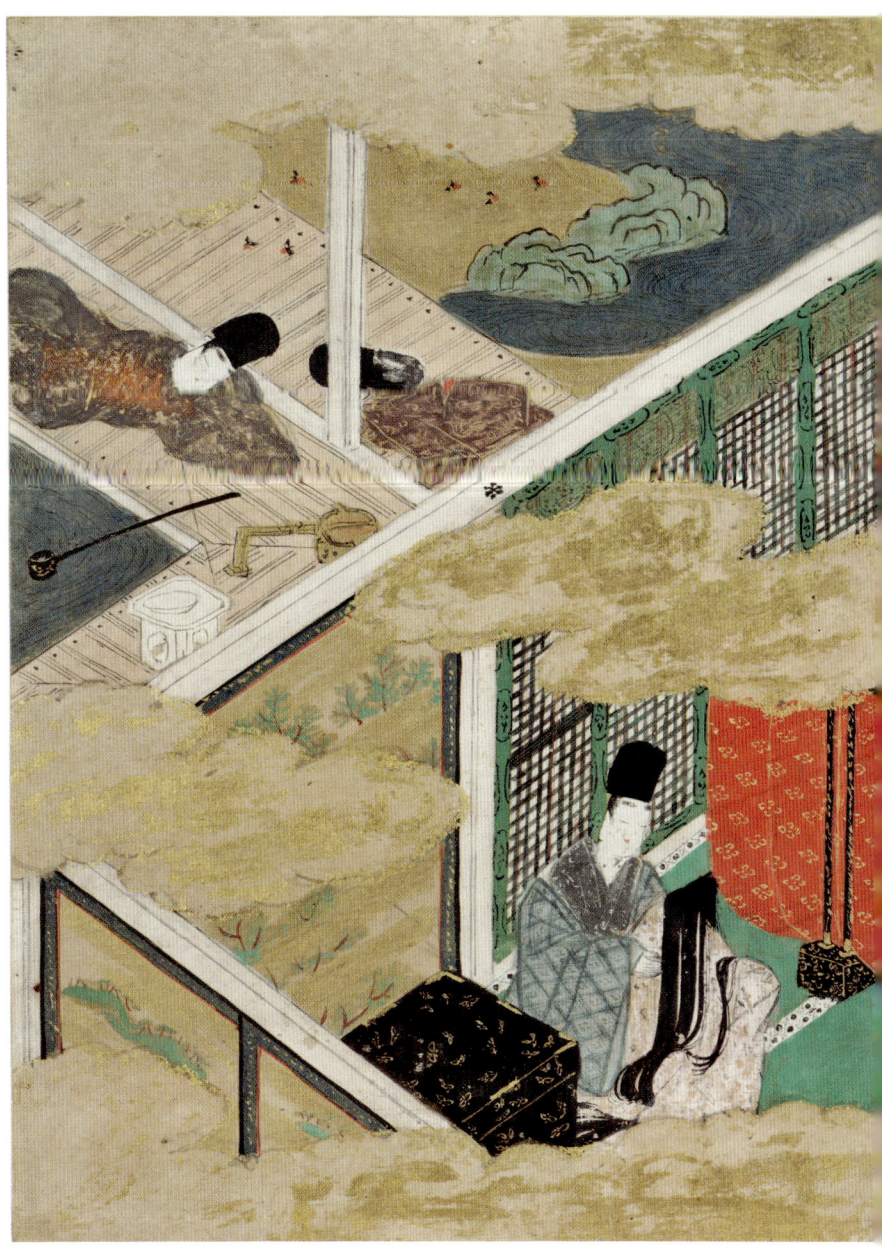

    Now the breaking day
Finds me still sighing in the dark
      Of my misery,
For those unresting cries are torn
Not just from the cockrel's throat.

CRANSTON, P. 698

With the sky growing lighter
by the moment, Genji brought her
back to the entrance of her room.

2

帚木
Broom Cypress
Hahakigi

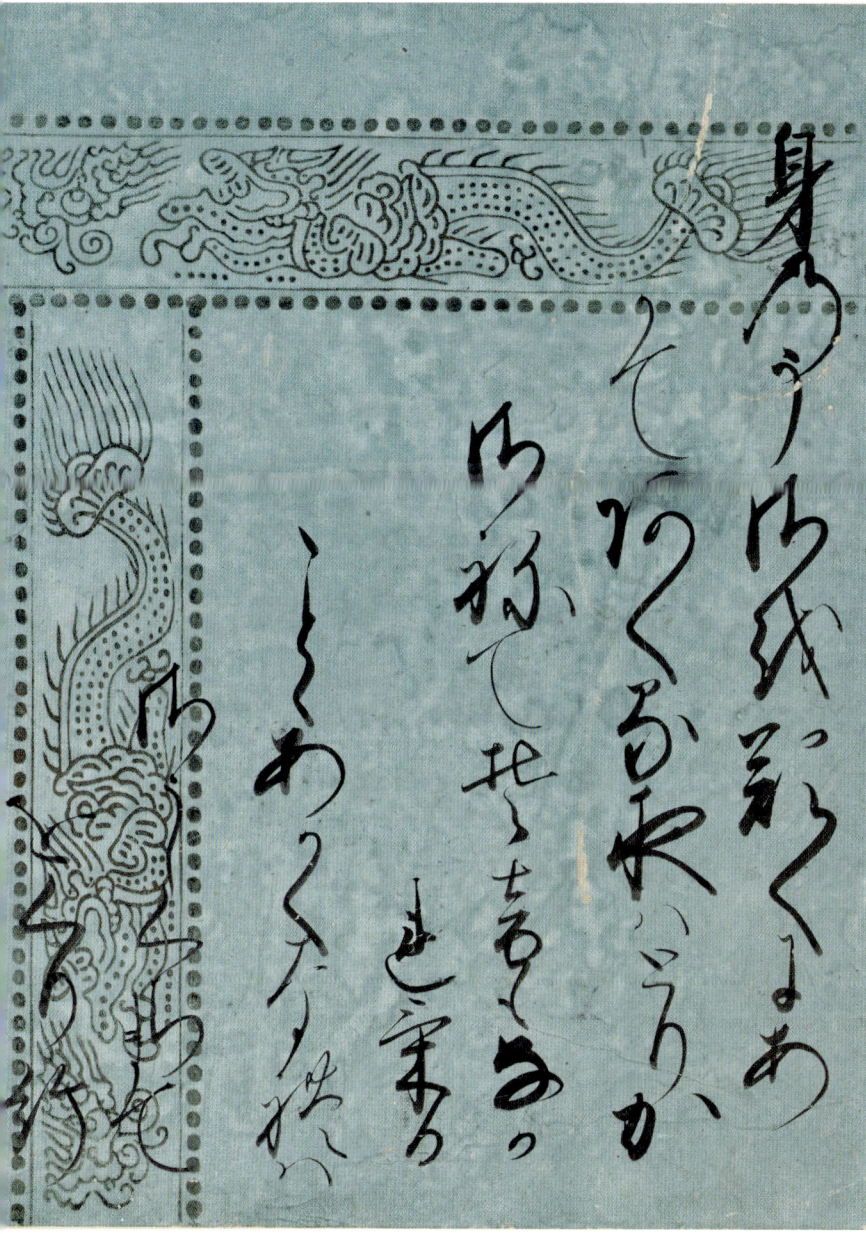

Mi no usa o
Nageku ni akade
　Akuru yo wa
Torikasanete zo
Ne mo nakarekeru

koto to akakunareba, shōjiguchi
made okuritamau.

身のうさを歎くにあ
かてあくる夜はとりか
さねてそ音もなか
れける
ことゝあかくなれは
さうしくちまて
をくり給

This second pair of leaves in the album, Hahakigi (Broom Cypress), takes us from the rarified atmosphere of the imperial court and aristocracy to the world of provincial governors and middle-ranking women. Genji, now seventeen, decides to spend the night at the city residence of the Governor of Kii Province. The painting is set amid the sweltering midsummer heat on the grounds of the governor's newly renovated villa, which is replete with shaded walkways traversing man-made streams, and a spring constructed by damming up part of the Nakagawa River. Sparks of red pigment suggest the intermittent radiance the fireflies are said to have cast on the banks of the garden stream, adding a magical quality to the scene. The burbling spring (*izumi*), with its associations of water delivered from the gods, and elixirs of youth, adds to the site's otherworldly air. In the top half of the painting, two attendants in courtiers' hats (*eboshi*) lie stretched out, asleep on a walkway. A black lacquered ladle bobs on the water, its long handle resting on the walkway, while the gold pitcher and white *sake* cup nearby suggest the night's revelry.

The wine has no soporific effect on Genji, who, unlike his men, is restless, and loath to sleep alone while at the governor's villa. The bottom half of the painting depicts the results of Genji's nocturnal wanderings—a dramatic encounter with the woman known as Utsusemi, the young stepmother of the Governor. Genji rises at the sound of voices and overhears a conversation between Utsusemi and her younger brother Kogimi. The stepmother was known to stay at the villa with her female attendants from time to time, and on this occasion was staying there while her husband ritually purified his own residence. She sparks Genji's interest, in part because her marriage to a man of the provincial governor class puts her beneath him within the "middle ranks" of the aristocracy. He has never had a liaison with a woman of middle rank, but their virtues were explained to him by three more romantically experienced men in a spirited and metaphorically rich conversation earlier in this chapter, the famous "rainy night appraisal" (*amayo no shinasadame*). Genji hears the woman call for her attendant Chūjō, literally "Middle Captain," a name that matches his own courtier's title at the time. Finding the door unlatched, he approaches the prone woman and pulls back her coverlet, saying, "I heard you call for a Captain," implying that his audacious entrance was at her own request. Whatever playfulness might have been intended is lost on the woman, who cries out for help only to have her screams muffled by her own robes.

The precise moment depicted in the picture is unclear, but it appears to show the dawn after their encounter. Nevertheless, it could stand in quite well for his initial moment of contact. Given the indirectness of courtly painting, the portrayal here of Genji physically touching the woman is bold, perhaps recalling, as Noguchi Takeshi has suggested, the influence of erotic *Genji* paintings that were known to have circulated in medieval Japan. Genji places a hand on her upper back and guides her forward as she turns her head, her long hair cascading down her robes. Her diminutive frame is striking and alludes to the way Genji is said to sweep her up and carry her into an interior room. Genji returns the woman to where he found her in a crowded storage room, here indicated by the large lacquered chest

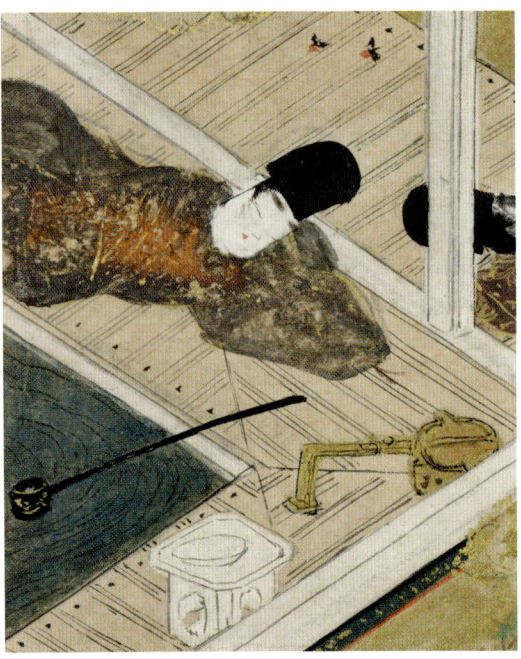

30 | *The Tale of Genji*

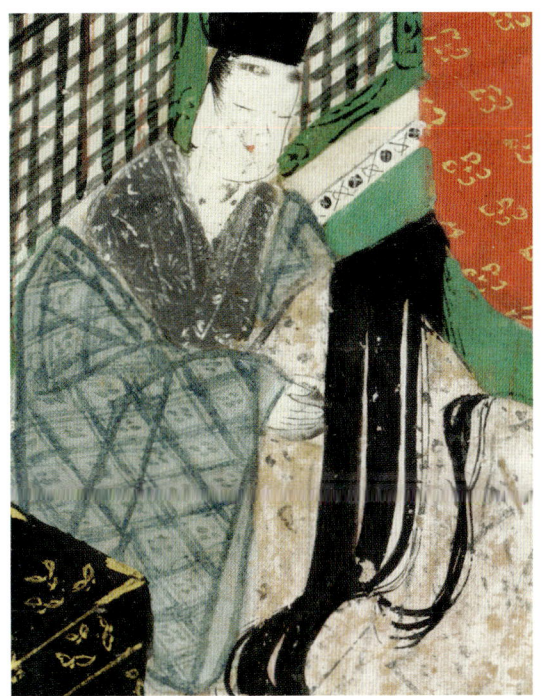

(*karabitsu*) decorated with golden butterflies in the foreground. The textual excerpt of the adjacent leaf also suggests a morning-after setting.

The painting's emphasis on Genji's figure and his amorous adventure is countered by the poem, which represents the woman's voice and her inner turmoil. Calligraphically the excerpt begins at the top right of the blue paper sheet with the darkly brushed character *mi*, which literally means "body" but more commonly refers to one's fate or station in life. The woman's misery and regret expressed in the verse capture not only the complexity of her feelings toward Genji (she is simultaneously attracted to him and upset at the way he has forced himself on her), but also her preoccupation with the disparity of their social standing. Her late father, a relatively high-ranking courtier, a Middle Counselor, intended to send her to court in the hopes that she would become a consort of the sovereign. When her father died before his dreams for her could be realized, she settled for the security of marrying the older (or as Genji repeatedly calls him, "over the hill") Vice Governor of Iyo, whom she seems to despise. That she should now be the object of attention by this handsome son of an emperor when she is no longer free causes her to regret the choices she has made in the past. At the same time, the overwhelming guilt she feels toward her husband prompts a concern that he may have witnessed the previous night's transgression in his dreams.

Given the hopelessness of her situation, she decides to maintain her dignity rather than risk becoming a trifle for a young man who has already garnered a reputation for promiscuity, and she resolves to resist any further advances. She is said to resemble the "supple bamboo" (*nayotake*) that bends but does not break under pressure. By the end of the chapter, when Genji is rejected after attempting another tryst, he feels humiliated but impressed by the strength of her character. The woman's ability to evade Genji prompts him to liken her in a poem to the "broom cypress" (*hahakigi*), legendary from earlier poems as a shrub that vanishes on approach. She similarly envisions herself as the ethereal tree in her reply poem to Genji and describes the "worthless hovel" where she, the broom cypress, was planted. This final poem in the chapter conveys the woman's preoccupation with her social status, while the mysterious image of the *hahakigi* epitomizes her characteristic elusiveness and gives the chapter its name.

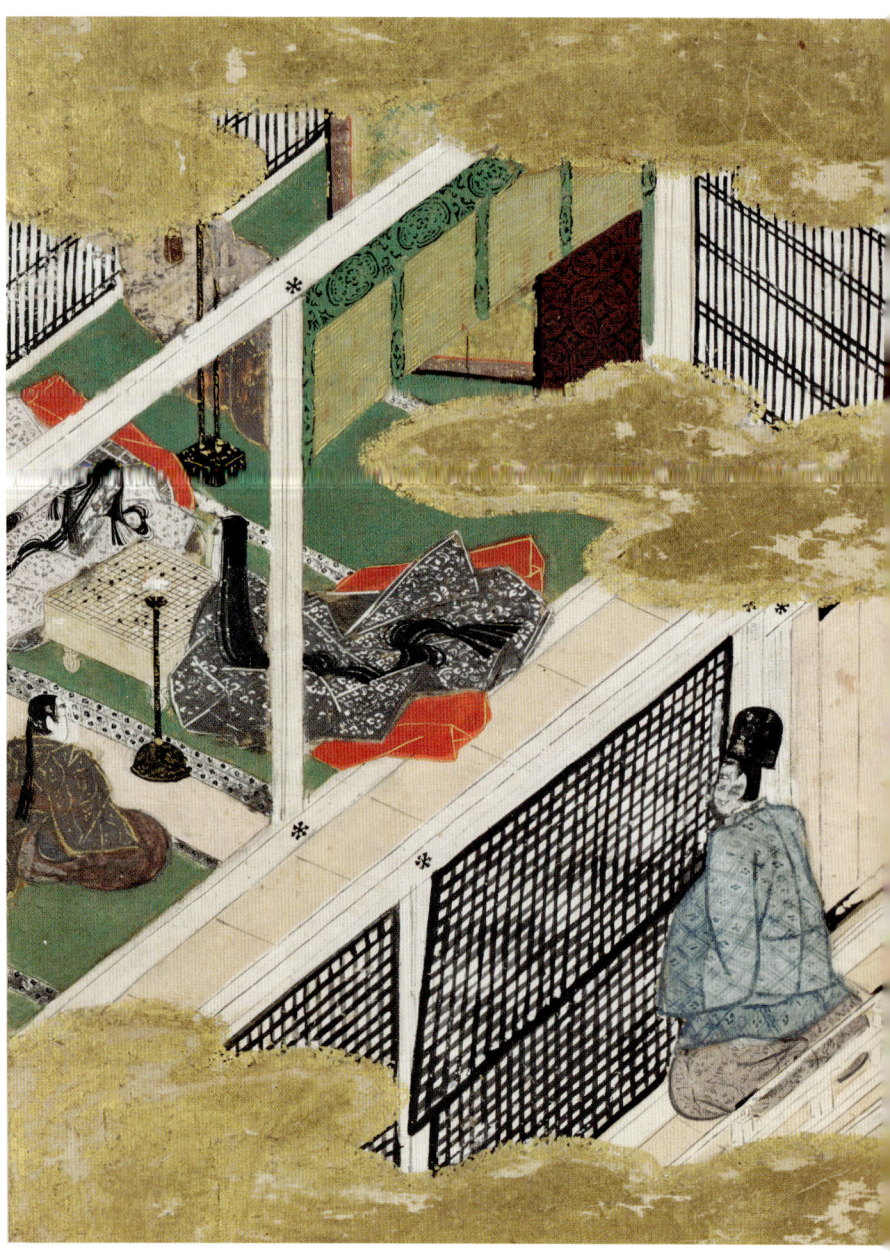

"The lady from the west wing has been here playing Go since noon," Genji heard someone say. Thinking that he would like to get a glimpse of the two women facing each other across the game board, he quietly stepped forward and stood in a space behind the blinds.

3

空蝉

A Molted Cicada Shell
Utsusemi

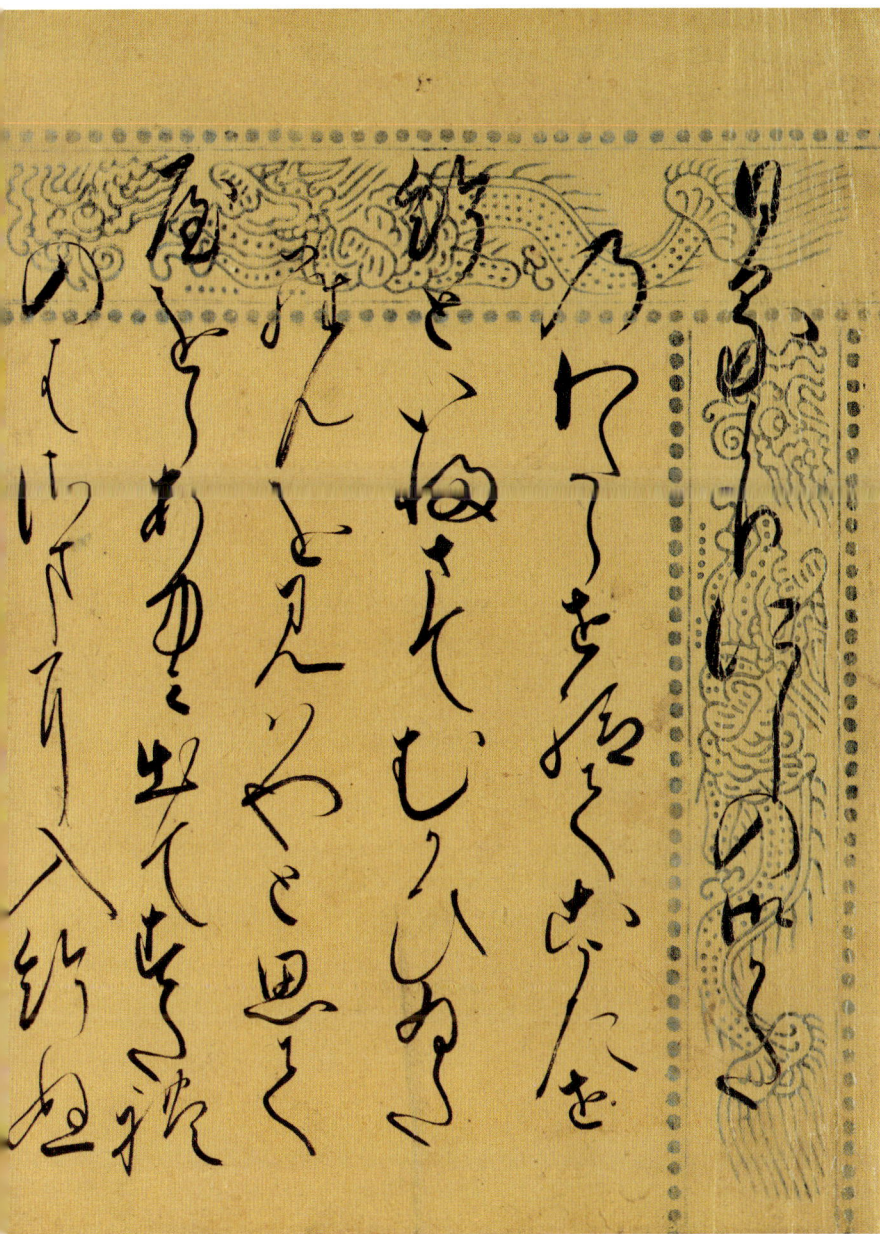

Hiru yori nishi no onkata no watarase tamaite, go utase tamau to iu. Sate mukai itaran o mibaya to omoite, yaora ayumi idete sudare no hasama ni iritamainu.

ひるよりにしの御かた
のわたらせ給てこうたせ
給といふさてむかひゐた
らんを見はやと思て
やをらあゆみ出てすたれ
のはさまに入給ぬ

Unable to free himself from thoughts of Utsusemi, Genji has her younger brother arrange yet another encounter for him at the governor's villa. Genji waits for the boy near outer wooden doors, allowing him to steal a glimpse inside the women's rooms. The painting depicts this moment of espionage with the top half of the black lattice shutters enclosing the aisle room raised ever so slightly for the peeping Genji. This is the first of six pictures in the album that depict the trope of voyeuristic peeking known as *kaimami* (literally "peeking through the fence"), in which male characters espy women who are ostensibly unaware of being observed. These fleeting moments of spectacle play important roles in the narrative: as plot pivots that incite male characters to engage in new sexual pursuits; as devices that reveal the mental world of a character through internal monologues inspired by the viewing of women; and as a means of drawing attention to particular female characters, whose physical features and personal attributes are deliberately discerned through the eyes of the male spectator.

Following the compositional pattern of other *kaimami* scenes, Genji, understood as a surrogate for the viewer, stands in the lower right corner and gazes leftward toward figures, usually women, immersed in their own activity and seemingly unaware that they are being watched. Spatial partitions including bamboo blinds (*sudare*), a standing curtain (*kichō*), and a folding screen (*byōbu*) are perfectly arranged so that nothing obstructs Genji's view. The composition artfully includes exposed architectural beams and interior furnishings to construct space cells within the scene. Three figures in the room are contained within one such cell, which includes an oil lamp with red flame, and a Go board with tiny black and white stones in play. Lamplight is a common feature of *kaimami* scenes, which are often nocturnal, drawing the voyeur to an object bathed in atmospheric light.

The scene within Genji's field of vision reveals striking contrasts between the two women facing off at the game board. His gaze first lands on the elusive Utsusemi, the woman he has been pursuing, and the figure closest to him in the image. He sees her only obliquely since she maintains a modest posture even in these private quarters when no one should be looking. He notes her extremely thin hands, which she attempts to keep hidden beneath her robes, and her narrow head. Apparently, his previous nocturnal encounter with the woman did not allow for such scrutiny, and he concludes that while she is far from a great beauty, her composure, elegance, and grace merit admiration.

In contrast, the attire of the other woman, described in the tale as directly in Genji's line of sight, leaves little to the imagination. She is said to be far more relaxed, to the point of dishabille, with her robes open to the waist of her red trousers and exposing her chest. Even if Tosa Mitsunobu, the decorous court painter, decided to forego this detail in the album leaf, his rendering of the figure's plump cheeks, bud-like red lips, and smiling eyes corresponds to the voluptuous and pretty features said to have captivated Genji. This young woman is the "lady from the west wing" mentioned in the first line of the album's calligraphic excerpt, the Governor of Kii's sister, who has spent the day in her stepmother's quarters. As the daughter of the provincial Iyo Vice Governor, she is described in

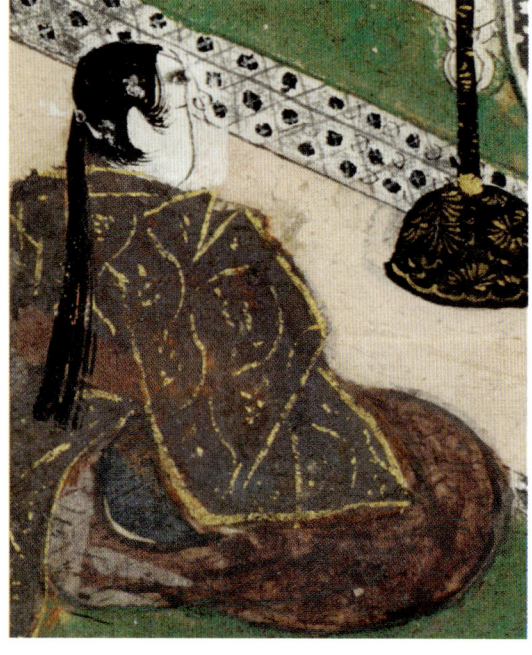

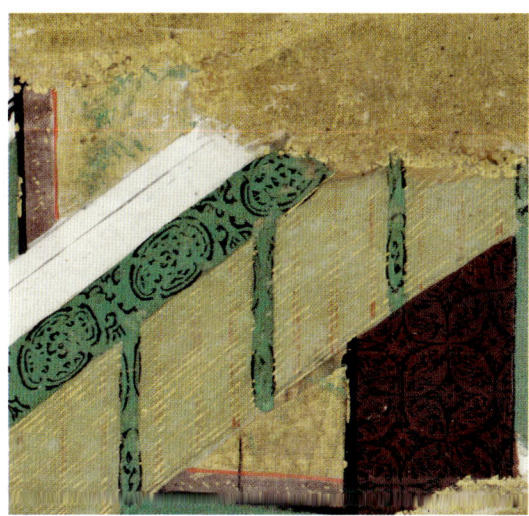

intermediary role in the episode. Although aware of his sister's determination never to meet with Genji again, Kogimi nevertheless admits Genji directly into her chambers after the ladies have retired for the night. Utsusemi, however, is too quick; she sees Genji's shadowy figure moving about in the darkness and slips away, leaving behind nothing but a sheer robe. Genji finds only the somnolent daughter of the Vice Governor. Despite being disappointed and embarrassed, he pretends that she was his intended target all along and makes the most of the situation.

When Genji returns to his Nijō mansion he takes with him the thin robe Utsusemi left behind and suggests its similarity to a cicada's empty shell in a poem he sends to her. The woman too uses the metaphor to characterize herself in a verse she inscribes on the margins of Genji's letter, hence the name "Utsusemi" by which this character and this chapter came to be known. Other *Genji* paintings illustrate the scene of Utsusemi in the act of fleeing and "molting her shell." This album instead showcases Genji's first act of voyeurism. At the same time, pictorial elements provide a subtle commentary that alludes to Genji's relationship to the two women. The folding screen in the inner chamber, shown here in a detail, depicts green bamboo on a gold ground, evoking Utsusemi's said similarity to "supple bamboo" because of her unyielding resistance to Genji's overtures. Meanwhile, a gold cloud hovering above Genji connects outside and inside, pointing past Utsusemi to her stepdaughter, with whom Genji will consummate this act of looking. The young girl serves as the negative counterpart to Utsusemi; she receives not even a single missive from Genji after their tryst, while Utsusemi will continue to fascinate him until they meet again in Chapter Sixteen.

the tale as having been raised with little attention to social decorum and appears rather uncouth to Genji's eyes, though not without charm. It is this guileless young woman who falls prey to Genji's advances when the savvier Utsusemi flees the scene and leaves her stepdaughter in her place.

Genji's field of vision also includes Kogimi, Utsusemi's younger brother. Seated on a tatami mat, he is depicted in profile with a longish face that resembles that of his sister. Indeed, this similarity provokes Genji's interest in the boy, and he spends the night in the company of the youth after being rejected by his sister. Here Kogimi wears the long ponytail of a boy who has not yet undergone a coming-of-age ceremony, reminiscent of images of young men known as *chigo*, acolytes and objects of affection for Buddhist monks in popular tales of the medieval period. The inclusion of the boy in the *kaimami* scene recalls the homoerotic leitmotif in these two chapters while acknowledging his

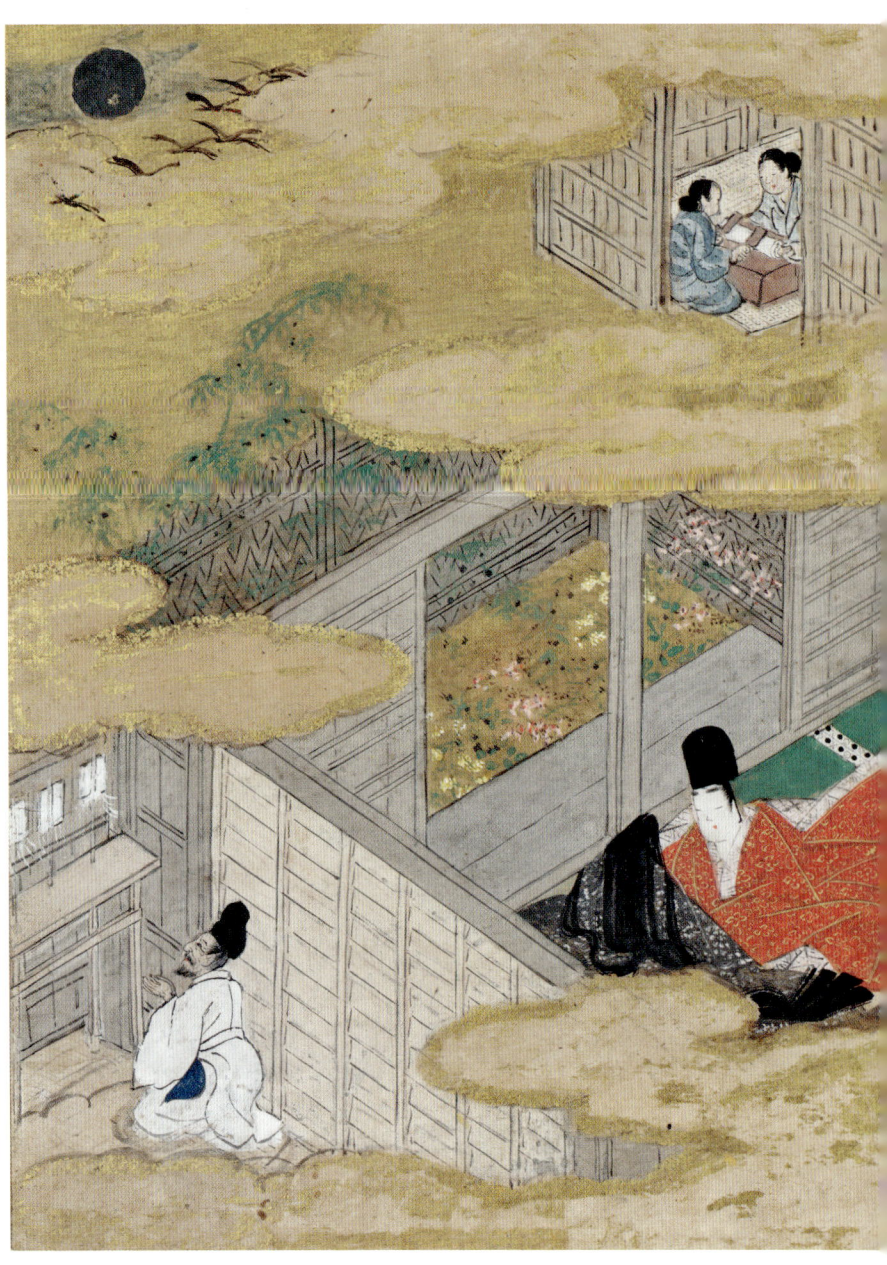

    This lay devotee
Practices the Way—oh, let
    It be our guide:
Even in the lives to come
Do not betray our deep vow.

CRANSTON, P. 702

4
夕顔
The Lady of the Evening Faces
Yūgao

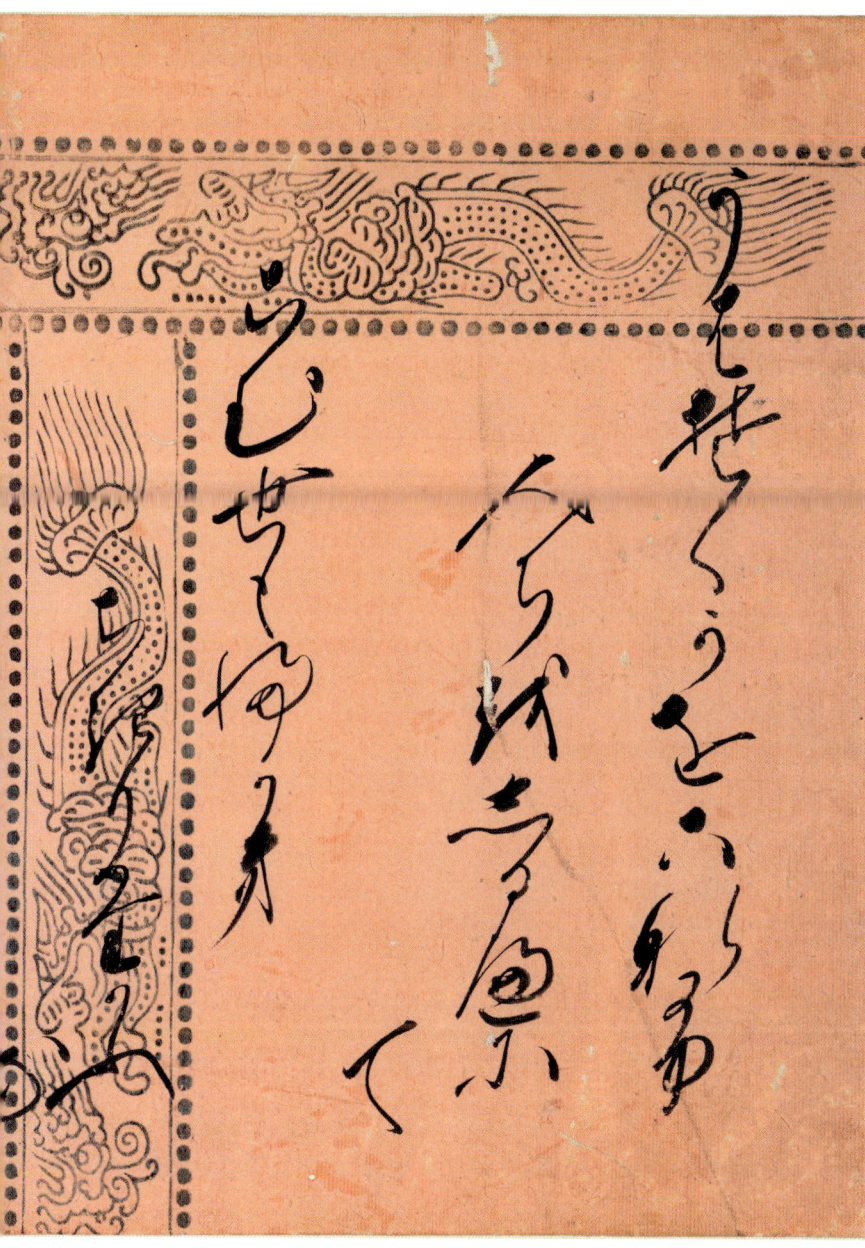

Ubasoku ga
 Okonau michi o
  Shirube ni te
Komu yo mo fukaki
Chigiri tagau na

うはそくかをこなふ
みちをしるへ
　　　て
こむ世もふかき
　ちきりたかふ
　　　な

The season turns to autumn and Genji, still in his seventeenth year, continues to pursue an array of women, including Lady Rokujō, a widow of exalted status with whom he has been carrying on a passionate affair. On his way to visit Rokujō he encounters a character of ambiguous origins known as Yūgao (Evening Faces), named after the white flowering vine that climbs the woven fence of her humble residence. Most illustrations of this chapter depict Yūgao's gift to Genji of a fan inscribed with a coquettish poem accompanied by a white blossom. The painting in this album instead represents a unique moment in the Yūgao chapter just before their affair takes a turn for the supernatural. As we shall see, this encounter culminates in one of the most spine-tingling episodes in Heian literature, with the young woman's sudden death caused by a malevolent spirit.

Genji is shown at Yūgao's residence on the fifteenth day of the eighth month. He has become utterly enchanted by Yūgao, in part because she may be the long-lost lover of Tō no Chūjō, his friend, brother-in-law, and rival. The reader first hears of this mysterious woman, and her daughter fathered by Tō no Chūjō, in Chapter Two, during the "rainy night appraisal." There, Tō no Chūjō explains that she suddenly disappeared after receiving threatening messages from his wife's family. In this image, it is before dawn, and the working-class neighborhood where the lady has been hiding fills with sounds to which Genji is unaccustomed: the rough voices of laborers, the thumping of a mortar and pestle hulling rice, and the dull rhythms of women pounding cloth. Gold clouds and architectural lines divide the painting into distinct quadrants bearing poetic motifs associated with the auditory landscape of autumn, namely the pounding of cloth (*kinuta*), and geese (*kari*). The garden teems with delicate pink and yellow flowers, and the painting evokes details cited by Genji in the tale, most notably Chinese bamboo, dew sparkling on the plants, and a cacophony of chirping insects. In keeping with a theme of hidden identity that runs throughout this chapter, Genji is said to disguise his status by wearing a hunting robe (*kariginu*), a garment rarely worn by someone of his stature. The striking red robe in the painting, embellished with a gold floral pattern, is far from understated, however, and it falls open casually to reveal the edge of a lightly colored undergarment. Yūgao faces Genji, her hair cascading down the back of her robe for the viewer to see.

What appears to be a romantic interlude between Genji and Yūgao is in fact suffused with religious overtones. As Genji pledges vows of love that will last into the next life, he overhears an old man intermittently intoning the name of the future Buddha Maitreya and thumping his forehead to the ground in ritual preparation for a pilgrimage to the Yoshino Mountains. Inspired by this hearing, Genji composes the poem that appears in the album leaf, a verse that deftly alludes to vows both romantic and Buddhist. The poem begins with the term *ubasoku*, a word derived from the Sanskrit term *upāsaka* that denotes a lay devotee who performs Buddhist austerities in the mountains and aims to acquire magico-religious powers. The pictorial counterpart

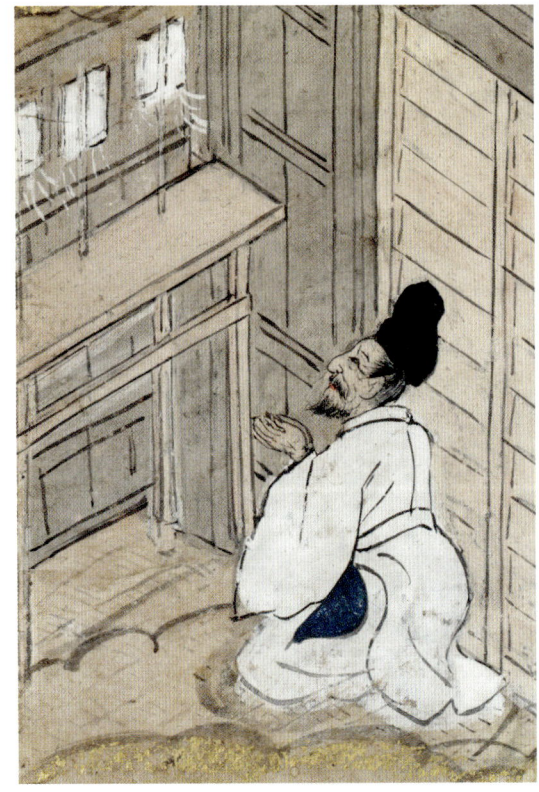

The Tale of Genji

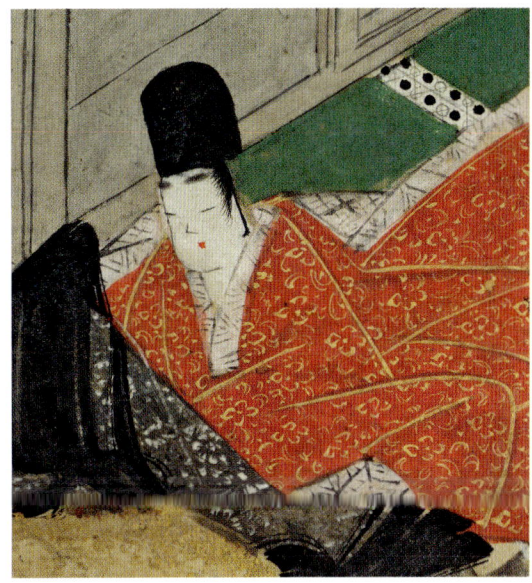

to this poem, the figure in the lower left of the painting, is unique among extant *Genji* paintings. The elderly figure clasps his hands in prayer and faces a simple wooden altar outfitted with white paper streamers (*gohei*) that signify ritual purification and sacred space. The mystical atmosphere conjured by his presence is echoed by the figure of Yūgao. At the time of the album's creation, Yūgao was the subject of a popular Noh play in which the character reappears after her death as a ghost seeking Buddhist salvation. The same poem that graces the calligraphy leaf here appears word for word near the climax of the play as Yūgao embarks on her spiritual path; its inclusion suggests how the theatrical, spectral version of this character found expression in medieval painting.

Genji's conspicuous red garment also foretells the death of Yūgao. According to the tale, after the scene depicted here, Genji whisks Yūgao away to a deserted villa, where he has a disturbing dream of a beautiful woman violently shaking his lover, only to awaken to discover Yūgao convulsing and near death. Her breathing stops and Genji begins to panic, drawing his sword and calling for his attendant Koremitsu. Yūgao has been attacked, it seems, by the angry spirit of Genji's lover Lady Rokujō. The language describing this scene is reminiscent of a ghost story, with a chilling wind that extinguishes the oil lamps, and creaking pines outside preceding another brush with the phantom woman as she sweeps in to deal the final blow to Yūgao. Genji must face the gruesome task of disposing of his lover's corpse and concealing his involvement in the tragic and potentially scandalous situation. He arranges for her body to be taken to a temple in the Eastern Hills of the capital for Buddhist rites and cremation, and later travels there incognito for one last glimpse of his lover. Despite taboos concerning contact with a dead body, Genji tenderly lifts her hand with no sense of repulsion, overcome with sadness and regret. He later reflects that lying there she looked no different from when he had last seen her, "still wrapped in my own crimson robe." The vibrant red robe Genji wears in the album painting is the same one that will be draped over the corpse of the young woman seated before him—a subtle and unsettling foreshadowing of events to come.

Like Utsusemi before her, Yūgao fretted over her low social status and refused to reveal her identity. At the same time, the text suggests an even more undistinguished status, likening her to a lady of the evening by associating her with the lowly "evening flower" that blossoms only after dark. Yūgao declares that she is "nothing but a fisher's child," an allusion to a famous poem associated with a category of peripatetic female entertainer. In fact, Yūgao's father was of high rank, but his death left her without support. When the phantom woman attacks in the abandoned villa, she rebukes Genji for dallying with a woman of such low status. Apparently Genji's gravest sin lay in his transgression of social boundaries. The chapter ends several weeks after Yūgao's passing. Its final scene witnesses Genji returning the robe likened to a "cicada shell" to Utsusemi, thus closing the curtain on two of the most famous amorous adventures of Genji's youth.

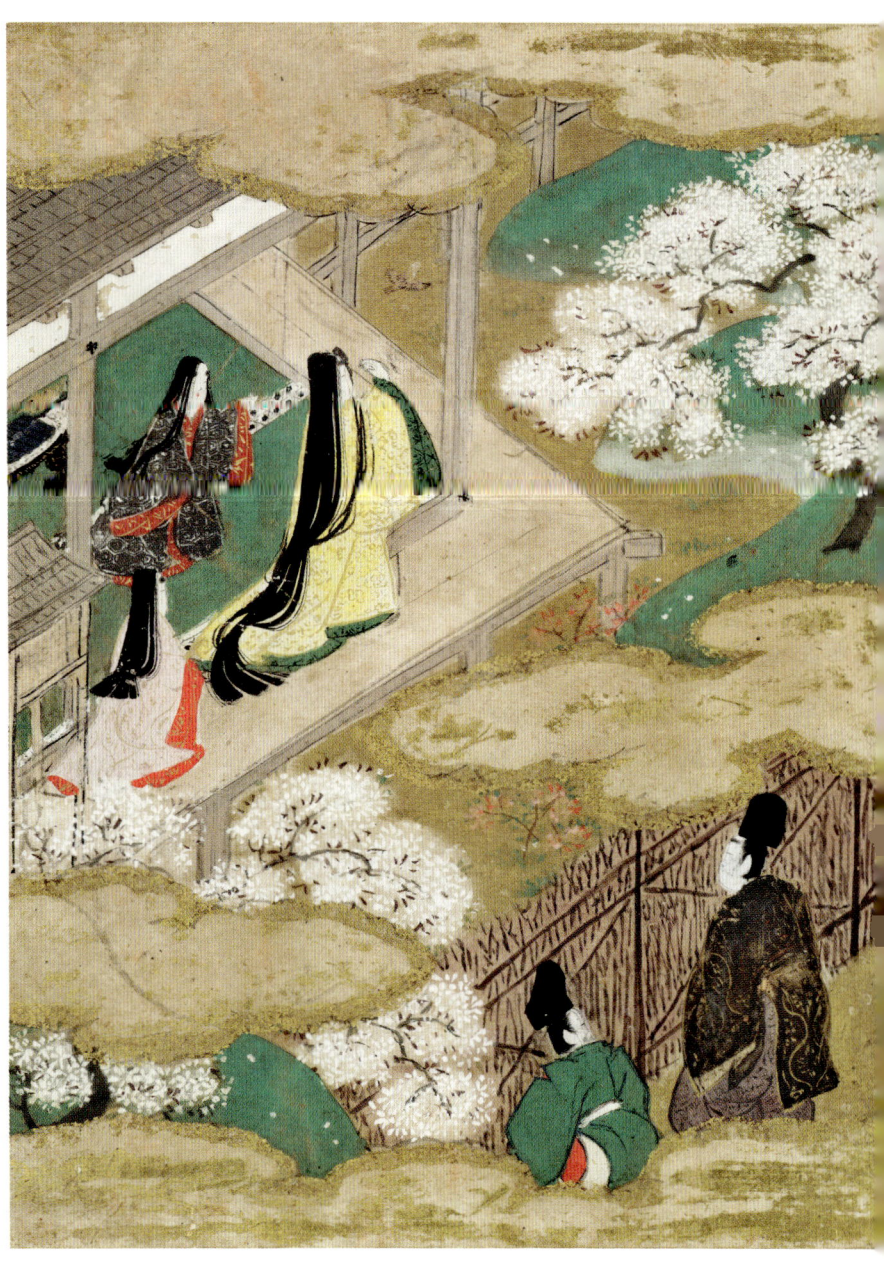

    Where is the garden
For this young grass to grow in?
    Since it cannot know,
The dewdrop that one day must leave
Finds no quiet space to fade.

CRANSTON, P. 708

5

若紫

Little Purple Gromwell

Wakamurasaki

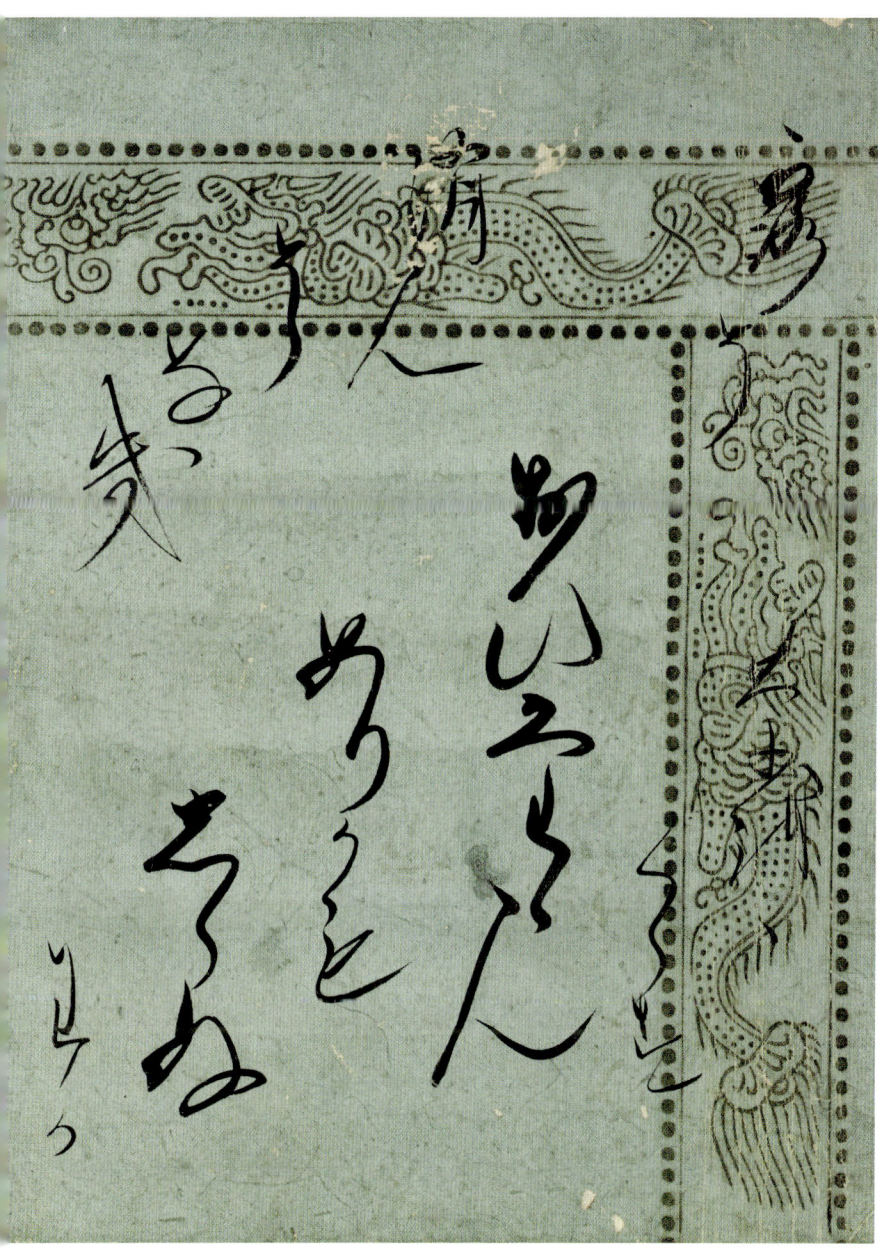

Oitatan
Arika mo shiranu
Wakakusa o
Okurasu tsuyu zo
Kien sora naki

露そ　くさを　
消ん　おひたゝん
　そら　ありかも
　な　しらぬ
　き　わか

Among the early chapters in *The Tale of Genji*, Chapter Five is notable for introducing Murasaki, the young woman who will go on to become Genji's primary companion and greatest love. Their encounter is initiated by a bout of fever that causes Genji to seek the healing powers of a Buddhist ascetic living in the northern mountains. His journey there gives rise to some of the most evocative descriptions in the tale and sets the stage for the scene depicted in the album. As if the ordinary rules of time do not pertain to this mountain site, the spring blossoms that have already faded in the capital burst back to life at higher altitudes. Hilltop vistas afford Genji a new and invigorating perspective of the surrounding landscape, views that are described with Buddhist imagery that resonates with larger themes in the tale. Genji's imperial parentage and right to ascend the throne, for example, is here manifest in references to divine rulership; the text equates Genji with a Buddhist ruler or Dharma King who only appears in the world once every three thousand years. The Buddhist nature of this chapter suggests that the worldly events and Genji's seemingly immoral acts are in fact being determined by unseen forces, all part of a preordained plan.

The spells of the healer whom Genji meets on the mountain, and his own meditations, prove effective, for soon he is well enough to investigate his surroundings, in particular an intriguing abode nestled amid the temple buildings and hermitages that dot the hills below. From far above, Genji sees the house, surrounded by a brushwood fence, as well as several page girls emerging to fetch water and flowers for Buddhist devotions. His interest piqued, the young courtier descends the mountainside for an eye-level view of the house, which is the moment captured in Mitsunobu's painting. The house is framed by two cherry trees in full bloom and connects to a temple building in the "overhanging style" (*kakezukuri*), the supporting columns of which are visible in the middle of the painting, while a shelf on the left with its own miniature roof is for holding Buddhist offerings, signaling that the house's inhabitants are devotees.

With his attendant Koremitsu at his side, Genji peers over the fence to behold a bustling scene in which three figures attempt to retrieve Murasaki's sparrow. The tiny bird has been let loose from its cage by the girl attendant Inuki, shown standing on the veranda in a pink robe. Genji watches as the older nursemaid Shōnagon jumps into the fray. Dressed in a bright yellow garment, she stands near the edge of the veranda raising a hand to call the bird depicted in mid-flight. While the attractiveness of all the ladies is duly noted, it is Mursasaki who leaves Genji mesmerized. She is the small girl facing him directly, whom Genji correctly surmises could be no more than ten years of age. He notes the way her hair falls loose against her shoulders, spreading out like a fan, and he finds her face, reddened from wiping away tears, utterly adorable.

But what attracts Genji to Murasaki most of all, and what drives his subsequent abduction of the child (an act deemed shocking by every character who witnesses it in the tale), is the girl's striking resemblance to Fujitsubo, the consort of Genji's father, the Emperor. Genji has been engaged in an affair with Fujitsubo, now pregnant with a child he rightly suspects to be his own. A familial tie substantiates the resemblance between the two women—Murasaki is the daughter of Fujitsubo's older brother, Prince Hyōbu, and thus her niece. Although Murasaki will become one of the most central figures in the tale, thoughts of her frequently mingle with those of Fujitsubo in Genji's

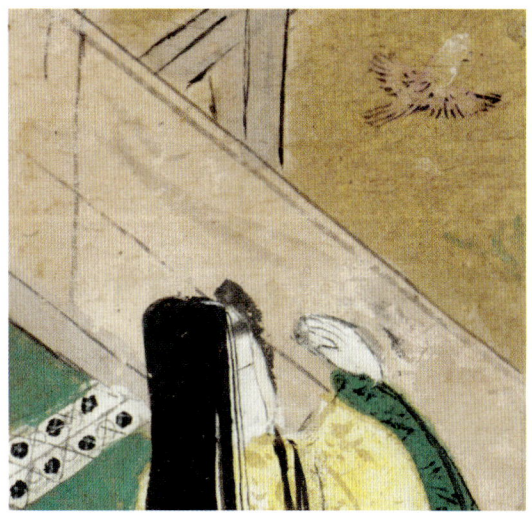

mind, and here she seems almost to materialize out of his intense desire for the great lady.

The young Murasaki has been residing with her maternal grandmother, an ailing nun who has been charged with the girl's care since her mother's death. It is the grandmother's voice that is captured in the painting's accompanying poem. There she expresses a desire to leave the world in a spiritually elevated manner, free from attachment, as well as a reluctance to do so while the fate of her granddaughter remains undecided. The calligraphy is inscribed on green paper evoking a field of grass, and begins with a boldly brushed sequence of *kana* with the word "to grow" (*oitatan*), a reference to the "young grass" (*wakakusa*) in the nun's care. The inscription jumps from the undecorated center of the sheet to the vertical dragon border on the right, where our eye is led above to the word "dew" (*tsuyu*) in the upper right corner. The nun uses this poetic metaphor to refer to herself, a fragile drop that should have evaporated but that clings stubbornly to the young grass. The word "dew" is brushed conspicuously as a logograph instead of in *kana* at the highest spot on the paper. Yet in another sense it is also diminished in size and hidden in the border, conveying the ambiguous position of the nun who utters the verse while longing for her own nonexistence. The final line of the poem laments her inability to "vanish into the sky," a sentiment conveyed with brushstrokes that trail across the top of the paper like smoke from a funeral pyre. Later, as Genji pines for Fujitsubo, his desire to possess Murasaki intensifies, whereupon he intones the closing line from this very poem about the nun's departure from the world. To Genji's ears, the verse must suggest a certain justification for taking the girl and lends authority to his own stated belief that such

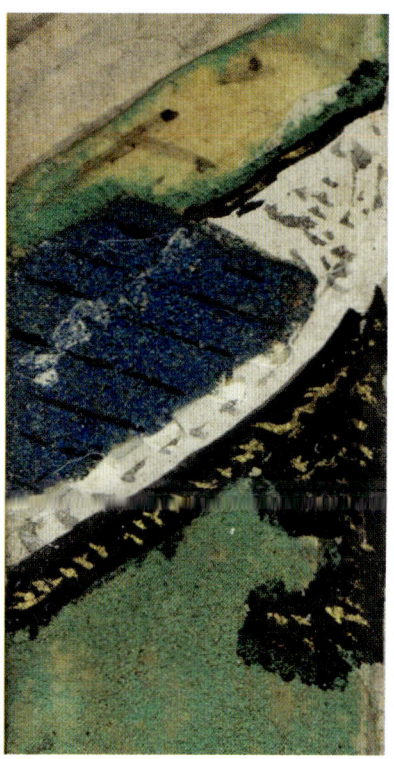

an action is karmically determined. Soon he learns that the nun has passed away, making the circumstances right for him "to pluck the young flower."

The painting anticipates the girl's fate by removing the nun from the scene and placing six indigo-colored sutra scrolls on an armrest as her metonymic replacement. In the tale, the nun reads from a sutra while Genji observes her, and the vast majority of pictorial representations of this scene include the grandmother. Her absence transforms the accompanying poem into the voice-over narration of an absent figure, the vanished dew that has left its little plant behind.

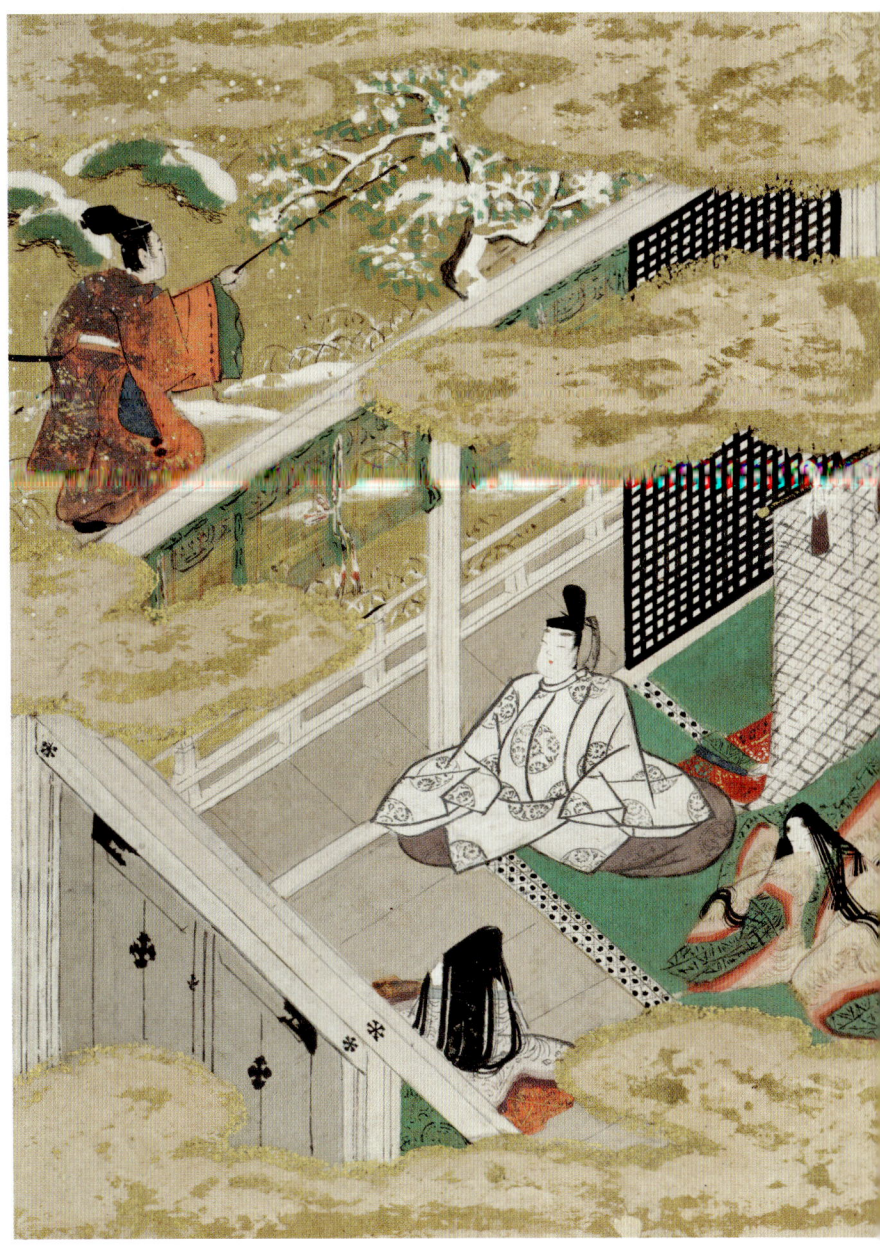

Noticing a mandarin orange tree covered in snow, Genji ordered one of his men to clear it off. A neighboring pine, seemingly out of envy, rose up and shook off its own heavy branches. The cascades of snow that suddenly came crashing down reminded him of those famous waves of Sue.

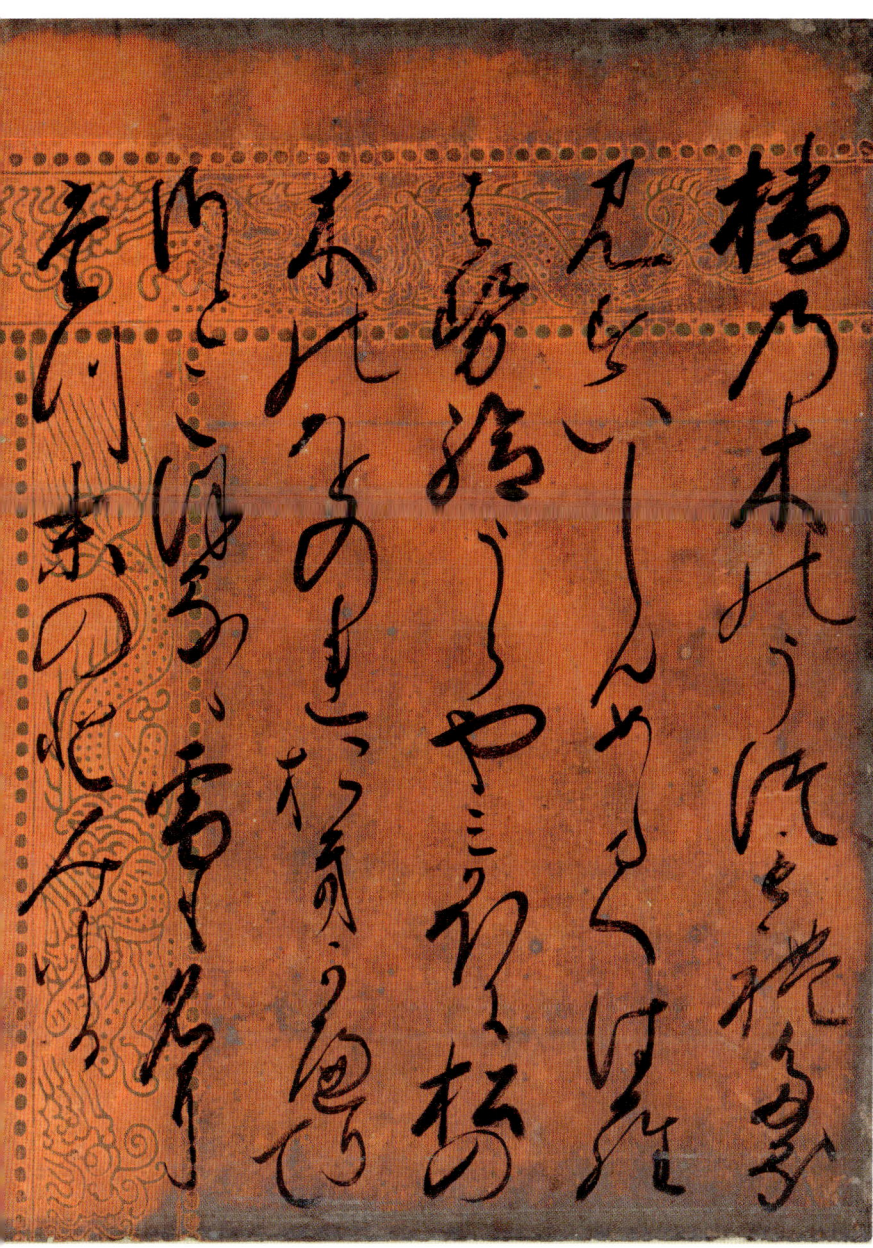

6
末摘花
The Safflower
Suetsumuhana

Tachibana no ki no uzumoretaru, mizuijin meshite harawasetamau. Urayami gao ni, matsu no ki no onore okikaerite sato koboruru yuki mo, na ni tatsu Sue no to miyuru.

橘の木のうつもれたる
みすいしんめしてはら
はせ給うらやみかほに松の
木のをのれおきかへりて
さとこほるゝ雪も名に
たつ末のとみゆる

The first chapters in *The Tale of Genji* present a series of remarkable female characters encountered by the young Genji, and Chapter Six is no exception, introducing the incomparable Suetsumuhana, the daughter of the late Hitachi Prince, eking out a meager existence in her father's desolate old mansion. When the chapter begins, Genji is still mourning the loss of Yūgao and is susceptible to hints of possible women who might console him. When the court lady Taifu no Myōbu, who as the daughter of Genji's childhood nurse relates to him like a sister, speaks of a princess skilled at the *koto* and living alone in straitened circumstances, Genji lets his imagination get the best of him. In an encounter staged by Myōbu, Genji does not get a glimpse of the woman but overhears a few strains of her music. When in addition he discovers his friend and rival Tō no Chūjō lurking in the princess's garden at the same time, he is spurred into romantic action. He begins sending poetic missives and enters into the rituals of courtship with nighttime visits, clearly intrigued by the woman's royal bloodline. After long periods of utter silence on her part, or disappointing letters written by proxy, he begins to fear that her reticence may reflect nothing more than ineptitude with the brush and versification. And yet, because their late-night encounters have not afforded him a good look at her, he visits once more, leading to the climactic moment in the chapter.

In the stark light of a winter morning, with the sun reflecting off the snow, Genji gets a clear view of the woman's features only to wish they could have remained hidden. He tries but fails to turn away and instead fixates on her attributes, giving the reader a unique and near clinical description of the character's physical appearance. Her torso is said to be overly long, her complexion so white that it looks bluish, and her bone structure, the line of her jaw and forehead, disconcertingly angular and broad. Most shocking to the young courtier, however, is her enormous nose, which prompts him to invoke in comparison the proboscis of the bodhisattva Fugen's elephant mount. The nose is lengthy enough to extend outward and then curl under, ending with a hideous bright red tip. Genji later conjures up this image in a cruel poem, privately scribbled to himself, lamenting his association with the "safflower," known for being picked by its bulbous red blossom:

Natsukashiki	Not for this color
Iro to mo nashi ni	Do I yearn, remembering
Nani ni kono	Some cozy love;
Suetsumuhana o	Why did I brush against my sleeve
Sode ni furekemu	The pinch-bright safflower bloom?

CRANSTON, PP. 720–21

The album painting depicts Genji in the princess's company on that bright winter morning, but while the tale's prose may have been harsh, the court painter avoids picturing the woman's unattractiveness. Indeed, she resembles most of the women in the album, with a nose as petite as any other and a forehead and jaw just as pleasantly round. Visual cues do, however, indicate that this is none other than the woman nicknamed the Safflower Princess. The hand raised to her mouth recalls the unattractive giggle she issues in lieu of a thoughtful response to Genji's banter. Meanwhile, a close look at the woman's robe reveals short strokes of brown pigment and gold paint on the surface that connote her sable fur jacket, a hopelessly outdated and inappropriate garment that keeps her from freezing in her dilapidated old house. The painting thus alludes to her unsightly appearance and ruinous living conditions, but still emphasizes Genji. Depicted beneath a prominent gold cloud, he glances outside at an attendant brushing snow from a mandarin orange tree. The exterior scene is described in a charming manner in the accompanying text, in which the chain reaction of falling snow from tree to anthropomorphized tree reminds Genji of a famous line of poetry. In the old poem, the speaker likens his drenched sleeves to waves of tumultuous rain pouring down on the "pine-laden mountain of Sue" (*Sue no matsuyama*). Gazing on the tableau in Suetsumuhana's garden, Genji revels in his own erudition and longs for a companion to understand the reference, someone other than the dim-witted princess.

Although the passage in the tale has Genji glimpsing the snow shower from inside his carriage while departing the residence, the album painting

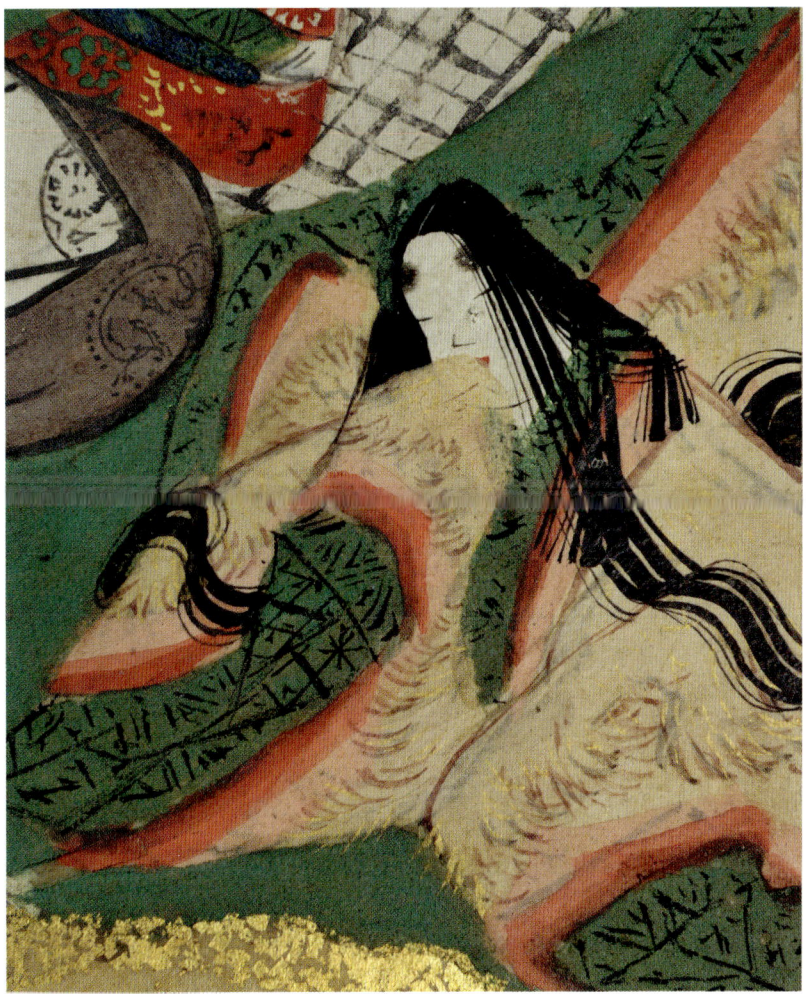

keeps him in the company of the princess during this moment of poetic allusion. The reason for this pictorial conflation may simply represent an economy of pictorial means, allowing for two scenes within the narrow format of the album leaf. But the impetus to combine these moments may also have come from the album's patron. Note that a line in the calligraphic excerpt, "the renowned Sue," contains a homophone for the surname of the Sue family, who commissioned the album. In the era when the album was made, it was common practice at poetic gatherings to compose a line of verse that embedded within it the host's surname. Ending the calligraphic passage in the album not only with the homophone for "sue" but also with a line that literally means "the renowned Sue" (*na ni tatsu Sue*) is likely more than coincidental. Viewed this way, the hybrid image does double duty, emphasizing the snow scene while including Suetsumuhana, the namesake of the chapter, depicted here with only a hint of unsightliness, so as not to detract from the commemoration of the patron. The image in the album depicts a seemingly jovial couple, obscuring the disappointment the princess engenders, but perhaps also pointing to Genji's compassion. Ultimately the misfortunes of the Safflower Princess only highlight the benevolence of the young man as he overcomes his repulsion and commits to looking after the woman, bestowing his radiance on her household for years to come.

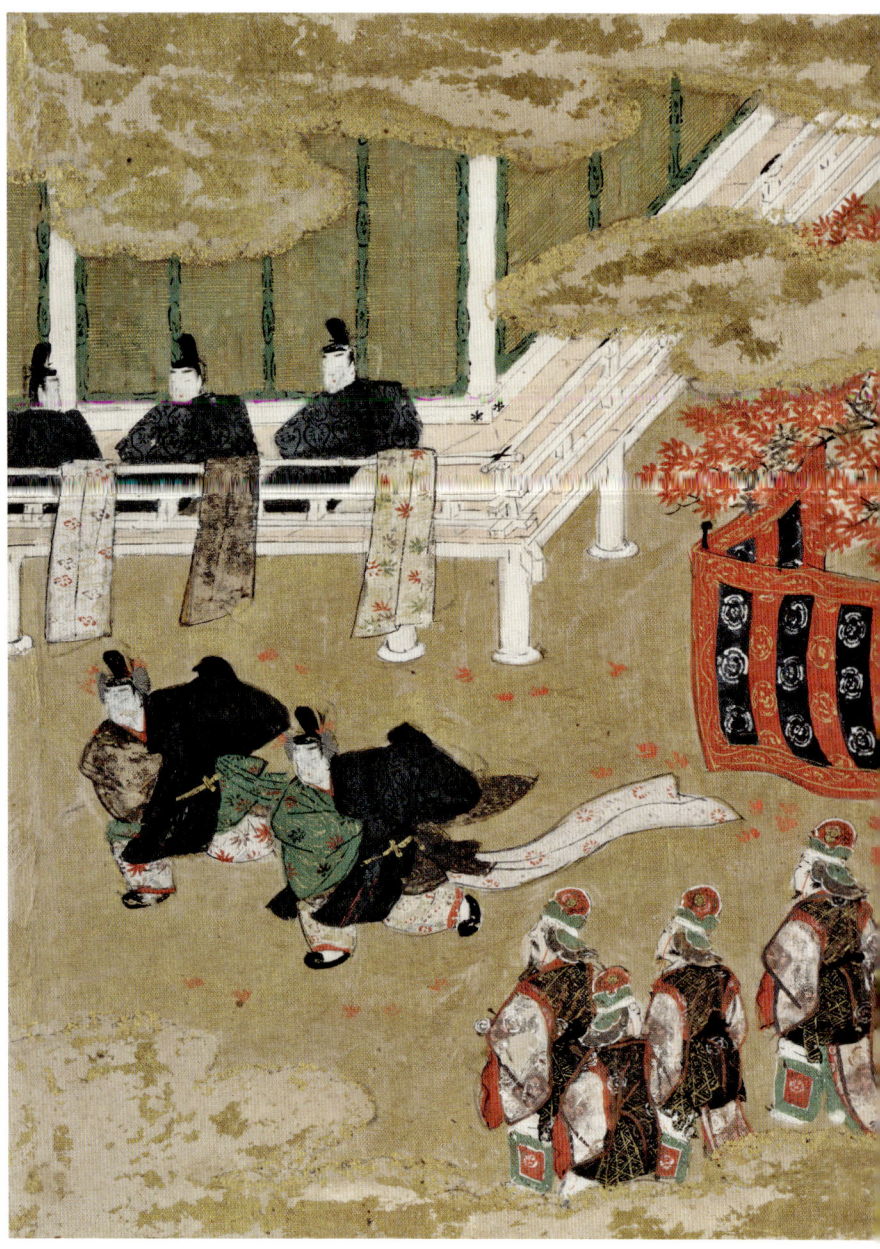

Amidst the colorful shades of falling autumn leaves, "Waves of the Blue Sea" shone forth with a frightening beauty.

7

紅葉賀

An Imperial Celebration of Autumn Foliage

Momiji no ga

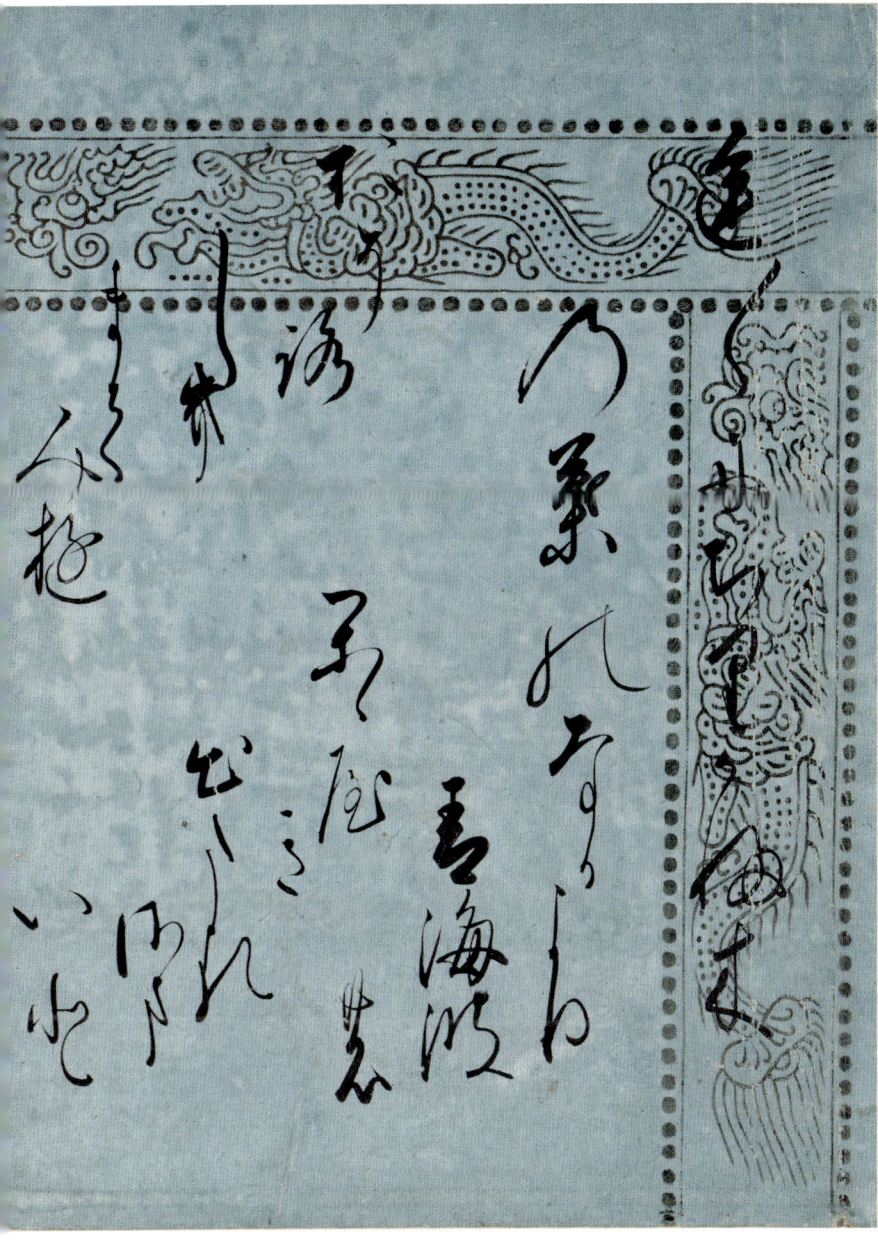

Iroiro ni chirikau ko no ha no naka yori, Seigaiha no kagayaki idetaru sama ito osoroshiki made miyu.

色々にちりかふ木の葉のなかより青海波のかかやき出たるさまいとおそろしきまて見ゆ

During the late autumn of Genji's eighteenth year, against a seasonal backdrop of fall colors and falling crimson leaves, a grand event is held at the palace of the Retired Emperor to celebrate his longevity. With the reigning Kiritsubo Emperor (Genji's father), and the Crown Prince (Genji's half brother) both in attendance, the audience for the event includes three generations of the imperial line. Lavish performances take place before them as festive decorated boats float across the pond, and as many as forty musicians perform throughout the day. The most spectacular and moving presentation of the festivities is said to be *Waves of the Blue Sea* (*Seigaiha* 青海波), a dance and song recitation set to Chinese-style music performed by Genji and Tō no Chūjō. The calligraphy leaf for Chapter Seven was fittingly brushed by the only imperial family member among the album's calligraphers, which augments the subject matter of the painting. The blue background of the sheet evokes the watery imagery of the dance, the title of which appears near the bottom of the sheet, like rippling water that buoys the calligraphy above. The final words of the excerpt hover at the top of the sheet and describe the beauty of Genji's performance as "frightening" (*osoroshiki*) in its sublimity.

In the album painting all eyes are on Genji and Tō no Chūjō, depicted in mid-performance. The three men of the imperial house, as custom dictates, do not appear, but are assumed to be within the building to the left, concealed behind blinds. Acting as their visual proxy, three noblemen seated on the veranda in black formal attire, their trains draped over the balustrade, turn to gaze at the pair. Meanwhile, in the lower right corner a group of musicians appear mesmerized by the display. The branches of a maple tree at the height of its autumn foliage enter the scene from the far right and seem to be the source of the red leaves that have scattered on the ground and that decorate the men's headdresses. In most paintings of this scene by later artists, the musicians stand behind a black and red curtain (*manmaku*), which here surrounds the tree, and the ensemble is usually shown with members playing the drum (*dadaiko*), reed pipe (*shō*), and small oboe (*hichiriki*). This painting instead shows at least some of the musicians pausing to watch the performance. Following the choreography of this particular dance, both Genji and Tō no Chūjō lunge forward holding their right arm close to the body, while fluttering the voluminous sleeves of the left to evoke the rolling waves of the sea.

The two men appear to be nearly identical in the painting, despite the description in the tale that Tō no Chūjō, although handsome and talented, is to Genji as an average mountain tree is to a cherry tree in full bloom. In terms of bloodlines and rank, Tō no Chūjō is Genji's near equal: the two men are cousins, sons respectively of the Kiritsubo Emperor and his sister Ōmiya, sharing a common imperial grandfather. They are also brothers-in-law, after Genji's betrothal to Tō no Chūjō's sister Aoi in Chapter One, a marriage that is the root cause of resentments for both parties. By marrying Genji, a commoner, Aoi cannot become a Consort to the Crown Prince, which prevents this Fujiwara Ministerial family from

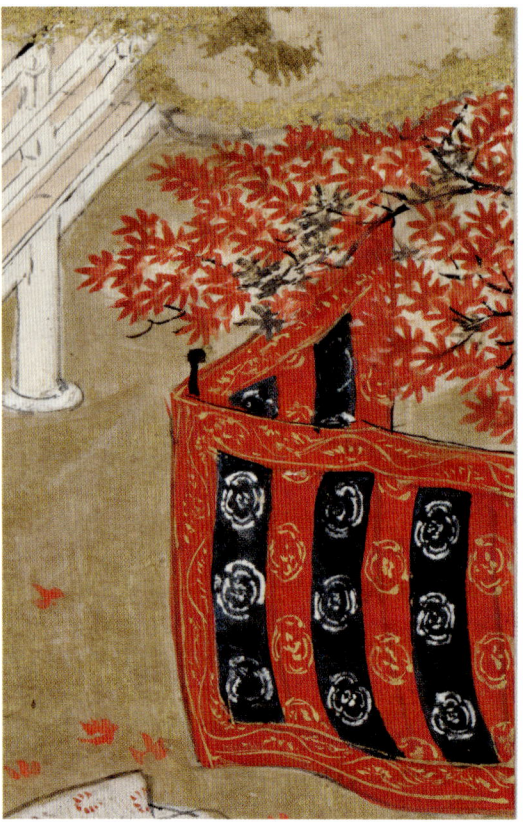

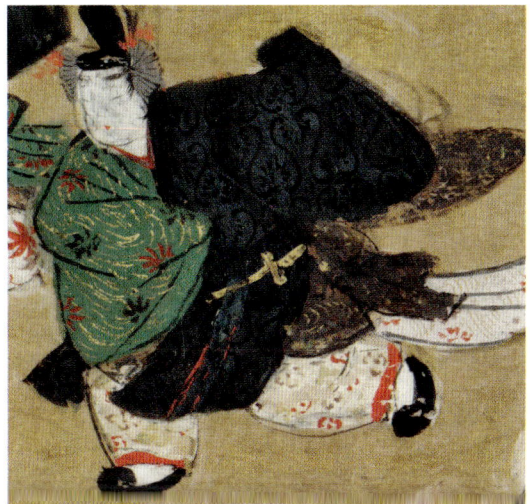

wielding control over the imperial matriline, at least for this generation. Beacuse she is his only sister, this has ramifications for Tō no Chūjō's own aspirations. The tale's depiction of the rivalry between the two young men never dwells too long on its political basis, however, representing it instead through a veneer of a jocular gamesmanship with homosocial overtones. Such deflection finds perfect expression in another episode in this chapter, when both men engage in a flirtation with one of the Emperor's older handmaidens named Naishi. Tō no Chūjō pranks Genji by donning a disguise and catching him in the act with the old woman, brandishing a sword and feigning to be a jealous lover. Genji catches on to the ruse and horseplay ensues as the men pull at each other's robes, both departing the woman's quarters in disarray. Naishi, although an interesting character in her own right, becomes the butt of a joke over which the two men continue to bond.

The lighthearted interlude allays the somber undertones of Chapter Seven in the representation of the relationship between Genji and Fujitsubo, and their sexual transgression against the Emperor. The performance of *Waves of the Blue Sea* depicted in the album painting is the second rendition of the dance, the first being a private rehearsal of the piece arranged by the Kiritsubo Emperor for Fujitsubo, who would be unable to see it otherwise. What the Emperor stages, seemingly unwittingly, is an encounter between Genji and Fujitsubo, who is at that moment pregnant with Genji's child. As Genji makes clear in a poem he sends to Fujitsubo the next day, he twirled his sleeves for her:

Mono omou ni	Deep in this longing,
Tachimaubeku mo	How I was to rise and dance
Aranu mi no	I could not think;
Sode uchifurishi	Did you guess the heart that beckoned
Kokoro shiriki ya	In the shaking sleeve I waved?
	"In fear and trembling."

CRANSTON, P. 722

By the end of this chapter Fujitsubo has given birth to Genji's son, the future Emperor Reizei, and has been promoted to Empress, rising above the station occupied by the Kokiden Consort. Descriptive terms for radiance in the tale are used exclusively for Genji, Fujitsubo, and now their newborn son, who is described as the moon to Genji's sun, and who resembles his real father to an unsettling degree. Genji is at a remove from the imperial line as he dances *Waves of the Blue Sea* for the lineage of emperors inside the building, but by the end of the chapter, he has fathered a son whom he will watch ascend the throne.

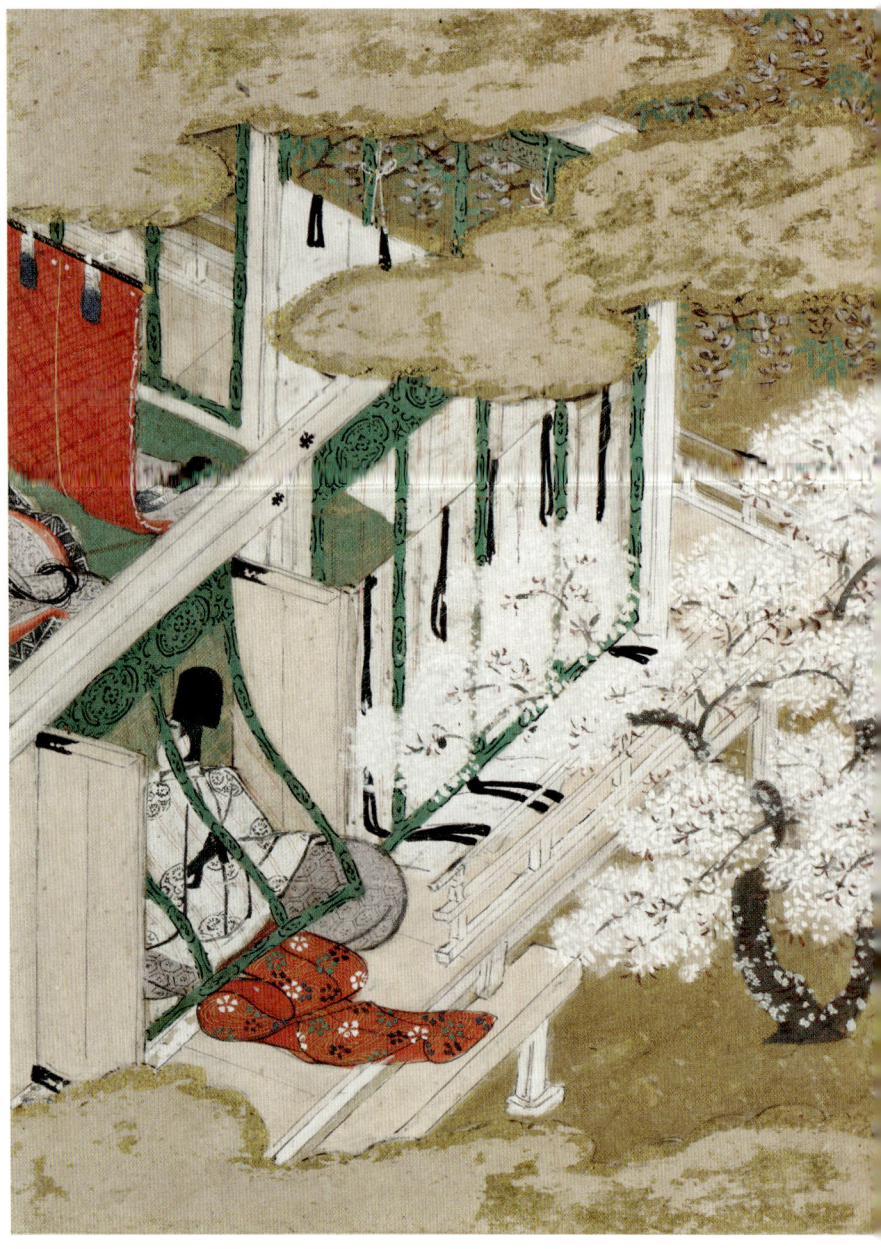

He reached through the curtain and
took her hand,

    Flown like an arrow
Shot from a catalpa bow,
    Lost on Irusa
Longing for Moonset Mountain
To betray the light I glimpsed.

CRANSTON, P. 731

8

花宴

A Banquet Celebrating Cherry Blossoms

Hana no en

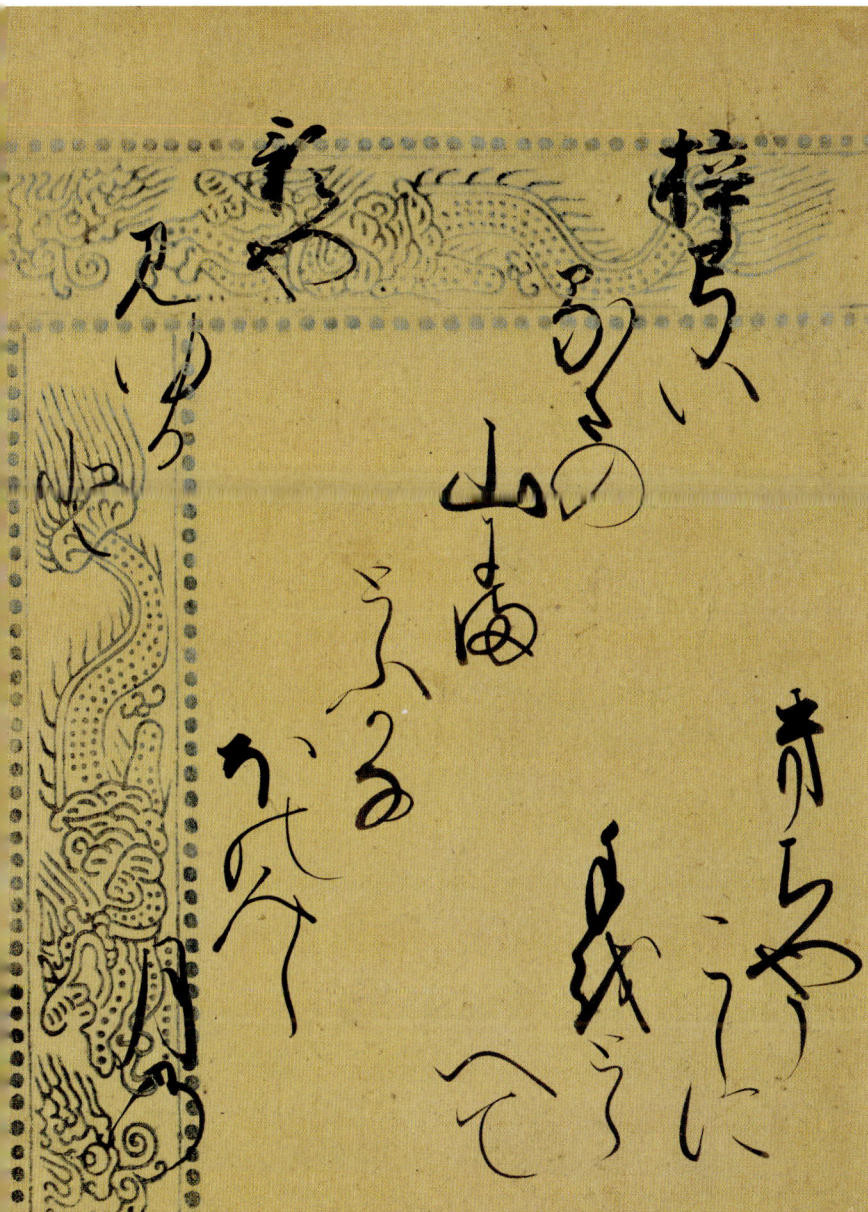

Kichōgoshi ni te o toraete,

    Azusayumi
    Irusa no yama ni
    Madou kana
Honomishi tsuki no
Kage ya miyuru to

梓弓
いるさの山にまとふかな
影やみゆる
ほのみし月の
と

きちやうこしに手をとらへて

Chapter Eight is one of the most sensual in the tale, full of evocative sensory experiences from the lavish performances that take place amid fragrant spring blossoms, to a dreamlike sexual encounter for a libidinous young Genji. Driving much of the behavior in this chapter, however, is an underlying political rivalry between the Minister of the Left and the Minister of the Right, both members of the Fujiwara house with different plans for the imperial succession. The Minister of the Right, father to six daughters, including the senior Kokiden Consort, aims to control the government by manipulating the imperial matriline and the grandsons who inherit the throne. The Minister of the Left, with his only daughter Aoi having married a "genji," can no longer hope for such a form of power and is thus more favorably disposed toward direct imperial rule. During the cherry blossom celebration at the palace that opens this chapter, the Kokiden Consort understandably seethes (personally, and on behalf of her family) when she is forced to watch from afar as Fujitsubo, newly appointed above her as Empress, sits alongside the sovereign, with the Crown Prince, her own son. Kokiden's position will improve as soon as her son ascends the throne, but in the meantime the Minister of the Right arranges marriages for his other daughters to expand his political reach. His fourth daughter is married to Tō no Chūjō, for example, infiltrating the Minister of the Left's faction. And, most important, he intends for his sixth daughter to become the consort of the current Crown Prince, in effect marrying his daughter to her own nephew, but providing him with yet another means to influence the throne.

Enter Genji who consistently manages to thwart well-wrought plans for imperial control by Fujiwara Ministers. After everyone has retired following the blossom banquet at the palace, Genji attempts to access Fujitsubo's quarters but finds the entrance securely locked, leaving him to try his luck among the women in the Kokiden Consort's quarters. There he discovers the alluring sixth daughter of the Minister of the Right, alone and singing a famous line of poetry about the peerless beauty of a misty moon on a spring night. Genji is captivated and acts immediately on his desire, startling the woman, who tries to resist, but gives in when she realizes that he is someone of high rank. In the context of the politics of the chapter, the flowery language of romantic seduction thinly veils an act of sexual aggression against the Minister's family, beginning with the pretense of Genji's ignorance of which sister he has encountered. He leaves the woman without learning her identity, but takes her fan, which bears an image of a moon reflected on the water. This, combined with her earlier poetic invocation, resulted in her nickname, Oborozukiyo, "Lady of the Misty Moon."

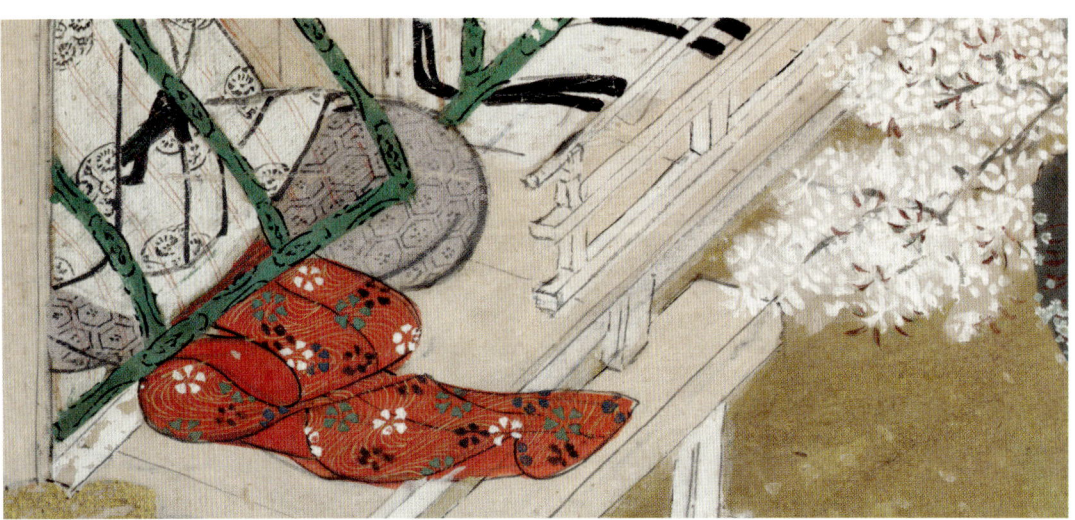

54 | *The Tale of Genji*

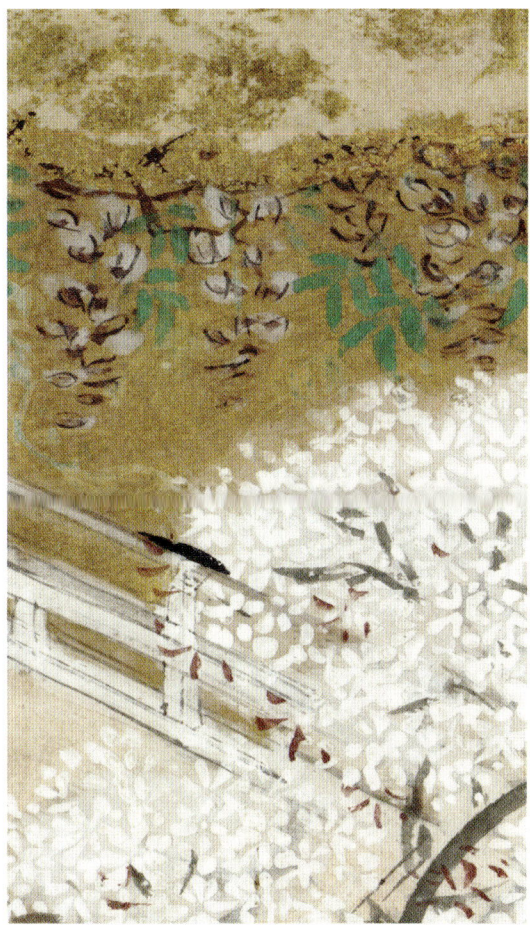

Although the Minister of the Right considers Genji something of a nemesis, he goes out of his way to ensure the young man's presence at his own blossom banquet the following month, unaware that Genji has slept with his treasured daughter intended for court service. The painting in the album depicts Genji at the Minister's residence dressed in what can only be described as an audacious choice of attire. Every other man in attendance wears formal robes (hō), but Genji takes great care in donning an informal white cloak (nōshi) of an elegant Chinese-style weave with a cherry blossom pattern. His costume is a less-than-subtle display of independence, as he exercises the prerogative of a prince to dress in an abbreviated style. Genji takes the display even further by pairing his informal robe with a brightly patterned train of extraordinary length. Here the train is depicted to be of bright red fabric pattered with multicolored flowers floating on a stream of rippling water in gold. The brash ensemble and his late arrival after sunset make for quite an entrance, prompting those in attendance to say he outshone even the Minister's wisteria (fuji), symbol of the Fujiwara house, and the very pretense for the gathering.

To add insult to injury, Genji excuses himself early and steals into the women's quarters at the Minister's home to find his Misty Moon. This is where we find him in the album painting entering beneath the blinds, with Oborozukiyo represented by nothing more than a strand of her hair and the edge of her robe. The painting's concealment of the woman's figure is an ideal pictorial counterpart to Genji's presumed ignorance of her identity. Outside, the flowering branches of a luminescent cherry tree parallel the movement of the lover as he advances into the woman's room. The cherry tree's anthropomorphized form even recalls ancient stories of otherworldly flower spirits, who, in the guise of dashing courtiers, approach unsuspecting young ladies. And the thick application of shell white for the flower petals makes this tree seem exceptionally tactile. The pendulant purple clusters of wisteria appear on the other side of the building, visible through the translucent bamboo blinds and between golden clouds. As the pride of the Minister and the symbol of the Fujiwara, the wisteria's inclusion affirms Genji's audacity, reminding the viewer that the transgression occurs right under the nose of the girl's father. The single poem by Genji chosen to accompany this painting in the calligraphy text enhances the romantic innuendo of the image. Playing on the event of the archery contest, another reason for the gathering at the Minister's residence, Genji likens himself to an arrow shot from a bow. The meandering arrow in the dark is lost, just like Genji, who longs to glimpse that misty moon he once saw. The chapter ends on one of the most puzzling lines in the tale, the nuances of which have been endlessly debated: as Genji recognizes the woman's voice, the narrator says, "he was delighted, and yet…" Something about the situation or the woman seems less than perfect.

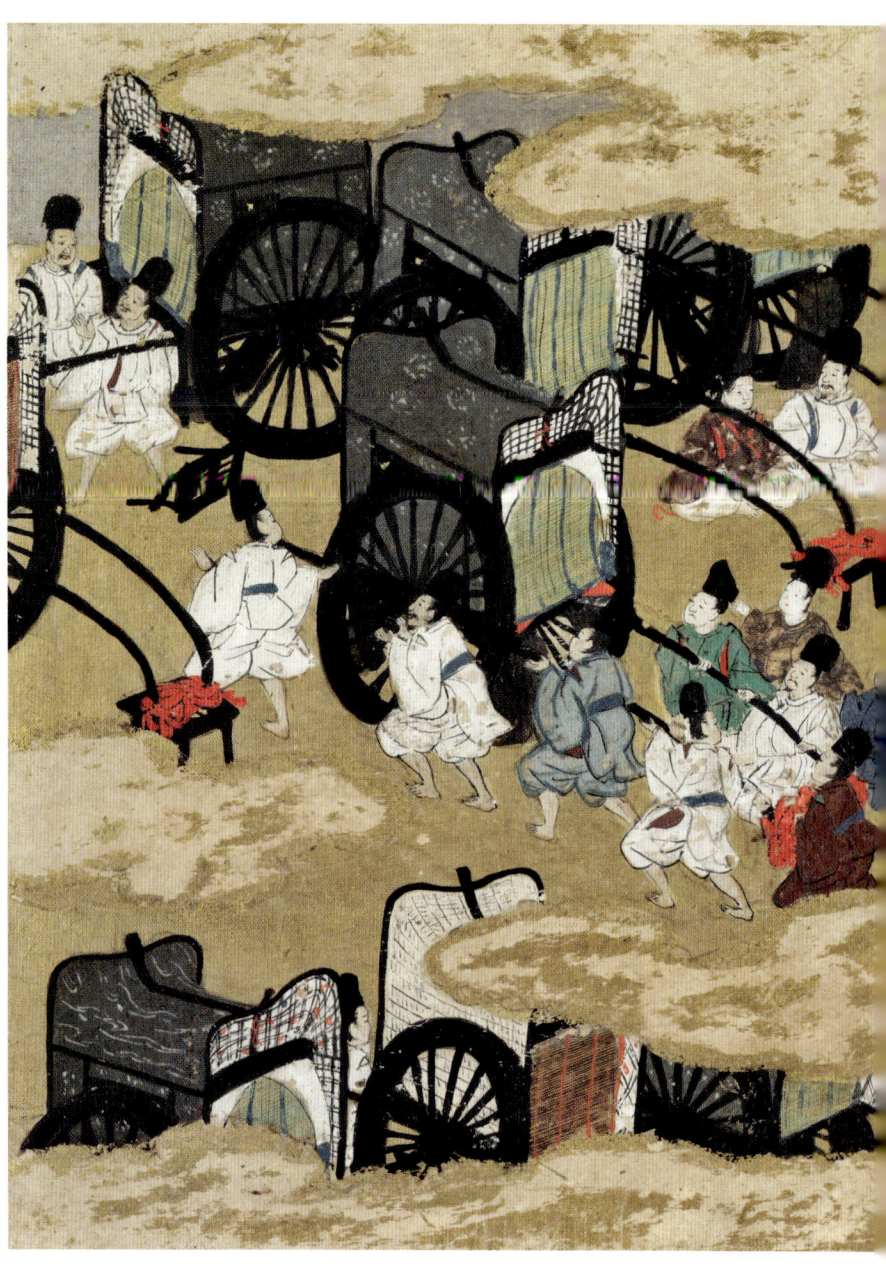

    Only a shining
Shadow on the cleansing stream—
    Hands dipped in vain
From these cold depths I learn
What foul mud clings to me.

CRANSTON, P. 732

9

葵

Leaves of
Wild Ginger

Aoi

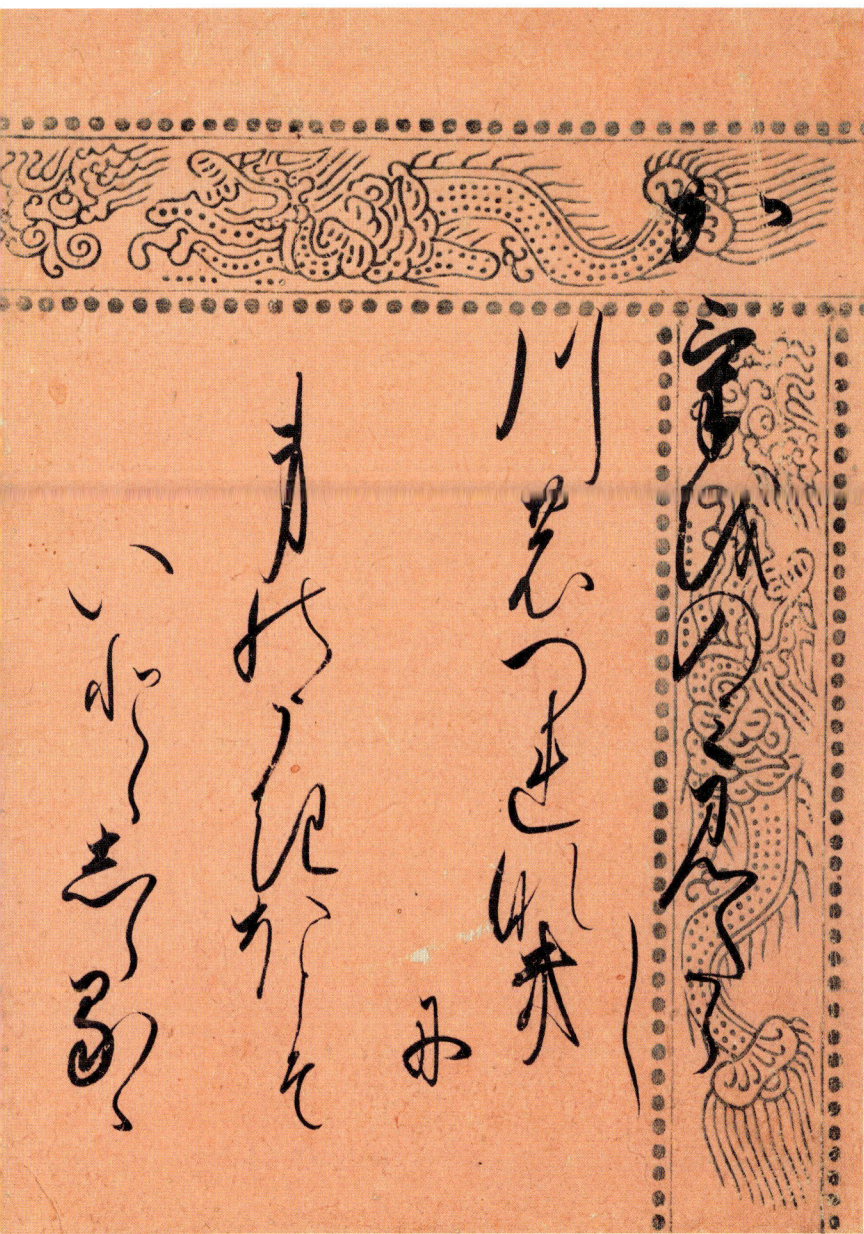

Kage o nomi
Mitarashigawa no
Tsurenaki ni
Mi no uki hodo zo
Itodo shiraruru

かげをのみみたら
し
川のつれなき
に
身のうきほどぞ
いとゞしらるゝ

Genji's wife, whom he officially married after coming of age, takes her name from the title of this chapter, Aoi, the Japanese name for wild ginger, also translated as "heartvine." The plant, which grows two heart-shaped leaves to a single stalk, was used to decorate the carriages and courtier caps of those who attended the annual Aoi Festival of the two Kamo shrines in the capital, an event depicted at the start of Chapter Nine. Lady Aoi bears no poetic relationship to the plant as Yūgao did to the evening flower or Oborozukiyo did to the misty moon, but her fate is sealed during incidents that transpire leading up to the Aoi Festival. Of the eight carriages depicted in the album painting for Chapter Nine, the one that marks the very center of the image belongs to her. As with other high-ranking ladies who traveled by carriage, she remains out of sight, but her identity may be surmised by the details of her vehicle and the distinct edges of colorful robes poking out from beneath its drawn bamboo blinds. This painting lacks the multicolored sleeves described in the tale as emerging from the other carriages, and only a small portion of fabric appears from beneath the blinds of Aoi's carriage, making for a more subdued display. The nine men in Aoi's entourage grasp the shafts of the cart, backing it into an empty spot among a line of other carriages along First Avenue to form a diagonal line across the picture plane. What seems to be a rather orderly maneuver by the Minister of the Left's men in fact represents the aftermath of one of the most famous and only scenes of an altercation in the tale, known as the "confrontation of carriages" (*kuruma no arasoi*).

It is a few days before the Festival proper and Aoi, now pregnant with Genji's child (his son Yūgiri), decides at the last minute to view one of the preliminary events. She ventures out to see the customary procession of the newly appointed priestess of the Kamo Shrines heading to her purification ritual at the Kamo River. The Kamo Shrines (Kamigamo and Shimogamo Shrines), located north of the imperial palace along the banks of the Kamo River and near the sacred Tadasu Forest, housed deities who protected the capital city against malevolent forces. An unmarried princess, often a daughter of the Emperor, was appointed Shrine priestess at the start of a new reign to perform various rites from her official residence, the Sai'in. The reign has changed since Genji's father has abdicated, and the Kokiden Consort's son, Emperor Suzaku, now occupies the throne. The Kokiden Consort herself holds the lofty title of Imperial Mother, and one of her daughters is the new Kamo Priestess. To ensure an impressive retinue to escort the Priestess to her Purification Rites, the Emperor has selected an elite group of the most admired and attractive courtiers, including Genji, who is said to outshine them all. People from all walks of life crowd the procession route to claim a spot that will afford a view of the radiant Genji. Among these onlookers is the Rokujō Lady, Genji's long-standing and neglected lover and a woman of exalted rank. It pains her to have to view him from a distance like a mere onlooker, but she cannot resist the chance to see him in his finery. She travels incognito in a subdued carriage and successfully secures a prime spot along the procession route. That is, until the official wife of Genji shows up and the inebriated men in her retinue shove Rokujō's carriage out of the way to make room for Aoi. An unruly brawl ensues among the men, insults are traded, and someone yells out a comment about Rokujō's affair with Genji that reveals her identity.

Hemmed in by other vehicles, and with her view blocked by Aoi's carriage, Lady Rokujō can only sit and wait, humiliated and seething with resentment. To add to the indignity, the pedestal on which her carriage shafts would normally rest after being unhitched from the oxen has been destroyed in the scuffle. Notice how the other carriages in the image have shafts that rest neatly on stands with red rope coiled around their ends. Without a stand, Rokujō's men must rest the shafts on the wheel hub of a neighboring carriage, lest they lower them to the ground and risk their Lady tumbling forward due to the resulting incline. The whole episode is unbearable for someone of Rokujō's status; she is the widow of an imperial prince, and the mother of a princess, who at that very moment is preparing for her role as Shrine Priestess at Ise, a counterpart to the Kamo Priestess and an honor rarely bestowed.

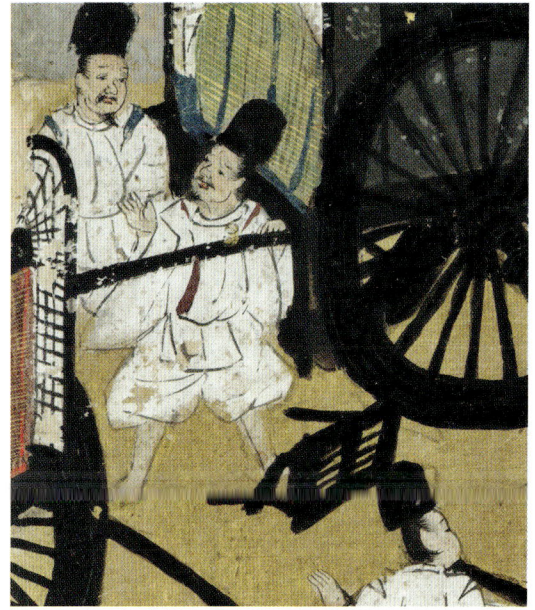

Rokujō has long worried that her affair with the dashing young Genji, seven years her junior, without the recognition of marriage, would destroy her reputation and leave her a laughingstock. The poem in the calligraphic excerpt paired with the painting in the album gives voice to Rokujō's despair as she sits in the carriage. She expresses her sadness that Genji is as inaccessible to her as the fleeting reflection across the waters of "the cleansing stream" of the Kamo River, reminiscent of her own miserable fate (*mi no uki*).

This humiliation at the hands of Aoi, her younger niece by marriage, sets the subsequent events of the chapter in motion. Rokujō's longing for Genji becomes obsessive, and her heart is thrown into so much turmoil that her feelings take the form of a wrathful spirit that torments her rival. The spirit attacks when Aoi is most vulnerable—as she goes into labor with Genji's son—and it displays a tenacity and ferocity that presents the exorcists and spirit mediums with an unprecedented challenge. Rokujō seems to be a victim of her own excessive passions as she recollects in horror a dream in which she violently attacks Genji's wife. The identity of the malignant spirit reveals itself to Genji while he sits at the bedside of his wife, who lies with her belly distended and in the throes of suffering. He hears the chilling voice of Rokujō emerging from Aoi's mouth, asking him to call off the exorcists. The full force of the spirit-taming community is mobilized, and somehow Aoi survives to deliver a healthy baby boy. Days later, when the family assumes Aoi is recovering and all is well, they leave her unattended, allowing the evil spirit to swoop in and deal one final, fatal blow to the young woman. Heart-wrenching scenes of parental grief and spousal mourning follow. The Minister of the Left and his wife Ōmiya must deal not only with the loss of their only daughter but with the inevitable disappearance of Genji from their household as his visits become few and far between.

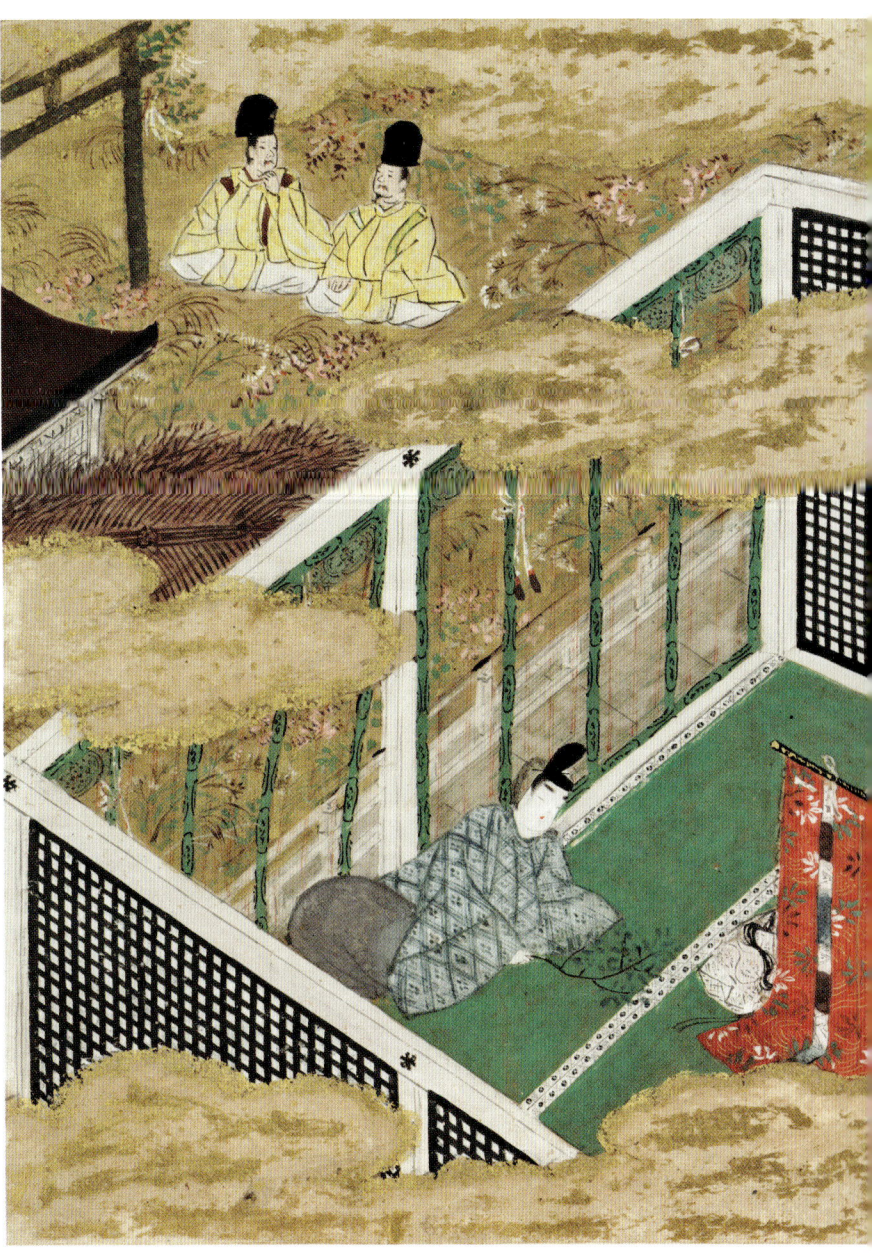

The fence of the gods
Has no signpost cedar tree
　　Standing by its gate;
How then can you have strayed here
To break this *sakaki* branch?

On hearing this Genji replied:

　　When I remembered
Here was where the maiden dwelt,
　　Drawn by my longing
I sought and broke the *sakaki*
For the fragrance of its leaves.

CRANSTON, P. 741

10

賢木

A Branch of Sacred Evergreen
Sakaki

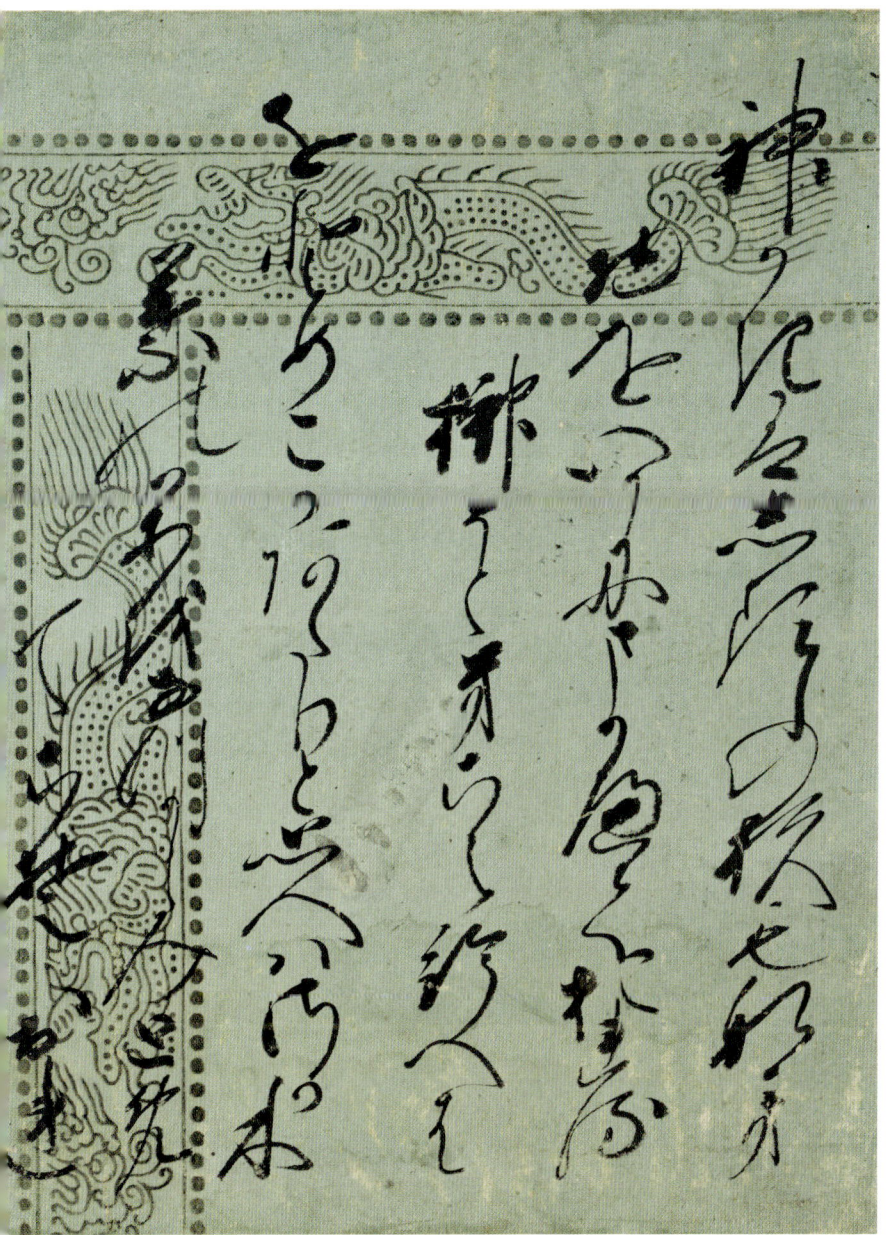

Kamigaki wa
Shirushi no sugi mo
Naki mono o
Ika ni magaete
Oreru sakaki zo

to kikoetamaeba,

Otomego ga
Atari to omoeba
Sakakiba no
Ka o natsukashimi
Tomete koso ore

神かきはしるしの杉もなき
物をいかにまかへておれる
榊そときこえ給へは
をとめこかあたりと思へはさ
か木
葉のかをなつかしみとめ
てこそおれ

Despite all that transpired in the previous chapter, Chapter Ten begins with the general assumption that, given her status, Rokujō will be appointed Genji's official wife, replacing the deceased Aoi. Having encountered the chilling voice of his lover emerging from the possessed body of his wife, however, Genji makes no such overtures, and Rokujō decides that the only course open to her is to leave the capital. She begins making plans to accompany her young daughter, newly appointed as the High Priestess of Ise, to the faraway shrine, which is dedicated to the goddess Amaterasu. Rokujō spends months at the "shrine in the fields" (*nonomiya*), a temporary lodging just west of the capital, where, according to custom, her daughter is to engage in rites of purification before her departure to Ise. The stage is thus set amid this hushed, sacred precinct for a final encounter between Genji and Rokujō, one of the most celebrated scenes in the tale, immortalized in Noh plays from the fifteenth century onward.

Genji crosses the plains of Sagano and basks in the austere scenery on that moonlit night—the withered autumn flowers and thickets of satin-tail grass on route, the chirping of crickets and the sparse strains of a *koto* carried on the wind. The simple wooden structures of the shrine soon come into view surrounded by low-lying brushwood fences and rough-hewn shrine gates made of tree trunks with their bark still intact. The main gate appears in the upper left corner of the album painting, a pictorial motif that makes this famous scene immediately identifiable. It stands amid a dense field of autumn wildflowers—maiden flowers (*ominaeshi*), bush clover (*hagi*), and pampas grass (*susuki*). A delicate vine of green ivy winds its way around the dark brown gateposts. Affixed to the crossbeam is a branch of *sakaki* and a cluster of white paper streamers used for purification and blessing. This is one of four representations of *sakaki* in this pair of album leaves if both text and image are taken into account. The most conspicuous extends from Genji's hand as he leans in toward Rokujō, offering her the evergreen and likening its unfading color to his unchanging feelings for her. Rokujō sits behind a brightly patterned red curtain, only the edge of her white robe and a curling strand of black hair hinting at her presence. In response to Genji's gesture, she speaks the first of two poems inscribed on the album leaf, hers beginning with the word for "deity" (*kami* 神) brushed at the highest point on the green-colored sheet. The darkly brushed character appears on the same visual register as the shrine gate in the upper left corner of the painting and acts as its graphic counterpart, establishing a sacred perimeter around the text-image pairing. The word *sakaki* (榊) appears at the top of the third line, highly visible on an undecorated portion of the paper just below the decorative border. Its placement at the head of a column despite the lack of a natural break in the poetry is the calligrapher's way of announcing the word's thematic importance. This particular logograph, which combines the radical for "tree" and the graph for "deity," resonates with the first character in the excerpt. Another option for the calligrapher would have been to express the word *sakaki* phonetically, as it appears at the bottom of the fourth line in Genji's poem, through two separate *kana* and the character for "tree" (さか木). Instead, the visually dense logograph in the center of the sheet calls attention both

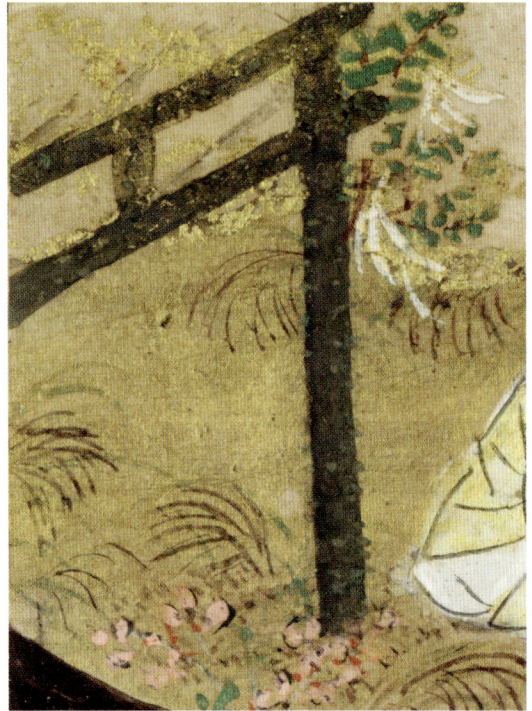

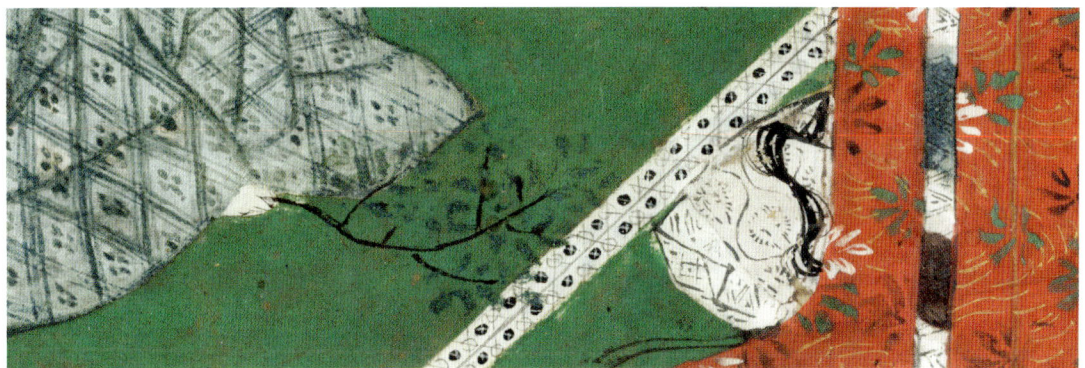

to the word's sacrality and its "thingness," triggering the viewer to search for the object it signifies in the image to the left. There, the painted *sakaki* branch appears at the culmination of a descending diagonal that begins with the sloping tops of the calligraphy and continues with the white borders of the tatami. Both the graphic and pictorial representations of the *sakaki* branch function as centripetal presences in their respective leaves.

Genji's foray into a hallowed precinct of the *kami* and his offering of a sacred branch in the opening scene of this chapter functions as a kind of purification after the death and haunting spirit possession of Chapter Nine, and specifically of the malignancies associated with Lady Rokujō. By this point Rokujō has been rejected by her young lover, subjected to public humiliation and gossip, and she has suffered viscerally while her tormented psyche took malevolent shape to lash out against Aoi. In a culminating scene of the dramatic arc of her story in the last chapter, she finds herself reeking of the poppy seeds characteristically burned at an exorcism, realizes in horror what her wandering spirit has been up to, and tries but fails to wash the smoky smell from her hair and clothing. The representation of Rokujō in this painting by a small portion of a white robe hints at her previous incarnation as a spirit, but also communicates her general reserve, her contrition, and her hesitation to meet with Genji. At the same time, her decision to remove herself from the capital allows for a recasting of the pair's relationship that puts Genji in the position of the rejected lover while allowing Rokujō to recuperate a modicum of dignity and to tame her angry spirit. As dawn breaks they exchange poems of parting, and Genji tenderly takes her hand, hesitating to leave, sensing this will be the last time they see each other. The scene ends with a touching image of Rokujō, her heart full of regret, staring at the empty place where her lover sat just moments before.

Once Lady Rokujō and her daughter have departed for Ise, Chapter Ten takes a dramatic turn, becoming one of the most politically consequential chapters in the book. Genji's father, the retired Emperor, passes away and the political center of gravity radically shifts in the direction of the faction of the Minister of the Right and his daughter Kokiden, the mother of the reigning emperor. The court becomes a hostile, even treacherous place for Genji, and with his status in free-fall, he acts up more recklessly than ever. He forces his way into the quarters of Fujitsubo, the widowed Empress, risking the exposure of their previous affair and thence the legitimacy of the imperial line. Fujitsubo so fears that people will realize that the Crown Prince is their son that she takes Buddhist vows. Meanwhile, Genji continues his affair with Kokiden's sister, Oborozukiyo, who is promised to the reigning Emperor Suzaku, leading to a farcical scene in which the Minister of the Right discovers Genji sprawled out brazenly inside his daughter's curtained bed. At the same time, the tale's masterful use of references to ancient Chinese history and classical figures lends weight to the court intrigue in this chapter, as well as Genji's attempts at resistance, and the events about to unfold.

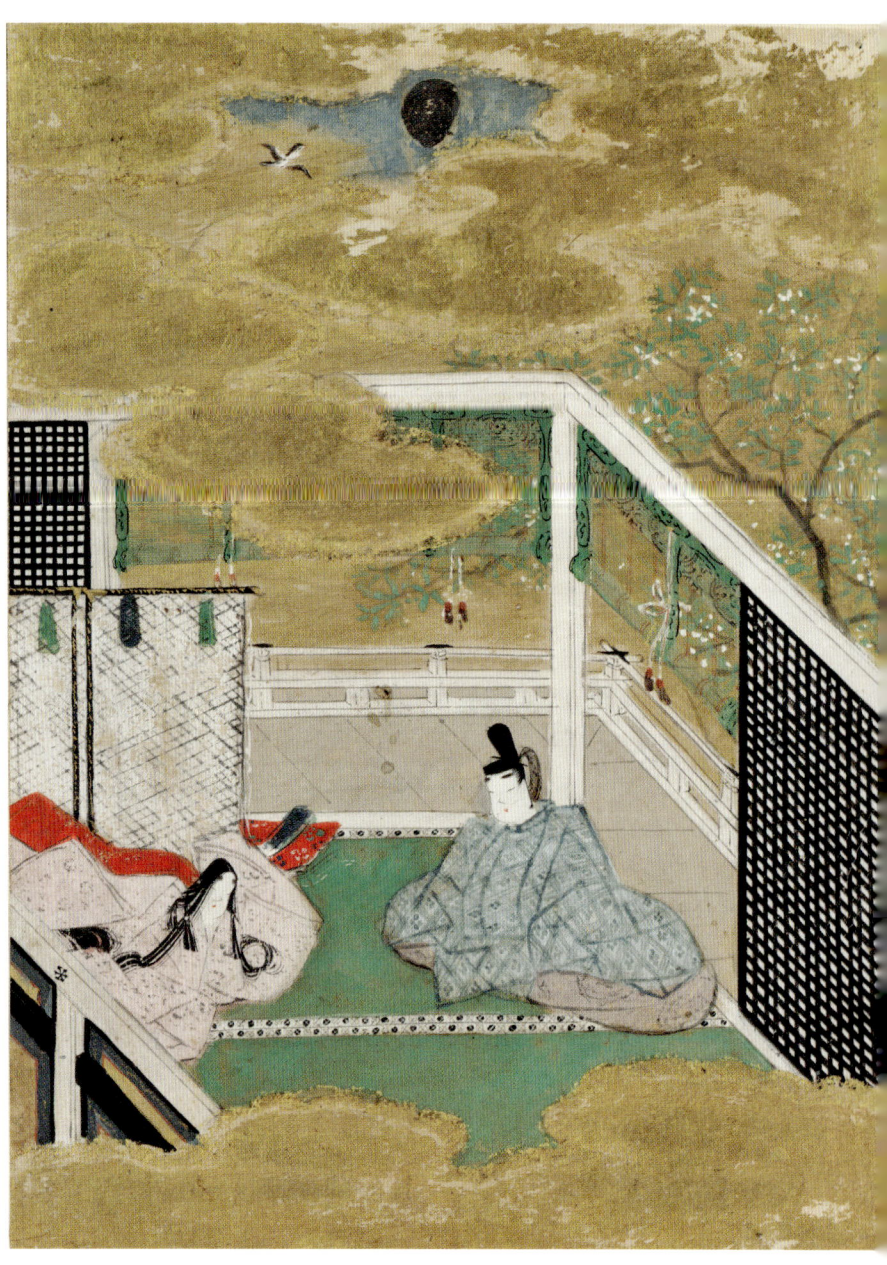

    In nostalgia
For the scent of orange bloom
    The cuckoo comes,
Visiting with its inquiries
The village where the flowers fall.

CRANSTON, P. 753

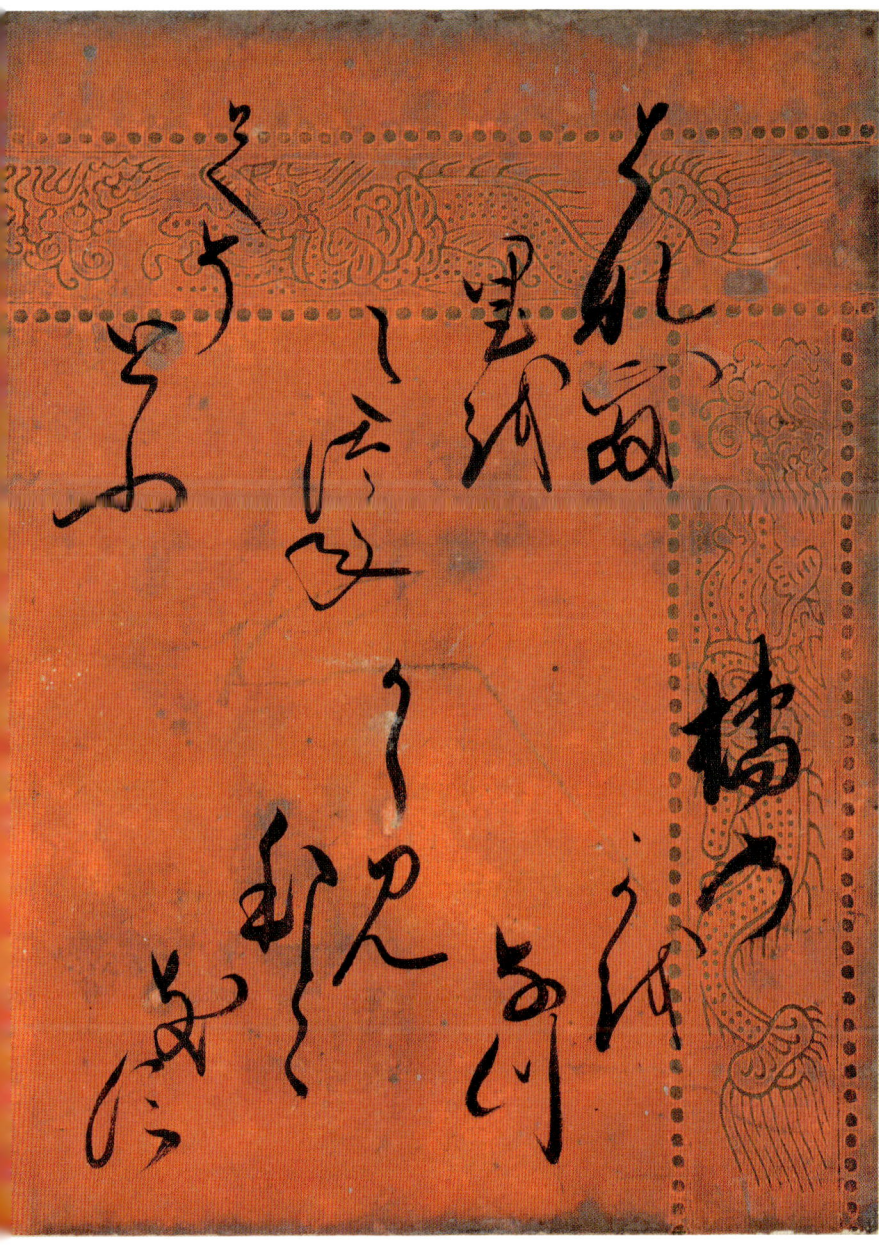

11

花散里

The Lady at the Villa of Scattering Orange Blossoms

Hanachirusato

Tachibana no
Ka o natsukashimi
Hototogisu
Hana chiru sato o
Tazunete zo tou

はな散
里を
たづね かしみ
てぞ ほとゝ
とふ きす

橘の
か を
な つ
か し み

In *waka* poetry, and in prose passages in *The Tale of Genji*, the invocation of the fragrance of the orange blossoms was often associated with a remembrance of things past, especially of lost loved ones. As if attempting to lure the viewer into a scent-triggered state of wistfulness, the calligraphic excerpt for this chapter begins toward the edge of the paper on the lower right with the words, "the fragrance of the orange" (*tachibana no ka* 橘のか). The brushwork of the poem gently lilts leftward and leads the eye directly to an image of an orange tree in the adjacent painting, where green branches, punctuated by delicate white blossoms, create a perfumed canopy over the couple below who converse about their longing for the past. Genji sits in the center of the room addressing a former consort of his father, a woman who occupied the Reikeiden quarters at the palace, and who was thus on par with the Kokiden Consort. The lady of the Reikeiden bore no children to succeed to the throne, however, and following the emperor's abdication and his recent death, has been living in relative isolation, her once grand life at court now seeming like a dream. As someone connected to the former reign and an intimate of his father, the Reikeiden Consort provides just the kind of solace and commiseration Genji needs after the tumultuous events of the last chapter. They both represent individuals out of favor politically, and their conversation is nostalgic for the previous reign, but their exchange is wrapped in the language of romance and longing.

The poem in the album is Genji's, and he speaks it to the Reikeiden Lady on hearing the call of the cuckoo, *hototogisu* in Japanese, a summer bird that sings at night like a suitor. The inquiring lovebird could stand for Genji; while he may have turned to the older Reikeiden Lady for commiseration, this night he also seeks an intimate encounter with her younger sister, a former lover. This younger sister comes to be known as Hanachirusato, the "Lady at the Villa of Scattered Blossoms," a name taken from a line in this poem, and she becomes forever linked to nostalgic memory and Genji's youth at the palace. Although this is Hanachirusato's first appearance in the tale, Genji's familiarity with her suggests that he must have been meeting her over the time period covered in previous chapters even though no such liaisons were ever described. Likewise, the chapter refers in its first lines to even more women from Genji's past who were never fully introduced, a narrative shorthand implying that Genji's affairs have outpaced Murasaki Shikibu's ability to record them.

Rather than Genji's romantic encounter with Hanachirusato on this summer night, the album painting focuses on his conversation with her older sister Reikeiden, placing the two of them directly in the center of the composition, their heads sympathetically tilting toward each other. A soft gold cloud gently floats above the pair and leads our eye upward to the night sky where a waning gibbous moon, once silver and now blackened from oxidation, appears between parted clouds. The fifth-month moon rises late, in utter darkness, its small size providing only faint illumination. Both poem and picture play with the idea of darkness creating a heightened sense of smell and sound; the smell of the orange blossom wafts in through the blinds and is evoked in the calligraphy, while above, the *hototogisu* spreads its wings in mid-flight. Murasaki Shikibu's contemporary, Sei Shōnagon, and other poets often envisioned this bird amid the branches of the orange tree, making the two a common pairing.

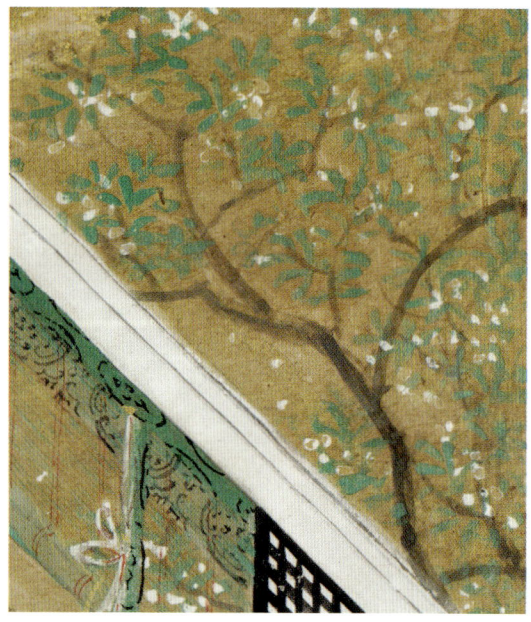

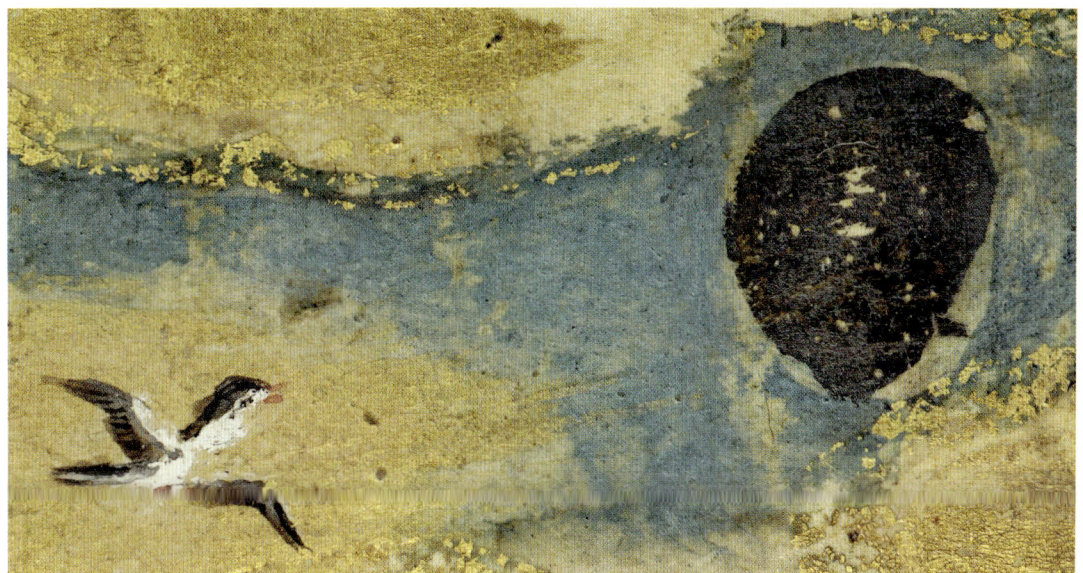

Here, however, the bird flies toward the moon, suggesting its role is not merely that of a lovebird, but that of an avian mediator between the living and the deceased lover or loved one. Genji's poem that appears on the album leaf is an allusion to one from the first imperially commissioned anthology of Japanese poetry, the *Kokinshū* (Book III, poem 139):

Satsuki matsu	Fragrance of the orange
Hanatachibana no	Flowering at last in June
Ka o kageba	Wafts through the summer night
Mukashi no hito no	The memory of scented sleeves
Sode no ka zo suru	Of someone long ago.

CRANSTON, PP. 142–43

The *hototogisu* in Genji's poem may represent Genji himself seeking solace among these women who share his sense of loss, but the allusion to the *Kokinshū* poem with its "scented sleeves of someone long ago" implies his deceased father, the Kiritsubo Emperor. A *tachibana* tree stood permanently in the courtyard of the Shishinden, the official ceremonial hall of the imperial palace, providing an associative link between the memory of sleeves scented with orange blossoms and the ruler now gone.

Chapter 11 | The Lady at the Villa of Scattering Orange Blossoms

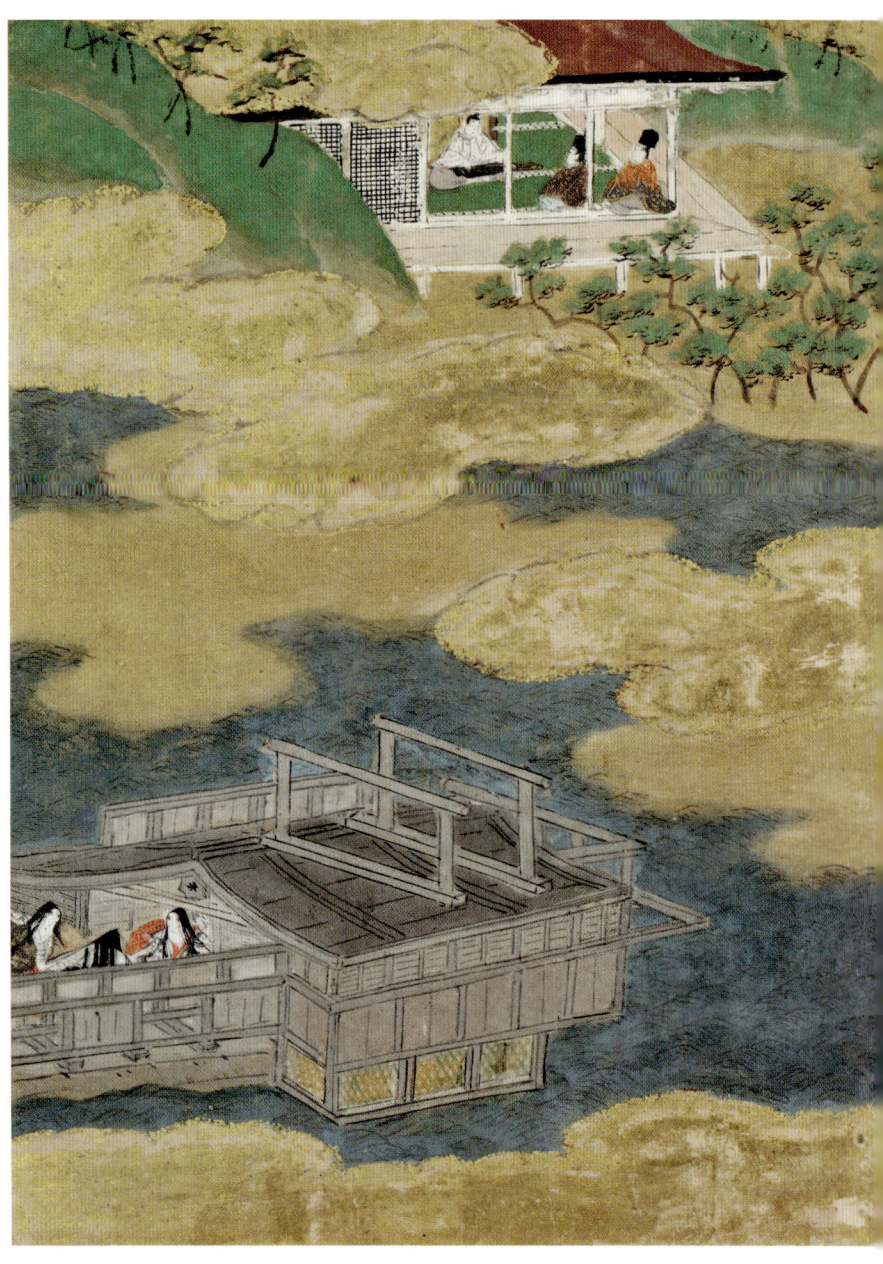

>How by *koto* strains
>Pulled, tugged to a stopping,
>   Rides on the rolling waves
>In the slack of our towlines
>A seasick heart, can you guess?

CRANSTON, P. 765

12

須磨
Exile to Suma
Suma

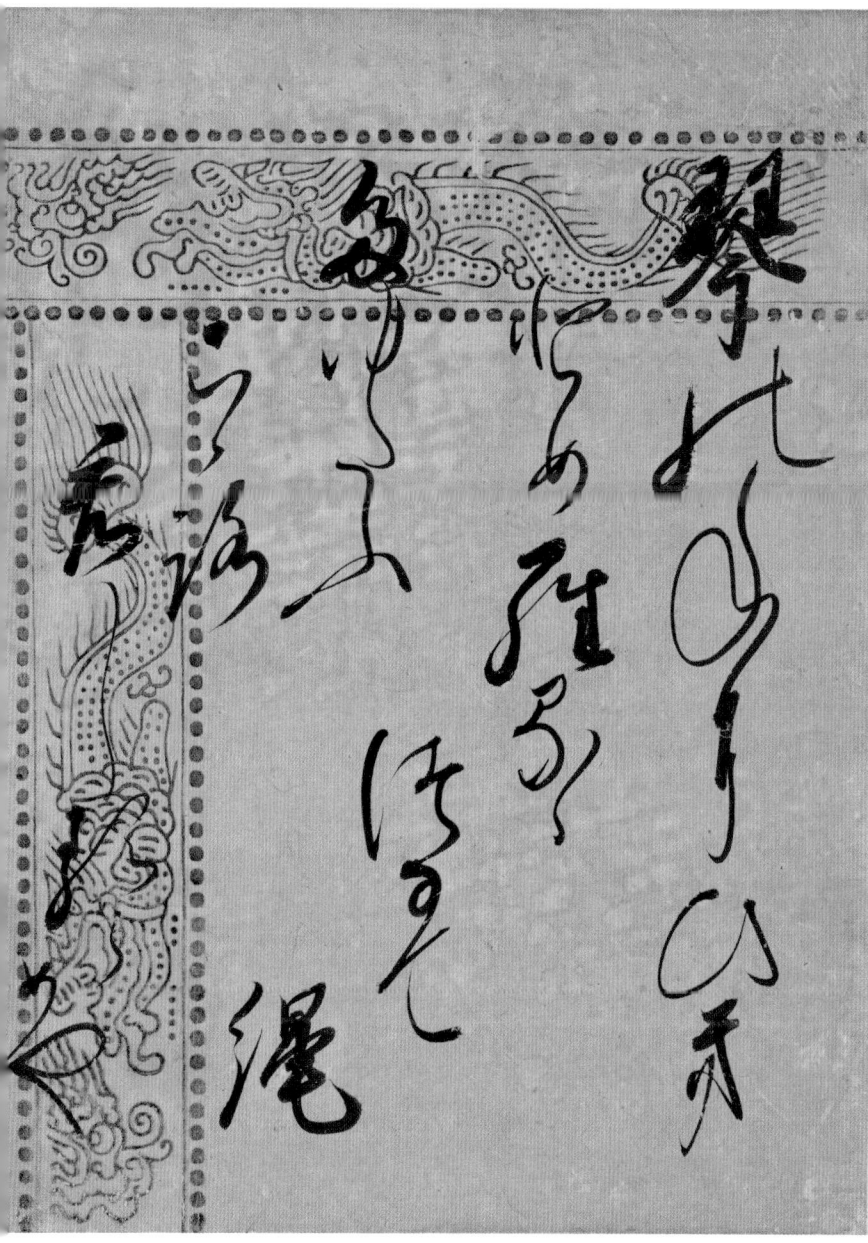

Koto no ne ni
Hikitomeraruru
   Tsunadenawa
Tayutau kokoro
Kimi shirurame ya

琴のねにひき
　とめらるゝ
　　つなて
たゆたふ　縄
こゝろ
　君しるらめや

With the Minister of the Right's faction fully in power, Genji is stripped of court rank and on the verge of censure for his alleged slights against the throne, as was threatened by the Kokiden Consort, now the Imperial Mother of the reigning sovereign. He preempts the embarrassment of official exile by leaving for the shore of Suma of his own accord, fearing both for the well-being of his secret son, the Crown Prince, and the possible revelation of the boy's true parentage. His affair with his father's consort Fujitsubo, which produced the child, weighs heavily on him, and the associated guilt, it is suggested, becomes another reason he has chosen to leave. Thus begins the tale's first extended foray into lands beyond the capital. The settings turn rustic, exotic, and are crafted in the poetic language of celebrated exiles from the Chinese and Japanese past. Genji's date of departure, the twenty-sixth of the third month, is exactly that of another dispossessed "genji" prince, Minamoto no Taka'akira (914–982), who was exiled to Dazaifu by a scheming Minister of the Right of his own day. Moreover, Genji's temporary residence in Suma, in present-day Kōbe on the Seto Inland Sea, would be near that of another famous exile, Ariwara no Yukihira (818–893), brother to Narihira, who famously described the "briny water drips from seaweed tangles" at Suma (*Kokinshū* Book XVIII, 863). Throughout the chapter are references to China's most famous exile, Bai Juyi (772–846), whose collected poems Genji takes with him, along with a seven-string Chinese *koto* (*kin*). That trusted instrument, his companion in isolation, figures prominently in this pair of album leaves in both text and image.

The single poem that appears on the album leaf for Chapter Twelve begins with the large, darkly inked characters for the "sound of the *koto*" (*koto no ne* 琴の音) in the upper right, then continues with the verb "to pull," or "pluck" (*hiki*). The poem is composed by the so-called Gosechi Dancer, a woman who once had a dalliance with Genji. And it is her heartstrings that are being plucked by the sound of Genji's seven-string *koto*, which she likens to the towrope that pulls her boat. Like sound reverberating across the water, the marks of the calligraphy resonate across the blue ground of the paper to echo the visual dynamic in the adjacent painting. Instead of focusing on Genji's point of

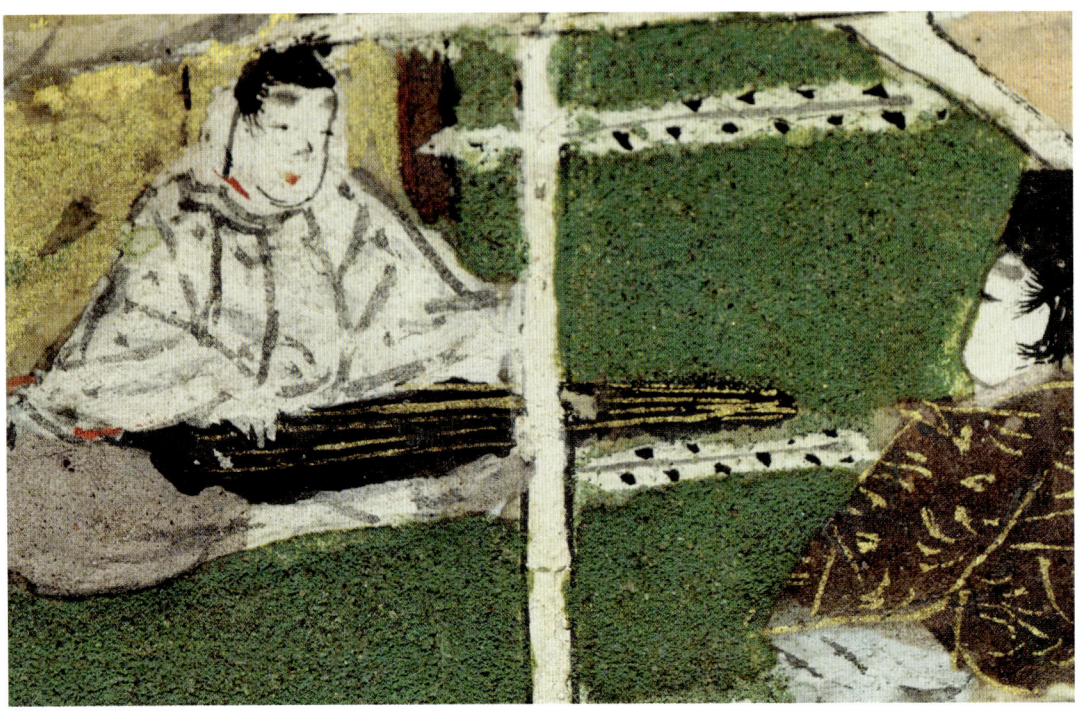

70 | *The Tale of Genji*

view, as many of the images in the album do, the painting foregrounds the Gosechi Dancer seated in the large boat listening to the elegant musical strains coming from the distant shore. Genji's abode is perched between golden clouds, a green hill on the far left, and a golden shore populated by spindly beach pines guarding against the wind and salty spray of the sea on the right. The open structure of the house reveals two retainers inside facing Genji, who appears with his back to a golden screen, playing the seven-string *koto* resting in his lap. Despite the miniature size, details are clearly articulated, including the white fingers of Genji's right hand plucking the instrument's golden strings.

Punctuating the watery stretch of blue waves that separate Genji and the Gosechi Dancer are floating gold clouds with mottled edges, and two wonderfully ambiguous cloud-like shapes that suggest shadows of the clouds above, or the sandbars that have appeared in Japanese art since the Heian period, and which here prefigure the shoreline paintings of Tawaraya Sōtatsu (d. 1643). The Gosechi Dancer, accompanied by her mother and sisters, is returning to the capital by boat while her father, the Assistant Governor of Kyūshū, travels overland. The women swoon when they hear of Genji's presence nearby and regret that the boat cannot stop, the Gosechi Dancer most of all. In a rather audacious move, she finds a messenger to deliver her poem to Genji and is soon rewarded with a reply. Genji compares his flirting to a man fishing with a line by alluding to a classical poem of exile by Ono no Takamura (*Kokinshū* 961):

Omoiki ya	Could I have thought it?
Hina no wakare ni	That I would come down to this,
Otoroete	In rude banishment
Ama no nawa taki	To haul a line with the seafolk
Isari semu to wa	And cast my hook for fish?

CRANSTON, P. 764

The playful exchange seems like an excuse for Murasaki Shikibu to include as many verses as possible from the canon of exile poems.

The most remarkable visual element of this painting is the representation of the Gosechi

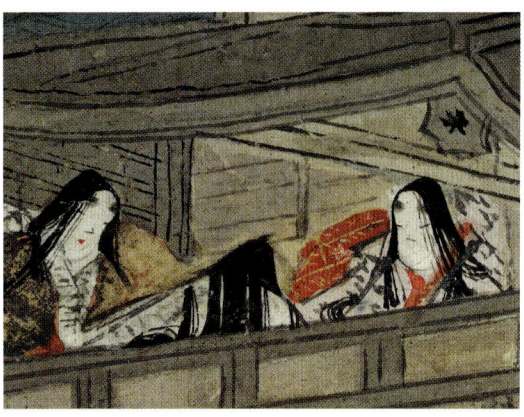

Dancer's boat, an impressionistic assemblage perhaps informed by shipbuilding techniques from the album's sixteenth-century time period. The vessel appears to be made, for example, with planks joined lengthwise to build the hull, which enabled greater width. Emphasizing the boat's size is its large cabin with a gabled roof that encompasses the entire stern. Two post and lintel frames are perched precariously atop the roof; in actuality, they should span the width of the cabin and provide stability for sailors manning the boat from atop the roof. The boat recalls domestic merchant ships that in the Muromachi period plied the waters around the bustling ports of Hyōgo and Sakai, gateways to the capital. A distinctive wooden barrier (*kakidatsu*) designed to guard against the waves juts out from the hull, here covered with a rhombus-patterned lattice, originally green, but now yellow where the pigment has fallen away. Boats with this unique feature were called "diamond guard cargo ships" (*higaki kaisen*) and were thought to have only been in use from the seventeenth century. The album painting thus suggests an earlier date for such boats and may represent vessels that were employed by the patrons of the *Genji* album, the Sue and their lords, the Ōuchi, as they traversed the waters going to and from their western home provinces. By bringing a sixteenth-century vessel into the *Genji* storyworld, this depiction of Genji's exile to Suma offered its original viewers a more topographically immediate and personalized version of *The Tale of Genji*.

Chapter 12 | Exile to Suma | 71

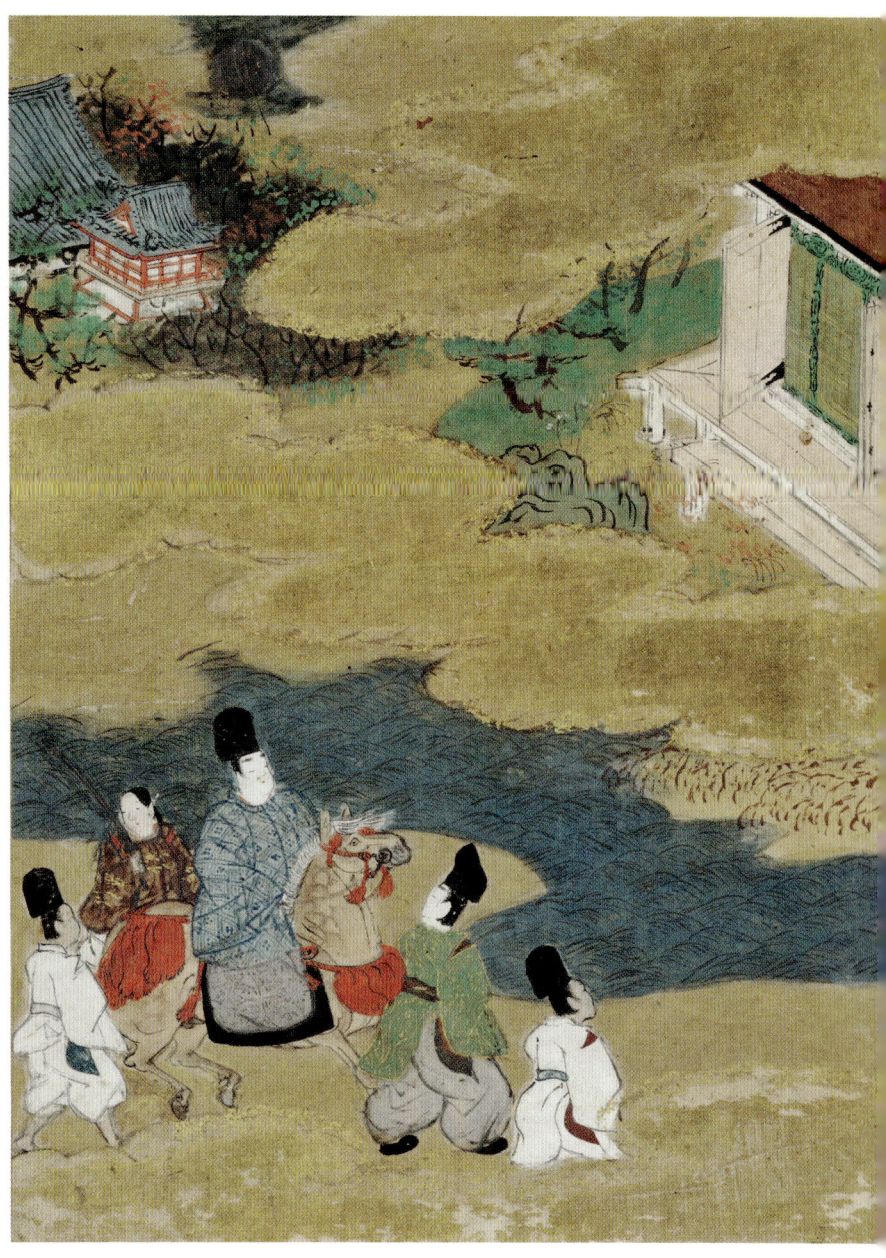

    Moonlight sorrel,
Stallion of the autumn night,
    Take me to my love,
Course the clouds to her dwelling—
For one hour let us meet.

CRANSTON, P. 772

13

明石
The Lady at Akashi
Akashi

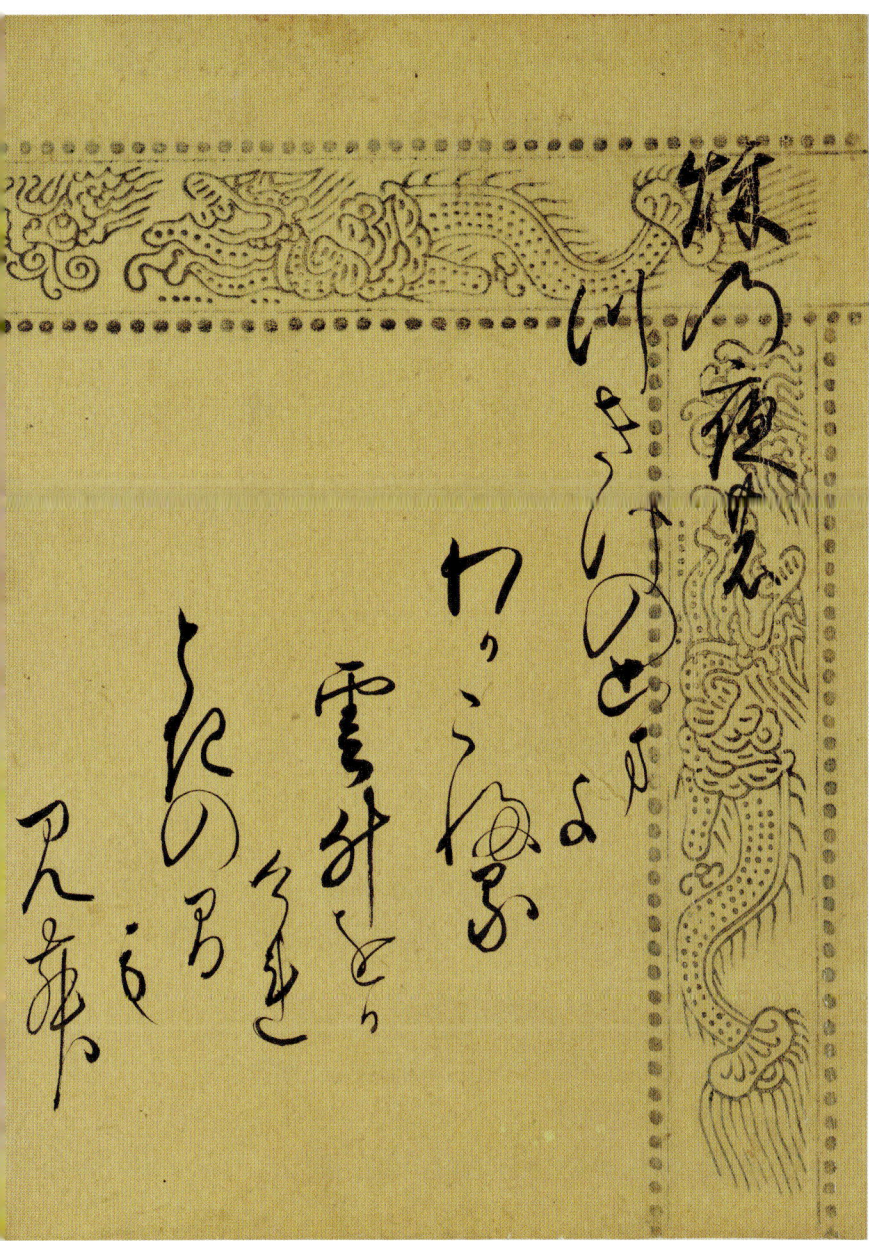

Aki no yo no
Tsukige no koma yo
Wa ga kouru
Kumoi o kakere
Toki no ma mo min

秋の夜の
つきけのこま
よ
わかこふる
雲ゐをか
けれ
ときの間
も
見む

On a moonlit autumn evening "too precious to waste," Genji sets out on horseback, as depicted in this album leaf, for his first romantic tryst with the woman known as the Akashi Lady. She is the daughter of a Buddhist lay monk, the Novitiate, a former Governor of Harima Province of aristocratic origins who fell in status and subsequently left the capital for the Bay of Akashi. The Novitiate turns out to be the cousin of Genji's deceased mother, the Kiritsubo Consort. Ever since his daughter's birth, he has aimed to restore his lineage, inspired by a dream of cosmic proportions in which he grasped the glowing orbs of the sun and moon. His hopes hinge on the marriage of his daughter to someone of royal descent, making Genji's presence just a few miles east along the shore in Suma seem like karmic destiny and an answer to his fervent prayers to the Sumiyoshi gods. In the midst of a raging tempest that blackens the sky and sends driving rain and violent winds and roiling waves, the Novitiate readies a small boat, intent on fetching the young noble. He miraculously makes it ashore unscathed, and Genji boards the boat, having received several omens himself, including a visitation in a dream by the ghost of his father exhorting him to leave.

Throughout the tale, the Akashi Novitiate is likened to the Dragon King, a mythical creature in possession of a powerful wish-fulfilling jewel who resides in a palace beneath the sea. The spectacular residence of the Novitiate, its extensive grounds that extend from the shore to the foothills and its numerous luxuries, resembles a palatial lair, and with its proximity to the sea, it suggests that Genji has crossed into a mythical realm. Indeed, the Akashi family will play a pivotal role in augmenting Genji's aura of rulership later in the tale, as the Akashi Lady bears his only daughter, who in turn becomes an imperial Consort and mother to a future emperor. Through the matriline of the Akashi Lady, therefore, Genji achieves one of the pinnacles of Heian courtly political success by becoming the grandfather of an emperor. The Akashi family experiences the most dramatic elevation of all, by moving from a forgotten household in the distant provinces to being firmly ensconced in the imperial line.

On the evening depicted in the album leaf, however, the future is far from certain and Genji waivers as he approaches the woman's residence, as captured in the album's poem. At first, he refused to travel to the woman's villa in the foothills, some distance from his quarters near the shore. To do so would acknowledge the Akashi Lady as an official wife, which Genji is loath to do because of his commitment to Murasaki back in the capital. Instead, Genji insists that the woman visit him. The Novitiate with his grandiose plans, however, understands that such a visit by his daughter would ruin her chances of being taken seriously by Genji. He stands his ground and succeeds in beguiling Genji with talk of the Akashi Lady's skill on the *biwa* and the thirteen-string *koto*, and he orchestrates a secret meeting for Genji to hear her play. In the poem recited by Genji in the album, however, Genji still imagines commanding his horse, with its lustrous coat reflecting the light of the autumn moon (*aki no yo no tsukige no koma*), to race through the sky straight back to the capital. On the verge of commencing and consummating his relationship with the Akashi Lady, Genji's expression of longing for Murasaki hints that his subsequent intimacy with the new lady is not motivated by his own desire; never before has Genji shown such reluctance for a liaison. His eventual acquiescence suggests that he views the relationship as a matter of fate that cannot be denied, while his invocation of Murasaki precisely at this moment foreshadows how her story will be intertwined with that of the Akashi family.

The painting shows Genji making his way from the shore to the Lady's villa, his face tilted toward the upper right where a wooden step leads to her veranda, and two doors, made of "exceptional wood," beckon him inside. The open doors also seem to represent Genji's thoughts at that moment, as expressed in the tale, that they must be ajar to allow the large autumn moon, nearly full on this night, to filter through the slats of the bamboo blinds. When Genji reaches the Lady's villa, he remarks on the beauty of its surroundings amid the pines, the roots of which cling to craggy rocks, and he notes the chirping of insects in the garden.

74 | *The Tale of Genji*

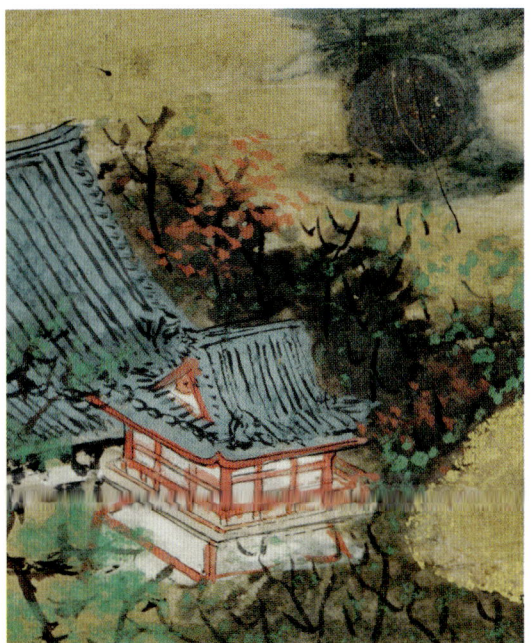

Touches of white, pink, and green pigment near the veranda connote the autumn flowers and grasses, which in turn suggest the sound of the chirping insects among them. As Genji surveys the touching isolation of the scene, he ponders the sadness of life and hears the sound of a temple bell reverberating on the wind.

The source of that sound appears in the upper left corner of the painting, a large Buddhist temple hall with an imposing gabled roof of gray tiles and an adjacent red and white bell tower. This cluster of buildings represents the Sanmaidō, a type of hall for performing *Lotus Sutra samādhi* meditative practice, which Genji first saw when coming to shore in Akashi. He noted its magnificence and its secluded site next to a stream flowing down from the hills, perfect for concentrating the mind on the next world. Here it is depicted beneath a low hanging autumn moon rendered in silver paint that has oxidized since the album was produced. The woman's villa on the right, and the meditation hall with the moon on the left, occupy distinct space cells in the album leaf, cordoned off by gold clouds, but they are interconnected by the sound of the bell and the light of the moon. Both structures are devoid of figures, but they act metonymically as the absent presences of the Lady and the Novitiate, each emitting a distinct sound heard by Genji: the ringing of the bell and the sound of the woman's *koto*. In the latter case, Genji hears strains from the instrument played not by the Lady but by the tassels of a curtain that accidentally brush across the strings. Indeed, it will be nearly a year before Genji actually hears her play, later in this chapter. By then Genji has been pardoned by the Suzaku Emperor and summoned back, the Akashi Lady is pregnant with his child and experiencing morning sickness, and Genji is vowing to bring her and their child to the capital.

Chapter 13 | The Lady at Akashi | 75

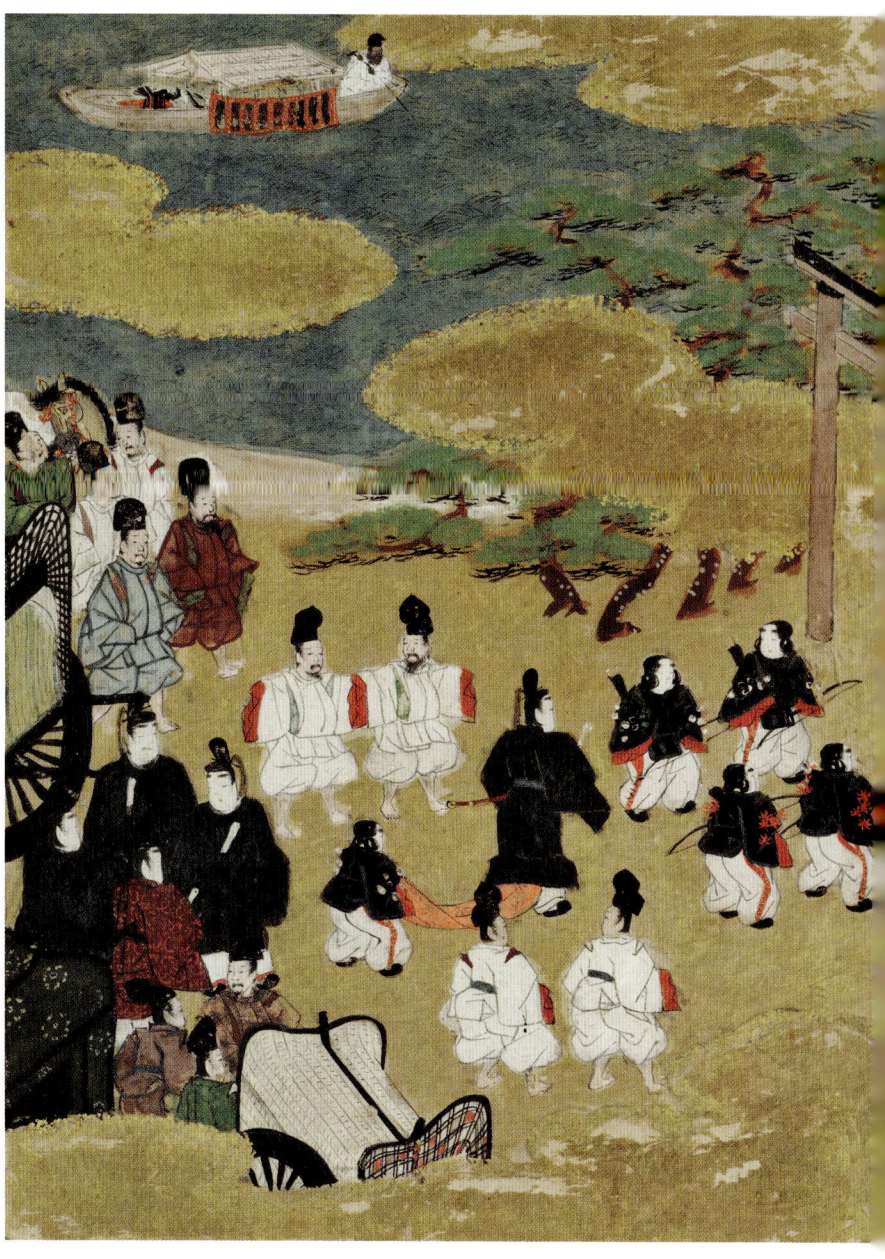

Our old sorrows come
With the first glimpse of the pines
   Of Sumiyoshi,
As in the rush of memory
I think of the Age of the Gods.

"Truly," thought Genji, remembering....

   In the rush of waves
We lived, lost in such tempest
   As the god alone
Could calm—Sumiyoshi,
Shall I ever forgive thee?

CRANSTON, P. 782

14

澪標
Channel Markers
Miotsukushi

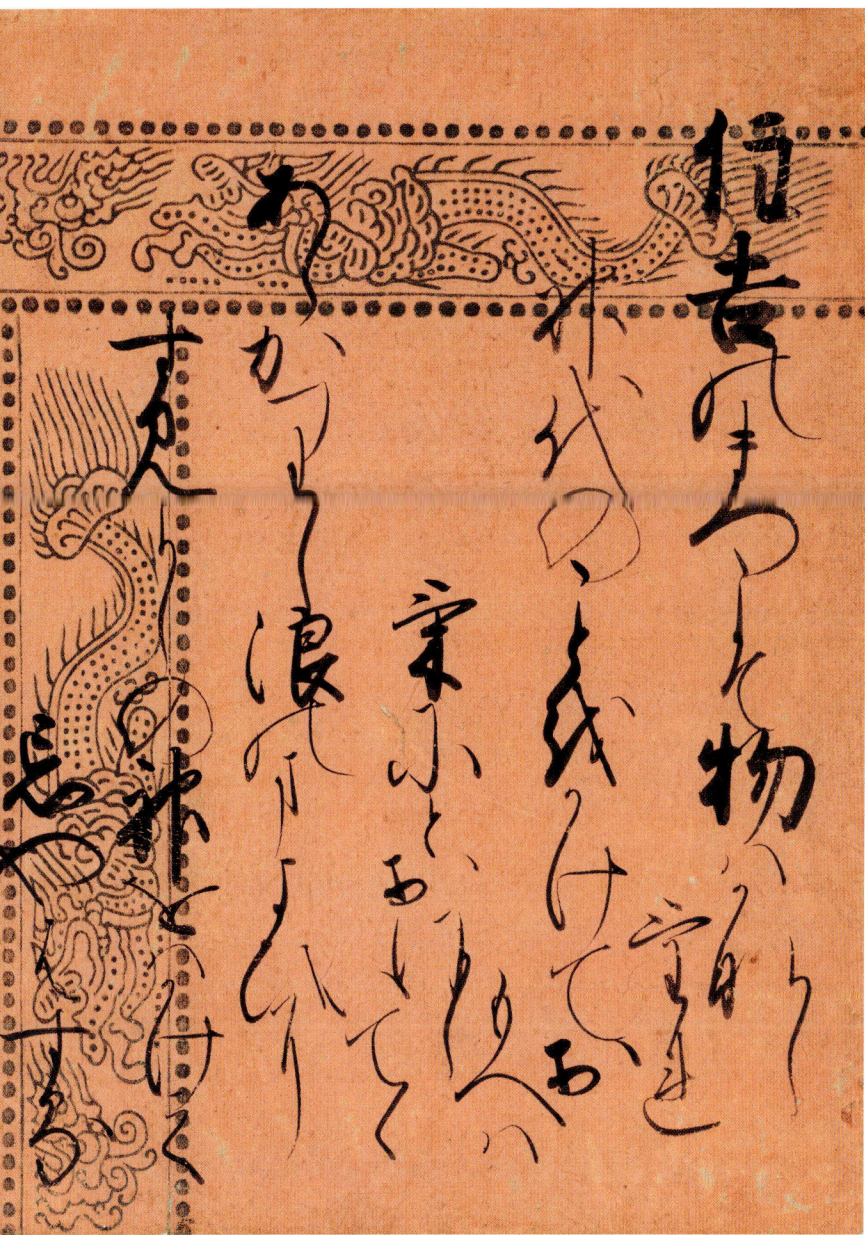

Sumiyoshi no
Matsu koso mono wa
Kanashikere
Kamiyo no koto o
Kakete omoeba

Ge ni to oboshiidete

Arakarishi
Nami no mayoi ni
Sumiyoshi no
Kami o ba kakete
Wasure ya wa suru

住吉のまつこそ物はかなし
　　　　　　　　　　けれ
神代のことをかけておも
　　　　　　　　　へば
　げにとおほしいでゝ
あらかりし浪のまよひに
すみよしの神をばかけて
　　　忘やはする

Exonerated from any wrongdoing and now on the path to political supremacy back in the capital with his own (secret) son on the throne after Emperor Suzaku's abdication, Genji decides to honor the gods for his good fortune and makes a pilgrimage to Sumiyoshi. The Channel Markers chapter, the title of which refers to wooden posts that warn seafarers of shallow water, describes a painfully poignant encounter between the Akashi Lady and Genji's entourage at the Sumiyoshi Shrine. In the album painting, her miniature figure, barely visible in the boat at the top of the painting, appears framed between the edge of the vessel and the bamboo blinds hanging from its wooden roof. She wears a white robe and faces the direction of the shore, partially revealing her face and long tresses. A female attendant in a red robe with gold accents accompanies her, sitting outside the roofed shelter of the boat and facing her mistress. From this seaward vantage point, the Akashi Lady gazes across rippling blue waves to view something entirely unexpected—the magnificent procession of Genji, newly elevated to the position of palace minister (*naidaijin*), on his visit to Sumiyoshi. The spectacle gives her a glimpse of Genji's glorious life at court, as she sees several men familiar from their time in exile, now donning fine robes of various hues appropriate to their recent promotions. Locals have gathered for a glimpse of Genji, but the Akashi Lady, uninformed of his visit and unrecognized as his wife, can only lurk on the surrounding waters. Although she has just given birth to Genji's daughter, she has not yet been brought to the city as he promised and must regard him from afar as if he were a mere stranger.

A lengthy passage in the tale describes the spectacle of Genji at Sumiyoshi through the eyes of the Akashi Lady, which the painting manages to convey in detail. A row of dark green shore pines and a *torii* shrine gate mark the sacred precinct of the Sumiyoshi shrine. Genji occupies the center of the painting, processing directly toward the gate led by four page boys with hair tied up in loops, dressed identically in white pants with a red and gold stripe, and carrying bows and arrows. Their dark upper garments, with red undersleeves, are festooned with flowers and maple leaves, hinting at the colorful display the Lady is said to witness. A fifth page boy follows behind, holding Genji's long, orange-colored train, which is decorated with a pattern of autumn leaves floating in a stream painted in gold. Genji is depicted in one of his most formal ensembles anywhere in the album: the courtly costume of civil officials (*sokutai*), consisting of a belted black robe, a crown-style courtier's hat (*kanmuri*), and a wooden baton (*shaku*). His high rank places him in an exalted group, the members of which are, like military officials of the court, allowed to wear a sword, which here extends from his left side.

The formality of Genji's costume and the solemnity of his pose reflect the awe in which the Sumiyoshi deity was held but also underscore the importance of its role throughout the tale. Just prior to his visit to the Shrine, Genji comes to the realization that his fate has been guided all along by the gods of Sumiyoshi. They are the deities to whom the Akashi Novitiate has long prayed, and whom Genji entreated in his darkest hours amid the storm at Suma. The catalyst for Genji's realization is not only his dramatic change in political fortune but also his recollection of a prophecy he received in childhood. Genji was told that he would one day

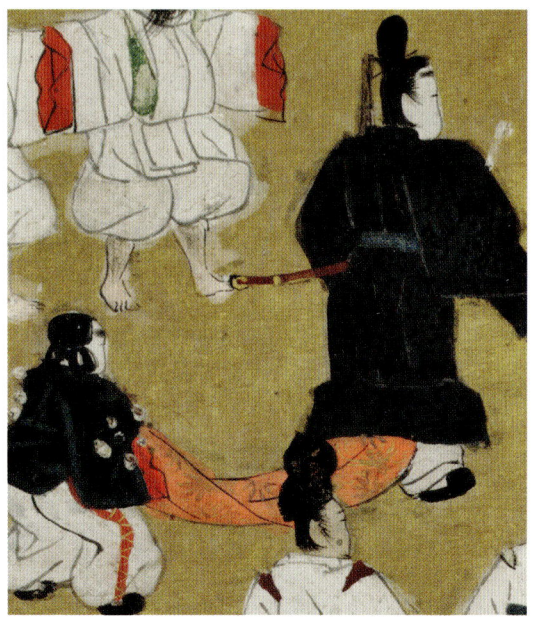

78 | *The Tale of Genji*

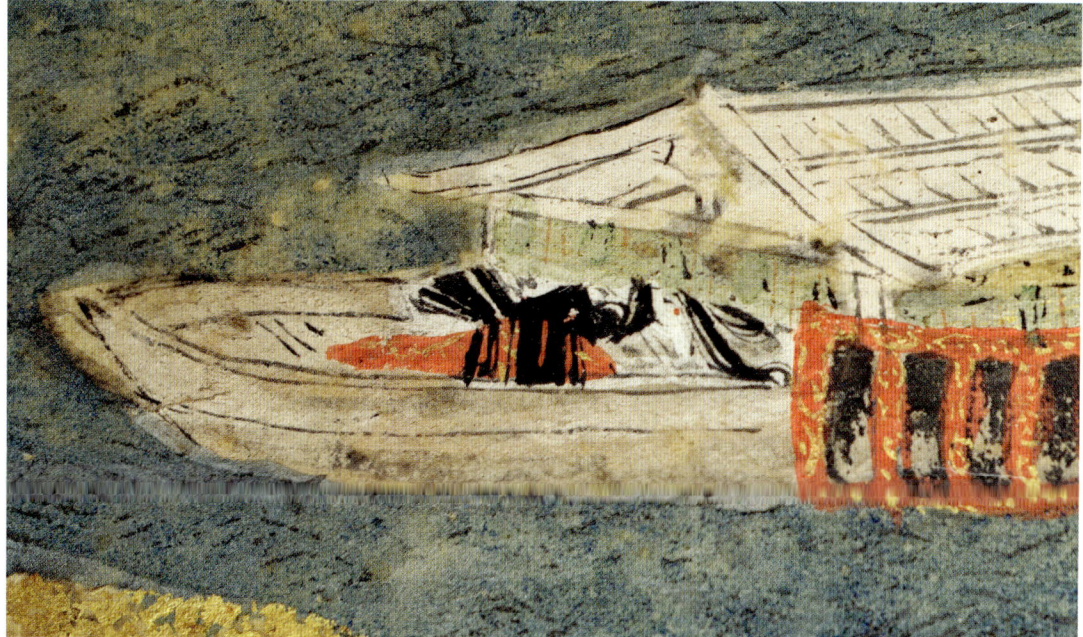

father three children: a son who would become sovereign of the realm (Emperor Reizei), another who would reach the position of Chancellor (Yūgiri), and a daughter who would bring him his greatest glory by becoming an imperial consort, giving birth to a crown prince, and thus making Genji the grandfather of an emperor. In the Channel Markers chapter, when the Akashi Lady gives birth to Genji's only biological daughter, Genji's fate appears to be following the prophecy. Although the focus of the painting seems to be on Genji and his entourage, the Akashi Lady hovers above the scene as if in recognition of her role in this predetermined series of events. The horizontal beams of the shrine gate are positioned as if to point upward in her direction, and she in turn directs her gaze toward Genji, linking the two characters and suggesting the intervention of the gods in this fateful relationship. Against this backdrop of predestination, however, the author of the tale emphasizes the Akashi Lady's painful longing and humility, which become the twin hallmarks of her character.

In place of the poetic exchange between Genji and the Akashi Lady that eventually occurs in this chapter, the album includes two poems by Genji and his loyal attendant Koremitsu that highlight the debt owed to the Sumiyoshi gods. Koremitsu had followed Genji into exile, leaving everything behind in the capital to serve his lord in Suma and Akashi. Here he offers a verse reminding Genji of their time in isolation, a time he refers to as the "age of the gods," suggesting their dependence on the deity as well as the primeval, transcendent time evoked by the Sumiyoshi pines. Genji's reply recalls the storms they endured while explaining his pilgrimage by asking rhetorically, "How could I forsake the god now?" The calligraphy in the album highlights the incantatory power of the poem; as if attempting to conjure the presence of the Sumiyoshi deity, it begins in the upper right corner with darkly inked characters reading *"Sumiyoshi no"* (住吉の), while the word for "deity" appears at the top of the next line in the compound for "age of the gods" (kami yo 神代). The name is invoked again in the penultimate column of verse, where *"sumiyoshi no kami"* (すみよしの神) constitutes a vertical column of *kana* that visually completes the shrine gate and marks the presence of the god, imbricating word and image into a powerful presentation of the deity.

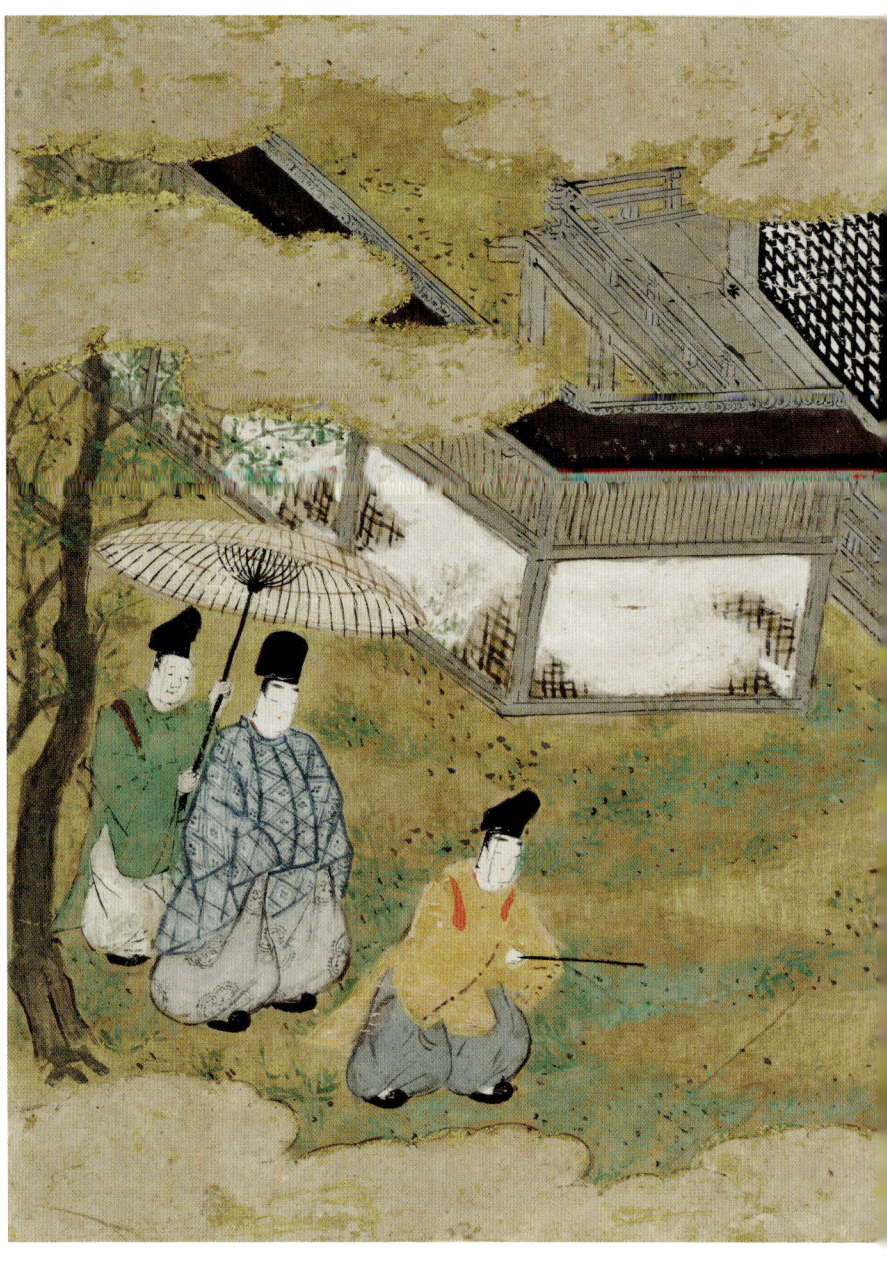

　　Let me be the one,
　Then, to worm my way in
　　　To this deep wormwood,
　That I may call and find again
　The unchanged heart of the grove.
CRANSTON, P. 785

He recited this to himself as he stepped down from the carriage. Koremitsu walked in front, brushing away the dew with a riding crop as his lord entered. The drops of rain falling from the trees above felt like a cold autumn shower. "I have an umbrella."

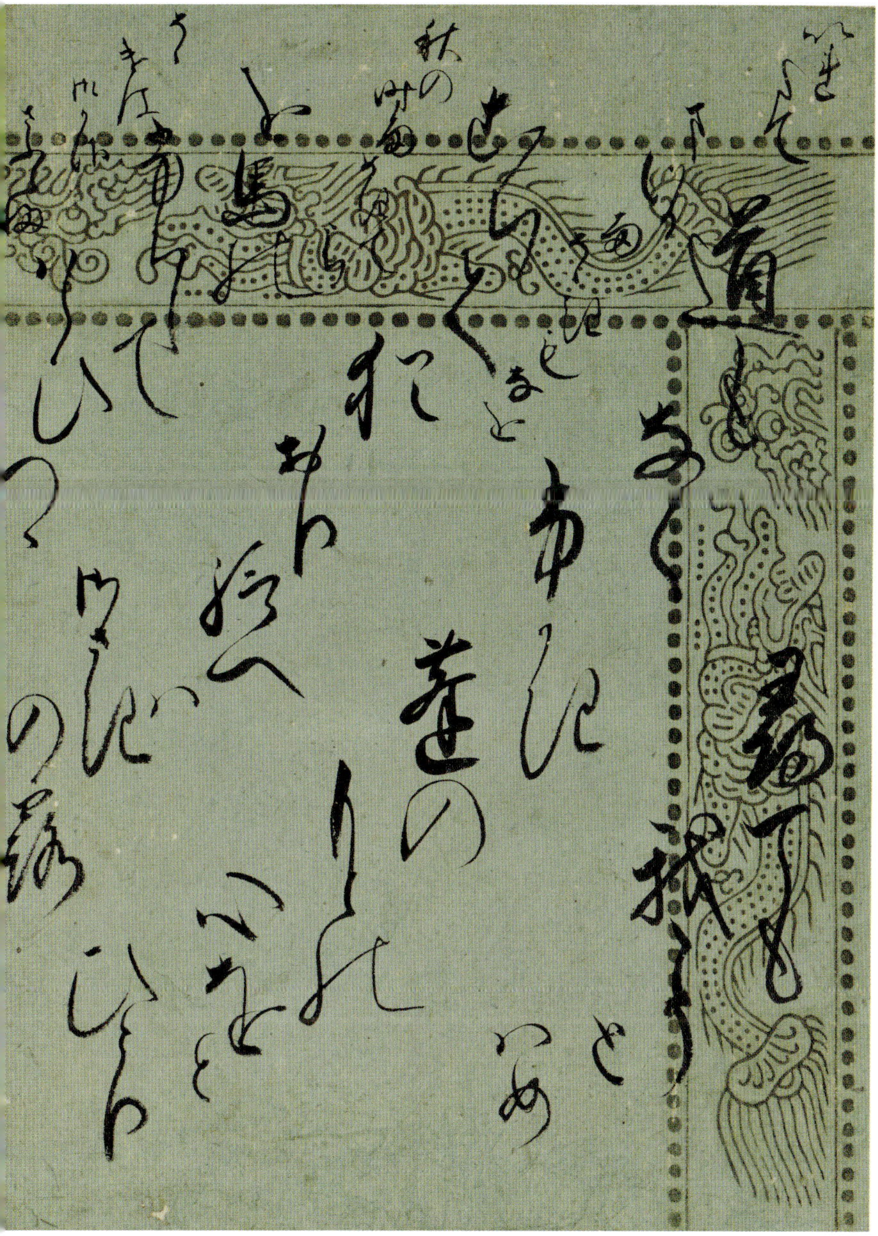

15

蓬生

A Ruined Villa of Tangled Gardens
Yomogiu

Tazunete mo
Ware koso towame
　Michi mo naku
Fukaki yomogi no
Moto no kokoro o

to hitorigochite nao oritamaeba,
onsaki no tsuyu o muma no buchi
shite haraitsutsu iretatematsuru. Ama
sosogi mo, nao aki no shigure mekite
uchisososogeba, "Mikasa saburau."

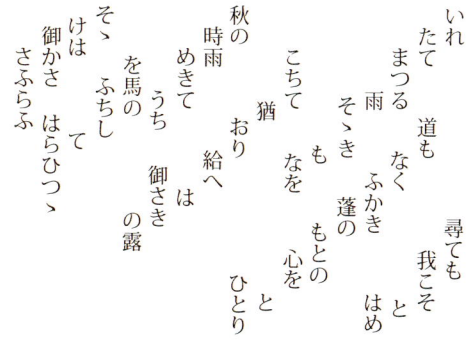

The detailed description of the physical appearance of Suetsumuhana earlier in the tale finds a counterpart in several passages in Chapter Fifteen that vividly evoke the ruinous state of disrepair into which the lady's estate has fallen during Genji's exile. The princess's residence, inherited from her deceased father, the Hitachi Prince, is described as completely dilapidated: wooden roof planks over the servants' quarters have fallen away, while the garden outside has become wild and overgrown. Teeming vines threaten to overcome the house, and waist-high satin-tail grasses and tangles of mugwort, or "wormwood" (*yomogi*), obscure any sign of the paths and gardens that were once artfully maintained. Amid this dereliction, markers of order and propriety are transgressed; parts of the earthen wall surrounding the property have crumbled, allowing horses and oxen to trample through the garden and graze. The lack of human activity has emboldened foxes and screech owls as well as, the narrator tells us, tree spirits, which roam the grounds. This frightening, gothic description is also paired with imagery that evokes the hermitage of the classic Chinese poet-scholar, through allusion to poems by Bai Juyi and Du Fu (712–770). Other descriptive phrases make the house and gardens metaphors for the abandoned, aging woman. Indeed, as the younger attendants begin to depart, seeing no hope of Genji's return, Suetsumuhana is left alone with a handful of women described as ancient, gravelly voiced, and unkempt. In contrast to the house's wild exterior, however, there are hints of lost grandeur inside, in the furnishings and valuable possessions handed down from the Hitachi Prince, but these too are described as dusty and old, and associate the Princess by extension with musty obsolescence. And yet through a combination of obstinacy, pride, and loyalty to her father, the Princess perseveres against a torrent of mounting pressure to abandon her home. The situation reaches a nadir when even her longtime attendant Jijū leaves, and Suetsumuhana spends a lonely winter and spring enduring months alone in a gloomy house.

In early summer, Genji decides to visit the woman at the "village of scattering blossoms,"

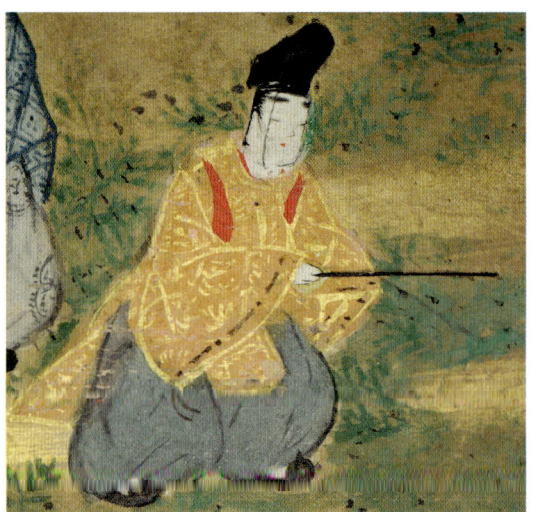

Hanachirusato, but fate intervenes when along the way he notices a distinctive grove of trees and is struck by the scent of wisteria flowers, which he sees hanging from a large pine. The wisteria-wrapped pine, a long-standing auspicious motif associated with regal lineages, seems to have a magical effect on Genji and spurs him into action. Koremitsu confirms that this is indeed the Hitachi Villa, unrecognizable as it is, and Genji alights from his carriage to venture into the dense thicket. Meanwhile, Suetsumuhana experiences her own magical intervention when a daytime slumber brings a dream of her father, which inspires her to have her surroundings cleaned, and to soliloquize about the absence of her father:

Naki hito o	Sleeves of my yearning
Kouru tamoto no	For the one who is no more
Hima naki ni	Have no time to dry,
Aretaru noki no	And now are added the drippings
Shizuku sae sou	That leak from my broken eaves.

CRANSTON, P. 785

As if in response, Genji recites to himself his own poem as he emerges from his carriage, the verse inscribed on the album leaf. The character for "wormwood" (*yomogi* 蓬) occupies the center of the green colored poetry sheet, complementing the image of the overgrown garden depicted in the painting to its left. Genji makes his way toward the house, its dilapidation conveyed by the exposed wattle of its white plastered wall, while Koremitsu clears away the dew-drenched grasses for his lord. Clumps of green, weed-like plants cover the ground while flecks of silver on the painting simulate the glistening effect of the dew said to drench the cuffs of the men's trousers. A slender tree frames the trio on the left edge of the composition, but conspicuously absent is the intertwined wisteria and pine found in nearly every rendition of this popular scene, including the oldest extant version in the twelfth-century *Genji Scrolls*.

The umbrella does call to mind, however, the same motif found in the *Genji Scrolls* version of this scene, perhaps evoking the parasol that hovers above the Buddha in traditional painting and sculpture. While Genji is likened to a Buddha elsewhere in the tale, Misumi Yōichi has argued that this chapter in particular structures its events according to a story of redemption in which Genji's eventual rescue of Suetsumuhana is akin to Buddhist salvation. Genji is said to appear "unexpectedly, like a god or the Buddha," to bestow his gracious attention on the Princess, and is later described as a *bosatsu*, and "the very incarnation of the Buddha," leaving people to wonder how "he came to be born into this world of corruption." Meanwhile, the "Rite of the Eight Lectures" commissioned by Genji takes place at his residence, which is said to "equal in every way the sublime beauty (*shōgon*) of the Pure Land of Supreme Bliss (*gokuraku jōdo*)." And when Genji begins his acts of compassion, which will transform the Princess's current squalor into splendor, the ladies-in-waiting "looked up to the sky, and facing in the direction of Genji's residence, offered joyful prayers of thankgivings" (Washburn, p. 354), as if in gratitude to a Buddha or deity.

Suetsumuhana, on the other hand, is presented as an anti-Buddhist figure, a woman who spurns Buddhist practice and the chanting of sutras, who offers an ironic retort when she hears Genji celebrated in Buddhistic terms, and who perhaps puts more faith in the rightness of the lifestyle of a Confucian Chinese recluse than that of a Buddhist renunciate. Suetsumuhana thus seems particularly unredeemable; as observed earlier, Chapter Six even described her in inhuman terms, with a nose as long and deformed as the Bodhisattva Fugen's elephant mount. In much the same way that the Buddha's compassion has the capacity to redeem even the nonhuman, Genji's ability to accept Suetsumuhana despite her appearance contains shades of bodhisattva-like mercy. As expressed in Genji's poem, he sees within Suetsumuhana the virtue of her devoted, "unchanged heart" (*moto no kokoro*), even though the (religious) "path may be hidden" (*michi mo naku*). He thus spreads his radiance like the Buddha, whose indiscriminate compassion, the *Lotus Sutra* says, touches all like the spring rain. In this way, Murasaki Shikibu frames Genji's relationship with the Hitachi Princess in terms of a central motif and belief found in Buddhist literature, and so hints at layers of possible meanings behind the tale's romantic redemptions.

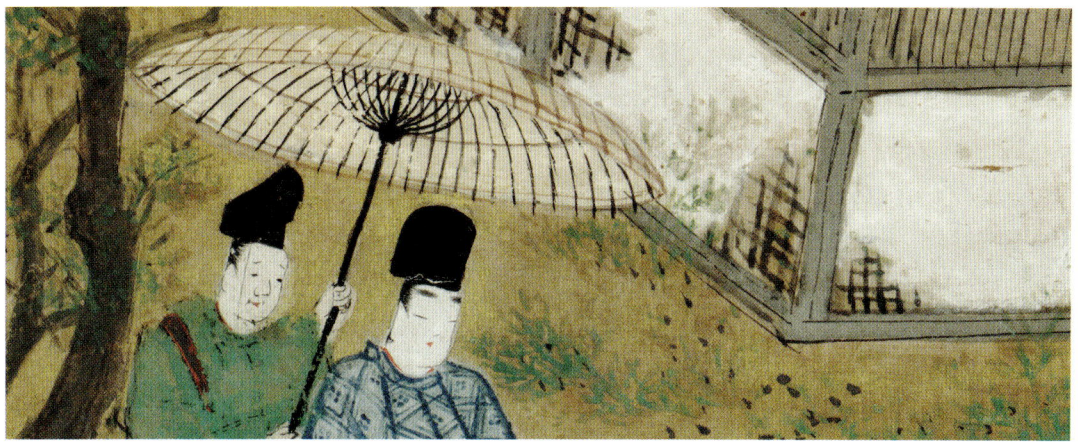

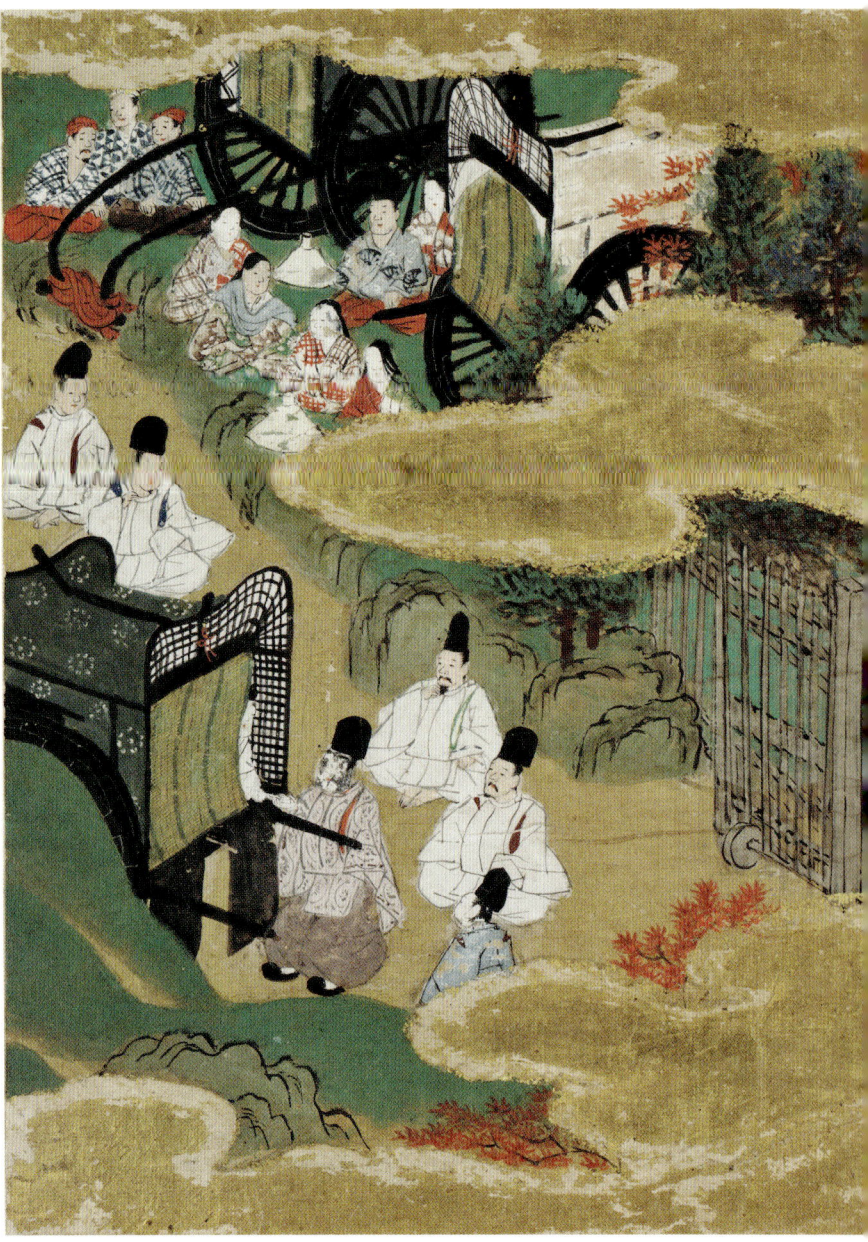

It was the end of the ninth month, and the autumn foliage was a blaze of color. Clumps of grass withered by the frost—some darker in hue, some lighter—stretched out delightfully all around as far as the eye could see. As the figures in their traveling outfits came streaming past the barrier gate, they looked ever so appealing in the harmonious embroidery and resist dyed cloth of their colorful robes.

WASHBURN, P. 357, MODIFIED

16

関屋
The Barrier Gate
Sekiya

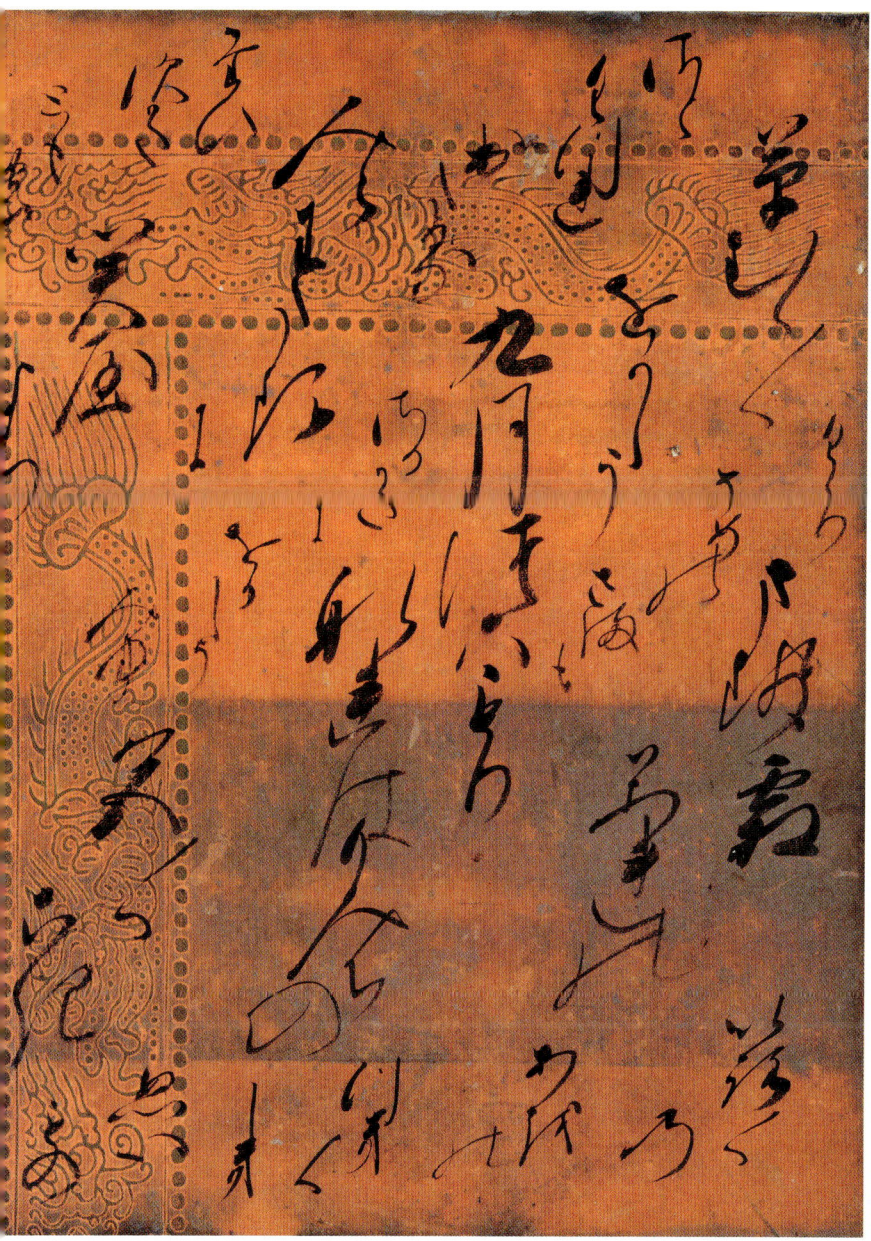

Nagatsuki tsugomori nareba, momiji no iroiro kokimaze, shimogare no kusa muramura okashiu miewataru ni, Sekiya yori sato kuzureidetaru tabisugatadomo no, iroiro no ao no tsukizukishiki nuimono, kukurizome no sama mo saru kata ni okashiu miyu.

草むらくませ霜 いろくさとをかしう そめの かれのくれ のあをの
出　　　　　さま も
たる　九月つごもり つきくさるかた なれはもみちのみえわたる にをかにしき
たひ　　　　　　　　色く
すかた　関屋　　　みゆ
ともの　より　　 ぬいもの

Twelve years have passed since the seventeen-year-old Genji's affair with the married woman Utsusemi, his "lady of the discarded locust shell." In Chapter Sixteen they happen upon each other again, as their traveling processions pass, heading in different directions, the gatehouse (*sekiya*) at Ōsaka, the famous place in Ōmi Province the name of which literally means the "slope of meeting" (*ausaka*). Having accompanied her husband, now the Governor of Hitachi Province, to his post in the eastern provinces, Utsusemi is returning to the capital after a four-year absence and is making her way westward. Her party has heard that Genji will pass through the same barrier gate on a pilgrimage to the temple of Ishiyamadera, and they cede the busy road to him, taking seats along the embankment. Their resting carriages are depicted with their shafts touching the ground, a thick, red rope coiled around the ends of one connoting unhitched oxen. The tale describes a substantial group of ten women's carriages, and in the album the diagonal placement of the vehicles and the obfuscating gold clouds imply a larger retinue beyond the border of the picture. Members of the traveling party seated on the slope include two women with their white, conical travel hats on the ground beside them as they watch the procession of Genji's carriages below.

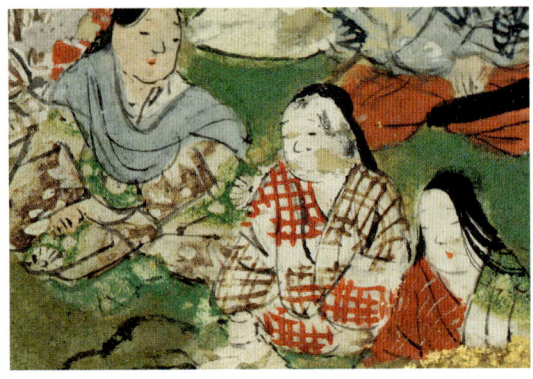

The album's calligraphy is brushed on crimson colored paper as if to suit the autumnal "ninth month" (*nagatsuki*), a word that is featured in the text and highlighted by its central location on the sheet, complementing the tinted fall leaves and red motifs in the adjacent painting. The text also focuses on the embroidered and dyed travel robes (*tabi sugata*), which in this painting are worn by members of Utsusemi's entourage. Rather than Heian-period robes, however, Mitsunobu painted the fabrics of his day, reflecting the range of patterns and dyeing techniques popular at the time of the album's creation in the early sixteenth century. The robes include those with a crosshatched pattern in blue and white, or red and brown, and a resist-dyed robe of blue triangles. One man, seated between the two parked carriages, wears a light blue robe decorated with black and white carriage wheels. The garment on the woman behind him is equally striking, with alternating bands of red and brown, a different pattern and color on each shoulder. Floral roundels of differing sizes appear within the bands, with traces of a purplish color delineating the center and petals of the blossoms. Conspicuous garments appear on women below this couple as well. One worn by a figure with a light blue cloth draped across her chest bears a complicated pattern of painted flowers and leaves recalling the decorative technique known as "flowers at the crossroads" (*tsujigahana*). The robe on the other, on the far right, is decorated with a striated red ground on the right shoulder and a band of green with minute brown strokes. This last woman is the only one in the group with features typical of

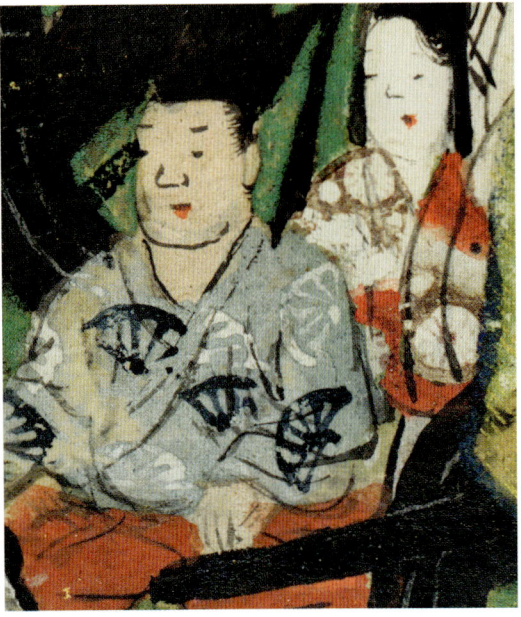

aristocratic figures in Mitsunobu's paintings, and although custom dictates that Utsusemi not emerge from her carriage, it is tempting to interpret her as a stand-in for Genji's regretful paramour. Her particularly intense focus on the spectacle below evokes a poem composed by Utsusemi to herself at precisely this moment:

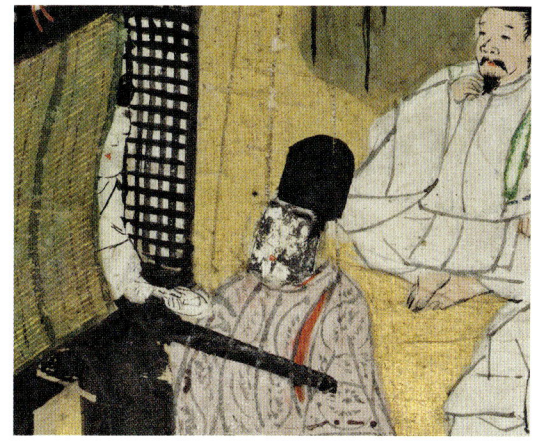

Yuku to ku to	Going and coming
Sekitomegataki	There has been no barrier
Namida o ya	For these my tears;
Taenu Shimizu to	Do others look upon them
Hito wa miruramu	As water from flowing wells?
	CRANSTON, P. 786

The sense of movement within this poem—the back and forth through the barrier gate, the downward torrent of the woman's tears—resembles the visual dynamics of the painting, with its zigzagging composition and precipitous diagonal leading the eye to the focal point of the scene: Genji's interaction with Utsusemi's younger brother Kogimi.

Genji's carriage has just passed through the barrier gate, which is rendered with unique detail, including the wheel at its base that allows it to swing open. Only the rear of the carriage is visible, and there Genji leans out from behind the hanging blinds to hand a message to Kogimi. The young boy who arranged his sister's liaison with Genji in Chapters Two and Three, and who became the nobleman's nocturnal companion when Genji's overtures to his sister failed, is now an Assistant Commander in the Right Gate Guard. Despite the damage to the white pigment of his face, his elegant features are still discernible, and his importance in the scene is marked by his full and stately representation in courtly hat, pink and red robe, pantaloons, and black lacquered slippers, which stand out amid the plain robes of Genji's retainers. Kogimi's prominence suggests that the drama of this scene occurs not only between Genji and Utsusemi but also between these two men, whose relationship is not without tension. The young man accompanied his sister to Hitachi rather than loyally following Genji into exile, as others had done, who at this point in the story are being rewarded.

Taken together, Chapter Sixteen, and Fifteen before it, starkly juxtapose the life choices of Utsusemi and Suetsumuhana. Sakamoto Tomonobu has suggested that Utsusemi's father, a Middle Counselor of high rank, was likely a son of the emperor who reigned before Genji's father. Although Utsusemi is presented as a woman of middle rank, as she has married a provincial governor, her bloodline could be identical to that of Suetsumuhana, whose father, Prince Hitachi, was a son of the same emperor. Both women thus exemplify contrasting paths; one chose immediate stability, while the other refused to settle and instead decided to wait for Genji. Utsusemi's pangs of regret over a lowering marriage to an uncouth man become understandable if we consider that her family pedigree would have enabled her to enter court service or to become Genji's wife. Her decisions continue to haunt her later on in the chapter when her husband's death brings untold "hardships," implying acts of sexual aggression by her dead husband's son. Her only option is to become a nun, which she does by the end of the chapter, but her relationship with Genji continues when she joins Suetsumuhana under Genji's roof in Chapter Twenty-Three.

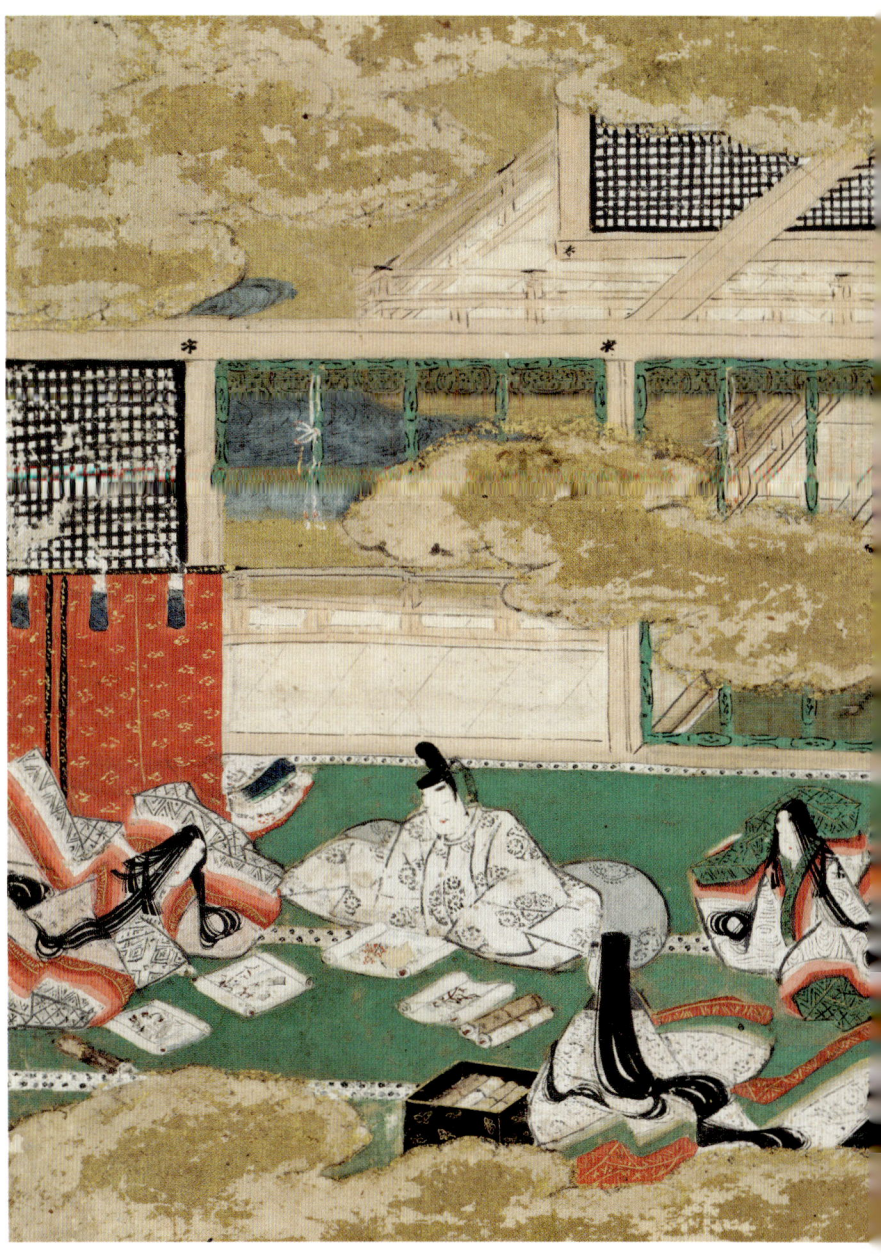

Narihira [Zai chūjō]'s fame cannot be sullied," argued Fujitsubo, composing:

> To the casual eye
> The bay with its burden of seaweed
>   May seem an old story,
> Yet shall we so easily scuttle
> The Ise fisher's ancient fame?

CRANSTON, PP. 789–90

17

絵合

A Contest of Illustrations

Eawase

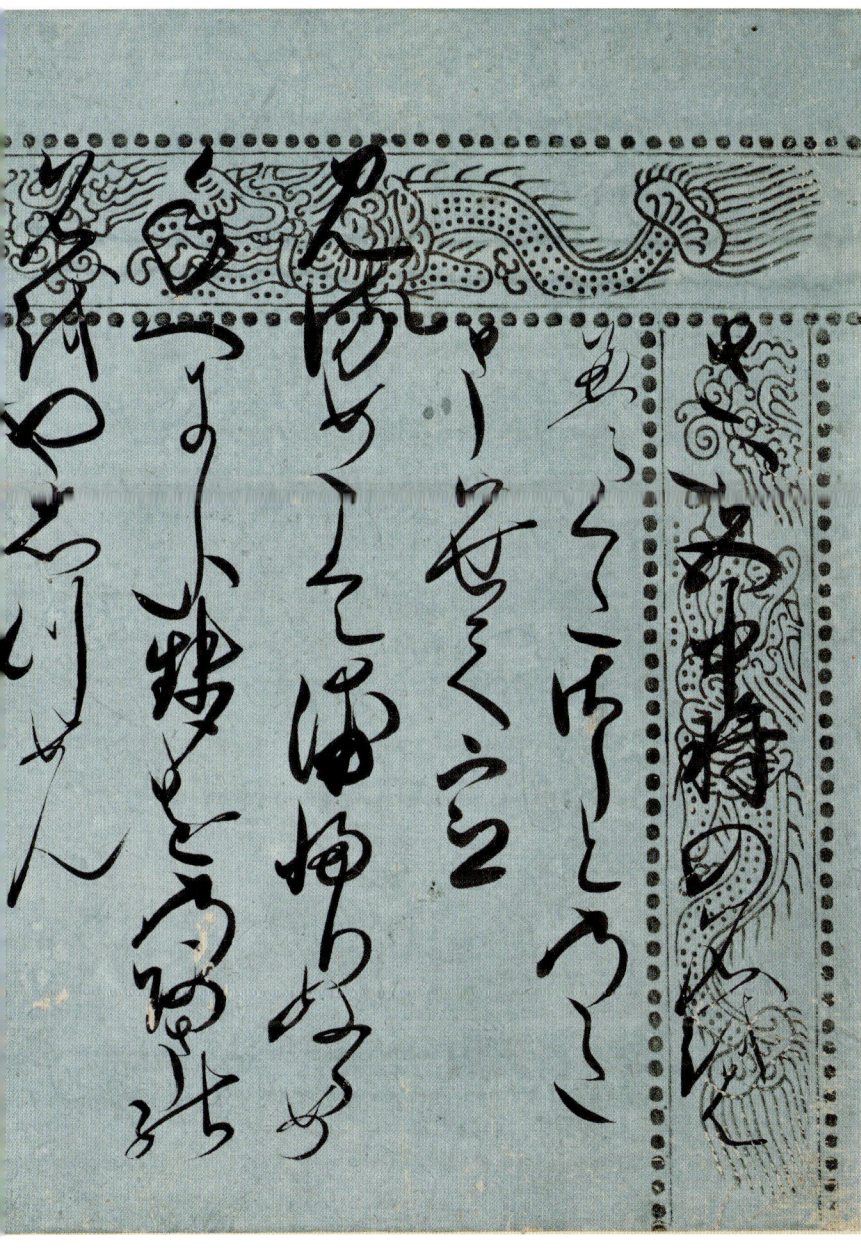

"Zaigochūjō no na o ba ekutasaji"
to notamawasete, Miya,

   Mirume koso
   Ura furinurame
     Toshi henishi
   Iseo no ama no
   Na o ya shizumen

さい五中将の名をば
えくたさしとのた
まはせて宮
見るめこそ浦ふりぬらめ
年へにしい勢をのあまの
名をやしつめん

The "contest of illustrations" in Chapter Seventeen consists of two matches: one among the ladies-in-waiting at the palace, presided over by Fujitsubo, and a more formal event before Emperor Reizei. The matches take place after Tō no Chūjō commissions modish new narrative illustrations for his daughter, the new Kokiden Consort, in order to entice young Emperor Reizei—who is fascinated with tales and paintings. Genji and Fujitsubo, who are supporting the Umetsubo Consort (daughter of the deceased Lady Rokujō) and aim to help her win the favor of Reizei, their secret son, soon learn of Tō no Chūjō's scheme and set out to thwart it. Genji inspects his collection of illustrated scrolls in order to supply the Umetsubo Consort with her own arsenal of amusing tales, and he consults Murasaki in the process.

The scene in the album depicts Genji and Murasaki examining his library for this purpose, having pulled several scrolls from the black lacquered box in the foreground, which is decorated with a gold butterfly design and filled with numerous works yet to be unrolled. Genji occupies the center of the composition, a gold cloud hovering overhead emphasizing his presence, as he contemplates a painting. Murasaki sits to his right, absorbed in a separate painting, her diminutive right hand pressed against the ground to steady herself as she leans in for a closer look. The painted scroll before her depicts scenes from the Suma seascape: a figure pulls a long rake across the space in the foreground, while behind him distinctive shore pines and the gray roofs of distant huts peek out between blue horizontal mist bands. The motifs in this "painting-within-a-painting" correspond to poetic tropes associated with the Suma shore that predate *The Tale of Genji*: fisherfolk (*ama*), seaweed (*mirume, ukime, moshio*), salt burning and brine (*shio*), and pines (*matsu*) on the bay (*ura*). These same word-motifs saturate the numerous poems from the Suma chapter composed by Genji and his women back in the capital, many of them functioning as homophones for expressions of isolation, passionate longing, and regret. This scroll surely represents one of the pictorial diaries that Genji made during his exile at Suma. Genji's sketches are singled out for the highest praise by the narrator; they not only capture pictorially the desolate and exotic landscape of his place of exile but also his innermost thoughts through the poems in *kana* that are interspersed among the pictures. As Ii Haruki has discussed, Genji created the scrolls originally with the intention of one day showing them to Murasaki, envisioning her adding her own poems to his, and deliberately leaving space for her to do so. And yet, this is the first time she views the intimate picture diaries, nearly three years after his return, having been shown them only incidentally. The images trigger memories of lonely days in Genji's absence, and she is said to feel distant from him even now. At the same time, Genji's thoughts turn not to the woman beside him, but to Fujitsubo, whose poem appears in the calligraphic excerpt adjacent to the painting, as if reflecting the content of his wandering mind. This poem by Fujitsubo appears later in the chapter, spoken as she reviews scrolls from the contesting sides at the first of the picture contests, where the ladies-in-waiting of the respective Consorts, divided into teams of Left and Right, debate the merits of each work. Genji's side, the Left, puts forth an illustrated scroll of the *Tales of Ise*, a collection of anecdotes about the ninth-century courtier Ariwara no Narihira, while the Kokiden Consort's faction on the Right submits a new illustrated tale. Fujitsubo speaks up for the *Tales of Ise* scrolls, lauding the work's pro-

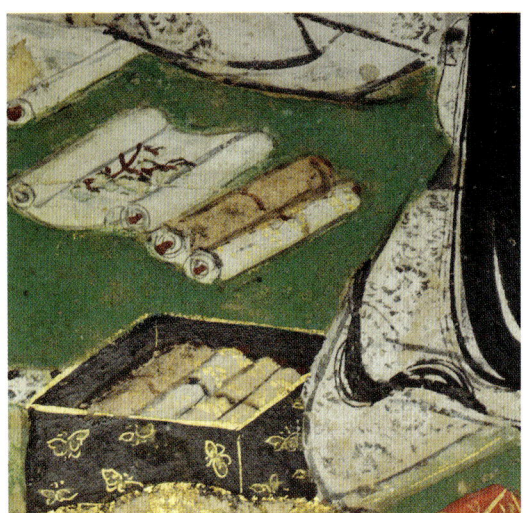

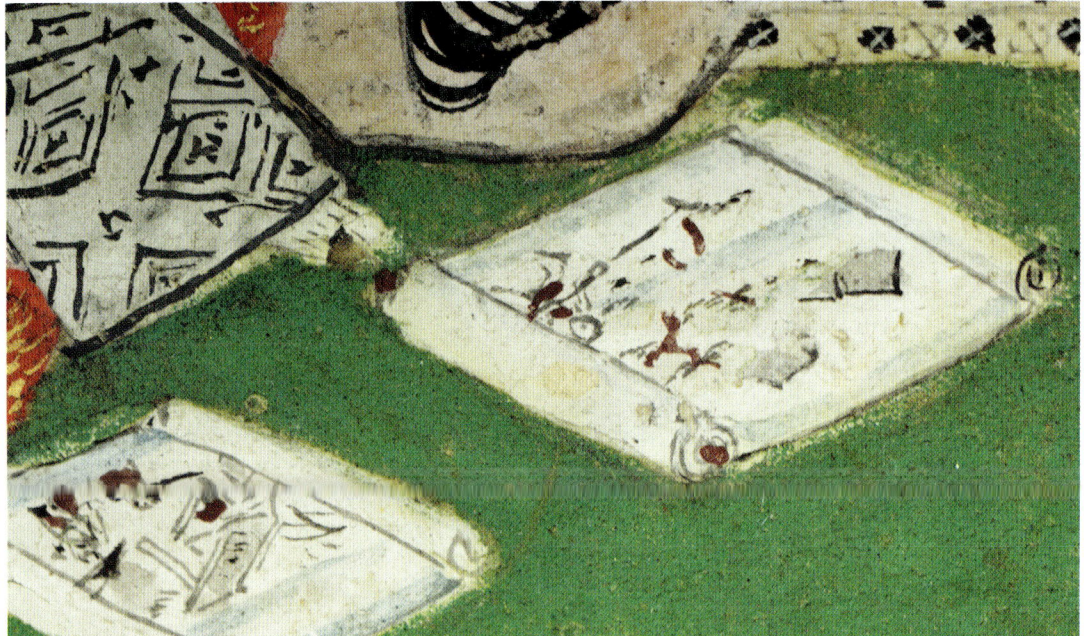

tagonist Narihira, himself a famous exile, and using seashore imagery to express sympathy for Genji's period of isolation.

Deliberations over the merits of various tales continue apace among the women until Genji suggests that the contest be brought before Reizei. A magnificent formal matching of illustrations ensues before the Emperor and his courtiers, emulating the pageantry and ceremony of court poetry contests. The subject matter and connotations of each illustrated story that comes up for debate serves a rhetorical purpose, and each side attempts to advance its case through the interpretation of prose, poetry, and painting. The seemingly lighthearted competition thus enables long-standing political foes to engage each other through the language of aesthetic debate. With the contest coming to a close, as its final maneuver Genji's side unveils his scroll from Suma. Its vivid evocation of his exile moves everyone to tears, bringing victory for Genji's side along with an implicit acknowledgment of the injustice he suffered. Considering the supernatural elements of the exile chapters—the invocation of the miraculous workings of the Sumiyoshi deity, the oneiric visitation from the deceased Kiritsubo Emperor, and the tempest that brings Genji to the Akashi shores—the Suma scroll in this moment of political triumphalism resembles an oracle. As it is revealed, Genji describes the spontaneity of its creation, confirming for those assembled Genji's righteousness and the otherworldly forces that brought him back to power.

The picture contests in this chapter can be seen as a pretext for an aesthetic pronouncement on naturalism and spontaneity, as well as literary genre. Genji's unmediated, personal renderings prove to be more powerful than the works of professional court artists, a stance that echoes the author's view, expressed in Chapter Twenty-Five, that tales (*monogatari*) relate human experiences of the past more compellingly than official histories. Genji's Suma diaries, rendered in pictures combined with *kana*, are the antithesis of official *kanbun* diaries, but they secure him this victory and suggest the author's understanding of the power of writing in the vernacular.

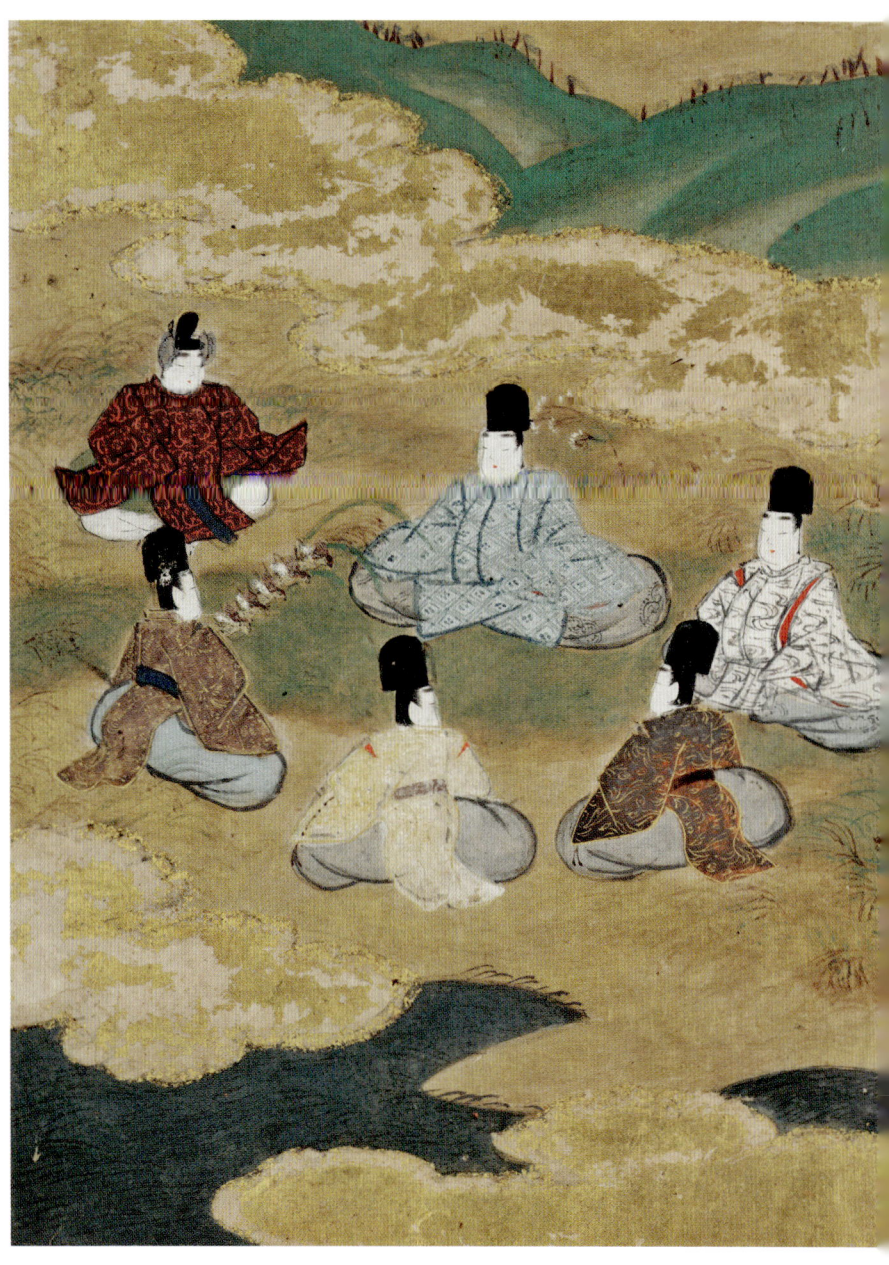

> Over the river
> Where the lambent moon does dwell
> Your village lies—
> Small wonder that the Katsura
> Should glow with a light serene.
>
> CRANSTON, P. 794

"How enviable," Reizei added.

18

松風
Wind in the Pines
Matsukaze

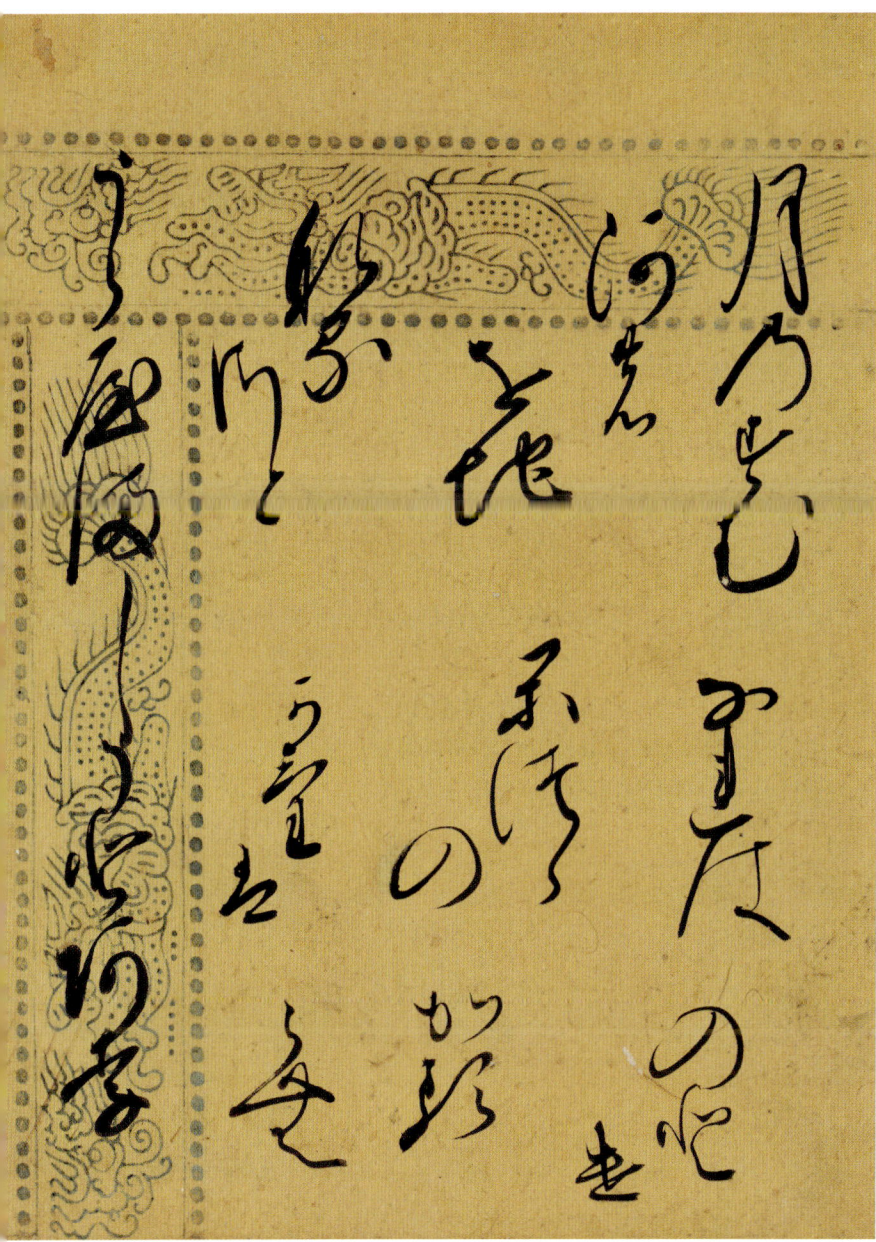

Tsuki no sumu
Kawa no ochi naru
Sato nareba
Katsura no kage wa
Nodokekaruramu

"Urayamashiu" to ari.

月のすむ なれは　のと
河の　　かつら　け
をち　　のかる
なる　　かけ　ら
さと　　は　　む
うらやましうとあり

In the only painting in the album that depicts a scene entirely outdoors without any architectural motifs, Genji sits amid a group of five other courtiers and devoted retainers, once again taking center stage with a gold cloud hovering above him that emphasizes his primacy. The group sits near the river's edge occupying a clearing among tall autumn grasses and mistflowers (*fujibakama*), with pine-tree-dotted green hills in the distance. This particular episode from Chapter Eighteen takes place in an area known as Katsura in the western part of the capital, where Genji has recently constructed a new villa for himself to be near the Akashi Lady, who is currently living upriver in Ōi with her mother and young daughter in the home in which the Akashi Nun was raised. Although Genji's Katsura villa was meant to be a secluded residence for him to use on his visits to the Akashi Lady, his whereabouts have become known, and numerous courtiers have traveled from the imperial palace to be in his company. One such man, a prince leading a hunting party, has spent the night in the fields on the way. In this scene, the party arrives, represented by the three men in the foreground bearing a token of the hunt—five small game fowl attached to a branch of bush clover. Their offering, along with their upturned gazes and location in the lower register of the image, clearly communicates deference toward Genji, the Palace Minister. The figures on either side of Genji appear to be the two men said to have accompanied him in his carriage from the Akashi Lady's villa in Ōi to Katsura: a Commander from the War Ministry (*hyōe no kami*), wearing the distinctive fan-shaped ornaments (*oikake*) on his *kanmuri* hat that indicate a member of the palace guard, and a Middle Captain (*tō no chūjō*) seated to Genji's left. The gathering begins in midday and continues late into the night as the men imbibe several rounds of wine, compose verses in Chinese-style quatrains (*zekku*), and offer musical compositions on the *biwa*, seven-stringed *koto*, and the flute, engaging in revelry beneath the autumn moon that rivals that at the imperial palace. In fact, despite the frivolity, this chapter and this particular scene have much to do with Genji's growing authority and claim to imperial legitimacy, the banquet functioning as a site for the demonstration of fealty and obligatory praise of a reign.

The poems in this section connote imperial sovereignty, beginning with the verse included in the album, composed by Emperor Reizei, who regrets Genji's absence from his own moon-viewing banquet at the palace. The young emperor's poem puns on "Katsura," which is the name of the place where Genji is, and also the name of a mythical tree said

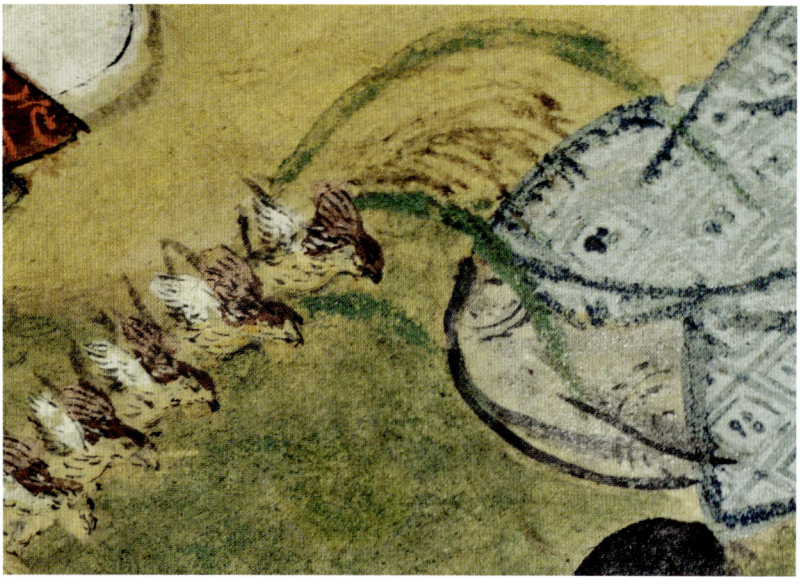

94 | *The Tale of Genji*

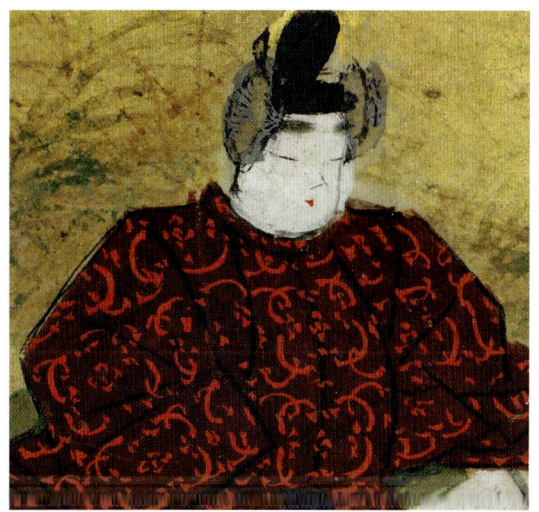

to grow on the moon. He compliments Genji, linking him with the *katsura* tree bathed in the radiance of the moon, while expressing frustration that he cannot leave the palace freely to be in Genji's luminous presence. The poem is unusually deferential for one composed by a sovereign to his own Palace Minister. But, as the reader knows, Genji is not just any Palace Minister—he is in fact Emperor Reizei's true father. Although Reizei will not learn the truth of his parentage until the next chapter, the inclusion of the poem introduces the tension apparent in all interactions between Genji and Reizei in which their hierarchical father-son relationship, although covert, puts into disarray the expected power dynamic of sovereign over subject.

The poetic entreaty subtly suggests that despite Reizei's status, Genji is somehow superior, a sentiment that Genji skillfully deflects in his response:

Hisakata no	Here in the mountains
Hikari ni chikaki	Morn and evening our village
Na nomi shite	Lies in unclearing mist;
Asayū kiri mo	Only an empty name implies
Harenu yamazato	Closeness to light everlasting.

CRANSTON, P. 794

The light of the moon, which can be taken as a symbol for the radiance of the emperor, resides in Katsura "in name only" (*na nomi shite*), says Genji. He posits Reizei as the real source of imperial light,

and, as Takada Hirohiko has argued, later seems to request an official visit (*gyōkō*) usually made by a reigning emperor to a retired emperor, normally the sovereign's father. While reinforcing Reizei's primacy as emperor, the text makes Genji into a figure with the exalted status of a pseudo retired emperor, which he will soon acquire. The final three poems by Genji and his retainers in the chapter use the imagery of the moon as a metaphor for Genji's exile and return and the glory of the current reign, and present Genji and Reizei as the true heirs to the late Kiritsubo Emperor (instead of Suzaku, Kokiden's son). Genji takes on a symbolic sovereignty, surpassing whoever occupies the actual throne in the narrative by the sheer force of his supremacy in all ways that matter, including in his enactment of ritualized revelry. The gathering at the end of "Wind in the Pines" evokes an imperial banquet in which praise poems and musical performances instantiate the harmony of the realm.

Although Chapter Eighteen concludes by confirming the supremacy of the Kiritsubo Emperor's line, specifically as it runs through Genji and Reizei, the majority of this chapter concerns the Akashi family, as does the chapter title. Much space is devoted to the decision to relocate the Akashi Lady, her young daughter, and the Akashi Nun to the capital as a part of the Novitiate's divinely inspired plan to elevate his lineage. A villa owned by the Nun's family near the Ōi river where she lived in her youth in Sagano enables the family to create a simulacrum of the Akashi shore in the capital. There the Nun hears her daughter's *koto* music and recalls the "wind blowing through the pines" (*matsukaze*), a sound that conjures up images of life on the shore and memories of her past. Rather than depict any number of episodes from this chapter concerning the Akashi family, however, the editors of the album chose a scene that highlights Genji's patrilineal claims to imperial authority. Such an image of loyal men paying obeisance to a leader amid the wild fields must have appealed to the album's sixteenth-century commissioners, men of the Sue house, themselves immersed in the world of homosocial bonds and the rituals that reified them.

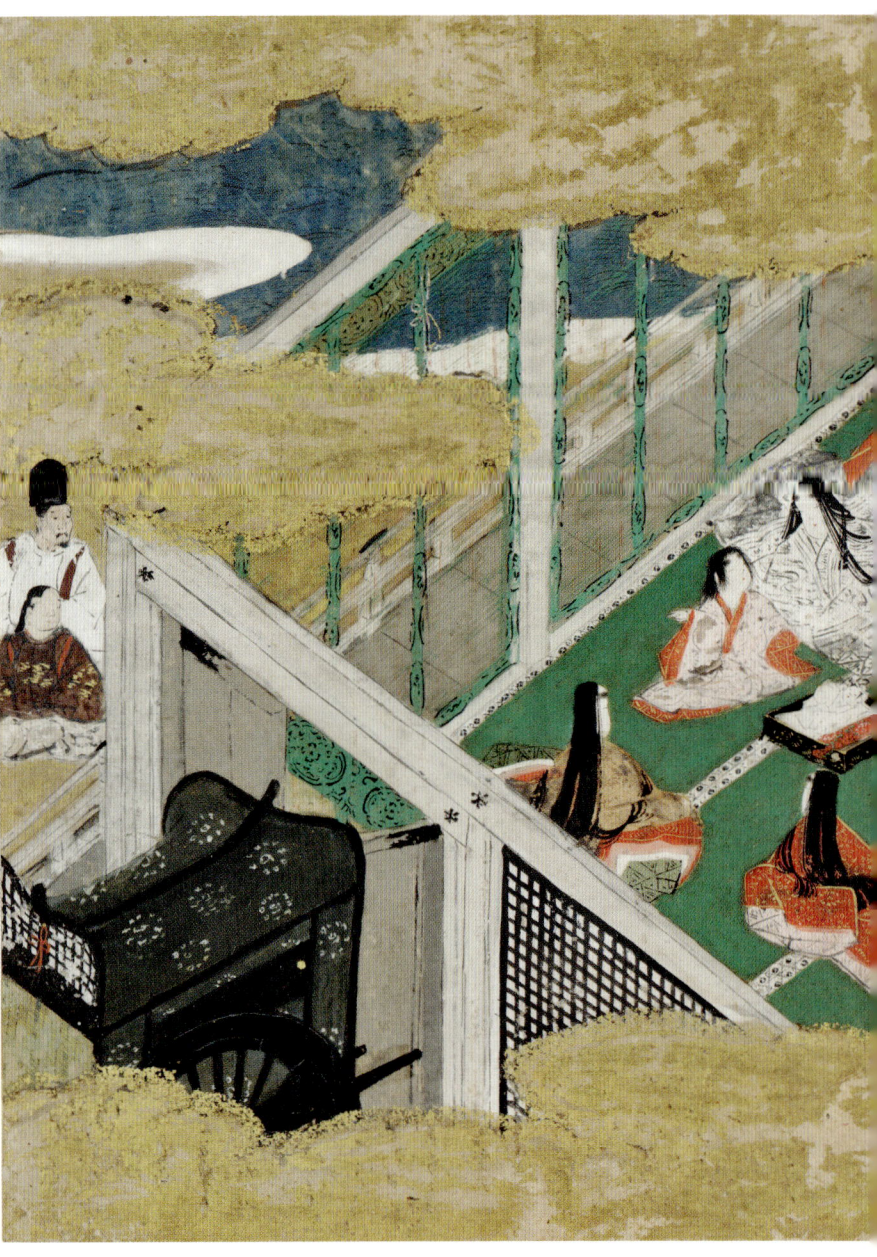

Her childish babbling was adorable as she tugged on her mother's sleeve. "Let's get in!" This was too much for her mother.

WASHBURN, P. 392

    Whose ends are far,
The twin-leaf little pine
    Now torn away—
I wonder when the day will come
To gaze on its lofty shade.

CRANSTON, P. 796

19

薄雲

A Thin Veil of Clouds

Usugumo

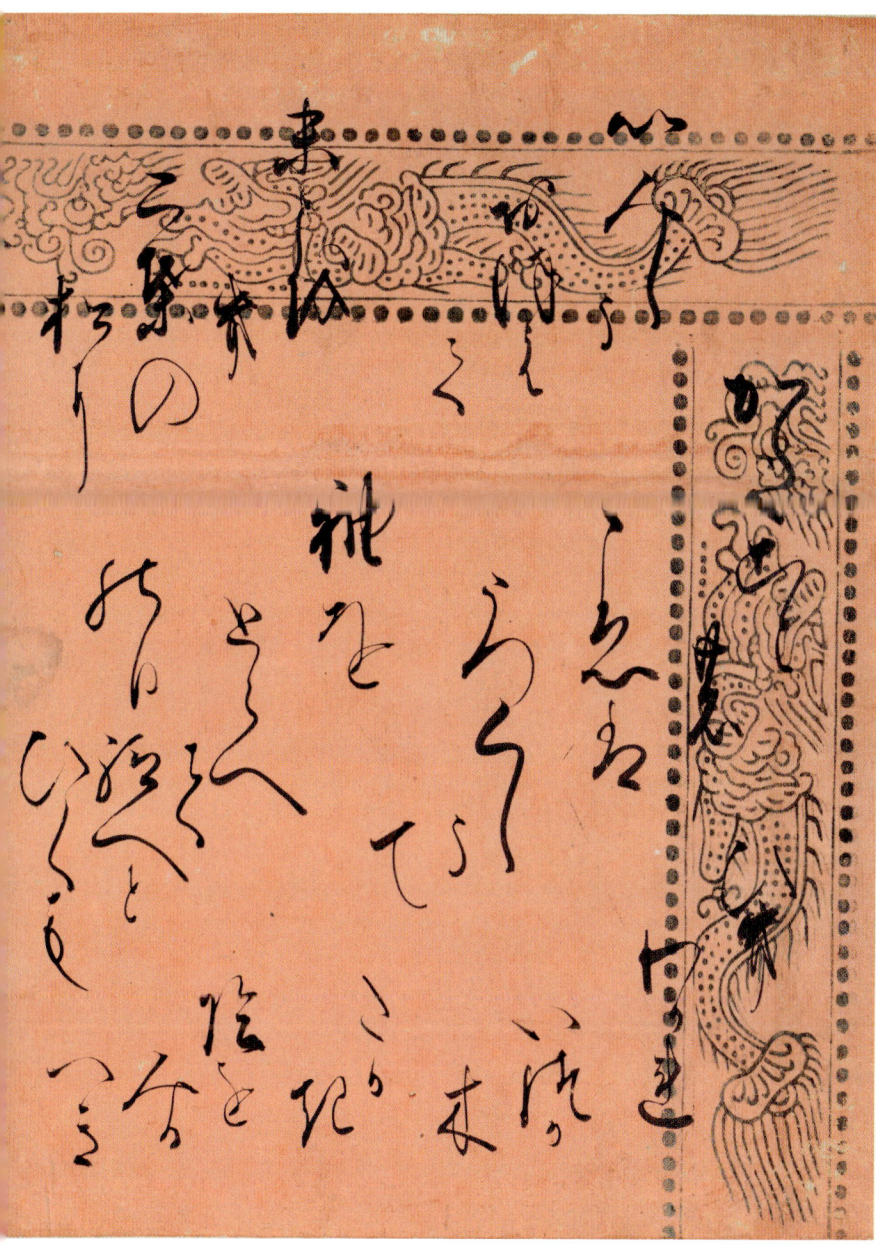

Katakoto no, koe wa utsukushiute, sode o toraete, "Noritamae," to hiku mo imijiu oboete,

Sue tōki
Futaba no matsu ni
Hikiwakare
Itsu ka kodakaki
Kage o mirubeki

かたことの こゑは うつくしうて 袖を とらへて のり給へと ひくも いみじう おぼえて

末とほき
二葉の松に
ひきわかれ
いつか木たかき
陰を みるへき

97

The painting for Chapter Nineteen depicts one of the most heart-wrenching scenes in the tale: when the Akashi Lady sends her three-year-old daughter to live with her father, Genji, and to be raised by Lady Murasaki. Given the Akashi Lady's provincial upbringing, she needs someone of Murasaki's status and pedigree to enable her daughter to ascend to the highest levels of court society and to achieve the greatness to which all believe she is destined. The decision torments the Akashi Lady, whose affection for her daughter is described in touching detail. In the cold days of winter leading up to the separation, she strokes the little girl's hair and sits gazing at her, as if attempting to commit her features to memory. She envisions how quickly her daughter's appearance will change through the stages of childhood that she will never witness—by spring, she muses, the girl's short hair will have grown long enough to brush charmingly across her shoulders, in the manner of a woman who has taken Buddhist vows. The line recalls the list of "Adorable Things" (*utsukushiu mono*) from the *Pillow Book* (*Makura no sōshi*, ca 1002) of Murasaki Shikibu's contemporary, Sei Shōnagon, which describes: "a child whose hair has been cut like a nun's, tilting her head to one side to see, rather than brushing away the hair from her eyes." The painting in the album puts us in the position of appreciating these thoughts of the Akashi Lady through its deliberate depiction of the girl's amorphous toddler hairstyle. In this and other ways, the painting emphasizes the bond between the Akashi Lady and her child, excluding Genji from the picture altogether, though he is present in this scene in the tale.

The line of prose and single poem in the accompanying calligraphy leaf follow suit by containing only the voices of mother and daughter. The innocent child, unaware that she is about to be separated from her mother, excitedly demands to enter the carriage. The text begins in the middle of three horizontal, slightly diagonally oriented registers, with the "adorable" voice of the little girl, as she tugs at her mother's sleeve urging them to ride together, saying "let's get in." In the painting, this eagerness is communicated by the girl's raised hand pointing to the carriage. The vehicle has been brought to the veranda, where the large open wooden door of the residence connects to it for direct and private access. Two female attendants in the foreground represent the girl's nurse and a woman named Shōshō, who will accompany her to Genji's Nijō residence. Yet the Akashi Lady is said to carry her child into the carriage herself, her action described with honorific language never before applied to this character, as if to acknowledge the nobility of her sacrifice. Precisely at this moment she speaks the poem included in the album, which uses the image of a "twin-leaf pine" torn in half to express her anguish, a sentiment captured by the calligrapher who has ripped the poem apart graphically. It begins in the upper portion of the sheet with an introductory phrase, "feeling overwhelming sadness" (*imijiu oboete*), and continues through the first twelve syllables of the verse, ending with the "twin-leaf pine." The poem splits here, not after the seventeen syllables of the "upper phrase" of the poem, but at an unnatural point. It continues along the very bottom of the sheet with the sharp consonants of the word for "torn apart" (*hikiwakare*) and trails off with the mother wondering if she will ever see her daughter again.

Genji is not without guilt for separating the mother and child, and he attempts to comfort the Akashi Lady with a poetic response not included in the album leaf:

Oisomeshi	Since its roots go deep
Ne mo fukakereba	That long since began to grow,
Takekuma no	The little pine tree
Matsu ni komatsu no	By the Takekuma pines
Chiyo o naraben	For a thousand years shall stand.
	CRANSTON, P. 796

He refers to legendary twin pines growing at Takekuma to suggest that this child born of their two lineages will lead to a flourishing of their descendants for "a thousand years to come." The Akashi girl, Genji's only daughter, is of course destined to become Empress and to fulfill the prophecy of the seers who predicted Genji's future, and to realize the Akashi Novitiate's portentous dreams.

In addition to accentuating the emotional intensity of the scene, the painting in the album

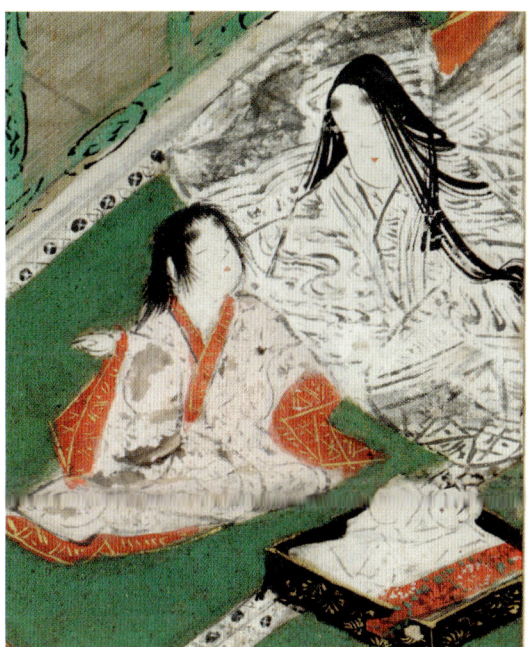

surrounds the Akashi Lady with imagery associated with winter, the season with which she will become associated, while calling attention to her daughter's lineage within the Akashi house. In a passage in the tale that leads up to the scene depicted in the album, the lady stares out at the frozen edges of the garden pond at the Ōi villa, while the morning skies darken amid falling snow. She wears robes of soft white silk, and appears to be, in the opinion of her ladies-in-waiting, the equal in beauty of any noblewoman at court. The painting references that melancholy morning through small but powerful touches, such as the bright white edges around the pond that connote ice and snow, and the white robes of the Akashi Lady, mentioned explicitly in the text. White robes are appropriate for the winter season, but they also evoke the uniquely achromatic garments traditionally worn by women during childbirth. In this way, the Akashi Lady's robe emphasizes her identity as the girl's biological mother, especially when viewed in conjunction with two other prominent motifs in the painting, the ceremonial dagger, and the doll (*amagatsu*), which both rest in the black lacquered box on the ground. The dagger was a gift sent from Genji on the fiftieth day after his daughter's birth while she was still in Akashi. The doll would have been handmade by the Akashi Lady as a protective talisman for her child. Although the girl is now three and at the age when the doll could have been put aside, it is specifically placed in the carriage and taken to Nijō. The artist paid great attention to the depiction of these objects, down to the detailed floral design of the red fabric covering the dagger and the white swaddled doll with its two strands of hair emulating that of a newborn. As Kurata Minoru has suggested, the objects will embody a memory of the rituals surrounding the girl's birth in Akashi and her true lineage even after her guardianship is relinquished to Murasaki. Biological and adoptive motherhood will continue to be represented, as in a later scene when ladies-in-waiting mention Murasaki's childlessness, emphasized when Murasaki attempts to soothe the Akashi girl with a breast that has no milk. The painting thus reflects an important theme of the tale, namely, the Akashi family's matrilineal claim to the imperial line through the girl, a glory in which Murasaki will partake, albeit in a limited way, as the official adoptive mother.

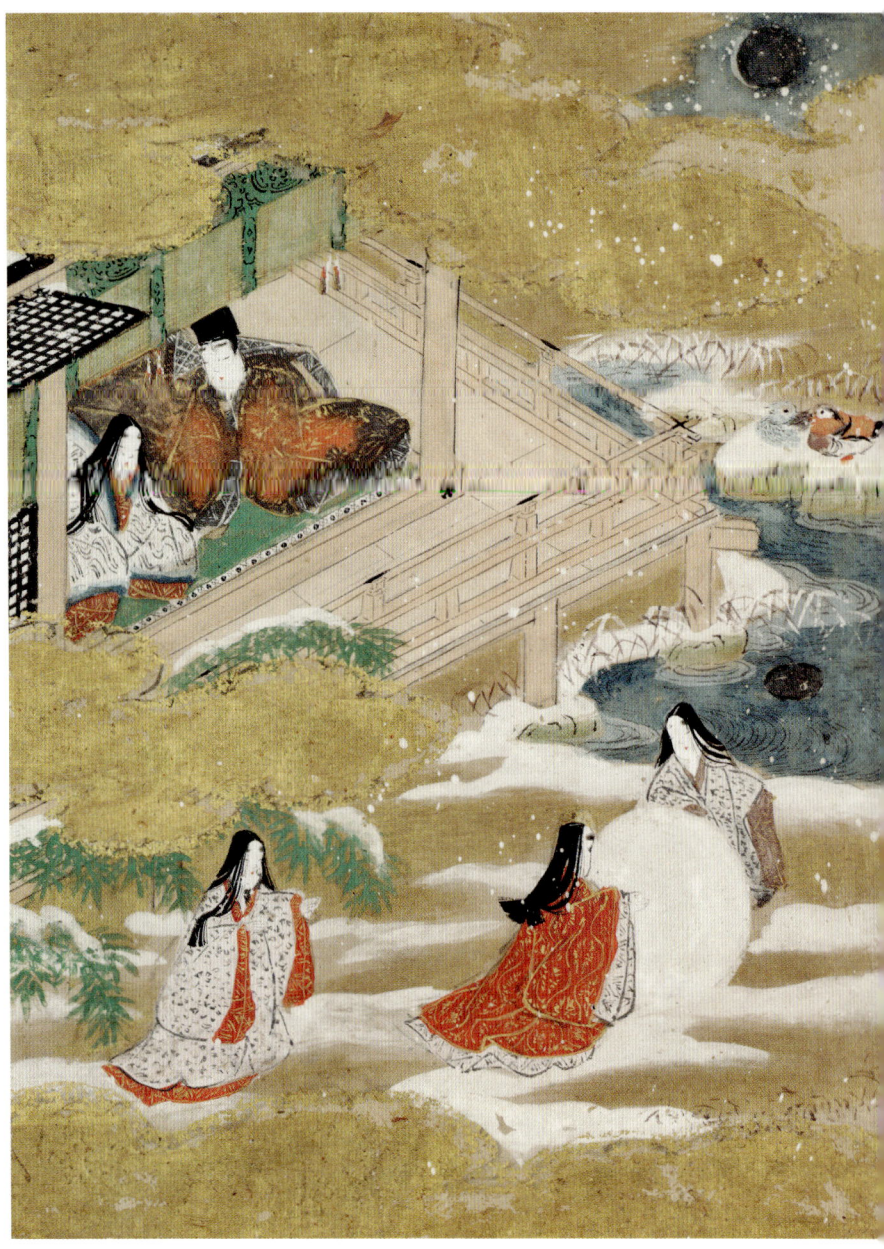

The poor withered plants in the garden were sagging beneath the weight of the snow, the burbling of the garden stream sounded as if it were sobbing in grief, and the ice on the pond was indescribably desolate. Genji sent the page girls out into the garden to roll snowballs.

WASHBURN, P. 420

20

朝顔
Bellflowers
Asagao

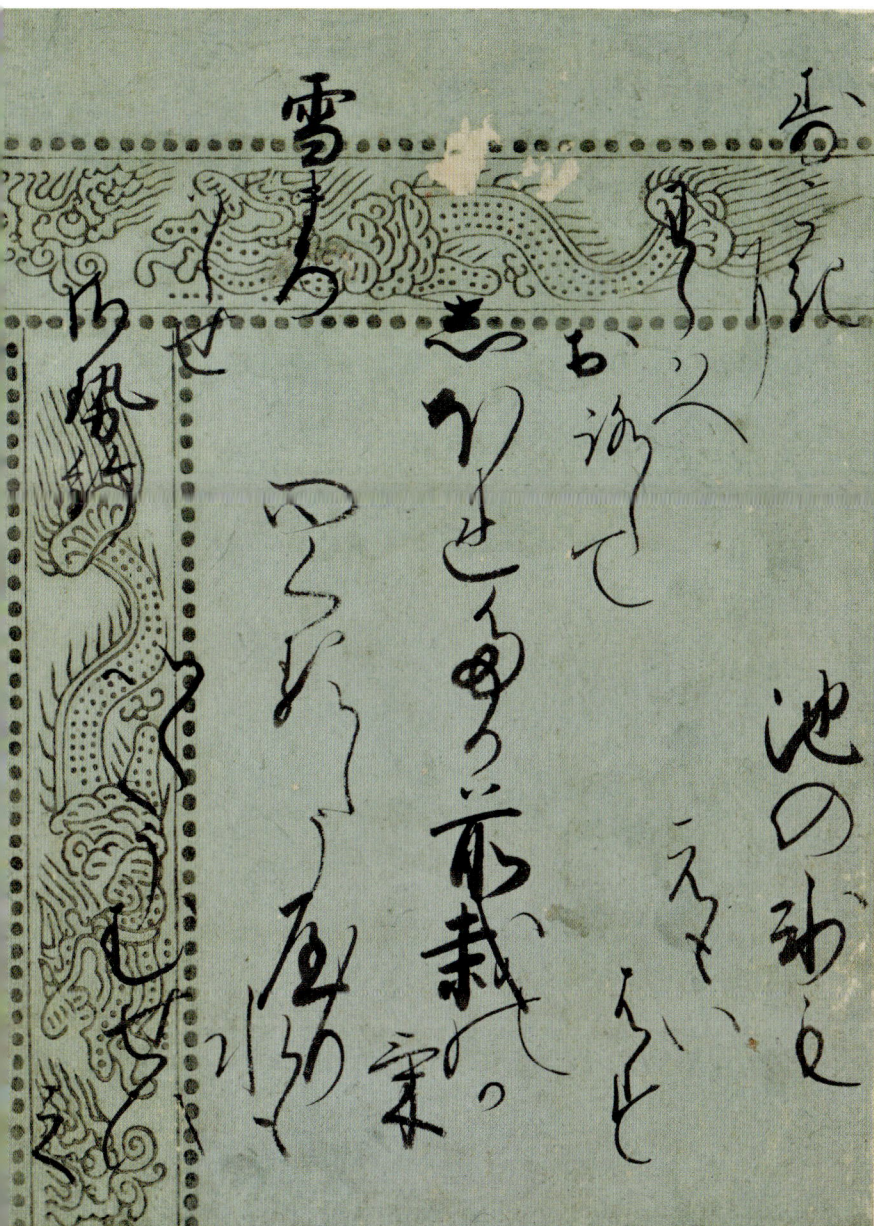

Shioretaru senzai no kage kokorogurushiu, yarimizu mo itau musebite, ike no kōri mo e mo iwazu sugoki ni, warawabe oroshite yuki marobashi sesasetamau.

すこき　池の氷も
に　　　えもい
わらはへ　はす
おろして
しほれたる前栽のかけ
心くるしうやり
雪まろ　　水も
はしせ　いたうむせひ
させ給　　て

On a moonlit evening in Genji's thirty-second year, he and Murasaki lie near the veranda of the Nijō residence looking out over a snow-laden garden in a scene of domestic serenity. In the tale, the narrator describes the perfection of the couple and the austere winter beauty of the evening as so ideal that it should be captured in a painting. Tosa Mitsunobu rises to the occasion and depicts the pair dressed in informally elegant, gold-patterned robes, indicating the luxury of their daily existence. The intimacy of the moment is emphasized by the absence of any watchful attendant figures and a tight frame around the couple made up of columns and a blind above, which Genji has just raised, allowing moonlight to flood the room. The source of the light appears in the upper right corner of the composition, a silvery moon with its illusory reflection floating on the pond below. Bright white snow covers the ground and weighs down the bamboo and the reeds at the water's edge, while soft flurries scatter across the gold clouds. Pale blue paint limning the otherwise dark blue water represents the ice just beginning to form on the edges of the pond, creating the sense of a chilly exterior in contrast to a warm interior occupied by the couple. Inside, Genji focuses intently on Murasaki as he turns toward her, affectionately scrutinizing her features, as described in the tale. The gold cloud that so often hovers above Genji's figure in the album as if to mark his status as the protagonist here floats over the two of them, edging closer to Murasaki. The lady's attention is not on Genji, however, but on the page girls outside, whose dark hair juxtaposed against their white robes and the glistening snow is said in the tale to be mesmerizing. The girls have rolled a snowball too large to push any farther, as suggested by the figure who leans her elbow on the orb as though resting in defeat. Another page seems eager to keep rolling, while a third girl enters from the left gesturing with her hands to offer advice.

The pictorial motifs depicted in the garden, which at first seem merely to embellish the elegant atmosphere, when read in conjunction with the chapter's poetry, reflect the restless thoughts of the characters looking out at them. Murasaki's poem,

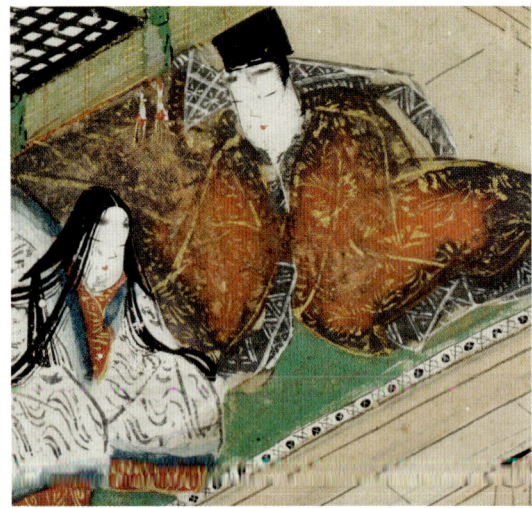

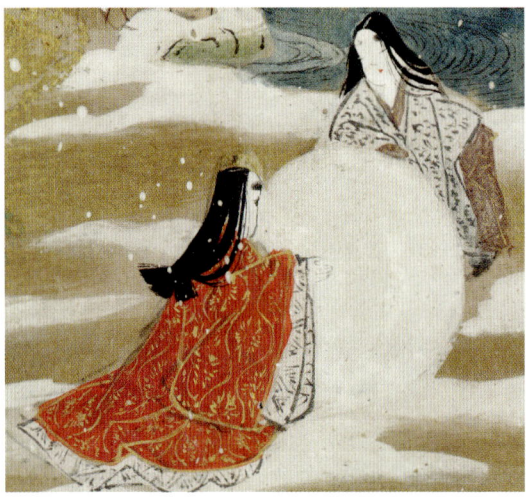

ostensibly about the frozen pond, indicates feelings of profound discontent:

Kōri toji	Locked in by ice,
Ishima no mizu wa	The water in between the stones
Yukinayami	Runs but poorly now;
Sora sumu tsuki no	It is the clear moon, sky-dwelling,
Kage zo nagaruru	That flows in a shining stream.

CRANSTON, P. 803

The anxiety expressed in the poem derives from Murasaki's knowledge that Genji has been pursuing the former Kamo Priestess, his cousin known as Princess Asagao. Genji first courted this woman when he was a young man in Chapter Two; with her royal pedigree, she represents a unique threat to Murasaki.

Although Genji has never been presented as a flawless hero, in this chapter the author begins to depict him in middle age and to complicate his portrayal in new ways. He continues to be politically ascendant, but the text criticizes his attempts to relive the amorous adventures of his youth in ways both subtle and humorous. Elderly female characters from Genji's past are reintroduced, such as Naishi, his father's handmaid, whose presence calls attention to the passage of time and Genji's own aging. Even Princess Asagao is not a young woman, but Genji's contemporary; he likens her in a poem to a bellflower (giving the chapter its name) past its prime. At the same time, Asagao's steadfast rejection of Genji's advances implies that his amatory powers may be in decline. In the scene depicted in the album, Genji has returned home after being rebuffed by Asagao and lavishes attention on Murasaki, attempting to console her. But his words quickly turn into a disquisition on the qualities of the various women he has known, Murasaki among them, giving her yet another reason to compose the poem above with its metaphor of the ice-locked pond.

For Genji, the image of the page girls playing in the snow triggers a memory of his greatest love, the recently deceased Fujitsubo, who had long ago staged a similar scene with a snow mountain. Once Genji makes the association, thoughts of Fujitsubo preoccupy him, and he notices anew Murasaki's uncanny resemblance to her aunt, and her beauty. He recalls the purple roots of the gromwell, Murasaki's namesake flower, which had always been a metaphor for her affinity with the Fujitsubo Consort, and the purple wisteria to which that name refers. At that moment, he composes a poem that reflects the joining of the two women and the merging of past and present in his mind:

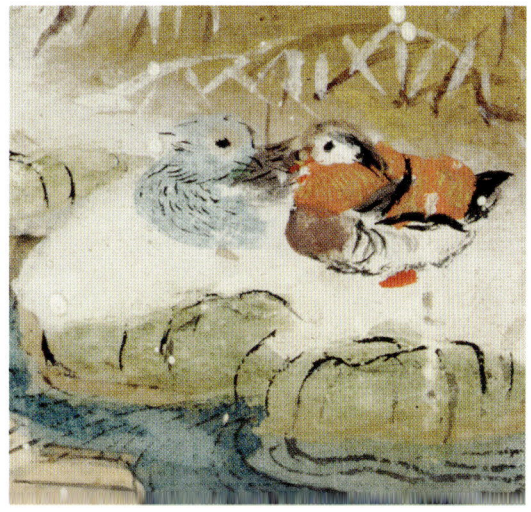

Kakitsumete	Over snow the past
Mukashi koishiki	Longings now gathered together
Yuki mo yo ni	In tonight's raking…
Aware o souru	A new note of sadness floats
Oshi no ukine ka	In the pond ducks' restless cry.

CRANSTON, P. 803

The mandarin duck, usually a symbol of auspicious marital fidelity, cries out over the snows that evoke the past. In the lines that follow, Genji falls asleep and dreams of Fujitsubo, who chastises him for exposing their secret affair while revealing that she has been suffering in the afterworld. Genji awakens to Murasaki beside him, who has heard him crying out in his sleep. The chapter concludes with Genji commissioning sutra readings for his deceased love's tormented soul. While the brightly painted pair of mandarin ducks in the album leaf echoes the apparent harmony of the couple inside, the scene is only superficially joyous. Beneath the surface of the picture's hibernal beauty is a melancholic, even ominous tone, with the shadow of Fujitsubo looming over the perfect couple.

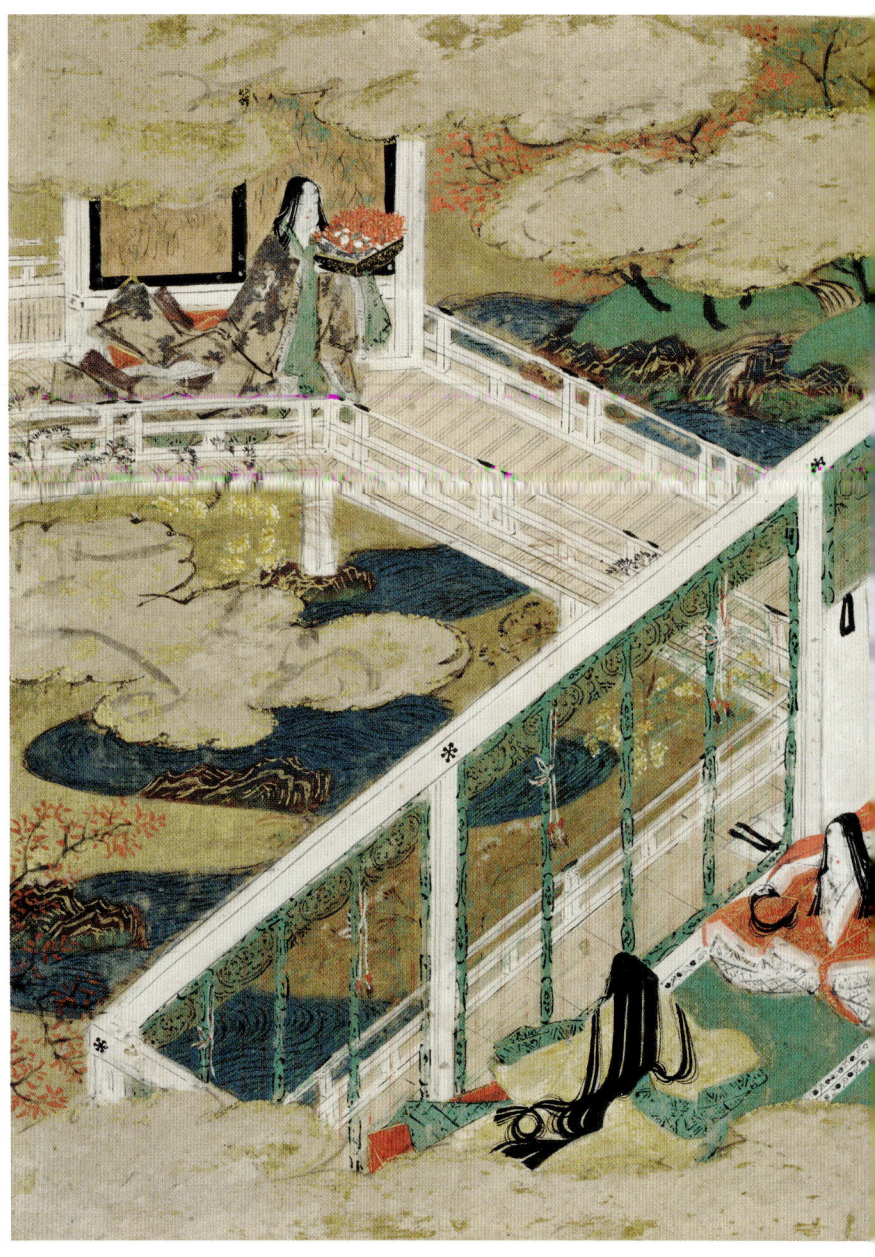

    May the flower garden
That awaits with all its heart
    The coming of spring
Still regard our crimson leaves
At least as offerings of the wind.

CRANSTON, P. 810

21

少女
Maidens of the Dance
Otome

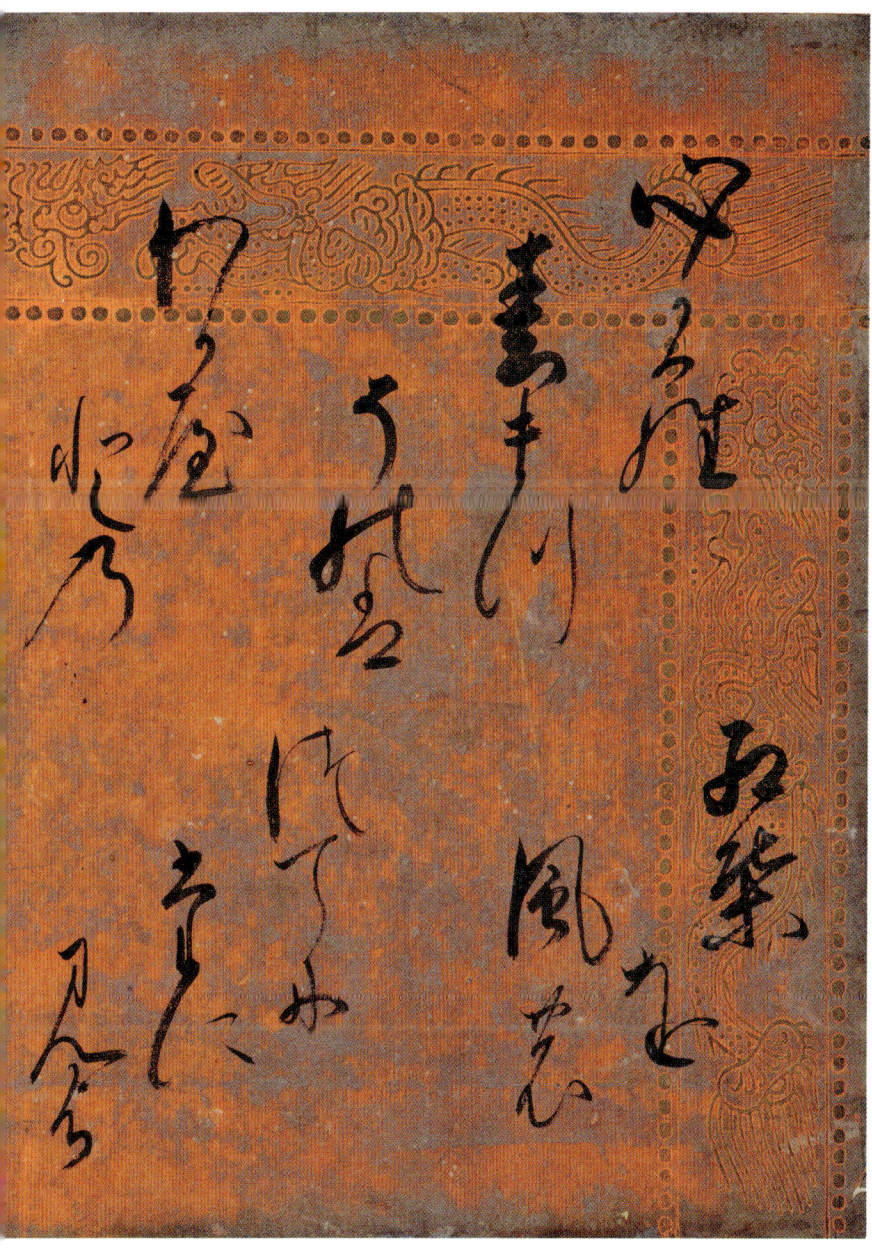

Kokoro kara
Haru matsu sono wa
  Wa ga yado no
Momiji o kaze no
Tsute ni dani miyo

心から
春まつその は
　わが 風の
　　やど つてに
　　紅葉 たに
　　を 見よ

In his thirty-fifth year Genji acquires four square parcels of land in the capital and unites them to construct a grand estate with separate structures in each quadrant to house his various women. The residence is known as the Rokujō estate (Rokujōin), named for its location on Rokujō, or Sixth Avenue, on land inherited by the Umetsubo Consort, daughter of the late Rokujō Lady. The finished estate is an architectural marvel in scale and design, arranged according to geomantic principles with each quadrant aligned with one of the four seasons. Genji has the grounds excavated, installs lakes and hills, and orders plantings to ensure each designated season is perfectly expressed in its respective quadrant. The Umetsubo Consort, named Empress in this chapter, occupies the southwest quadrant when home from her duties at the palace. Her garden flourishes in autumn, earning her the nickname "Akikonomu," literally "one who loves the autumn." Murasaki occupies the spring corner in the southeast, with its cherry trees, wisteria, azalea, and mountain rose. She is joined by the Akashi girl, whom she is raising, and Genji himself. Hanachirusato, the lady associated with orange blossoms, as seen in Chapter Eleven, lives in the summer quadrant in the northeast corner of the complex. Having been asked by Genji to look after Yūgiri, Hanachirusato shares her summer quadrant with the young man. And finally, Genji relocates the Akashi Lady from the distant Ōi villa in Sagano, bringing her within close proximity to her daughter, although convention still prevents them from meeting directly. The Akashi Lady resides in the northeast corner, which boasts an elegant winter garden with hills and pines that promise a picturesque snow scene when the season arrives. Her quadrant is the only one without its own lake, and her residence consists of merely two small structures that resemble the adjacent wings (tai no ya) of a main hall (shinden) without the central hall itself, as found in the structures of the other ladies. Such disparity in the opulence of her accommodations results from the Akashi Lady's lower status as the daughter of a provincial governor. And yet her role as mother to a future empress is quietly suggested in other ways, by the conspicuous chrysanthemum in her garden, which has long been associated with imperial offspring, and by its position in the northern half of the estate, as the northern direction is linked to belief in the realm of the Dragon King, to which the site of Akashi was likened, a clear symbol for the claims of the Akashi family to the throne.

Although the four mansions of the Rokujō Estate are divided by walls and landscaping, a network of elevated bridges and covered walkways connect them to enable a degree of interaction between residents in different quadrants. This is precisely what is happening in the scene depicted in the album, in which a messenger sent by the Empress traverses a corridor leading to Murasaki's quarters. The woman appears as if she is processing in a formal

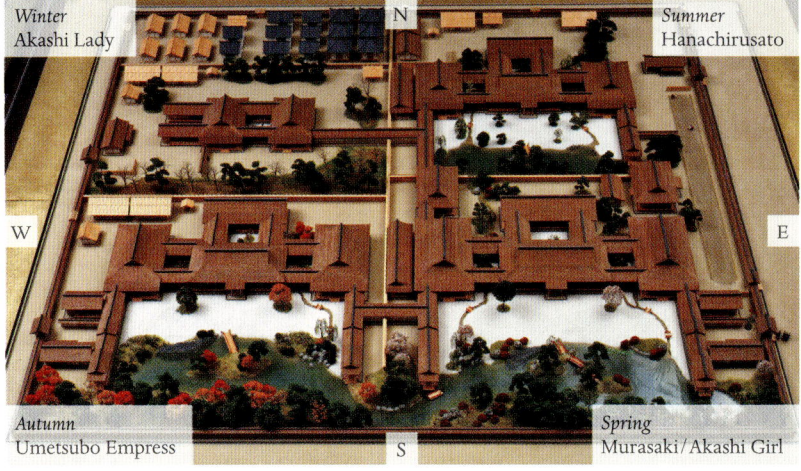

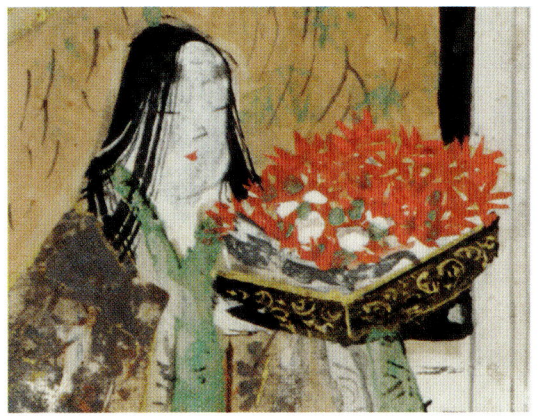

manner, appropriate for an empress's attendant, and indeed her regal comportment and the subdued purple colors and the intricate details of her robes are richly described in the tale. She carries a black and gold box lid, which contains a dense collection of autumn flowers, bright crimson leaves, and a letter with a single poem by the Empress. That same poem appears in the adjacent calligraphy in the album, allowing the viewer to read the missive that Murasaki is about to receive. The calligraphy is brushed in a straightforward manner, while the crimson color of the paper seems carefully matched with the autumn foliage referenced in both text and image. The Empress's poem is a deferential greeting that acknowledges Murasaki's place within Genji's household as the mistress of the spring, but it also speculates that Murasaki must be awaiting the glory of her garden, which is now out of season. Murasaki responds with her own poem championing the spring over the autumn, a provocation that initiates a seasonal competition between them lasting for several chapters. Outside, a small number of autumn plants appear: yellow maiden flowers (*ominaeshi*), mistflowers (*fujibakama*), and red-tinged leaves, as though the Empress, likened to Tatsuta-hime, the goddess of autumn, has animated Murasaki's garden.

Of the two women in the foreground, Murasaki sits in the more interior part of the room with a white standing curtain beside her suggesting her higher status. The other woman is an attendant, but a striking one in a bright yellow robe with exceptionally long tresses flowing down her back. She turns toward Murasaki while peering through the bamboo blinds as if reporting the messenger's approach. The viewer looks down at the scene from a high vantage point and over the sharp diagonal lines of the building to see the winding garden stream marking a central diagonal swath through the composition. A low-lying waterfall in the upper right corner is the source of this stream, which cascades over a rocky bank and meanders downward, hinting at the extensive artificial lakes and watercourses that flow throughout the estate. The detail in this upper part of the painting echoes the description of the Empress's autumn garden in the tale, for which Genji constructed a waterfall, diverted and rechanneled springs, and strategically placed rocks to trip the stream and enhance the sound of burbling water. Although the primary setting of the painting is Murasaki's spring garden, these motifs suggest that it may represent a conflated image of two gardens at once.

The architectural fantasy that is the Rokujōin is not without historical or literary precedent in terms of grand palatial residences constructed by men with imperial aspirations in Heian Japan, but it is unique in its configuration. Its seasonal spatial layout is a mismatch with the temporal order of the seasons, which may derive from Chinese precedents. The conceit of all four seasons blooming also recalls representations of Buddhist paradise, as well as the Dragon Palace beneath the sea. Whatever the case may be, by placing all of his women in one vast complex, Genji creates a simulacrum of an imperial palace. Chapter Twenty-One also marks a shift to the next generation, with the coming-of-age ceremony of Genji's only son, Yūgiri, at the age of twelve. Yūgiri engages in his first act of voyeurism, espying the daughter of Genji's former manservant Koremitsu, who performs at the Feast of Glowing Harvest (Toyo no Akari) in the Dance of the Heavenly Maidens, or Otome, from which the chapter takes its name. This harvest banquet, a central ritual related to imperial enthronement, provides an interesting backdrop against which Genji constructs his pseudo-imperial palace at Rokujō.

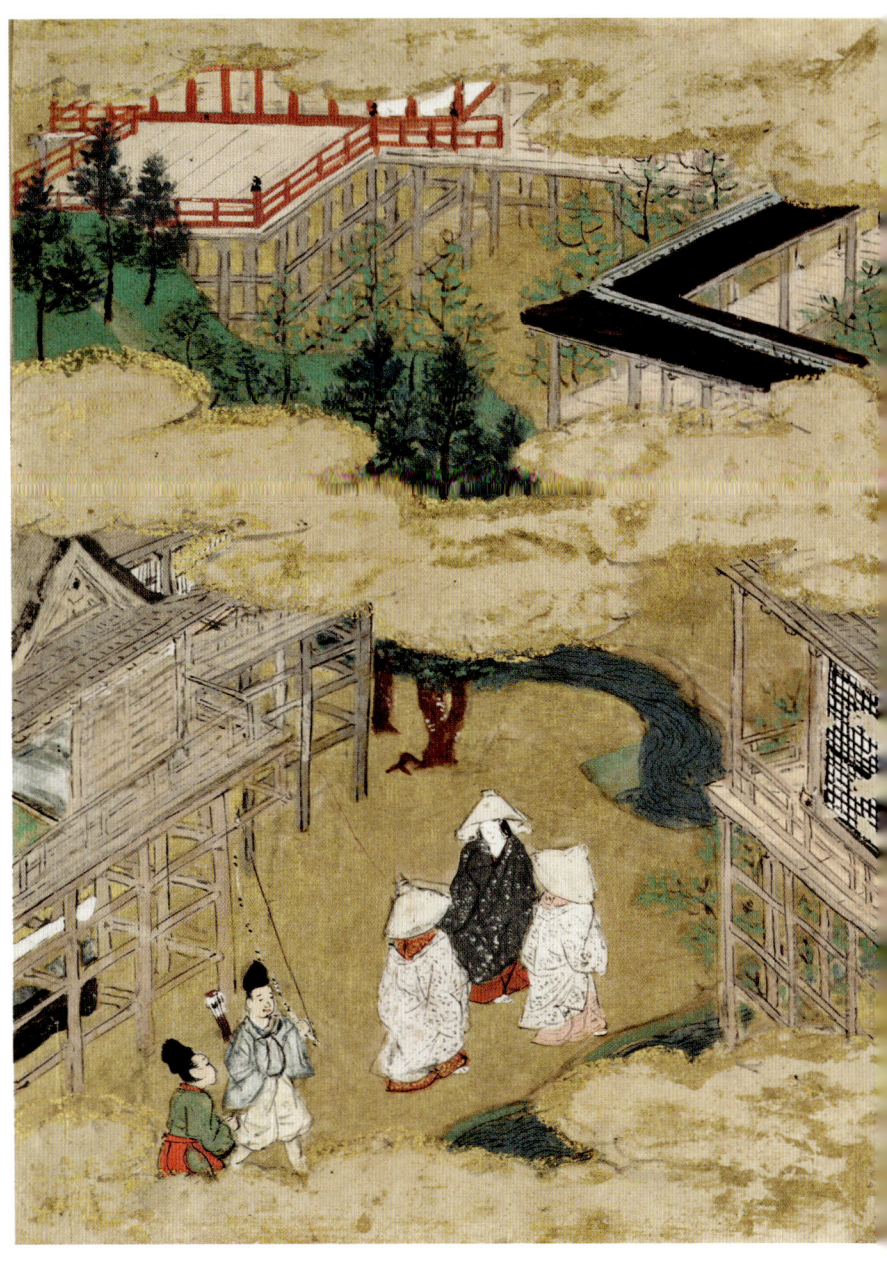

    If we had not come
Seeing out the place where stand
    The twin cedar trees,
How would we ever have found you
On the banks of the old river?

"At the rapids of joyous meeting!"

CRANSTON, P. 813

22

玉鬘

A Lovely Garland
Tamakazura

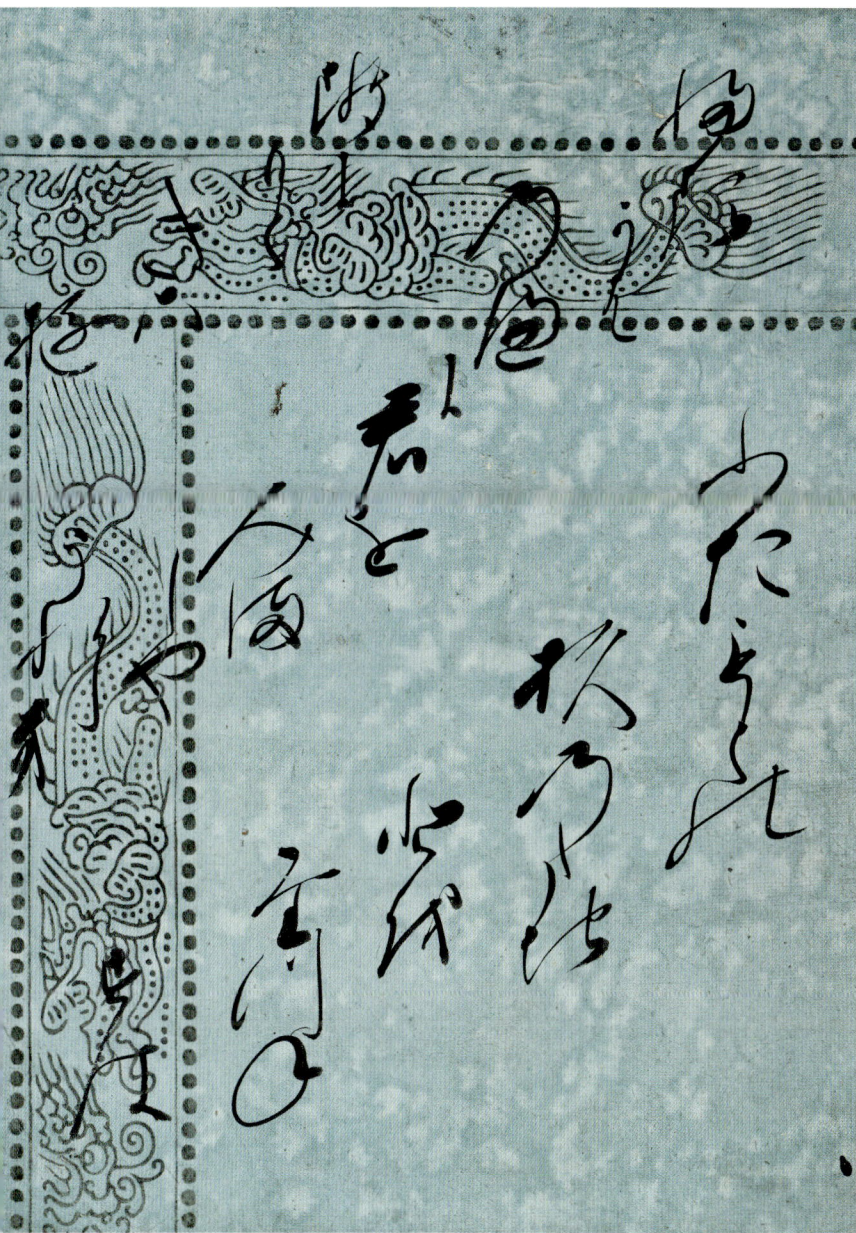

Futamoto no
Sugi no tachido o
Tazunezu wa
Furukawanobe ni
Kimi o mimashi ya

"*Ureshiki se ni mo*" *to kikoyu.*

ふる　ふたもとの
かは　　杉のたち
のへ　　　　とを
に　君を　　たつね
瀬に　み　　　すは
　もと　ま
　き　　し
　こ　　や
　ゆ　うれしき

Twenty years have passed since Yūgao died in Genji's arms in Chapter Four, but Genji has not forgotten his "lady of the evening faces." Chapter Twenty-Two turns to the fate of Yūgao's daughter, Tamakazura. Yūgao's death long remained a secret, known only to Genji, his retainer Koremitsu, and Ukon, the female attendant who accompanied the couple on that fateful night. Tō no Chūjō, Tamakazura's real father, was never told of Yūgao's passing or of his daughter's whereabouts. Even the nurse who was left to care for Tamakazura believed only that the girl's mother had disappeared. And she rejected the idea of sending the girl to her father Tō no Chūjō, acutely aware that threats by his wife's family had driven Yūgao into hiding in the first place. Instead, the nurse decided to take Tamakazura with her to Kyūshū, where her husband had received a government post. There she raised the girl alongside her own two daughters and three sons for sixteen years. Tamakazura grew into a beautiful young woman who attracted numerous suitors, much to the dismay of the nurse, who believed these provincial men entirely unsuitable for the daughter of a nobleman. She did her best to discourage them, but when an aggressive warrior named Taifu no Gen demanded the young woman's hand in marriage, the nurse and Tamakazura, as well as her oldest son and daughter, were forced to escape by fast boat through the Inland Sea to the capital.

The album painting for Chapter Twenty-Two shows them having departed again to offer prayers at the Buddhist temple of Hasedera, some fifty miles south of the capital, in Nara. They make the arduous pilgrimage on foot, traveling for four days in order to worship before the temple's icon of the Eleven-Headed Kannon, housed in the main hall of Hasedera, which looms over the scene between bands of gold clouds in the upper portion of the painting. The building is immediately identifiable by its distinctive main hall and protruding stage, supported by tall, horizontally tied columns in the overhanging style (*kakezukuri*). The vermilion railing and architectural details stand out amid the green hills and blue and green trees surrounding the structure, nestled as it is on the eastern side of Mount Miwa. One corner of

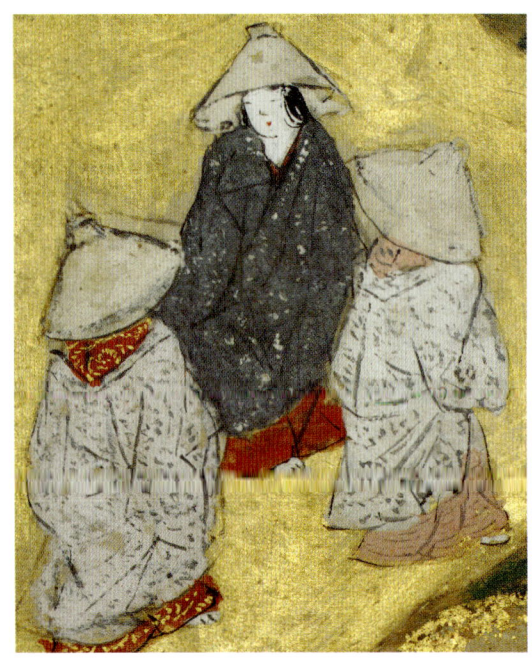

Hasedera's famous cypress roofed staircase stands in here for the hundreds of steps that zigzag down the mountain. In the painting, the v-shaped line of the brown roof and its central tiled ridge leads the eye to the scene below, where elevated timber-frame structures on either side of the painting point diagonally toward the center of the composition. Buildings to the right and left frame the focal point of the image: a group of three women in large conical hats and travel robes, representing Tamakazura, her nurse, and her nurse's daughter, Hyōbu. The women are unaccustomed to walking such a distance, and the glimpse we get of sandaled feet poking out from beneath their robes suggests their exhausted, footsore state as described in the tale. As luck would have it, Ukon, now a well-respected attendant in service to the Chancellor, Genji, and Murasaki, has come to Hasedera to pray for help in finding Tamakazura and is staying at the same lodgings the party from Kyūshū occupy. Ukon recognizes one of the attendants, and a joyful but bittersweet reunion ensues as Ukon confirms Yūgao's death. A now lost *Genji* book cover painting of this same scene by Tosa Mitsunobu (shown opposite) introduced by Ryūsawa Aya, helps make sense of the lodgings depicted in the album

110 | *The Tale of Genji*

painting. It reveals how the ground level spaces of these elevated structures were used as stables for travelers' horses, partitioned with curtains for attendants, in this case an escort armed with bow and arrows for protection.

After the reunion, both parties make their way up to the temple where they sit before the Buddha offering prayers and chanting sutras through the night. They remain on pilgrimage for three days, during which time Ukon composes the verse that appears in the album's calligraphy, and which draws inspiration from the scenery around them. They gaze upon the Hatsuse River, which is mentioned in the poem (referred to as the "ancient river" *furukawa*), as is the famous "twin-trunked cedar" (*futamoto no sugi*), represented by a conspicuous image of a tree with two trunks standing directly behind the central group of women on the banks of the river that flows around them. The painting thus masterfully combines elements from disparate temporal moments into one image: the traveling party, which alludes to both the long journey and their arrival; the temple lodgings for pilgrims, shown empty and anticipating the miraculous meeting that will take place within their walls; the poetic motifs of cedar tree and river from a poem composed after the meeting; and finally, the sacred temple that floats above the scene in a vista that is topographically impossible but made coherent through the use of gold clouds. Like other landscapes depicted in the album, the pictorial motifs work as word-images from the chapter's poems, arranged in a naturalistic way, to create a landscape of the mind and of poetic memory. The painting is an amalgamation of pictorial images associated with Hasedera, artfully arranged to foreshadow the most fateful moment in Tamakazura's story.

Mitsunobu's emphasis on the famous landmarks of Hasedera is unique among *Genji* paintings of this scene, and it invokes another pictorial genre popular in the sixteenth century: illustrated scrolls of temple-origin tales (*engi-e*). Such paintings provided details about the buildings and famous sites associated with a temple or shrine to which viewers might make a virtual pilgrimage. The album painting also highlights the phenomenon of female pilgrimage by abbreviating the male participants in the group, which matches Chapter Twenty-Two's emphasis on the actions of female attendants. The tale captures the sense of independence women enjoyed when visiting a temple, an activity engaged in by Murasaki Shikibu and by women throughout the medieval period. Amid their prayers, Ukon regales the women from the provinces with accounts of the glorious couple, Genji and Murasaki, playing the role of storyteller, an oblique nod to the female authorship of *The Tale of Genji*.

At the same time, the author advances the plot by having female attendants make decisions that at times seem detrimental to the women in their care. In Tamakazura's case, her women keep her existence a secret from Tō no Chūjō and allow Genji to install her in the Rokujōin estate. Tamakazura knows instinctively the perils that await her in the home of a man who is not her father, but she has no other option. To explain his decision to shelter Tamakazura, Genji claims that she is a long-lost daughter from a past affair. He places her in Hanachirusato's quarters, residence of his son Yūgiri, who believes she is his half sister. The cruelties to which Genji later subjects Tamakazura stem once again from the author's narrative structure in which the Kokiden faction and potential competitors to the throne are brought to heel. Tō no Chūjō, who is aligned by marriage with Kokiden's family, continues in the tale as Genji's great rival and as an object of obsessive homosocial competition. Genji's treatment of Tamakazura becomes yet another means for him to assert his dominance over her father Tō no Chūjō.

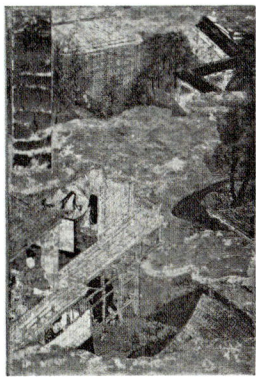 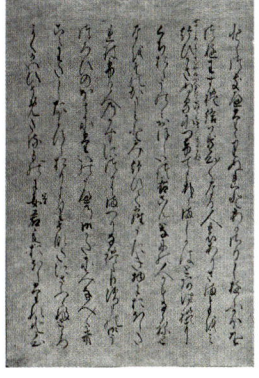

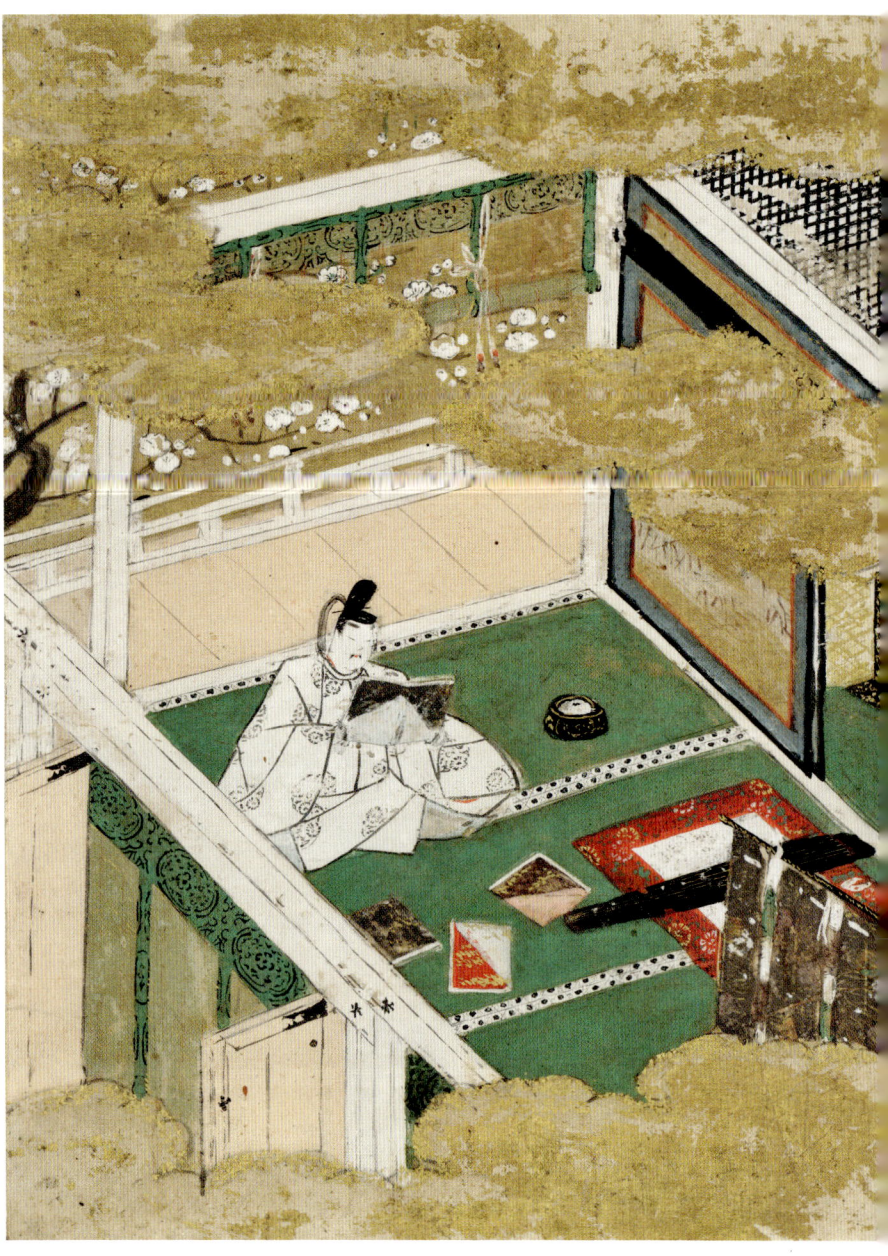

      How adorable!
From among its flowery roosts,
    Flitting from tree to tree,
To its old nest in the valley
A-calling comes the warbler.
"And how I have waited for that voice!"

CRANSTON, P. 817

23

初音
First Song of Spring
Hatsune

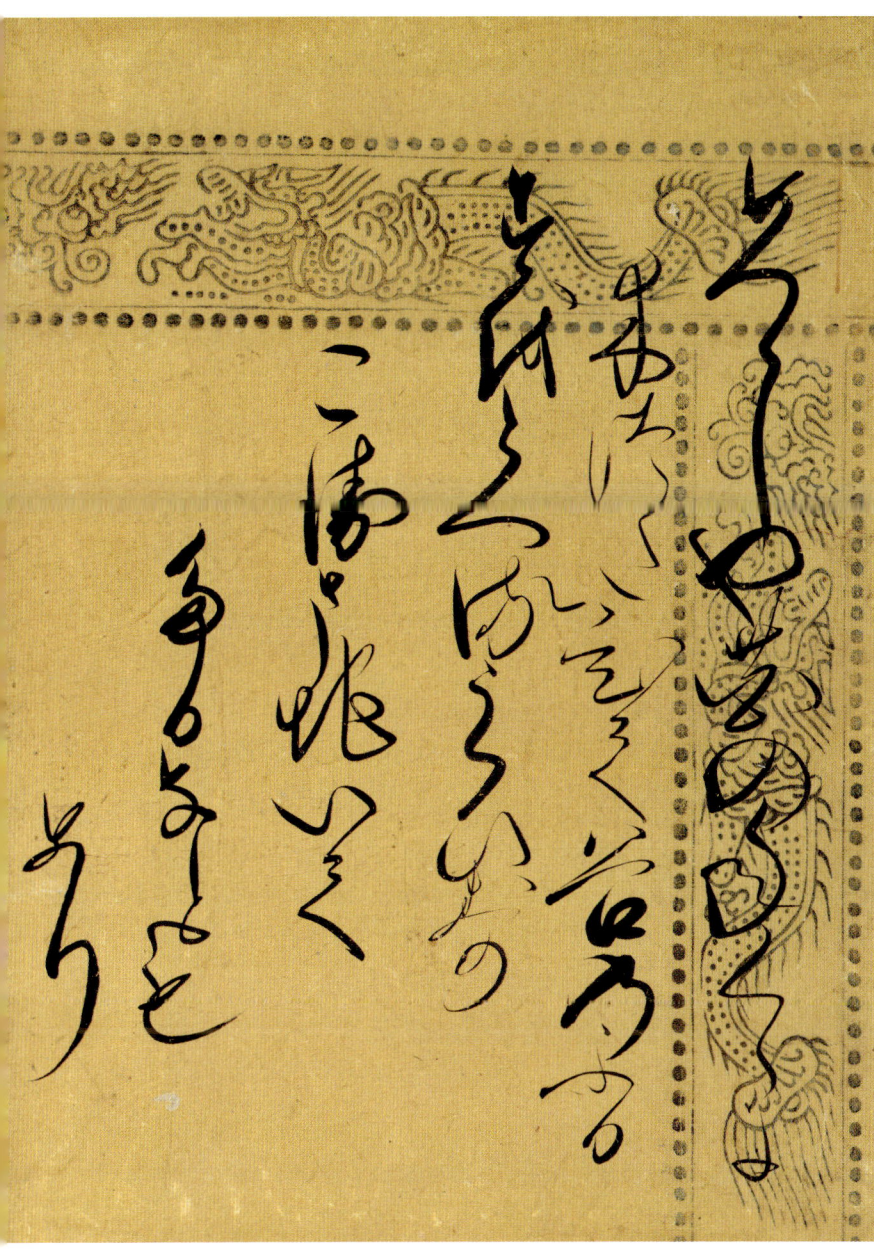

Mezurashi ya
Hana no negura ni
Kozutaite
Tani no furusu o
Toeru uguisu

"*Koe machiidetaru*" *nado mo ari.*

めつらしや花のねくらに
木つたひて谷のふる
すをとへるうくひす
こゑまちいて
たるなとも
　　　あり

It is New Year's Day, the start of spring in the lunar calendar, and amid the splendor and festivity at the Rokujōin estate, Genji visits all of his women in their respective seasonal quarters. The album painting for Chapter Twenty-Three depicts him that evening in the winter rooms of the Akashi Lady, where he will spend the night. His progression through the seasons began, however, in Murasaki's spring quarters where the garden has just begun to flourish. The tale relates how the couple exchange verses, taking up the motif of the icy pond (as in Chapter Twenty) but transforming it into an auspicious symbol—a mirror reflecting their beautiful visages and a harmoniousness that will last for "a thousand years," as Murasaki intones. The poetic communication that occurs on this day, and even the banter between Genji and his various ladies-in-waiting, references a long history of ritualistic court poetry that praises a beneficent ruler and offers wishes for a long-lasting reign. In this way, Genji's survey of his private domain resembles a ruler receiving felicitations from his subjects. Yet the author never takes this conceit too far, making sure that all of the women's comments or poetic offerings leave room for other interpretations, including those that even make light of Genji's grandeur. From Murasaki's rooms Genji moves to another wing in the spring quarter occupied by his daughter, the Akashi girl. Gifts from her biological mother, the Akashi Lady, have just arrived: artfully crafted woven baskets and boxes of delicacies, an artificial warbler perched on a fabricated pine branch, and a poem from which the chapter gets its name.

Toshitsuki o	Through the months and years,
Matsu ni hikarete	Ever drawn to the seedling pine,
Furu hito ni	Waits the aged one;
Kyō uguisu no	Today permit her to listen
Hatsune kikase yo	To the warbler's first spring song.

CRANSTON, P. 816

The Akashi Lady writes beneath her poem the phrase, "In this village where no warbler sings," making clear that the bird represents her little girl, whose voice she no longer hears. Although the letter is kept carefully within the confines of what is seasonally appropriate, it also unmistakably registers the Akashi Lady's sadness about her inability to meet with her daughter. The sent gifts express her feelings as well, as she switches the warbler's perch from its conventional plum, a symbol of spring and of the girl's home with Murasaki, to a five-needled pine, a tree of winter, suggesting the Akashi Lady's northern quarters.

The guilt of separating mother and daughter seems to be too much for Genji as he insists that his daughter reply to her mother immediately, and then personally visits the Akashi Lady's rooms, where we find him in the album painting. White plum blossoms, the quintessential flower of spring, fill the outside space behind Genji and evoke Murasaki's garden, which is also her daughter's "flowery roost." Inside, however, everything points to the Akashi Lady. An alluring scent wafting from her room beckons him as he approaches, suggested in the painting by the round lacquered incense brazier. In the tale it is described as just lit and smoldering *jijū* incense, a mixture of aloeswood, clove, sandalwood, musk, and the aromatic resin of the Mediterranean evergreen, mingling with the earlier scent of *Melia azedarach*, or Persian lilac. However, the lady herself is nowhere to be seen, and he finds only the sensuous presence of her things, which seem still animated by her touch. A Chinese-style *koto*, or *kin*, with its clearly articulated seven strings, rests on a richly pattered silk mat, with an embroidered border of continental brocade. The image of the *kin* calls to mind the instrument's pivotal role in originally bringing the couple together, the Akashi Lady's renowned musical skill in a style of play passed down from Emperor Daigo, and the seven-stringed *koto* that Genji brought with him into exile and that he gave to the Akashi Lady on his return to the capital. Scattered around the room Genji also finds the lady's writings—sheets of paper with jottings of calligraphy, and notebooks of her poetry. The painting depicts four notebooks, all with decorative covers in striking diagonal color blocks that anticipate book design of the early seventeenth century. Genji holds one volume in his hands, entirely absorbed, seemingly intoxicated by the atmosphere, and unaware of himself. He reads a poem written

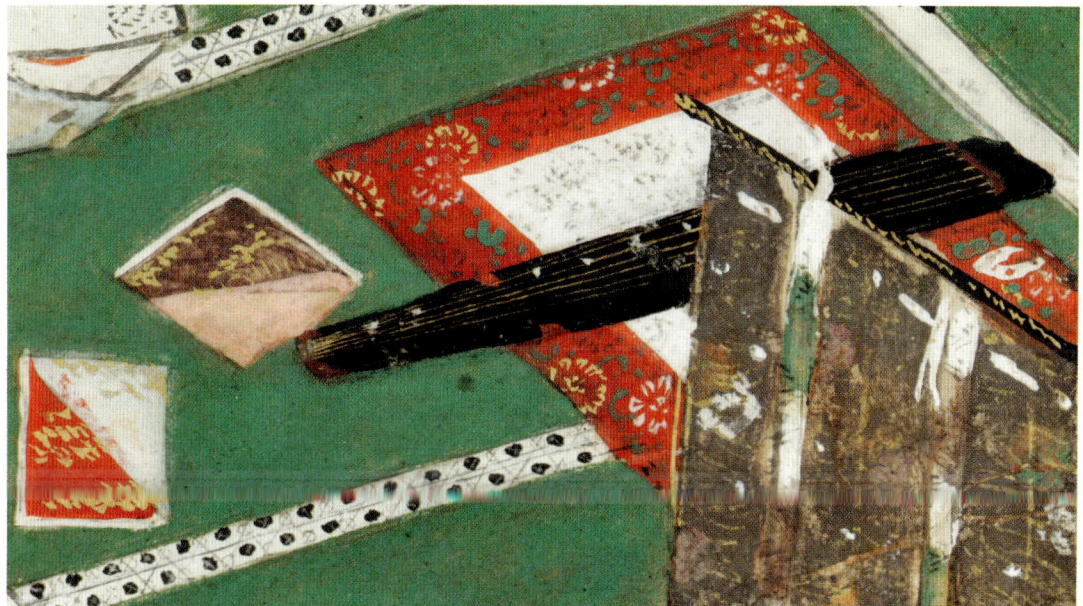

by the Akashi Lady, the same one included in the album's calligraphy, which is a personal response to the letter and poem she has just received from her daughter. As elsewhere in the album, the calligraphy captures the words or thoughts of a figure absent from the painting and has the effect of voice-over narration for the viewer.

The Akashi Lady does, however, appear as an "absent presence" in this scene, not only through the depiction of possessions that are unmistakably hers but also through motifs that suggest her impending return. The sliding door on the right side of the composition, for example, stands open just enough to reveal the adjacent room, which contains a gold and black lacquered stand supporting a fabric curtain. In the tale, the lady discreetly enters the room only moments after the scene depicted in the album painting, so that the curtain suggests her offstage presence, and perhaps even a deliberate contrivance of the tableau that Genji discovers. The room is full of elements that elicit Genji's memories of Akashi, including the Chinese touches of the surroundings that are similar to those of the Novitiate's residence, which must remind him of the Akashi family's wealth and crucial role in his success by providing him with his only daughter. The enchanting atmosphere in the Akashi Lady's quarters, and the subtle demand for recognition encoded in its trappings, compels Genji to spend the first night of the year with her rather than with Murasaki, a decision for which he will have to endure Murasaki's resentment. The gesture acknowledges the Akashi Lady's role as the future Empress's biological mother, as well as Genji's deep connection to the Akashi family. Despite the sadness of living apart from her daughter, in a "village where no warbler sings," the Akashi Lady's sacrifice ensures the recuperation of her family line and Genji's success in redeeming his own matriline. It was perhaps for this reason, in part, that the verse cited above, and the pictorial symbols of Chapter Twenty-Three—the warbler, the plum, the pine—were emblazoned on the luxurious lacquer sets of bridal trousseaus in the early modern period. The auspiciousness of the New Year, the scenes of Genji's prosperity at the Rokujōin estate, and the lessons contained in the moral fortitude of the Akashi Lady made for a powerful combination, useful for instructing young brides, and for expressing their families' wishes for powerful and successful marital unions.

Chapter 23 | First Song of Spring | 115

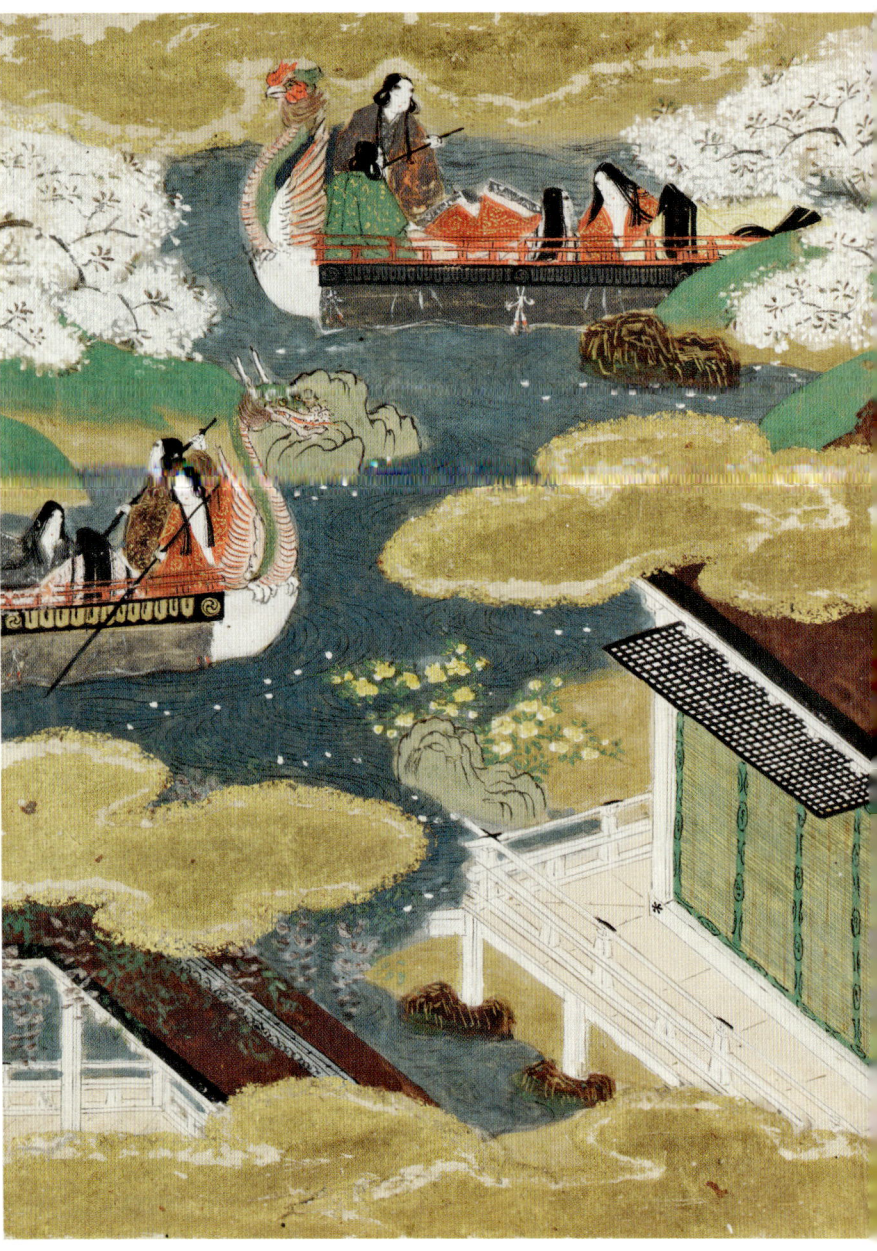

Not for me the mountain
Mounted on the turtle's back;
   No, I shall stay
Here in our boat and leave behind
A name for never aging.

On a bright spring day
All across the bay the boat
   Moves to the pole,
And the droplets scattering
Are blossoms in the shining sun.

CRANSTON, P. 818

24

胡蝶
Butterflies
Kochō

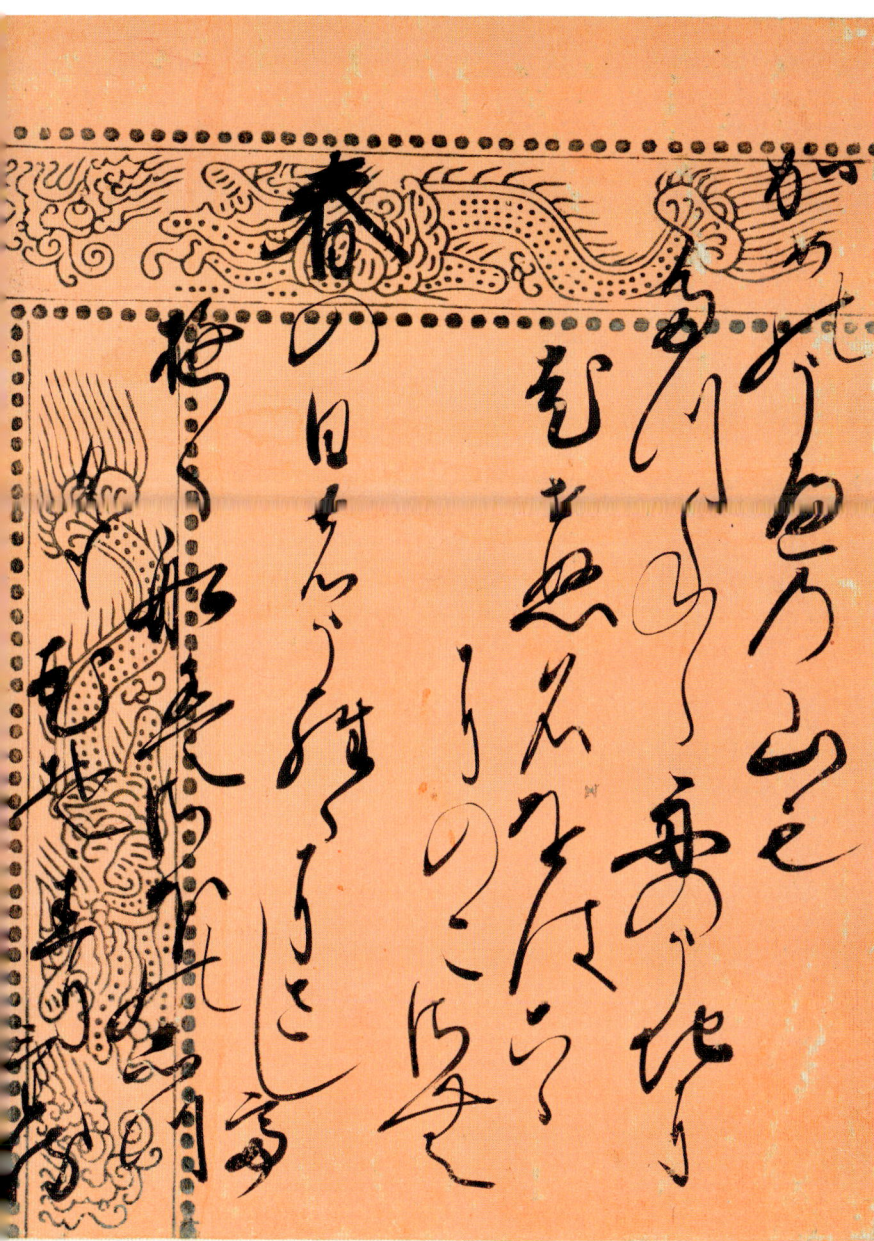

Kame no ue no
Yama mo tazuneji
Fune no uchi ni
Oi senu na o ba
Koko ni nokosan

Haru no hi no
Urara ni sashite
Yuku fune wa
Sao no shizuku mo
Hana zo chirikeru

かめのうへの山も
たづねし舟のうちに
老せぬ名をはこゝ
にのこさむ
春の日のうらゝにさして
ゆく船はさほのしつ
くも花そちりける

Although it is now late spring, the cherry blossoms in Murasaki's garden that should have waned continue to flourish, just like the flowers that defied the season in the northern mountains where Genji first discovered the "little purple gromwell" in Chapter Five. That earlier description signaled Genji's entry into an otherworldly realm in the hills above the capital, and in the "Butterflies" chapter, the Rokujōin is similarly marked as it is likened to paradise (a "land of living Buddhas"). In the first poem included with this chapter's album painting, the estate is said to rival even "the mountain on the turtle's back," that is, the immortal realm of Mount Hōrai. The speaker of the poem is one of the several ladies-in-waiting from the Umetsubo Empress's autumn quarters whom Genji has invited to view Murasaki's garden. The women will act as surrogates for the Empress, since her elevated position precludes a visit merely to view the garden and enjoy its delights. The women travel in Chinese-style wooden boats that Genji has constructed to navigate the vast pond that connects the autumn and spring quarters (see Chapter 21)—the prow of each boat has been carved in the shape of a different mythical animal, a large water bird (*geki*), and a dragon (*ryū*), associated respectively with the elements of wind and water. Setting out for the spring, they row beyond a rocky promontory that divides the two residences to behold a fresh new vista, as though they had entered a foreign land.

The ladies dock at an islet in the center of the pond and view Murasaki's grounds from a distance, glimpsing the cherries through veils of thick spring mist and noting the purple wisteria wrapping around the covered walkways. The purple blossoms appear in the lower left corner of the painting, with five clusters of the pendulous flowers hanging over the roofed corridor. The other emblematic flower of Murasaki's garden is the kerria (*yamabuki*), the deep yellow flower of late spring. In the painting, it occupies a place in the center of the composition, poking out from behind a green rock on the edge of the pond. Layers of shell white, yellow pigment, and gold paint make up the blossoms, while thin gold lines define the veins of the plant's bright green leaves. The conspicuous flower appears in two of four total poems by the ladies-in-waiting composed aboard the boats, but not included in the album calligraphy text. In one, Murasaki's kerria becomes the famous "Cape of Yamabuki" (Yamabukinosaki) in nearby Ōmi Province, which seems to have informed Mitsunobu's depiction of the flower paired with a craggy rock. In another poem, a yellow blossom on the banks of the Ide River lends its golden hue to the water when the wind scatters its petals on the surface. In juxtaposing the blossoms directly over the dark blue pond with its swirling waves delineated in black ink, the painter seems to have responded to this poetic image as well. The conceit of the water's surface as a place of magical metamorphosis appears throughout this passage in the tale; it is likened to a brocade in which the ripples made by paddling ducks weave new patterns, or as in the second poem featured in the album's calligraphy, to a place where concentric circles made by the dipping of the rowers' oars become blossoming flowers (*sao no shizuku mo, hana zo chirikeru*).

The passage in the tale presents Murasaki's garden as it is seen through the eyes of the ladies-in-waiting, but the painting takes a different vantage point, that of the occupant of the building in the foreground, an implied Murasaki, gazing out from behind lowered bamboo blinds toward the spectacle on the water. Motifs are stacked and staggered to suggest recession into the distance across the pond, and the vividly painted dragon and bird-headed boats, touches of gold paint on their eyes for enlivenment, appear to float back and forth. The page girls make "water blossoms" with their oars as mentioned above, stirring up white cherry petals that

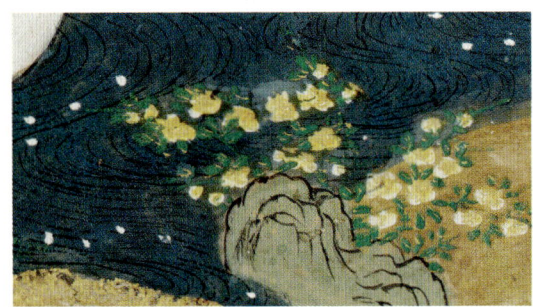

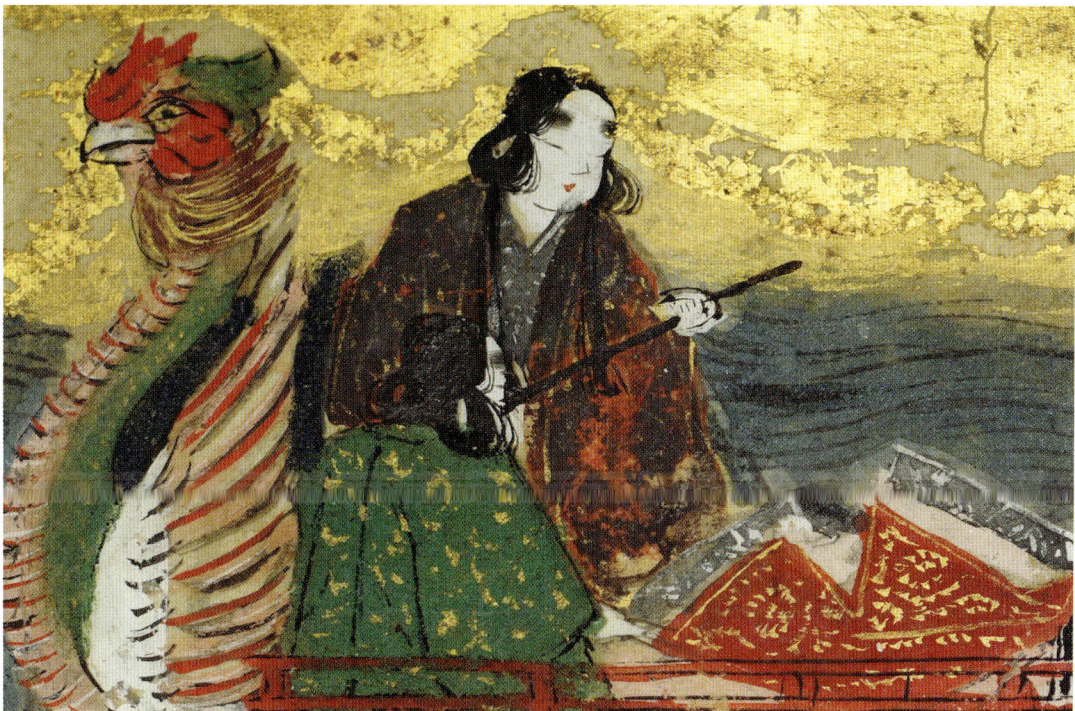

float on the water. The girls are dressed like boys, with their tresses tied into loops in the Chinese style, like Genji wore his hair before he came of age in the first leaf of the album. The women will disembark from their boats and enter the mansion through the fishing pavilion of the southeastern abode. There they will be treated to music and dance, which will continue until early morning.

The next day, Murasaki sends her own messengers across the pond, offering the Empress a hint at the splendors of her spring realm. The Empress has sponsored a grand sutra reading that day attended by the entire court and officiated by numerous Buddhist priests. Murasaki uses the exotic boats docked in her pond to transport eight page girls to the ceremony spectacularly costumed as the paradisal kalavinka birds and butterflies of court *bugaku* dance. The narrative describes the girls dressed in their feathered capes, headdresses, and multicolored wings disembarking and moving through a spring haze toward the main hall of the residence before the priests and the noble spectators who line the verandas and walkways. The tableau is again otherworldly and appropriately tuned to the Buddhist ceremony, as the cry of the kalavinka in paradise is said to give voice to the dharma. The pretense for the visit is to offer flowers to the Buddha, and in the tale the silver and gold vessels of cherry blossoms and kerria brought by the girls are dutifully placed on the altar.

The scene is magical and participates in the overall effect of these middle chapters, which is to present the Rokujōin as a site that rivals the imperial palace. At the same time, the private nature of Genji's estate allows the mistresses of the seasons to act as the protagonists of these events. But not all is peaceful in this paradise. The spring season has aroused memories in Genji of his youth, his affair with Yūgao, and a longing for Yūgao's daughter Tamakazura residing in his summer quarter. The chapter ends with an episode of sexual aggression by Genji toward Tamakazura, heightened in its intensity and perversity by their pretend father-daughter relationship. Tamakazura's precarious existence at the Rokujō Estate will continue as the story progresses into the summer months.

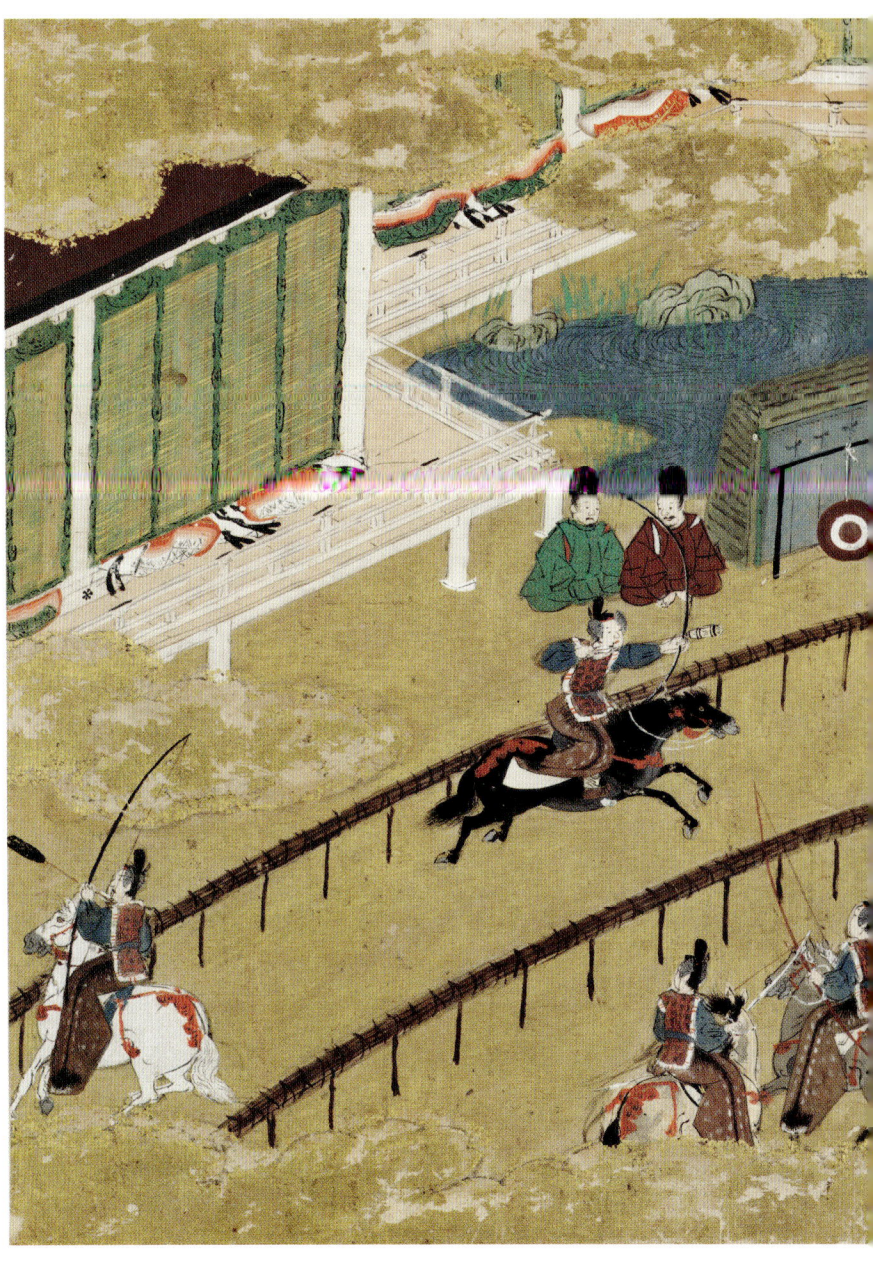

That well-known pony
Will not forage on such grass—
    So poor its fame—
But today it draws your favor,
The sweet flag by the waterside.

CRANSTON, P. 824

25

蛍
Fireflies

Hotaru

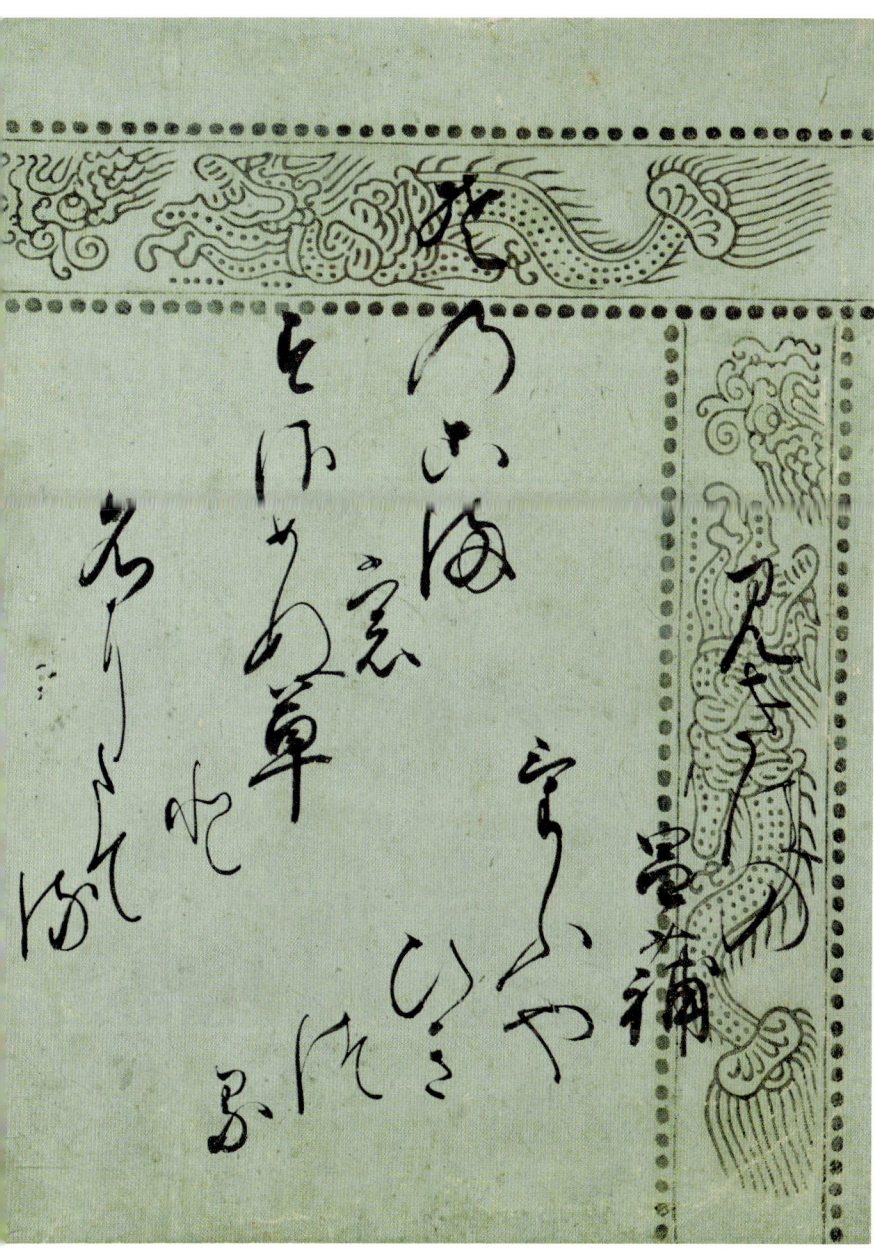

Sono koma mo
Susamenu kusa to
Na ni tateru
Migiwa no ayame
Kyō ya hikitsuru

そのこま も
すさめぬ草 と
名にたて る
みきはの菖蒲
けふや ひきつ る

It is easy to imagine the patron of the *Genji Album*, a warrior from Suo province who had just followed the powerful military leader Ōuchi Yoshioki into Kyoto, appreciating the particular scene selected to represent Chapter Twenty-Five. The painting focuses on the skills of court military officials in a mounted archery competition that takes place on the grounds of the Rokujōin. At the center of the composition a single archer is depicted with his horse in mid-stride, galloping between the guardrails of a causeway while drawing his whistling bulb arrow (*kaburaya*) across his chest and aiming for a target that is not shown, though a typical one is included in the painting, just above this figure and to the right. A marksman was required to hit three such targets in rapid succession. The disc of the target with its three concentric circles hangs from a black bar supported by two posts and is held still by a white cord at three points. A blue-gray, five-panel fabric curtain hangs behind the target, attached to a sturdy wooden wall, which is intended to deflect any stray arrows. The archers wear the fan-shaped wings on their caps seen in the painting for Chapter Eighteen, Matsukaze, but the rest of their costumes are unique to this painting. Most striking are the chaps made of white-spotted deer pelts, which anachronistically cover their entire legs, a detail that may suggest the patron's interest in depictions of a more contemporary warrior culture. A dark stripe runs down the center of the garment, which originally marked the spine of the deer, while a tuft of white and black fur marks its tail, which now covers the riders' feet. One can see that each man is wearing the equivalent of two slain animals. The rider on the black steed moves at such a clip that the right leg of his fur chaps is blown upward, flipping over slightly to reveal its tanned leather underside as well as a zigzag patterned pant leg. The archers' upper garments consist of short, sleeveless tunics with a red interlocking pattern bordered in white with green and red stripes and cinched with a cord at the waist. Blue-gray garments underneath with billowed sleeves allow for a range of arm motion. Three other archers depicted in the painting illus-

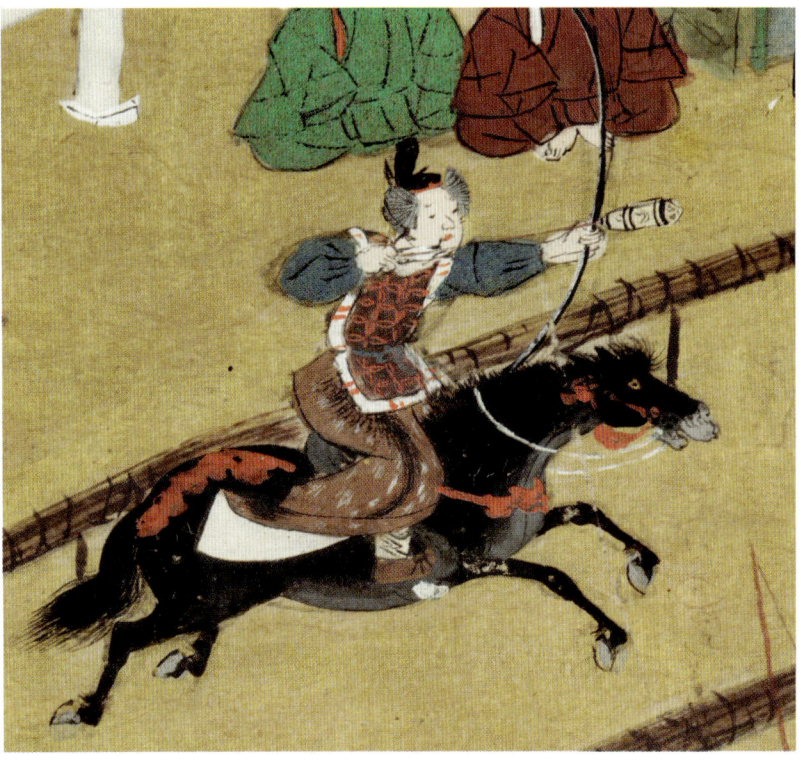

122 | *The Tale of Genji*

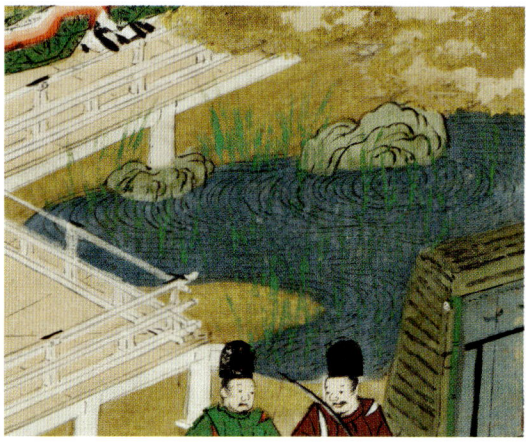

trate the various stages of the competition. Two riders in the lower right corner focus on the action in the center, while a third waits on the causeway readying his bow and arrow as his white horse rears slightly, as if ready to charge forth.

The Rokujōin was built to host such displays of martial skill, as is clear from the inclusion of riding grounds along the eastern side of the property, technically in the summer quarter overseen by Hanachirusato. The occasion for the archery event is the Sweet Flag Festival (*tango no sechie*), which takes place on the fifth day of the fifth month, the second month of summer in the lunar calendar. On this day, tall green water plants (*ayamegusa*), which because of their length, deep roots, and medicinal properties symbolized longevity, were offered to the emperor along with prayers for longevity and the avoidance of calamity. The festivities included an imperial appearance at the martial facilities within the palace compound, along with horse racing, archery, music, and dance. The event at the Rokujōin occurs after the one at the palace concludes, but as usual, Genji's event is hailed as superior and innovative, especially in its spontaneity and lack of excessive formality. The sweet flag plants that figure prominently in the chapter's poetry appear in the painting, growing in the shallow waters around Hanachirusato's residence. In an instance of complete cohesion between picture and poem, the calligraphic excerpt in the album begins with the word for "horse" (*sono koma*), then describes the grass, disdained as too withered for the horse's liking (*susamenu kusa*). It is a humble poem spoken by Hanachirusato to Genji in which she likens herself to the withered plant. It explicitly alludes to a verse from the *Kokinshū* (Book XVII, no. 892) that laments the absence of foraging horses from a field of aging grass. Hanachirusato's poem then goes on to suggest that on this day of the Sweet Flag, the plant by the waterside might be plucked after all. Genji replies by comparing himself to the faithful grebe, who mates for life and who would never desert the water plant. Unexpectedly, Genji spends the night in her quarters. She offers her bed to him, and he takes it, but cordons himself off with a curtain without inviting her inside.

Hanachirusato and her attendants are suggested in the painting by the multicolored robes that peek out from beneath the bamboo blinds of the residence, a formal mode of decoration called *uchide*. The tale's elaborate description of the robes of Hanachirusato's page girls is striking and suggests her prowess in creating and arranging textiles, but their appearance is also meant to attract the men in the Left Guard. Genji's own amatory interests lie elsewhere in the summer residence, in the wing occupied by Tamakazura, and this chapter continues to depict his desire as well as his efforts to arrange liaisons between her and other men. In particular he lures in his half brother Sochinomiya, better known as Prince Hotaru (literally "firefly"), nicknamed after the scene in this chapter in which he espies Tamakazura illuminated suddenly by a flash of firefly light. The encounter is entirely orchestrated by Genji, who waits until his brother is nearby and then pulls away Tamakazura's curtain while releasing the fireflies. The scene is one of many in which Genji torments Tamakazura, but the young woman maintains her composure and holds out hope for escaping from her predicament. By the end of the chapter the long summer rains have begun, during which Tamakazura immerses herself in illustrated tales (*monogatari*), leading to a discussion between Genji and Tamakazura concerning the merits of fiction. It is a metafictional set piece within the narrative, that among other things, defends the value of tales.

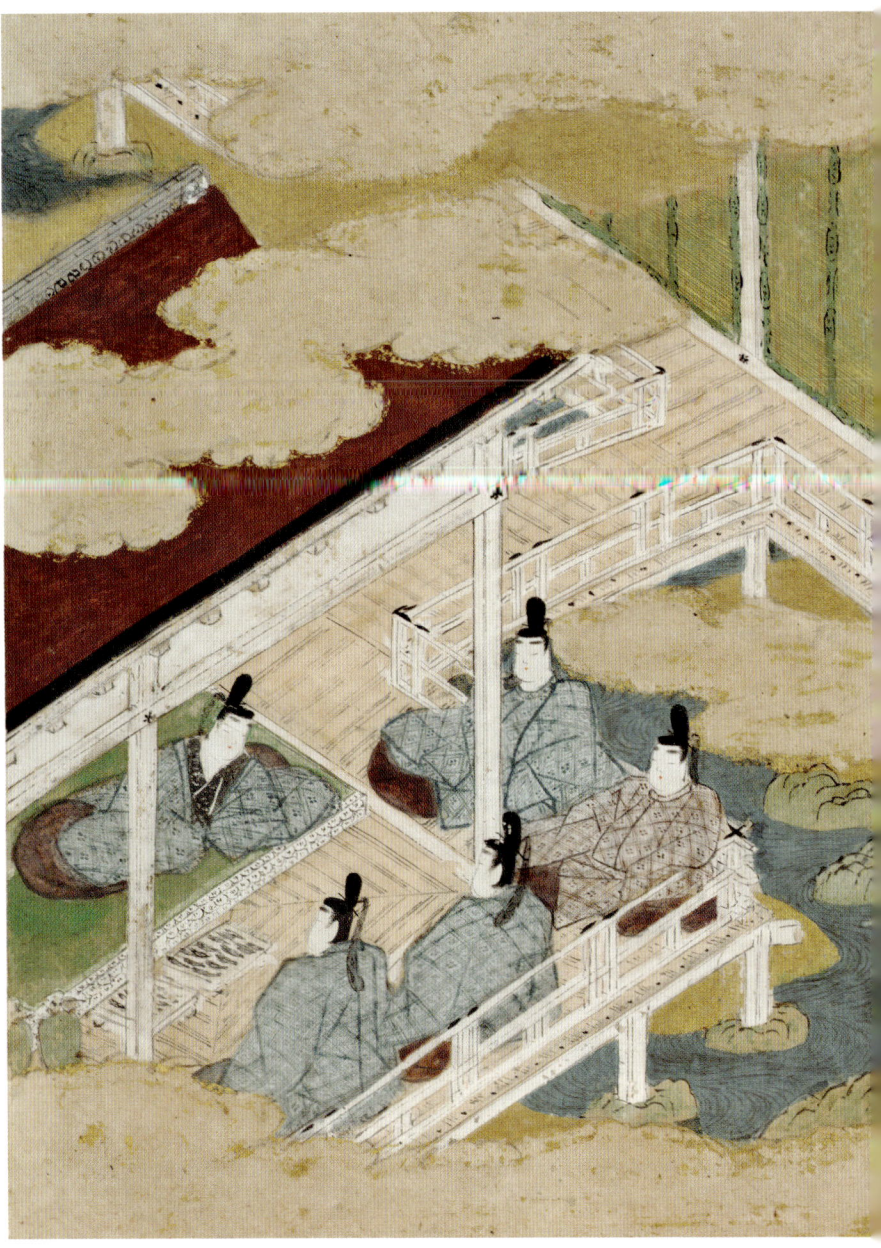

A refreshing breeze was blowing through the pavilion, and as the sun slowly followed its westerly course through a cloudless sky, the raucous cries of cicadas screeched unpleasantly.

"It's so hot today, it doesn't do much good even to be on the water. Excuse me if I'm being discourteous, but…" Genji apologized as he stretched out on his side.

WASHBURN P. 524

26

常夏
Wild Pinks
Tokonatsu

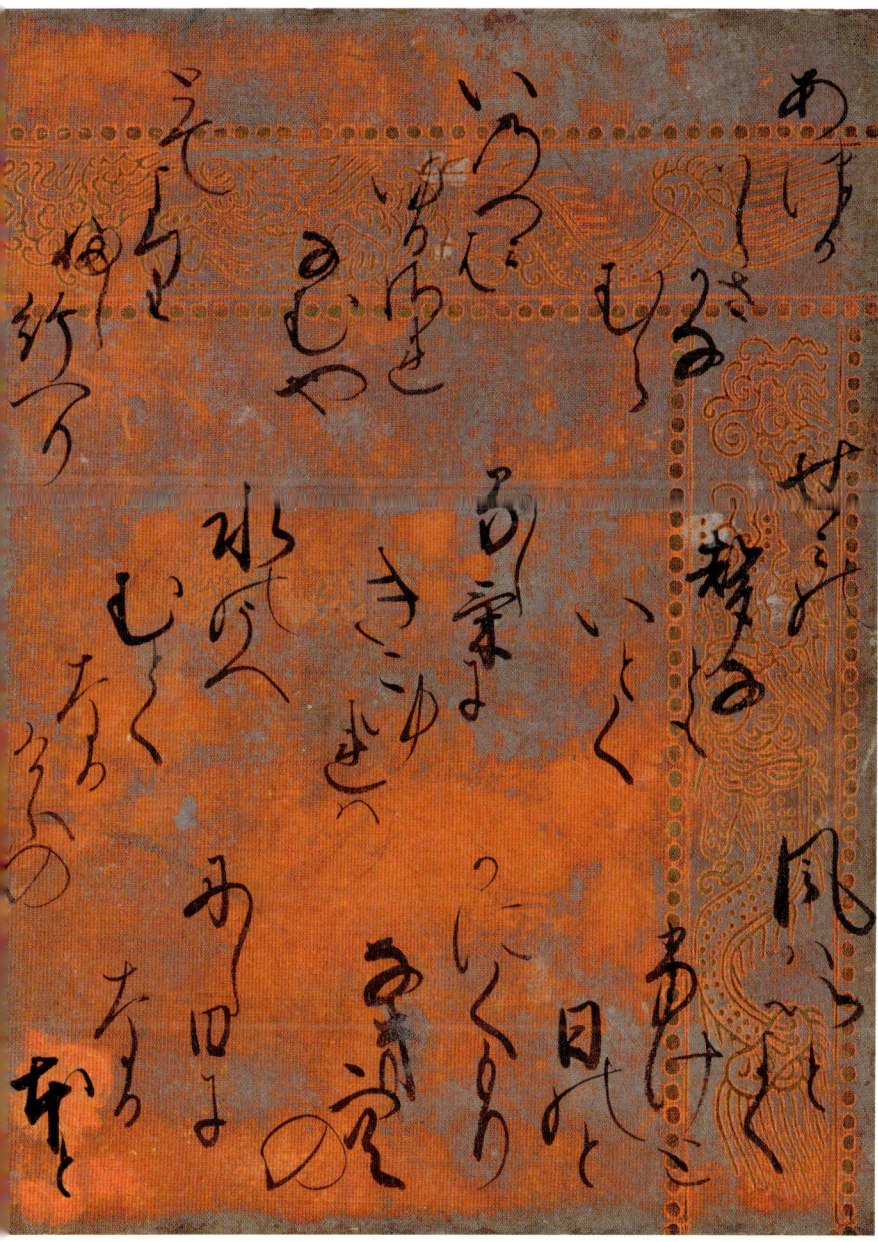

Kaze wa ito yoku fukedo, hi nodoka ni kumori naki sora no nishibi ni naru hodo, semi no koe nado mo ito kurushige ni kikoyureba, "Mizu no ue mutoku naru kyō no atsukawashisa kana. Murai no tsumi wa yurusarenan ya," tote, yorifushitamaeri.

あつかはしさかな　声なども　ふけど
せみの　いとく　日のと
風はいとよく
むらるしけに　かにくもり
いのつみは　きこゆ　なき空
ゆるされ　れは
なむや　水のうへ　にし日に
むとく　なる
とてより　なる　ほと
ふし給へり　けふの

The album painting for Chapter Twenty-Six depicts Genji and several young men in the fishing pavilion (*tsuridono*) at the Rokujō Estate attempting to escape the oppressive summer heat. The residences at Rokujō equipped with large ponds all include fishing pavilions, which extend out over the water from the southern walkways of one or both of the flanking wings of the main buildings. In Chapter Twenty-Four, the pavilion in the spring quarter of Rokujō was used as a boat launch as well as the point of arrival for the ladies sent by boat from the Umetsubo Consort's quarters. With a roof supported only by columns and removable walls, the southeastern residence's fishing pavilion is completely open to the exterior, as in the illustration. Cool waters flowing directly below the structure make for an ideal place to seek a respite from the heat. The degree to which actual fishing took place in these buildings is unclear, but the design enabled access to the water below through removable central floorboards, creating a hole into which lures could be dropped or vessels of refreshments could be chilled on strategically placed rocks. In the album painting, Genji's green tatami mat covers the spot where such an opening would be, but the distinctive concentric squares of the floorboards are clearly visible. The bridge that arches over the water signals that the pavilion is located at a slight remove from the residence, while enabling the viewer to imagine how the figures arrived at the site.

Genji is once again the center of attention, on a raised tatami mat, in the middle of the building—his placement and his relaxed pose and dress clearly convey his elevated status. He is depicted in a semireclined pose, with his outer robe untied and worn loosely on his shoulders, opening slightly to reveal an inner garment, and the white of his neck and chest. The text in the album's calligraphy has him stretching out his legs in front of his guests, feeling too listless from the heat to maintain a formal posture. Only someone in a superior position would take such a liberty, and indeed he is not only of such a status and older than the men encircling him on the veranda, but he is also quite familiar with them. The group of young men consists of Tō no Chūjō's many sons, including his second son known as Kōbai, although the eldest, Kashiwagi, who will play a prominent role later in the narrative, is notably absent. The young courtiers have come to call on Genji's son, Yūgiri, who is differentiated in the painting by his light-colored robe, conspicuous amid the blue garments the others have donned. Like his father, Yūgiri assumes a more relaxed pose, with one arm draped over the railing

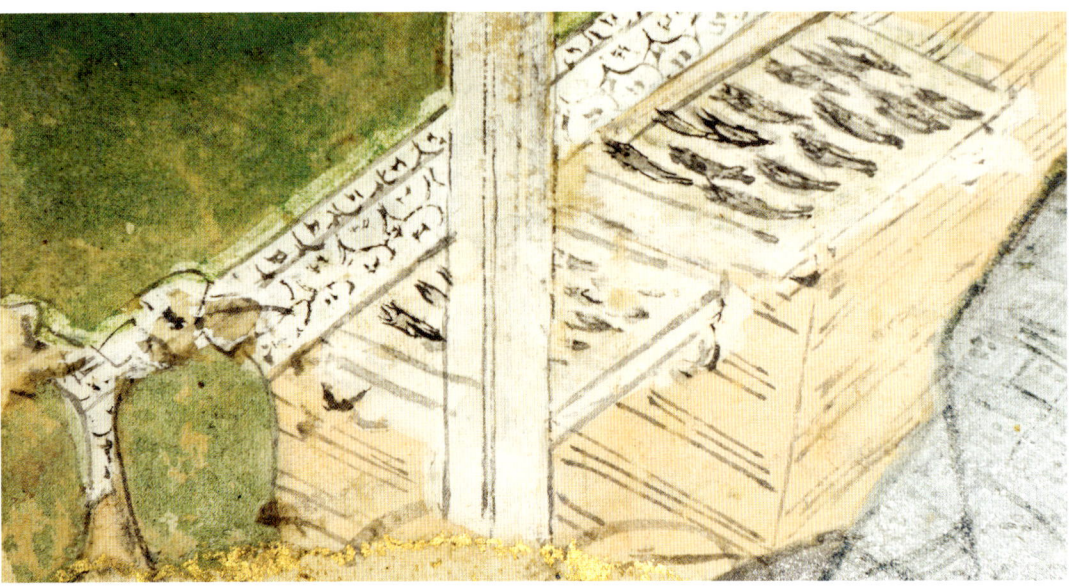

as he leans back into the corner of the veranda. Among the refreshments that Genji offers his guests are bullhead fish (*ishibushi* or *kawa kajika*) caught from the Kamo River, and sweetfish (*ayu*), best in the summer, and which is specifically described in the tale as having been caught from the "western river," meaning the Katsura River. Because only fishing intended for imperial offerings was allowed in this river, the reference seems to be another nod to Genji's prestige and position and the ongoing theme of kingship within his symbolic realm. The men also partake of sake, ice water, and dried rice in chilled water, which represent the height of luxury given that access to ice in midsummer was only for the most privileged in society and was often only represented in literature in scenes taking place at the imperial palace.

The gathering of young courtiers offers a pleasant distraction from the heat, and Genji asks to be regaled with news of the court, since he has largely turned over his official duties to Tō no Chūjō, who has become Palace Minister. The scene recalls one from Genji's youth, the famous "rainy night debate" from Chapter Two, when men sequestered at court because of an imperial taboo told tales of amorous adventures and offered definitive statements on the merits and demerits of various types of women. Tō no Chūjō recounted one of the most consequential stories that night long ago, when he spoke of his lost love, the woman Yūgao whom he called his "wild pink" (*tokonatsu*), after the summer flower. Always intrigued by the possibility of besting Tō no Chūjō, the story of the mystery woman and her daughter led to Genji's own affair with Yūgao and ultimately his decision to harbor her grown daughter, Tamakazura, secretly in the summer quarter of the Rokujōin. In this scene, Tō no Chūjō's sons tell Genji of yet another long-lost daughter of their father, a girl living in the provinces whom he recently brought to the capital. This new character, the "girl from Ōmi," is no Tamakazura, however, and in fact picks up where Suetsumuhana left off in the tale as an object of derision. It turns out that the Ōmi daughter is embarrassingly uncouth, from looks to intellect and manners. Although both she and Tamakazura were raised in the provinces, only one of them was raised well, with the dignity befitting their father's noble pedigree. The second half of Chapter Twenty-Six becomes a study in contrasts between the two women and their situations, redolent of behavioral primers for young ladies that often tempered their didacticism with comedy.

At the same time, the story of the daughter from Ōmi is woven into the plotline and the development of Tamakazura's relationship with Genji, whose infatuation with Tamakazura has only intensified. Summer is Tamakazura's season, stationed as she is in the summer quarters, and the sultry days exacerbate Genji's longing, as he is drawn frequently to her residence. Although still disturbed by the sexual tone of his overtures and the physical contact between them that he insists on, she begins to warm to Genji, believing that he has saved her from becoming a laughingstock like her half sister from Ōmi. Tamakazura and Genji exchange poems that reference Tamakazura's mother the "wild pink" (*tokonatsu*), Tō no Chūjō's nickname for Yūgao, and the title of the chapter. The word is a homophone for "endless summer" as well as for the phrase "remembered bed" (*toko natsukashiki*), as it is used in Genji's poem. The allusions are to Genji's past affair with Yūgao and suggest how mother and daughter mingle in his mind, as he is reminded of his youthful passion. The young men depicted in the album painting are roughly the age Genji was when he met Yūgao and provide yet another connection between past and present. These sons of Tō no Chūjō know that Genji has a long-lost "daughter" living in his estate, but like their father, they are unaware that she is in fact their half sister. Despite Genji's attraction to Tamakazura, he knows that he cannot keep her for himself and discusses potential husbands with her, all the while envisioning different scenarios in his mind and intending to postpone her departure as long as possible.

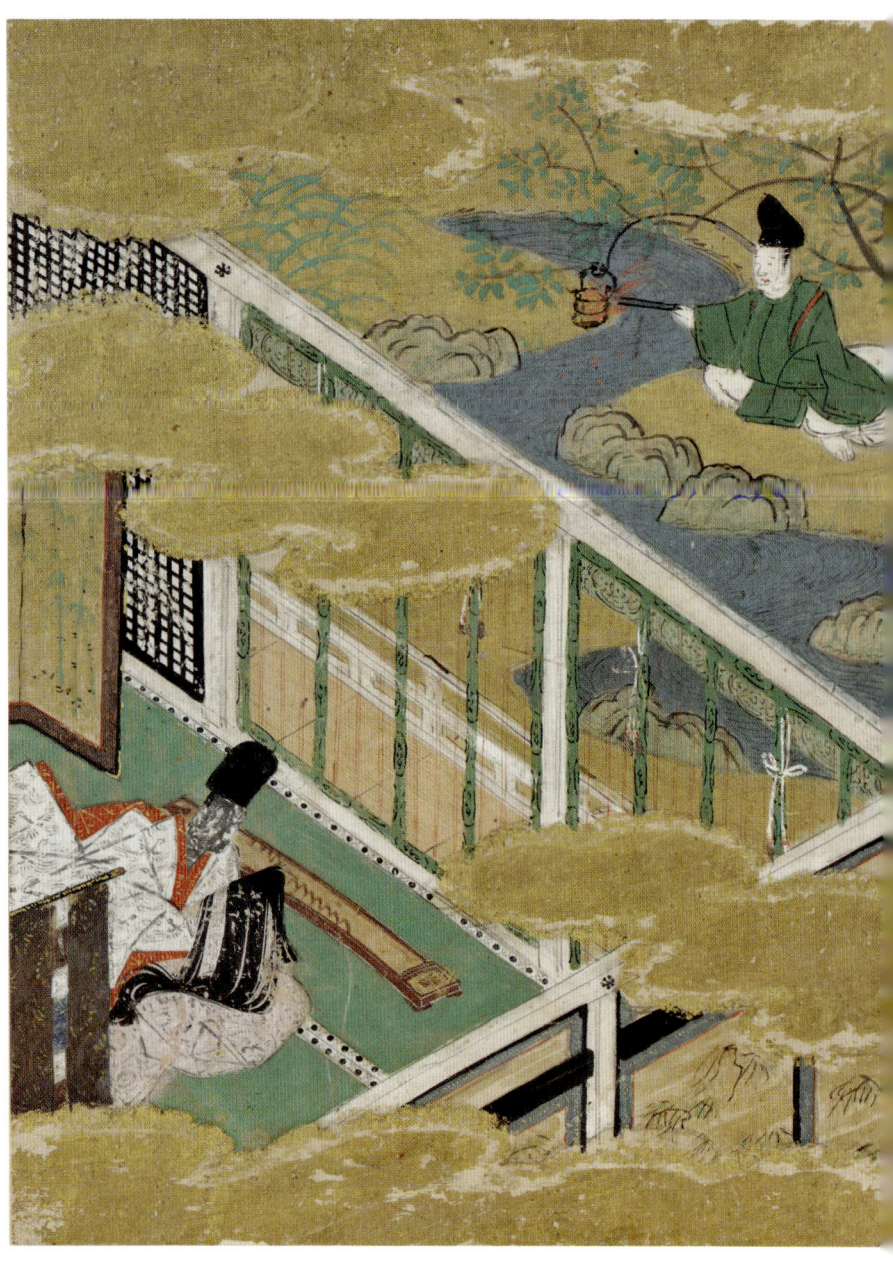

    The fire of longing
That rises beside these cage-flares
    Is the one whose smoke,
Now I know it, never dies—
That flame of all nights of the world.

CRANSTON, PP. 827–28

27

篝火
Cresset Fires
Kagaribi

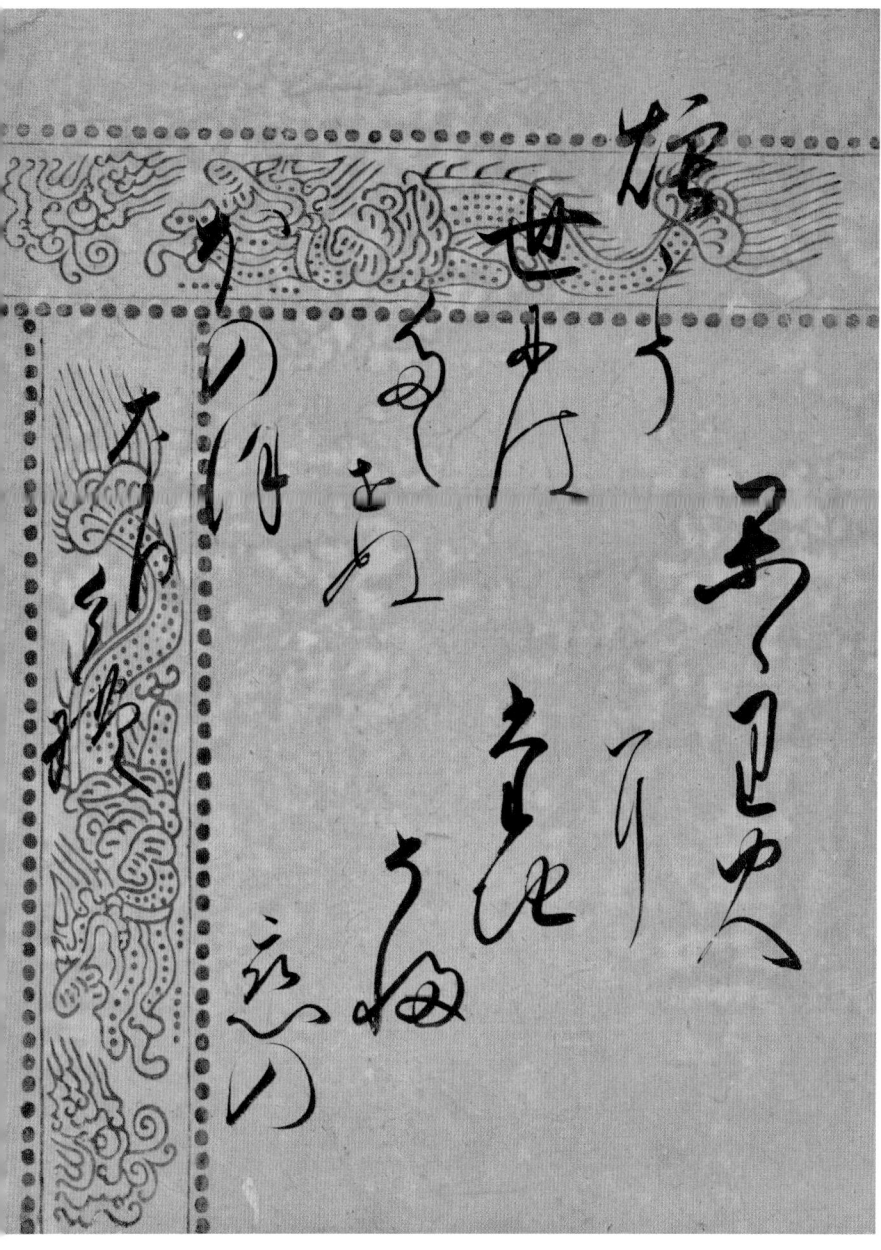

Kagaribi ni
Tachisou koi no
Keburi koso
Yo ni wa tae senu
Honō narikere

かゝり火に
たちそふ恋の
煙こそ
世にはたえせぬ
ほのほなりけれ

The season turns to fall at the start of Chapter Twenty-Seven, the air turns chilly and the atmosphere melancholy, as Tamakazura's saga continues, with Genji becoming increasingly enthralled by her beauty. He frequently goes to her wing of the northeast residence, where the garden with its nostalgia-inducing *tachibana* tree and flowers bring back memories of youthful adventures. Episodes from the earliest chapters begin to feel distant at this point in the tale, making the passage of narrative time and Genji's transition into the next stage of life seem convincing. Genji, all too aware of how a man of his age and stature should behave, decides against pursuing a sexual relationship with Tamakazura, and yet he cannot abstain from visiting her chambers. His poem to her, included in the album's calligraphy excerpt, speaks of his "smoldering passion," a reference to his pent-up desire. The first word of his poem, "*kagaribi*," "cresset fire," also the title of this chapter, refers to a fire in a metal cage (a "cresset"), and is used as a metaphor for Genji's passion. Genji has just ordered one of his men to relight a lantern in Tamakazura's garden that has died out, which inspires his choice of poetic imagery. In the album painting the servant appears in the upper right corner, using a pair of black tongs to stoke the fire. The metal cage of the cresset, filled with kindling pine, hangs from a bent pole beneath a spindle tree (*mayumi no ki*), from which sparks fly and flames flicker beyond the confines of the cage. The lantern hangs directly over the garden stream (*yarimizu*), where the water's reflection will maximize its light. Once the fires are relit, the garden is bathed in a beautiful light, as is Tamakazura in Genji's eyes, reminiscent of her illumination by firefly light in Chapter Twenty-Five.

Turning to the album painting's depiction of the interior of the residence, we find Genji and Tamakazura in one of the most intimate scenes in the album. The two lie together, just as described in the tale, with a "koto as a pillow" (*on koto wo makura nite*), meaning that the instrument rests near their heads. Tamakazura is depicted with her back to the viewer to highlight the beauty of her abundant hair as it falls over her garment. Throughout the chapters that feature Tamakazura, Genji is frequently described as stroking her hair, and in this scene, he finds it to be elegantly cool to the touch. The painting has unfortunately been damaged, leaving Genji's facial features only just visible, but the rest of his figure is intact. Dressed in an informal robe and *eboshi* hat, he reaches his right arm across her back, his body enveloping hers. The intimate pose is reminiscent of the painting for Chapter Two, the only other image in the album that shows Genji in the middle of an embrace. While in the earlier scene Genji was shown placing his hand on Utsusemi's back, the painting for "Cresset Fires" depicts the pair lying side by side. In another nod to the Utsusemi sequence, the folding screen behind Genji and Tamakazura depicts a tall stand of bright green bamboo. This summer plant reminds the viewer that Tamakazura's home, the northeast residence, is aligned with the summer season, despite the autumnal frame of the current scene. But it also echoes the bamboo screen in Utsusemi's room from Chapter Three in the album, a possible reference to Utsusemi's resemblance to "supple bamboo" because of her gentle resistance to Genji's advances. Tamakazura has managed to fend off Genji as best she can, while deftly showing him her gratitude. Before reciting the poem included in the album, Genji remarks how the world has never seen

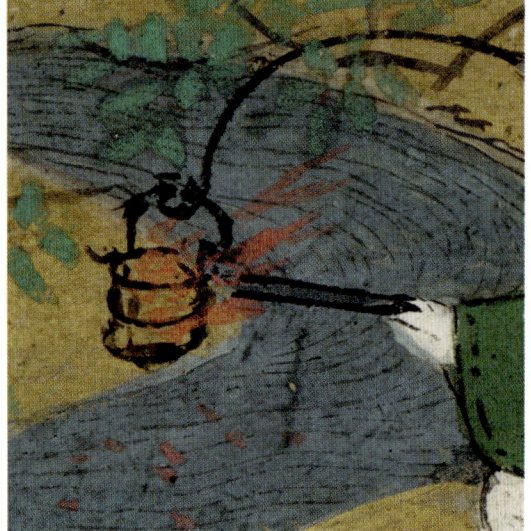

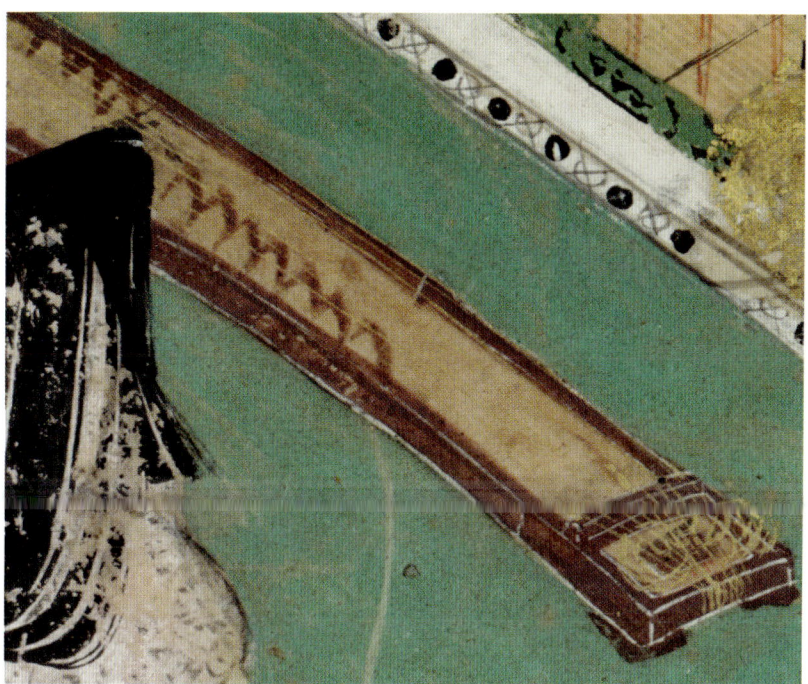

a relationship such as theirs, meaning a relationship in which two people so close do nothing more physical than lie together. The description also refers to their pseudo-father-daughter relationship, a facade that Genji insists on maintaining but that he perhaps realizes cannot go on forever. The unusual situation creates an atmosphere of narrative tension, as readers wonder, along with Genji, how he will ever admit to Tō no Chūjō that the woman he has been harboring is in fact his daughter.

The final paragraphs of Chapter Twenty-Seven continue ushering in the next generation of characters, such as young men whose enthusiastic but superficial passions are juxtaposed with Genji's professed depth of feeling, among them Tō no Chūjō's sons. While visiting Tamakazura's rooms in the northeast quadrant, Genji hears music being played by these young men calling on Genji's son Yūgiri. The young courtiers join Genji on Tamakazura's veranda, and after Genji briefly plays the seven-string *koto*, the very "pillow" seen in the painting, he turns the instrument over to Kashiwagi, Tō no Chūjō's son, as though passing the baton. Kashiwagi plays with liveliness and remarkable skill, and within the earshot of Tamakazura, whom all the men are trying to impress. Of course, the scenario Genji has staged is perverse, since he hastens the development of Kashiwagi's infatuation with a woman who, unbeknownst to the young man, is his own half sister. Kashiwagi's misguided fascination foreshadows the future romantic hardships that are in store for him.

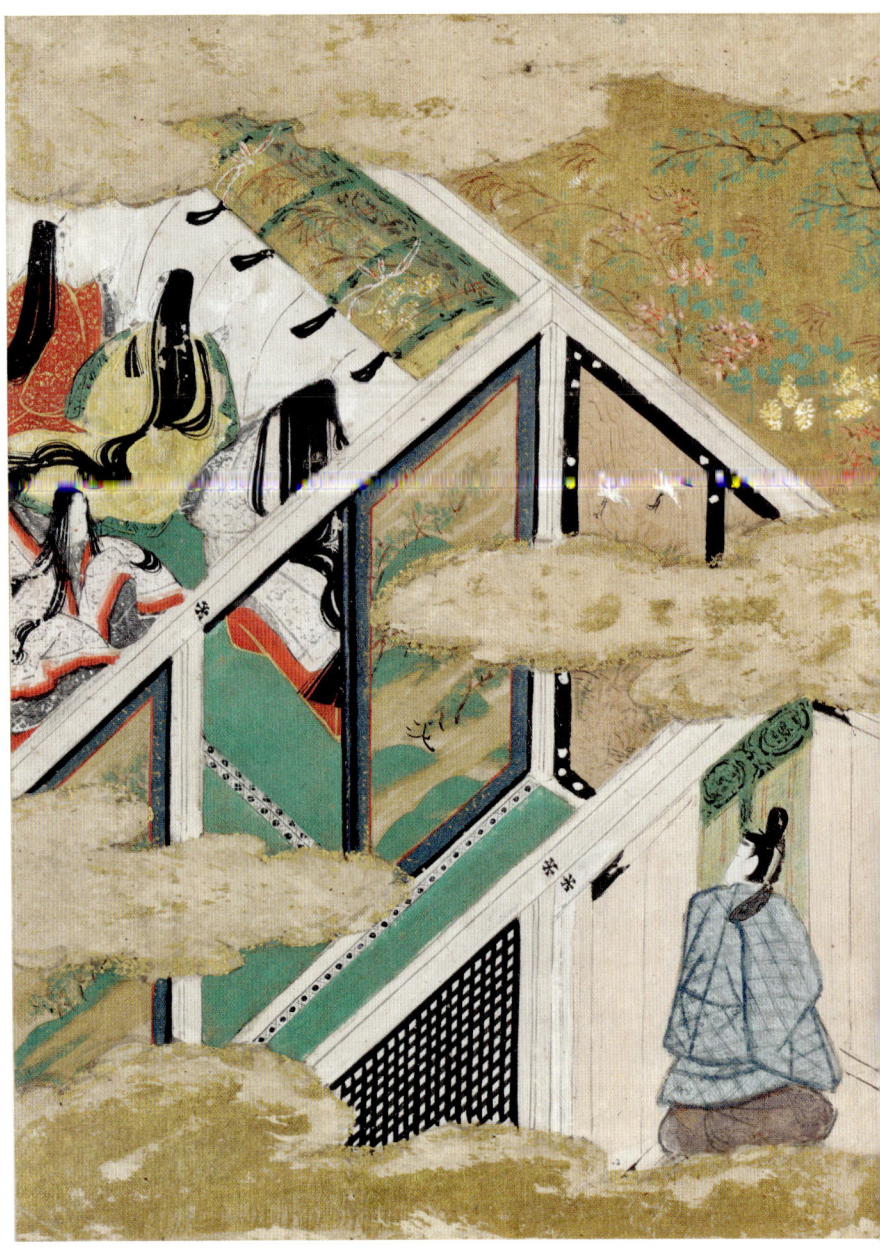

There could be no mistaking the person seated in the room off the corridor. Her refined grace and radiant beauty put him in mind of a mountain cherry tree, its wild profusion of blossoms dimly visible through the mists of a spring dawn.

WASHBURN, P. 543, MODIFIED

28

野分

An Autumn Tempest

Nowaki

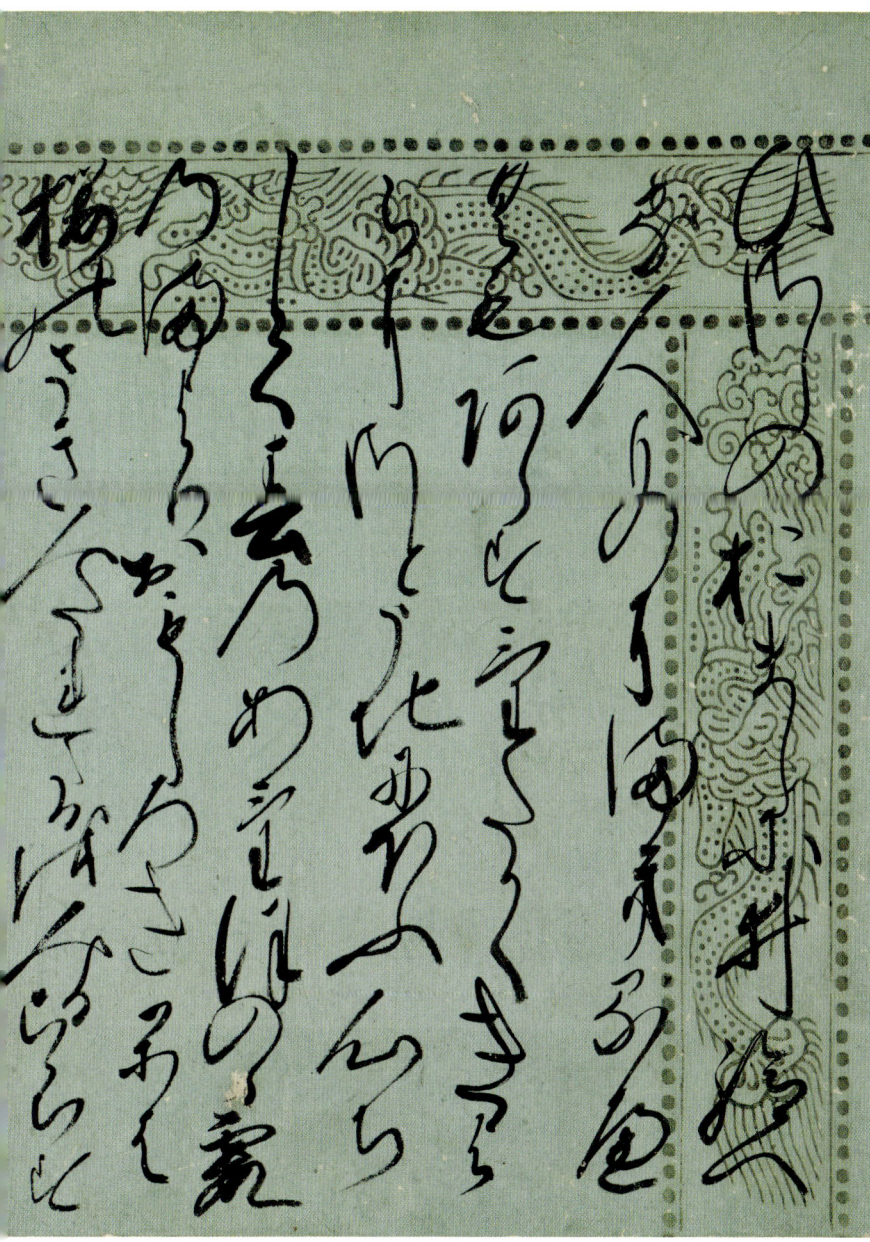

Hisashi no omashi ni itamaeru hito, mono ni magirubeku mo arazu, kedakaku kiyora ni, sa to uchiniou kokochishite, haru no akebono no kasumi no ma yori, omoshiroki kabazakura no sakimidaretaru o miru kokochisu.

ひさしのおましにゐ給へ
る人ものにまきるべ
くもあらすけたかくきよ
らにさとうちにほふ心ち
して春のあけほのゝ霞
のまよりおもしろきかは
桜のさきみたれたるをみる
こゝちす

Chapter Twenty-Eight marks the midpoint of the tale, and for the first time in the album the lone male figure highlighted in the painting is not Genji, but his fifteen-year-old son, Yūgiri, who is the protagonist of this chapter. The narration of this episode seems to provide us with unfettered access to Yūgiri's inner thoughts, a kind of interiority common to scenes of *kaimami*, in which the hero of the tale steals a glimpse of a woman who supposedly is unaware that she is being observed. Such scenes are characterized by long prose passages that describe the object of the gaze from the voyeur's perspective, and this chapter includes three of them, with Yūgiri either gazing on or visiting nearly every woman residing at Rokujō. To the extent that acts of looking are linked with desire, and that within the genre of the courtly romance, surreptitious observation can lead to sexual possession, this chapter uses the trope of *kaimami* to represent Yūgiri's coming of age. Indeed, *kaimami* scenes that eventually result in romantic conquests have already been depicted in the album, as in Chapters Three and Five, where Genji was the voyeur. But Yūgiri is a serious and filial young man, consigned to a life of commoner status and regular officialdom by his father, and unlike Genji, he does not consummate his voyeuristic adventures. And so rather than an initiation into the amorous lifestyle of Genji, the chapter represents Yūgiri's emotional maturation and self-reflection alongside a growing awareness of the oddities and uniqueness of his father's relationships with women.

The first and most pivotal of Yūgiri's *kaimami* episodes is the one depicted in the album painting, in which he views for the first time his father's most beloved companion, Lady Murasaki. The accidental glimpse is occasioned by a violent autumn storm, a typhoon (*nowaki*) that wreaks havoc on each of the seasonal gardens at Rokujō and that serves as a master metaphor for the inner turmoil Yūgiri experiences. Amid the chaos brought on by the storm, the outer wooden doors and sliding panels of Murasaki's rooms have been left open, and the folding screens and fabric curtains that would normally obstruct the view have been stored away, leaving her exposed. As Yūgiri approaches his father's rooms, he stops on the covered walkway connecting the east wing to the main hall and is presented with a view of several women inside Murasaki's chambers. At that moment he notices one woman separate from the others sitting in the corridor (*hisashi*) and realizes that it is none other than Murasaki, as reflected in the album's text excerpt. To heighten the sense of interiority, the passage eliminates the use of honorifics, which normally indicate deference by the narrator toward characters of high rank and signal that the character is being observed from the outside. Without the honorifics and the distancing effect they create, the reader gets the sense of being in the mind of the male character as he scrutinizes the woman before him. Yūgiri likens Murasaki's appearance to a mountain cherry tree (*kabazakura*), a kind of weeping rosebud cherry, which recalls imagery the album employed for Genji's first glimpse of young Murasaki in the northern hills in Chapter Five, where she is shown framed between two cherry trees teeming with white blossoms. At that time Genji referred to Murasaki as a mountain cherry (*yamazakura*) and likened himself to the spring mist wishing to cling to its flowers. In this scene, now eighteen years later, Yūgiri glimpses the same beauty that captivated his father, describing his experience as like "seeing a flowering cherry through a gap in the spring mists." In the painting, Murasaki sits on the green tatami of a room adja-

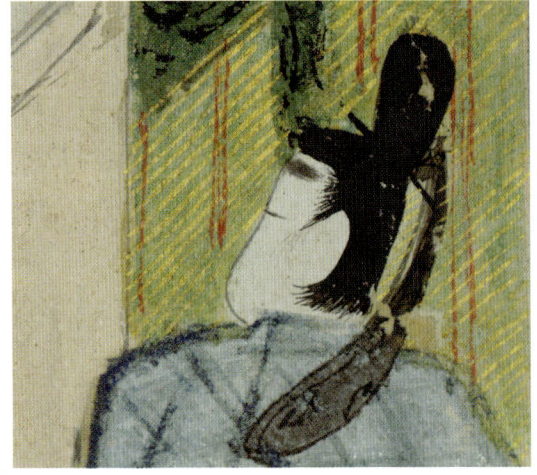

134 | *The Tale of Genji*

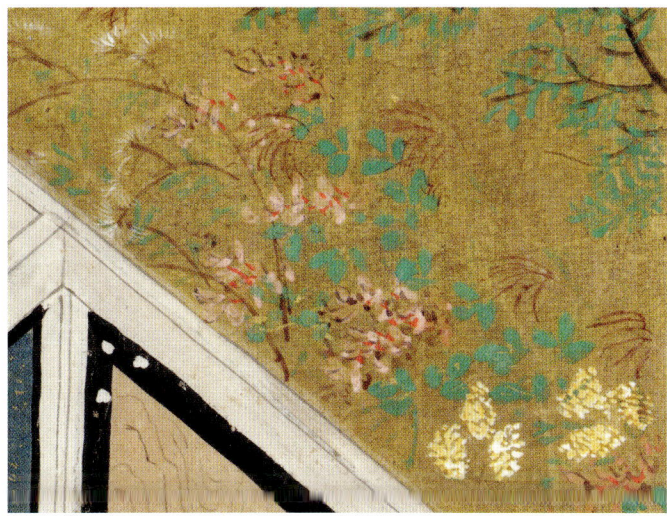

cent to the corridor, framed for the young voyeur between sliding panels left wide open. Each sliding panel bears paintings of verdant green hills and trees ringed with gold mists as though creating a landscape setting for Murasaki the mountain blossom.

Yūgiri is depicted as having a direct frontal view of Murasaki's face as he stands at the outer threshold of the residence on the veranda connected to the walkway. He hides his body behind one of the large wooden exterior doors (*tsumado*) as he extends his head into the gap left open by the other. A bamboo blind hangs on the inside of the door, allowing him to go undetected. The emphatic gold cloud that usually punctuates Genji's presence in these paintings hovers over Yūgiri and extends toward Murasaki as if linking the two figures. Outside a disordered profusion of yellow maiden flowers (*ominaeshi*), mistflowers (*fujibakama*), and pink blossoms signify the beauty of Murasaki's garden now in disarray. As described in the passage in the tale, a number of attractive ladies-in-waiting populate Murasaki's quarters, and here three do battle against the raging wind as they attempt to secure the blinds and curtains billowing inward, their small white hands outstretched toward the fabric. Despite the commotion of the other women, Yūgiri's eyes remain fixed on Murasaki, and when he sees her looking distressed at the damage done to her garden, her expression of sentiment entrances him.

The image of her beauty is imprinted in his mind and torments him when he realizes the powerful feelings he has for his father's wife. The predicament parallels Genji's own attraction to his father's consort Fujitsubo, but history does not repeat itself as Yūgiri chastises himself for his infatuation and channels his energies into longing for a wife who might approach Murasaki's perfection.

Although Yūgiri's *kaimami* of Murasaki may have started out as accidental, he indulges in several more deliberate acts of voyeurism in the rest of the chapter, beginning with an extended observation of his father interacting with Murasaki, where he sees a scene of laughter and domestic marital contentment. He then goes on to witness his father with Tamakazura, an episode that upends his understanding of the world, when he sees Genji engaged in behavior entirely inappropriate for a father toward a daughter. Still believing that Tamakazura is Genji's daughter, Yūgiri can only conclude that they have an incestuous relationship, which repulses him, try as he might to rationalize what he sees. By the end of the chapter Yūgiri, either on his own initiative or shadowing his father, has visited every woman living at Rokujō, assessing the extensive damage done by the storm to each garden. The vision of the once paradisal grounds in ruins prompts Yūgiri to shed a tear, which, given the context of the chapter, seems to be over his loss of innocence.

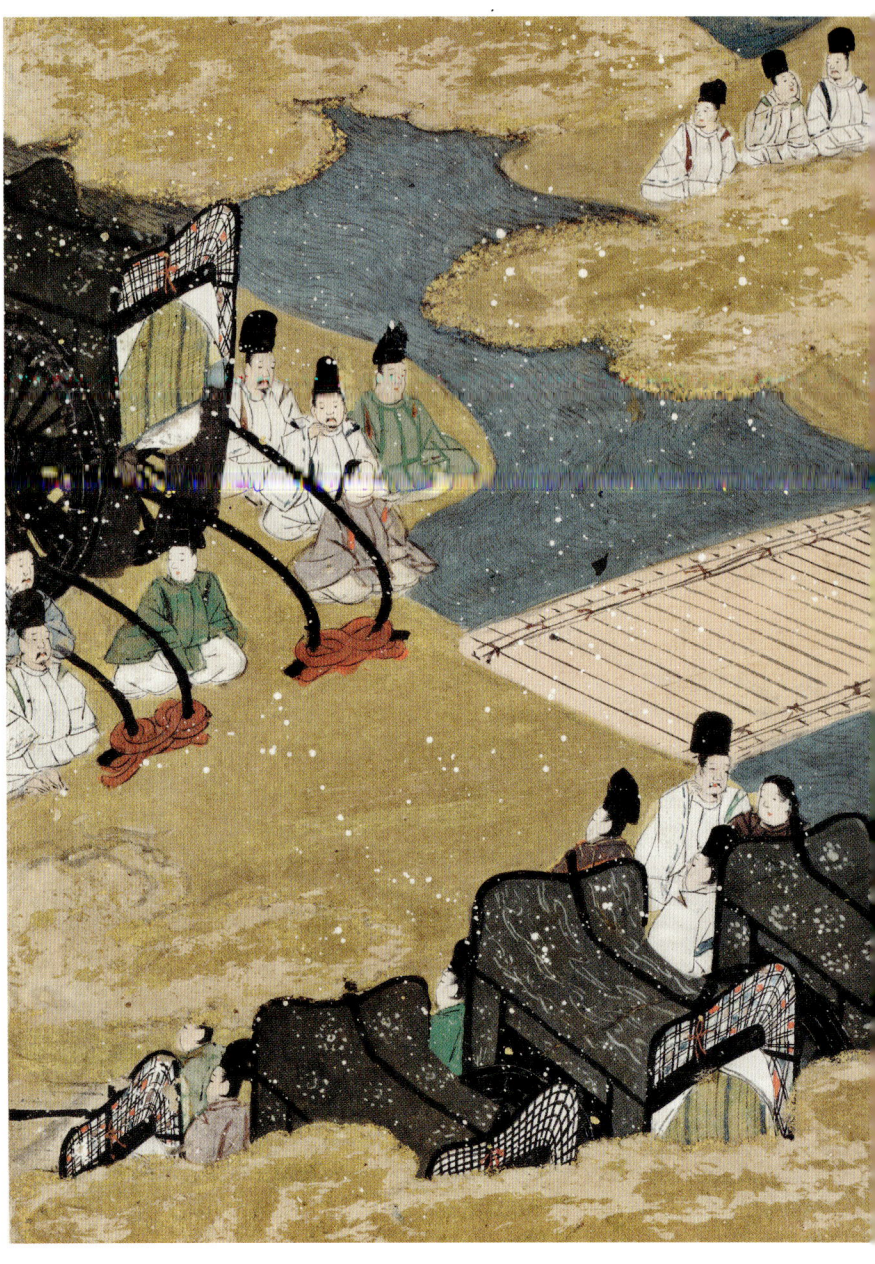

Here on Oshio
Where the ground lies deep in snow
　　The pheasants start up;
Seek, I bid you, the old tracks
Of the bygone hunts today.

CRANSTON, P. 830

Had there ever been an example of a Chancellor participating in an imperial excursion to Ōharano?

WASHBURN, P. 556, MODIFIED

29

行幸

An Imperial Excursion
Miyuki

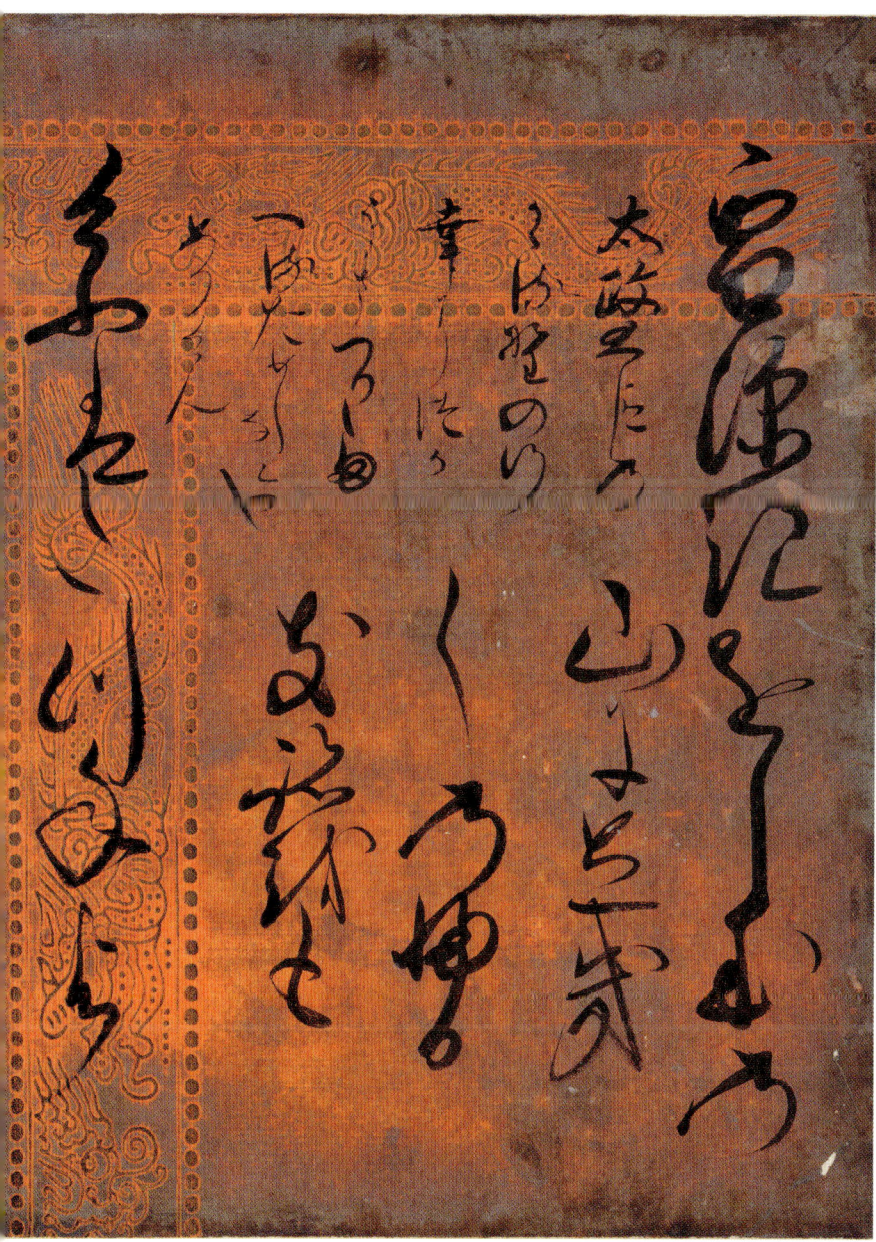

Yuki fukaki
Oshio no yama ni
　Tatsu kiji no
Furuki ato o mo
Kyō wa tazune yo

Ōkiotodo no, kakaru no no miyuki ni tsukaumatsuritamaeru tameshi nado ya ariken.

雪深きをしほの
　太政大臣の
　かゝる野の行　山に立き
　幸につか　しのふる
　うまつりたま　き跡をも
　へるためしなとや
　ありけん　けふはたつねよ

After six successive painting scenes in the album set within the various corners of the Rokujō Estate, which together cycled us through the seasons of one year, Chapter Twenty-Nine takes us outside and onto the streets of the capital during the twelfth month. Sightseers in carriages have lined the city streets as far west as the edge of the Katsura River in the hopes of catching a glimpse of Emperor Reizei's procession, the "imperial excursion" of the chapter title. The party will stop for a hunting expedition on the way to Ōharano Shrine, which is located in the western outskirts of the capital at the base of Mount Oshio, and which enshrined the tutelary deity of the Fujiwara house and the imperial lineage. The route through the city is congested with onlookers, in a manner that recalls the "battle of the carriages" episode in Chapter Nine, because the spectacle is well worth a wait: the imperial escort consists of men from the highest levels of the senior nobility to courtiers of the fifth and sixth ranks, all dressed in their finest attire, riding impressively caparisoned horses, while the costumes of princes and other officials readied for falconry add a colorful flair to the entourage. The album painting captures the moment when snow flurries begin to fall, said to further enhance the elegance of the event. The artist has sprinkled a dusting of shell white over the image to emulate the gentle snowfall, with iridescent flecks appearing especially striking against the rich blue color of the water. No members of the imperial entourage are included in the painting—the makers of the album opting instead to depict a moment pregnant with anticipation before the Emperor has reached the banks of the Katsura River. His Majesty's impending arrival and the direction of the procession is suggested by the conspicuous empty bridge that spans the water, a temporary, floating bridge constructed of planks of wood bound together. The far edge of the bridge is cropped but seems to extend beyond the visible portion of the picture, lending it a mysterious air, especially as it connects the golden shores. Three attendants dressed in white on the far shore, however, bring the bridge motif down to earth and imply another throng of onlookers or escorts waiting across the river.

The most prestigious carriages are said in the tale to line the immediate approach to the bridge for the best view of the imperial procession, and among them is the carriage of Tamakazura. She more than anyone has a good reason for wanting to see the Emperor, since Genji has decided to send her to the imperial palace to assume the coveted position of Reizei's Principal Handmaid. (And with this act, Genji finally reveals Tamakazura's identity to Tō no Chūjō, claiming that he was ignorant of her true origins until he investigated her background in preparation for her role at the palace.) The tale's description of the Emperor's procession, and of his physical appearance, is told from Tamakazura's point of view as she sits in her carriage, in a passage that represents an unusually lengthy indulgence in the pleasures of looking by a female character. It is unclear which carriage in the painting belongs to Tamakazura, but one with visible bamboo blinds seems a likely candidate, especially given the gold cloud floating above it, which has drawn attention to the protagonists throughout the album. From her vantage point Tamakazura observes not only His Majesty but also her true father, the Palace Minister, Tō no Chūjō, and the various men who have vied for her hand, and she critiques their appearance and demeanors. Although we are not treated to a depiction of this in the painting, in the tale, she finds the Emperor to be "handsome and resolute in his crimson cloak." In fact, the only representation of a sovereign in the entire album appears in the painting for Chapter One, where the Kiritsubo Emperor appears from the waist down, his face obscured by hanging blinds. By the Muromachi period, it was common to avoid overt representations of the Emperor out of deference, and Reizei's absence in this painting may be explained by that deference as well. At the same time, the artist's decision to anticipate his entourage rather than depict it outright lends an emotional intensity to the scene, especially when examined in conjunction with the adjacent calligraphy leaf.

The single poem selected for inclusion on this chapter's calligraphy leaf belongs to Emperor Reizei, who sends the verse to Genji after arriving in

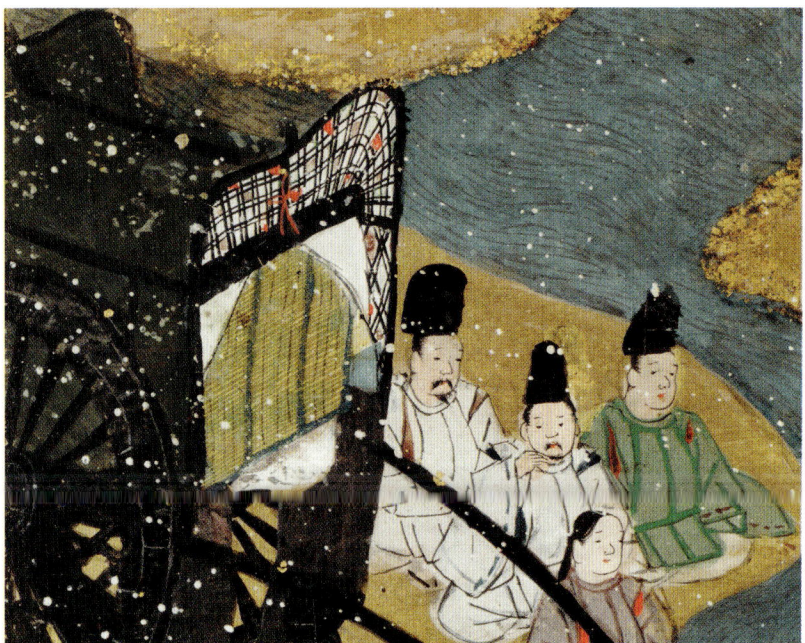

Ōharano. Genji does not attend the festivities that day, and Reizei deeply regrets his absence. As in the poem in the album representing Chapter Eighteen, once again the Emperor initiates communication with Genji, his loyal subject and (unbeknownst to the world at large) his father, except this time Reizei knows the truth of his parentage. This particular poem appears slightly later in the chapter than the scene depicted in the adjacent painting, but its inclusion floats the voice of the Emperor over the scene of the spectators at the bridge, inserting the poignancy of Reizei's longing for his absent father into the episode. The composition of the calligraphy is unusual: the first and final lines of five darkly inked and boldly brushed columns extend the full length of the paper, while the middle three lines occupy only half the height; filling in the space above the shorter lines of the poem are six lines of prose, consisting of a question posed in the voice of the narrator. She asks, rhetorically of course, whether or not there was a precedent for a Chancellor (Genji) attending an imperial excursion to Ōharano, with the intended question being rather, "Why did he not attend?" It seems like an odd fragment to include, but it provides viewers of the album an example of the tale's frequent use of oblique historical references to develop the narrative. Reizei's fictional hunting excursion equals in scale and atmosphere one that occurred in 928 under the real Emperor Daigo (885–930), while another during the reign of Emperor Kōkō (830–887) to a different location was indeed attended by the Chancellor at the time, Fujiwara no Mototsune (836–891). The historical answer to the narrator's question seems to be that, yes, a Chancellor does attend such events. The question suggests that readers reconsider Genji's motives for not joining his son-emperor on this occasion. In fact, Genji's absence from such events with Reizei allows him to avoid a public display of obeisance to his own son. The insertion of the narrator's voice takes what could be a straightforward exultation of Emperor Reizei and turns it into a more complicated scene that reminds readers of the ruler's parentage, and the false pretense at the heart of Reizei's reign.

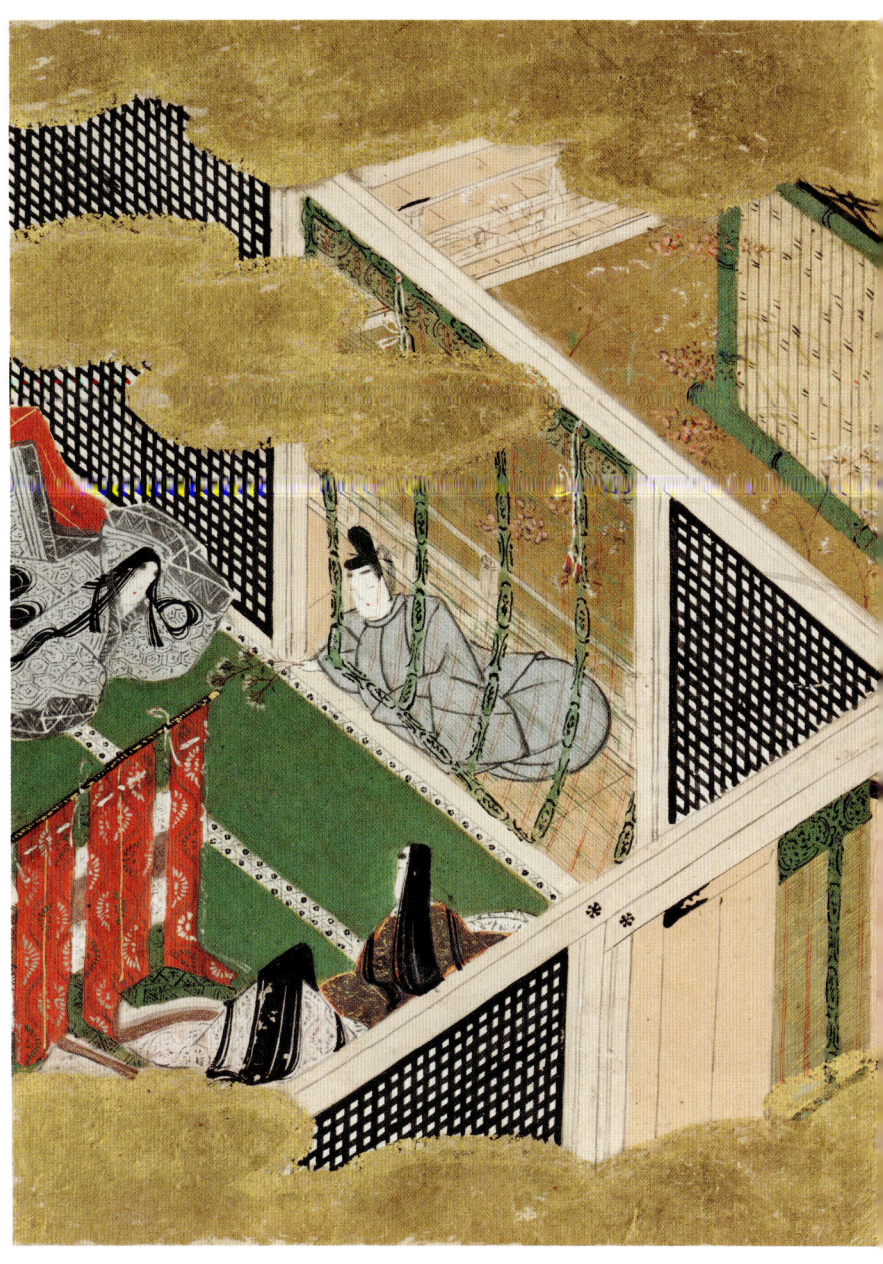

    Dew from the same field
Has given these purple trousers
    Their humbled air;
Bestow your pity on them—
One little moment, I beg.

CRANSTON, P. 834

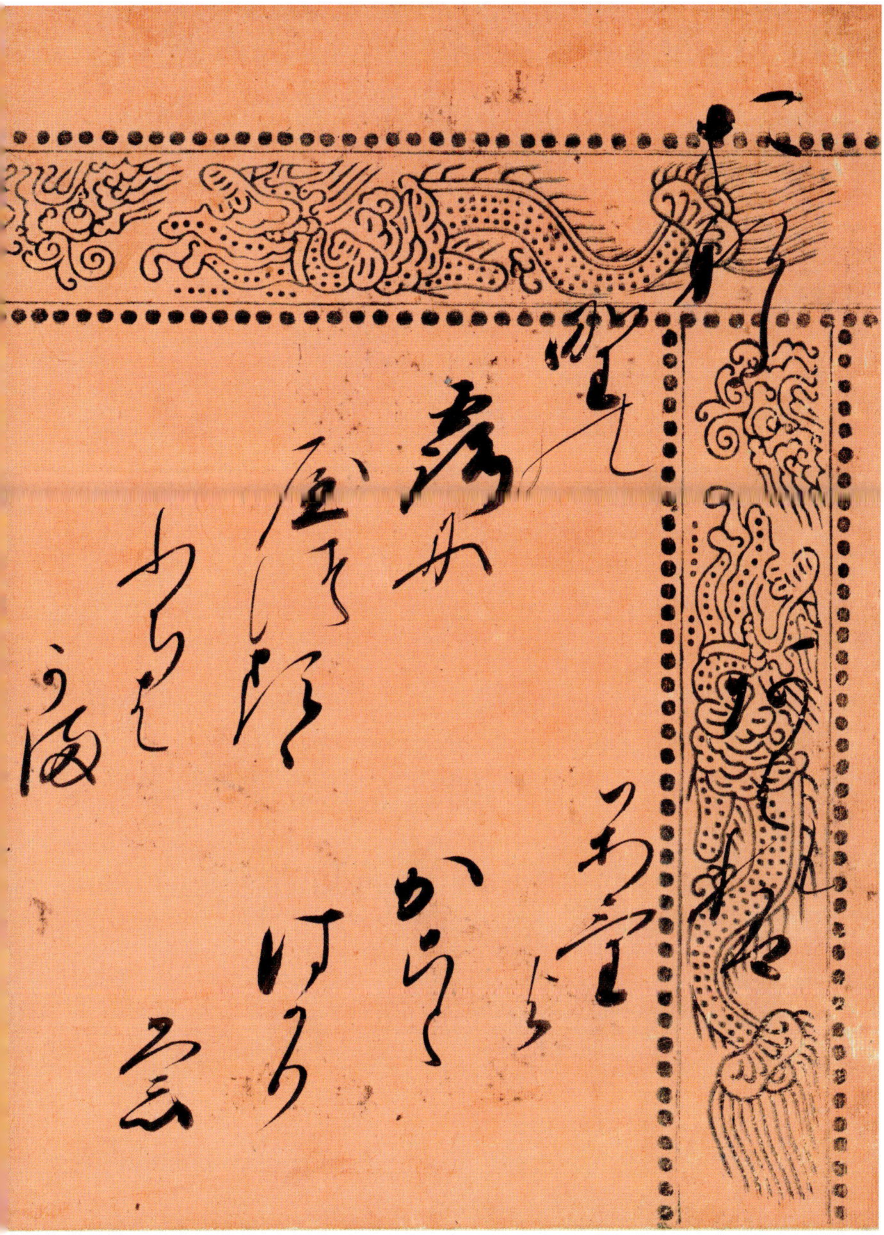

30

藤袴
Mistflowers
Fujibakama

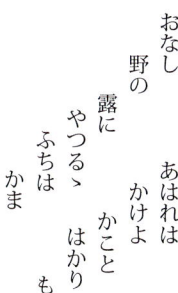

Onaji no no
Tsuyu ni yatsururu
Fujibakama
Aware wa kake yo
Kagoto bakari mo

おなし　あはれは
野の　かけよ
　露に　かこと
　やつるゝ　はかり
　ふちは　も
　　かま

At the start of Chapter Thirty, Princess Ōmiya, mother of Tō no Chūjō and Aoi and so grandmother to both Tamakazura (Tō no Chūjō's daughter) and Yūgiri (son of Aoi and Genji), has passed away, and Tamakazura and Yūgiri are in mourning. Princess Ōmiya, a sister of the Kiritsubo Emperor and thus a member of Genji's royal house, always seemed to bear an allegiance to her blood relations despite her marriage to the Fujiwara Minister of the Left. After the death of her daughter Aoi in childbirth, she took care of Yūgiri and raised him in the Minister of the Left's household. There Yūgiri grew up in close proximity to his uncle Tō no Chūjō, and Yūgiri's many cousins. Ōmiya's death is thus especially significant to Yūgiri. As an expression of his grief, he wears the deepest-hue variety of mourning robe and does so for longer than is necessary following the death of a maternal relative. Newly aware that Tamakazura is not his half sister, but his cousin and a grandchild of Ōmiya, he sees their mutual loss as the basis of a new potential bond between them. In the painting depicted in the album for Chapter Thirty, Yūgiri arrives at Tamakazura's quarters at Rokujō to deliver a message concerning her new appointment as Handmaid (Naishi) to Emperor Reizei. It is a task that the responsible young man, now sixteen and a Consultant in the Council of State (Saishō no chūjō), should be able to carry out without difficulty. The painting depicts him in a plain steel-blue garment meant to represent the dark gray robes of mourning, also known as "purple robes," or "wisteria robes" (*fujigoromo*), named after the lavender-dyed threads with which they were woven. Tamakazura wears robes of a lighter gray, having only recently been in contact with her grandmother, and perhaps wishing to avoid declaring her connection to her Fujiwara family out of deference to her "foster father," Genji. In the picture, her robes are the same color as those worn by Yūgiri, although they also feature a honeycomb design and a zigzagging pattern on the sleeves, and she wears red trousers outlined in gold as well.

Although Yūgiri should strictly convey the message dictated by Reizei and Genji about Tamakazura's new post, instead he ends up confessing his feelings of affection for her, which have become more than brotherly. Just before he does so, the tale describes Yūgiri remembering the erotic encounter between Genji and Tamakazura that he witnessed taking place in these very rooms in the Autumn Tempest chapter, an image that seems imprinted on his mind. As if taking a cue from the sexual aggressiveness he observed on the part of his father, he makes an overture to Tamakazura. Taking a branch of mistflower (*fujibakama*), literally "wisteria" or "purple trousers," from the garden, he pushes the plant beneath her blinds, stating that it demonstrates their deep bond. By this he means their shared gray robes and grief for Princess Ōmiya, and their Fujiwara lineage through their common grandfather, the late Minister of the Left, Princess Ōmiya's husband and father of Tō no Chūjō. But the offering also becomes a lure when Yūgiri grasps at Tamakazura's sleeve as soon as she reaches for the flowers. At that moment, he speaks the poem included in the calligraphy leaf, which on the surface seems innocent enough. Tamakazura has been educated well, however, and recognizes immediately the poetic allusions that give his verse a romantic double entendre. The phrase "one little bit" (*kagoto bakari*) in Yūgiri's poem alludes to an ancient love poem from the *Kokin rokujō* (5:3 360) that refers to the two sashes of prospective mates being ceremonially tied together in hopes of marriage. The allusion to sashes is clever in the context of mourning robes, a flower with "trousers" in its name (*fujibakama*), and the idea of a shared Fujiwara lineage, but Tamakazura is not swayed and rejects the overture immediately. Her poetic reply is decisive:

Tazunuru ni	If on inquiry
Harukeki nobe no	The dewdrop has turned out to be
Tsuyu naraba	One from a distant field,
Usumurasaki ya	This pale purple must surely
Kagoto naramashi	Color some deeper design
	CRANSTON, P. 834

She correctly interprets his poem about their deep familial bond as a pretense for ulterior romantic motives, stating that the plant is a "pale purple" (*usumurasaki*) and thinly veils a "deeper design,"

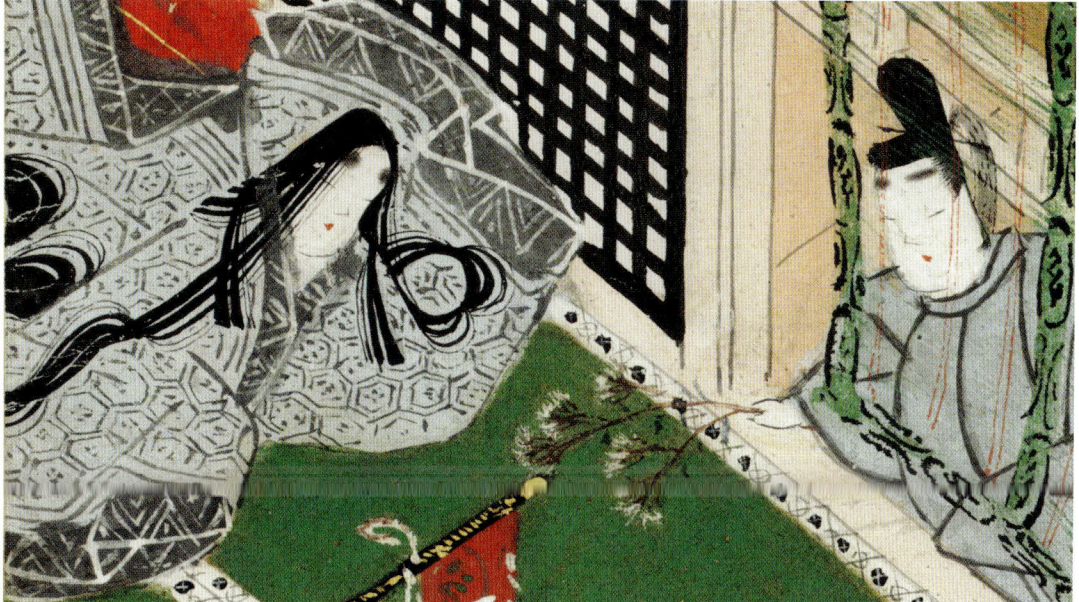

or *kagoto*, which as Edwin Cranston points out, can mean "an excuse." Having fended off Genji's advances for close to two years, Tamakazura knows how to escape from this encounter, which she does by feigning illness, leaving the young Yūgiri to regret his attempt to become one of her suitors.

All of those suitors are still in engaged in a heated competition to win her over, and Yūgiri had hoped to take the place of Kashiwagi, now out of the running as her true biological brother. With so many men vying for her attention, Tamakazura worries that accepting a position as Handmaid at the Palace, where she will not be an official wife and thus still accessible to other men, could lead to scandal. Even Genji seems to be planning to maintain his intimacy with her after the appointment by maintaining her quarters at Rokujō. As the day of her departure for the Palace approaches, missives from the various suitors intensify, with three men in particular pleading their case: Genji's brother Prince Sochinomiya (commonly known as Prince Hotaru), a Major Captain nicknamed Higekuro or "Blackbeard" for his distinctive facial hair, and a Commander of the Left Palace Guard. Just as the comparison between Tamakazura and the daughter from Ōmi seemed to embed within the narrative a didactic set piece, here too the description of these various suitors and the way they each pursue Tamakazura bear similarities to didactic tales of courtship written for young women of marriageable age.

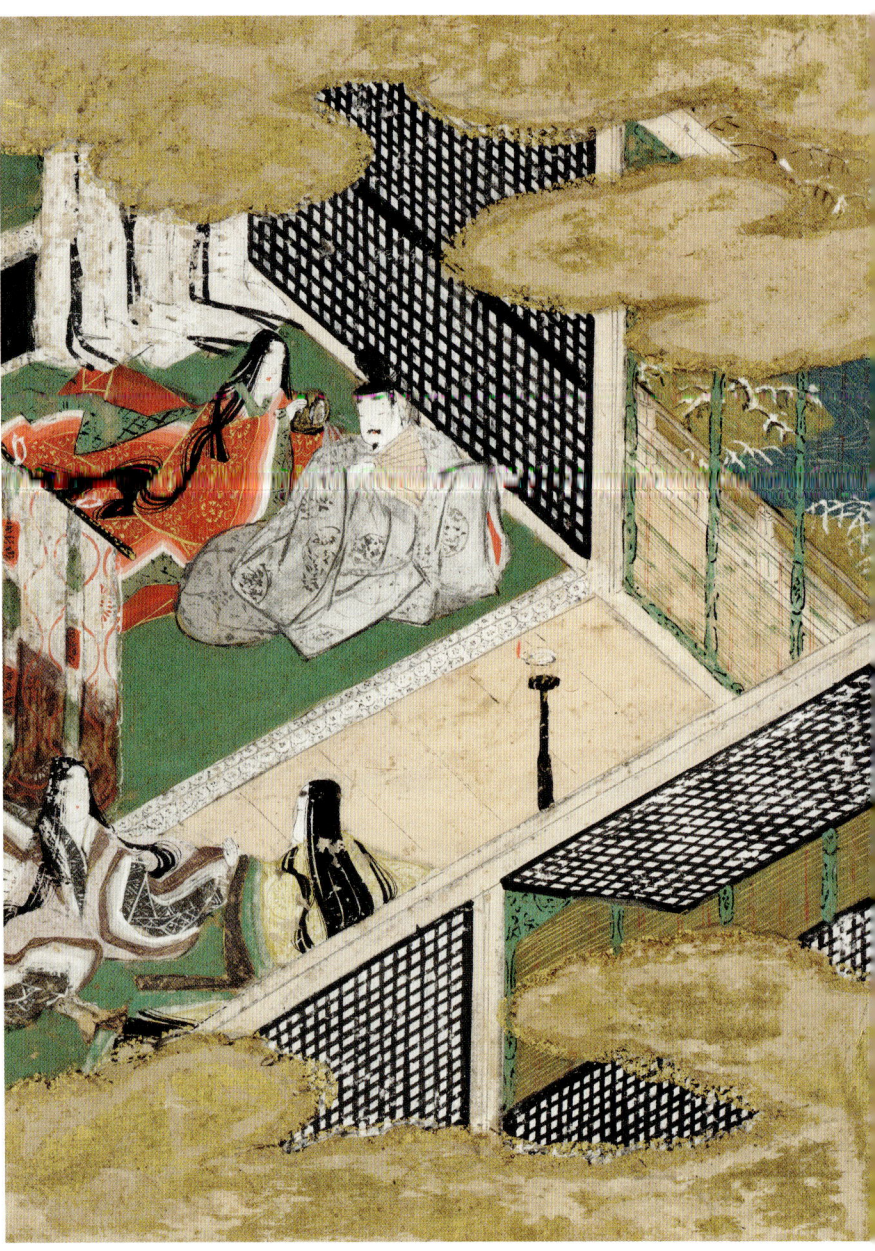

The voices of the retainers in his escort were audible.

"The snow is letting up…"

"It's getting late…"

They coughed and cleared their throats, urging him as discreetly as possible to set off, aware that their lord's principal wife was there.

WASHBURN, P. 589

31

真木柱

A Beloved Pillar of Cypress

Makibashira

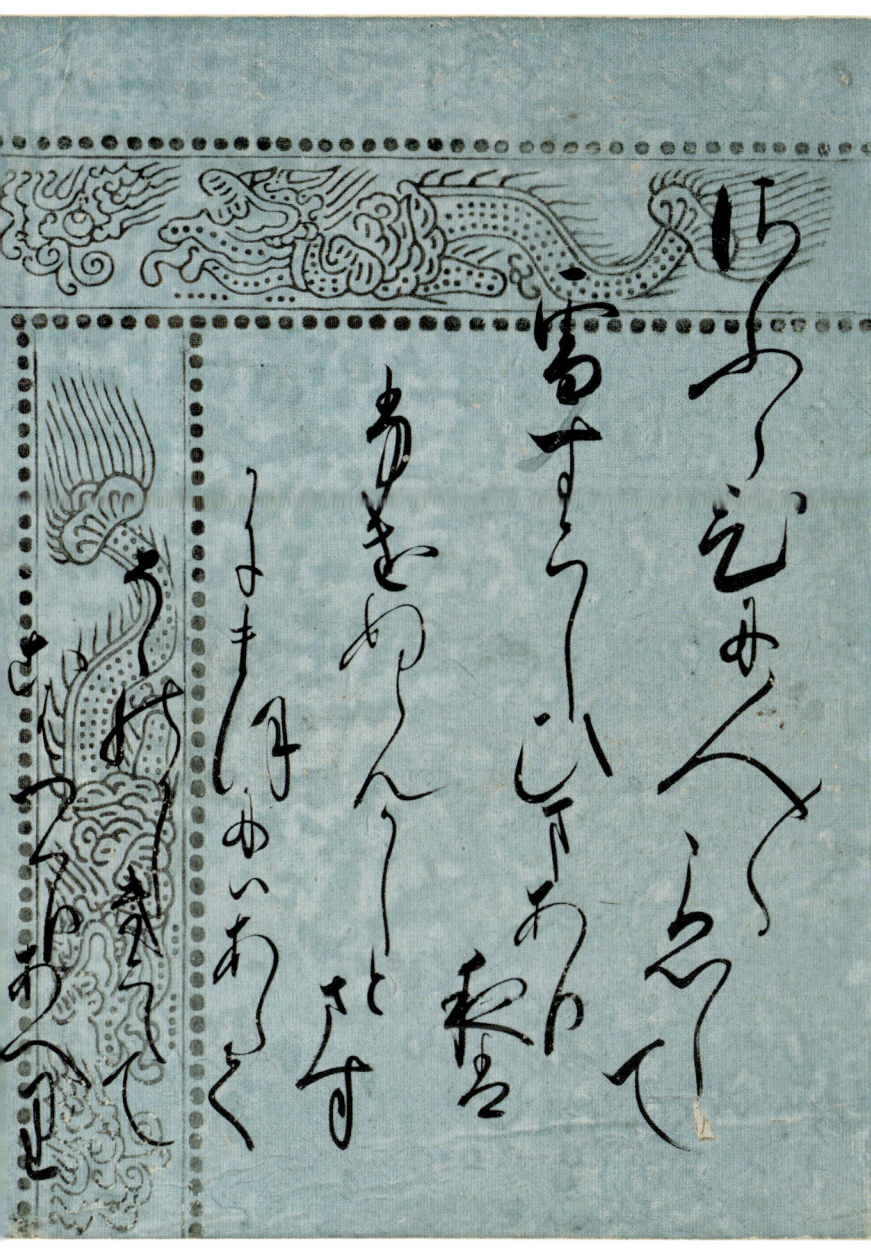

Saburai ni hitobito koe shite,
"Yuki sukoshi hima ari.
Yo wa fukenuran kashi," to sasuga
ni maho ni wa arade, sosonokashi
kikoete, kowazukuri aeri.

さぶらひに人〴〵こゑして
雪すこしひまあり
夜は
ふけぬらんかしと
さすがにまほにはあらて
そゝのかしきこえて
こはつくりあへり

Of all the male suitors of Tamakazura, the one who seemed least likely to win her hand was the Major Captain of the Right Guard, the hirsute courtier known as Higekuro (Blackbeard), and yet at the start of Chapter Thirty-One preparations are being made for the "third night ceremony" that will mark their formal union. The details of how this came about are never explicitly given, but apparently Higekuro manipulated one of Tamakazura's female attendants in order to gain access to Tamakazura's chambers, and then began an intimate relationship with her that made a formal marriage with him the only option for the young woman. Tamakazura is distraught at the turn of events, feeling no attraction to this man and realizing how poorly he compares to Genji and her other previous options, including Prince Sochinomiya and Emperor Reizei, who with their familial connections to Genji possessed shades of his radiant appeal. Instead she is left with a man who is no blood relation to Genji, technically respectable as his pedigree may be, and whose current household situation is a cause for concern. Higekuro already has a principal wife, a woman of distinction, to whom he has been married for many years and with whom he has a daughter and two sons. The wife is in fact a princess, the daughter of Prince Hyōbu, Murasaki's father, by his principal wife. She is described as suffering from an unspecified malady that prompts her to engage in unruly behavior and that makes her prone to verbal outbursts; some suspect a malignant spirit at work. Higekuro's amorous feelings for his wife have long faded, as a result of these "episodes" of hers, prompting him to consider dissolving the marriage. In the meantime, he plans to move Tamakazura out of Rokujō and into the home that he shares with his wife and children. The narrator describes Higekuro as an exemplar of dignified courtly behavior, who is now suddenly acting like a lovesick young man, visiting Tamakazura every night at the Rokujō estate.

The painting for Chapter Thirty-One depicts one such night when Higekuro is about to depart for an evening with Tamakazura and is at his home fastidiously primping and adjusting his wardrobe in preparation. His wife's sadness, anger, and feelings of humiliation over the imminent introduction of a new wife into the household have been made known, but on this night, she is eerily calm. It has begun to snow heavily, as the painting suggests through the depiction of reeds laden with white near an icy-looking pond. As the storm intensifies, Higekuro worries that braving the elements on a night like this might be too disrespectful to his wife, but she encourages him to go, playing the martyr and acting like the ideal obedient wife in a polygynous marriage. She even assists him in perfuming his garments for his new bride. All seems well; Higekuro's escort outside begins to urge him to depart, as is related in the album's text, while the female attendants, Moku and Chūjō, sit at ease. The wife too has been seated calmly but suddenly she retrieves the censer of burning incense being used to scent the robes, walks up behind her husband, and dumps a mound of ash all over him. This shocking act of pique by a noblewoman is unique in the tale, and the artist of the album seems to revel in capturing precisely this dramatic moment. Higekuro looks over his shoulder in surprise, as he lurches to the side, raising his folding fan in a useless attempt to shield himself. The ash from the censer, depicted in long lines of gray pigment, covers his robe and fan. In the tale, the ash does far worse damage, getting in his eyes and ears so that he is temporarily blinded and confused. Higekuro's wife, dressed in a lavish multicolored robe with a delicate floral pattern in gold, seems rather calm as she tilts the censer over her husband in her act of retribution. According to the codes of courtly painting, any depiction of a noblewoman standing in an interior, however, is usually a sign that things have gone awry. The inclusion of the couple's white curtained bed in the room seems to function as a symbol of their marital bond, now broken, and the wife's sense of betrayal. In the foreground, one female attendant with a view of the shocking incident responds with alarm, a hand extending from her outstretched sleeve, while her counterpart with her back to the couple still seems blissfully unaware of the confrontation taking place. If Higekuro's wife intended to prevent his tryst, the ash dumping did the trick, as the smoky odor

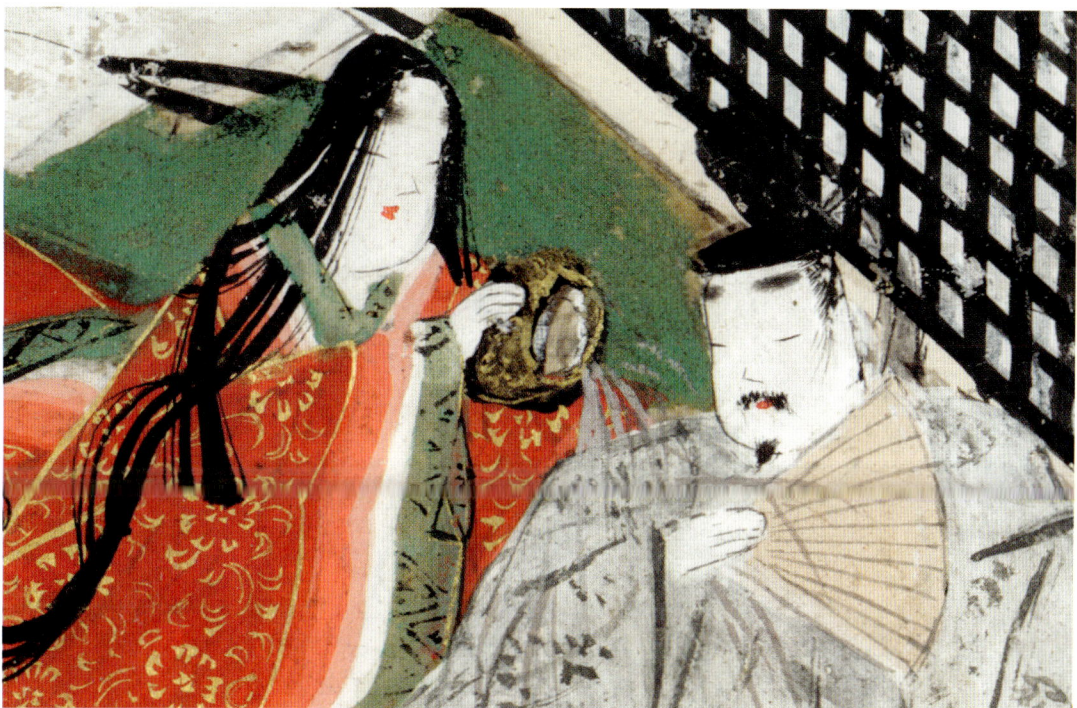

permeates his undergarments, lingers on his body, and makes a visit to Rokujō impossible. While the episode is dramatic, and is not without its moments of high comedy, especially in the description of the ashen Higekuro, it results in the husband summoning priests and exorcists to purge his wife of the demons to which he attributes her actions. The narrator describes the wife crying out in anguish during the exorcism, which continues for days in what can only be interpreted, at least on some level, as a punishment meted out by her husband for her bad behavior.

The chapter goes on to record the details of the couple's divorce, the wife's return to her parents' home, and her decision to take her daughter, called Makibashira, with her, leaving her two sons to be raised by Higekuro. The chapter title derives from a poem by the daughter, who is reluctant to part from her beloved father; she leaves the poem in the house attached to her favorite "cypress pillar" (*makibashira*), a metaphor for her father as her stalwart supporter. By the end of the chapter Tamakazura has moved in with Higekuro and his boys, and soon she gives birth to her first son. Her life as an exalted overseer of the handmaid staff at the palace, a job she accepted even though she was in the process of marrying Higekuro, then comes to an end. Although Tamakazura will reappear later as a mother arranging the futures of her children, Chapter Thirty-One brings the so-called "ten Tamakazura books" (*Tamakazura jūjō*, Chapters 22–31) to a close, having traced Tamakazura's story from the provinces to the very center of courtly life in the capital.

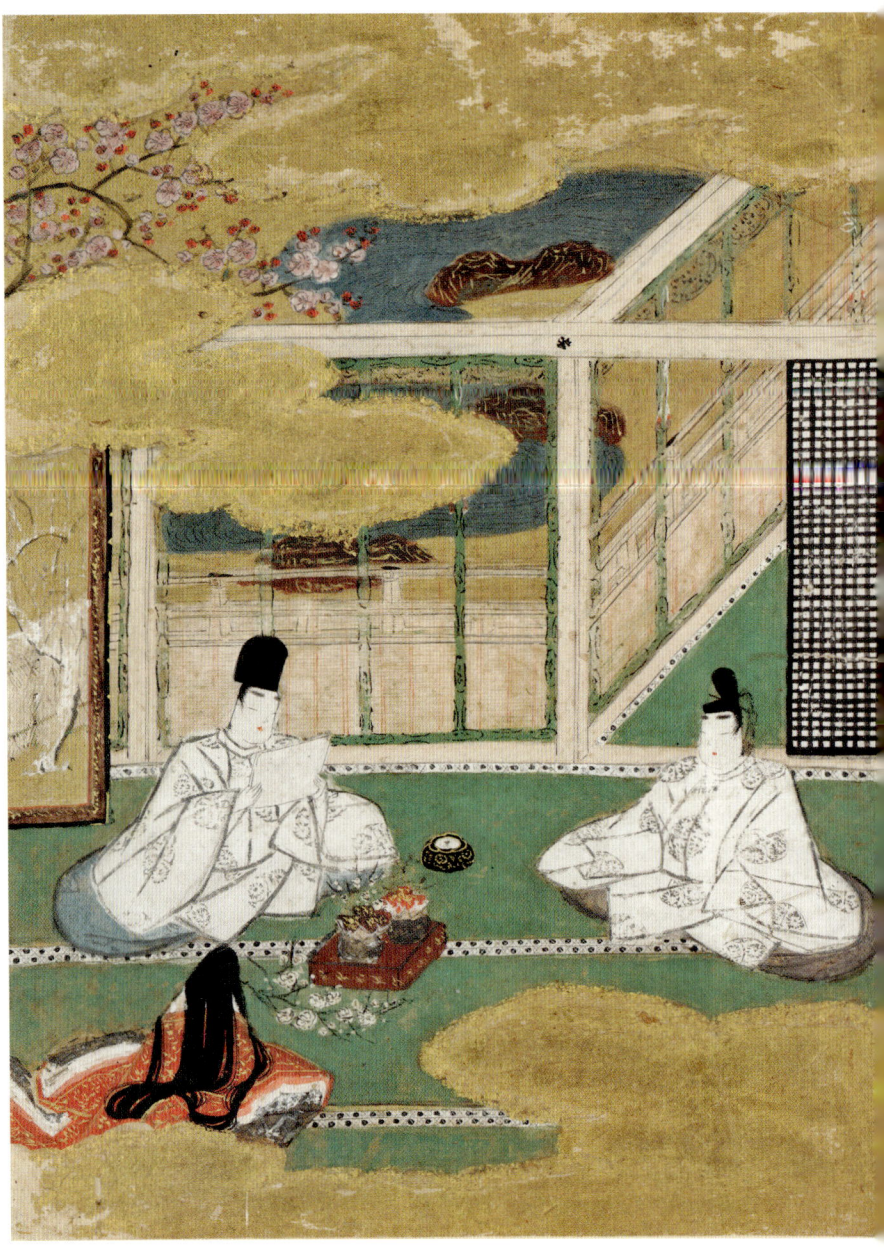

What an elegant presentation, he thought. He noticed a poem:

WASHBURN, P. 610, MODIFIED

Fragrance of the bloom
Does not linger on the branch
Whence the flowers fall,
But will it be but shallowly
It perfumes the receptive sleeve?

CRANSTON, P. 845

32

梅枝

A Branch of Plum

Umegae

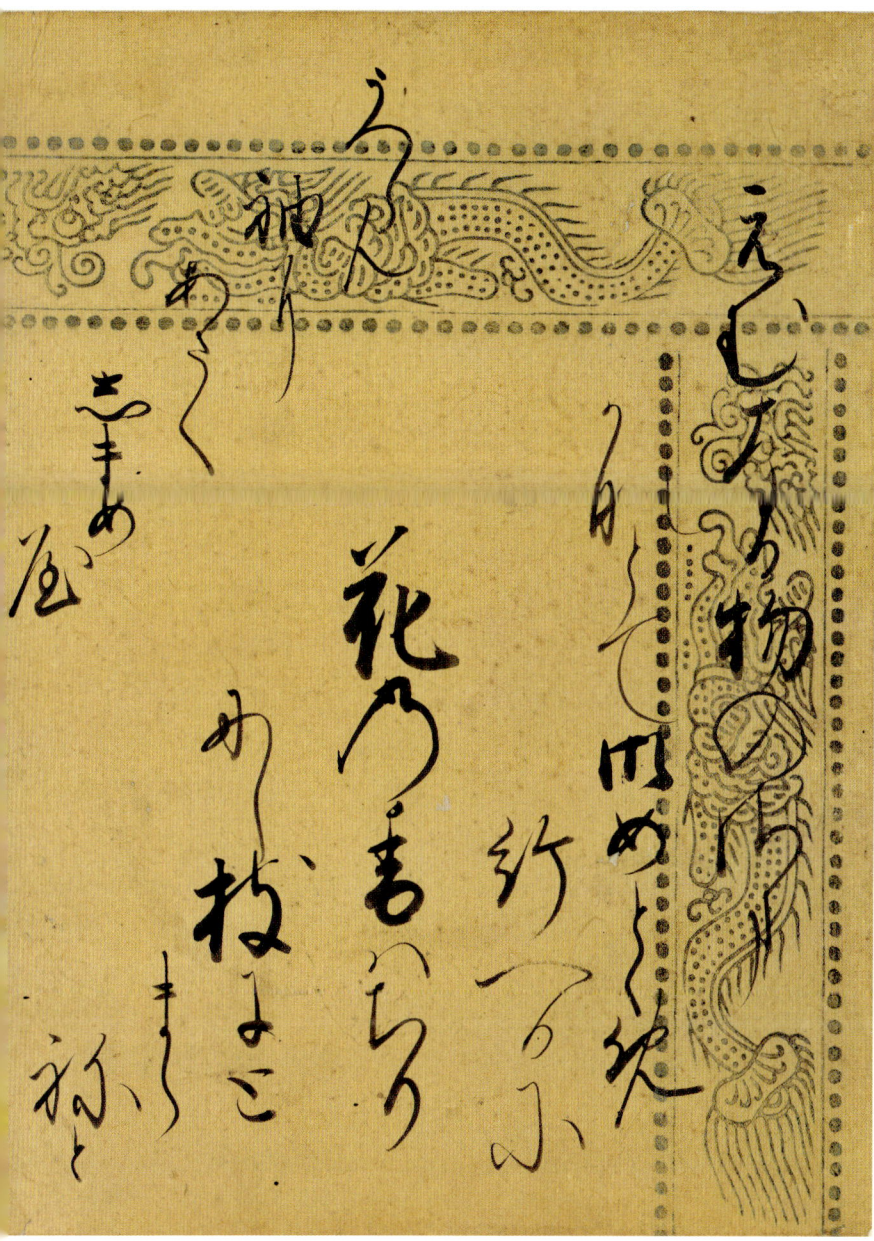

"Ennaru mono no
sama kana" tote, onme
todometamaeru ni,

   Hana no ka wa
   Chirinishi eda ni
     Tomaranedo
   Utsuran sode ni
   Asaku shimame ya

えむなる物のさま
かなとて御めとゝめ
給へるに
うつらん　花の香はちり
袖に　にし枝にと
あさく　まら
しまめ　ねと
や

Although the Akashi girl is only eleven years of age, in Chapter Thirty-Two, Genji holds her coming-of-age ceremony, the so-called donning of the skirt (*mogi*), which will precipitate her entry into the imperial palace. If all goes as planned, she will win over the Crown Prince, become Empress, as prophesied long ago, and give birth to an imperial heir. To outfit her palace quarters, which will be within the Kiritsubo court of his late mother, Genji begins putting together a thoughtfully arranged trousseau. He throws open his storehouses to procure the best furnishings and textiles, such as brocades and damasks from China and Korea, as well as books and scrolls, and he commissions new paintings and copybooks of exemplary calligraphy. He even briefly considers including in her library the precious Suma scrolls, his picture-poem records of exile that won him the important symbolic victory of the picture match in Chapter Seventeen. In the end, Genji decides not to turn them over just yet, but the reference to them reminds readers of the Akashi girl's role in carrying out the legacy of her family. Next Genji turns to the task of gathering incense for his daughter, which she will need for scenting robes and perfuming her chambers. To concoct an alluring scent required the utmost skill and access to exotic aromatic woods, along with the best instructions, which often took the form of closely guarded recipes handed down within families. Genji blends certain fragrances himself, and he enlists the help of his most trusted women: Murasaki, Princess Asagao, Hanachirusato, and the Akashi Lady.

The album painting for Chapter Thirty-Two depicts the arrival of Asagao's two fragrances, in front of Genji, on the left, and Sochinomiya (a.k.a. Prince Hotaru), on the right. Sochinomiya is dressed in formal attire to call on his esteemed half brother at Rokujō. Outside, a canopy of plum branches, profuse with pink blossoms and red buds, arches over the blue stream that winds its way into the background through Murasaki's celebrated spring garden. Genji is absorbed in reading a letter from Princess Asagao, who formerly was the Kamo Priestess and is a cousin to him and Sochinomiya, her father having been a brother of the Kiritsubo Emperor. Asagao is also the one woman who always eluded Genji, despite numerous advances and flirtations on Genji's part, and deliberately chose not to marry. In their poetry exchange in Chapter Twenty, the chapter that bears her name, she rejected Genji outright, leading him to respond by implying that she was past her prime. In this scene, ever hopeful, he excitedly reads her letter, as Sochinomiya's eyes turn to the remarkable gifts she has sent. As described in the album's calligraphy text, Sochinomiya marvels at the "elegance," or "allure" (*en*) of the presentation. Her two glass jars of incense rest within a Chinese box made of fragrant agarwood (*jinkō*), itself a source of incense. She prepared one, containing the color of blue lapis lazuli (*konruri*), for incense of the black variety (*kurobō*) associated with winter, which she decorated with an artificial sprig of five-needle pine. Some loss of pigment has occurred in the album painting, but the jar with the silvery blue color and red fabric corresponds to this description; traces of the brown pigment of pine branches, and green needles, are still slightly visible. Traces of white pigment appear on the body of the other jar, while a decorative white plum branch emerges from its center. The term used to describe this jar in the tale, "white lapis" (*haku ruri*), calls to mind the cloudy white shards of glass of possible Persian origin, found in the ancient Shōsōin imperial storehouse. The allusion to such exotic materials evokes ancient trade

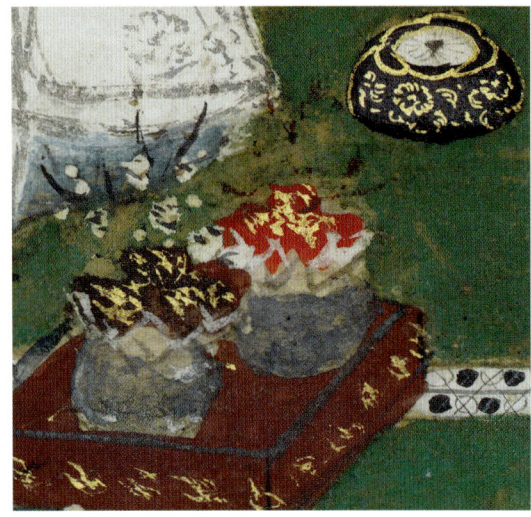

routes that linked central Asia to the Japanese royal courts; Genji mentions the fabrics he was given by Chinese and Korean envoys, and Asagao, as a princess, has in her possession precious objects the likes of which were primarily owned by individuals with royal bloodlines.

While scrutinizing Asagao's elegant gifts, Sochinomiya notices a poem from the lady attached to the ensemble, which is the verse featured in the calligraphy sheet in the album. It alludes to the bare plum branch she attached to her letter, using it as a metaphor for herself, no longer in the spring of her youth, as she graciously cedes its flowers to the Akashi girl, hoping that their scent permeates the young girl's robes. The artist has chosen to include a plum branch with its white blossoms still intact, however, lying adjacent to the incense. One final object included in the composition is a censer for burning incense, which alludes to an incense competition that follows this scene, during which Sochimoniya acts as the judge and complains of the smoke he must endure. As Inamoto Mariko has suggested, the black lacquered censer with its elegant gold pattern is also a visual echo of the censer wielded by the wife of Higekuro in the previous album painting. Its conspicuousness in the center of the composition marks a contrast between the two households: one in the midst of chaos, and the other the epitome of order and harmony, at least for now.

A painting within the album painting—a folding screen that appears behind Genji—depicts a snow-covered tree standing beside a rustic fence and seems anomalous in the context of the spring rains and the humid air described in this chapter. But of course, early spring in the lunar calendar coincided with lingering winter snow, and indeed the hearty plum tree blooming in winter was a symbol of perseverance. Winter is also associated with the Akashi Lady, deprived of seeing her daughter on the occasion of donning the train, and the image may allude to her as the mother of the girl whose entry to the

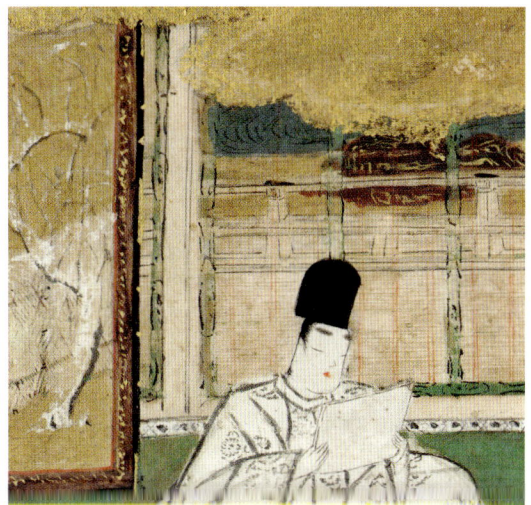

palace is at the heart of the scene. Another more likely interpretation, however, is that the snow is an oblique allusion to the title of the chapter. Following the scene illustrated in the album painting, Genji and Sochinomiya are joined by Tō no Chūjō's sons and Yūgiri for a musical soiree where Ben no Shōshō (Kōbai), well known for his beautiful voice, sings the folk song (saibara) "A Branch of Plum" (Umegae):

> To the plum tree branch the warbler comes, to sing
> all spring long, all spring long, yet snow is still falling.
> Look, how lovely! snow is falling.
> TYLER, P. 550

Both Genji and Sochinomiya join in the singing, which is followed by rounds of rice wine and the exchange of auspicious poetry by all the men present. Sochinomiya's poem praises his brother and host, starting off the rounds of ritualized versification by complementing the voice of the warbler (Kōbai) amid the glorious spring blossoms. The sound sends his heart soaring for the proverbial "thousand years," a phrase common to imperial banquet poetry, and felicitations appropriate on this eve of the Akashi girl's donning of the train, which will ultimately lead to her elevation as Empress.

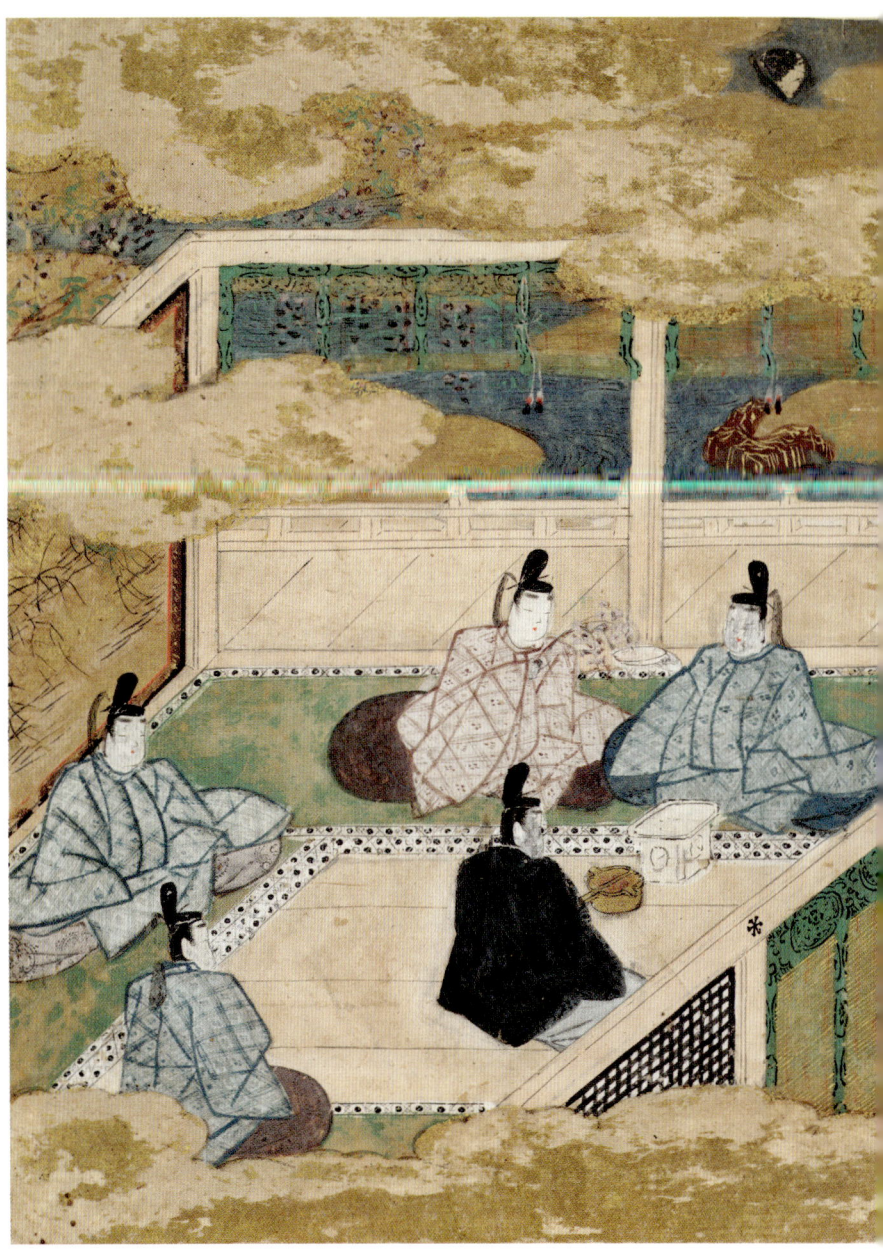

The Palace Minister spoke a line of verse: "Shoots of wisteria leaves…" Taking that as his cue, Kashiwagi broke off an extremely long, full cluster of richly hued blossoms adding it to the guest of honor's cup.

WASHBURN, P. 627, MODIFIED

33

藤裏葉
Shoots of Wisteria Leaves
Fuji no uraba

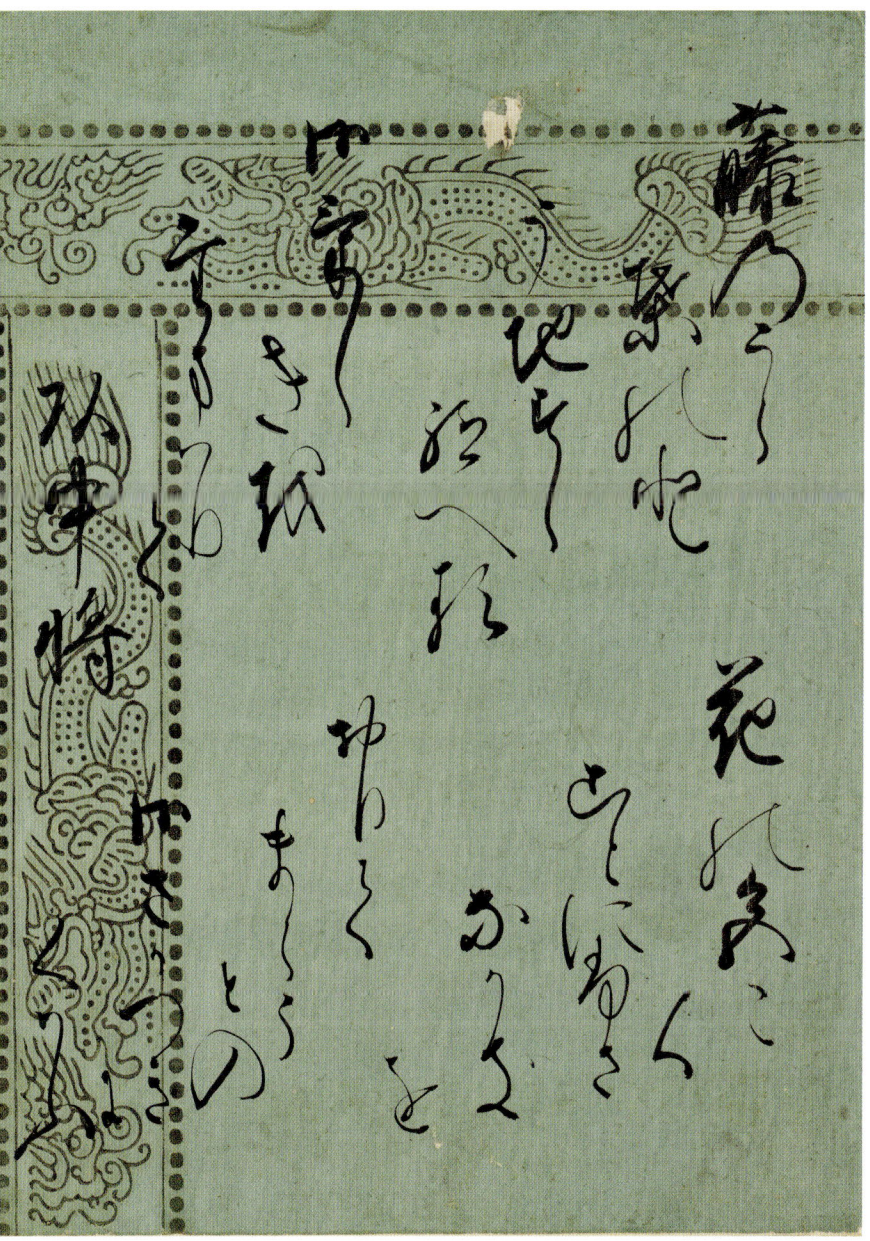

"Fuji no uraba no," to uchizujitamaeru, mikeshiki o tamawarite, Tō no Chūjō, hana no iro koku koto ni fusa nagaki o orite, marōdo no onsakazuki ni kuwau.

藤のうら葉の　花の色こ
葉のと　　ことにふさ
うちすし　　なかき
給へる　　おりて
御けし　　まらう
きを　　　との
たまはり　御さかつきに
頭中将　　くはふ

Three events take place in Chapter Thirty-Three that mark the pinnacle of Genji's success: the marriage of Genji's son, Yūgiri; the Akashi girl's official entry into the imperial palace; and Genji's elevation to the status of retired emperor. The album painting depicts the first of these three events, showing the eighteen-year-old Yūgiri on his wedding night, engaging in a ritualized toast and poetry exchange with his new in-laws. His bride is the young woman known as Kumoinokari, twenty years of age, and a daughter of Tō no Chūjō, whom Yūgiri has been in love with since childhood. Both were raised at the knee of Princess Ōmiya, their shared grandmother, to Yūgi, the childhood home of Aoi (Yūgiri's mother) and Tō no Chūjō. The cousins were constant companions until they were precautionarily separated at around age ten by Tō no Chūjō. Kumoinokari's mother was a princess of royal blood, giving her father great hope that she might one day become an imperial consort. In this way, Tō no Chūjō embodies the institution of the Fujiwara Regency, in which commoners controlled the throne by marrying their daughters into the imperial family. Yet nothing has gone according to plan. Genji, the son of an emperor, made a commoner not of his own volition, has consistently usurped the prerogatives of the Fujiwara Regents by sending his own daughters to court to become empress consorts. This was the nature of the competition underlying the picture contest in Chapter Seventeen in which the Umetsubo Consort (Genji's adopted daughter) prevailed over the Kokiden Consort (Tō no Chūjō's daughter). Tō no Chūjō hoped to try again with Kumoinokari and thus did his best to keep her away from Genji's son, a commoner. When, in Chapter Twenty-One, Tō no Chūjō learned that despite their young age the two had already been intimate, his hopes were dashed again. At the same time, comments by Kumoinokari's serving lady regarding Yūgiri's low rank deeply offended the young man, which led to a lull in the romance for several years, although both Yūgiri and Kumoinokari continued to pine for each other.

When Yūgiri is promoted to Consultant (Chūnagon) in Chapter Thirty-Three, and it becomes clear that others want him as a son-in-law, Tō no Chūjō sends his eldest son Kashiwagi with a message for Yūgiri, an invitation to his home for a banquet celebrating the wisteria blossoms in his garden. The invitation tells Yūgiri to arrive at twilight when the flowers are most luminous, the first of many wisteria and flower images in the chapter that function as metaphors for both the Fujiwara house and the daughter on offer, Kumoinokari. Yūgiri arrives late, in a noteworthy parallel with Genji's tardy appearance at the wisteria banquet in Chapter Eight. The similarities end there, however; whereas Genji appeared at the party dressed in an audacious costume and flagrantly pursued the Minister of the Right's daughter Oborozukiyo, Yūgiri, ever the filial son and upstanding courtier educated in Confucian ethics, shows the utmost respect to his prospective father-in-law. All the men dress up for the occasion by pairing their informal robes (*nōshi*) with formal caps (*kanmuri*). The painting makes it clear that it is no longer twilight—the moon has risen, represented by a silver half circle in the upper right, and it casts a glow on the rocks in the garden, which are highlighted by lines of gold pigment. The perspective of the painting is such that we see over the veranda and through translucent bamboo blinds to the wisteria in the garden. These elements recall the moment in the tale when Tō no Chūjō escorts the nervous young groom to the veranda where he praises the purple wisteria, reminding Yūgiri of their shared Fujiwara/purple roots (*iro mo, hata, natsukashiki yukari*).

The festivities for the guest of honor begin as Yūgiri's hosts press wine on him, and Tō no Chūjō feigns inebriation in order to voice sentiments that might otherwise be awkward and to make the marriage proposal. The painting situates Yūgiri to the far right, while a figure in a *kanmuri* cap and a black patterned cloak sits on the floor holding a golden sake pitcher at the ready for the guest. As the host and most senior figure in the room, Tō no Chūjō is likely the figure with his back to the wall painting on the far left. When the timing is right, he utters a line from which the chapter title derives, "shoots of wisteria leaves" (*fuji no uraba*). The fragment is from a verse in the *Gosenshū* spoken by a woman who has finally realized the trustworthiness of her lover:

Haruhi sasu	Rays of the spring sun
Fuji no uraba no	Cast the last leaves on the vine tips
Ura tokete	Of wisteria:
Kimi shi omowaba	Caught up in the glow of melting words,
Ware mo tanomamu	I'll trust in your true love.

CRANSTON, P. 254

Although this marriage proposal is a transactional one between men, with no women in the room, Tō no Chūjō alludes to a poem spoken by a woman acquiescing to a marriage proposal. The base poem is not only appropriate in terms of the betrothal and the faithfulness to be expected of the groom, but it also includes the wisteria, the symbol of the Fujiwara house; even the first word, *haruhi*, the characters of which can also be read *kasuga*, invokes the name of the most important tutelary shrine of the Fujiwara clan. Kashiwagi, sitting in between his father and Yūgiri, turns toward his friend in a pose that exudes eagerness as he holds up a glorious branch of wisteria. While most translations of the tale say that he "laid the branch on the floor alongside the cup," the artist interprets Kashiwagi's "adding" (*kuwau*) of the wisteria to the cup as a ritualized gesture, more like a blessing or a toast. Traces of green pigment around the branch show that the painting originally included those "shoots of wisteria leaves" as well. Kashiwagi holds out the branch awkwardly until his father chimes in with a poem that alludes to the wisteria (his daughter) and the pine (Yūgiri) as both having waited too long to unite. Yūgri responds by raising his cup, bowing his head, and expressing his joy at the marriage in his own poem. A number of off-color references by the men follow, suggesting that the bride is a flirtatious woman, a characterization that Kumoinokari hears from Yūgiri, making her less than welcoming to him on their first night together, but things progress and the narrator confirms their unbreakable bond.

The marriage of Genji's son to Tō no Chūjo's daughter, taking Kumoinokari out of contention as an imperial wife, is a victory for Genji over his long-standing rival. After the Akashi girl enters the palace in a grand ceremony, Genji is promoted to a status "equivalent" (*nazurau*) to that of retired emperor (*daijō tennō*), which is unprecedented for a commoner, while his son, Emperor Reizei, still wishes to abdicate and make his real father the sovereign. In the stunning final scene of the chapter, both retired Emperor Suzaku and Emperor Reizei pay an official visit to Genji at Rokujōin, now the symbolic retirement villa (*in*) of an ex-emperor. Interestingly, Mitsunobu depicted precisely this scene of the imperial visitation to Rokujō for the back cover of a bound booklet of Chapter Thirty-Three (shown here), now in the collection of the Idemitsu Museum. The front cover depicts Yūgiri's betrothal, virtually identically to the album leaf, demonstrating how these two scenes were viewed as the most emblematic of the chapter. The scene of festivities taking place amid autumn leaves recalls the one in Chapter Nine where Genji and Tō no Chūjō, then nearly on equal footing, danced before three generations of emperors. Now, however, Genji has taken his seat among the sovereigns. In a final stroke, Genji sends Tō no Chūjō a poem with a chrysanthemum (symbolic of heirs to the throne), to which his long-standing rival can only respond with praise. This chapter named for the Fujiwara wisteria thus ends with an image of imperial chrysanthemum, but with hints that all is not settled between these two intertwined houses.

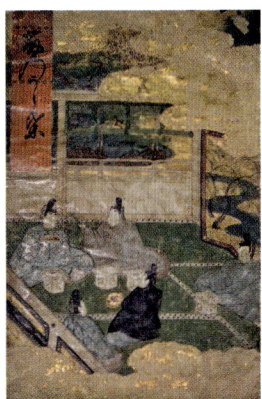 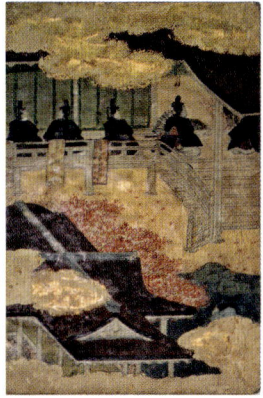

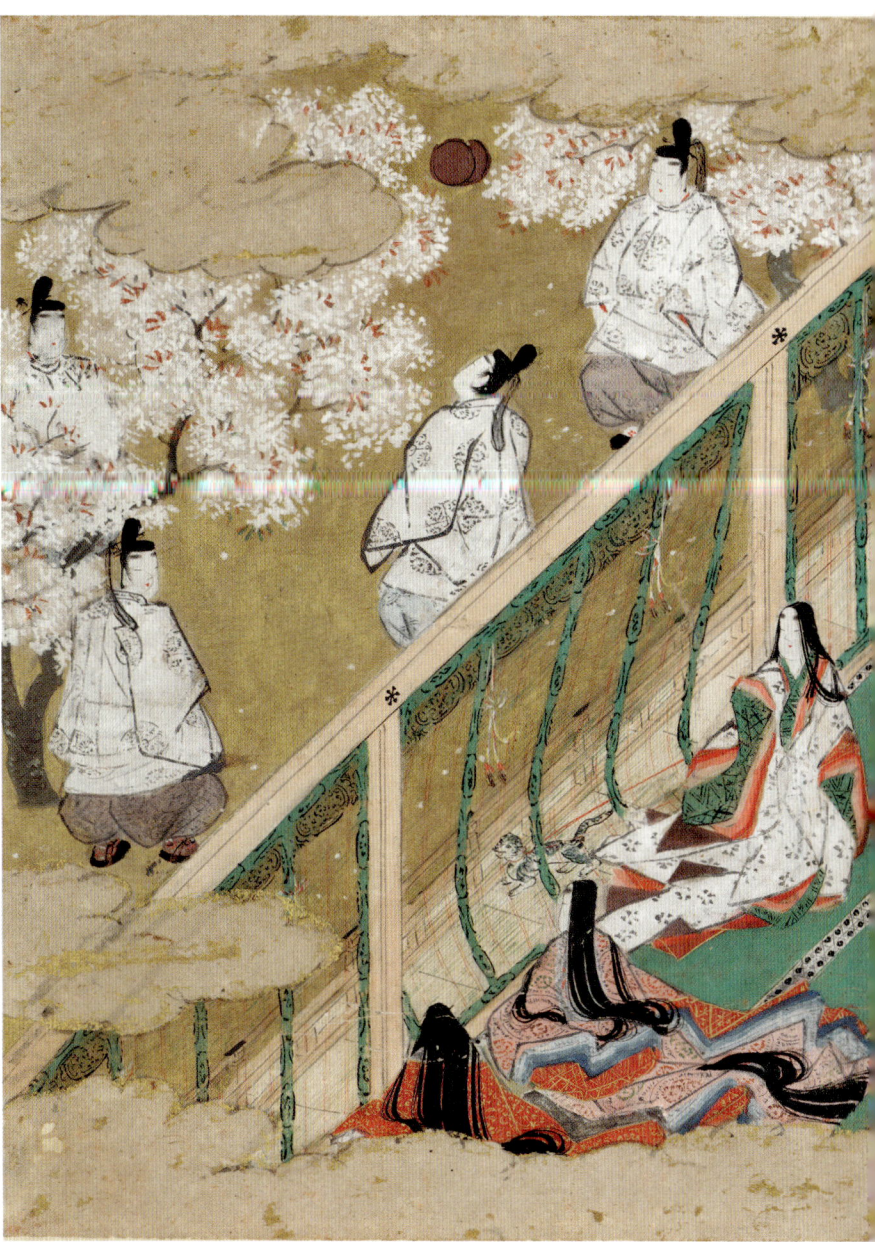

"We should stay clear of the cherry tree."

As he was speaking, he cast a sidelong glance over at the quarters of the Third Princess. From what he could tell, some of the more forward ladies-in-waiting had apparently stepped into the south outer aisle room, as was their wont. The various colors of their robes were faintly visible through the translucent blinds, and their sleeves were spilling out onto the veranda. It resembled those bright cloth pouches filled with offerings.

WASHBURN, P. 696, MODIFIED

34

若菜上
Early Spring Greens: Part One
Wakana jō

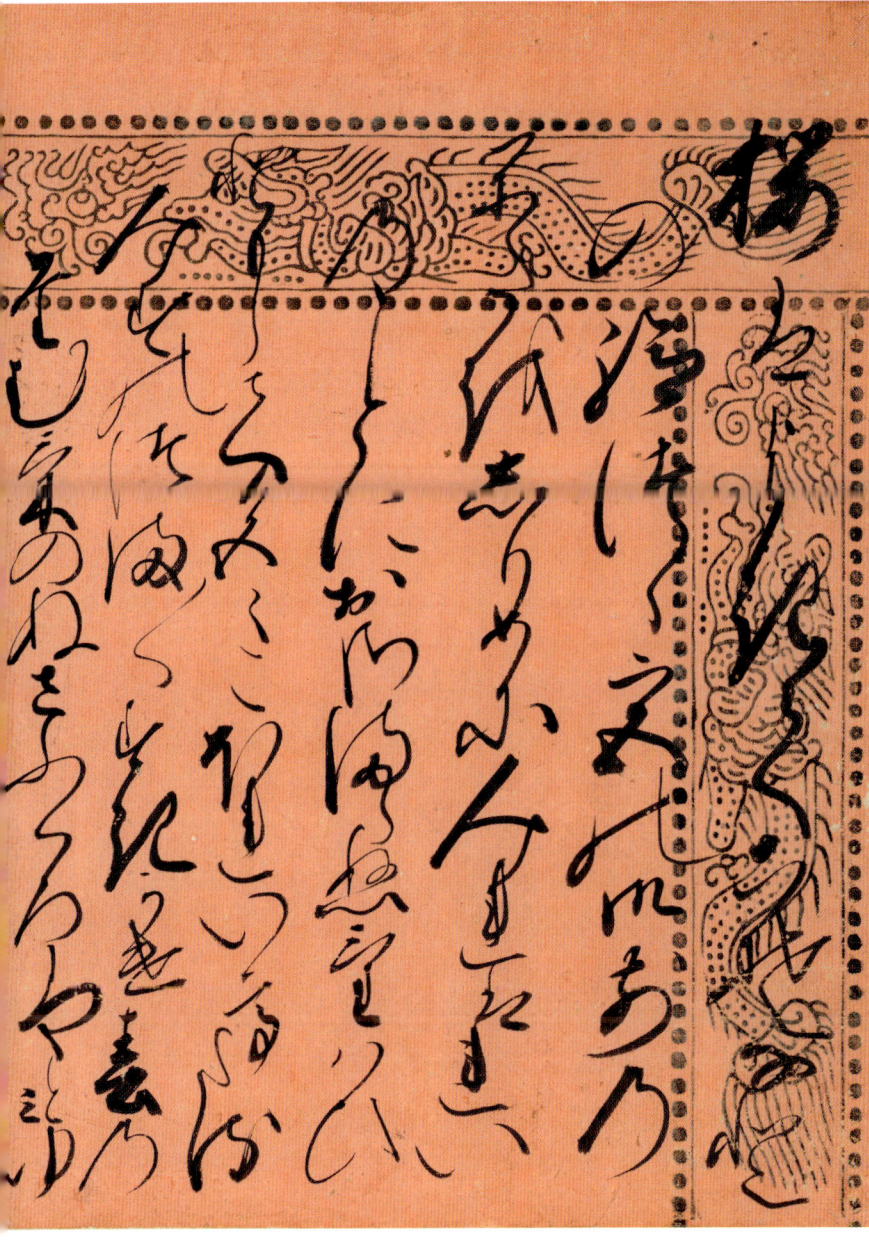

"Sakura wa yokite koso" nado notamaitsutsu, Miya no omae no kata o shirime ni mireba, rei no, koto ni osamaranu kewaidomo shite, iroiro kobore idetaru misu no tsumazuma sukikage, haru no tamuke no nusabukuro ni ya to miyu.

桜はよきてこそなど
の給ひつゝ宮の御前
のかたをしりめにみれはれい
のことにおさまらぬけはひ
ともして色々こほれいて
たるみすのつまく〉すきかけ春の
たむけのぬさふくろにやと
みゆ

The chapters *Early Spring Greens* Parts One and Two together cover several years, their titles referring to the green plants offered at celebrations commemorating Genji's fortieth year (Chapter Thirty-Four), and his half brother, the Retired Emperor Suzaku's fiftieth year (Chapter Thirty-Five). Genji's daughter and Retired Emperor Suzaku's daughter, sponsors of the celebrations, present the spring greens, symbolizing youthful vitality, to each man. Father-daughter issues are the central theme of both chapters, beginning in Chapter Thirty-Four with Emperor Suzaku's concerns over the future of his youngest and favorite daughter, the Third Princess, age fourteen. With a temple under construction and plans to take Buddhist vows and withdraw from the world, Suzaku frets over the young girl's marriage. Several potential husbands are considered and rejected: Genji's son Yūgiri (already married to the Chancellor's daughter), Kashiwagi (not yet of high enough rank), and Prince Sochinomiya (deemed too fickle). Suzaku finally decides on Genji himself, despite the substantial age difference and the complicated personal history between the two men. At first Genji seems disinclined to accept the proposal, but when he remembers a familial connection between the mother of the Third Princess and the late Fujitsubo (both were daughters of the emperor who reigned before Genji's father), he is intrigued. Only after accepting the proposal does he realize the devastating effect the new marriage will have on Murasaki, who had long feared being replaced by a woman of higher social status. The Third Princess soon moves into the Rokujō Estate with all the pageantry befitting a princess and becomes Genji's official principal wife. She also usurps Murasaki's position as mistress of the spring quarter by taking over the southeastern residence, occupying the western half of the main hall and the western wing, while Murasaki is moved into the eastern wing. The harmony that had once characterized the Rokujōin is in jeopardy, but Murasaki refuses to display any signs of jealousy, only acting supportive, even during the new couple's three nights of wedding festivities. Genji is soon disappointed in his new bride, finding her not only immature but also lacking in judgment and talent. The Third Princess is consistently described as childish, and her carelessness is blamed for the fateful event depicted in the album painting for Chapter Thirty-Four— Kashiwagi's surreptitious observation of the Princess.

The *kaimami* scene takes place on a bright spring day amid blooming cherry blossoms, when a number of courtiers join Genji's son Yūgiri at Rokujō for a game of *kemari* football, in the northeastern quarter. Genji hears of the young men's activity and insists that they bring the game to the southeast residence where he can watch. Although they are both of a rank that usually precludes joining in such rollicking, Kashiwagi and Yūgiri take part, and as the game grows more intense the players move to the south garden of the residence. Although the tale describes Yūgiri and Kashiwagi breaking off the branch of a cherry tree and taking a seat on

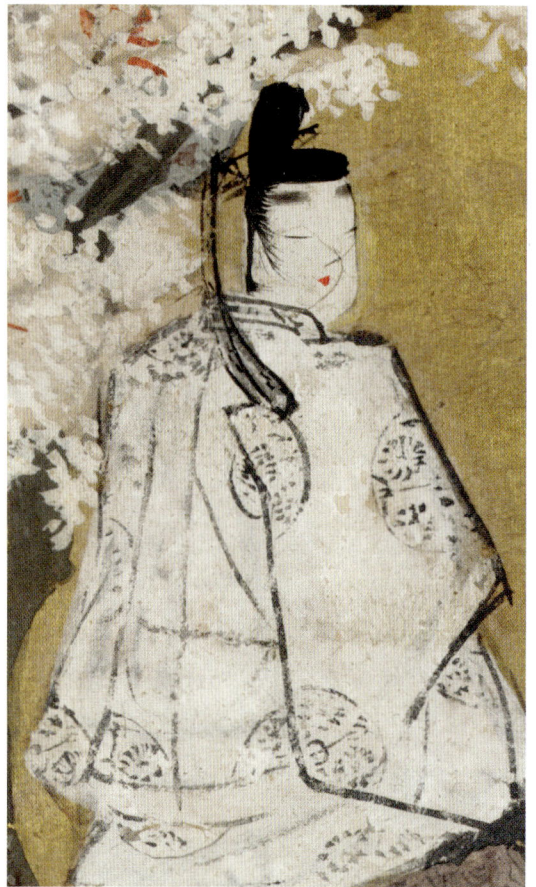

158 | *The Tale of Genji*

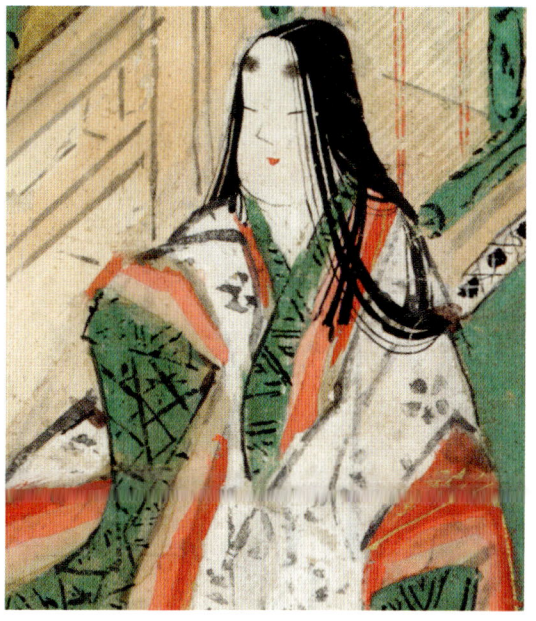

the stairs to the veranda, the album painting shows all the men still in the middle of play, attending to the ball suspended in the air. As Kashiwagi turns his head to gaze at the women's sleeves poking out from beneath the blinds, suddenly one of the panels floats upward, revealing the women's rooms on the other side. A kitten is to blame, lifting the blind as it dashes out to the veranda fleeing a larger cat (which is not depicted in the painting). The kitten's long red leash, said to have been tangled in the blinds, leads directly to the Third Princess, who stands in the gap left open. In the album painting, both the cat and the Princess look toward Kashiwagi, the one courtier in the group looking at them directly. Kashiwagi realizes that the woman in the interior must be the Princess, as she stands out in the casualness of her dress: a long white outer robe of patterned silk in the cherry blossom style, over multicolored robes. As in other examples of *kaimami*, it is when the woman makes an interesting facial expression that the voyeur becomes truly moved, and here Kashiwagi is said to be touched by her expression when she hears the cat mewing in discomfort, still caught in the cords.

The Chinese cat (*kara neko*) is untamed, and prone to trouble, and it becomes a metaphor for the Third Princess, who is characterized by similar qualities. The painting depicts the young woman in a standing pose, which tends to signal an unruly woman, as it did in the case of the ash-dumping wife of Higekuro in Chapter Thirty-One. The cat breaks free from the blinds and Kashiwagi picks it up. He smells the young woman's perfume permeating its fur and fantasizes that he is caressing the Princess as it purrs pleasantly, beginning a strange attachment between him and the feline. The composition of the painting allows the viewer to see inside and outside at once, positioning the principal figures so that they are engaged in a mutual face-to-face encounter. The woman, and the cat for that matter, look directly at the young man, connoting Kashiwagi's belief that their relationship was somehow meant to be. From this point on, Kashiwagi becomes obsessed with the Princess and begins justifying to himself his desire for Genji's wife while regularly entreating her lady-in-waiting Kojijū to arrange a meeting. He will eventually find a way into her chambers in Genji's absence and force himself on the Princess in the next chapter. Before these events, however, he bides his time and contrives to take possession of the cat; he has it brought to the palace for the Crown Prince to admire and then leaves with it himself. He keeps it as a memento of the Princess and willfully refuses to return it when requested. It even appears in Kashiwagi's dreams, the meaning of which he will not be able to decipher until several other tragic events unfold.

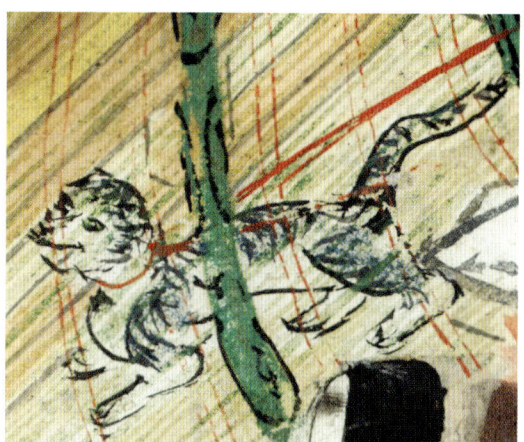

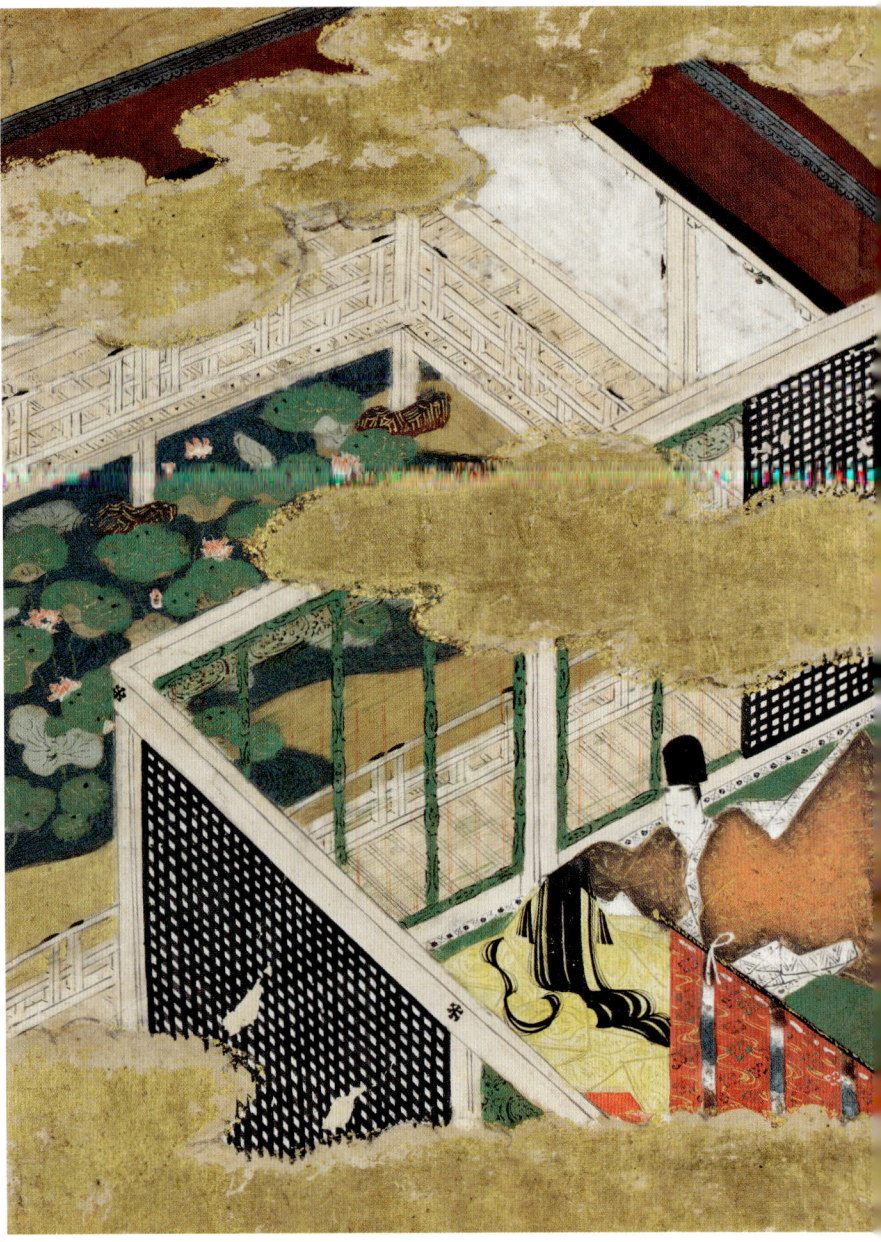

Before the dew dries
That has clung to the lotus—
　O fragile fortune—
Surely it would be foolish
To think I shall not be gone,

Murasaki said.

Bind we by an oath:
Let us be as two dewdrops
　On one lotus leaf;
Do not let us be apart,
Dear heart, though not in this world.

CRANSTON, P. 870

35

若菜下

Early Spring Greens: Part Two

Wakana ge

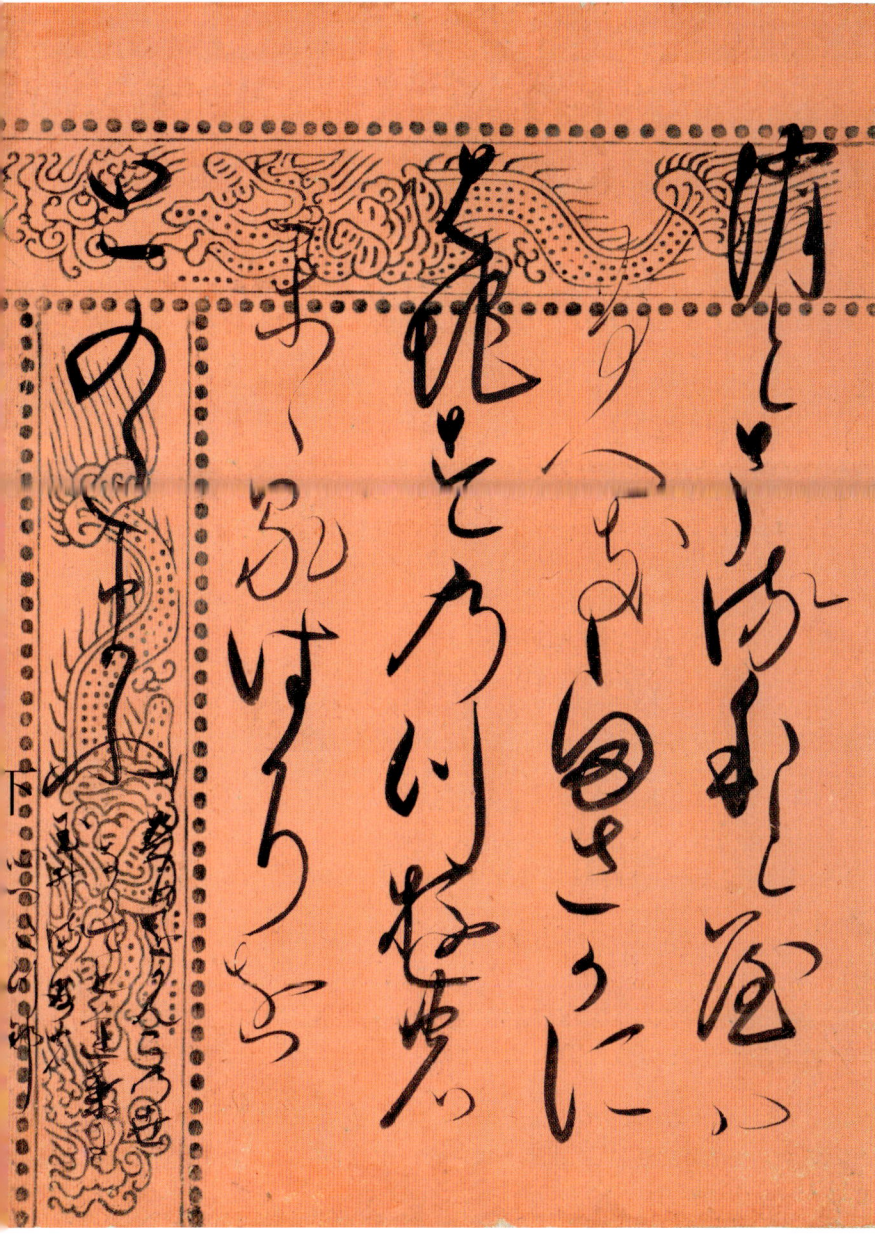

Kietomaru
Hodo ya wa fubeki
Tamasaka ni
Hachisu no tsuyu no
Kakaru bakari o

to notamau.

Chigiriokan
Kono yo narade mo
Hachisuba ni
Tama iru tsuyu no
Kokoro hedatsu na

消とまるほとやは
ふへきたまさかに
はちすのつゆの
かゝるはかりを
とのたまふ

契りをかんこの世
ならても蓮葉に
玉ゐるつゆの
心へたつな

The setting is the Nijō villa, where Murasaki first lived with Genji and which she still considers her true home. Genji has moved her there, away from Rokujō, to care for her during a sudden and severe illness. In the scene depicted in the album, she has improved just slightly after several months of precarious health, battling fevers and seizures, even a cessation of breathing that led to premature rumors of her passing. The onset of Murasaki's illness occurs midway in Chapter Thirty-Five, after she has played her role in one of the tale's most important subplots: the rise of the Akashi house. The Akashi girl, now an Imperial Consort, has given birth to a son who has been appointed Crown Prince, the first of many royal offspring to come. As her foster mother, Murasaki occupies a position of honor when the Akashi women and Genji perform a pilgrimage to the Sumiyoshi Shrine. In doing so, they fulfill a sacred vow made by the Akashi Novitiate, whose portentous dream in which he grasped in his hand Mount Sumeru, the axis mundi of the Buddhist cosmos, has seemingly come to fruition. Murasaki is still well enough to perform at another event that occurs in Chapter Thirty-Five, a musical concert at Rokujō—a rehearsal for Emperor Suzaku's fiftieth-year celebration. Four of Genji's women play together in harmony: Murasaki on the six-string *koto*, the Akashi Lady on the *biwa*, the Akashi Consort on the thirteen-string *koto*, and the Third Princess on the seven-string *koto*. In a postconcert conversation with Murasaki about the various women in his life, echoing the scene in the Asagao chapter, Genji makes the mistake of invoking the deceased Rokujō Lady in less than flattering terms. Murasaki's fever then quickly returns, and her illness intensifies, prompting Genji to commission Buddhist rites and prayers, and exorcisms. Finally, in a chilling scene, a possessing spirit moves into the body of a page girl at Murasaki's bedside and reveals herself as Lady Rokujō, now suffering the torments of the afterworld. She pleads for Buddhist prayers to be said on her behalf, and Genji complies, ordering a full reading of the *Lotus Sutra* by the capital's most skillful orator-priests. During the sixth month, the height of summer, Murasaki finally begins to improve.

In the painting, Genji faces toward the viewer while looking directly at Murasaki; he is positioned at an angle slightly above her, wearing an informal hat and a russet-colored robe with a phoenix pattern in gold, seen before in the leaf for Chapter Twenty, another tableau of domestic intimacy between the two. As in the previous painting, Genji gazes at her with great affection. Here, however, her back is turned toward the viewer, appropriately, given the emphasis on her hair in this passage in the tale, where it is described as just washed, lustrous, and perfectly combed as it spreads out behind her to dry. The painting represents her black hair falling in undulating waves down the back of her bright yellow robe, in long striations, with slight parts between strands, and shorter sidelocks that fan over her shoulders. The hair defines Murasaki's beauty, as does her porcelain pale skin and her figure, described in the tale as especially delicate and frail from illness. Murasaki has already requested multiple times Genji's permission to become a Buddhist nun, an act that entails cutting the beautiful locks seen in the painting. Genji finally agrees, but only to a partial tonsure. A small portion of her hair is cut from the top of her head, and she is administered the "five precepts" rather than the full ten. Genji's acquiescence results from his frightening vision of Rokujō's spirit; no longer the "living spirit" that attacked his wife Aoi, the one he encounters this time is hideous in death. His reaction mimics

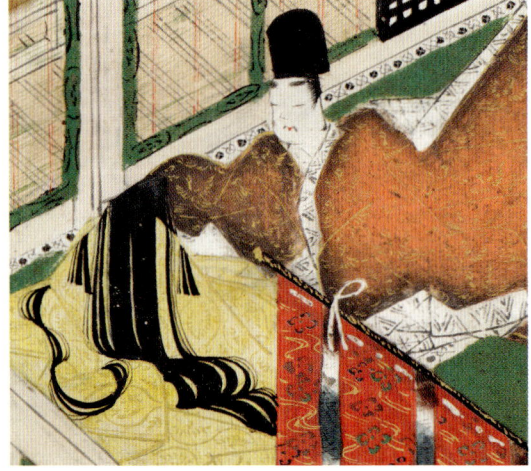

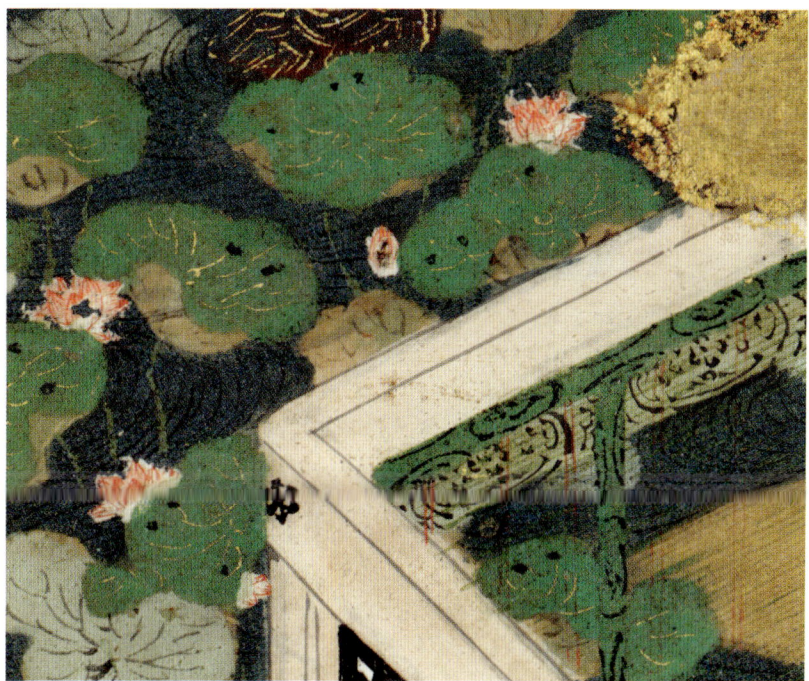

the Buddhist practice of meditating on a decaying corpse, used by monks and layman as a means to spur an awareness of the illusive nature of reality. Genji mentions the sin and contamination of the female body (*onna no mi wa mina onaji tsumi fukaki*), declares that sex between men and women is repugnant, and then allows Murasaki to take Buddhist vows. As though taking Genji with her on a path toward contemplation of the afterlife, they both call the Buddha's name together "with one heart" and commission the recitation of the entire *Lotus Sutra*.

The album painting depicts a moment of peacefulness after Murasaki has received the precepts, while the calligraphy records the poems exchanged by the couple as they sit near the cool garden pond with its abundant summer lotus flowers. Murasaki initiates the poetic exchange, with a poem that expresses her acceptance of a short life, which she likens to the fragile dew on the lotus leaf. In his verse, Genji resists the idea of their separation, using the trope of two dew drops on the same lotus to pledge an eternal vow of love. The lotus, which emerges from murky waters to reveal exquisite blossoms, is the most sacred plant in Buddhism.

Its use in this scene is perfectly in keeping with the tale's overall language of flowers, and the floral metaphors of Buddhist literature. Genji's poem and the composition of the painting also evoke images of pious believers being reborn by emerging from lotus flowers before the Buddha in paradise. The lotus plants in the painting teem with life. The pink flowers, outlined and tipped in darker red, include both blossoms about to open fully and closed pink buds. Thin black lines represent ripples in the water, and as they are painted over the green stems of the plants, give viewers the sensation that they are looking at stems beneath the water's surface. The curling edges of the lotus leaves in different shades of dark and light green allow us to see both surfaces and undersides of the plants, while delicate lines of gold limn the veins of the broad leaves, suggesting an otherworldly constitution. Even the gems of dew (*tama iru tsuyu*) glistening on the lotus leaves in Genji's poem are included, rendered by tiny dots of silver, now oxidized, that would have made the pond sparkle, evoking the jeweled, gilt atmosphere of paradise imagined and articulated in Buddhist sutras.

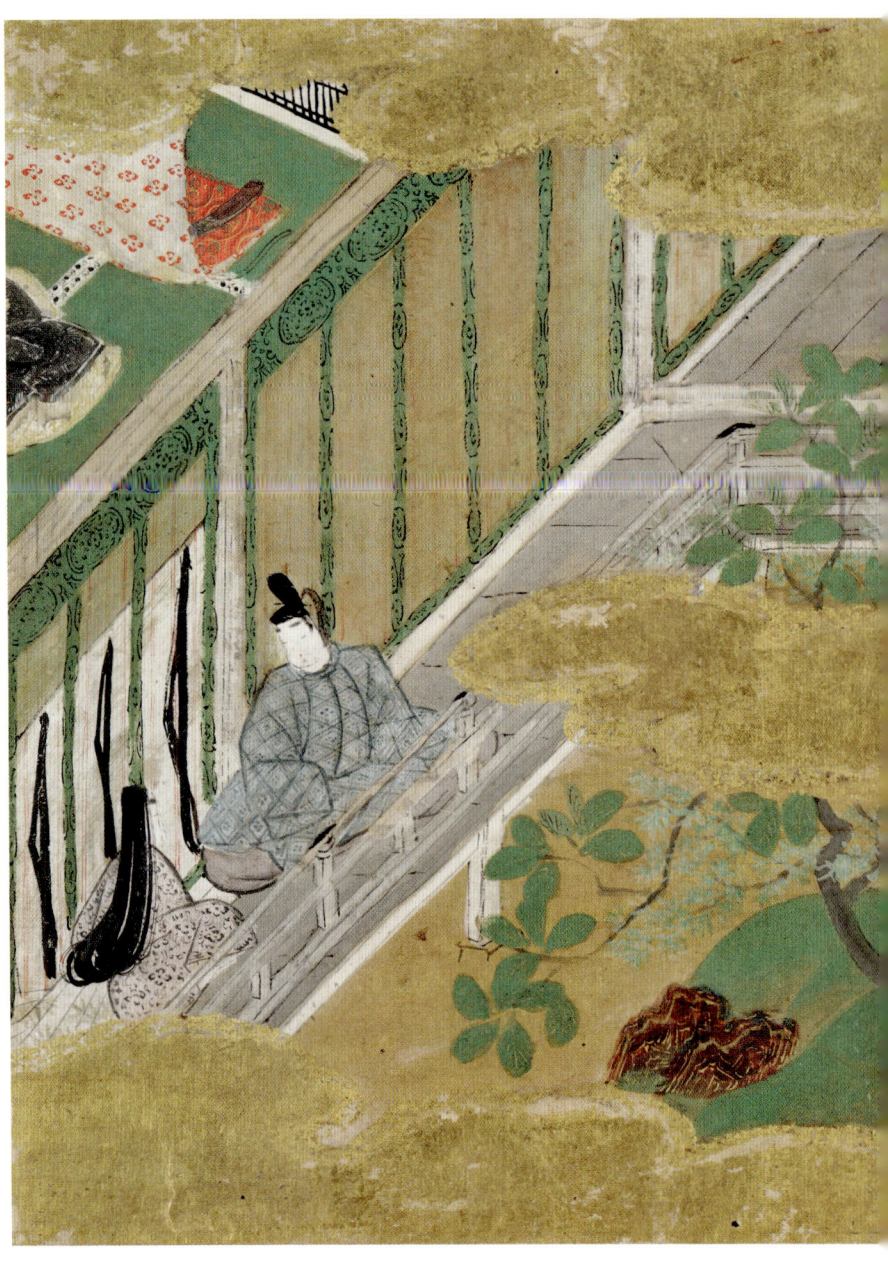

    Though in the oak tree
The god the guardian of leaves
      No longer dwells,
Do its branches trail so low
That strangers may find rest thereon?

CRANSTON, P. 875

36

柏木
The Oak Tree
Kashiwagi

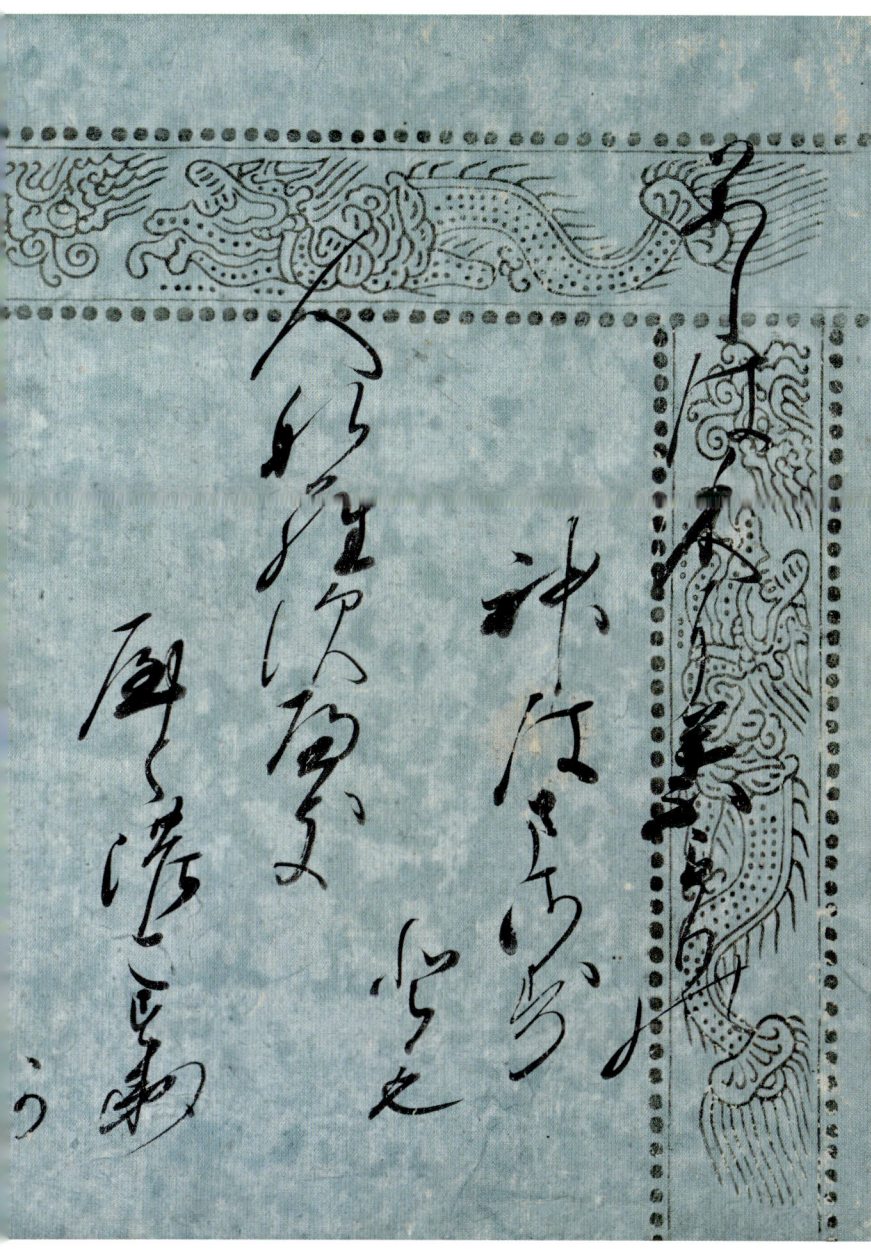

Kashiwagi ni
Hamori no kami wa
Masazu to mo
Hito narasubeki
Yado no kozue ka

かしは木に葉もりの
　神はまさす
　　とも
人ならすへき
　やとのこすゑ
　　か

At the start of Chapter Thirty-Six, both Kashiwagi and the Third Princess are tormented by feelings of guilt over their transgression against Genji: in the previous chapter, while Genji cared for Murasaki at Nijō, Kashiwagi, abetted by Kojijū, finally slept with the Third Princess. Not only is the Third Princess now carrying Kashiwagi's child (a pregnancy foretold by Kashiwagi's dream of a cat), but it has also become clear to both of them that Genji knows of the affair. Kashiwagi's health deteriorates as a result of his guilt, shame, and continued longing for the Princess. Despite the prayers commissioned by his father, Tō no Chūjō, Kashiwagi succumbs to his illness soon after hearing that the Third Princess has safely delivered a son. The Third Princess insists on becoming a nun, and her father, Retired Emperor Suzaku, having taken vows himself, administers the rites.

Before Kashiwagi passes away, he requests two favors from his friend and brother-in-law, Yūgiri: to convey his remorse to Genji (for a sin Yūgiri does not understand), and to look after his official wife, the Retired Emperor Suzaku's other daughter, the Second Princess, a character known as Ochiba. The album painting depicts Yūgiri seated on the veranda of the villa at Ichijō Avenue where the Second Princess lives with her mother. It is late spring, and Yūgiri has already visited several times since Kashiwagi's death. Ochiba's mother, a lower ranking consort of the Retired Emperor, ever mindful of her daughter's status as an imperial princess, opposed the marriage to Kashiwagi, a commoner. For his part, Kashiwagi only married Ochiba because he failed to win her half sister, the Third Princess, before she was wed to Genji. The marriage was thus not an ideal one for either party, but the young widow and her mother still mourn him as they attempt to recover from the unexpected turn of events. Yūgiri's attentions are not unwelcome, especially given the Major Counselor's stature, but the Princess's mother remains vigilant and keeps Yūgiri at a distance, on this occasion restricting him to the veranda, where he must communicate through an intermediary.

Until the scene depicted in the album painting, Yūgiri had only spoken with Ochiba's mother, but the sight of two trees in the garden, an oak (*kashiwa*) and a maple (*kaede*), with intertwined branches, inspires him to send a poem to the Princess:

Koto naraba	Pray let it please you
Narashi no eda ni	That these branches rest amidst
Narasanamu	Those welcoming boughs,
Hamori no kami no	Remembering his consent who was
Yurushi ariki to	The god the guardian of leaves.

This fencing me off outside your blinds—I do find cause for resentment.

CRANSTON, P. 875

Yūgiri uses the image of intertwining branches to suggest that he take the place of Ochiba's husband, and that she, like the bright green leaves, emerge from the somber colors of mourning. He makes his case by saying that the "deity who guards the leaves" (*hamori no kami*), a homonym for the title that her husband held, has given his consent.

Ochiba responds to Yūgiri with the poem included in the album leaf, which is spoken to him by the lady-in-waiting Shōshō no kimi, who faces him on the veranda. The white pleated apron trailing behind her signals her status as a serving woman. Yūgiri is seated cross-legged with his back to the outer post of the building, as described in the tale. The blinds have been partially raised in one bay of the building, but a white curtain blocks Yūgiri's view of the interior. Inside the residence, Ochiba sits near a vibrantly patterned red and white standing curtain, which is out of keeping with the funereal atmosphere described in the tale. She is represented by a mere corner of her dark gray mourning robe, and a single curl of long hair. Such partial images of female characters appear elsewhere in the album in ways that reflect the meaning of a scene (Chapters Eight and Ten). Here, the minimal representation of Ochiba through a mere sliver of her robe reflects her guardedness and hesitation to meet with Yūgiri, the man waiting for her. It also complements the way the painting stages the ventriloquism of the poem's delivery; the Princess is nearly absent, while the female attendant acts as her proxy reciting the verse to Yūgiri on her mistress's behalf. In the

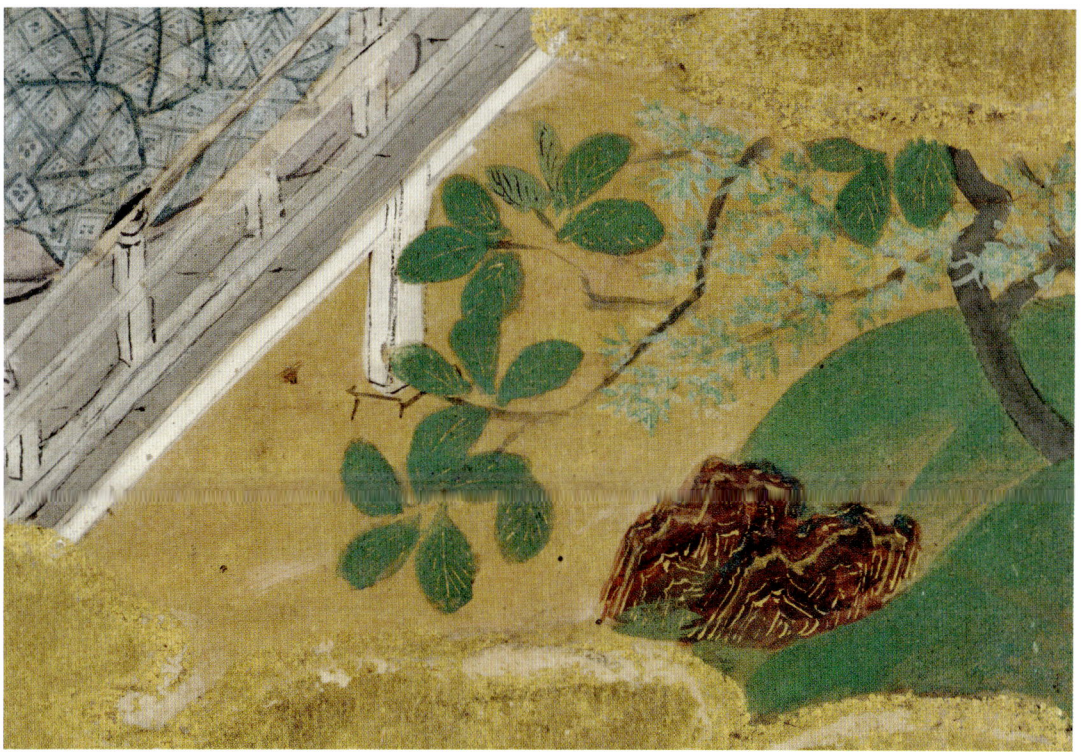

poem, Ochiba uses the word *kashiwagi* (oak tree), which gives her deceased husband his name, and the chapter its title, to assert that the "deity of the leaves" (Kashiwagi) does not grant his consent to the relationship Yūgiri desires. She refuses to be the "welcoming branches" (*narashi no eda*) of Yūgiri's poem, instead asking rhetorically whether "branch tips" (*kozue*) should shelter a stranger.

In the painting, the oak tree dominates the right side of the composition, with its slender but sturdy trunk and its broad leaves, the veins of which are outlined in gold pigment. The image of the oak tree announces the title of the chapter and the importance of the character of Kashiwagi, as both the individual being mourned over in the household and as the link between Yūgiri and Ochiba. The branches of oak and maple trees are interwoven, as in the poetry, but they are not equally represented. The maple leaves are faint in comparison, rendered in a lighter shade of green, with branches overlaying those of the oak in a tentative manner. The image of the trees pictorializes the metaphors in the poems, suggesting that the maple (the Second Princess) still clings to the oak tree.

Chapter Thirty-Six is part of a subplot within the larger story that essentially tells the tale of two sisters: the Second Princess (Ochiba), married to Kashiwagi, and the Third Princess, ravaged by him. Neither sister fares well after their father takes Buddhist vows and retires from the world. The naive Third Princess, with no female relatives to rely on at Rokujō, is manipulated by her soubrettish attendant Kojijū, who flirted with Kashiwagi and granted him access to her lady's chambers. In Chapter Thirty-Six, the Second Princess, with her mother as a bulwark, and her attendants largely under control, manages to keep Yūgiri, sent by Kashiwagi, temporarily at bay. From the Retired Emperor Suzaku's point of view, however, both of his daughters' lives have taken a tragic turn, with one woman having become a nun and the other widowed by Kashiwagi, protected only by her mother and thus susceptible to rumor and scandal no matter how well she comports herself.

Chapter 36 | The Oak Tree | 167

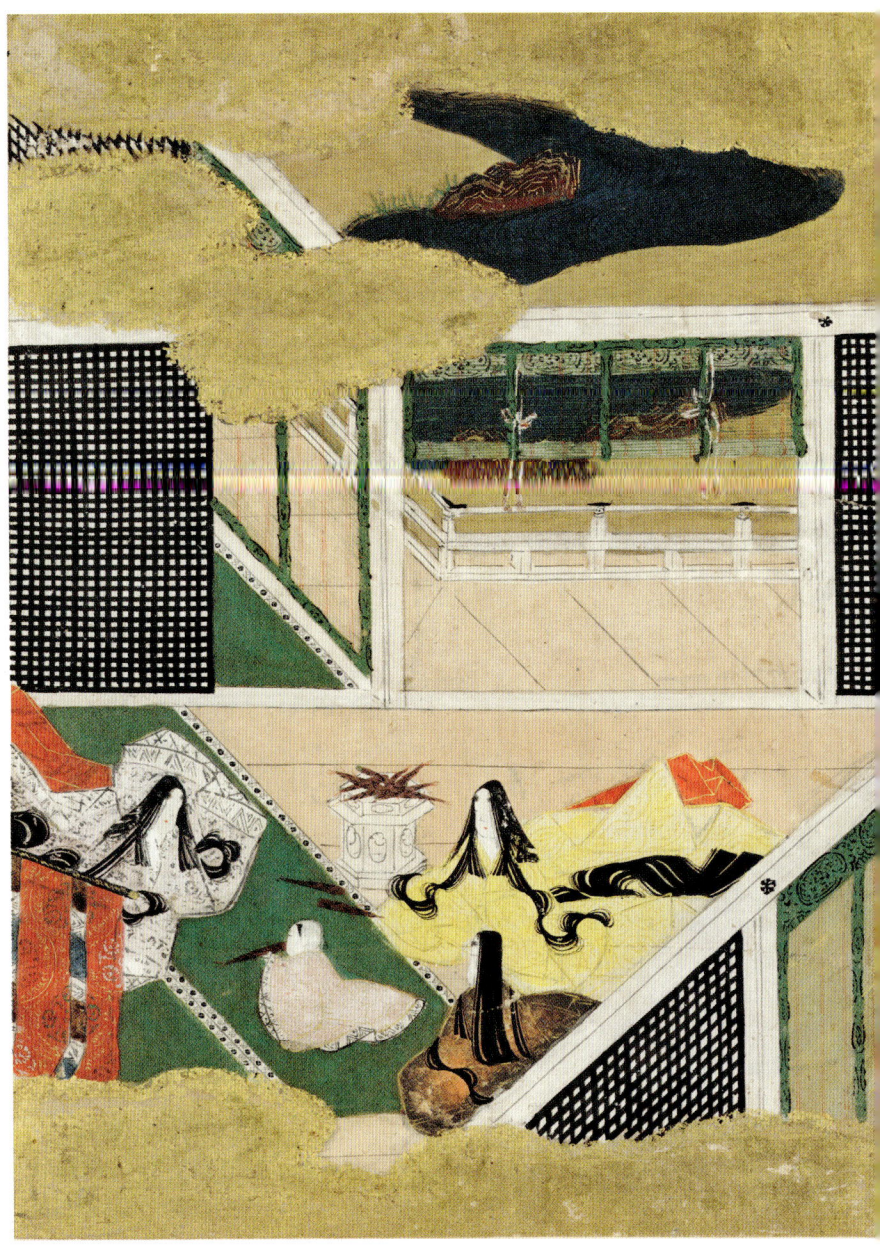

    I've not forgotten
That painful segment of our life,
    But the black bamboo
Grows this time in a tender shoot
I should find it hard to cast aside.

CRANSTON, P. 876

37

横笛
The Transverse Flute
Yokobue

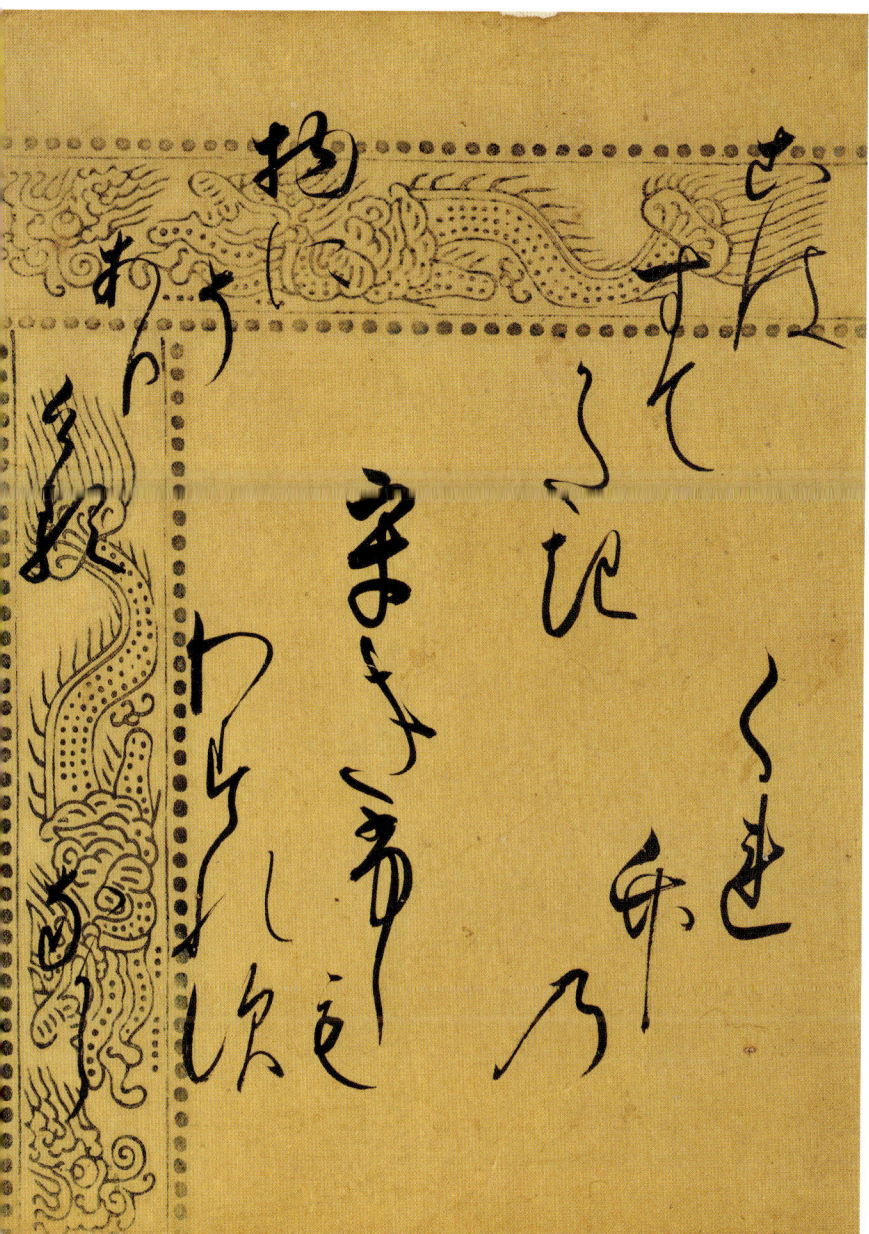

Ukifushi mo
Wasurezu nagara
Kuretake no
Ko wa sutegataki
Mono ni zo arikeru

こは
すて
かたき
物に そ
 ありわすれす
 けるなから
くれ
竹
の
うきふしも

Genji is absent from the painting for Chapter Thirty-Seven, but the scene in the tale is narrated from his perspective and his words appear in the adjacent calligraphy in the album. He converses with the Third Princess, who as a Buddhist initiate is off limits to her husband Genji sexually, but who at Genji's insistence still resides at the Rokujō Estate. On entering the Third Princess's room, Genji is surprised to see an unusual tray of bamboo shoots. It is a gift from her father, Retired Emperor Suzaku, now referred to in the original text as "the mountain emperor" (*yama no mikado*) after his current abode at a temple in the western hills. The Third Princess is referred to as the "Princess Initiate" (*nyūdo no miya*), which resonates with the epithet now applied to her father, though by looking only at the painting, it would be difficult to identify her as such. She is the only female figure seated on the green tatami, with a curtain to her side, and her hair shows no sign of tonsure. This follows the description in the previous chapter of her hair as only minimally cut and looking much as it did before taking vows. Her robes, pale pink over white, are somewhat subdued compared to the garments of the two female attendants in the room. Suzaku's gift is a show of sympathy, and his poem refers to their mutual pursuit of the Buddhist path. The bamboo shoots and taro roots were taken from the forest beside his mountain abode and are intended to symbolize the eremitic lifestyle that he imagines she desires as well.

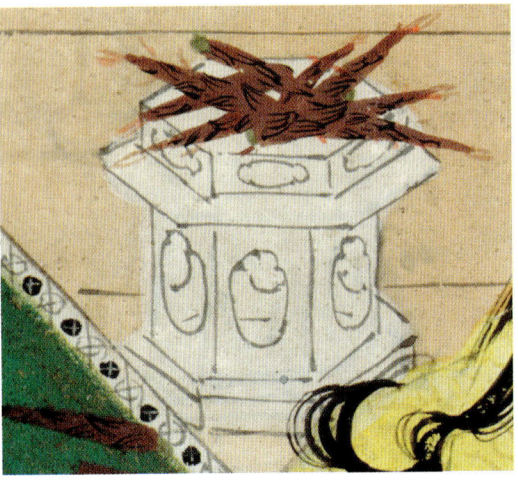

Suzaku's poem, and one that his daughter writes in response, both use coded language to suggest that a departure from Rokujō might be best in order to pursue her Buddhist devotions in earnest—a suggestion that annoys Genji when he discovers the exchange.

In crawls the son of the Third Princess and Kashiwagi, the character who later becomes known as Kaoru, thought by the world to be Genji's son. In the tale, the two-year-old boy's appearance and behavior are described in great detail in the mind of Genji, whose attitude toward the boy is at once jovial and fraught with ambivalence given his knowledge of Kashiwagi's betrayal. Genji's mixed feelings are perfectly expressed in the poem included in the album, which begins with the assertion that the Third Princess's infidelity with Kashiwagi will never be forgotten, expressed as that "painful segment" (*ukifushi* 憂き節) in Cranston's skillful rendering, which captures the pun on *fushi*, a word that means "time," but also the "joint" or "segment" of a bamboo stalk. The poem continues, however, with Genji conceding that the bamboo shoot (*kuretake no ko*), in other words the child (*ko*) before him, Kaoru, is too endearing to disavow. Genji expressed the same ambivalence in the previous chapter when he first held the newborn, his feelings for the innocent child mingling with trepidation over the resemblance to Kashiwagi and the possibility that his turn as a cuckold would become known.

Kaoru's physical appearance is described in the tale as having its own special radiance, and his long and supple body as though it had been delicately carved from the pale inner wood of a willow tree. His head, as seen in the painting, is shaved according to the custom for children under the age of three and gives off a bluish tint, the color of "dewflowers" (*tsuyukusa*). The artist uses an underlayer of blue pigment that does indeed make the child's head seem paler than white. Genji marvels at the child's appealing facial features that seem to emanate a warm glow but feels uneasy as he considers the possible dangers that lie ahead as the boy is raised under the same roof as his granddaughter, the First Princess of the Akashi Consort, who has been put in

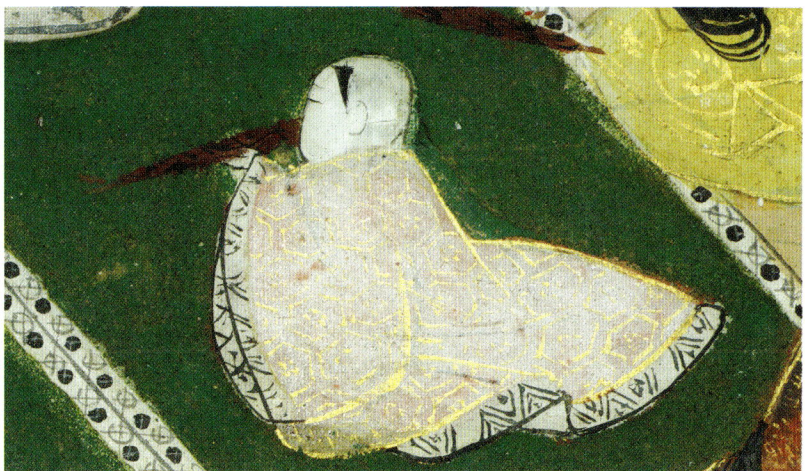

Murasaki's care. Genji succumbs to Kaoru's charming antics as he toddles into the room and makes a beeline for the bamboo shoots, soothing his new teeth and his curiosity by gnawing on one, then immediately discarding it for another. In the painting, Kaoru holds a long, rugged, brown shoot up to his mouth, with two others lying on the tatami mat already tasted and cast aside. He continues to nibble away, his own drool dripping excessively (*shizuku mo yoyo to*), leading Genji to exclaim that the boy has strange "desires," or *irogonomi*. The word is used most often to describe sexual desire, signaling Genji's inability to see him as merely an innocent child rather than the offspring of a father whose desires overcame him. The scene concludes when Genji takes the bamboo away, and the toddler blithely scampers off.

It is difficult to regard the bamboo in Mitsunobu's painting, which is excessively long and horizontally held, as anything but a suggestive allusion to the bamboo flute, the *Yokobue* of the chapter title. As the chapter continues, the mother of Kashiwagi's widow bestows on Yūgiri a transverse flute that once belonged to the deceased courtier. As an instrument that symbolizes patrilineal transmission, the gift is significant and causes the vexed ghost of Kashiwagi to visit Yūgiri in a dream and inform him that the flute was intended for someone else. The ghost appears eerily in the same garb that Kashiwagi wore the last time Yūgiri saw him, as he lay on his sickbed in Chapter Thirty-Six. In the dream, Kashiwagi's ghost picks up the flute and composes:

Fuetake ni	May the wind that blows
Fukiyoru kaze no	In the flute bamboo oblige—
Koto naraba	Be there no other strain—
Sue no yo nagaki	Long years yet I would desire
Ne ni tsutaenamu	These notes passed on through the air.
	CRANSTON, P. 878

In the ghost's poem, because "notes" or "sound" (*ne*) is a homonym for "root," the idea of Kashiwagi's descendants playing the flute into the future shares imagery with the lengthy bamboo, which is perpetuated by means of its root. Phallic connotations are also implied, with the word for "root" (*ne*), a term for genitalia, reflecting the paternity anxiety inherent in the Kashiwagi storyline. And as Cranston states, his use of the word "air" in translation is intended to suggest "heir" to reflect the underlying meaning of the poem. When Yūgiri confronts his father about the dream and the flute's rightful heir, Genji admits nothing but understands the import of the dream. The chapter ends with Genji trying to take possession of the bamboo flute to give to Kaoru, as though reversing his earlier actions of removing the bamboo shoot from Kaoru's hands. Although Genji goes unrepresented in the album painting, his voice in the poem inserts him into the scene and allows him to hover over the spectacle of this illegitimate son with his faux bamboo flute.

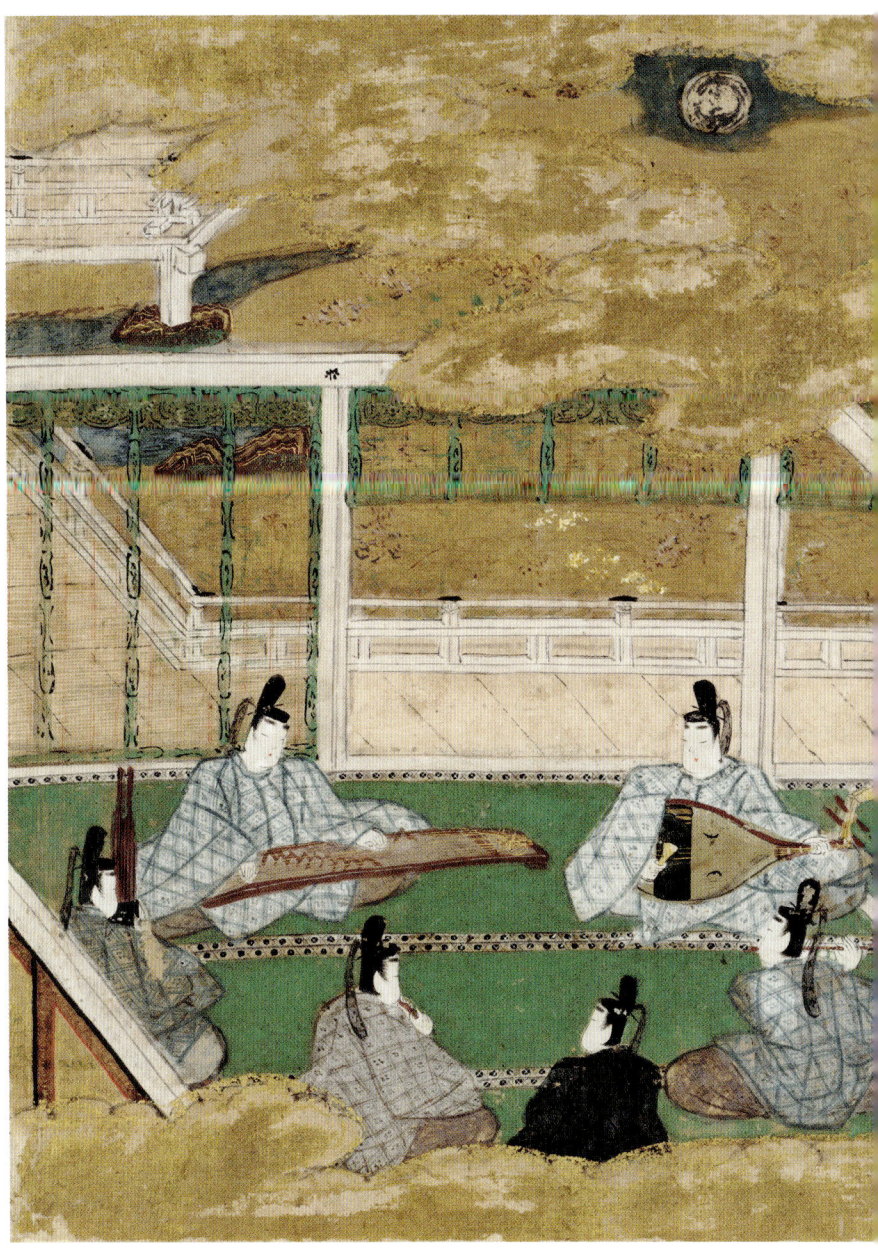

>   Moonlight as ever
> In a cloudland not other
>   Than it was before...
> Yes, the fault lies in my house
> That this autumn is so changed.

CRANSTON, P. 880

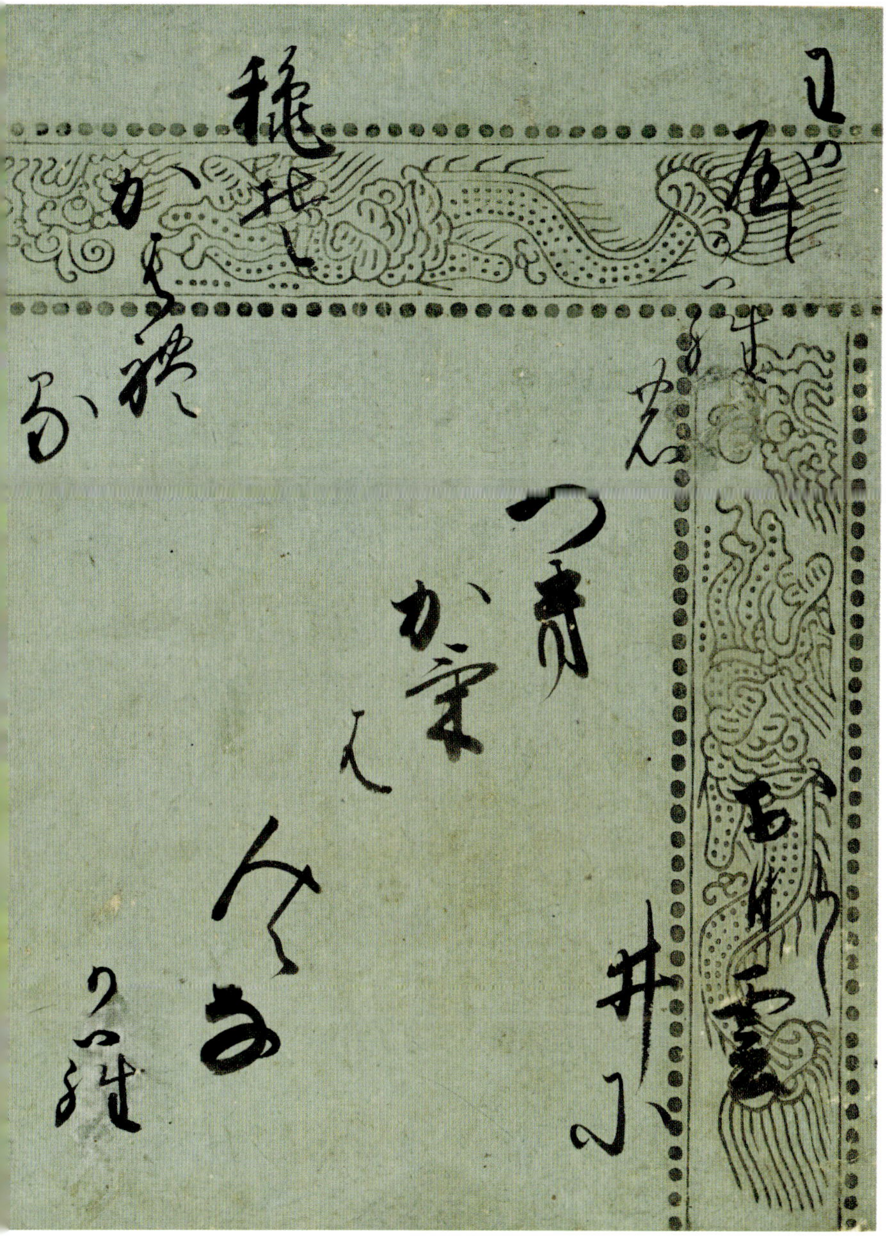

38

鈴虫

Bell Crickets

Suzumushi

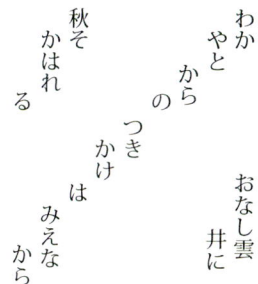

Tsukikage wa
Onaji kumoi ni
Mienagara
Wa ga yado kara no
Aki zo kawareru

The setting, as in the previous leaf, is the quarters of the Third Princess in the southeastern residence at Rokujō, on the fifteenth of the eighth month, the night of the harvest moon. The moon-viewing banquet at the imperial palace is canceled for reasons that go unexplained, and courtiers descend on Genji's villa. They find him playing the thirteen-string *koto* (*sō no koto*), and a musical concert ensues. The courtiers' arrival at Rokujō follows an extended passage in the tale that describes the elaborate Buddhist ceremonies, sutra readings, and dedications that Genji commissioned to transform the Third Princess's residence into a chapel befitting her new status as a nun. He ordered statues of Buddhist deities, paintings, and a shelf for offerings. He even transcribed the *Amida Sutra* himself, so that the Third Princess would always have a copy at her disposal. It took Genji weeks of diligent work to write out the sutra, and his calligraphic transcription is said to be magnificent. Given the power of handwriting in the tale to invoke a person's presence, Genji's transcription of the sacred text ensures that the Third Princess will have him in mind even during her Buddhist practice. That he should wish to remain in her thoughts this way is in keeping with the description of their tension-filled relationship, in which Genji insists on professing his attraction to his young tonsured wife. The elaborate transformation of the Third Princess's quarters justifies keeping her at Rokujō and preempts Suzaku's plan to move his daughter to his Sanjō residence. Genji has created a veritable nunnery in miniature for the Princess, complete with disciple nuns and a renovated spring garden, which before was too ostentatious for a place of meditation on the sorrows of the world. The western half of the spring garden has been fenced off from Murasaki's eastern wing and transformed into a subdued autumn moor. Into the grassy field Genji has introduced bell crickets, which give the chapter its name, and to which he likens the Third Princess, saying that her voice is similarly bright and clear. For her part, the Third Princess seems somewhat less than entirely committed to rigorous meditation on the afterlife; just before the scene depicted, Genji plucks the *koto*, and the Third Princess stops rubbing her prayer beads in order to listen more attentively, drawn to the pleasures of his music. Knowing he has her attention, Genji has welcomed the courtiers from the palace to join him in a concert "to celebrate the bell cricket."

The painting depicts the musical diversion taking place beneath the full moon, with all of the musicians situated in the bottom third of the painting. Through raised bamboo blinds, we see the newly created moor, full of autumn grasses and flowers, which are home to the bell crickets whose chirping

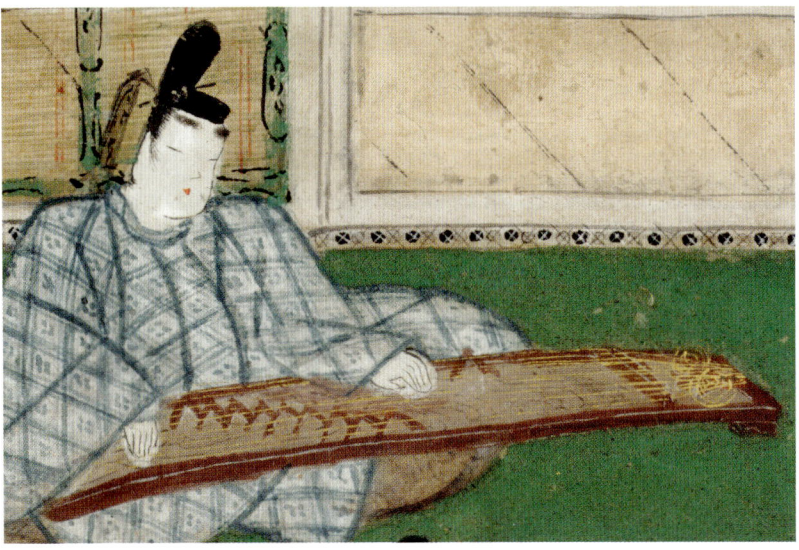

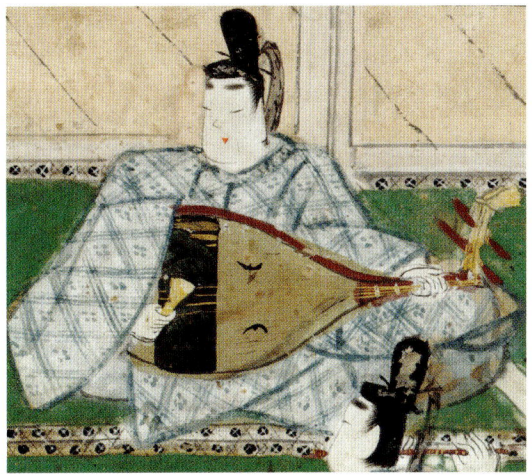

Just as the gathering is at its peak, a message from retired Emperor Reizei arrives with a poem that laments Genji's absence on this moonlit night:

Kumo no ue o	Once above the clouds,
Kakehanaretaru	Now my dwelling is far off,
Sumika ni mo	But even this abode
Monowasure senu	Receives unforgotten the splendor
Aki no yo no tsuki	Of the moon on an autumn night.

CRANSTON, P. 880

It is the third time Reizei has written to his father wishing to be with him. The previous instances were in Chapter Eighteen of the album, where Genji was shown occupied with his men in Katsura, and in Chapter Twenty-Nine, where Genji decides against participating in Reizei's royal excursion. The single poem included in the album's calligraphy for this chapter is Genji's response to the above poem in which he honors Reizei's reign and modestly alludes to his own waning glory, but instead of avoiding an encounter with his son this time, Genji subsequently makes an impromptu visit, taking along with him the musical entourage depicted in the painting.

Only after Genji achieves the status of Retired Emperor (Chapter Thirty-Three) does the narrative describe him visiting his son, the Emperor. To do so beforehand would have necessitated placing Genji in an inferior position. Instead, the one grand imperial visitation in the tale, which takes place in Chapter Thirty-Three, presents Retired Emperor Suzaku and Emperor Reizei paying Genji the highest show of respect by visiting *him* at the Rokujō Estate. When Genji finally does visit Reizei in the scene following the one depicted in this album painting, the visit is marked by informality; the men do not wear formal cloaks, but simply add trains to their regular robes, as if Murasaki Shikibu is wary of presenting Genji, the symbolic Retired Emperor, as beneath his son. The meeting on this moonlit night will in fact be the last one between Genji and Reizei.

is said to mingle with the music. Visible beyond the blinds are the veranda, a walkway, and the adjacent wing of the southeastern residence, perhaps an allusion to the hidden presence of the Third Princess. She is said to be just behind a blind, within earshot of Genji's words and the musical concert put on in her name. Only the *koto* is mentioned in this passage in the tale, but the album leaf depicts a variety of instruments in detail, beginning with the striking *koto* in Genji's lap. It has thirteen golden strings tied and looped at the end, ten wooden bridges, and a pattern to suggest the grain of its paulownia wood. Yūgiri is most likely the figure on the transverse flute (*yokobue*), while one of Tō no Chūjō's sons plays the small oboe (*hichiriki*). On the far left a figure plays the mouth organ (*shō*), consisting of seventeen vertical bamboo pipes, which rounds out the wind instruments. To Genji's left, a figure, most likely his half brother Sochimomiya (Prince Hotaru), strums with his plectrum a four-stringed *biwa* with a painting of a mountain landscape and gold clouds on its front. The inclusion of so many instruments is unique among renditions of this scene, and it complements the emphasis on sound in this short chapter, from the intoning of sutras, to the chirping of crickets, to the courtly music.

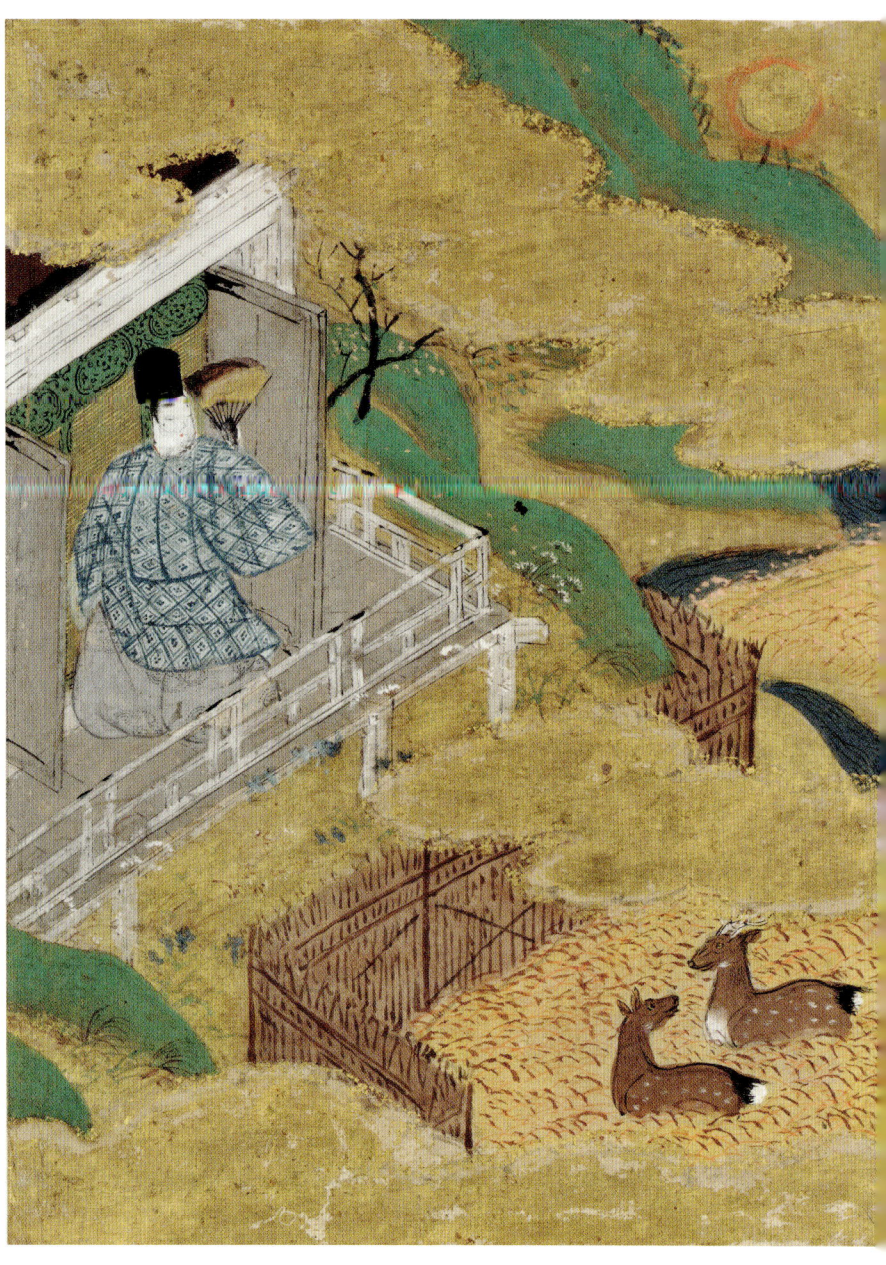

As the cold wintry wind blew, deer were standing stock-still near the brushwood fence and would not scare despite the sharp reports of wooden clappers intended to drive them away from the fields. A stag was belling in a rice field amidst dark golden stalks of grain, calling out plaintively for his mate.

WASHBURN, P. 832, MODIFIED

39

夕霧
Evening Mist
Yūgiri

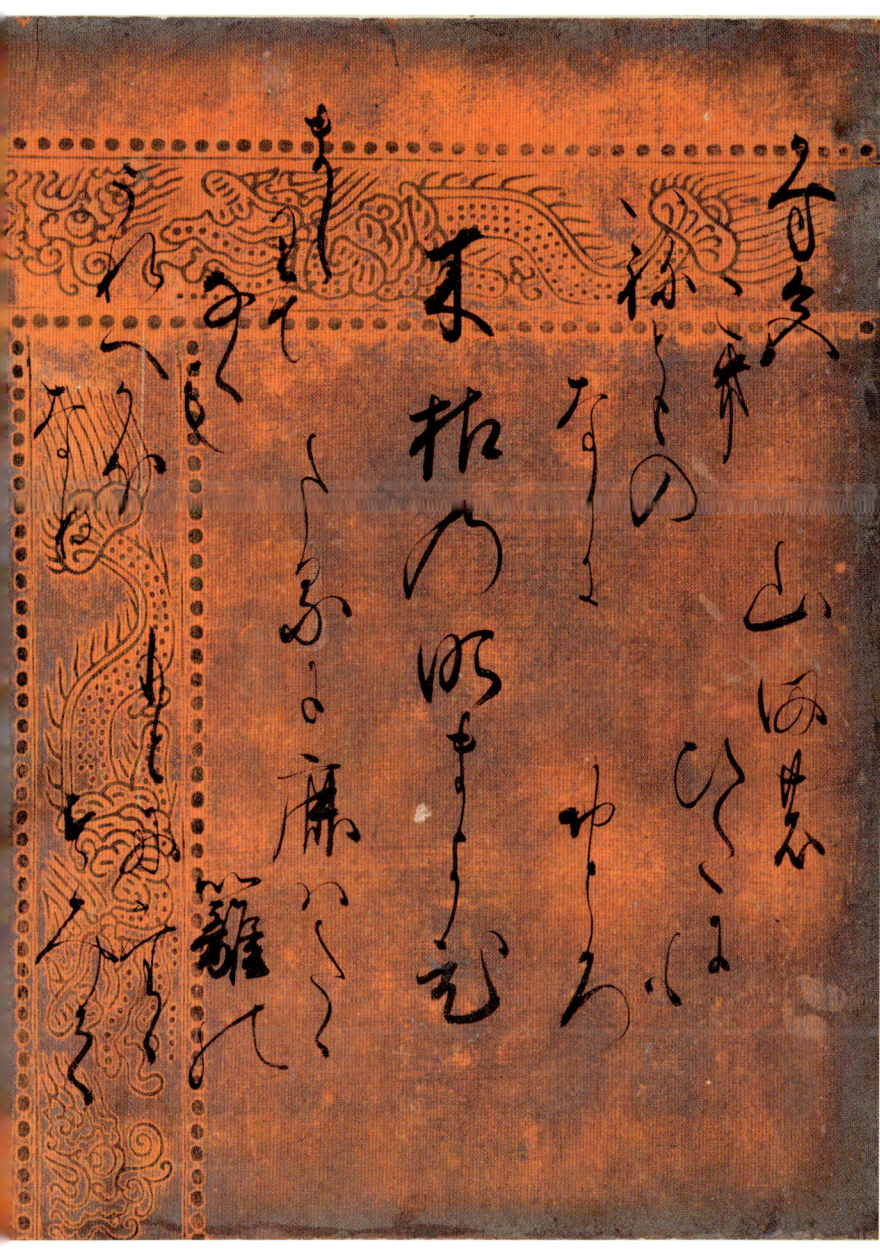

Kogarashi no fukimayoitaru ni, shika wa tada magaki no moto ni tatazumite, yamada no hita ni mo odorokazu, iro koki ine domo no naka ni majirite naku mo urēgao nari.

かす色　山田のひたに
いねともこき
なかにも
まし　木枯の　吹まよひ
りて　たるに鹿はた〵
なく　籬の
うれへかほ　もとにた〽
なり　すみて

Yūgiri's romantic pursuit of Kashiwagi's widow, Ochiba, Suzaku's Second Princess, starts up again in Chapter Thirty-Nine, and the location of action shifts to the village of Ono, where the Princess and her mother are now residing. Ochiba's mother has been suffering from an illness that seems attributable to a malignant spirit and has sought the help of a priest from Mount Hiei to perform healing rites and incantations. The villa at Ono, at the base of the famous mountain, is remote for Yūgiri, but he visits several times in this chapter, providing the pretense for passages dense with descriptions of desolate autumn scenery and allusions to classical poetry. His character's nickname derives from the thick "evening mist" (*yūgiri*) that blankets the Ono foothills, which he uses in this chapter as an excuse to stay the night at the villa and to declare his romantic intentions to Ochiba. Reflecting this allusiveness, the painting in the album is like a primer of autumnal poetic motifs, visualizing several keywords found in the accompanying prose excerpt. The calligraphic text (on red paper that complements the autumn colors) begins with the word for "chilly wind" (*kogarashi*), the wind that rustles through the remaining leaves on the trees, harbinger of the winter to come. The brushwood fence (*magaki*), which zigzags through the center of the image, signals the rusticity of the site and marks the boundary of the rice fields (*ine*) where the deer (*shika*) stand "stock-still." The rice stalks are depicted with a combination of red and brown pigments to delineate the long stems of the grasses and the oblong spikelets containing their grains, all against a yellow ground that lends the entire image a subtle glow. The album text describes the deer as indifferent to the sound of clappers (*hita*), not depicted in the image, but that would have been suspended on strings across the fields and sounded to scare them off. Instead, the stag and doe seem preoccupied, looking "forlorn" (*uregao*) as described in the album excerpt. In a subsequent poem (quoting *Kokinshū* 582 and 505) to Ochiba's lady in waiting, Yūgiri likens himself to the stag, whose call in Heian poetry is a metaphor for the plaintive cries of a lover:

Sato tōmi	Far from the homes of men,
Ono no shinohara	Over the Ono bamboo fields,
Wakete kite	I have made my way,
Ware mo shika koso	For I too, O dear one, thus
Koe mo oshimane	Cannot restrain my call.

CRANSTON, P. 885

By the time of the visit depicted in the painting, Ochiba's mother has passed away and all at the house are grieving, which prompts the attendant to reply on her lady's behalf with a poem about the Princess's deep gray "mourning robes" (*fujig-*

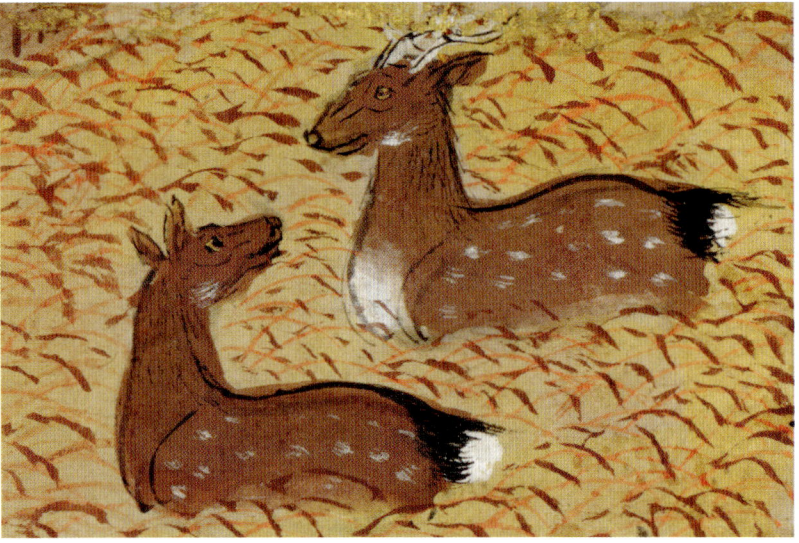

oromo). The word is evocative of the "mistflower" (*fujibakama*), which can be seen in the image growing around the veranda. Also growing at the foot of the house are blue autumn bellflowers, gentians (*rindō*), which were mentioned in Sei Shōnagon's *Pillow Book*, for the way their "brilliant color perseveres when the other flowers have withered in the autumn frost." Besides the cry of the deer, motifs in the album painting help us imagine the other sounds mentioned in the tale, such as the faint chirping of the crickets from beneath the clumps of grass and the roar of a waterfall that pierces the silence, loud enough to "bring anyone lost in sorrowful thoughts back to themselves" (Washburn p. 833).

Standing on the narrow veranda of Ochiba's villa, Yūgiri is conspicuously large as he gazes out over the landscape. The fence and deer are within Yūgiri's field of vision, but their small scale suggests that they stand at some distance from the villa. The landscape representation is not contiguous but structured according to poetic and semantic emphases. The gold clouds, which compartmentalize the composition, provide cover for spatial elisions between the motifs, while the image of the sun helps unify the composition. It is a golden orb outlined in a circle of red pigment to indicate twilight (*yūhi*), which casts a warm glow over the entire golden-toned painting. But while the poignant autumnal atmosphere is presented from Yūgiri's point of view in the painting, the perspective in the tale suddenly shifts to that of the women inside the residence. They watch Yūgiri on the veranda as he nonchalantly raises a fan to his face to shade his eyes from the rays of the setting sun. He gazes in the direction of the sun, moving the fan with a flourish in such a way that it does not hide him but, as in the painting, shows off his face. To the ladies observing inside, the gesture recalls that of a woman coyly attempting to conceal herself. They concede, however, that even a woman may not have executed the gesture so well. The painting thus captures a moment of rare stylishness for the usually stilted Yūgiri, as he strikes a pose, framed by the wooden doors, standing tall in his courtier's costume.

In previous chapters Yūgiri had been characterized as "masculine" (*ooshi*), an adjective also applied to figures like the hirsute Blackbeard, the husband of Tamakazura we met in Chapter Thirty-One. In Yūgiri's case, his identity as a student of Chinese learning and court bureaucracy aligned him with ideas of conventional masculinity, and it distanced him from the gender ideal achieved by his father. Genji's ability to transcend the societal boundaries associated with masculinity and femininity, and to figure in the romantic imaginations of both men and women, set him apart with a spiritually suffused physicality reserved for those in the imperial line. Yūgiri, though admired, and called handsome by many an onlooker, never exuded such gender-ambiguous radiance until now. The characterization reflects Yūgiri's transition to a romantic protagonist in this chapter, in pursuit of a Princess, as Genji prepares to exit the narrative. And yet his attempts to emulate the polygamous behavior of his father rarely succeed, and if they do, result in complications. Playing out simultaneously with his pursuit of Ochiba is an ongoing domestic drama occurring with his primary wife, Kumoinokari. As his love and companion since childhood, daughter of the powerful Tō no Chūjō, and mother to seven of Yūgiri's twelve children, Kumoinokari speaks her mind and rebels against her husband's desire for another wife. To be clear, Yūgiri also has six children by a daughter of Koremitsu, Genji's loyal retainer. But as a woman of lower status, she posed no existential threat to Kumoinokari. In her opposition to Yūgiri's marriage to Ochiba, Kumoinokari offers the most fully articulated objection to polygamy in the tale. Ochiba's own sincere attempts to reject Yūgiri's advances epitomize how the relationships in this chapter are far from any romantic ideal. Even Murasaki makes an appearance and gives voice to the plight of women while in conversation with Genji about Ochiba's difficult situation as a vulnerable widow. By the end of Chapter Thirty-Nine, Yūgiri has relocated Ochiba to the capital, but his relationship with Kumoinokari is on the brink of dissolution. Yūgiri never comfortably occupies the persona of his father and fails to produce the kind of amity between his own wives and lovers that apparently existed between the women at Genji's Rokujō estate.

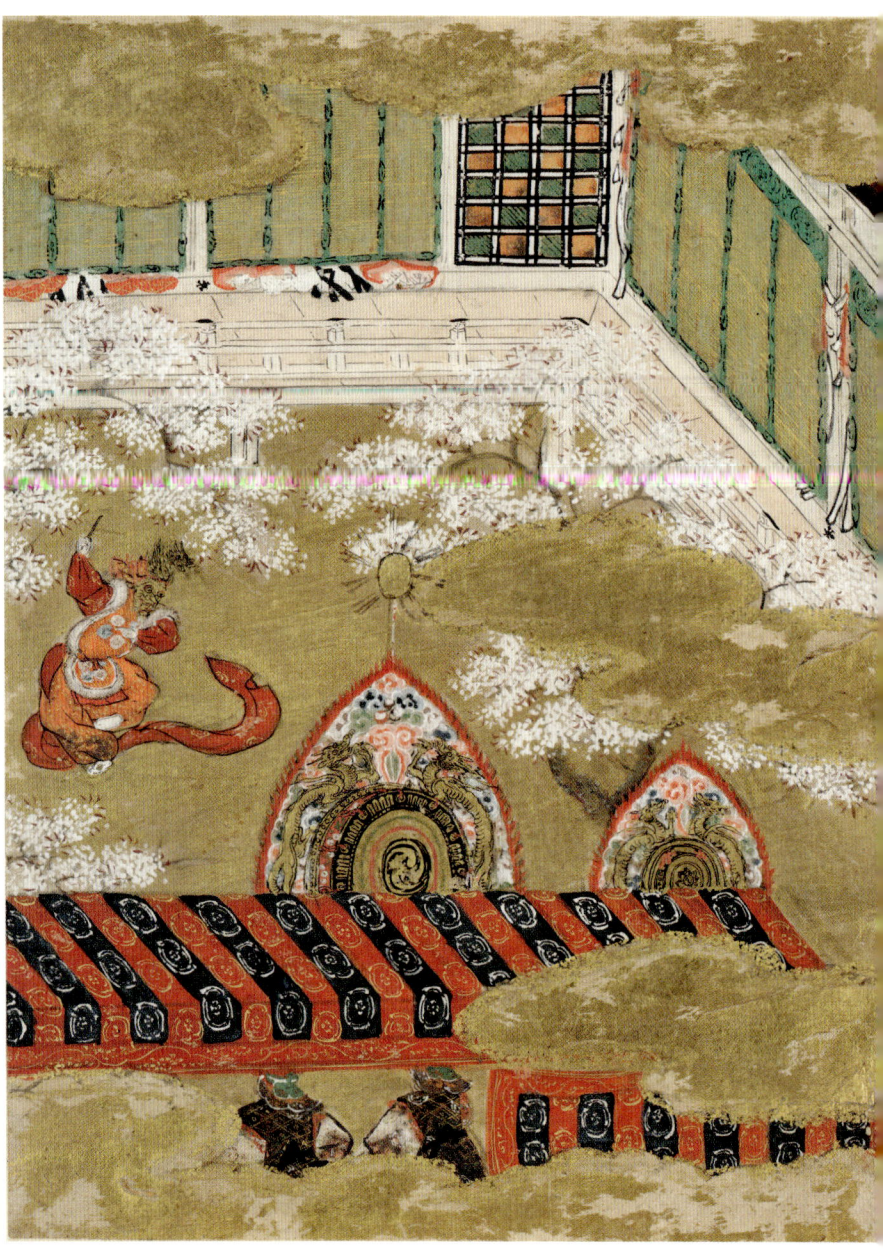

    To cut firewood—
Only today has it begun,
    Your new resolve,
And the Dharma is distant
That we pray for in this world.

CRANSTON, P. 890

40

御法

Rites of the Sacred Law

Minori

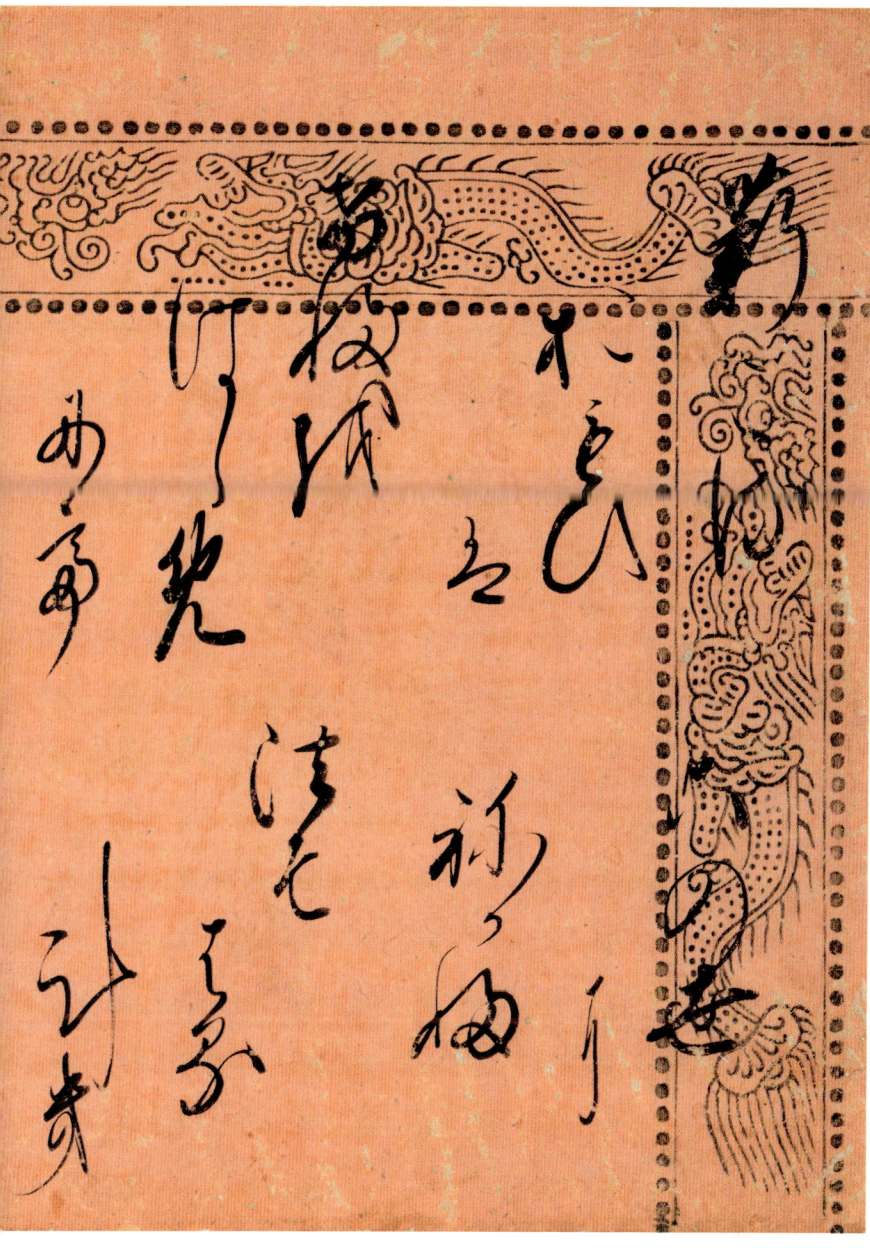

Takigi koru
Omoi wa kyō o
　Hajime nite
Kono yo ni negau
Nori zo harukeki

薪こる
おもひは けふを
　はしめ にて
この世に ねかふ
法そ はるけき

It is spring and the cherry blossoms are at their peak at the start of Chapter Forty, a chapter famous for recounting the death of Lady Murasaki. The setting is the Nijō villa, the residence Murasaki considers to be her true home, and where she was last seen in the album with Genji, gazing on the paradisal lotus blossoms in the garden pond (Chapter Thirty-Five). She narrowly escapes death in that chapter and lives on to raise two of the Akashi daughter's children, but she never fully recovers. Realizing that her illness has advanced and that her life is actually drawing to a close, she asks again to receive the full tonsure of a nun that she has long desired in order to ease her way in the afterlife, but Genji refuses. She takes steps on her own, however, to aid her own salvation, including the sponsorship of an elaborate Buddhist ceremony at Nijō—the dedication of one thousand copies of the *Lotus Sutra*, which culminates in offerings of music and dance, as depicted in the album leaf. The expertise with which she arranges every detail of the ceremony, from copying and mounting precious sutra scrolls to preparing robes for the many priests officiating at the event, demonstrates a profound knowledge of Buddhist ritual and doctrine. Genji is astounded that "a mere woman" is able to accomplish all this without his help. The tale's description of the success and beauty of the ceremony is in keeping with observations about Murasaki's character throughout the book, in which she is lauded for her good judgment and taste. But this final endeavor provides a glimpse of a new sense of autonomy on her part; her work on the ceremony is equal to that performed by Genji for the dedication of the Third Princess's chapel in Chapter Thirty-Eight, and it affords her a sense of agency and dignity as she orchestrates her own departure from the world.

During the course of the ceremony, Murasaki hears the monks chanting a famous verse by the priest Gyōki (668–749) that is related to the Devadatta chapter of the *Lotus Sutra*, which praises how the Buddha humbled himself in a former life. Although an exalted king in that former life, the Buddha served a Dharma preacher by "gathering firewood, picking herbs, and drawing his water."

Inspired by the line, Murasaki sends a poem to the Akashi Lady, also in attendance at the event:

Oshikaranu	Nothing to regret
Kono mi nagara mo	I am only this, and this
Kagiri tote	Must reach an end;
Takigi tsukinan	And yet there is a sadness when
Koto no kanashisa	The firewood at last burns out.

CRANSTON, P. 890

Murasaki's poignant verse puts herself in the position of the Buddha-king subservient to the Dharma; her good works and dedications of the *Lotus Sutra*, akin to gathering firewood, have now sadly come to an end. The Akashi Lady's reply, the poem included in the album leaf, expresses her refusal to accept the idea of Murasaki's death by transforming the "firewood's depletion" (*takigi tsukusu*) in Murasaki's poem into the "cutting of firewood" (*takigi koru*), which, she hopes, Murasaki will continue to do.

The poem is paired in the album with an image that depicts a dancer performing the *bugaku* dance called "The Masked Warrior King" (*Ryōō*), which occurs at dawn, amid fragrant blossoms bathed in mist and early morning light. The painting positions the viewer high above a canopy of ethereal cherry trees in Murasaki's courtyard, looking down on a solitary dancer standing on a gold ground. The

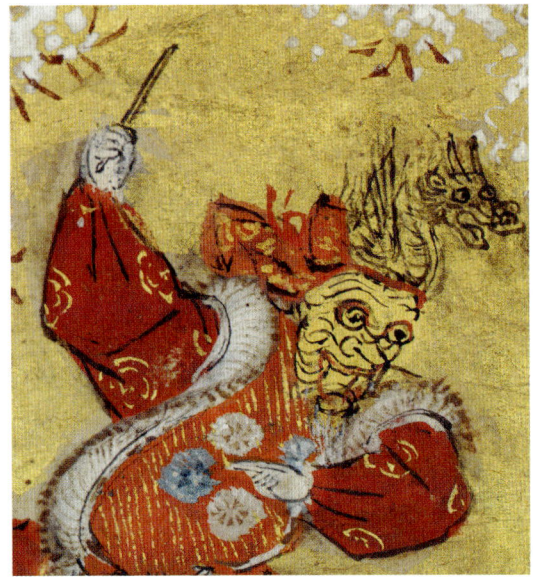

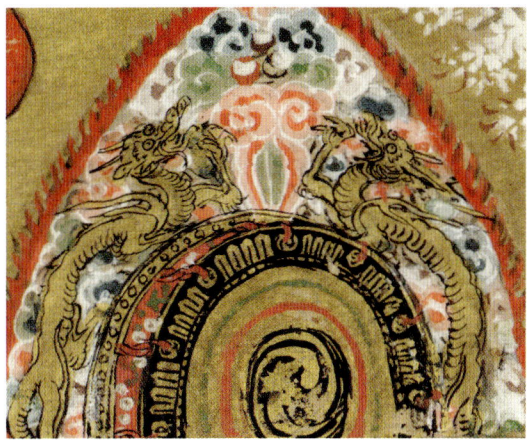

perspective encompasses a vision of the dancer, the musicians beneath the tent in the foreground with their elaborately decorated drums, and a wing of the residence. The spectators sit behind drawn bamboo blinds, and are suggested by the brightly colored sleeves that poke out from beneath the blinds in two bays of the residence.

Wherever Murasaki may be, the artist has created a composition in which the focus is on the dancer and his relationship to the drums in the foreground as he seems to move in time to the rhythm. The dancer wears a striking costume of bright orange trousers, a red garment (*hō*) cinched at the wrists, a white fur-lined orange campaign jacket (*ryōtō*) with gold stripes and blue and white floral medallions, and a large, red train that snakes behind him and upward with a flourish. He raises a gold baton in his right hand and reaches across his body with his left arm as he lifts his bent left leg, revealing the underside of his white shoe. The distinctive dragon-headed mask used in this particular dance alludes to the story of the Chinese king of Lanling, who entered battle wearing a dragon mask and long beard in order to hide his own features, which were too handsome to intimidate his adversaries. In Mitsunobu's painting, the headdress includes the neck of the dragon and part of a ribbed wing, while the mask itself has red-rimmed eyes, a long nose, and a white beard. The dancer turns his body toward two spectacular drums encircled by decorative wooden flame-rimmed halos containing images of five-colored clouds and pairs of golden dragons. In the larger of the two drums the dragons reach for three jewels in the center, while a radiating golden disk finial rises from the drum into the gold clouds. The dragon imagery on the mask may derive from that of the Eight Dragon Kings (*hachidai ryūo*) in Buddhism, while the dragon and jewel motif on the drum references the Dragon King beneath the sea, protector of the Dharma and owner of the wish-fulfilling jewel. The Dragon King has already been mentioned (Chapter Thirteen) in relation to the Akashi Novitiate, who resembles this mythical ruler of the sea. The Akashi Lady and the Akashi girl, now an Empress, figure prominently in this chapter: the women share a significant moment alone with Murasaki, the Akashi Empress holds Murasaki's hand as she dies, and the Empress's sadness at her foster mother's death concludes the chapter. The image of the dancer, as an old man Dragon King, staring up at the flaming sun-disk, recalls the Akashi Novitiate and his wishes for his lineage, which, thanks to Murasaki, have come to fruition.

The Dragon King imagery is also relevant, however, to the Devadatta chapter of the *Lotus Sutra*, which is alluded to in the poems above. In addition to depicting a ruler's subservience to the Dharma, that chapter was famous for its representation of a young daughter of the Dragon King, who became an emblem for female Buddhist salvation in the face of obstacles said to obscure a woman's path. The story of the dragon girl was the section of the *Lotus Sutra* most commonly read at women's funerals and inscribed on their grave markers. Taken together, the poem and painting in the album can therefore be seen as representing both halves of the Devadatta chapter and reflecting the tale's emphasis on Murasaki's noble death. Her passing occurs in autumn, marked by a series of three touching poems by her, Genji, and the Akashi Empress, which all liken her to the fragile dew drop and lament the ephemerality of life.

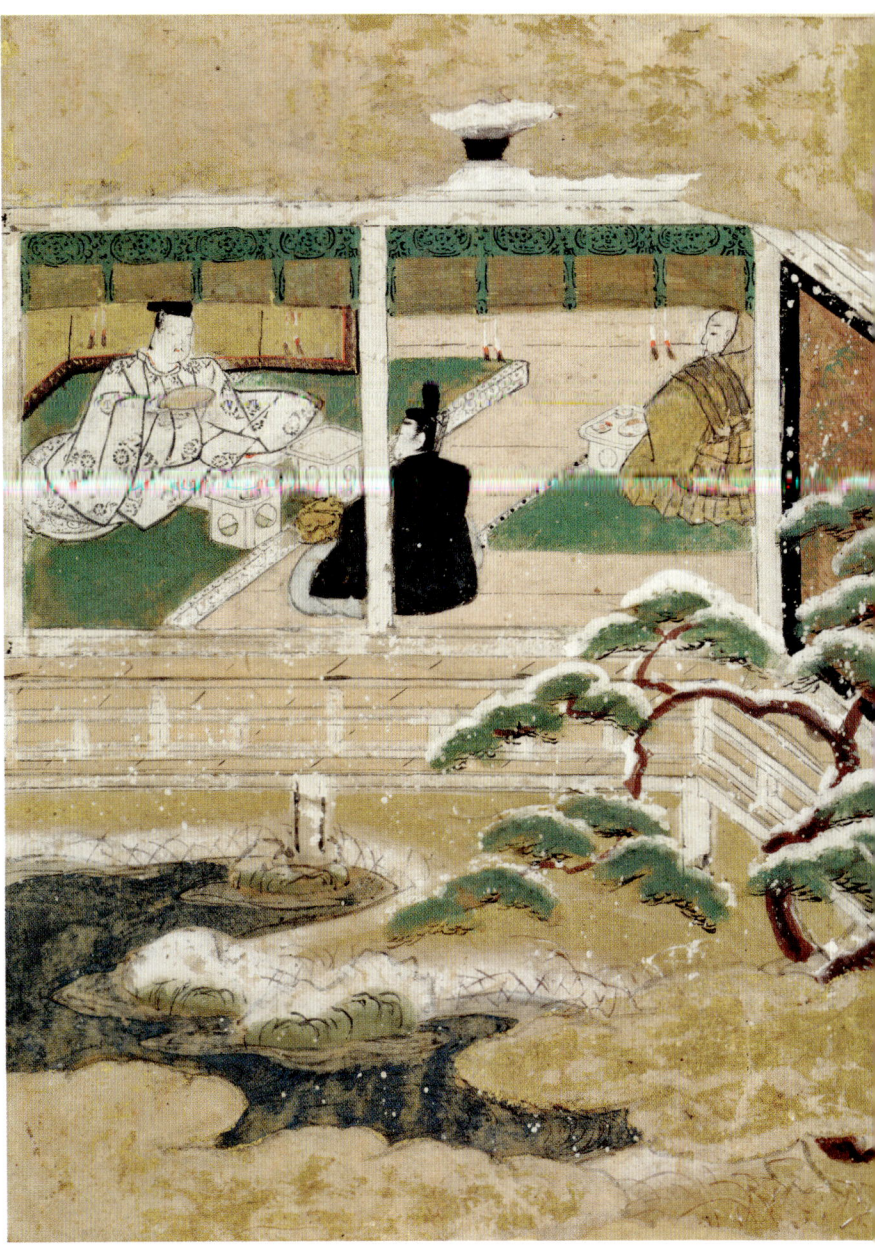

Spring may come too late
For a life one cannot know—
   Amid snow today
Let us find the time to deck
Our brows with the reddening plum.

His Holiness responded,

Let us see this flower
In springtime for a thousand years,
I make my prayer;
Mine is the body fallen
With snow in the drifts of age.

CRANSTON, PP. 901–2

41

幻
Spirit Summoner
Maboroshi

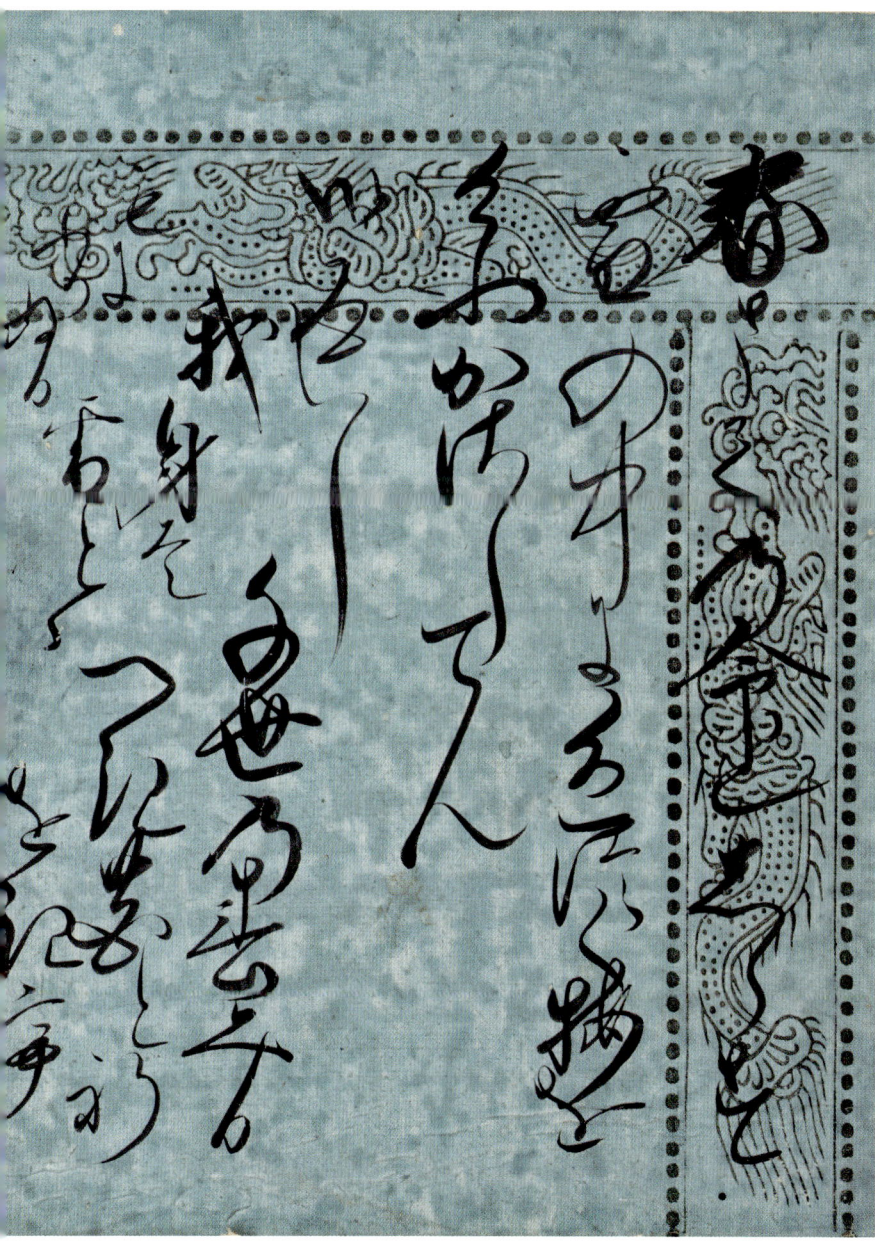

Haru made no
Inochi mo shirazu
　Yuki no uchi ni
Irozuku ume o
Kyō kazashiten

Onkaeshi

　Chiyo no haru
Mirubeki hana to
　Inoriokite
Wa ga mi zo yuki to
Tomo ni furinuru

It is the spring after Murasaki's death and Genji's grief is all-consuming. The Maboroshi chapter depicts the twelve months after Murasaki's death and beyond, accounting for every stage of Genji's grief and self-reflection after his loss. He lingers on at Nijō immediately after Murasaki's death, and then he visits the women at Rokujō; they are plain by comparison and give him no comfort and only depressingly remind him of Murasaki's perfection. He withdraws from society, has no visitors aside from members of his immediate circle, and sleeps alone, seemingly on the verge of renouncing the world to focus on Buddhist prayer and his own rebirth. Things always arise to prevent him from taking religious vows, however, from a supposedly deep attachment to his grandchildren at one point, to an obligation to others who rely on him at another. Eventually Genji admits to himself that he is simply not strong enough to do it. That self-reflection is expressed within a chapter structured in a unique manner as twelve months pass in rapid succession. Each month brings a new revelation and stage of mourning in tune with seasonal markers and calendrical events. Within that compressed year we see the microcosm of an entire life lived, as a flood of memories sparked by seasonal change interweave the past with the present in Genji's mind. Much of this is accomplished through the chapter's abundant poetry—nineteen poems by Genji, twelve of them lamentations for Murasaki expressed as soliloquies. As the year comes to a close, Genji gathers all of Murasaki's letters and examines them, startled by the emotional power of seeing her handwriting, and then instructs her women to burn every one of them. As if it is a symbolic re-cremation with utterly final effect, the destruction of this last trace of Murasaki seems to purge Genji of her memory and to free him to exit the world and the story.

The album painting depicts Genji with the year of mourning behind him, making his final appearance before the world of the court. It is the twelfth month and time for the annual chanting of *The Sutra on the Names of the Buddhas* (*Butsumyō kyō*), a ceremony in which the names of three thousand Buddhas of the past, present, and future would have been intoned by an assembly of priests. The rite included the confession of sins committed during the past year (*sange*) as well as prayers for longevity. At the end of the ceremony, as the participants are leaving, Genji spots the main officiant, a monk he has known for many years, offers him wine and delicacies, and bestows on him the gifts that protocol dictated priests receive, which Genji makes unexpectedly grand. The two men sit across from each other in the painting, with the priest depicted on the right in the regal robes of an abbot, patterned in gold with a pointed hood, and a surplice (*kesa*) draped across his body. He appears in profile, with a tall tray of dishes before him containing food and wine, the attendant in black having already used the golden sake ewer to fill the priest's cup. Genji sits opposite the priest looking as imposing as ever, in voluminous white robes and trousers, physically larger than the other two figures. He sits on a mat with a gold screen behind him, in a manner appropriate for a man with the status of retired emperor.

The painting shows Genji with his full cup raised as if capturing the very moment when the first

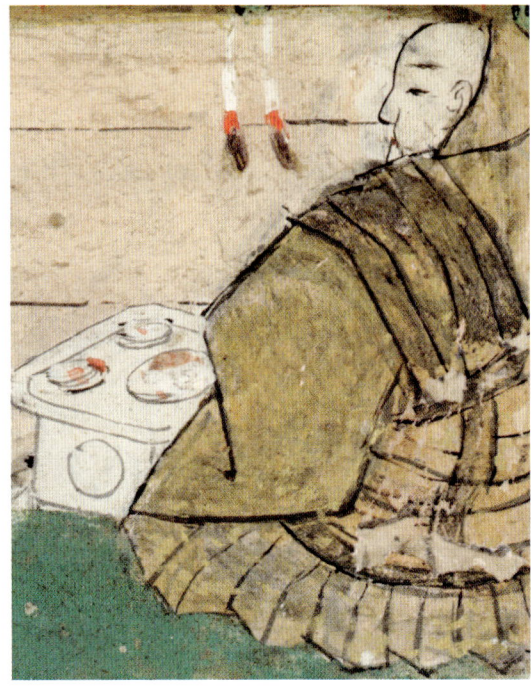

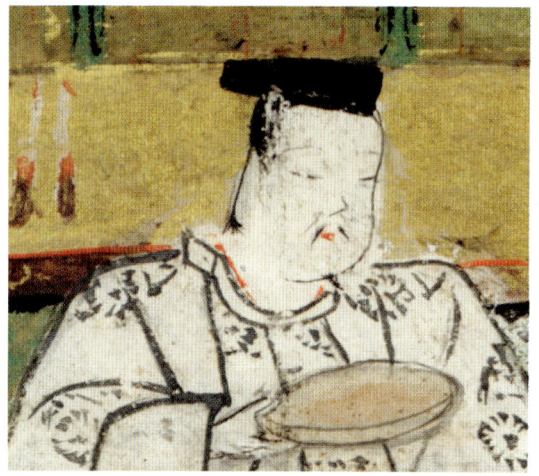

poem in the accompanying calligraphy leaf is spoken. The verse expresses Genji's doubt that he will live long enough into the spring to see the plum blossoms flower again, and it records his contentment to settle instead for a simple appreciation of their reddening buds amid the snow. No plum trees appear in the painting, but the artist made sure to include a slight blush of color in the men's wine cups. Genji notices how the priest has aged over the years, observing that the tint of his shaved head has turned white. The red plum and white snow in Genji's poem play on the trope of two old men whose heads have gone white while they have been enjoying their wine. While Genji's hair remains dark in the image, for the first time in twenty-five depictions of the protagonist in the album, the artist has included wrinkle lines on either side of his mustache to show his age. The priest in his poem refuses to accept Genji's prediction of his impending death and prays instead for a thousand more years for Genji while likening his own aged self to the drifts of snow around them. The artist uses motifs such as the tufts of pine tree branches capped with snow, the icy pond rimmed with frozen reeds, the bamboo in snow depicted on the wooden door to the residence, and the falling snow outside to create a withered wintry scene.

Why did Murasaki Shikibu make this exchange between Genji and an unnamed priest her protagonist's final poetic exchange in the tale, and why was this particular scene emphasized in the album painting? One clue may be the way in which this chapter mimics in lyrical form the structure of the third volume of a Heian-period Buddhist text that predates *The Tale of Genji* known as *The Three Jewels* (*Sanbōe*). The third volume of that work concerns the Buddhist clergy and presents an entire year of Buddhist rites and ceremonies, beginning with the first month and ending, like the Maboroshi chapter, with the ceremony for intoning *The Sutra on the Names of the Buddhas* in the twelfth month. Among other things the description of the ceremony explains that "When you hear the names of the Buddhas...the sins you have accumulated in countless kalpas will be erased" (Kamens, p. 366). And it ends intriguingly by citing a poem by Bai Juyi:

> With but one burner for incense and one lone candle,
> The white-haired monk passes each night, worshipping
> The Sutra of the Buddhas' Names.
>
> KAMENS, P. 367

The similarities with the ending of the Maboroshi chapter are striking, down to the inclusion of poems that pun on the white hair of an old monk. The monthly "rites and ceremonies" depicted in the Maboroshi chapter are not the Buddhist ones of *The Three Jewels* but romantic equivalents that eulogize Murasaki and touch on the events and themes of the tale. By alluding to the words and structure of *The Three Jewels*, the author sums up the story of Genji in a way that asserts her tale's identity as a work of literature infused with Buddhist spirituality. Having absolved Genji of his sins, the author ends the chapter with the shouts of his grandson, the six-year-old Niou, chasing out demons, and with Genji preparing for the New Year, positing a recurring cycle of life. Genji's final poem lets the reader know that the cycle will continue, but without Genji himself.

> | *Mono omou to* | One thing on my mind, |
> |---|---|
> | *Suguru tsukihi mo* | I never knew the passing |
> | *Shiranu ma ni* | Of the months and days, |
> | *Toshi mo wa ga yo mo* | But now it seems today at last |
> | *Kyō ya tsukinuru* | The year and my time are over. |
>
> CRANSTON, P. 902

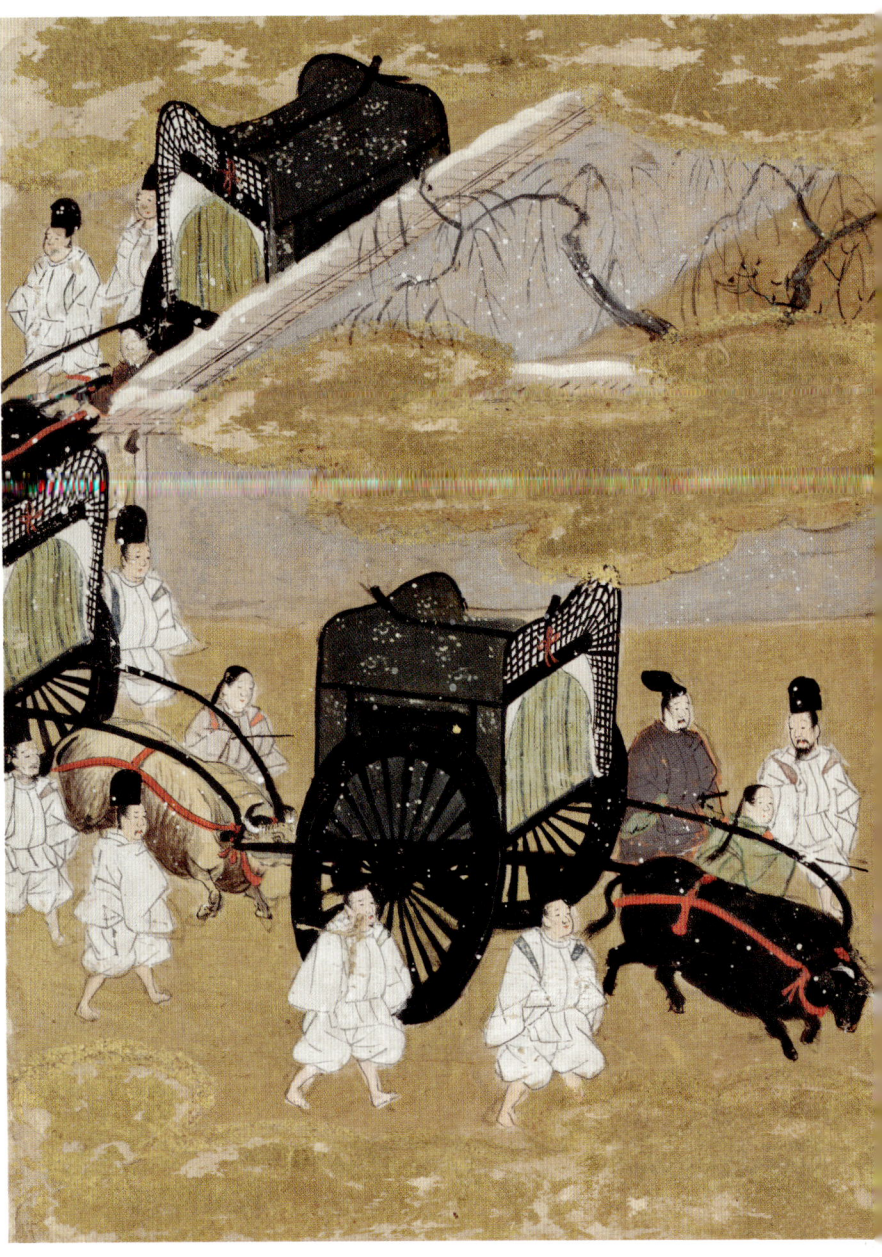

The procession included several of the Minister's sons—the Commander of the Guards, the Acting Middle Counselor, the Major Controller of the Right, as well as many senior nobles and officials. Soon, the assembled party was heading for the Rokujō Estate. The excursion took some time. A light snow was falling along the way, and the twilight had a fabulous glow.

WASHBURN, P. 891, MODIFIED

42

匂宮
The Fragrant Prince
Niou miya

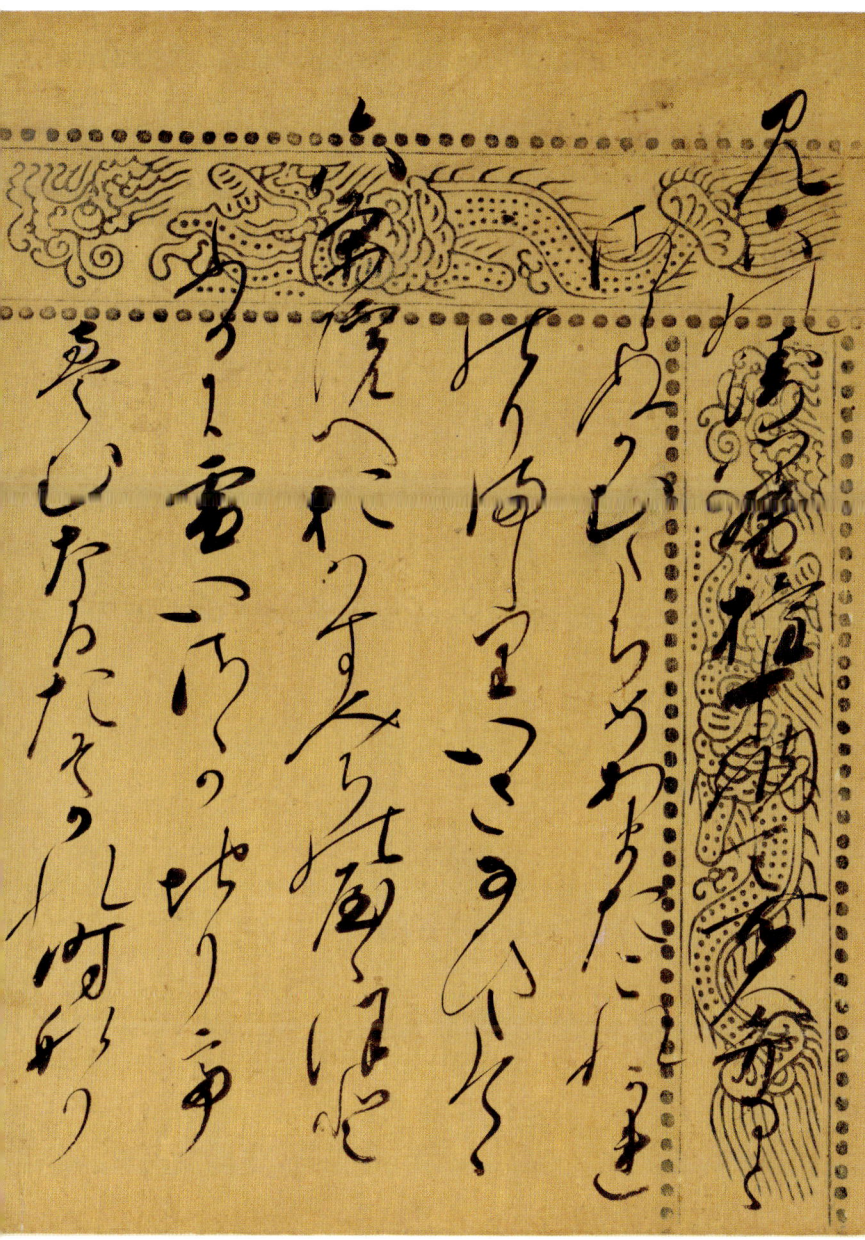

Miko no Emon no Kami, Gon no Chūnagon, Udaiben nado, saranu kandachime amata kore kare norimajiri, izanaitatete, Rokujōin e owasu. Michi no yaya hodo furu ni, yuki isasaka chirite, ennaru tasogaredoki nari.

みこの衛門督権中納言右大弁なと
さらぬかむたちめあまたこれかれ
のりましりいさなひたてゝ
六条院へおはすみちのやゝほと
ふるに雪いさゝかちりて
えむなるたそかれ時なり

Chapter Forty-Two opens eight years after Genji's death—the so-called eclipse of radiance (*hikari kakuretamai*)—and all under heaven have been left feeling that a "light has been extinguished" (*hi wo kechitaru yō ni*). This phrase is borrowed from the description of the death of the Buddha in *The Lotus Sutra* and conveys the magnitude of Genji's passing for the characters in the tale. Two male protagonists take Genji's place from this point on: Kaoru, who is believed by the world to be Genji's son but is in fact Kashiwagi's son by Genji's wife, the Third Princess, and Niou, the Akashi Empress's third son and Genji's grandson. In a world gone dark from Genji's absence, visual form recedes and other senses come to the fore, and indeed the personas of these two young protagonists are characterized by their distinctive aromas. Kaoru (meaning "scent," "smell") exudes a scent that is natural, uncontrived, and that mingles organically with that of the flowers around him to intoxicating effect. Niou (meaning "fragrance"), on the other hand, must concoct his own fragrances to perfume himself, an enterprise he undertakes with determination as he attempts to outdo his rival Kaoru, much like Genji competed with Tō no Chūjō. Niou's fragrances are derived not from ordinary flowers but from those such as the chrysanthemum and the wisteria, flowers with connotations of the highest imperial pedigree, a pedigree to which Niou, as a prince and Genji's grandson, can legitimately lay claim. Kaoru's scent is ethereal and of his essence, while Niou's is superficial, but sensual, and stirring. Chapter Forty-Two, despite its title, reintroduces both Prince Niou and Kaoru, last seen as young children living together at Rokujō, now around twenty years of age and eligible bachelors.

Their marriageability motivates the episode depicted in the album leaf, as Yūgiri, now a powerful Minister and inheritor of the Rokujō Estate, leads a procession of young courtiers in ox-drawn carts from the palace for a postarchery banquet at his residence. Among the women now living at Rokujō is Yūgiri's sixth and youngest daughter by the Principal Handmaid (Koremitsu's daughter), Rokunokimi, who is being raised by Yūgiri's wife Ochiba. Both women live in the northeast quarter, which was previously Yūgiri's home with his caregiver Hanachirusato, and which is where a similar postarchery event occurred in Chapter Twenty-Five. The setting for the event is thus the sixth daughter's residence, and Yūgiri's ulterior motive in sponsoring the event is to entice potential sons-in-law, primarily Prince Niou. Yūgiri has already triumphed in the marriage politics of the day, having betrothed his first two daughters to Niou's two older brothers, imperial princes born to Yūgiri's half sister, the Akashi Empress. Prince Niou differs from his older brothers, however, and openly expresses his lack of interest in Yūgiri's daughter. Doted on by Murasaki and Genji and raised separately at Rokujō, he has grown into something of a dandy and prefers to keep his options open. The one woman who has caught his eye is the only child of Emperor Reizei, a daughter born to his Kokiden Consort. Kaoru, on the other hand, has numerous affairs, but has somehow managed to avoid commitments to particular women without accumulating any ill will.

Rather than depicting the banquet at the Rokujō estate, the album painting focuses on a moment of transition as the party moves from the palace to Genji's former residence on the way to the banquet, symbolically leading the reader into a new era of characters and their interrelationships. Snow

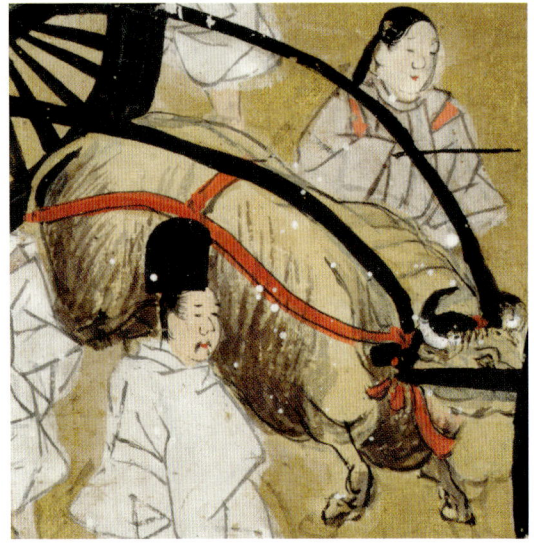

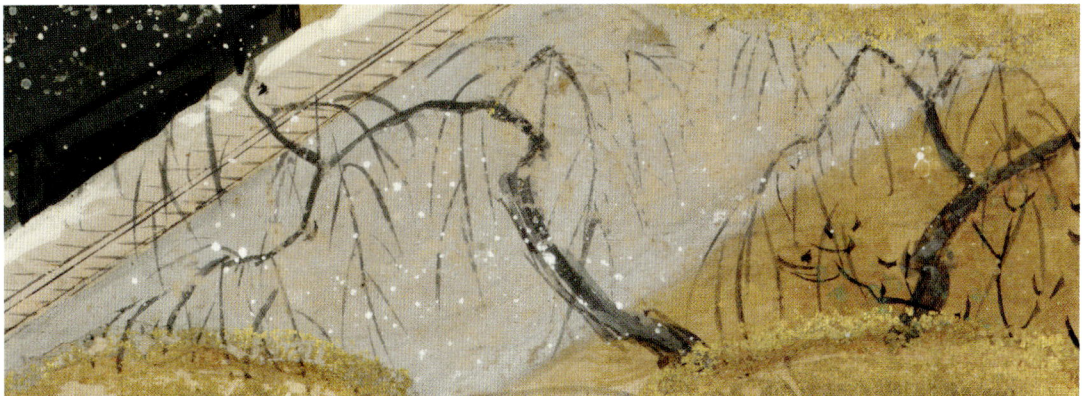

scenes in the tale often triggered remembrances for Genji, the drifting flakes having a dreamlike effect, bringing associations with different moments in time. Eight years have passed since the last scene in the album, but it seems as though the snow continues to fall from the previous leaf, an effect that is enhanced by the image of the solemn, stately march of the courtiers en route, characters moving onward without Genji. Three black carts pulled by black and brown oxen march through the city streets, taking a sharp turn at the corner of a walled residence in the center of the composition. The sides of the wall are covered in silver paint, which stands out against the gold-covered ground, producing a luminous effect for this twilight snow scene. As described in the calligraphy excerpt, the drifting snow at dusk gives the scene a seductive glowing appeal (*ennaru*). Each cart is escorted by two or three attendants in white garments. Managing each animal is an oxherd with a stick in hand; they are identifiable by their darker robes and long hair, which is cinched in the style of a juvenile. Only the first cart in the procession, the one in the foreground, includes an attendant with a sword, indicating that this is the vehicle belonging to Yūgiri, the Minister. This would also then indicate the presence of Prince Niou, and his two younger brothers, whom the tale tells us share Yūgiri's carriage. Kaoru sits in one of the other carriages, since Yūgiri invited him to join the procession after spotting him attempting to depart the palace unnoticed.

The figures of the young men remain obscured behind the drawn blinds of the carts in which they ride, a fitting approach to the introduction of two characters who are known principally by their scents. Seemingly standing in for them is the plum tree in this painting, which is growing in the courtyard around which the procession turns. Mitsunobu eschews painting the buds on the tree limbs, opting instead for a barren tree as if it was still the middle of winter in the story. The flowerless plum in effect creates a visual echo with the tree in the previous album painting, which marked Genji's last appearance in the album.

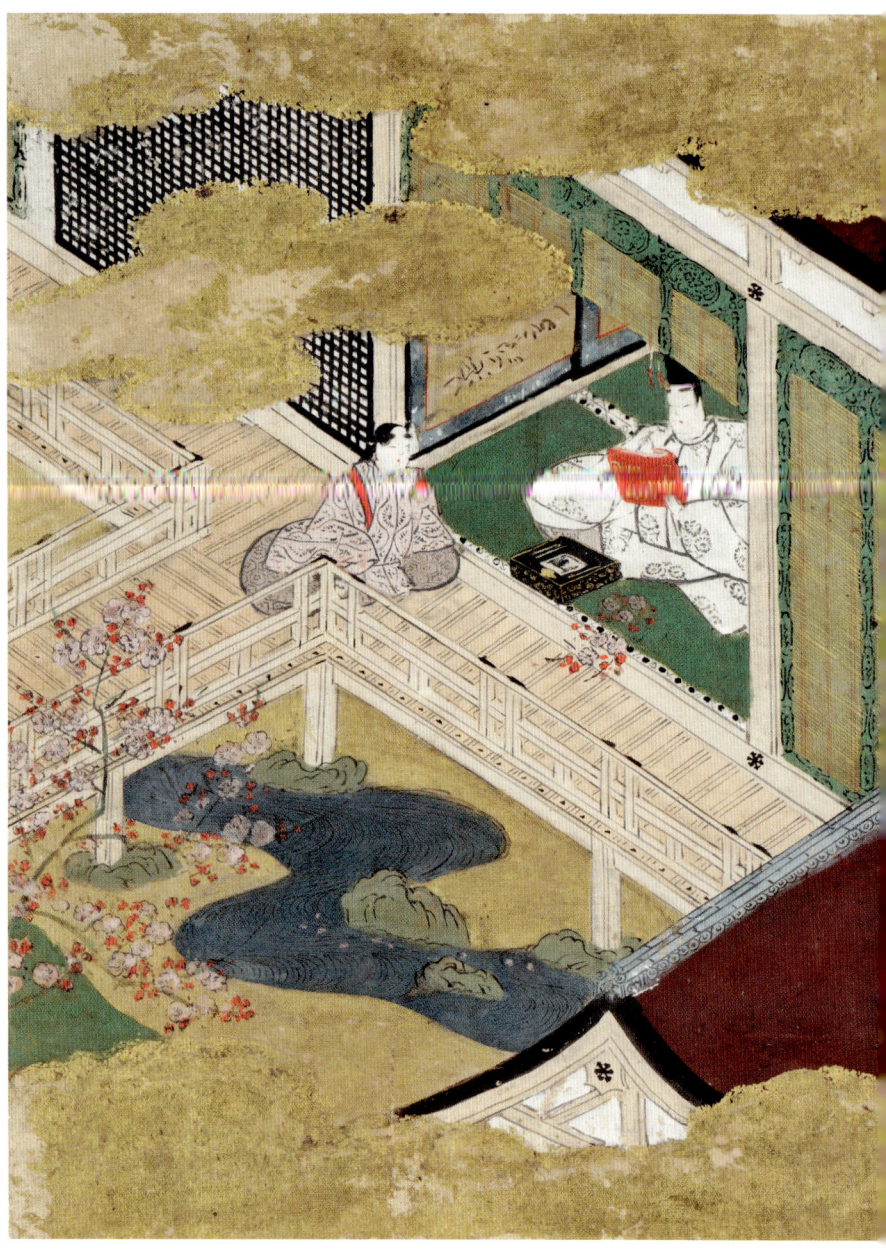

    Something on its mind,
The wind wafting the fragrance
    Of the garden plum
Wonders why the warbler thinks
Not yet of coming to call.

CRANSTON, P. 903

43

紅梅

Red Plum

Kōbai

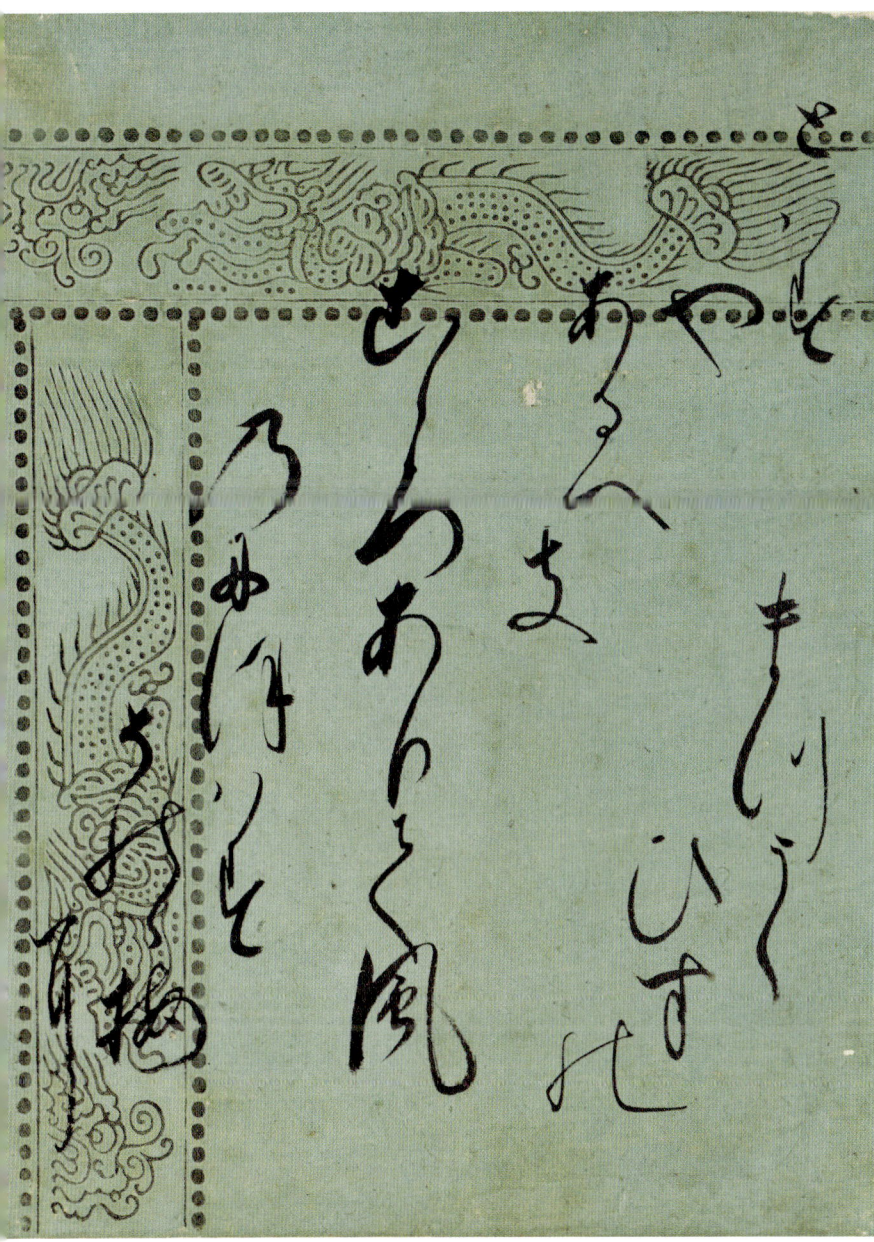

Kokoro arite
Kaze no niowasu
　Sono no ume ni
Mazu uguisu no
Towazu ya arubeki

とはすやあるへき
　まつうくひすの
　　こゝろありて風
　のにほはす
　　そのゝ梅
　　　に

Chapter Forty-Three tells the story of Kōbai, Tō no Chūjō's second son and Kashiwagi's younger brother, who in his earlier appearances in the tale was often lauded for his beautiful singing voice. As a young boy in Chapter Ten (Sakaki), he performed the *saibara* folk song "Takasago" and received generous gifts and accolades from Genji. Thereafter he was often required to lend his voice to the musical entertainments of Genji's banquets, and he was compared in poems to the warbler, and the bell cricket (as in the Hatsune, Kagaribi, Umegae, and Fujinouraba chapters). Now, in his mid-fifties, he is a high-ranking Major Counselor and remarried to Makibashira, as his first wife is deceased. Makibashira, the daughter of Higekuro and the ash-dumping lady from Chapter Thirty-One, suffered from her parents' divorce and ensuing separation from her brothers and her family home. Before marrying Kōbai, she had reluctantly married Genji's half brother, the late Sochinomiya (Prince Hotaru), with whom she had one daughter. Kōbai thus has a blended household: with two daughters from his first marriage, and a new stepdaughter from Makibashira, Kōbai has three young women under his roof, whose marital options occupy much of his attention.

Kōbai's matchmaking provides the background for the scene depicted in the album painting, which shows him composing a letter to Prince Niou, whom he is trying to entice into a relationship with his second daughter. He raises his brush in his right hand as he writes out the single poem that appears in the adjacent calligraphy leaf in the album. In the painting, the letter is brushed on paper with a red backing embellished with designs in gold. Kōbai concentrates as he wields his brush, freshly inked from the well in the elegant writing box before him. The poem speaks suggestively of the fragrant plum in his garden (his daughter), waiting for the warbler (Niou) to land on its branches. He plans to send it with the sprig of blossoms lying on the floor, all the better to tempt the "fragrant prince." In contrast to the barren winter plum tree shown in the previous album painting, the red plum tree in Kōbai's garden is represented at its peak. Spikey branches lean in from the left of the composition toward the veranda of the luxurious residence, presenting clusters of fully opened pink blossoms and round, red buds, that are evocative of the alluring fragrance noted in the tale's description of the tree. The scent's delivery on the wind is mentioned in the poem and visualized in the painting by a few pink petals that have wafted down on the breeze and float on the surface of the garden stream.

The pivotal figure in this painting, however, is the youth on the veranda, the only biological child born to Makibashira and Kōbai as a couple, a young man who has earned the favor of both the Crown Prince and Prince Niou while serving as a palace page. He acts as an intermediary, delivering his father's letters and Niou's responses about his sister, similar to the role Utsusemi's younger brother Kogimi played in Chapter Two. The conspicuous gold cloud hovering above him, which is used so often in the album to highlight Genji and his prominence as the protagonist, suggests, however, that he is more than a go-between, as Joshua Mostow has pointed out.

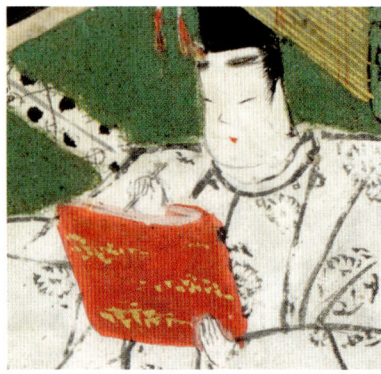
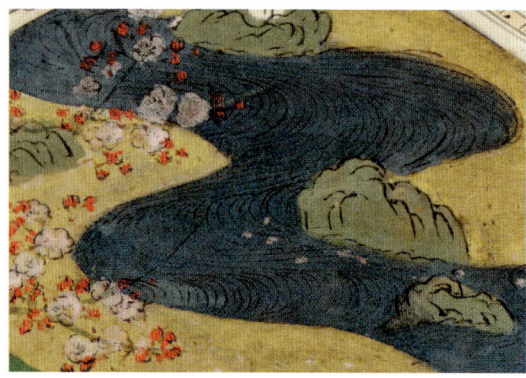

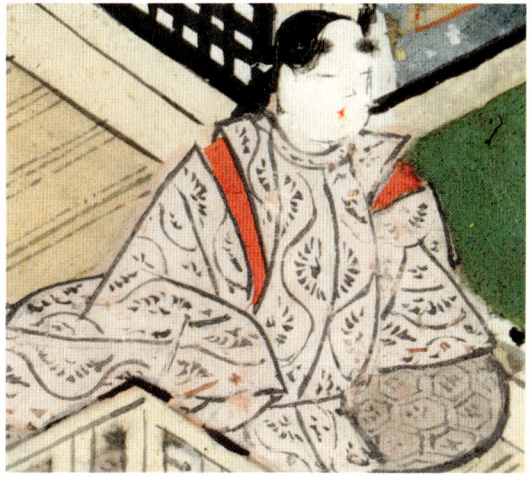

The boy is as visually stunning as the plum blossoms, which are positioned on either side of him, framing his figure. He wears distinctive apparel: purplish trousers with a tortoise shell pattern covered in shimmering mica, and a pink tinted robe with a bright red undergarment peeking out from between the arm seams. The colors of the boy's dress mimic the pink and red of the plum blossoms and buds and suggest that they be interpreted as a symbol for the youth himself. The plum was in fact a common symbol for beautiful boys, known as *chigo* in stories popular in the fifteenth and sixteenth centuries, in which they figured as the objects of affection by older men, usually Buddhist priests. Tosa Mitsunobu knew such illustrated tales and employed their conventions for beauty in depicting the boy, giving him full eyebrows, wisps of hair on the side of the face, and delicate features on a white, thickly powdered face. The text mentions that Kōbai in this scene admires his son's hair, which he wears loose rather than in the twin loops appropriate for service as a page. Interestingly, Mitsunobu chooses neither of those options for the painting, but depicts the boy's long tresses cinched in the back, a style typical of *chigo* characters. In so doing, the artist emphasizes the implicit content of the Heian period text in a sixteenth-century visual language.

When Kōbai looks at his son, he sees a vision of himself at the same age, a time that he fondly recalls as having been spent in Genji's service. He reflects on Prince Niou's charms and decides that he alone is the true inheritor of Genji's radiance, likening him to Ananda, first disciple of the Buddha. His desire for Niou as a son-in-law for his second daughter mingles with his own desire for a memento of Genji, and for the pleasure of Niou's company in his household. That pleasure can also be experienced vicariously, through his son's relationship with the prince. The boy seems to find Niou just as attractive as his father does, and the narration directly expresses his "delight at being able to lie so intimately with him" (*ke chikaku fusetamaeru wo...tagui naku ureshiku natsukashu omoi kikoyu*). While similar interactions occurred between Genji and Kogimi earlier in the tale, Kōbai's son seems more demonstrative of his desire. The depiction of physical attraction by other men to Prince Niou heightens his appeal and shows him to be Genji-like in his ability to cross gender lines as an object of desire.

Relationships between men outside the confines of marriage also work to define the primary importance of heterosexual marriage in terms of the perpetuation of a lineage. Lineal concerns often dictate attractions between men and women in subterranean ways in the tale. Niou, for example, inherits Genji's aversion to women who represent Fujiwara control over the imperial line. He rather curtly dismisses Kōbai's overtures proposing a match with his second daughter, preferring instead Kōbai's stepdaughter by Makibashira, who shares with Niou the same imperial "ancient bloodline" (*furumekashiki onaji suji nite*). She is the granddaughter of a prince on Makibashira's side, and the great-granddaughter of the Kiritsubo Emperor through her biological father. For her own part, however, she has no desire to marry, a sentiment with which her mother sympathizes. While previous female characters, such as Princess Asagao, were able to opt out of marriage, none expressed the desire to do so as explicitly as the stepdaughter in this chapter. In this way, both Kōbai's son's expression of desire for Niou and the stepdaughter's clear assertion that she wants to remain single stand out as independent voices in this chapter that throw into high relief the conventional nature of marriage in the narrative.

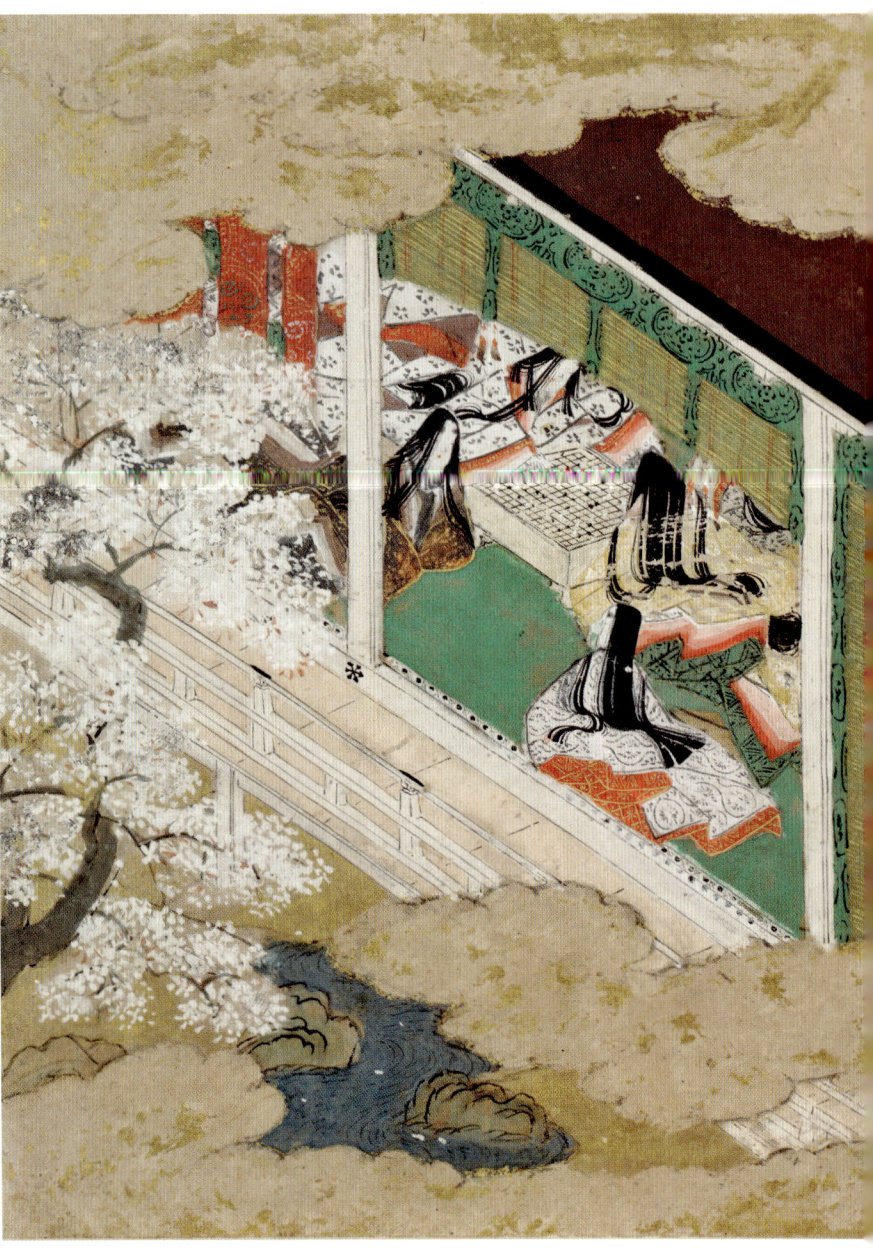

The older sister on the losing side:

All for the cherry
Was my heart in a tumult
Over the wind—
And yet I had to own these blossoms
Wasted little thought on me.

Saishō replied in consolation:

Now they are in bloom,
Now they scatter on the wind—
Such are these blossoms;
Losing cannot bring so deep
Regret for contested flowers.

CRANSTON, PP. 906–7

44

竹河
Bamboo River
Takekawa

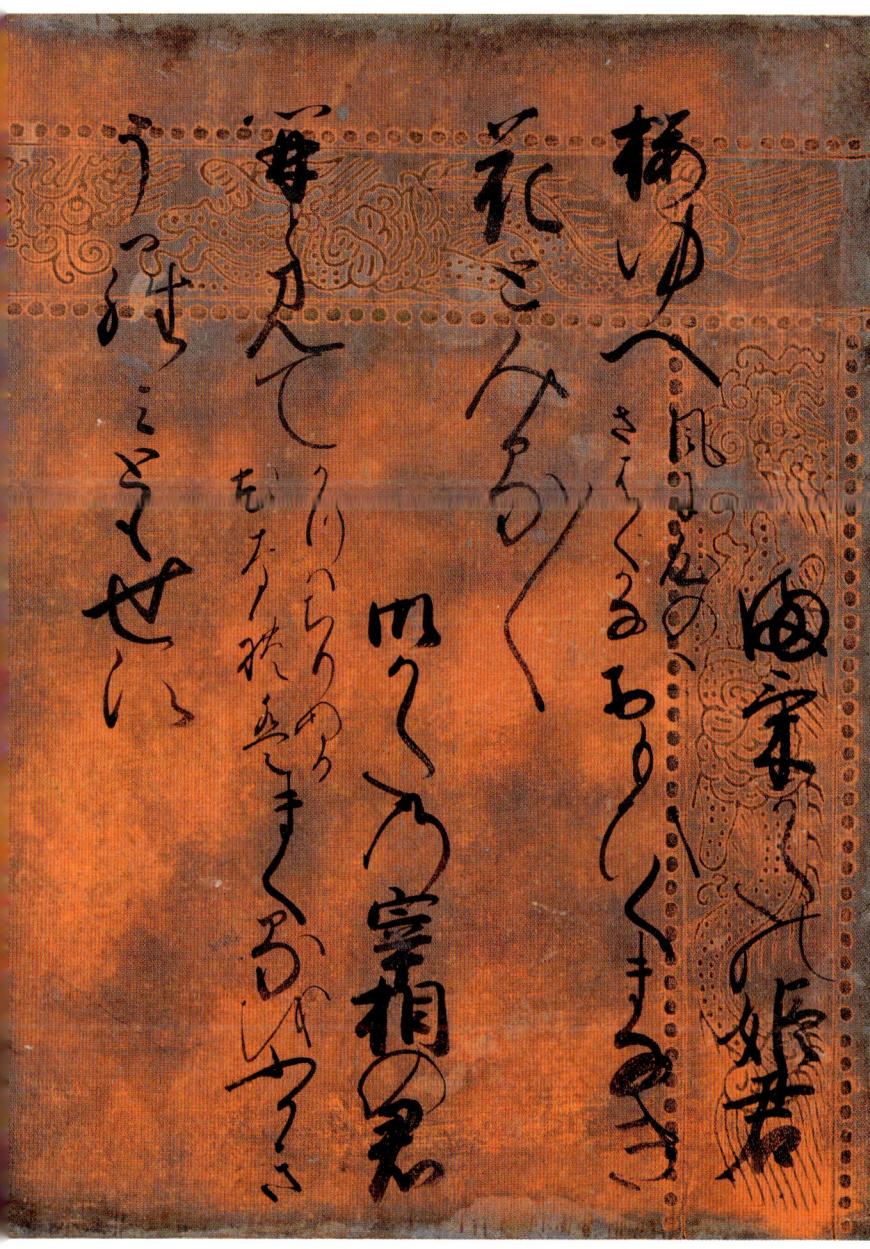

Makegata no Himegimi,	Onkata no Saishō no Kimi,
Sakura yue	Saku to mite
Kaze ni kokoro no	Katsu wa chirinuru
Sawagu kana	Hana nareba
Omoigumanaki	Makuru o fukaki
Hana to miru miru	Urami to mo sezu

　まけかたの姫君
桜ゆへ
　風に心の
おもひくまなき
花とみるみる

　御かたの宰相の君
さくとみて
　かつはちりぬる
花なれば
まくるをふかき
うらみともせず

While the previous chapter concerned Kōbai's attempt to arrange marriages for his daughters, Chapter Forty-Four focuses on the efforts of Tamakazura, now forty-seven and a widow of Higekuro, to secure the futures of her two daughters without any male backing at court. Like Kōbai, her half brother, her decisions are driven by memories of events from her personal history and lingering romantic regrets. At the start of the chapter, numerous suitors vie for the hand of her older daughter, most persistently Yūgiri's youngest son, called the Lesser Captain. He befriends Tamakazura's youngest son, making himself a fixture at the household in the hopes of catching a glimpse of the girl, which he finally gets one spring evening. The scene shown in the album painting takes place on that same evening and depicts the two sisters sitting across from each other at a Go board in the shadow of a cherry tree in full bloom. In a composition similar to that of Chapter Forty-Three's painting, the activity is framed within a single bay of the residence from a high vantage point, through floating gold clouds and over the blossoms of the tree on the left. The cherry tree is the thematic subject of this picture and of the poems in the album's calligraphy, just as the plum functioned symbolically in the previous painting in the album. The sisters have wagered possession of the tree as the winner's reward. Apparently, ownership of the cherry tree has been contested between them since childhood, and they eagerly compete cheered on boisterously by respective teams of ladies-in-waiting. The older sister, the figure facing outward, wears robes in the "cherry blossom style,"

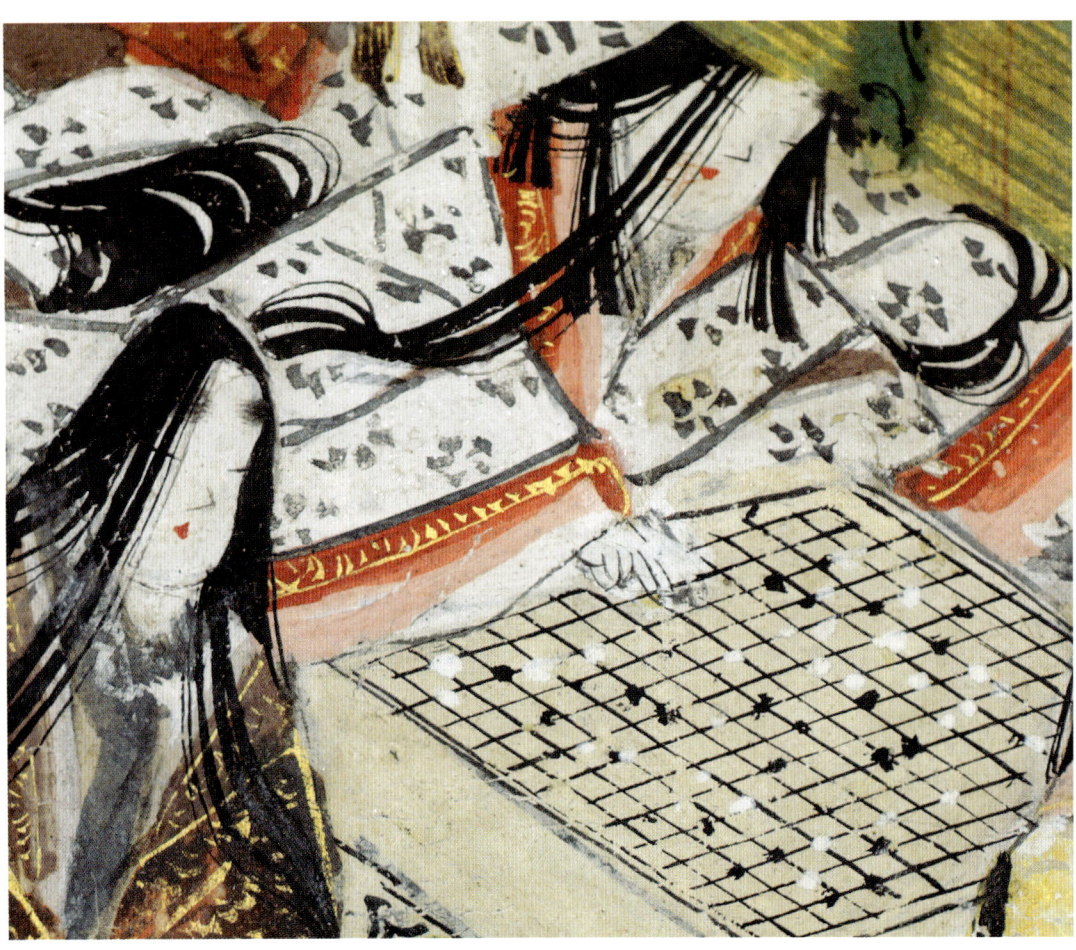

with a white, diaphanous robe layered over fabrics of reds in varying tones to produce the pink tinted hue of a cherry blossom. Her garment spreads out voluminously behind her as she leans forward, intently pushing a stone across the board with two fingers. Although she seems to embody the cherry tree, alas, it is the younger sister, dressed in the beautiful yellow robe embellished with patterns in gold, who emerges victorious. Some of the ladies' supporters are seated alongside them, closer to the veranda, while a glimpse of a third attendant's robe and hair to the right of the younger sister suggests yet more figures inside.

The majority of *Genji* paintings that illustrate this scene include a voyeur—the abovementioned Lesser Captain, who loses his heart to the older sister. According to the passage in the tale, the Lesser Captain glimpses the older sister in her cherry-blossom attire and imagines her as a living memento of the flowers after they fall, alluding to a classical poem to articulate her beauty. In this painting, the artist has eliminated the figure of the voyeur entirely and has painted the scene from a perspective too high for it to be taken as approximating the Lesser Captain's view. Instead, the composition encourages the viewer to see the sisters from a wider angle and a context broader than that of one moment of infatuation. Ultimately, nothing of consequence comes from the young man's gaze in the narrative, as this son of Yūgiri does not act as aggressively on his desire as Genji did after espying two women playing Go (Chapter Three), or as Kashiwagi did after fatefully glimpsing the Third Princess among similar cherry blossoms (Chapter Thirty-Five). The scene also differs from most *kaimami* scenes in that the peeping courtier quietly withdraws, while the women express no concern that they may have been seen. Instead, the action in the tale stays focused on the dynamics of the two sisters for several days and includes a lengthy sequence of six poems composed on the subject of cherry branches, which have become endangered by the wind.

The six poems, the first two of which are included in the album's calligraphy, represent an unusual moment of female-centered group poetry composition, which we have not encountered since the Akashi women's pilgrimage to Sumiyoshi in Chapter Thirty-Five. The poets are not only the sisters but also the ladies-in-waiting, Saishō and Taifu, and even two pages—one unnamed girl who goes into the garden to retrieve fallen blossoms and a girl named Nareki. The lively round of spoken poetry matches the tenor of an unusual prologue to this chapter, unique among *Genji* chapters, in which the narrator directly addresses the reader, explaining that the story she is about to tell was related to her by former female attendants from Tamakazura's household. The series of cherry-blossom poems re-create a primal scene of female literary production by ladies-in-waiting, the storytellers and narrators of *Genji* itself. The focus on the sisters and their attendants in the poems that are included in the album also seems fitting for a chapter exploring one mother's nuptial negotiations for her daughters. The results of Tamakazura's efforts, however, leave much to be desired. Requests for her eldest daughter from Retired Emperor Reizei prove impossible for Tamakazura to dismiss. She ends up infuriating numerous suitors and their fathers when she sends the girl to be Reizei's new consort. By doing so, she appeases the man to whom she herself was once promised by Genji until Higekuro intervened. The oldest sister bears Reizei a princess and prince, but her children never ascend the throne, and the attention they all receive from Reizei disturbs his senior Umetsubo and Kokiden Consorts. Tamakazura sends the younger sister to serve as the Principal Handmaid of the reigning Emperor, where the young lady is said to enjoy a stylish lifestyle and moderate success. Of the two sisters, then, the eldest finds herself in the less favorable marital circumstances, a situation foreshadowed by the outcome of the Go match depicted in the album painting.

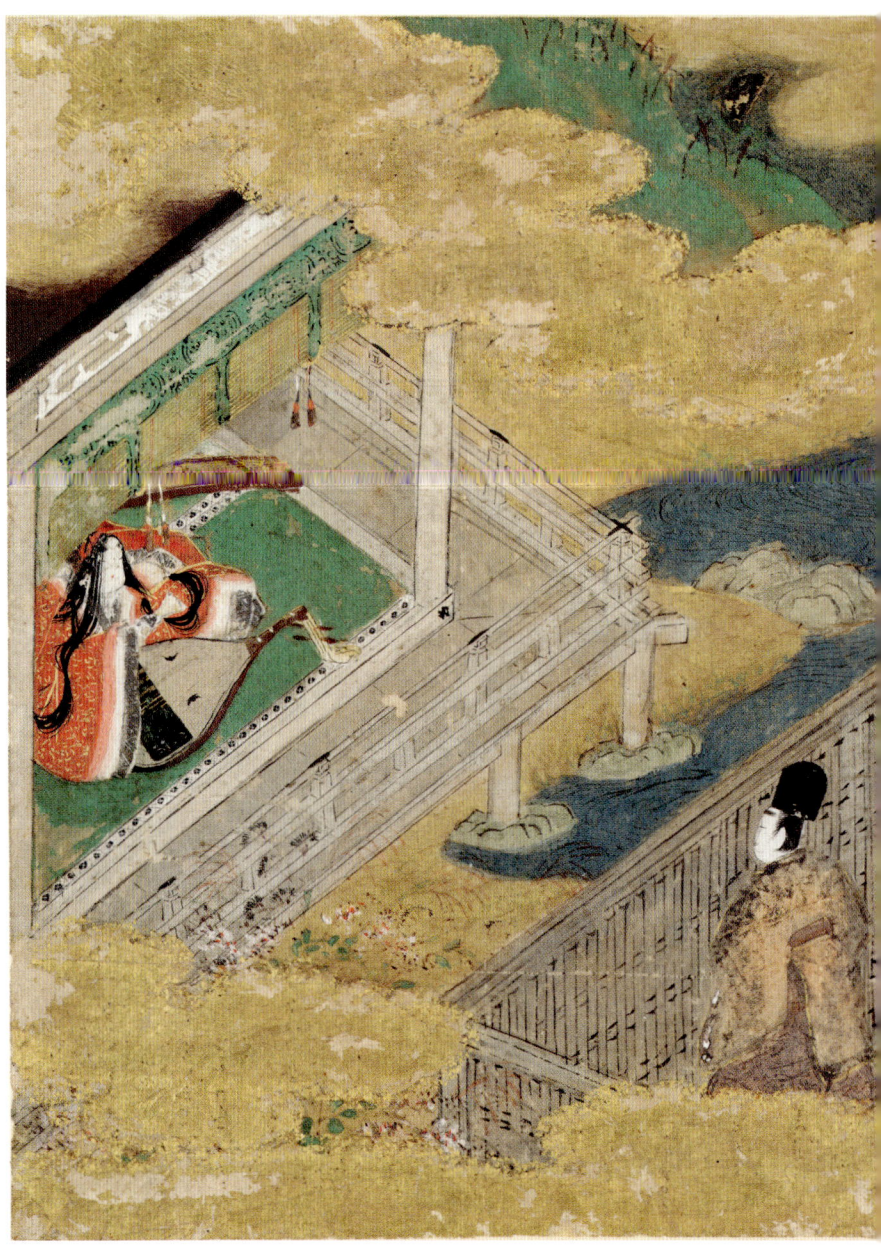

A *biwa* lute was set out in front of her and she was turning over the plectrum with her fingertips, toying with it. When the moon suddenly emerged from behind a cloud and brightly lit up the scene, she said, "I may not have a fan, but I can still call forth the moon with this." The lovely glow of her face, which peeked out from behind the plectrum, was utterly adorable.

WASHBURN, P. 942

45

橋姫

The Divine Princess at Uji Bridge

Hashihime

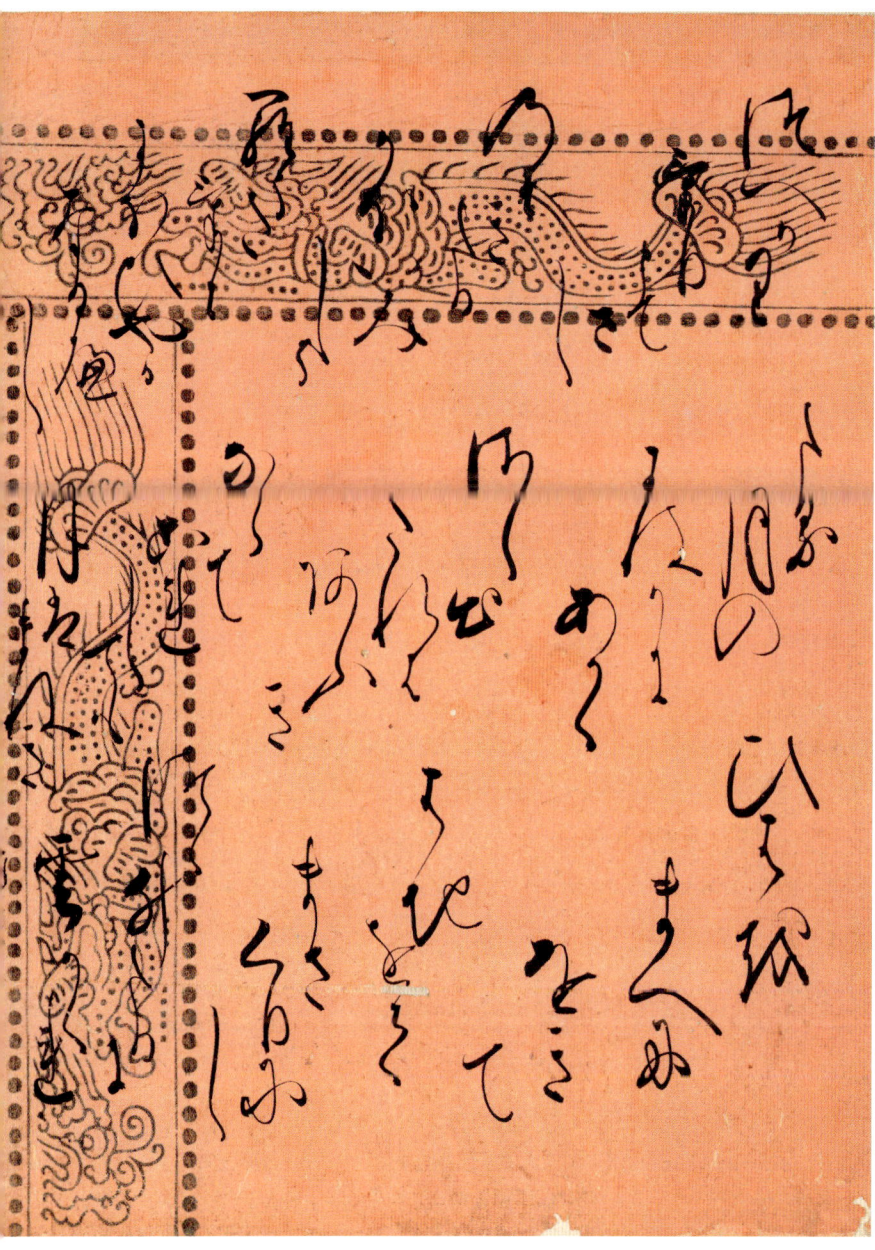

つへかりけりとて さしのそきたる かほいみしう らうたけにならて にほひやかなるへし

ひはをまへにおきて はちをてまさくりにしつゐたるに月はまねき

月のにはかにあかくさし出たれはあふきにこれしても雲かくれ

Biwa o mae ni okite, bachi o temasaguri ni shitsutsu itaru ni, kumogakuretaru tsuki no niwaka ni akaku sashiidetareba, "Ōgi narade, kore shite mo tsuki wa maneki tsubekarikeri," tote, sashinozokitaru kao, imijiu rōtage ni nioiyaka narubeshi.

Chapter Forty-Five is the first of ten chapters in the tale set partially in a locale south of the capital called Uji, a name that can also mean "gloom," or "sadness" (*ushi*). Uji is near the banks of a noisy, turbulent river, and is described in the tale as mist-covered and rustic. There Kaoru discovers two sisters, princesses, living an isolated existence with only their father to care for them. The father is Prince Hachinomiya, who is said to be a devout Buddhist practitioner living an awakened existence without taking formal Buddhist vows. Of the two post-Genji protagonists in the tale, Kaoru and Niou, Kaoru is the spiritual, introspective one, ever seeking philosophical guidance. When he first hears of the prince and his daughters, Kaoru is intrigued by the possibility that the prince could become his religious guide. With his royal pedigree—as the eighth son of the Kiritsubo Emperor, Hachinomiya is Genji's half brother—Hachinomiya proves to be a kindred spirit, a nobleman with a similar sensibility as well as profound Buddhist insights. His elegant demeanor and poignant surroundings only add to his mystique. Kaoru begins moving between his secular life at court and this spiritual realm he has discovered in Uji, forging a bond of friendship with the prince. One autumn night after he has been visiting for three years, Kaoru approaches the residence and hears strains of *koto* and *biwa* music. He learns that Hachinomiya has left for a seven-day retreat at a temple in the Uji mountains but realizing that the

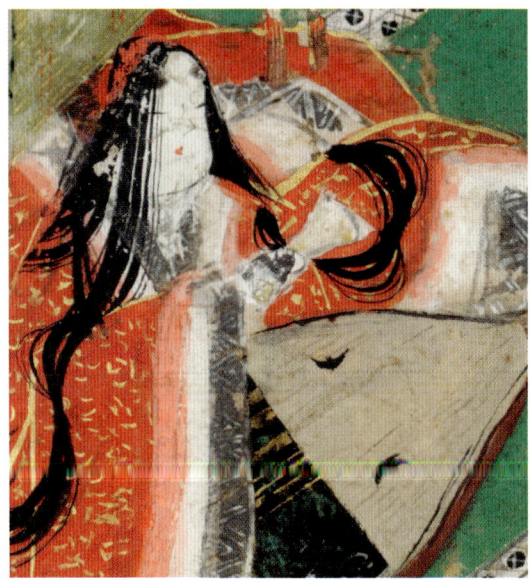

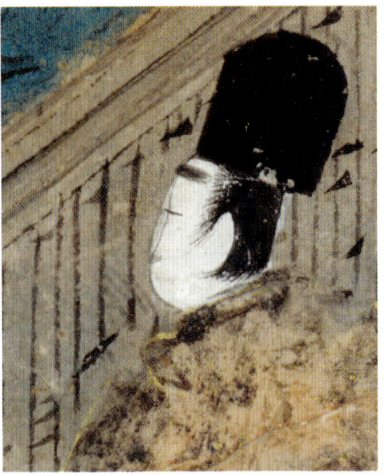

musicians are none other than the prince's daughters, he continues listening surreptitiously, leading to the most famous *kaimami* scene in the tale.

The album painting shows Kaoru standing before a bamboo fence near the sisters' room, having been led there by a watchman, in the familiar pose of the voyeur occupying the lower right corner of the composition. Shown in profile and dressed in informal hunting robes and a tall cap, he presses up against the fence, enthralled by what he sees. A loss of pigment has resulted in an underdrawing of Kaoru's left hand appearing near his face and touching the fence. The hand conveys Kaoru's degree of absorption, while also referencing the original text in which he is said to "push open" a door in the fence. A hazy mist hangs over the garden, but he spots women on the veranda and in the interior room, framed by blinds only partially raised.

The narration in the tale describes how suddenly the moon emerges from behind the clouds, lighting the scene with brilliant clarity. Kaoru watches and listens as one of the sisters reacts to the sudden illumination. She likens the plectrum in her right hand to a fan, which it resembles in shape, alluding to a poem from the eleventh-century *Wakan rōei shū* that was itself was derived from a phrase in the Tendai meditational treatise *The Great Stillness and Contemplation*

(*Maka shikan*). The *Wakan rōei shū* poem uses the hidden moon as a metaphor for veiled truth, which could be revealed through the device of the fan that acts as its double and thus suggests the teachings of Buddhist nonduality. Here the sister misquotes the original poem and makes her plectrum-fan not a substitute for the moon but a device to "call forth" the actual moon, and she playfully takes credit for eliciting the moon's sudden emergence.

Although the other sister is not depicted in the album painting, in the tale she is said to be lying over her *koto* in the same room, and she teases her sibling about her poetic allusion. A *biwa* plectrum (*bachi*) does not call forth the moon, she states, but a dancer's baton (also called a *bachi*) does bring on the "setting sun." Her reference is to the *bugaku* dance of "The Masked Warrior King," the climax of which involves the dragon-headed performer gazing up toward the sun while lifting his baton in the air, in time with the beating of the drum. (Remarkably, the producers of the album included precisely this moment of the dance in the painting for Chapter Forty of Murasaki's sutra dedication ceremony, showing the dancer with baton in hand, beckoning the radiant sun as represented by the finial of the drum.)

The *biwa*-playing sister defends herself after her sister's comment, pointing out that there is indeed a connection between the *biwa* and the moon, referring to the "half-moon" acoustic holes in her instrument. The painting helps make this connection to the fuller text of the tale by prominently including the details of the *biwa*. The two half-moon holes on either side of the instrument's golden strings appear just beneath the sister's raised hand, while the woman's upturned face and the plectrum point toward the silver moon in the upper right corner of the composition, directly above Kaoru's head. Unlike other artists' renditions of this scene, the moon is not a full autumn moon, but a half-moon, as if to match the sister's comment and the holes on the *biwa*. Meanwhile, the inclusion of the *koto* in the painting, without its player, alludes to the continued dialogue between the sisters in the tale.

The conversation between the sisters resembles other instances in the tale in which serious content is tempered through its presentation within light-hearted contexts, and in this case accompanied by endearing smiles. Here the banter, stemming from esoteric poems and commentaries, reflects the influence of the girl's upbringing by a father immersed in Buddhist texts, as Dennis Washburn points out, and it also provides an appropriate method to arouse the interest of the spiritually oriented Kaoru. The moon as a symbol of enlightenment is integrated into a standard *kaimami* template for an awakening of desire, again fittingly for a character who lacks the usual worldly inclinations. Accordingly, the *kaimami* scene does not result in an erotic encounter, but to a revelation that leaves Kaoru existentially unsettled. After Kaoru awkwardly attempts to exchange words with the sisters, an old female attendant comes forward to deal with the unexpected visitor. The woman is Bennokimi, who happens to be the daughter of the late Kashiwagi's wet nurse, and thus is the milk-sibling of Kaoru's true father. She was present at Kashiwagi's deathbed and became the confidante to whom he disclosed that he was actually the father of Kaoru, believed by the world to be Genji's son. Bennokimi reveals all of this to the young man on a subsequent visit, handing over several old letters between his mother the Third Princess and Kashiwagi. Kaoru goes to see his mother, observes her with a critical eye, and ultimately decides to keep his newfound knowledge of his parentage to himself.

The identity of the sisters (the elder, known as Oigimi, and the younger, known as Nakanokimi) remains ambiguous throughout this chapter, leading to a long-standing debate over the identity of the *biwa* player in this scene. The album painting shows Kaoru focusing on only one sister, who is most likely Oigimi, with whom he later develops a deeper bond. She is also the sister most commonly identified as "the divine princess at Uji Bridge" (Hashihime), the person referred to in the title of this chapter. The name comes from a poem by Kaoru in which he likens himself to a ferryman who is adrift between the secular world and the far shore of the next life, and who pines romantically for the mythical female guardian deity of the floating bridge that spans the two realms.

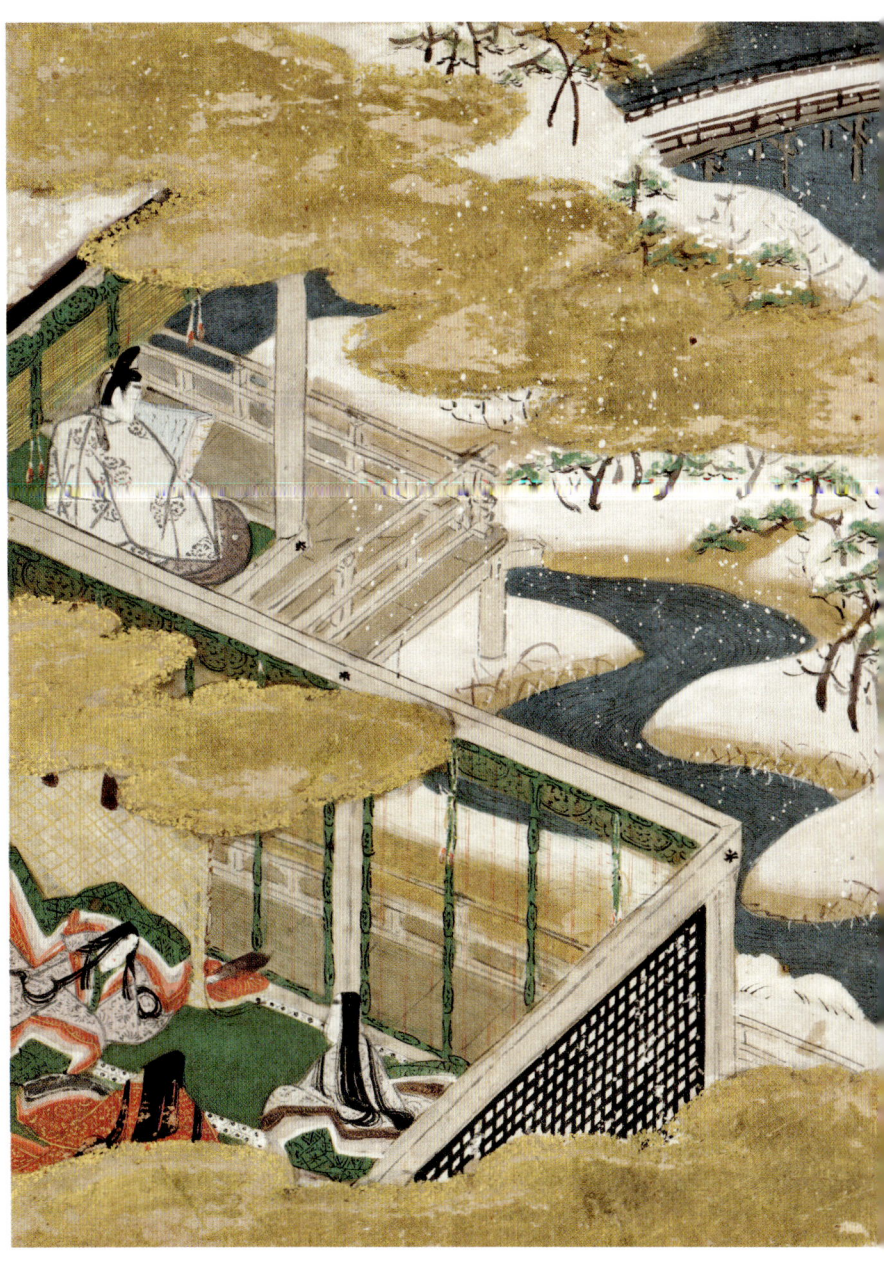

The great bole of oak
Into whose sweet shade I thought
    To come for shelter
Has become, alas, a space
Empty of its seat of prayer.

CRANSTON, P. 922

46

椎本

At the Foot of the Oak Tree

Shiigamoto

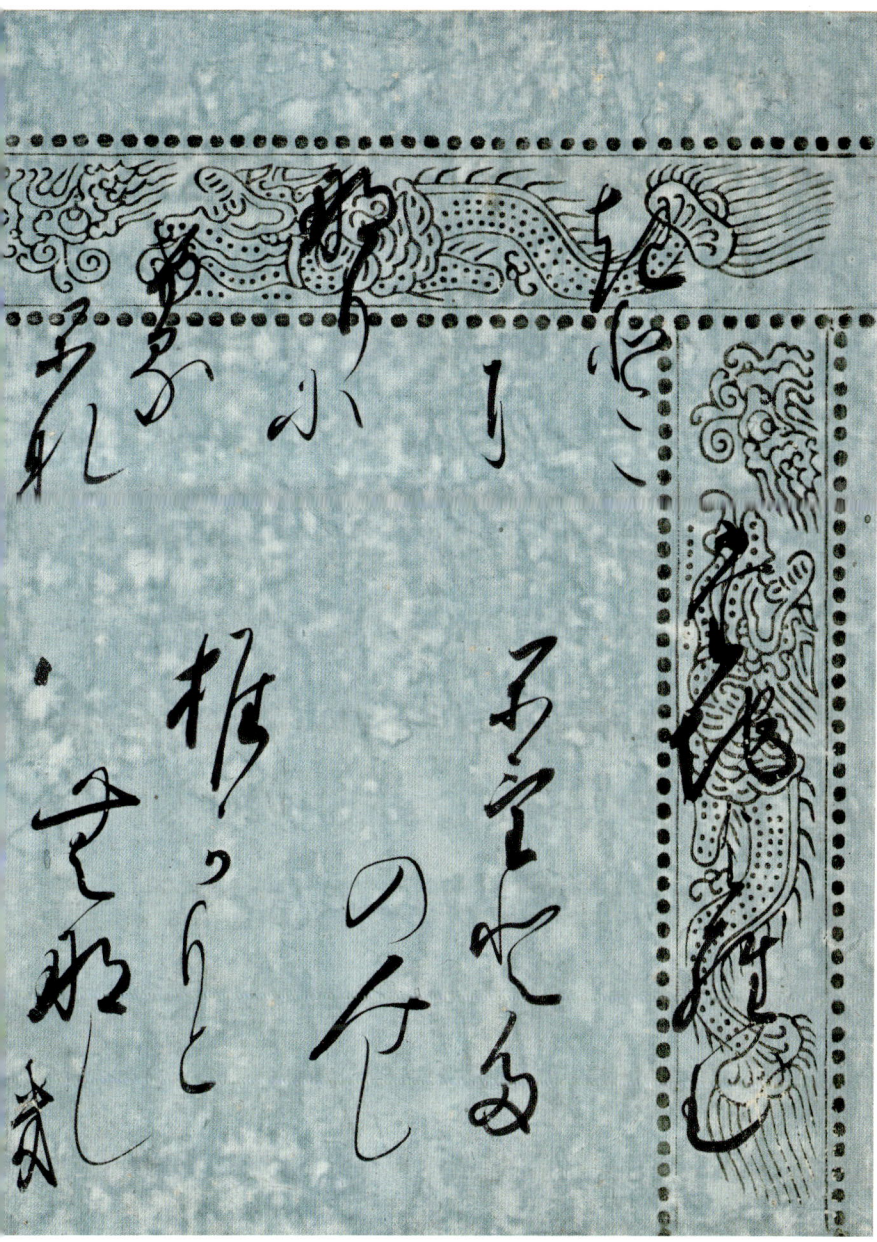

Tachiyoramu
Kage to tanomishi
Shii ga moto
Munashiki kitoko ni
Narinikeru kana

たちよらむ
かげとたのみし
椎がもと
むなしき
きとこに
なりにける
かな

In one of the most beautiful and well-preserved paintings in the album, Mitsunobu's artistry with snow scenes is on full display in the picture's medley of shimmering gold, luminescent shell white, and dark mineral blue, combined with a visually striking and unique design. It is just before the New Year in the twelfth month and the landscape at Uji is blanketed in powdery white snow. The banks on opposite sides of the undulating stream alongside the sisters' villa are soft, rounded mounds shaped as if they interlock like a puzzle. The gold ground beneath the dusting of white does the work of the bright winter sun, its refulgence capturing the crispness of a visual world in high resolution. Ink lines in the water suggest the ripples of a fast-moving stream, but the frosty reeds at the edge of the shore foretell the freezing of the water soon to come. Adding to the sense of a chilly but not quite frigid atmosphere are the gentle flurries of white flakes, which stand out against the mineral blue pigment used to depict the water. The snowbanks and land formations on the right side of the composition, dotted by snow-covered pine trees, lead the eye upward past a large gold cloud that extends across the entire width of the painting, to the rim of a snow-covered mountain. There, in the upper right corner, is the Uji bridge, spanning from behind the mountain to an unseen shore beyond the picture plane. The image participates in the long-standing symbolism of bridges as linking this world and the next, integral to the overall characterization of the otherworldly atmosphere of Uji. At the same time, it recalls the "maiden of the bridge," the elder sister Oigimi, as in the previous chapter.

The visible span of the bridge is covered in freshly fallen snow between its brown-colored railings and is free of tracks or traces of travelers. Its pristine state calls to mind a poem by Oigimi in the tale (different from the one in the calligraphy leaf), a reply she gives to Kaoru during a visit in which he asks her whether she has ever corresponded with Prince Niou. She seeks to reassure him with her verse:

Yuki fukaki	Over the bridges
Yama no kakehashi	Clinging to the cliffs along
Kimi narade	Our deep-snow mountains
Mata fumikayou	No letter-bearer leaves his trace:
Ato o minu kana	Those footprints are yours alone.

CRANSTON, P. 921

The painting for Chapter Forty-Six works with this poem as a "poem-picture" (*uta-e*), more so than the verse actually included in the album's calligraphy, as Katagiri Yayoi has pointed out. Keywords in Oigimi's poem find direct visual counterparts in the image, beginning with the most obvious "deep snow" (*yuki fukaki*), and the "mountain spanning bridge" (*yama no kakehashi*), in the first part of the *waka*. Even the last part of the poem is visualized through a pun on the word "*fumi*," which can mean both "letter" and "to step" (*fumu*). In a corner of the residence, Kaoru sits with his head tilted downward, engrossed in reading a letter held in his hands. The missive, with its pink and gold back, and light blue surface bearing lines of writing, is unusually large,

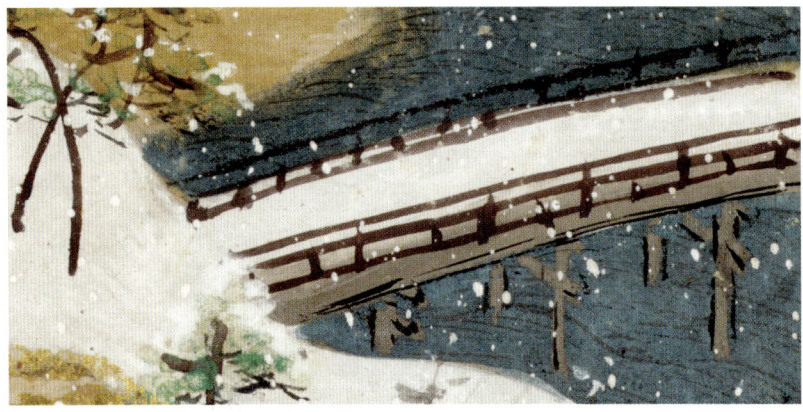

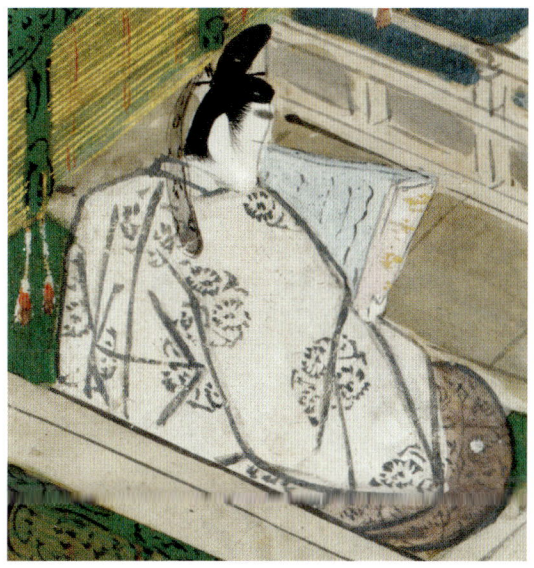

as if signaling its status as a word-image for corresponding components in Oigimi's poem: "letter" (*fumi*) and "traces" (*ato*) of writing. The letter in Kaoru's hand and the pristine snow on the bridge suggest that Kaoru's competitor, Prince Niou, has not "stepped" (*fumu*) here, as he has left no "tracks" (*ato*) either in snow or in writing.

The sender of the letter, Oigimi, appears in the large room near the bottom of the zigzagging architectural structure, highlighted by a bright red standing curtain to her side decorated with a gold crisscross design on its reverse. She is dressed in elaborate robes with layers of pink and red sleeves, and a dark green underlayer, as she leans forward facing two female attendants. The young lady's face is downturned and shows a troubled expression, while a gold cloud hovers above, emphasizing her importance in the scene. Although she has reassured Kaoru that she has never written to Niou, the reader knows better. She has in fact sent the prince a poem on behalf of her sister who had been corresponding with him, but who was too grief-stricken by the death of their father to reply. Niou was fascinated by Oigimi's writing, and according to the narration in the tale, he stared at the letter, unable to put it down, in much the same posture, one might imagine, as Kaoru in this painting. Kaoru's figure calls to mind Niou as a suitor with whom the women must now contend without their father. Kaoru's presence at the house in Uji, however, represents the fulfimment of a promise he made to Hachinomiya to look after the princesses.

The calligraphic excerpt chosen for this chapter does not match the picture, as mentioned, but it does provide the verse from which the chapter title derives, which also reflects Kaoru's sadness over the passing of Hachimomiya, his friend and spiritual mentor. The poem is a lament composed by the young man after he enters the room of the deceased Hachinomiya. He sees that the chambers are already covered in dust and emptied of all the ritual implements and Buddhist statues and paintings that had aided the prince in his devotions. The place where Kaoru once studied with Hachinomiya is "beneath the oak" (*shii ga moto*), the tree being a symbol for the old prince, a space now empty (*munashiki toko*) in both the literal and Buddhistic sense of "emptiness." Reading the image in conjunction with this poem, regardless of its fit with the precise temporal moment of the scene, encourages the viewer to understand the figure of Kaoru in the painting as a character contemplating more than just romance. With the inclusion of this poetic lament, the painting can function as a depiction of another step in Kaoru's ill-fated relationship with the princesses and as a vision of him grieving the loss of his religious teacher and friend, allowing the bridge at the top of the painting to symbolize the link to the mythical maiden and to the otherworld.

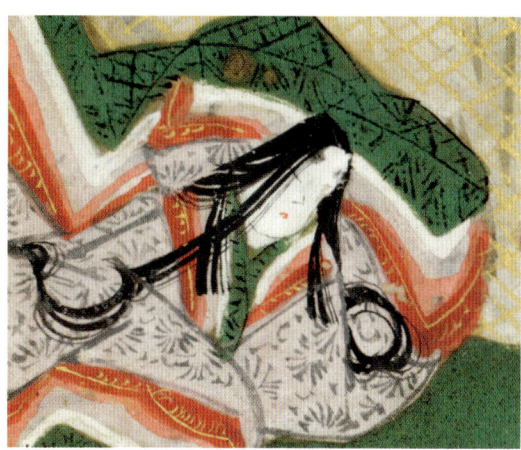

Chapter 46 | At the Foot of the Oak Tree | 207

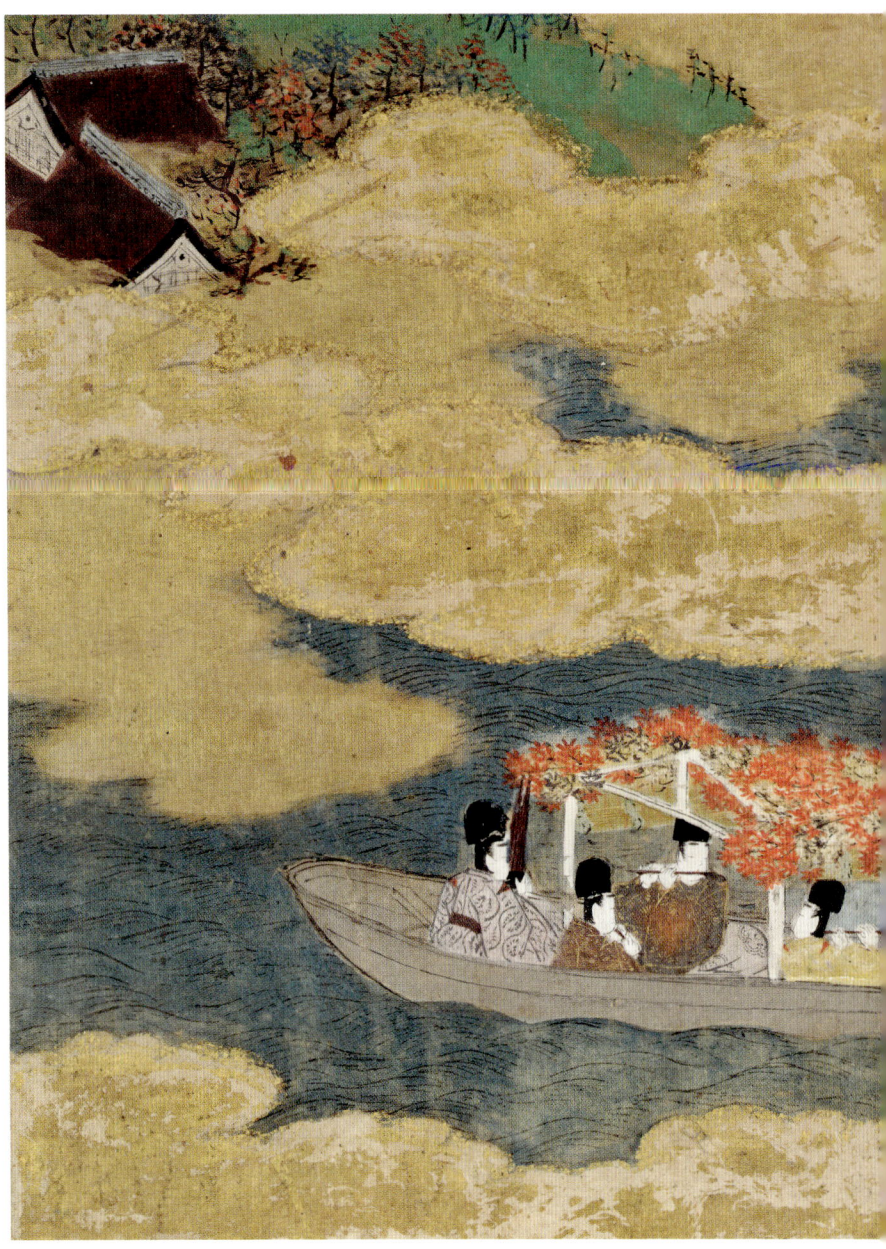

They could make out the brocade-like thatch of autumn leaves that decorated the roof of the boat and were surprised by the extravagant, lively sound of musical instruments in concert that came wafting toward them on the wind.

WASHBURN, P. 1016

47

総角

A Bowknot Tied in Maiden's Loops
Agemaki

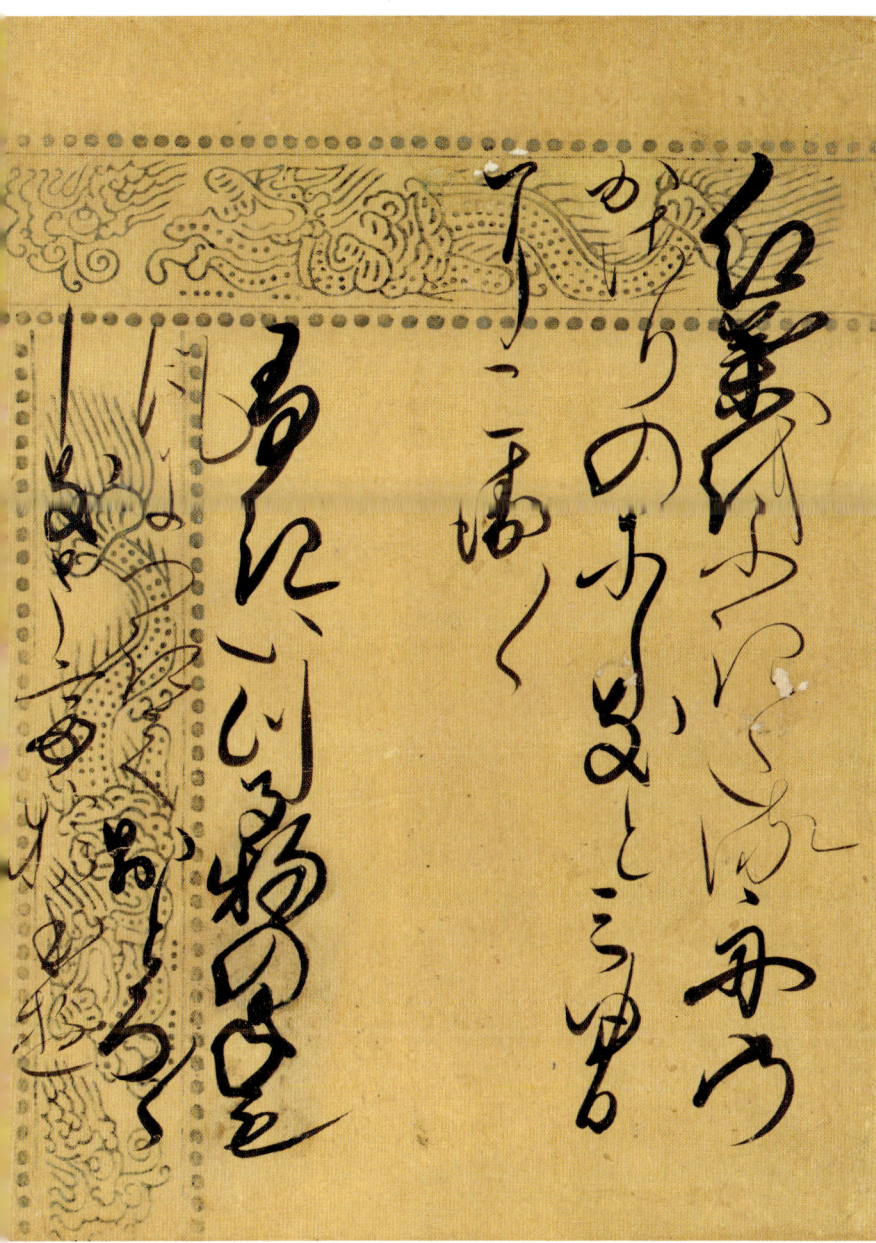

Momiji o fukitaru fune no
kazari no nishiki to miyuru
ni, koegoe fukiizuru mono
no ne mo, kaze ni tsukite
odoroodoroshiki made oboyu

紅葉をふきたる舟の
かさりのにしきとみゆる
にこゑく
ふきいつる物のねも
風につきておとろく
しきまておほゆ

Drawn to women of royal status, Niou ignores the plans made for him to marry the sixth daughter of his commoner uncle, Yūgiri, and in Chapter Forty-Seven, he secretly weds the second princess at Uji, Nakanokimi. As Niou is a favorite son of the Akashi Empress, and it is presumed he will one day become Crown Prince, Niou's movements and behavior are strictly circumscribed by protocol and scrutinized by the watchful eyes of his parents and relatives. His visits to Nakanokimi, after having been introduced to the Uji sisters by Kaoru in the last chapter, have only been conducted with great effort on Niou's part and careful scheming by Kaoru. Niou manages to make the arduous trip south of the capital for the obligatory three consecutive nights that constitute a wedding, but with no one else's knowledge or acknowledgment, the union still feels tenuous to Nakanokimi and her sister. Oigimi, burdened by her father's admonitions not to shame the family or marry beneath her station, coupled with her own aversion to marriage and deep-seated feelings of inadequacy, persists in rejecting Kaoru. And yet for a brief moment after Niou spends his third night with Nakanokimi, both sisters seem hopeful.

The album painting depicts the moment, however, just as events take an unfortunate turn, leading Oigimi to fear that the couple is indeed star-crossed, and that her sister may be headed for neglect and ridicule after all. It has been weeks since Niou wed Nakanokimi and having been subjected to court duties and constraints placed on him by vigilant parents suspicious of his philanderings, he has been unable to visit his secret bride at Uji. Finally, under the public pretense of an autumn excursion, he travels by boat, one extravagantly decorated and festooned with fall leaves. The painting shows the boat transporting four courtiers playing the "lively music carried on the wind," as the text in the album's excerpt describes. The instruments include the reed pipe (*shō*), the small oboe (*hichiriki*), and two horizontal flutes (*yokobue*). Only one figure faces the viewer, a flute player, who seems to be Prince Niou. He wears elegant robes and sits directly beneath the pinnacle of the boat's roof. A golden-lined bamboo blind hangs behind him, and a profusion of crimson leaves encircle his face. The figure playing the short vertical flute is dressed in similarly elegant robes and might be Kaoru. As in the album painting for Suma (Chapter Twelve), sound travels over the waves and across golden forms that evoke sandbars, or the shadows of the mottled gold clouds hovering above. The musical strains reach the villa, which is represented by two grand structures poking through the clouds in the upper left corner. The buildings have gray-tiled ridges that top hipped and gabled cypress roofs. Trees with leaves painted in red, green, and blue signify the canopy of colorful autumn foliage that blends in with the green hills said to be visible to Niou and Kaoru from the boat.

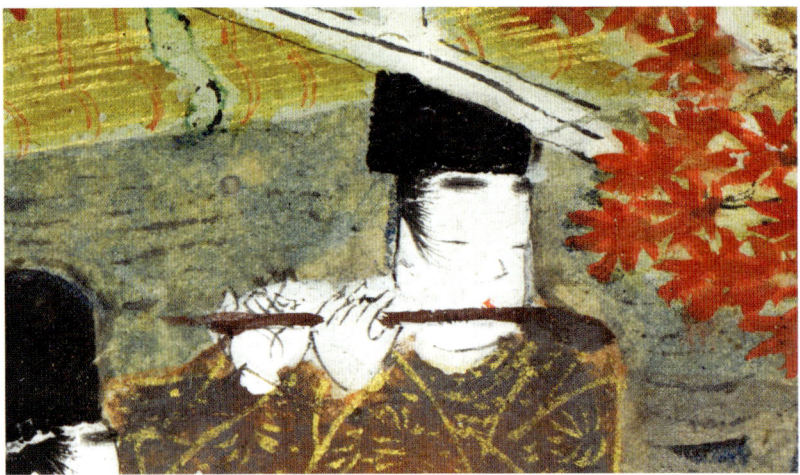

210 | *The Tale of Genji*

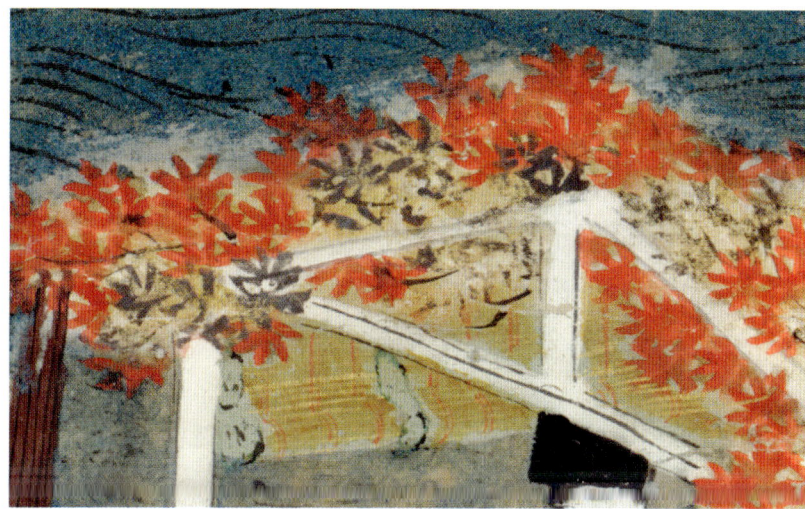

The passage in the tale also describes the boat from the perspective of the female attendants at the Uji villa who have crowded onto the veranda to get a glimpse of their lady's new husband. They cannot spot Niou himself through the heavy mist suspended over the water, but they are struck by the lavishness of the entourage and the colorful red leaves, "brocade-like," floating through the haze. The women find the vision of Niou's floating spectacle so magnificent that they liken him to Hikoboshi, the celestial oxherd (the star Altair), who only meets his lover the celestial weaver maiden, Orihime (the star Vega), once a year. The women decide that if he were Hikoboshi, Niou's celestial light would be worth the wait for Tanabata, the autumn festival during which the two stars cross the "River of Heaven" (Ama no Kawa), the band of stars known as the Milky Way that otherwise keeps them apart. In this way, the Uji River can be viewed as the River of Heaven that separates the two lovers. During Tanabata the mythical couple reunites by crossing a bridge of autumn leaves, as beautifully expressed in a *Kokinshū* poem (IV: 175), which explains why the weaver maiden has been known to long for fall. From the perspective of the ladies at the Uji villa, the boat bobbing on the waves through mist could easily be taken for that ethereal floating bridge of woven brocade-like leaves that will unite the lovers once more. And reinforcing the idea of Prince Niou as Hikoboshi in the painting, the artist makes him a flute player, the instrument long associated with the oxherd.

But while natural forces conspire to bring the two stars together in poetry, in this episode, higher powers, namely Prince Niou's mother and father, keep Niou and Nakanokimi apart. Not only is Niou surrounded by young men who would be his future brothers-in-law (sons of Yūgiri), he is also soon joined by a vast contingent of palace officials sent by the Akashi Empress. The excursion becomes a grand courtly event, making a visit for Niou across the river to the Uji villa impossible. Meanwhile, the sisters, even though they have been told to prepare for the prince's visit, can only watch in humiliation as the fanfare and revelry exceeds anything they have witnessed before, and Niou simply ignores them. Oigimi had already been doubtful of Niou's intentions, but this indignity shames her to the core. She wants nothing more than to disappear, a goal she finally accomplishes by the end of the chapter when she loses all will to live and simply stops eating. Kaoru rushes to her sickbed, commissions Buddhist rites to heal her, but is forced to witness her demise, and he remains at the household for the full forty-nine days of mourning. Meanwhile Niou visits the grieving Nakanokimi and finally makes plans to move his bride to the capital, to Nijō, the home he inherited from Murasaki.

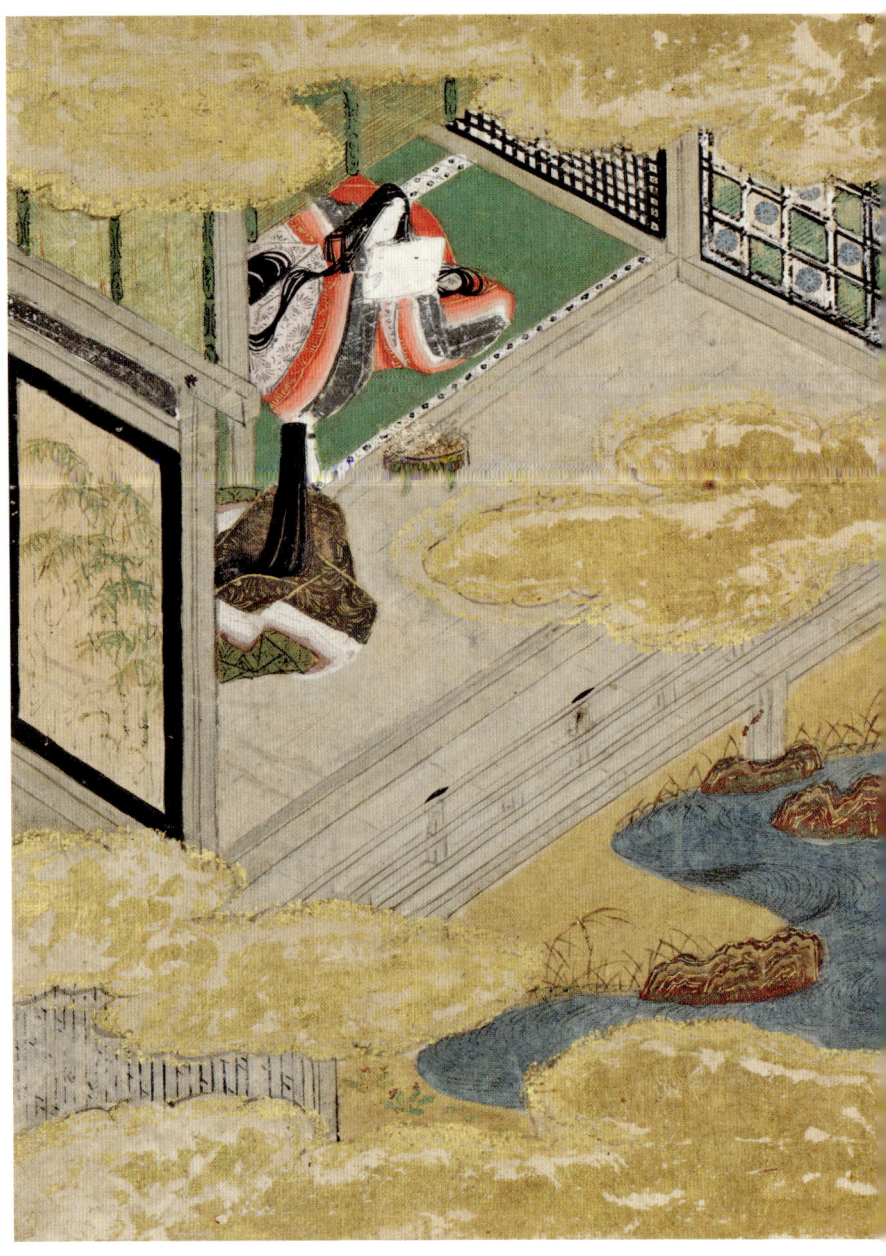

    These are now for you
(Many springs have I picked them
      Through drifting years for *him*),
These first shoots of the bracken
In a custom we won't forget.

CRANSTON, P. 934

48

早蕨

Early Fiddlehead Greens
Sawarabi

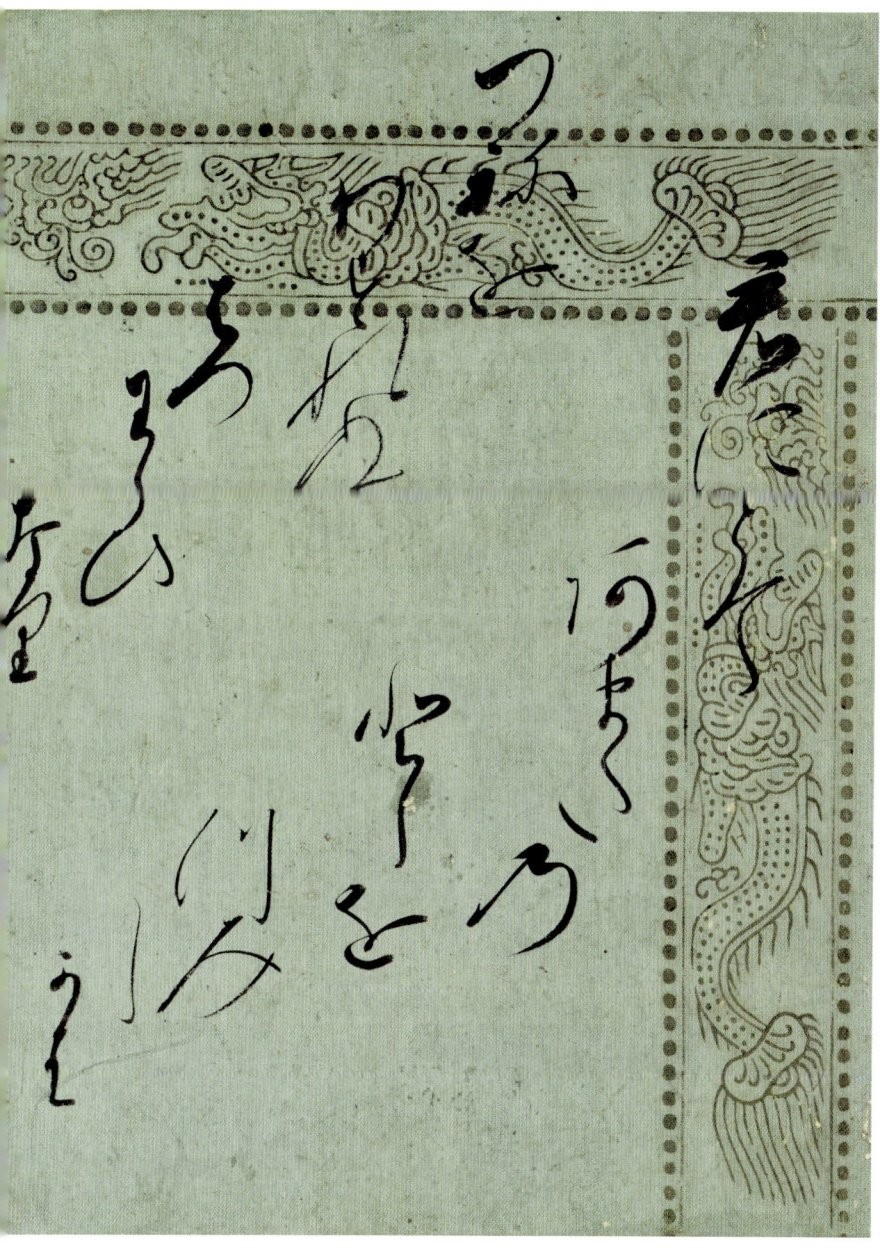

Kimi ni tote
Amata no toshi o
Tsumishikaba
Tsune o wasurenu
Hatsuwarabi nari

君にとて
あまた の
つねを としを
わすれぬ つみ
はつ し
わらひ かは
なり

Chapter Forty-Eight opens with Nakanokimi still mourning her older sister and in the midst of examining a gift from a character known as "the ascetic" (*azari*), a priest who had been her late father's religious guide. It being spring and the start of the New Year, the ascetic has sent a basket filled with plants recently picked near his temple in the Uji mountains. The basket that has been gifted is a focal point in the album painting, shown on the floor directly in front of Nakanokimi. It contains both horsetail shoots (*tsukushi*), with their distinctive brown circles on beige-colored spore cones, and fiddleheads (*warabi*), most of the green pigment of which has disappeared from the surface of the painting. The ascetic has also sent a letter through the princess's female attendant inquiring about the young lady's well-being. The attendant appears in the painting, seated in the aisle room in profile, seemingly having just delivered the gift and the ascetic's note, which Nakanokimi holds in two hands as she reads intently. In a trope that we have seen before in the album, the poem inscribed on the adjacent calligraphy sheet is the very one being read by the figure in the image. It may have taken some effort for Nakanokimi to decipher the ascetic's writing—the narrator makes a point of noting the roughness of his *kana* calligraphy and the clumsy indentation of his poem amid the prose of the letter. Nevertheless, Nakanokimi is grateful for the sentiments expressed and contrasts them to the superficial content and florid language of Niou's letters.

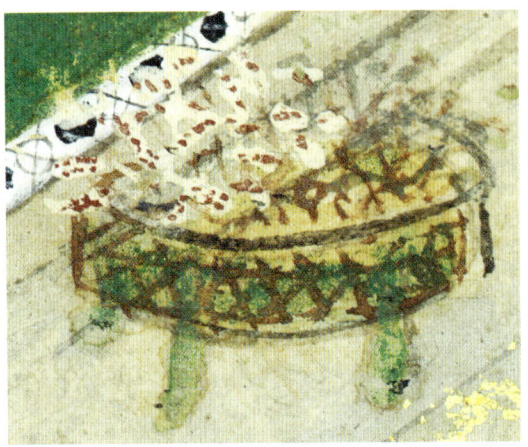

The poem in fact touchingly recalls for Nakanokimi a time one year ago when she and her now deceased sister both mourned the death of their father, Hachinomiya. The sisters received a similar delivery of spring bracken from the ascetic at that time (narrated in the Shiigamoto chapter), which inspired a verse that Oigimi sent to the ascetic in response:

> *Kimi ga oru*   Could we but view it
> *Mine no warabi to*   As the bracken Father plucked
> *Mimashikaba*   On the peak where he dwelt,
> *Shirare ya semashi*   We might find in it a sign
> *Haru no shirushi mo* That spring has come again.
>   CRANSTON, P. 922

The word *kimi* refers to Hachinomiya, as Oigimi wished the plants were ones their father himself had picked—Hachinomiya died while on a retreat at the ascetic's mountain temple after suddenly becoming ill, and the sisters were never allowed to see him. Oigimi's poem suggests an imagining on her part that her father lived on, like an immortal on his mountain peak, and her wish that the plants provided a confirmation of his eternal return. The ascetic's poem, included with his gift and reproduced in the album leaf, reuses the first word *kimi* ("him," which referred to Hachinomiya) to echo Oigimi's previous verse, but now refers to Nakanokimi (sent to "you"). The last two lines of the verse pay tribute to the deceased Oigimi, the "*first shoots of bracken*" (*hatsu-warabi*), the elder, firstborn sister. In this way, the ascetic's words bring all three family members together. In response, Nakanokimi sends the following poem (not included in the album leaf):

> *Kono haru wa*   Whom this year in spring
> *Tare ni misemu*   Shall I show the shoots you've picked,
> *Naki hito no*   These remembrances
> *Katami ni tsumeru*   Of one who is no more,
> *Mine no sawarabi*   Early bracken from the hill?
>   CRANSTON, P. 935

She laments the loss of her one true companion in life, her grief over her sister's death surpassing even that for her father. Nakanokimi uses "early bracken" (*sawarabi*), the title for this chapter, altering the priest's "first bracken," as if to say that the elder sister was taken too soon.

For all of the expressions of paralyzing grief, the first line of the Sawarabi chapter hopefully announces the change in season from winter to spring after Oigimi's death, explaining that "the radiance of spring illuminates even the darkest of thickets." Life will go on, as it indeed does when the story soon turns to Nakanokimi's move to the capital, and into Niou's magnificent Nijō residence. Chapter Forty-Eight marks Nakanokimi's emergence as the sole remaining heroine of the Uji storyline, and the album painting depicts her taking her sister's place. She is situated at an angle within the architecture identical to that of Oigimi in the painting for Chapter Forty-Five, for example, visualizing the theme of their interchangeability. The bamboo fence of the residence that figured so prominently in the *kaimami* passage in the Hashihime chapter appears in this image as well, between golden clouds in the lower left corner, a subtle reminder of all that has happened since Kaoru first glimpsed the sisters from the other side of the fence on that moonlit night in Chapter Forty-Five. Nakanokimi is depicted wearing a transparent white singlet, with its pink tone created by layers of red garments underneath. Her eyebrows point inward and upward registering her sorrow as she reads the ascetic's mournful poem, while her black tresses are full and luxurious. The narrative stresses the closeness and similarity of the sisters, and yet when directly compared, Nakanokimi is said to be more cheerful and yielding than her sister.

The decor of the sister's room also hints at Nakanokimi's new life to come in the capital as a princess married to Prince Niou. One of the wooden panels enclosing the aisle of her residence includes a colorful lattice wall, resembling a freestanding lattice panel (*tatejitomi*). Its squares are painted alternatively in green and white in a checkerboard pattern, with blue chrysanthemums, each with ten petals, adorning the center of the white squares. The chrysanthemum could be a symbol for offspring of the imperial house and may suggest Nakanokimi's marriage to Prince Niou. Meanwhile, a second wooden panel directly opposite this one bears a painting of tall green bamboo overlaid with conspicuous ink lines that indicate the panel's wood grain. Nakanokimi sits directly between these two visual symbols, the regal chrysanthemum (Niou) and the sturdy, austere bamboo (Kaoru). The only flowers shown in the Uji garden are violets (*sumire*), which are never mentioned in the narration of *The Tale of Genji* but are alluded to indirectly by Niou, when he sends Nakanokimi a suggestive message and refers to a poet who sleeps among a field of violets. The delicate purple petals connote spring but also Niou's attraction to Nakanokimi, an attraction that is said to be mutual. Despite this suggestion that the newlywed's union is a promising one, Kaoru is tempted to believe that the younger sister should be for him a living memento of Oigimi, creating a complicated romantic triangle that Nakanokimi will be forced to negotiate on her own.

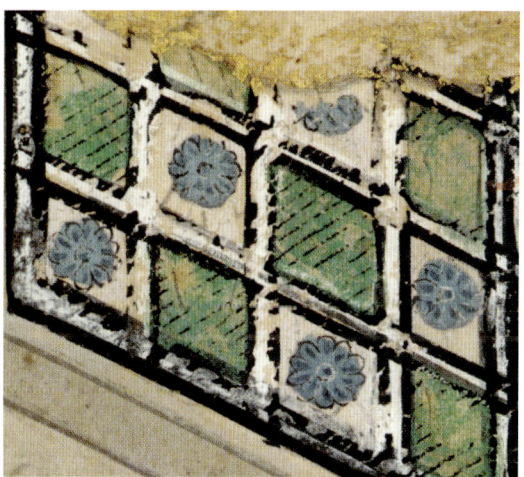

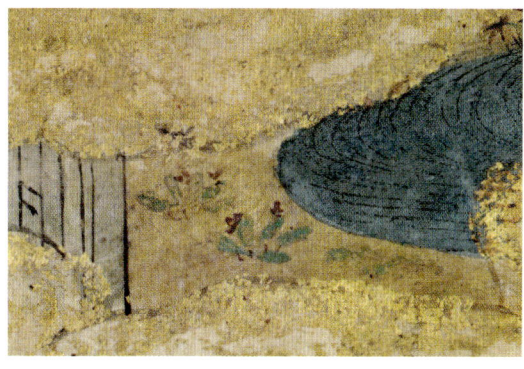

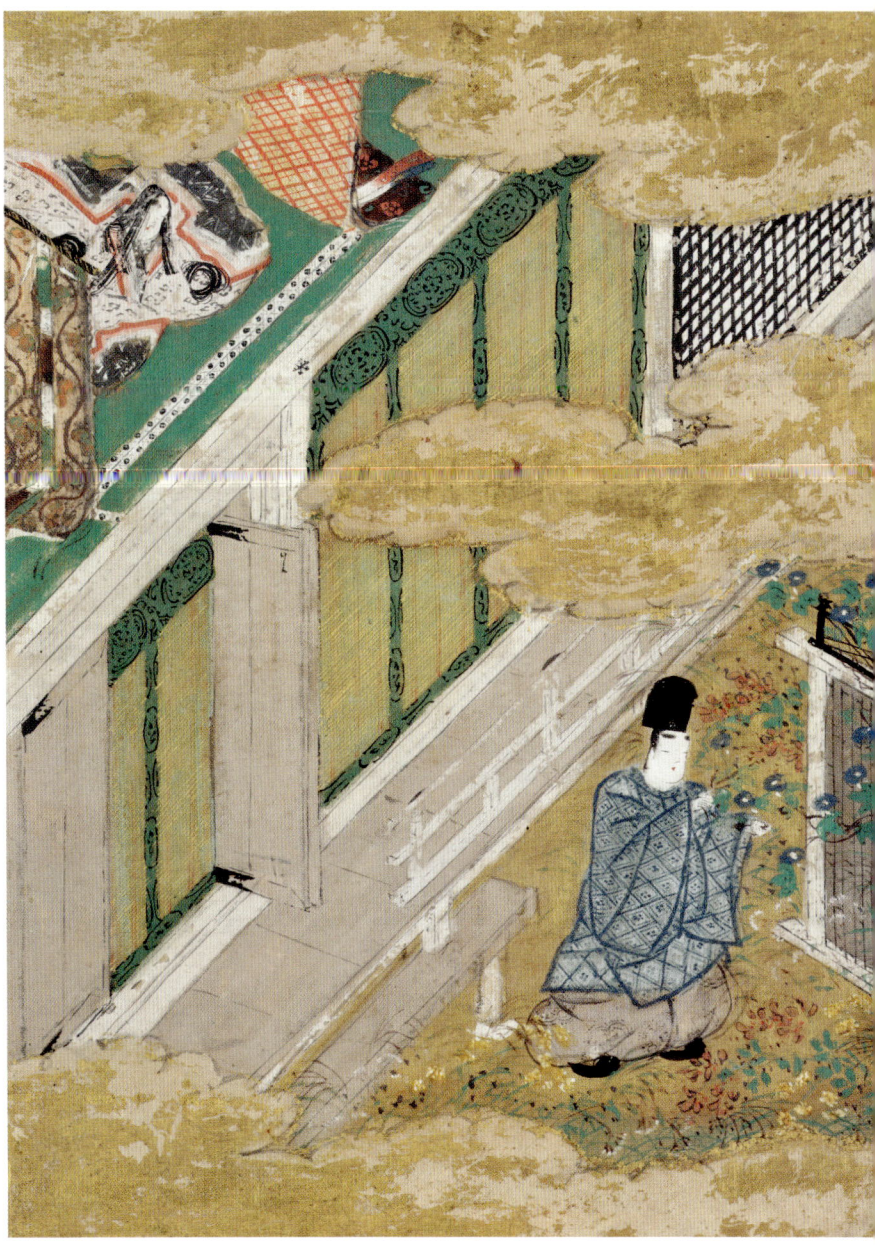

He pulled a tendril of the
morning glory toward him,
causing a cascade of dew to fall.

WASHBURN, P. 1063

    Shall I give my glance
Admiring to this morning's hue,
    Knowing all the while
I but rely on a flower
Lustrous til the dewdrops dry?

CRANSTON, P. 940

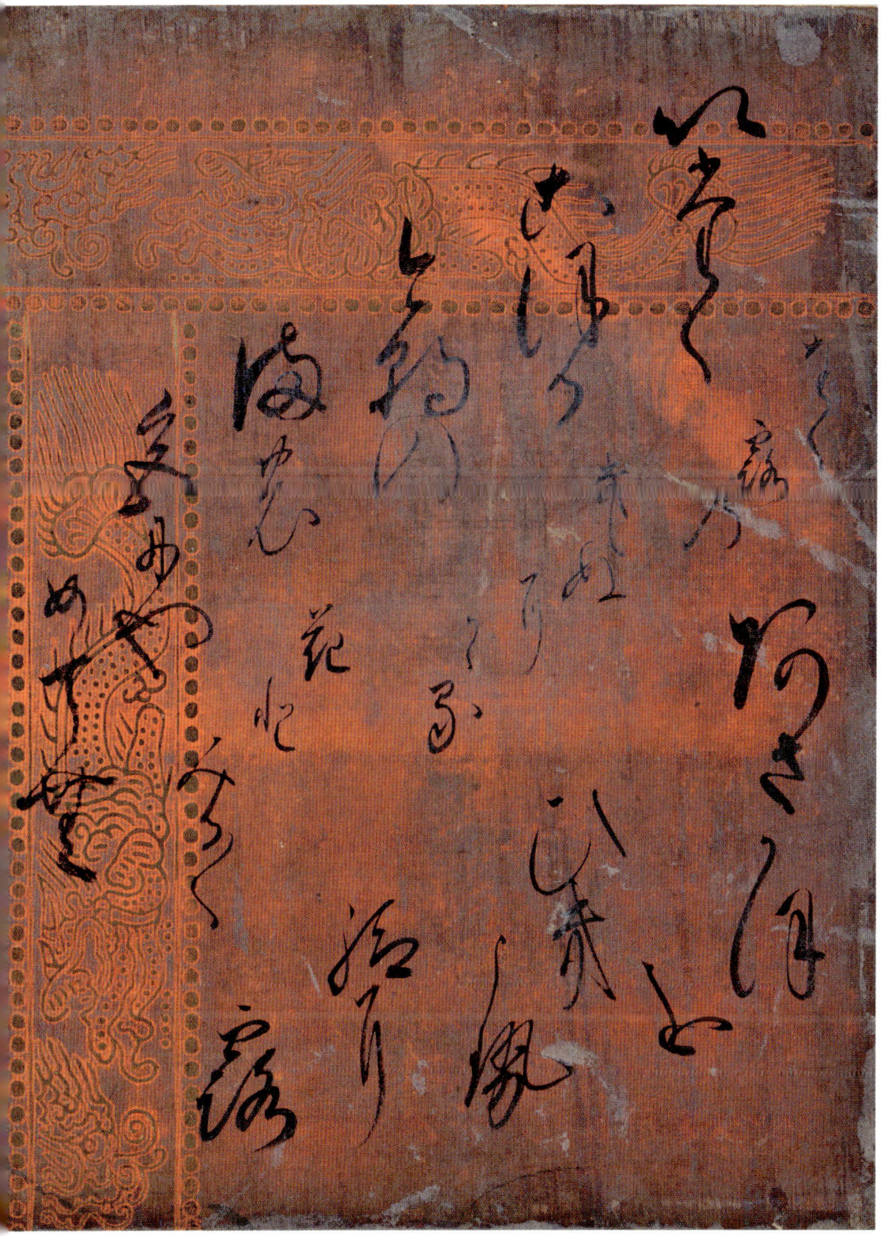

49

宿木
Trees Encoiled in Vines of Ivy

Yadoriki

Asagao o hikiyose tamau
ni tsuyu itaku koboru.

    Kesa no ma no
    Iro ni ya medemu
      Oku tsuyu no
    Kienu ni kakaru
    Hana to miru miru

をく あさかほ
いたく 露の を
こほる きえぬ ひきよせ
今朝の にかゝる 給に
まの 花と 露
色にや みる
めてむ

In the painting for Chapter Forty-Nine, Kaoru stands amid a garden teeming with autumn flowers—pampas grass, bush clover, white-tipped mistflowers, and yellow maiden flowers—accented by dots of silver to evoke the glistening morning dew. As in the text of the album's calligraphy, Kaoru pulls a tendril of morning glory toward him; the painting shows him firmly taking the dew-drenched vine in both hands. The vines of the jaunty blue flowers wind around a wood-framed bamboo fence and a black, open-work design atop its lintel. The fence is called "mist-enshrouded" in the preceding passage in the tale, and Kaoru first spots it, along with the blue morning glories, from inside his Sanjō residence. He has spent a sleepless night still tormented over the loss of Oigimi and filled with regret for not pursuing Nakanokimi when he had the chance. Niou has recently succumbed to relentless pressure by his parents and the Minister, Yūgiri, to take Rokunokimi (Yūgiri's sixth daughter) as a second wife. The news devastates Nakanokimi, who has just learned she is pregnant with Niou's first child, and it encourages Kaoru to rationalize acting on his attraction to Nakanokimi. At the same time, Kaoru himself has finally agreed to marry, after having received a personal invitation from the Emperor to wed his daughter by his Fujitsubo Consort. Although it is a great privilege for a commoner to marry a princess, Kaoru remains conflicted given his spiritual aspirations and aversion to commitments that would hinder his later withdrawal from the world. The morning glory, blooming only briefly, captures Kaoru's sentiment at this moment, as a metaphor for life's ephemerality. Before plucking the flower, the narrative describes Kaoru as lying alone, staring out into the garden through raised shutters, watching the flowers as they open with the coming of dawn. He decides to visit Nakanokimi, breaks off the morning glory, and intones the verse in the album on his way to the Nijō villa. In the poem Kaoru questions his own tendency to be drawn to such fleeting beauties, referring, it seems, to both the short-lived Oigimi and her unattainable younger sister.

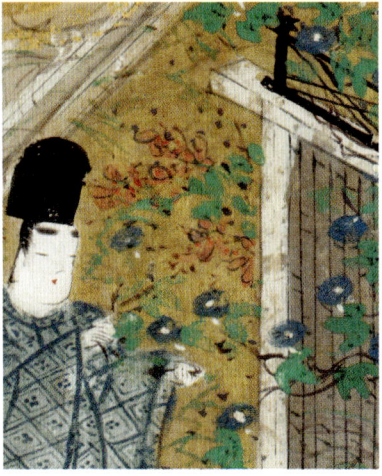

While the image of Kaoru and the morning glory that so aptly expresses his ethereal persona and the sentiment of his verse seems rather straightforward, the painting's inclusion of a female figure inside the residence complicates the identification of the scene's subject matter. Although Kaoru is said to gaze at the garden alone in the early morning hours, and although he is presented as the chaste foil to the libidinous Niou, he is far from abstinent. In fact, the prelude to his plucking of the morning glory is a passage that describes his relations with a number of women in his service, women of distinguished lineages, but to whom he never develops a strong attachment. These women seem to be like the proverbial "showy maiden flowers" noted in the tale (Washburn, p. 1024), an allusion to three different *Kokinshū* poems by Bishop Henjō, in which the priest-poet spurns the seductive charms of flowers that threaten the single-minded purpose of the religious devotee. Kaoru prefers the morning glory, symbol of transience, a point underscored by the painting, which has him nearly trampling the yellow maiden flowers underfoot, and turning his back to the beautiful woman inside, while focusing his attention on the waning beauty in his hands. He leaves the garden, it is said in the tale, "without so much as a glance at the maiden flowers."

The woman in the painting could be an example of the kind of alluring beauty who lacks the sensitivity and thoughtfulness that attracted Kaoru to Oigimi. The visual tropes that convey social status in narrative painting, however, make this identification unlikely. Luxurious curtains framing the woman, her location deep within the interior of the room, and the gold cloud above her, all suggest someone specific and prominent. The album painting most likely combines two scenes: Kaoru in the garden at Sanjō and his subsequent visit to Nijō just moments later, in which case the woman depicted in the interior is none other than Nakanokimi. The residential facade that diagonally bisects the painting can refer to the building at Sanjō from which Kaoru emerged as well as to the veranda at Nijō to which he will next ascend. The architectural features recall Kaoru's early morning visit to Nakanokimi at Nijō—one of the wooden exterior doors has been swung outward, with a metal latch hanging in its upper right corner emphasizing how it was opened to provide access to the princess. In the narrative of this visit to Nakanokimi, the attendants eventually lay out a mat on the veranda for Kaoru so that he keeps his distance from their lady, and he converses with her through drawn bamboo blinds and layers of standing curtains. Irritated by such restrictions given his familiarity and history with the family, Kaoru is tempted to cross the threshold, leaning on the door frame (*shimo-nageshi*) as he contemplates lifting the blinds to speak to Nakanokimi face to face. He restrains himself, however, and instead pushes beneath the blinds the morning glory from his garden, placed on a fan. In a poem Kaoru likens the flower to Nakanokimi and the dew on its surface to her sister. But as Dennis Washburn notes, Nakanokimi reverses the identification in her reply. She claims to be the dew with nothing to cling to, now that her sister is gone, faded like the wilted maiden flower that has already changed color since being removed from Kaoru's garden.

One other woman is referred to as a maiden flower in this chapter—Rokunokimi, the new wife of Niou, who with her powerful paternal backing, stands in stark contrast to the solitary Uji Princess. Nakanokimi fears that she will be abandoned by a husband on whom she is wholly dependent but finds ways to assert her position and to occupy Niou's attention even over the course of the three successive wedding nights and the early days of his marriage to Rokunokimi. First, she provokes his jealous nature by writing to Kaoru and requesting a meeting, leading to an unusually bold move by Kaoru, in which he gets close enough to leave his indelible scent on her body for Niou to detect. The prospect of cuckoldry keeps Niou from staying too long with his new bride. Later, the birth of a son to Nakanokimi results in Niou sequestering himself with her for an even longer period, much to the irritation of Rokunokimi's father Yūgiri. At the same time, Nakanokimi must manage Kaoru's increasing passion for her, which she does by revealing the existence of a secret half sister, the character known as Ukifune. Although born to a servant woman related to Hachinomiya's late wife, the girl is still the flesh and blood of the prince and apparently the living image of Kaoru's deceased love Oigimi. By the end of the chapter Kaoru has confirmed the resemblance during an extended *kaimami* scene at the Uji villa where the young woman stops on her return from a pilgrimage to Hasedera. Ukifune is introduced in the context of Kaoru's desire to create an effigy and painted portrait of Oigimi. Despite her being characterized as merely a "living doll" for Kaoru to remind himself of his deceased beloved, Ukifune will emerge as the most remarkable heroine of the remaining chapters in the tale.

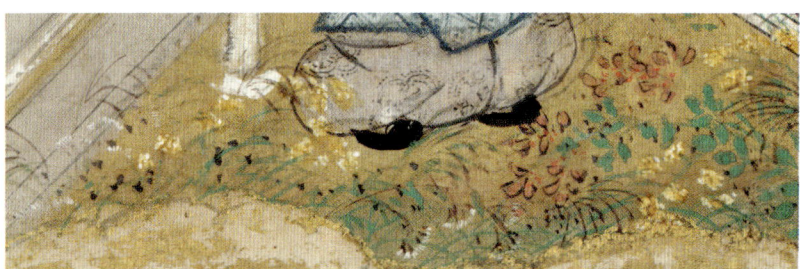

Chapter 49 | Trees Encoiled in Vines of Ivy | 219

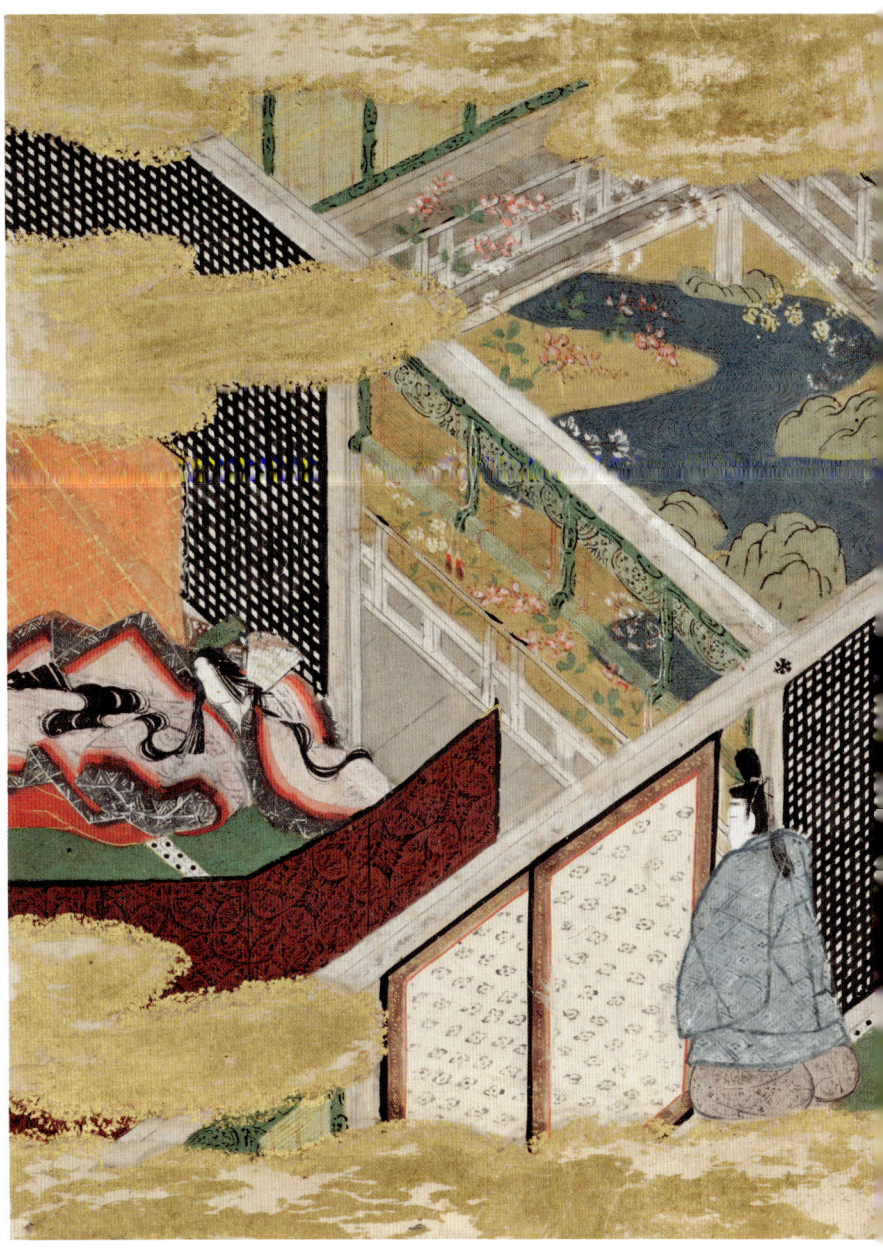

The young lady was reclining near the veranda as she gazed out at the courtyard framed by the passageways on the west side of the villa. She was evidently captivated by the extraordinary beauty of the flowers blooming there in a riot of colors and by the charm of the tall stones that lined the garden stream.

WASHBURN, P. 1144, MODIFIED

50

東屋

A Hut in the Eastern Provinces

Azumaya

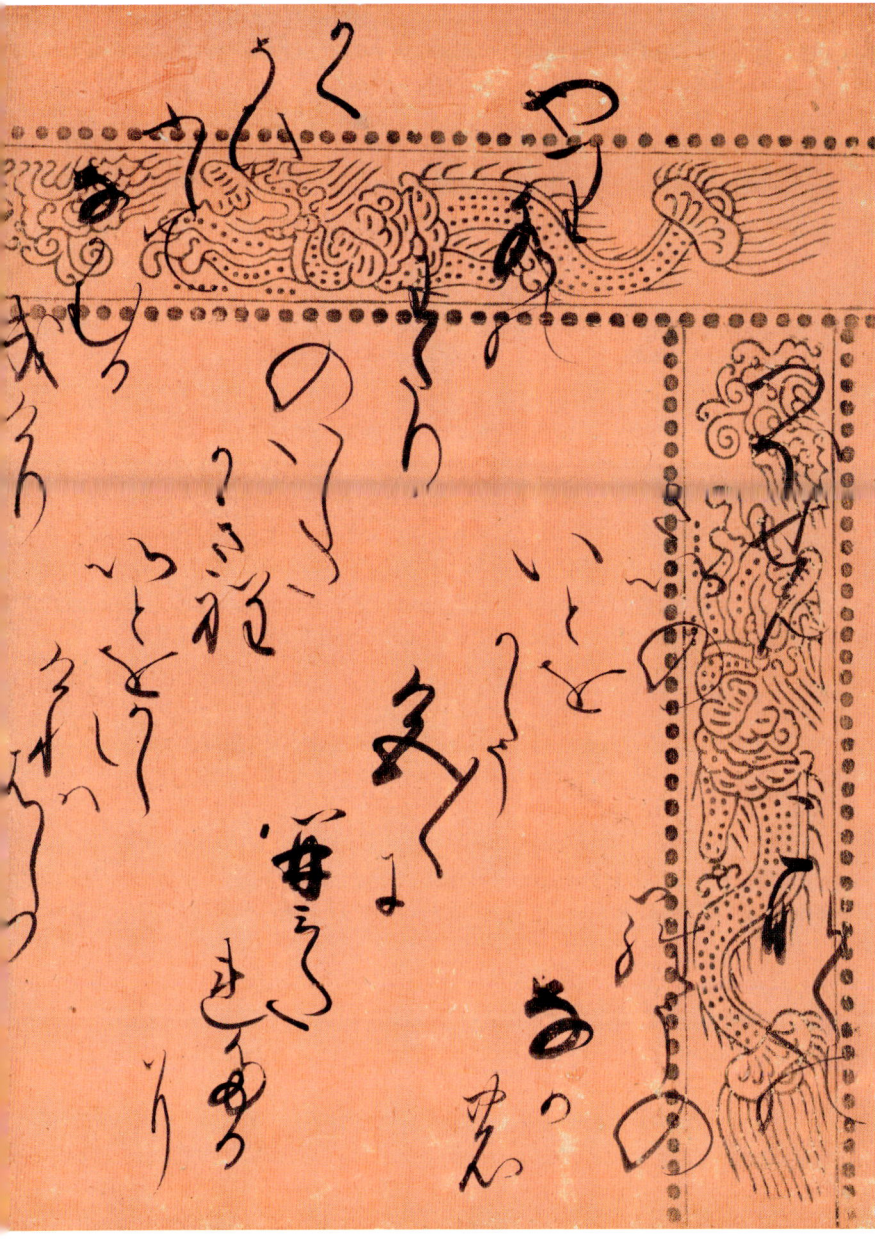

Konata no rō no naka no tsubosenzai no ito okashiu iroiro ni Hirakimidaretaru ni, yarimizu no watari no ishi takaki hodo ito okashikereba, hashi chikaku soifushite nagamuru narikeri.

つほせん こなたの らうの
さいの なか の
いとを かしう の
かく わたり のいした
やり水の かしう 色〻に 開みた
のわたり の いし 開みた れたる
かく たかき程 いとをかし に
そひ ふして けれは はしち
ふして いとを かし に
なかむる けれは
成けり

The painting for Chapter Fifty depicts Ukifune at the Nijō residence of her half sister, Nakanokimi, after she has left the home of her stepfather, the Vice Governor of Hitachi. Ukifune's mother has secretly attempted and failed to marry Ukifune to a nobleman, in the process prioritizing her over her other daughter with the Governor and making her no longer welcome in the household. Ukifune's mother turns for assistance to Nakanokimi, who agrees to hide Ukifune temporarily in a remote corner of Nijō, all the while never informing Niou that the half sister exists, let alone that she is living in his house. One evening, after Niou returns from the palace where he has been attending to his ailing mother, the Akashi Empress, he seeks out his wife's company in the west wing of Nijō only to find that she is occupied with the laborious process of having her hair washed. He teasingly scolds her for leaving him bored and lonely and wanders about, when he suddenly spots a young serving girl he has never seen before (a woman who has accompanied Ukifune) in the western aisle room of Nakanokimi's quarters. His curiosity piqued, he looks through the crack of a sliding door that had been left open, assuming the usual *kaimami* pose. The narrative describes how he quietly widens the sliding panel to see around a folding screen in front of the door and stealthily enters the room. The text in the adjacent calligraphy sheet describes Niou watching Ukifune as she gazes out at the beautiful courtyard garden (*tsubo senzai*), represented in the painting by an array of colorful small flowers near the veranda and around the winding garden stream. The lattice shutters in Ukifune's room have been opened for her, and the horizontal bamboo blinds with their colorful tassels have been raised, showing the unobstructed view that she peacefully enjoys. Walkways and railings of the adjacent buildings define the square enclosure of the private and protected courtyard space. Caught completely off guard, Ukifune is startled and confused when Niou enters her room, and she raises her fan to hide her face. Niou then grabs hold of her robes and her hand clasping the fan, asking her who she is while keeping his own identity secret.

Without any idea that his wife's half sibling has been staying at his home, Niou assumes the mysterious woman he discovers to be a new lady-in-waiting. In the world of the tale, dalliances with such women by a man of Niou's status are considered inconsequential if they pose no social threat to the principal wife and her family. Niou's assumption that Ukifune is of low status also foreshadows the ambiguous position this new heroine will continue to occupy throughout the rest of the story. After Ukifune's mother was shunned by Hachinomiya and married the Vice Governor of Hitachi, she was forced to raise Ukifune in the provinces, but she views her daughter as worthy of an auspicious marriage. Even if the girl's true father, Hachinomiya, never acknowledged her, she is the daughter of a prince, and the granddaughter of the Kiritsubo Emperor in whose reign the tale began. Ukifune is therefore like

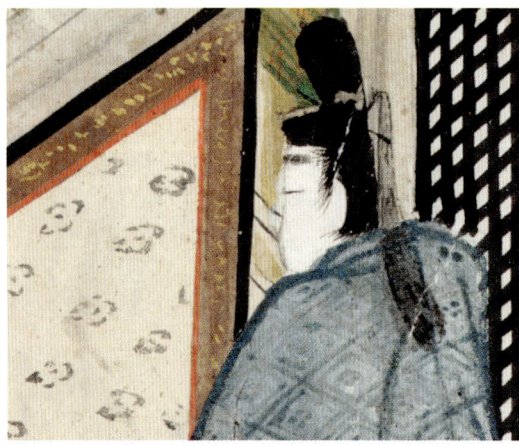
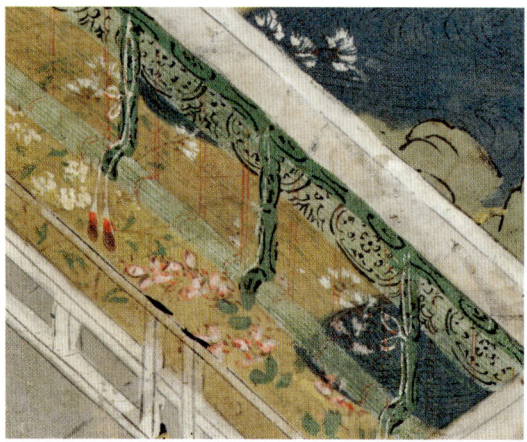

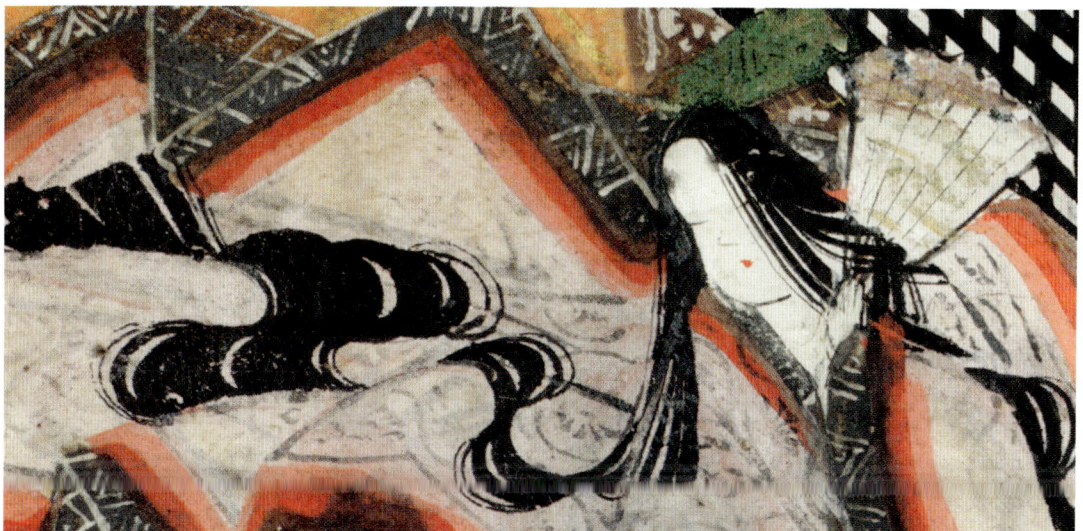

Genji—she is a figure of royal lineage who is denied the full benefits of her heritage, yet who still retains the inherent radiant appeal of her bloodline, which attracts men like Kaoru and Niou.

After hearing about Niou's advances on her daughter, which were apparently prevented from going too far by the girl's stalwart nurse who intervenes, Ukifune's mother moves her to a small house she is having constructed in the capital. The character of Ukifune's mother and the staff of the household into which she has married provide the tale's first extended look at nouveau riche members of the governing class (*zuryō*), along with glimpses of the warriors rising in power in the eastern provinces. The watchmen at the small abode speak in "vulgar eastern accents" (*iyashiki azumagoe*), startling Kaoru, who visits the small house soon after discovering Ukifune's whereabouts. Kaoru then composes a poem referring to Ukifune's new hideaway as the "Eastern Abode" (Azumaya), giving the chapter its title. In a show of uncharacteristic decisiveness, at the end of the chapter the usually hesitant lover forces his way into Ukifune's chambers at the "Eastern Abode" and spends the night amid the strange surroundings. The scene recalls the night Genji spent with Yūgao in Chapter Four, as Kaoru overhears the exotic sounds of peddlers and workers at dawn when he awakes, which are said to be completely unfamiliar to him. In another echo of the Yūgao episode, Kaoru suddenly whisks Ukifune away by carriage, this time to the Uji villa, setting the stage for the remaining chapters and a return to the territory of old romantic pursuits for both Kaoru and Niou.

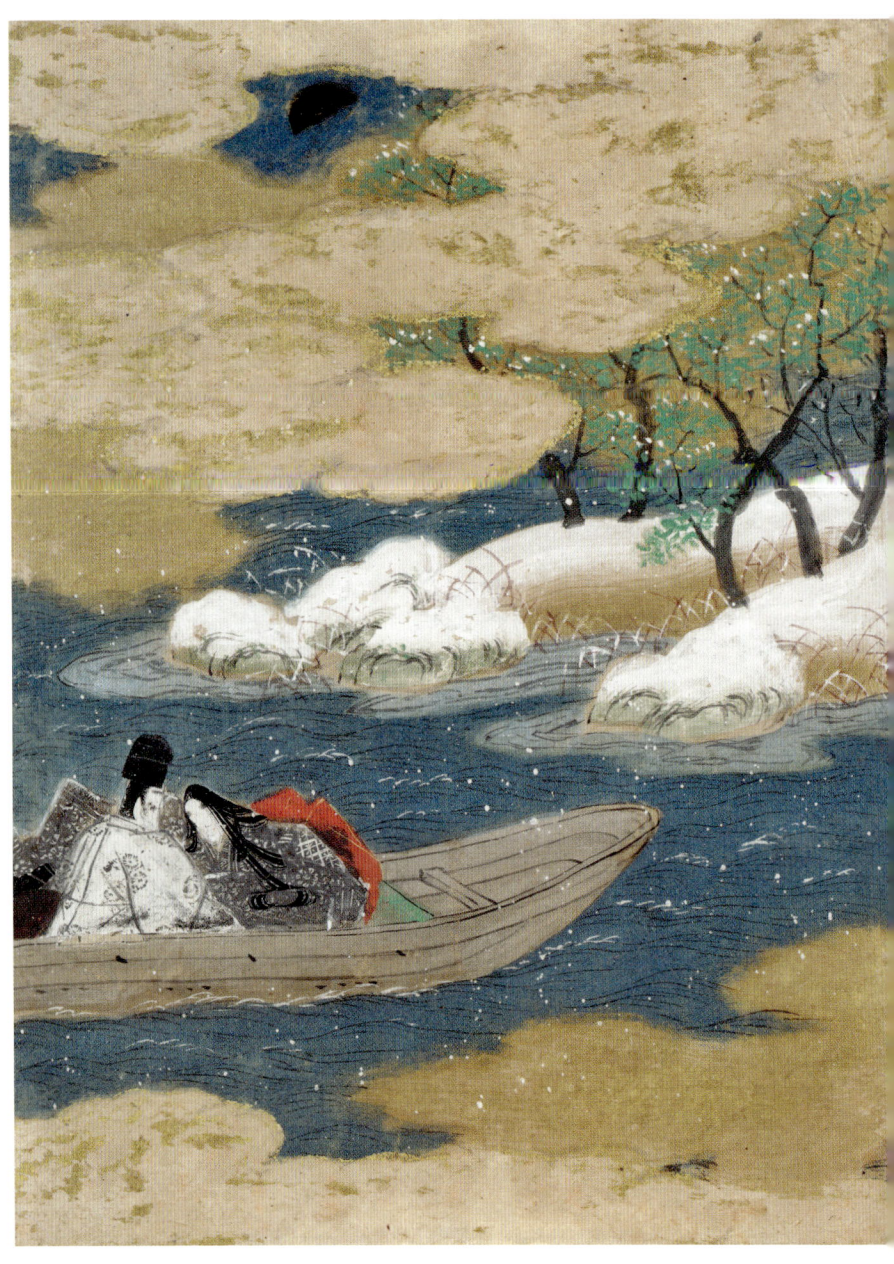

    Though the orange-tree isle
Remain fast in its color,
    'Tis not such change,
But this drifting boat's whither
That is beyond all knowing.

CRANSTON, P. 956

51

浮舟
A Boat Cast Adrift
Ukifune

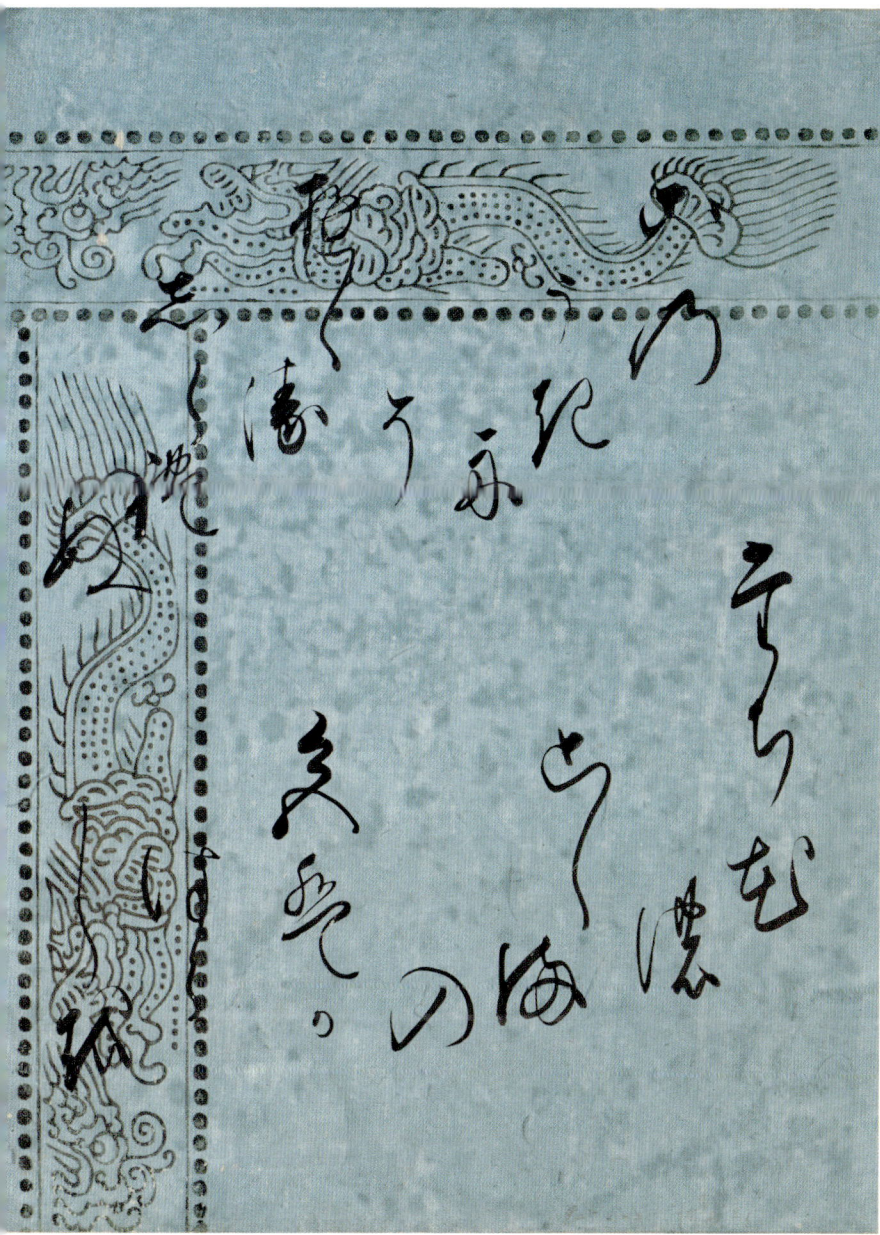

Tachibana no
Kojima no iro wa
Kawaraji o
Kono ukifune zo
Yukue shirarenu

たち花の
こしまの
色はかはらを
この
うき舟そ
ゆくゑ
しられぬ

Niou cannot stop thinking about his encounter with Ukifune and enlists a network of retainers, some in Kaoru's employ, to discover her location and help him arrange a clandestine trip to Uji. Visits to Uji from both men begin in earnest, leaving Ukifune anxious and upset over the impossible entanglement with her sister's husband and the scandal that will inevitably ensue. Yet she finds herself drawn to the passionate Niou, while remaining dependent on the seemingly steadfast Kaoru. On his second visit, Niou disguises his lofty rank and travels on horseback through treacherous mountains and falling snow to reach Ukifune, risking discovery by the watchmen Kaoru has positioned at the villa. To avoid the prying eyes of staff loyal to Kaoru, Niou arranges to use an empty residence across the river where he and Ukifune can be together at their leisure. In the dramatic and evocative scene depicted in the album painting, Niou carries Ukifune off in the middle of the night, to a boat that will take them to the other shore. Images of their trip across the icy waters of the river, beneath the lingering moon in the dawn light, are among the most familiar in the history of *Genji* painting, with the version in the album being the oldest dated example currently known. As with the other winter scenes in the album, the painting evokes the quiet stillness of a chilly winter night. The shores of a small islet where the couple will stop temporarily extend into the composition from the right, and consist of two golden, low-lying land masses with a layer of thick white to show the accumulated snow. Green rocks at the tip of the shore meet the river, with mica-covered, light blue areas indicating the water's frozen edges. Bending reeds encased in white, flecks of white falling snow, and delicate white lines interspersed with the deep blue mineral pigment of the waves, all contribute to the desolate beauty of the scene.

The oblong boat carrying the two lovers enters the scene from the left, as if slowly gliding toward the shores of the islet. Although the passage in the tale has them accompanied by an oarsman and Ukifune's attendant Jijū, the painting crops out the stern of the vessel and depicts the couple alone. Overwhelmed by the experience of riding in one of the fragile boats she had always viewed from afar to a strange, distant shore, Ukifune leans into Niou, who embraces her. Mitsunobu depicts Ukifune turned toward Niou, her head tilted and her gaze lowered, with the shape of her head matching the contour of his profile as if to show their intimate connection. The painting gives us a full view of her face, which is shown with a few strands of her abundant tresses falling across her bushy eyebrows, while the length of her hair is suggested by the curlicues and ends that nearly reach the hem of her garment. Ukifune's voluminous silvery gray robes fill the part of the boat that extends beyond Niou to the left, while a red undergarment appears behind her outlined in gold. Niou, with his back to the viewer, perfectly complements the shape and weight of Ukifune's figure, his billowing trousers to the left and white robed form intermeshed with her garments. With his tall courtier's hat and downward gaze at Ukifune, Niou is an imposing presence, but his expression seems to reflect his thoughts as related in the tale—that he finds her most charming.

This depiction of the couple face to face also suggests the moment of their poetic exchange, one verse of which is included in the album's calligraphy. Their poems are prompted by the voice of the oarsman, who announces, "This is the Orange Tree Isle," referring to the rocky island before them covered in lush mandarin orange trees. Alluding to a *Kokinshū* poem, Niou likens his love to the evergreen orange trees, unchanging even in the midst of winter, and lasting for a thousand years. Ukifune's reply, in the adjacent calligraphy, echoes the sentiment about the steadfast orange tree, but introduces the subject of the "boat adrift" (*ukifune*), a metaphor for her own predicament, which gives the charac-

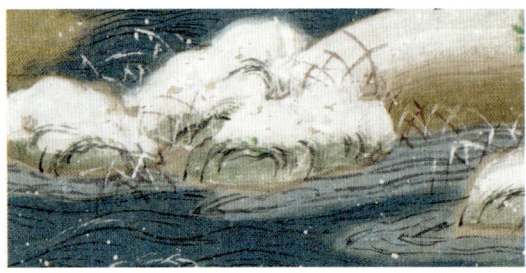

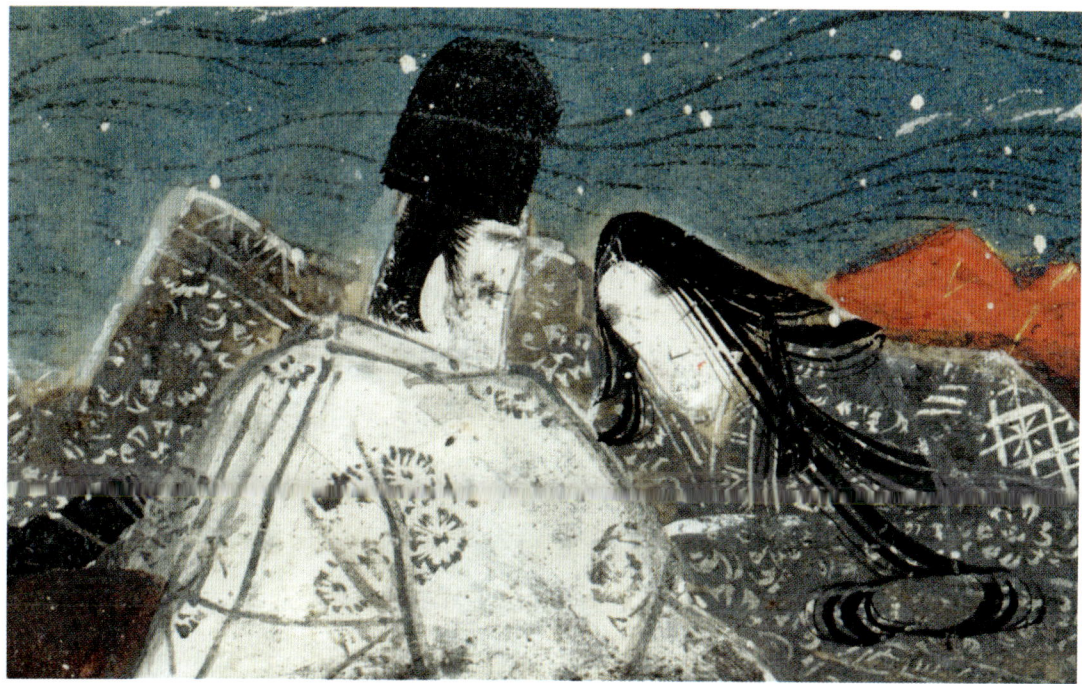

ter her name. Although the intimate scene aboard the boat has come to epitomize romance, Laura Allen has pointed out that Mitsunobu's rendition captures the turmoil beneath the surface and within Ukifune's heart. Even the falling snow in this painting hints at something more ominous, as suggested by the poem she composes the following day:

Furimidare	Sooner than the snow
Migiwa ni kōru	Blown in flurries but to freeze
Yuki yori mo	By the riverbank
Nakazora nite zo	Shall I vanish—still aloft
Ware wa kenubeki	In the midair of my falling.

CRANSTON, P. 956

Reflecting her persona as someone adrift and without a permanent home, the poem has her hovering in "midair" (*nakazora*) as she begins to articulate her desire to disappear. The desire to end it all becomes overwhelming after she is exposed to cautionary tales from her nurse about romantic triangles ending in murder and exile, and after she overhears her own mother, who is unaware of the relationship with Niou, ponder aloud how she would disown her were she to be involved in a scandal. Feeling as though she has no other options, Ukifune decides to drown herself in the Uji River, following a long line of heroines who met similar ends in ancient tales. The chapter concludes with a series of poems by Ukifune, composed as she steels herself and bids farewell to Niou, her mother, and the world. Her suicide attempt goes unrepresented in the tale, and the reader is left instead with a description of Ukifune lying with her sleeves pressed to her face, silently plotting to depart the villa and head to the riverbank as soon as her watchful women have fallen asleep. Her final parting poem is intended for her mother:

Kane no oto no	Joining my own cry
Tayuru hibiki ni	To the dying echoes
Ne o soete	Of the sounding bell,
Wa ga yo tsukinu to	Tell her my life has ended
Kimi ni tsutae yo	In this world of endless night.

CRANSTON, P. 961

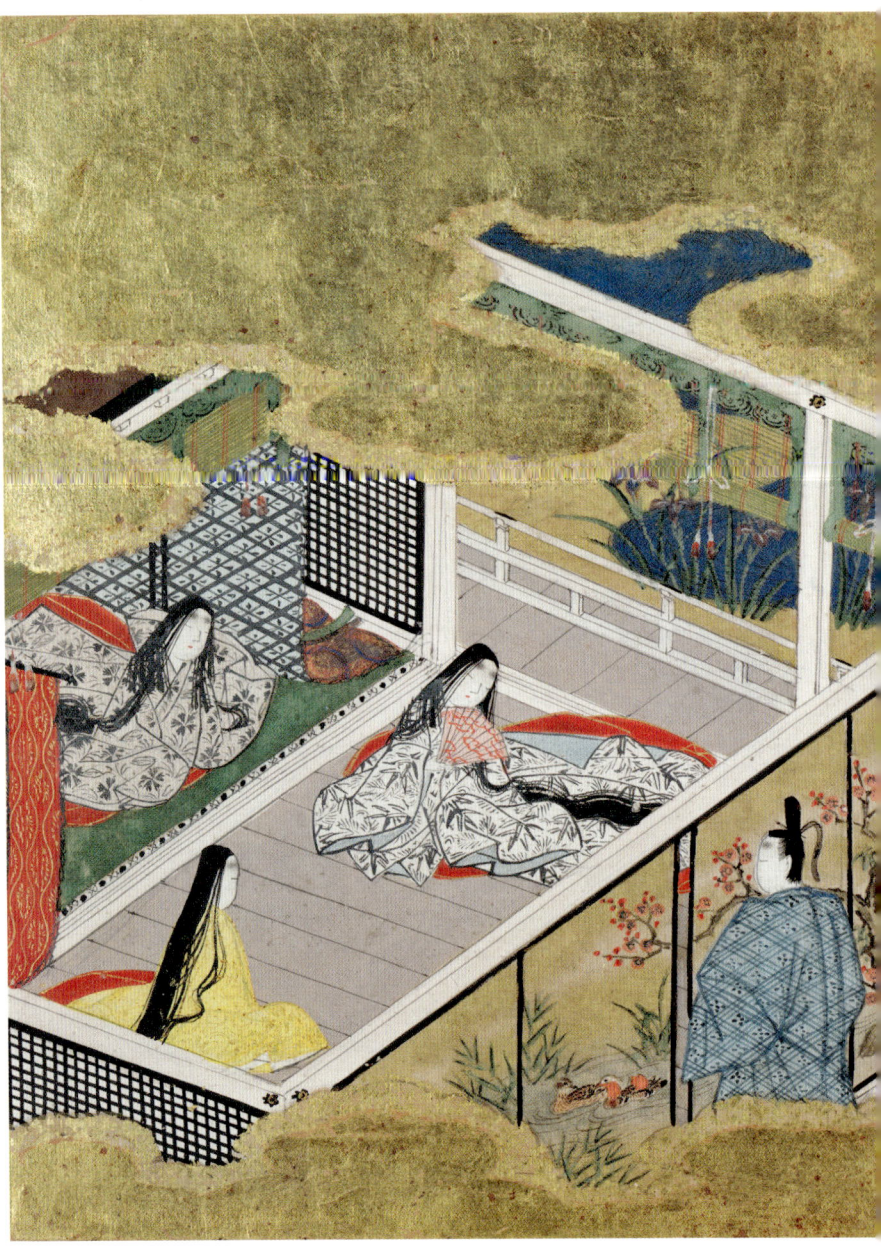

She had changed into a single white robe of sheer gauze and was holding a piece of ice in her hand, smiling faintly at the fuss her women were making. Her features were beautiful beyond description.

WASHBURN, P. 1242

52

蜻蛉
Ephemerids
Kagerō

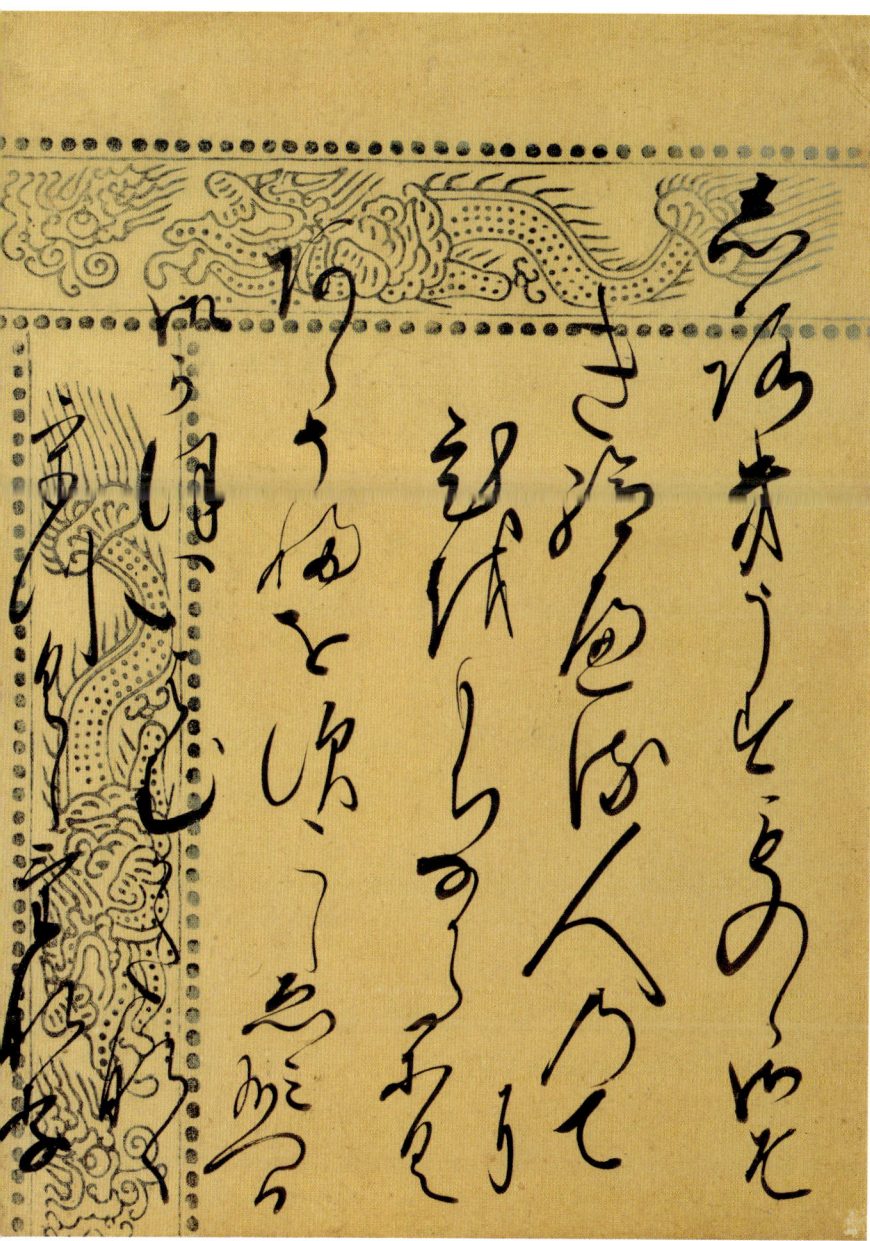

Shiroki usumono no onzo kitamaeru hito no, te ni hi o mochinagara, kaku arasō o sukoshi emitamaeru onkao, iwan kata naku utsukushige nari.

しろきうすものゝ御そ
き給へる人のて
にひをもちながらかく
あらそふをすこしゑみ
給へる御かほいはむかたなく
うつくしけなり

Chapter Fifty-Two begins with the entire Uji villa in an uproar after it has been discovered that Ukifune has vanished without a trace, and with Ukon and Jijū convinced that she has thrown herself into the river. They, along with Ukifune's mother, quickly arrange a funeral and faux cremation without a body, fearing that rumors of suicide would ruin the young lady's reputation postmortem, as people would infer that her suicide was the result of a scandalous affair. The women hide the truth from both Niou and Kaoru, who mourn her death, but who are not without doubts concerning her sudden demise, and who at first suspect each other of hiding her away. Their respective expressions of grief prove all too real, suspicions are allayed, and the two men together grapple with the loss of Ukifune. Unlike their literary predecessors, however, they do not follow their lover in death, but move on with their lives, which in this chapter means beginning a series of liaisons with female attendants and ladies-in-waiting. Kaoru also becomes fixated on the First Princess, who is Niou's older sister and the Akashi Empress's firstborn daughter. The First Princess has always intrigued Kaoru, and in this chapter, he begins indulging his fantasy, as depicted in the album painting, in which he gazes on the lady during a particularly unguarded moment.

The scene takes place at the Rokujō estate, where the Akashi Empress resides during a temporary leave from the palace, and where she sponsors the Eight Lectures on the *Lotus Sutra*, an elaborate five-day ceremony. On an intensely warm summer morning, after the ceremonies have concluded, Kaoru is prowling around the estate, seeking the refreshing breezes of the fishing pavilion, when he notices an open door near the First Princess's quarters. Peeking in, he observes a group of women who have removed their outermost layers of clothing as they chip away at a block of ice brought in to alleviate the heat. Kaoru is surprised to see even the Princess wearing only a gauzy white singlet as she holds a piece of ice in her hand, looking incomparably beautiful, as the calligraphy text says. Her thick hair has been gathered to one side because of the heat, giving Kaoru a full view of her face. He is entranced and believes the other ladies pale in comparison, although one other stands out, a woman named Kosaishō with whom he has been intimate. She is said to be wearing a diaphanous yellow singlet and an apron of pale purple and sits fanning herself. The other ladies take the broken ice chips and apply them to their foreheads and chests, in an unseemly manner, thinks Kaoru. But the First Princess does not take the piece of ice presented to her by Kosaishō, and instead holds out a dainty little hand and has it wiped by her ladies. Kaoru is enchanted. So much so that the next day he attempts to recreate the identical tableau with his wife, the Second Princess. He goes so far as to have the ladies prepare a gossamer singlet for his wife, which he puts on her himself, and bring in a block of ice, a piece of which he offers to the Princess. The simulation ultimately disappoints, however, as the Second Princess fails in Kaoru's opinion to live up to the standard set by her half sister. In the end Kaoru finds himself frustrated and pondering the mysterious blessings of the Akashi Bay, realizing that the First Princess with her Akashi lineage will remain unattainable to him and more admired than his own Second Princess.

The album painting corresponds to the scene described in the calligraphy, but it is a replacement painting by an unknown artist. At first glance the image approximates the others in the album, with its gold clouds and gold ground, its composition and perspective, and its inclusion of the typical voyeur figure in the lower right corner. The pristine condition of the leaf, however, stands out from the others, which almost always reveal something of the paper and sketching below the pigments, because of flaking and the more transparent quality of Mitsunobu's pigments. The architectural features differ as well—Mitsunobu never constructs a box as explicit as the one shown here, but instead tends to use gold clouds to mask corners and connections in order to create more suggestive architectural spaces. The artist of the replacement leaf has also mistakenly included the eave end of a brown cypress roof in the middle of the interior space, perhaps indicating a misunderstanding of the architecture seen in the other leaves. Given Mitsunobu's interest in small details, the absence of the ice block, surely something he would have included, is also a glaring omission. Kosaishō, however, does appear with her fan, as does the seasonal flower of the summer, the iris, outside, although it is not mentioned in the corresponding passage in the tale.

Kaoru engages in various flirtations in this chapter, but in the end his thoughts return to the women at Uji and the too-brief time he had with Ukifune. He ponders the ephemerality of it all and gazes out over the garden at Rokujō. Seeing ephemerids, or dayflies (*kagerō*), flitting about in the twilight, he composes a poem to himself that gives the chapter its title:

Ari to mite	There—you can see them,
Te ni wa torarezu	But not catch them in your hand,
Mireba mata	And when you look again
Yukusue mo shirazu	They have vanished, who knows where,
Kieshi kagerō	These ephemerids of dusk.

CRANSTON, P. 965

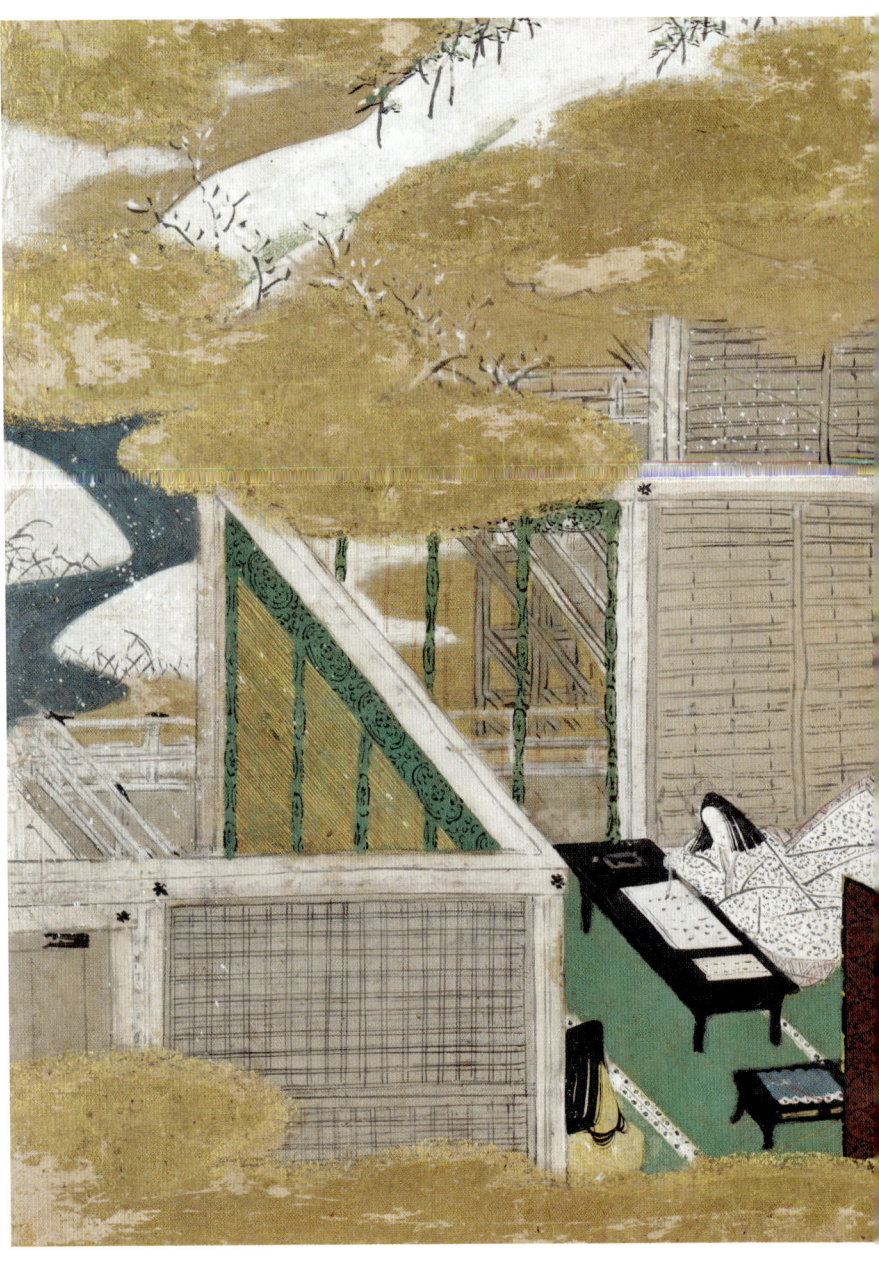

On the darkening hills,
On the wild fields lost in snow,
    I gaze today
And know again a sadness
For things buried long ago.

CRANSTON, PP. 972–73

As always, she wrote this down while practicing calligraphy, which served as a diversion for her during the breaks between her devotions.

WASHBURN, P. 1301

53

手習

Practicing Calligraphy

Tenarai

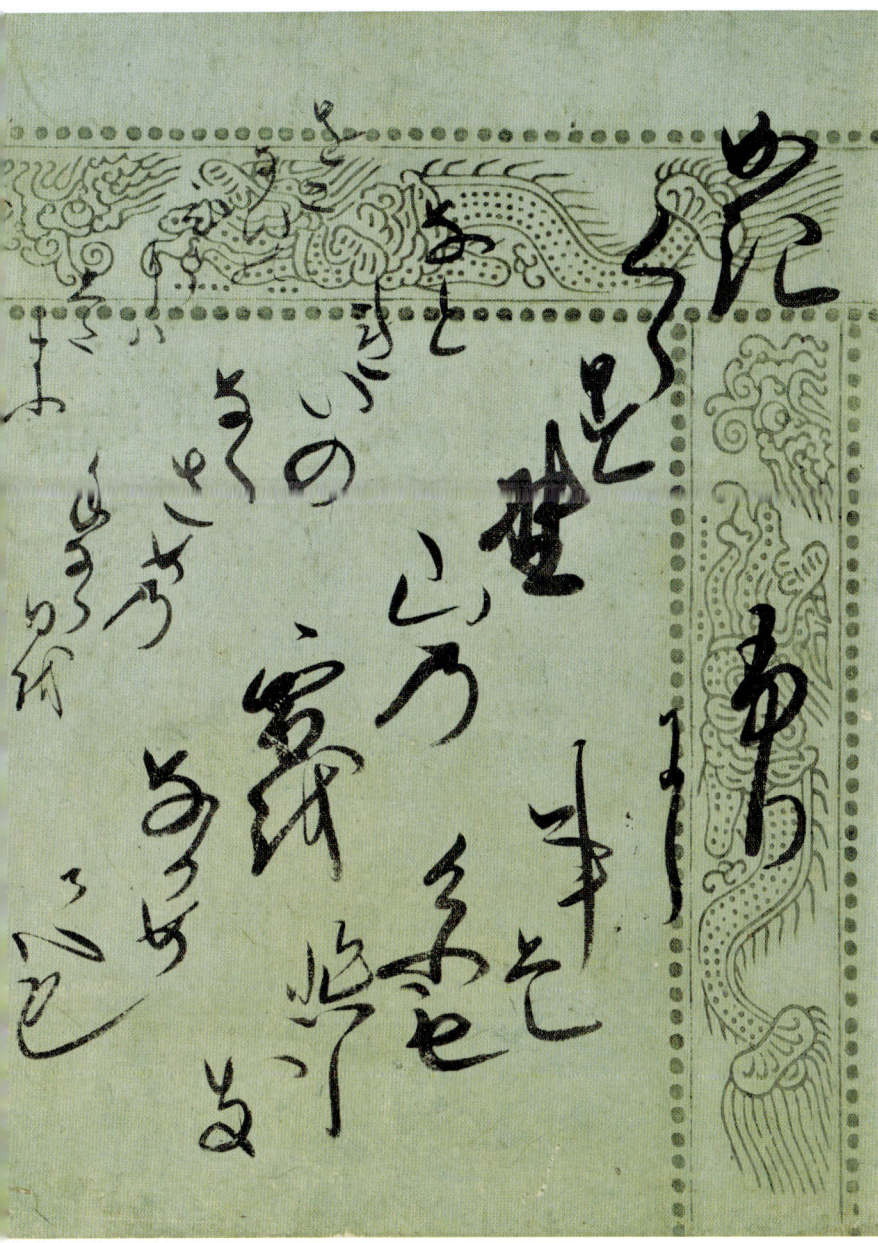

*Kakikurasu
Noyama no yuki o
Nagamete mo
Furinishi koto zo
Kyō mo kanashiki*

Nado, rei no, nagusame no tenarai o, okonai no hima ni wa shitamau.

かきくらす
野山の雪を
ながめても
ふりにし事ぞ
けふも悲しき

など れいの なぐさめの 手ならひを
おこなひの ひまには したまふ

Having recounted the various reactions to Ukifune's disappearance in the previous chapter, Chapter Fifty-Three takes the reader back in time to explain the course of events from another perspective, beginning with the discovery of Ukifune, on the night of her attempted suicide in Uji, by a Tendai prelate, the Bishop of Yokawa. The priest is in Uji preparing an empty villa there as a temporary rest stop for his ailing mother, an old nun, who is on her way home from a pilgrimage to Hasedera. He instructs a group of torch-wielding monks to investigate the grounds, and they soon happen on a weeping Ukifune lying amid a copse near the river. After much hesitation and suspecting that she may be a shape-shifting demon, they eventually bring her inside, where the Bishop's sister, a nun in her fifties who is mourning the loss of an adult daughter of her own, helps nurse Ukifune back to health and grows attached to the young woman. The nuns take Ukifune to their residence in Ono, in the foothills of the Bishop's temple, Enryakuji, on Mount Hiei. Ukifune professes amnesia, but her internal monologue provides to the reader fuller insight into her recollections, as she remembers wishing to drown in the river, and being led away by a radiant "prince," with the narration evoking images of Niou. What is consistent in her story as told to us and to the nun is her fervent desire to leave the mundane world, which now, in the company of the Bishop and his mother and sister, she hopes to realize by becoming a nun. Although the Bishop's sister is a nun herself, she discourages Ukifune from casting the world aside, seeing the young woman as a means to fulfill her own longings. She aims to match Ukifune with her deceased daughter's husband, a man who is more than eager to court the beautiful mystery woman. The son-in-law's increasingly ardent overtures, facilitated by the nuns at Ono, become yet another distressing obstacle to Ukifune's goal of renunciation. This time, though, Ukifune holds her ground, refusing to engage with the man, hoping meanwhile to take the full religious vows that she believes will finally allow her to rid her mind of thoughts and regrets about the past.

The album painting for Chapter Fifty-Three depicts Ukifune having achieved her goal of nun-

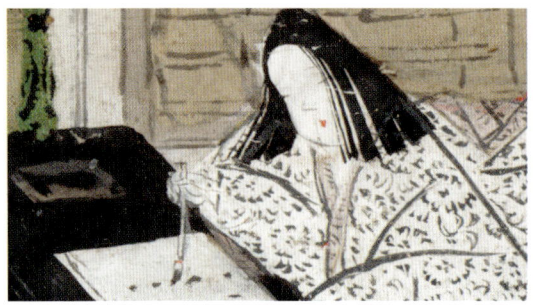

hood, as is evident from her newly cropped hair with its blunt edges that just skim the tops of her shoulders. To take the tonsure signaled a social death and an end to sexual activity. With the cutting of her hair, Ukifune finally reaches, at least temporarily, an equilibrium, by bringing her physical appearance into alignment with her psychological detachment from the secular world. The short hair in the image, the first time such a drastic "nun's cut" is depicted in the album, is particularly striking given the emphasis that Ukifune's long black tresses received until this point. The allure of her hair, extending the length of her body in the boat scene with Niou, for example, has captivated her suitors and delighted the women around her. In contemplating its loss Ukifune laments that her mother will never see it long again, alluding in her words to an earlier poem in which an old monk poet imagines his mother stroking his pitch-black hair as a child, never thinking that the same head would one day be the shaven head of a Buddhist priest. The beauty of Ukifune's hair even causes the Bishop to hesitate before he administers her vows, having been persuaded by her to perform the ceremony hastily during his sister's absence. In a show of resolve, Ukifune picks up the scissors herself and hands them to the Bishop. Her thick hair proves difficult to cut, but when the deed is done, Ukifune feels a joyous release and no longer burdened by concerns about the future.

As with many of the main characters who preceded her in taking the tonsure, Ukifune's thoughts about her momentous decision are complicated, and as she grapples with her new identity and tries to let go of her past, she turns to her writing practice (*tenarai*), the activity that gives its name to this chapter, to sort out her emotions. In addition to the copying of old poems in order to train the calligraphic hand, "writing practice" included composing new poems, which were not intended to be sent, or necessarily seen by someone else, but to be written as a means of airing one's innermost thoughts, working out ideas, or developing a poetic voice, all the time gaining practice in the allusive system of *waka*. In Chapter Fifty-Three Ukifune uses writing practice as a means of self-expression; six of her twelve poems in this chapter are composed in the context of writing practice. In the painting, she sits facing a large black desk that holds an inkstone and a text that she is copying. She wields her brush vertically in her small hand, making marks on the white paper spread out before her. She seems to be concentrating intently, and her thin eyebrows slant upward and inward, creating a facial expression that may reflect her melancholy mood that is described in the tale. It is the start of the New Year, and the remote house in Ono seems especially isolated as the snow piles up on the surrounding mountains. Rather than showing Ukifune in the company of the other nuns, Mitsunobu enhances the sense of her physical and psychological isolation by depicting her alone except for a single attendant in the foreground. She is dwarfed by the unusually tall walls that rise up around her, and this intensifies the sense of interiority that her soliloquized writing-practice poems evoke.

Outside, the distant snow-covered mountains suggest the route to Mount Hiei, and they are dotted with deciduous trees, their barren branches coated in white. The viewer sees above, beyond, and even through the walls that surround Ukifune, as the semitransparent bamboo blinds reveal the zigzagging verandas and horizontally tied columns of the large structure in which Ukifune resides. In her poem included in the album she describes herself gazing at the snowy landscape, but despite its brightness, fixating on the "ever darkening" (*kakikurasu*) atmosphere. As elsewhere in the tale, and as illustrated elsewhere in the album, snow scenes bring back memories, and here the falling snow, and the "frozen stream that makes no sound" (*kōri*

watareru mizu no oto senu) trigger a flashback to the snowy nighttime journey across the river and the intimate days Ukifune spent with Niou in Uji. Before composing the poem, she cites a line, "I am lost in you, my love," from a verse by Niou featured in that episode in Chapter Fifty-One:

Mine no yuki	Snow on the mountain
Migiwa no kōri	Ice along the riverbank—
Fumiwakete	I trudge through all:
Kimi ni zo madou	I am lost in you, my love,
Michi wa madowazu	But I never lose the path.

CRANSTON, P. 956

The poem in the album leaf makes it clear that Ukifune has achieved her goal of vanishing and burying the past, but her allusion to this one line shows that her "sadness" over Niou lingers. She next composes a verse about Kaoru, giving equal time to him, and we have in consequence a portrait of Ukifune as someone committed to renunciation, but still struggling with attachments. Thoughts of her former lovers arise intermittently when she is not occupied with her devotions and readings of the *Lotus Sutra* and other sacred texts. The deliberate inclusion of indigo-covered sutra scrolls in the lower right corner of the album painting shows this dichotomous nature of her inner world. As if in recognition of this tension, her separation from secular life proves tenuous; Kaoru has learned of the presence of a woman at Ono harbored by the Bishop of Yokawa who fits Ukifune's description. With one of Ukifune's own half-brothers in service as his page, and with personal connections to the Bishop to aid him, Kaoru begins to make his way to Mount Hiei to arrange a meeting.

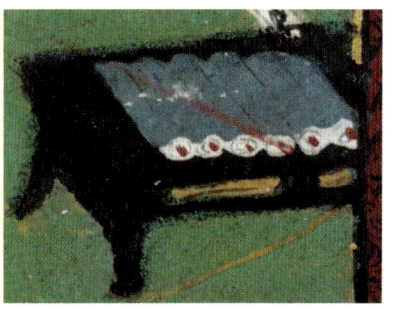

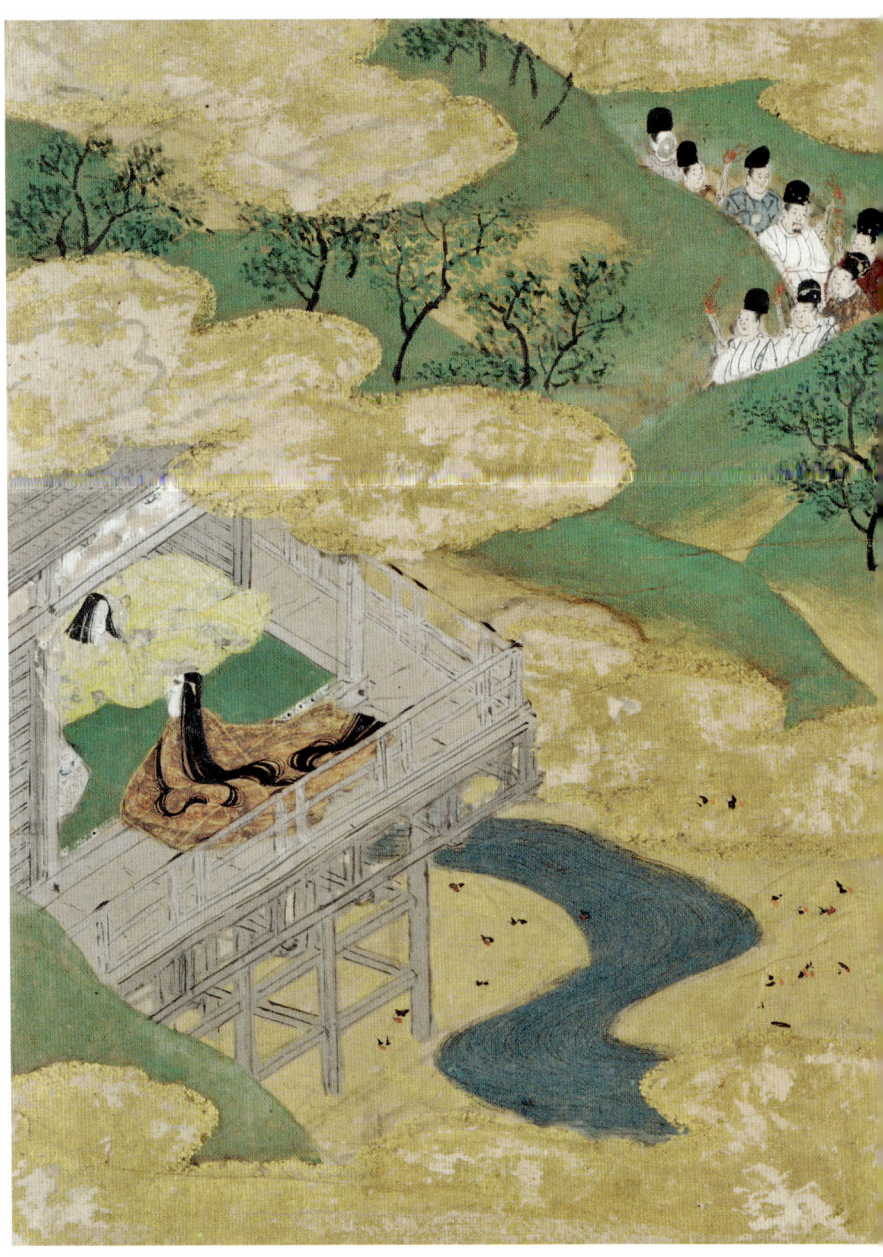

The house at Ono faced onto verdant mountains that were covered in deep, dense foliage—a place where there was nothing to distract the mind or heart. Ukifune sat gazing out pensively at the fireflies flitting over the garden stream. Such small things were her only solace, bringing back memories of the past.

WASHBURN, P. 1313, MODIFIED

54

夢浮橋

A Floating Bridge in a Dream

Yume no ukihashi

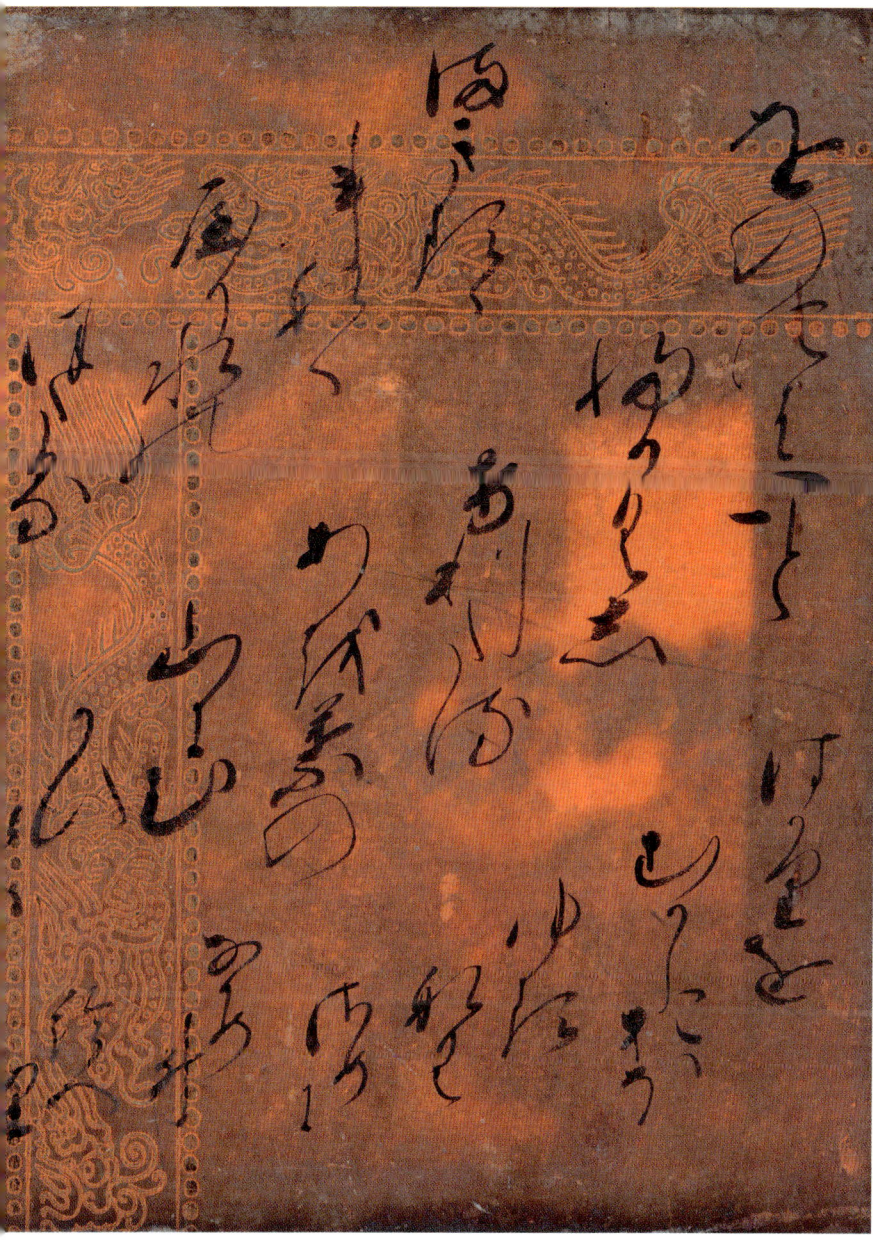

Ono ni wa, ito fukaku shigeritaru aoba no yama ni mukaite, magiruru koto naku, yarimizu no hotaru bakari o mukashi oboyuru nagusame ni nagame itamaeri.

をのにはいと　ふかくし　けりたる　あを葉の　山にむかひて　まきるゝ　事なく　やり水　の　ほたる　はかりを　むかしおほ　ゆる　さめに　なかめ　ゐ　給へり

The painting for Chapter Fifty-Four does not depict the final scene in the tale, but one that places Kaoru and Ukifune in proximity, while ultimately capturing the ambiguity of the tale's conclusion. By the time this scene takes place, Kaoru has made his way to see the Bishop at Yokawa and has confirmed that Ukifune is indeed alive and living as a nun in Ono. The Bishop, nervous that he has unknowingly administered the tonsure to a noble lady caught up in an affair of the heart, refuses to escort Kaoru to see the young woman, understanding that a reunion with the courtier may lead her to stray from the Buddhist Precepts she has sworn to follow, which could have implications for the priest's salvation. Nevertheless, Kaoru persuades the prelate of his own religious leanings and purity of intent, explaining that he only wishes to see Ukifune in order to be able to go back and comfort the girl's grieving mother. When Kaoru introduces the handsome page boy in his service, Ukifune's little brother, the Bishop is won over and finally acquiesces, writing a letter that chastises Ukifune for abandoning Kaoru and hinting that her destiny is with him rather than with the nuns in Ono. In characteristic fashion, however, Kaoru does not act immediately, deciding against delivering the letter himself, and opting instead to send the page boy (Ukifune's half-brother) to the nuns' abode the next day after he has returned to the capital. In the painting Ukifune has not yet seen the letter from the Bishop, but she and the nuns have been told that a certain Major Captain is visiting Yokawa. Soon they hear the shouts and see the torches of a large group of men coming down the rarely traveled mountain road, and Ukifune anxiously surmises that the Major Captain they heard about is none other than Kaoru.

The painting shows one corner of the Ono residence, which the Bishop describes as a rustic abode, with its basic wooden sliding doors and a simple wooden roof. As in the previous album painting, it rests atop an elaborate structure of tall, horizontally tied columns, for a commanding view of the valley. This style of overhanging architecture resembles the actual temple at Yokawa, making the paintings for Chapters Fifty-Three and Fifty-Four wonderfully suggestive of the locale of Mount Hiei. The exterior sliding panels are open to the veranda, revealing Ukifune in the interior seated above the green tatami, immediately recognizable by her cropped nun's hair. The bright, gold-painted robe is out of keeping with the simple gray nun's robes described in the tale, and considering the severity of visible damage to the layers of pigment on her garment, it may be a relatively rare example in this album of later retouching. The corner of another figure's robe appears to the left, peeking out from behind the wall, along with a delicate strand of long black hair, suggesting that Ukifune is shown in the company of two nontonsured female attendants. The other attendant, facing Ukifune, is one of those who in the tale went to the veranda for a view of the large group of travelers making their way down the mountain path. She seems to be reporting to Ukifune about what she has seen, her long tresses and bushy eyebrows contrasting with Ukifune's shorn appearance.

The calligraphy text describes the serenity of the landscape that surrounds Ukifune at Ono, a densely wooded forest that keeps everyone away except the

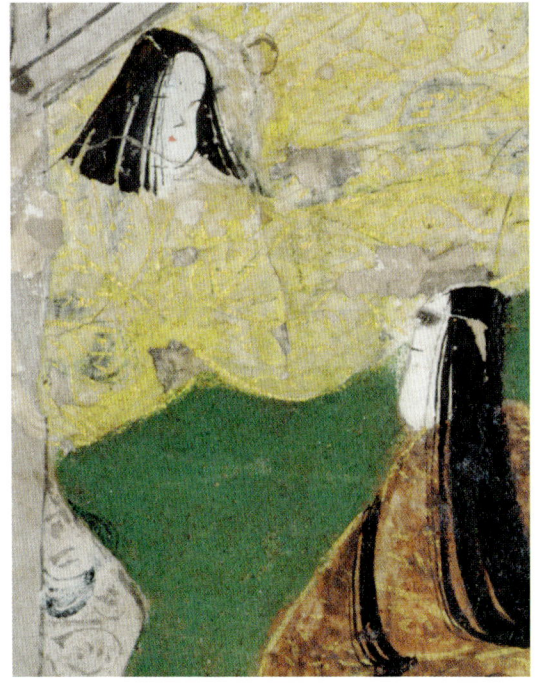

238 | *The Tale of Genji*

most determined and devout travelers to Yokawa, where there is nothing to distract her heart and mind (*magiruru koto naku*). From Ukifune's perspective, only the fireflies that flit about the garden stream remind her of the past, and she finds them somehow soothing. The brief text included with the painting stops there, describing the relative peace that Ukifune realizes at Ono, not mentioning the encroachment of Kaoru's men, which begins in the very next line in the tale. The painting, however, picks up where the calligraphy excerpt ends, showing the verdant green mountainside landscape, but also the man who will potentially disrupt the solace Ukifune has found. Red fireflies dot the golden shores of the stream, white the undulating blue line of the water and the winding green hills lead the eye to the top of the painting. Amid the hills that glow with brushed gold in their valleys, the tiny lights of the fireflies are echoed in the larger points of light, the flaming torches wielded by Kaoru's men. While the fireflies may bring only soothing memories, the torches represent the actual return of men from Ukifune's past that threaten her tranquility. She hears the voices of outrunners as they fan out across the mountainside and recognizes them as those of Kaoru's retainers, familiar to her from his visits to Uji. Mitsunobu depicts eight figures curving down the path to represent the group of men, five of them holding torches as they clear the way for their lord. Although it is unlikely that a man of Kaoru's status would be on foot, the thick white pigment that remains on the now damaged face of the final figure in the group represents someone of the courtier class, suggesting Kaoru. In this way, the painting juxtaposes Ukifune the nun with the man who represents all that she has renounced. On hearing the voices, Ukifune turns inward and meditates on the Amida Buddha's name (*Amida hotoke ni omoi magirawashite*), becoming profoundly silent.

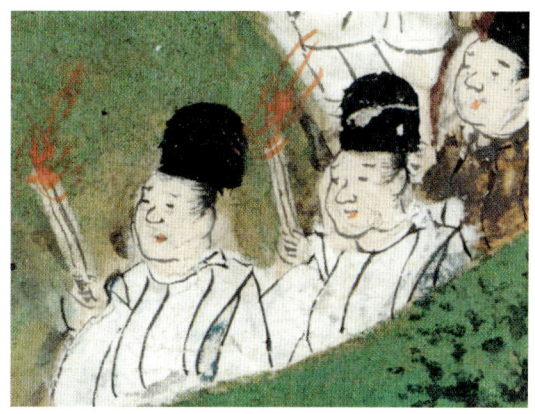

Ukifune is further tested in her resolve the following day and struggles with her emotions, when her younger brother, Kaoru's page, arrives just outside her blinds. His presence puts information about her mother's well-being within reach and makes her longing for her mother all the more acute. She knows, however, that any response to Kaoru will open the door to all the problems her drastic measures were meant to erase, and so she resists, pleading with the nuns to keep her hidden. The final scene in the tale describes Kaoru receiving word from the page that Ukifune has refused to answer his letter. Kaoru regrets sending such an inexperienced messenger and considers giving up on contacting her altogether, until he suddenly suspects that another man may be hiding her away, as he once did himself. Thus, imagining that her life among the nuns may be mere pretense, he dismisses the possibility that Ukifune genuinely renounced the world, something that for all of his professions of spirituality he has never been able to achieve himself. The final words of the tale suggest Kaoru's never-ending jealousy of perceived rival lovers and his unrequited longing, a metaphor for the samsaric cycle that turns on attachment and desire, itself an underlying theme of the book.

Appendix: Album Calligraphy Key

A Kunitaka Shinnō (1456–1532)
   伏見殿式部卿宮邦隆親王
   Chapters 1, 7, 13, 19, 25, 33, 39, 45, 51

B Konoe Hisamichi (1472–1544)
   近衛殿前大政大臣前関白尚道
   Chapters 2, 8, 14, 20, 26, 32, 38, 44, 50

C Sanjōnishi Sanetaka (1455–1537)
   三條西殿前内大臣実隆
   Chapters 3, 9, 15, 21, 27, 31, 37, 43, 49

D Jōhōji Kōjo (1453–1538)
   定法寺殿大僧正三条前左大臣実量公御息公助
   Chapters 4, 10, 16, 22, 30, 36, 42, 48, 54

E Reizei Tamehiro (1450–1526)
   上冷泉殿民部卿入道宗清
   Chapters 5, 11, 17, 23, 29, 35, 41, 47, 53

F Son'ō Jugō (d. 1514)
   青蓮院殿入道親王
   Chapters 6, 12, 18, 24, 28, 34, 40, 46, 52

Ch.	Title	Calligrapher	Color	Ch.	Title	Calligrapher	Color
1	Kiritsubo	A	Red	28	Nowaki	F	Yellow
2	Hahakigi	B	Blue	29	Miyuki	E	Red
3	Utsusemi	C	Yellow	30	Fujibakama	D	Pink
4	Yūgao	D	Pink	31	Makibashira	C	Blue
5	Wakana	E	Green	32	Umegae	B	Yellow
6	Suetsumuhana	F	Red	33	Fuji no uraba	A	Green
7	Momiji no ga	A	Blue	34	Wakana jō	F	Pink
8	Hana no en	B	Yellow	35	Wakana ge	E	Pink
9	Aoi	C	Pink	36	Kashiwagi	D	Blue
10	Sakaki	D	Green	37	Yokobue	C	Yellow
11	Hanachirusato	E	Red	38	Suzumushi	B	Green
12	Suma	F	Blue	39	Yūgiri	A	Red
13	Akashi	A	Yellow	40	Minori	F	Pink
14	Miotsukushi	B	Pink	41	Maboroshi	E	Blue
15	Yomogiu	C	Green	42	Niou	D	Yellow
16	Sekiya	D	Red	43	Kōbai	C	Green
17	Eawase	E	Blue	44	Takekawa	B	Red
18	Matsukaze	F	Yellow	45	Hashihime	A	Pink
19	Usugumo	A	Pink	46	Shiigamoto	F	Blue
20	Asagao	B	Green	47	Agemaki	E	Yellow
21	Otome	C	Red	48	Sawarabi	D	Green
22	Tamakazura	D	Blue	49	Yadorigi	C	Red
23	Hatsune	E	Yellow	50	Azumaya	B	Pink
24	Kochō	F	Pink	51	Ukifune	A	Blue
25	Hotaru	A	Green	52	Kagerō	F	Yellow
26	Tokonatsu	B	Red	53	Tenarai	E	Green
27	Kagaribi	C	Blue	54	Yume no ukihashi	D	Red

Glossary

Glossary of Japanese Words Used in Text
(Excludes chapter titles, personal names of characters, and words quoted from poems)

amagatsu 天倪
amayo no shinasadame 雨夜の品定め
ato 跡
araita 浄板
ayamegusa 菖蒲草
ayu 鮎
azari 阿闍梨
bachi 撥
biwa 琵琶
bosatsu 菩薩
bugaku 舞楽
Butsumyō kyō 仏名経
byōbu 屏風
chigo 児
dadaiko 大太鼓
daijō tennō 太上天皇
eboshi 烏帽子
en 艶
engie 縁起絵
ennaru 艶なる
fujibakama 藤袴
fujigoromo 藤衣
fumi 文
fumu 踏む
geki 鶏
gofun 胡粉
gohei 御幣
gokuraku jōdo 極楽浄土
gyōkō 行幸
hachidai ryūō 八大竜王
hagi 萩
haku ruri 白瑠璃
hamori no kami 葉守の神
hichiriki 篳篥

higaki kaisen 菱垣廻船
hiji 秘事
hiki 引き
hisashi 庇
hita 引板
hō 袍
hototogisu 時鳥
hyoe no kami 兵衛督
in 院
irogonomi 色好み
ishibushi 石伏
iyashiki azumagoe 卑しき東声
izumi 泉
jijū 侍従
jinkō 沈香
kabazakura 樺桜
kaburaya 鏑矢
kaede 楓
kakezukuri 懸造
kakidatsu 垣立
kaimami 垣間見
kana 仮名
kanmuri 冠
karabitsu 唐櫃
kara neko 唐猫
kari 雁
kariginu 狩衣
kashiwa 柏
kasuga 春日
kawa kajika 川鰍
kemari 蹴鞠
kesa 袈裟
kin (Chinese koto) 琴
kinuta 砧
konruri 紺瑠璃
koto 琴
koto no ne 琴の音
kurobō 黒方

kuruma no arasoi 車の争い
kuwau 加ふ
magaki 籬
Makura no sōshi 枕草子
manmaku 幔幕
mayumi no ki 檀の木
mogi 裳着
moya 母屋
naidaijin 内大臣
nakazora 中空
na ni tatsu Sue 名に立つ末
nayotake なよ竹
nazurau 準ふ
nonomiya 野々宮
nōshi 直衣
nyūdō no miya 入道の宮
oikake 緌
ominaeshi 女郎花
ooshi 雄雄し
osoroshiki 恐ろしき
rindō 竜胆
Rokujōin 六条院
Ryōō 陵王
ryōtō 裲襠
ryū 龍
saibara 催馬楽
Sai'in 斎院
Saishō no chūjō 宰相中将
sakaki 榊
Sanbōe 三宝絵
sange 懺悔
sanmaidō 三昧堂
sawarabi 早蕨
Seigaiha 青海波
shaku 笏
shika 鹿
shimo-nageshi 下長押
shinden 寝殿

shō 笙
shōgon 荘厳
Shōsōin 正倉院
sokutai 束帯
sō no koto 箏の琴
sudare 簾
Sue no matsuyama 末の松山
sumire 菫
susuki 薄
tachibana 橘
tachibana no ka 橘の香
tai no ya 対の屋
tango no sechie 端午節会
tatejitomi 立蔀
Tō no Chūjō 頭中将
torii 鳥居
Toyo no Akari 豊明
tsujigahana 辻が花
tsukushi 土筆/筆頭菜
tsuridono 釣殿
tsuyukusa 露草
ubasoku 優婆塞
uchide 打ち出
ukifushi 憂き節
ushi 憂し
uta-e 歌絵
utsukushiu mono 美う物
waka 和歌
wakakusa 若草
warabi 蕨
yamabuki 山吹
yama no kakehashi 山の掛け橋
yama no mikado 山の帝
yarimizu 遣り水
yokobue 横笛
yuki fukaki 雪深き
zekku 絶句
zuryō 受領

The Album: Works Cited and Consulted

1 Kiritsubo

Okada, H. Richard. "Narrating the Private: Kiritsubo." In *Figures of Resistance: Language, Poetry, and Narrating in The Tale of Genji and Other Mid-Heian Texts*, 183–96. Post-contemporary Interventions. Durham, NC: Duke University Press, 1991.

Tamagami Takuya. *Genji monogatari hyōshaku*. Vol. 1. Tokyo: Kadokawa Shoten, 1964.

2 Hahakigi

Noguchi Takeshi. "Hahakigi." In Chino Kaori et al., eds. "Tokushū Genji monogatari gajō (Hābādo Daigaku Bijutsukan zō)." *Kokka* no. 1222 (1997): 39.

Ōtsu Naoko. "Kii no Kami tei no suiryū—Genji monogatari naka no hina no josei henreki no shihatsu to izumi." *Kokugakuin Daigaku kiyō* 49 (2011): 23–41.

4 Yūgao

Abe Akio, et al. *Genji monogatari*, vol. 1, p. 180. Shinpen Nihon noten bungaku zenshū 20. Tokyo: Shōgakkan, 1994.

Goff, Janet Emily. *Noh Drama and The Tale of Genji: The Art of Allusion in Fifteen Classical Plays*. Princeton, NJ: Princeton University Press, 1991.

Phillips, Quitman E. "Yūgao." In Chino Kaori et al., eds. "Tokushū Genji monogatari gajō (Hābādo Daigaku Bijutsukan zō)." *Kokka* 1222 (1997): 39.

6 Suetsumuhana

Noguchi Takeshi. "Suetsumuhana." In Chino Kaori et al., eds. "Tokushū Genji monogatari gajō (Hābādo Daigaku Bijutsukan zō)." *Kokka* no. 1222 (1997): 40.

10 Sakaki

Goff, Janet Emily. *Noh Drama and The Tale of Genji: The Art of Allusion in Fifteen Classical Plays*. Princeton, NJ: Princeton University Press, 1991.

11 Hanachirusato

Cranston, Edwin A. *A Waka Anthology, II, pt. A: Grasses of Remembrance*, 142–43. Stanford, CA: Stanford University Press, 2006.

12 Suma

Akiyama Ken, et al. *Suma*. Vol. 12 of *Shūkan emaki de tanoshimu Genji monogatari gojūshijō*. Shūkan Asahi Hyakka. Tokyo: Asahi Shinbun Shuppan, 2011.

Murai Shōsuke, et al., eds. *Nichi-Min kankeishi kenkyū nyūmon: Ajia no naka no kenminsen*. Tokyo: Bensei Shuppan, 2015.

13 Akashi

Okada, H. Richard. "The Akashi Intertexts." In *Figures of Resistance: Language, Poetry, and Narrating in The Tale of Genji and Other Mid-Heian Texts*, 266–86. Durham, NC: Duke University Press, 1991.

Shirane, Haruo. "History, Myth, and Women's Literature: The Akashi Lady." In *The Bridge of Dreams: A Poetics of The Tale of Genji*, 73–87. Stanford, CA: Stanford University Press, 1987.

15 Yomogiu

Abe Akio, et al. *Genji monogatari*, vol. 2, p. 337. Shinpen Nihon koten bungaku zenshū 21. Tokyo: Shōgakkan, 1995.

Misumi Yōichi. "Yomogiu maki no tanpenteki shuhō." In *Genji Monogatari to Tendai Jōdokyō*, 35–69. Chūko bungaku kenkyū sōsho 1. Tokyo: Wakakusa Shobō, 1996.

Fukuda Toshiaki. "'Yomogiu' no maki ni mieru kanseki no kentō." In Suzuki Kazuo and Koyano Jun'ichi eds. *Genji monogatari no kanshō to kiso chishiki*, no. 36, *Yomogiu, Seikiya*, 155–69. Tokyo: Shibundō, 2004.

16 Sekiya

Sakamoto Tomonobu. "Suetsumuhana to Utsusemi." In Suzuki Kazuo and Koyano Jun'ichi, eds. *Genji monogatari no kanshō to kiso chishiki*, no. 36, *Yomogiu, Seikiya*, 207–22. Tokyo: Shibundō, 2004.

17 Eawase

Ii Haruki. "Suma no e-nikki kara e-awase no e-nikki e." *Chūko bungaku* 39 (1987): 41–52.

McCormick, Melissa. "Eawase." In Chino Kaori et al., eds. "Tokushū Genji monogatari gajō (Hābādo Daigaku Bijutsukan zō)." *Kokka* no. 1222 (1997): 43.

18 *Matsukaze*

Takada Hirohiko. "Hikaru Genji no fukkatsu—Matsukaze kara no shiten." In *Genji monogatari no bungakushi*, pt. 3, chap. 3, 319–41. Tokyo: Tokyo Daigaku Shuppankai, 2003.

19 *Usugumo*

Kurata Minoru. "Akashi no Himegimi no hakama gi—yōin to naru shidai." In Suzuki Kazuo and Koyama Toshihiko, eds. *Genji monogatari no kanshō to kiso chishiki*, no. 33, Asagao, Usugumo, 211–25. Tokyo: Shibundō, 2004.

21 *Otome*

Shirane, Haruo. "Flowering Fortunes." In *The Bridge of Dreams: A Poetics of The Tale of Genji*, 24–42. Stanford, CA: Stanford University Press, 1987.

22 *Tamakazura*

McCormick, Melissa. "Tamakazura." In Chino Kaori et al., eds. "Tokushū Genji monogatari gajō (Hābādo Daigaku Bijutsukan zō)." *Kokka* no. 1222 (1997): 44.
Ryūsawa Aya. "Tōkyō Kokuritsu Hakubutsukan zō 'Genji monogatari sasshi hyōshi-e mohon' ni tsuite." *Museum* 643 (2013): 25–50.

26 *Tokonatsu*

Takeuchi Masahiko. "Nie toshite tatematsurareru sakana, Nishikawa no ayu." In Akiyama Ken, et al. *Tokonatsu*, 11. Vol. 26 of *Shūkan emaki de tanoshimu Genji monogatari gojūshijō*. Shūkan Asahi Hyakka. Tokyo: Asahi Shinbun Shuppan, 2011.

29 *Miyuki*

Katō Shizuko. "Ōharano miyuki no junkyō to monogatarika." In Suzuki Kazuo et al., eds. *Genji monogatari no kanshō to kiso chishiki*, no. 30 Miyuki, Fujibakama, 235–46. Tokyo: Shibundō, 2003.

32 *Umegae*

Inamoto Mariko. "Genji-e ni egakareta kaori no sekai." In Akiyama Ken, et al. Umegae, 24. Vol. 32 of *Shūkan emaki de tanoshimu Genji monogatari gojūshijō*. Shūkan Asahi Hyakka. Tokyo: Asahi Shinbun Shuppan, 2012.

33 *Fuji no uraba*

Cranston, Edwin A. *A Waka Anthology, vol. 2, pt. A: Grasses of Remembrance*, 254. Stanford, CA: Stanford University Press, 2006.

39 *Yūgiri*

Fujii Yukiko. "Kanshōran: Dansei no joseiteki bi." In Suzuki Kazuo and Ii Haruki, eds. *Genji monogatari no kanshō to kiso chishiki*, no. 23, Yūgiri, 159. Tokyo: Shibundo, 1998.

41 *Maboroshi*

Kamens, Edward, and Tamenori Minamoto. *The Three Jewels: A Study and Translation of Minamoto Tamenori's Sanbōe*. Michigan Monograph Series in Japanese Studies 2. Ann Arbor, MI: Center for Japanese Studies, University of Michigan, 1988.

43 *Kōbai*

Mostow, Joshua. "Kōbai." In Chino Kaori et al., eds. "Tokushū Genji monogatari gajō (Hābādo Daigaku Bijutsukan zō)." *Kokka* no. 1222 (1997): 49.

45 *Hashihime*

Abe Akio, et al. *Genji monogatari*, vol. 5, 140–41. Shinpen Nihon koten bungaku zenshū 24. Tokyo: Shōgakkan, 1994–98.
Washburn, Dennis C. *The Tale of Genji*, p. 942, n. 13. 1st ed. New York: W. W. Norton, 2015.

46 *Shiigamoto*

Katagiri Yayoi. "Shiigamoto." In Chino Kaori et al., eds. "Tokushū Genji monogatari gajō (Hābādo Daigaku Bijutsukan zō)." *Kokka* no. 1222 (1997): 50.

51 *Ukifune*

Allen, Laura. "Ukifune." In Chino Kaori et al., eds. "Tokushū Genji monogatari gajō (Hābādo Daigaku Bijutsukan zō)." *Kokka* no. 1222 (1997): 51.

Bibliography

The Tale of Genji annotated text in Japanese consulted and cited

Abe Akio, et al. *Genji monogatari*. 6 vols. Shinpen Nihon koten bungaku zenshū, 20–25. Tokyo: Shōgakkan, 1994–98.
    Page numbers in this *Genji* edition corresponding to the album's chapter excerpts: Vol. 1: Ch. 1, 44–45; Ch. 2, 104; Ch. 3, 119; Ch. 4, 158; Ch. 5, 208; Ch. 6, 296; Ch. 7, 314–15; Ch. 8, 366. Vol. 2: Ch. 9, 24; Ch. 10, 87; Ch. 11, 156; Ch. 12, 205; Ch. 13, 255; Ch. 14, 305; Ch. 15, 348; Ch. 16, 360; Ch. 17, 382; Ch. 18, 419; Ch. 19, 434; Ch. 20, 490–91. Vol. 3: Ch. 21, 82; Ch. 22, 116; Ch. 23, 150; Ch. 24, 167; Ch. 25, 209; Ch. 26, 223; Ch. 27, 257; Ch. 28, 265; Ch. 29, 293; Ch. 30, 332; Ch. 31, 365; Ch. 32, 406; Ch. 33, 438. Vol. 4: Ch. 34, 140; Ch. 35, 245; Ch. 36, 338; Ch. 37, 351; Ch. 38, 385; Ch. 39, 448; Ch. 40, 497; Ch. 41, 549. Vol. 5: Ch. 42, 34; Ch. 43, 49; Ch. 44, 80; Ch. 45, 139; Ch. 46, 212; Ch. 47, 293; Ch. 48, 346; Ch. 49, 391. Vol. 6: Ch. 50, 60; Ch. 51, 151; Ch. 52, 248; Ch. 53, 355; Ch. 54, 382.

English translations consulted

Cranston, Edwin A. *A Waka Anthology, Volume Two: Grasses of Remembrance, Parts A and B*. Stanford, CA: Stanford University Press, 2006. Part B contains the translations of all 795 *waka* in *The Tale of Genji* introduced with informative headnotes.
Tyler, Royall. *The Tale of Genji*. New York: Viking, 2001.
Washburn, Dennis C. *The Tale of Genji*. 1st ed. New York: W. W. Norton, 2015.

Select reference series on the entire tale and compendia of illustrations

Akiyama Ken, et al. *Shūkan emaki de tanoshimu Genji monogatari gojūshijō*. 60 vols. Shūkan Asahi Hyakka. Tokyo: Asahi Shinbun Shuppan, 2011.
Sano Midori. *Genji shūsei*. Tokyo: Geika Shoin, 2011.
Sieffert, René, and Estelle Leggeri-Bauer. *Le Dit Du Genji*. Paris: D. De Selliers, 2008.
Suzuki Kazuo, Kameyama Kōichi, et al. *Genji monogatari no kanshō to kiso chishiki*. 43 vols. Koku bungaku kaishaku to kanshō bessatsu. Tokyo: Shibundō, 1998–2005.
Taguchi Eiichi, and Akiyama Ken. *Gōka "Genji-e" no sekai Genji Monogatari*. Tokyo: Gakushū Kenkyūsha, 1988.
Tamagami Takuya. *Genji monogatari hyōshaku*. 14 vols. Tokyo: Kadokawa Shoten, 1964–69.

Research publications on the 1510 Genji Album

Chino Kaori, Ikeda Shinobu, and Kamei Wakana. "Tokushū Genji monogatari gajō (Hābādo Daigaku Bijutsukan zō)." *Kokka* no. 1222 (1997). Special issue on the Harvard *Genji Album*.
Cranston, Fumiko E. "Hābādo Daigaku Bijutsukan zō 'Genji monogatari gajō' kotobagaki shakumon." *Kokka* no. 1222 (1997): 54–57.
Eremin, Katherine, Jens Stenger, and Melanie Li Green. "Raman Spectroscopy of Japanese Artists' Materials: *The Tale of Genji* by Tosa Mitsunobu." *Journal of Raman Spectroscopy* 37 (2006): 1119–24.
Kasashima Tadayuki. "Hābādo Daigaku Bijutsukan zō 'Genji monogatari gajō' kotobagaki no shofū to seisaku nendai." *Kokka* no. 1222 (1997): 53.
Kitagawa, Anne Rose. "Behind the Scenes of Harvard's Tale of Genji Album." *Apollo* 154, no. 477 (2001): 38–35.
McCormick, Melissa. "Genji Goes West: The 1510 *Genji Album* and the Visualization of Court and Capital." *Art Bulletin* 85, no. 1 (2003): 54–85.
———. "Hābādo Bijutsukan zō 'Genji monogatari gajō' to 'Sanetaka kōki' shosai no 'Genji-e shikishi.'" *Kokka* no. 1241 (1999): 27–28.
Oka Bokkōdō. *Shūfuku*. Vol. 6. Kyoto: Oka Bokkōdō, 2000.

Index

"absent presence," 43, 50, 114, 115, 138, 166–67, 191, 195; Buddhist "emptiness," 207; and deference to the Emperor, 138; scent and, 198; sound and, 75
acolytes, young boys *(chigo)*, 35, 195
adoption, 98–99, 154, 183
"adorable things" *(utsukushiu mono)*, 98
Agemaki (A Bowknot Tied in Maiden's Loops, *Genji*), 208–11
aging, 82, 102–3, 123, 187
Akashi Empress, (*Genji* character a.k.a Akashi girl and Akashi Consort), 74, 94–95; coming of age, 150–51; and death of Murasaki, 183; and Genji's rise to power, 98; Imperial marriage of, 154–55, 162; matriline of, 74; as mother of Crown Prince, 162; Murasaki's adoption of, 98–99, 106, 114–15, 150, 154, 162, 170–71, 183; prophecy concerning, 78–79, 98, 150
Akashi Lady (*Genji* character): as "absent presence," 114–15; Genji's reluctant courtship of, 74–75; importance to Genji's rise to power, 74, 94–95, 115; lineage of, 74; as mother of future empress, 74–75, 78–79, 98–99, 106, 114–15, 150–51; and Murasaki, 115, 162, 182–83; musical abilities of, 74–75, 114, 162; in Rokujō estate, 106; winter associated with, 99, 114, 151
Akashi Novitiate (*Genji* character): lineage and relationship to Genji's mother, 74; portentous dream of, 74, 94–95, 98–99, 162; symbolic relationship to Dragon King, 74
Akashi Nun (*Genji* character), 94–95
Akashi (The Lady at Akashi, *Genji*), 72–75
album format, 1 3
Allen, Laura, 227
allusion, 66, 71, 155, 178, 183, 235; in conversation, 46, 142; historical references, 139; structural, 187
Aoi, Lady (*Genji* character): betrothal and marriage to Genji, 26, 50–51, 54, 58; death of, 59; as mother of Yūgiri, 142; as Princess Ōmiya's daughter, 142, 154; Rokujō as rival of, 58–59, 62–63, 162–63
Aoi festival, 58
Aoi (Leaves of Wild Ginger, *Genji*), 9, 56–59
archery, 55, 122–23
architecture: and depiction of social relationships, 26–27, 107; fishing pavilions *(tsuridono)*, 126; hierarchical spaces within, 27; interior views and "blown off roof" *fukinuki yatai* perspective, 10; Mitsunobu's style of depicting, 230–31; model of Rokujō estate, 106; "overhanging style," 42, 110; and painting composition, 10, 27, 34, 219; temple architecture, 75, 110–11
Ariwara no Narihira, 70, 88, 90–91
Ariwara no Yukihira, 70
Asagao (Bellflowers, *Genji*), 100–103

Asagao Princess or Kamo Priestess (*Genji* character), 58; and fragrance, 150; gifts to the Akashi girl, 150–51; lineage of, 102, 150; rejection of Genji and of marriage, 103, 150, 195
"the ascetic" *(azari)*, 214
At the Foot of the Oak Tree (Shiigamoto, *Genji*), 204–7
audience for *Genji* and paratexts, 1, 3–5, 15–16, 18n4, 19n14, 21n52, 21n55, 47
auditory landscape, 38, 75, 107, 178–79; birdsong, 66, 114, 151; emphasis on sound, 174–75; musical instruments or performances, 79, 95, 175, 219
autumn: and depictions of the moon, 17, 74–75, 174, 203; flowers of, 75, 179, 218; foliage of, 50, 210; motifs of, 178; Tanabata festival, 211; Umetsubo Empress associated with, 106
An Autumn Tempest (Nowaki, *Genji*), 12, 132–35
Azumaya (A Hut in the Eastern Provinces, *Genji*), 220–23

backing papers, 5, 6, **6**, 19nn18–19
Bai Juyi, 70, 82, 187
bamboo *(nayotake)*, 31, 38, 130, 170–71; as painting motif, 35
Bamboo River (Takekawa, *Genji*), 196–99
A Banquet Celebrating Cherry Blossoms (Hana no en, *Genji*), 52–55
The Barrier Gate (Sekiya, *Genji*), 84–87
Bell Crickets (Suzumushi, *Genji*), 172–75
Bellflowers (Asagao, *Genji*), 100–103
A Beloved Pillar of Cypress (Makibashira, *Genji*), 144–47
Bennokimi, 203
Ben no Shōshō or Kōbai (*Genji* character), 126, 151, 194–95, 198
Bishop Henjō, 218
Bishop of Yokawa, 234–35
biwa (lute), 74, 94, 162, 175, 200, 202–3
A Boat Cast Adrift (Ukifune, *Genji*), 224–27; thread-bound chapter booklet, 4
boats, 78, 110, 210–11, 226–27; *higaki kaisen*, 71; prows, 118
book networks and circulation, 5
A Bowknot Tied in Maiden's Loops (Agemaki, *Genji*), 208–11
bracken fern, 214–15
"A Branch of Plum" (folksong, *saibara*), 151
A Branch of Plum (Umegae, *Genji*), 148–51
A Branch of Sacred Evergreen (Sakaki, *Genji*), 60–63
bridges, 126; of Rokujō estate, 106; symbolism of, 203, 206, 207; temporary floating, 138
Broom Cypress (Hahakigi, *Genji*), 28–31
Buddhism, 4, 38–39, 43, 218–19. *see also* Lotus Sutra; annual rites of, 187; *bosatsu* (bodhisattva), 83; calendar of rites and ceremonies, 187; celibacy, 39; and confession, 186; *Genji* as Buddhist narrative, 4–5, 16–17, 18n9, 83, 187–88, 239; karma and Genji's narrative, 43, 74; and nonduality, 4, 203;

Buddhism (continued)
    paradise as conceived in, 107, 118–19, 163; and radiance, 4, 83; Rite of Eight Lectures, 83, 230; and romantic love, 38–39; Suetsumuhana as anti-Buddhist figure, 83; Sutra on the Names of the Buddhas (*Butsumyō kyō*), 186; Tendai, 4, 202
bugaku dance, 119, 182–83, 203
"built-up pictures" *(tsukuri-e)*, 11
bush clover *(hagi)*, 62
butterflies, 30, 90, 119
Butterflies (Kochō, *Genji*), 116–19

calligraphy: attribution of, 20n37, 20nn51–52; calligraphic lineages, 9; covers for individual bound chapters, 13; as design element, 79, 139; distribution of pages to calligraphers, 9; imperial calligraphers, 10, 13, 50; *kana* script, 8–9; manuals guiding placement of, 9; modes of writing, 8–9; as representation of courtly culture, 5; by Sanetaka, 3, 6–8, 9, 12; "scattered writing," 8–9
cats (Chinese cat, *kara neko*), 159
cedar trees, 111
ceremonies, 118–19, 146, 299; coming-of-age, 14–15, 26–27, 107, 150; Genji's elevation to "retired emperor" status, 155; *Lotus Sutra*, 230; Rite of Eight Lectures, 83, 230; rites of confession *(sange)*, 186; vows of religious dedication, 234
Channel Markers (Miotsukushi, *Genji*), 76–79
chapters: individually bound booklets, 2, 12–15
chapter titles, 7
cherry trees or blossoms, 42, 50, 54–55, 106, 118–19, 134, 158–59, 182, 198–99; *kabazakura* (weeping mountain cherry), 134
chigo (acolytes), 35, 195
childbirth, 15, 99
Chinese literary or artistic influences, 8, 11, 20n35, 183
Chino Kaori, 10
chrysanthemums, 106, 155, 190, 215
clothing: abandoned robe as "molted shell," 35; anachronistic details in paintings, 122; "cherry blossom style," 159, 198–99; of civil officials *(sokutai)*, 78; courtiers' hats *(eboshi)*, 30, 130; courtiers' hats *(kanmuri)*, 78, 94, 154; of dragon dancer, 183; fabric patterns, 86; festival costume, 118–19; formal court, 78; formal robes *(hō)*, 55; hunting robes *(kariginu)*, 38; informal robes *(nōshi)*, 55, 154; and military status, 94; Mitsunobu and depiction of, 86; as momento, 35; mourning robes, 142; religious, 186; sashes, 142; and social status, 78, 99, 166; white robes, 99
collaborative production process, 21n44
Collection of Waka Old and New (*Kokinshū*), 5
coming of age: Genji's initiation, 26–27; *kaimami* and, 134; of the Akashi girl, 150
"confrontation of carriages" *(kuruma no arasoi)*, 58–59
Contest of Illustrations (Eawase, *Genji*), 12, 88–91
contests: archery, 55, 122–23; "contest of illustrations," 90–91, 154; incense competition, 151; poetry exchange, 107
covers: album, 16–17; chapter booklet, 12–15
Cranston, Edwin, ix
Cranston, Fumiko, ix
Cresset Fires (Kagaribi, *Genji*), 128–31

crickets, 62, 174–75, 179
cuckoos *(hototogisu)*, 66–67
cultural contexts, 5
curtains, 27, 34, 50, 61–62, 115, 123, 207, 219
cypress, "broom cypress" *(hahakigi)*, 31

dadaiko (drum), 50
Daigo, Emperor, 114, 139
dance: *bugaku*, 119, 182–83, 203; dancers' batons, 203; Waves of the Blue Sea (*Seigaiha*), 50
dayflies *(kagerō)*, 231
death. see also grief and mourning: Buddhist practice and belief, 162–63; corpse taboos, 39; funerary rites, 183
deer *(shika)*, 122, 178, 179
desire, sexual *(irogonomi)*, 171; gaze and, 134 (see also "peeking through the fence" voyeurism *(kaimami)*); male-male, 35, 195
dōri (tonjin), 43, 163, 165, 218, 219
digests, *Tale of Genji*, 3, 12
The Divine Princess at Uji Bridge (Hashihime, *Genji*), 200–203
dolls *(amagatsu)*, 99
Dragon Girl (*Lotus Sutra*), 183
Dragon King (mythical creature), 74, 106; in Buddhism (*hachidai ryūō*), 183
dragons *(ryū)*, 118; *bugaku* dance masks, 182–83, 203; motif on paper, 8–9
dreams, prophetic or supernatural, 39, 59, 74, 98–99, 103, 159, 162, 166, 171
ducks, 103, 118
Du Fu, 82

Early Fiddlehead Greens (Sawarabi, *Genji*), 212–15
Early Spring Greens I (Wakana jō, *Genji*), 156–59
Early Spring Greens II (Wakana ge, *Genji*), 160–63
Eawase (A Contest of Illustrations, *Genji*), 12, 88–91
en (elegance or allure), 150
engi-e (temple origin tales), 111
ennaru (seductive glow), 150
Ephemerids (Kagerō, *Genji*), 228–31
esoterica, hidden teachings *(hiji)*, 4–5, 12
Evening Mist (Yūgiri, *Genji*), 176–79
exile, 18n8, 70–71, 79, 82, 90–91, 95, 150
Exile to Suma (Suma, *Genji*), 68–71

faces: depiction of, 10; expression and *kaimami*, 159; Mitsunobu and individuality, 11; Mitsunobu's conventions for, 26
fate, 91; body *(mi)* as, 30–31; Genji's behavior as karma, 42, 43, 74, 98–99; Genji's realization and acceptance of, 78–79; mortality, 163; prophecies or portentous dreams, 78–79, 98, 150; relationships as predestined, 74, 78–79, 82
Feast of Glowing Harvest (*Toyo no Akari*), 107
female literary productivity, 114–15
fences, 62, 151, 178–79, 202, 215, 218; as dividers in images, 178; voyeuristic peeking (see "peeking through the fence" voyeurism *(kaimami)*)
fiddleheads, bracken *(warabi)*, 214–15
fire, 130–31

248 | *The Tale of Genji*

fireflies, 30, 123, 239
Fireflies (Hotaru, *Genji*), 120–23
firewood, 182
First Song of Spring (Hatsune, *Genji*), 12, 112–16
fishing pavilions (*tsuridono*), 119, 126
A Floating Bridge in a Dream (Yume no ukihashi, *Genji*), 236–39
flutes (*yokobue*), 170–71, 175, 210
folding screens, 6, 19nn18–19
footprints or steps (*fumu*), 206–7
formats, Japanese illustrated manuscript: albums, 1–3; handscrolls, 2
fragrance. *see also* incense: and allusion, 66; as character trait, 190, 191, 219; and memory, 66
The Fragrant Prince (Niou miya, *Genji*), 188–91
Fujibakama (Mistflowers, *Genji*), 140–43
Fuji no uraba (Shoots of Wisteria Leaves, *Genji*), 152–55
Fujitsubo Consort or Empress (*Genji* character): Buddhist vows taken by, 63; and the "contest of illustrations," 90–91; death of, 103; Genji's sexual relationship with, 42, 51, 63; as mother of Reizei, 51, 63, 70, 90; Murasaki's resemblance to, 42–43, 51; radiance of, 51
Fujiwara clan, 26, 50–51, 54–55, 138, 142, 154–55, 195; wisteria as emblem of, 55, 155
Fujiwara no Mototsune, 139
furnishing or decor, 26, 30, 82, 150, 215; blinds or curtains, 27, 34, 50, 61–62, 115, 123, 207, 219; and division of composition, 34; writing implements and, 235

games, 34–35, 158–59
gates, 62
geese (*kari*), 38
geki (mythical water birds), 118
gender: and audience for *Tale of Genji*, 15–16, 18n4, 18n8, 19n14, 21n55; Buddhist salvation and, 183; conventional masculinity, 179; female literary productivity, 21n55, 199, 234–35; gendered modes of writing, 8, 20n36; Genji as gender ambiguous, 179; homosociality, 21n56, 51, 95; and participation in literary gatherings, 15; and posture in paintings, 146–47, 159; religious pilgrimage and, 111; women as central characters, 5, 15–16, 46
Genji (*Genji* character): adoption of Umetsubo Consort, 90; aging and mortality of, 186–87; architectural cues to status of, 26–27; audience and identification with, 18n8; Buddhism and, 42, 83, 163, 174, 190; and centrality in paintings, 15; as commoner dispossessed of birthright, 4, 14, 26–27, 42, 70, 154; as competition to Fujiwara clan, 154; death of, 190; disguise and hidden identity of, 38; and divine rulership, 42; exile and loss of rank, 4, 18n8, 70–71; and gender ambiguity, 35, 179; gold clouds and emphasis on, 15, 35; name as significant, 26–27; as Palace Minister (*naidaijin*), 78; as "radiant," 1, 26–27, 51, 58, 83; and "retired emperor" status, 4, 27, 95, 154–55, 175, 186; as sexually aggressive, 31, 54, 119; as socially transgressive figure, 39; and voyeuristic peeking (*kaimami*), 34
Genji Scrolls, 2–3
Gensei, 6–8, 10, 20n24, 20n31, 21nn44–45

gentians (*rindō*), 179
ghosts, 39, 74, 171. *see also* spirit possession
Gleanings from the Rivers and Seas (Kakaishō), 8
Go-Kashiwabara, Emperor, 13
gold clouds, 55, 71, 75, 86, 110, 111, 215; and compartmentalization of the composition, 10, 111, 179, 210, 230; as pictorial convention, 26, 38; and visual emphasis, 15, 135, 138, 194–95, 207
Gosechi Dancer (*Genji* character), 70–71
grief and mourning, 59, 142, 186, 207, 214–15, 230
Gyōki, 182

Hachinomiya (*Genji* character), 202, 207, 214, 222
Hahakigi (Broom Cypress, *Genji*), 28–31
hairstyles, depiction of, 35, 195; age or gender and, 26, 98, 187; for children, 98, 170; hair as essential to beauty, 162; religious tonsure, 98, 162, 170, 234
Hanachirusato (*Genji* character), 66, 82, 106, 111, 123, 150, 190
Hanachirusato (The Lady at the Villa of Scattering Blossoms, *Genji*), 64–67
Hana no en (A Banquet Celebrating Cherry Blossoms, *Genji*), 52–55
handscrolls, 14
Hasedera temple, 110–11, 219, 234
Hashihime (The Divine Princess at Uji Bridge, *Genji*), 200–203
Hatsune (First Song of Spring, *Genji*), 12, 112–16
Henjō, Bishop, 218
hichiriki (small oboe), 50, 175, 210
Higekuro "Blackbeard" (*Genji* character), 143, 147, 199
Hofer, Philip, 1, 18n1, vii
homoeroticism, 35, 195
homosociality, 21n56, 51, 95
honorifics and narrative distance, 134
horses, 123
horsetail shoots (*tsukushi*), 214
Hotaru (Fireflies, *Genji*), 120–23
Hotaru (Sochinomiya) (*Genji* character), 123–24, 143, 146, 150–51, 158, 175, 194
hunting, 94
A Hut in the Eastern Provinces (Azumaya, *Genji*), 220–23

ice, 102–3, 114, 127, 230–31
iconographic tradition or convention, 2, 12–13, 15
identity, secret or hidden, 38–39, 54–55, 138, 203, 222, 234–35; of Kaoru, 170–71, 190, 203; of Reizei, 51, 70, 90, 95–96, 139; of Tamakazura, 138, 142–43, 146–47
Ii Haruki, 90
An Imperial Celebration of Autumn Foliage (Momiji no ga, *Genji*), 48–51
An Imperial Excursion (Miyuki, *Genji*), 136–39
Inamoto Mariko, 151
incense, 114, 146, 150–51, 190
incest, 119, 131, 135
initiation ceremonies, 26–27. *see also* coming of age
ink painting, 11
interiority, 1–2, 10, 134, 235
Inuki (*Genji* character), 42

Index | 249

Jijū (*Genji* character), 82, 226, 230
Jōtōmon'in, Empress (Fujiwara no Shōshi), 17

Kagaribi (Cresset Fires, *Genji*), 128–31
Kagerō (Ephemerids, *Genji*), 228–31
kaimami "peeking through the fence" voyeurism, 34–35, 134–35, 158–59, 199, 202–3, 215, 219, 222
kalavinka birds, 119
kana script, 8–9; depicted in paintings, 90–91; as gendered mode of writing, 20n36
Kanroji Motonaga, 13
Kaoru (*Genji* character), 190–91; First Princess and, 230; fragrance as characteristic of, 190; Nakanokimi and, 218–19; Ōigimi and, 202–3, 206–7, 210–11, 218–19; parentage of, 170–71, 190, 203; rivalry with Niou, 190, 202, 206–7, 218; spirituality of, 190–91, 202, 203, 207, 218, 238–39; Ukifune and, 219, 223, 230, 233, 238–39
karma. *see* fate
Kasashima Tadayuki, 20n37
Kashiwagi (*Genji* character), 126, 131, 143, 154–55, 158–59, 167–68, 170–71, 203
Kashiwagi (The Oak Tree, *Genji*), 164–67
Katsura River or region, 94–95, 127, 138
katsura trees, 94–95
kemari (football), 158–59
kerria (*yamabuki*) flowers, 118
Kiritsubo Consort (*Genji* character), 26, 74
Kiritsubo Emperor (*Genji* character), 91; depiction of, 138; as Genji's father, 26–27, 50, 67, 95; social status conveyed through depiction of, 26–27
Kiritsubo (The Lady of the Paulownia-Courtyard Chambers, *Genji*), 24–27
Kōbai or Ben no Shōshō (*Genji* character), 126, 151, 194–95, 198
Kōbai (Red Plum, *Genji*), 192–95
Kochō (Butterflies, *Genji*), 116–19
Kogimi (*Genji* character), 30, 35, 87, 195
Kojijū (*Genji* character), 159, 166, 167
Kokiden Consort (*Genji* character), 26, 51, 54, 58, 63, 70, 90, 154
Kokinshū, 123
Kōkō, Emperor, 139
Koremitsu (*Genji* character), 39, 42, 79, 110
Kosaishō (*Genji* character), 230–31
koto, 94–95, 114–15, 130–31, 162, 174–75, 202, 203; *kin* (Chinese *koto*), 70, 114; plectrums for *biwa*, 70, 202–3
Kumoinokari (*Genji* character), 154–55, 179

The Lady at Akashi (Akashi, *Genji*), 72–75
The Lady at the Villa of Scattering Blossoms (Hanachirusato, *Genji*), 64–67
Lady of the Evening Faces (Yūgao, *Genji*), 36–39
The Lady of the Paulownia-Courtyard Chambers (Kiritsubo, *Genji*), 24–27
Lake Biwa, 1, 17
Leaves of Wild Ginger (Aoi, *Genji*), 9, 56–59
lectures, *Genji* scholarship, 5–7, 15, 19n13, 20n25
Lesser Captain (*Genji* character), 198–99

letters, 46, 186, 194, 203, 206–7, 214
lineage: and adoption, 98–99; charts (*keizu*) of *Genji* characters, 20n24; flute as symbol of, 171; Genji as dispossessed, 4, 14, 26–27, 42, 70, 154; physical attractiveness and, 222–23
lineage charts (*keizu*), 20n24
Little Purple Gromwell (Wakamurasaki, *Genji*), 40–43
logographs, 8, 9, 43, 62–63
lotus, 163
Lotus Sutra, 83, 162–63, 182–83, 190, 230, 235
A Lovely Garland (Tamakazura, *Genji*), 108–11

Maboroshi (Spirit Summoner, *Genji*), 184–87
maiden flowers (*ominaeshi*), 62, 107, 135
The Maiden of the Bridge, Illustrated Handscrolls of the Tale of Genji (Hashimie), 3
Maidens of the Dance (Otome, *Genji*), 104–7
Makibashira (A Beloved Pillar of Cypress, *Genji*), 144–47
Makibashira (character, *Genji*), 147, 194–95
manuals, *Genji* painting, 9, 12–13
maple trees (*kaede*) or leaves, 50, 78, 166–67
marriage: ceremonies and rituals, 142; divorce or dissolution of, 146, 147, 194; extramarital liaisons, 51, 166; Fujiwara regency and, 154; *Genji* and ideology of, 15, 115, 143, 155, 195; and lineal concerns, 195–96; as political arrangement, 16, 26, 50–51, 54, 74, 142, 154–55, 166, 190, 195–96; resistance to or rejection of, 143–44, 146, 150, 179, 195–96, 210, 218, 234; status anxiety and rivalry within polygynous, 146–47, 151, 158, 179, 219
"The Masked Warrior King" *bugaku* dance (Ryōō), 182
Matsukaze (Wind in the Pines, *Genji*), 92–95
military themes, 122–23
Minamoto lineage, 4
Minamoto no Taka'akira, 70
Minister of the Left, 15, 26, 54, 58, 59, 142
Minister of the Right, 54–55, 63, 70
Minori (Rites of the Sacred Law, *Genji*), 180–83
Miotsukushi (Channel Markers, *Genji*), 76–79
mistflowers (*fujibakama*), 94, 107, 135, 142–43
Mistflowers (Fujibakama, *Genji*), 140–43
Misty Moon, Lady of the (Oborozukiyo) (*Genji* character), 54–55, 63, 154
Mitsunobu, Tosa, 10, 11, 118, 191, ix; Chinese painting influences on, 11, 20n35; and conventions of courtly narrative painting, 26, 195; covers for individual bound chapters, 12, 13–14, 118, 155; distinctive style of, 10, 11, 130, 230–31; fabric and clothing depicted by, 86; and the Painting Bureau, 10–15; and picture manuals as guide, 12; *Portrait Sketch of Sanjonishi Sanetaka*, 7; reputation and status of, 10, 12–13; screen painting and, 21n42; and "small scrolls" (*ko-e*) innovation, 21n42
Miyuki (An Imperial Excursion, *Genji*), 136–39
A Molted Cicada Shell (Utsusemi, *Genji*), 32–35
Momiji no ga (An Imperial Celebration of Autumn Foliage, *Genji*), 48–51
moon, 66, 102, 202–3; as inspiration for Murasaki's *Genji*, 5, 17; as symbol of enlightenment, 203

250 | The Tale of Genji

morning glory, 218–19
Mostow, Joshua, 195
motherhood, 99
mourning. *see* grief and mourning
Murasaki (*Genji* character): abduction of, 15, 42; adoption of Akashi girl, 98–99, 106, 114–15, 150, 154, 162, 170–71, 183; as child, 42; death of, 182–83; Genji as devoted to, 74; Genji's mourning and grief for, 186; Genji's neglect of, 115; illness and death of, 162, 182–83, 186; religious piety of, 162–63, 182–83; resemblance to Fujitsubo Consort, 42–43, 51; and rivals for Genji's affection, 102–3, 115, 158; spring associated with, 114
Murasaki Shikibu, author of *Genji*, 1–2, 7, 66, 90, 111, 134; and defense of fiction, 123; as divinely inspired, 18n9
music, 210–11. *see also specific instruments*
Myōeiji temple, 1, 5

Naishi (*Genji* character), 51, 103
Nakamikado Nobutane, 12n32
Nakanoin Michihide, 12
Nakanokimi (*Genji* character), 203, 210–11, 214–15, 222; as interchangeable with her sister Oigimi, 215; Kaoru and, 218–19; marriage to Niou, 218–19
Nareki (*Genji* character), 199
narrative modes, 1–2
narrative painting: conventions, 26; "psychological perspective" and visual emphasis, 10
New Wisteria Leaves (Kanroji Motonaga), 13
Nijō villa, 162
Niou, Prince (*Genji* character), 187; as desirable match, 194–95, 210–11; fragrance as character trait, 190; as Hikoboshi figure, 211; Kaoru as rival of, 190, 202, 206–7, 218; marriage to Rokunokimi, 219; similarities to Genji, 195; Ukifune and, 222, 226–27, 230, 234, 235; voyeurism and, 222
Niou miya (The Fragrant Prince, *Genji*), 188–91
Noguchi Takeshi, 30
nonduality, 4, 203
nostalgia, 66, 130, 195
Nowaki (An Autumn Tempest, *Genji*), 12, 132–35

The Oak Tree (Kashiwagi, *Genji*), 164–67
oak trees (*kashiwagi*), 166–67, 207
Oborozukiyo, Lady of the Misty Moon (*Genji* character), 54–55, 63, 154
Ochiba, Second Princess (*Genji* character), 166–67, 178–79, 190
official visits (*gyōkō*), 95
Oigimi (*Genji* character), 203, 206–7, 210–11, 214–15, 218–19
the Ōmi daughter (*Genji* character), 127
Ōmiya, Princess, 50, 59, 142, 154
orange trees or blossoms (*tachibana*), 46–47, 66–67, 130
Otome (Maidens of the Dance, *Genji*), 104–7
Ōuchi Yoshioki, 5, 122

Painting Bureau, 10–15
pampas grass (*susuki*), 62
paper: backing papers, 5, 6, **6**, 19nn18–19; borders, 9; Chinese dragon, 8; *shikishi* (colored), 6, 8–9

paper streamers (*gohei*), 39
parasols, 83
"peeking through the fence" voyeurism (*kaimami*), 34–35, 42, 134–35, 158–59, 199, 202–3, 215, 219, 222
perspective: visual emphasis and, 10, 179
The Picture Contest (Mitsunobu), 12
pigments, 10–11, 26, 28, 30, 71
Pillow Book (Sei Shōnagon), 98, 179
pine trees, 90, 95, 98, 114–15, 150, 154–55; as emblem of Sue clan, 46; entwined with wisteria, 82–83, 155; pines of Sumiyoshi, 78–79
plectrums, 70, 202–3
plum tree or plum blossoms, 114–15, 150–51, 187, 191, 194–95, 198
poetry. *see also specific forms*: court poetry contests, 91; poem-pictures (*uta-e*), 206; social status of poets, 8; *zekku* composition, 94
poverty, 46–47
Practicing Calligraphy (Tenarai, *Genji*), 232–37
provenance of Harvard album, 1–3
"psychological perspective," 10
purification rituals, 39, 58, 62–63, 187–88

radiance: and Buddhist monarchs, 4, 83, 95, 150; as descriptor for *Genji* characters, 51, 170, 179; *ennaru* (seductive glow), 150
"rainy night appraisal," 30
Red Plum (Kōbai, *Genji*), 192–95
reed pipe mouth organ (*shō*), 50, 175, 210
Reikeiden Lady, 66
Reizei Emperor (*Genji* character): as absent presence, 128–29; affection and respect for Genji, 94–95, 138–39, 142, 155, 175, 190; and the contest of illustrations, 90–91; as Genji's son, 51, 79, 90, 95, 139; prophecy concerning, 78–79; Tamakazura's daughter as consort of, 199
renga (linked verse), 5, 19n16; Genji and tradition of, 7–8; Hiroaki and, 7–8, 19n16
replacement paintings, 230–31
"retired emperor" status (*daijō tennō*), 4, 27, 155
retouched paintings, 238
Rites of the Sacred Law (Minori, *Genji*), 180–83
Rokujō estate (Rokujōin), 106–7, 175; Akashi Empress at, 230; fishing pavilions of, 126; as pseudo-imperial palace, 107, 119; as residence of Third Princess, 158, 170; Yūgiri as inheritor of, 190
Rokujō Lady (*Genji* character), 58–59; as mother of Umetsubo Consort, 90, 106; and spirit possession, 38–39, 59, 62–63, 162
Rokunokimi (*Genji* character), 190, 218–19
A Ruined Villa of Tangled Gardens (Yomogiu, *Genji*), 80–83

Safflower (Suetsumuhana, *Genji*), 44–47
Saishō (*Genji* character), 199
Sakaki (A Branch of Sacred Evergreen, *Genji*), 60–63
sakaki trees, 62–64
Sanbōe (The Three Jewels), 187
Sanjonishi Sanetaka, 3, 6–8, 12; calligraphy of, 9; portrait of, 7
The Sarashina Diary, 18
Sawarabi (Early Fiddlehead Greens, *Genji*), 212–15

screens, folding *(byōbu)*: album paintings mounted on, 6, 19n18, 19n20; as furnishing or architectural element, 34, 35, 130, 151
scrolls, 2–3, **3**; *ko-e* (small scrolls), 21n42
seasons. *see* specific
Sei Shōnagon, 66, 98, 179
Sekiya (The Barrier Gate, *Genji*), 84–87
sexual aggression, 15, 142, 223
Shiigamoto (At the Foot of the Oak Tree, *Genji*), 204–7
Shoots of Wisteria Leaves (Fuji no uraba, *Genji*), 152–55
shō (reed pipe mouth organ), 50
Shōshō no kimi, 166
"shrine in the fields" *(nonomiya)*, 62–63
sixth daughter of Minister of the Right (Oborozukiyo), 54–55, 63, 154
size (visual emphasis) and narrative importance, 10
"slope of meeting" *(ausaka)*, 86
snow, 46–47, 101–1, 100–01, 206, 215
Sochinomiya (Prince Hotaru) (*Genji* character), 123, 143, 146, 150–51, 158, 194
Sōgi, 8
Sōseki, 5–6, 7, 17, 19n15, 19n16
sound. *see* auditory landscape
sparrows, 42
spatial relationships: interiority and, 10
spirit possession, 39, 62–63, 146, 147, 162–63, 178
Spirit Summoner (Maboroshi, *Genji*), 184–87
spontaneity, 91, 123
spring: Akashi girl associated with, 106, 114, 150; birds of, 151; and cherry blossoms, 118–19, 134; flowers of, 54, 118, 215; and green plants as gifts or offerings, 158, 214; Murasaki associated with, 106–7, 114, 118–19, 134, 182; plum as symbol of, 114, 150, 151, 187; Third Princess associated with, 158
springs *(izumi)*, 30
stars, 210–11
status, social: adoption and, 98–99, 154; artistic conventions for depicting aristocracy, 10, 26, 85–86; calligraphy as inscription of, 9–10; civil officials *(sokutai)*, 78; clothing and representation of, 99, 166; commoners and court marriages, 154; and extramarital liasons, 30–31, 39; as fate, 30–31; food and prestige, 127; and incense fragrances, 190; insult and, 154; marriage as political transaction, 16, 26, 50–51, 54, 74, 142, 154–55, 166, 190, 195–96; nouveau riche among the governing class, 223; orphanhood or widowhood and diminished, 39, 87, 166, 167; of poets, 8; "rainy night appraisal" of middle rank women, 30; sexual dalliances and, 30, 54, 222; tō no chūjō (middle captain) rank, 94; and tropes in narrative painting, 218–19
storms, 74, 78–79, 91, 134–35, 146
Sue Hiroaki: as Governor of Hyōgō, 5, 19nn15–16; inscription of *Album* backing papers by, 5–6; as patron of 1510 *Genji Album*, 8, 18–19nn11–12, 47; as scholar and copyist of *Azuma Kagami*, 5
Sue Saburō (Okinari): as patron of 1510 *Genji Album*, 1, 5–8, 7–8, 47
Suetsumuhana (*Genji* character), 46–47, 82–83, 87, 127
Suetsumuhana (Safflower, *Genji*), 44–47

suicide, 211, 227, 230
Suma (Exile to Suma, *Genji*), 68–71
Sumiyoshi Gukei, handscroll by, 14
Sumiyoshi Shrine and deities, 74, 78–79, 91, 162, 199
summer: birds of, 66; flowers of, 127, 163, 231; green bamboo associated with, 130; Hanachirusato associated with, 106; Sweet Flag Festival, 123; Tamakazura associated with, 127, 130
The Sutra on the names of the Buddhas (Butsumyō kyō), 186–87
Sutras: dedication of *Lotus Sutra* by Murasaki, 182; *The Sutra on the names of the Buddhas (Butsumyō kyō)*, 186–87
Suzaku Emperor (*Genji* character), 27, 58, 63, 155; as "mountain emperor," 170; as Retired Emperor, 78, 155, 166, 167, 170, 175
Suzaku (*Genji* character), 27, **50**, **54**, 63, 123, 158
Suzumushi (Bell Crickets, *Genji*), 172–75
Sweet Flag Festival *(tango no sechie)*, 123

Taifu (*Genji* character), 199
Taifu no Myōbu (*Genji* character), 46
Takeda Hirohiko, 95
Takekawa (Bamboo River, *Genji*), 196–99
The Tale of Genji Album (1510): audience for, 3, 13, 47; "built-up pictures" *(tsukuri-e)* technique in, 11; coordination of project, 3, 6–10; diaries and documentation of creation process, 3, 7, 21n44, 21nn44–45; Mitsunobu as artist of, 10–14; patronage and commission of, 3, 5–6, 20n21; provenance of, 1; relationship of text and illustration in, 11, 62, 70–71, 82–83, 98, 191; replaced paintings in, 230–31; selection of scenes for illustration, 12, 15–17, 34, 238
The Tale of Genji (Murasaki Shikibu): as Buddhist narrative, 4–5, 16–17, 18n9, 83, 187–88, 239; composition and commission of, 17; handbooks, 7; narrative structure of, 1–2; as novel, 1–2; popularity of, 1, 3–4; as protest literature, 18n8
Tamakazura (*Genji* character), 123; as daughter of Yūgao and Tō no Chūjō, 110–11, 127; daughters of, 147, 198–99; Genji's cruelty to, 111, 119, 123, 135; Genji's sexual infatuation with, 123, 127, 130–31, 135; hidden identity of, 110–11, 138, 142–43, 146–47; marriage to Higekuro, 146–47, 179; at Rokujōin estate, 111, 119, 127
Tamakazura (Lovely Garland, *Genji*), 108–11
Tanabata festival, 19n17, 211
Tawaraya Sōtatsu, 71
temple-origin tales *(engi-e)*, 111
temples or shrines, 1, 5, 219, 234; architecture of, 75, 110–11; gates to, 78; "shrine in the fields" *(nonomiya)*, 62–63; Sumiyoshi Shrine and deities, 74, 78–79, 91, 162, 199; temple-origin tales *(engi-e)*, 111
Tenarai (Practicing Calligraphy, *Genji*), 232–35
Tendai Buddhism, 4, 202
A Thin Veil of Clouds (Usugumo, *Genji*), 96–99
Third Princess, Princess Initiate (*Genji* character): Buddhist vows taken by, 165, 170, 173–74; cat as symbolic of, 159; Genji's marriage to, 158–59, 174; Kashiwagi and, 158–59, 166–67, 170, 174–75, 199, 203; as mother of Kaoru, 165, 170, 190, 203
The Three Jewels (Sanbōe), 187

Tokonatsu (Wild Pinks, *Genji*), 124–27
Tō no Chūjō (*Genji* character): as Aoi's brother, 50; as father of Tamazakura, 110–11, 131, 138, 179; as Genji's friend and rival, 38, 46, 50–51, 54, 90, 126–27
Tosa Mitsuoki, 16–17
traces or tracks (*ato*), 206–7
translation, ix
The Transverse Flute (Yokobue, *Genji*), 168–71
Trees Encoiled in Vines of Ivy (Yadoriki, *Genji*), 216–19

Uji region, 202
Ukifune (Boat Cast Adrift, *Genji*), 224–27
Ukifune (*Genji* character): attempted suicide, 227, 230, 234; independence or autonomy of, 219, 234–35, 239; Niou and, 226–27; religious vows of, 234–35; as substitute for Oigimi, 219; and writing practice, 234–35
Ukon (*Genji* character), 110–11, 230
umbrellas, 69
Umegae (A Branch of Plum, *Genji*), 148–51
Umetsubo Consort or Empress (*Genji* character), 90–91, 106, 118, 126, 154, 199
Usugumo (Thin Veil of Clouds, *Genji*), 96–99
Utsusemi (*Genji* character), 30, 34–35, 39, 86–87, 130
Utsusemi (Molted Cicada Shell, *Genji*), 32–35

violets (*sumire*), 215
visual emphasis: gold clouds and, 15, 135, 138, 194–95, 207; size related to centrality of character, 10, 138, 179

A Waka Anthology (Cranston), ix
Wakamurasaki (Little Purple Gromwell, *Genji*), 40–43
wa-kan aesthetics (Chinese cultural influences), 8
Wakana ge (Early Spring Greens II, *Genji*), 160–63
Wakana jō (Early Spring Greens I, *Genji*), 156–59
waka poetry, 1–2, 7–8, 235, ix
warblers, 114–15, 151, 194
Washburn, Dennis, 203, 219, ix
water plants (*ayamegusa*), 123

Waves of the Blue Sea (Seigaiha), 50
widows or widowhood, 39, 87, 166, 167, 198
Wild Pinks (Tokonatsu, *Genji*), 124–27
Wind in the Pines (Matsukaze, *Genji*), 92–95
winter: Akashi Lady associated with, 99, 106, 114, 151; plum trees and endurance of, 151, 191; snow or ice as images, 46–47, 102–3, 190–91, 206, 235
wisteria, 190; as emblem of Fujiwara house, 55, 103, 154–55; entwined with pine, 82–83, 155; *fujigoromo* (lavender robes) associated with, 142; mourning robes as wisteria robes, 142; Murasaki and, 103, 118
wordplay, 142–43, 155, 171, 206; in conversation, 203; double entendre, 142; homophones, 47, 90, 127, 166; letter/footprint, 206–7

Yadoriki (Trees Encoiled in Vines of Ivy, *Genji*), 216–19
Yokawa, Bishop of, 234–35, 238
Yokobue (The Transverse Flute, *Genji*), 168–71
Yomogiu (A Ruined Villa of Tangled Gardens, *Genji*), 80–83
Yotsutsuji Yoshinari, 8
Yūgao, Lady of the Evening Faces (*Genji* character), 38–39, 46, 110, 119, 127, 223
Yūgao (Lady of the Evening Faces, *Genji*), 36–39
Yūgiri (Evening Mist, *Genji*), 176–79
Yūgiri (*Genji* character): Aoi as mother of, 58, 142; as central character, 134–35, 179, 190–91; and death of Ōmiya, 142; depiction of, 126–27, 154–55, 175; and infatuation with Murasaki, 134–35; and Kashiwagi, 158, 166–67, 171; marriage to Kumoinokari, 154–55, 179; and Ochiba, 166–67, 178–79, 190–91; as problematic romantic hero, 179; prophecy concerning, 78–79; and pursuit of Tamakazura, 142–43; at Rokujo estate, 106–7, 111, 126–27, 131; and Rokunokimi, 190, 219; voyeurism and, 107, 134–35
Yume no ukihashi (A Floating Bridge in a Dream, *Genji*), 236–39

zekku poetry, 94
zuryō (provincial governing class), 223

Image Credits

© Idemitsu Museum of Arts: p. 13, fig. 9; p. 155, ref. fig, Ch. 33.

Reproduced from auction catalog *Kōshaku Hachisuka-ke gozōhin nyūsatsu* (Tokyo: Tōkyō Bijutsu Kurabu, 1933): p. 111, ref. fig., Ch. 22.

© The Museum Yamato Bunkakan: p. 4, fig. 3.

© The Tale of Genji Museum: p. 106, ref. fig., Ch. 21.

© Tenri Central Library: p. 12, fig. 8.

© The Tokugawa Art Museum, Image Archives/DNPartcom: p. 3, fig. 2.

© The Tokyo National Museum, Image Archives/DNPartcom: p. 14, fig. 10.

All other figures from Imaging Department © President and Fellows of Harvard College

The Tale of Genji Album, 1510. Paintings by Tosa Mitsunobu (except for Ch. 52, anonymous, Edo period, 1615–1868). Calligraphy by Kunitaka Shinnō (1456–1532) (Chs. 1, 7, 13, 19, 25, 33, 39, 45, 51); Konoe Hisamichi (1472–1544) (Chs. 2, 8, 14, 20, 26, 32, 38, 44, 50); Sanjōnishi Sanetaka (1455–1537) (Chs. 3, 9, 15, 21, 27, 31, 37, 43, 49); Jōhōji Kōjo (1453–1538) (Chaps. 4, 10, 16, 22, 30, 36, 42, 48, 54); Reizei Tamehiro (1450–1526) (Chs. 5, 11, 17, 23, 29, 35, 41, 47, 53); Son'o Jugō (d. 1514) (Chs. 6, 12, 18, 24, 28, 34, 40, 46, 52). Harvard Art Museums, Cambridge. Harvard Art Museums/Arthur M. Sackler Museum, Bequest of the Hofer Collection of the Arts of Asia, 1985.352.